Industry & Financial Consulting Services

Industry Norms & Key Business Ratios

One Year Edition 1995-96

Agriculture, Mining, Construction, Transportation, Communication, Utilities

SIC #0100-1799 & 4000-4971

Dun & Bradstreet
Information Services

A Company of
The Dun & Bradstreet Corporation

See how a company measures up to its peers

with D&B's
Industry Norms & Key Business Ratios
on Diskette

When you need detailed information to evaluate your customers, your prospects and your business, Dun & Bradstreet can help. With D&B's Industry Norms & Key Business Ratios on diskette, you get industry norm statistics — on over 800 lines of business — right from your PC, to help you:

- Compare a company's financial condition to its peers'.

- Project a company's future performance by creating pro forma statements
- Determine standards of risk and performance for your own company
- Create a model statement to measure how a typical company's financials should look based on industry performance

**Dun & Bradstreet
Information Services**

D·B a company of
The Dun & Bradstreet Corporation

. . . .

For more information, complete and return this coupon...

By fax to 610-882-7269. By mail to: Dun & Bradstreet, PC Software Sales, 899 Eaton Avenue, Bethlehem PA 18025-0001.

For Academic Institutions and Public Libraries, return by fax to 201-605-6911. By mail to: Dun & Bradstreet, Business Reference Services, Three Sylvan Way, Parsippany NJ 07054.

Name _____

Title _____

Company _____

Address _____

City/State/ZIP _____

Telephone _____

YES! I want more information on D&B's Industry Norms & Key Business Ratios on Diskette:

☐ Have a D&B representative contact me.

☐ Send me a FREE demo diskette.

☐ Send me additional information.

Industry & Financial Consulting Services

Industry Norms and
Key Business Ratios
One Year

Agriculture, Mining, Construction, Transportation, Communications, Utilities
SIC #0100-1799 & 4000-4971

Dun&Bradstreet
Information Services

a company of
The Dun & Bradstreet Corporation

CONTENTS

INDUSTRY NORMS AND KEY BUSINESS RATIOS

Agriculture, Forestry and Fishing

Major Group SIC

Mining

Major Group SIC

Construction

Major Group SIC

Transportation, Communications and Public Utilities

Major Group SIC

APPENDIX - SIC Numbers Appearing in This Directory

INTRODUCTION

The Dun & Bradstreet Industry Norms and Key Business Ratios are made possible through over one million financial statements in the Dun & Bradstreet Financial Information Base. This file consists of U.S. corporations, partnerships and proprietorships both public and privately owned, in all size ranges, and includes over 800 different lines of business as defined by the U.S. Standard Industrial Classification (SIC) code numbers. Our data is collected weekly, maintained daily, and constantly edited and updated. All of these factors combine to make this financial information unequaled anywhere for scope and timeliness*.

The Industry Norms are published separately in the following five major industry segments:

1. **Agriculture, Mining, Construction/ Transportation/Communication/Utilities**
2. **Manufacturing**
3. **Wholesaling**
4. **Retailing**
5. **Finance/Real Estate/Services**

All five segments are available in three different formats. The three formats are as follows:

1. **Industry Norms and Key Business Ratios, Three Year Edition.**
   Directories and diskettes available.

2. **Industry Norms and Key Business Ratios, One Year Edition.**
   Directories and diskettes available.

3. **Key Business Ratios, One Year Edition.**
   Directories only.

Note that the Industry Norms contain "typical" balance sheets and income statements, and "common-size" financial figures, as well as Key Business Ratios. The Key Business Ratios books contain fourteen indicators of performance.

All entries are standardized into a concise, practical format and are well suited for both comparative analysis and trend analysis.

Each segment displays consolidated information by two-digit and four-digit SIC numbers, and then is subdivided into four geographic areas of the U.S. (for two-digit SICs only) and up to eight assets-size ranges (both two-digit and four-digit SICs).

The size groupings for each book are unique to that industry segment, based on a study of the particular sample size or "universe."

Occasionally, breakdowns will be omitted. This is due to insufficient data which prohibits a fair representation of that particular SIC category.

Four Geographic Area Breakdowns

Northeast	Central
Connecticut	Illinois
Delaware	Indiana
District of Columbia	Iowa
Maine	Kansas
Maryland	Michigan
Massachusetts	Minnesota
New Hampshire	Missouri
New Jersey	Nebraska
New York	North Dakota
Pennsylvania	Ohio
Rhode Island	South Dakota
Vermont	Wisconsin

South	West
Alabama	Alaska
Arkansas	Arizona
Florida	California
Georgia	Colorado
Kentucky	Hawaii
Louisiana	Idaho
Mississippi	Montana
North Carolina	Nevada
Oklahoma	New Mexico
South Carolina	Oregon
Tennessee	Utah
Texas	Washington
Virginia	Wyoming
West Virginia	

*To provide the most current information available, fiscal years July 1 - June 30 were utilized to calculate the Norms. Sample sizes for 1995 data may tend to be lower than the previous years because some firms, as of publication date, have not ended their fiscal periods.

INDUSTRY NORM FORMAT

At the top of each industry norm will be identifying information: SIC code number and short title. Beside the year date, in parenthesis, is the number of companies in the sample. The "typical" balance-sheet figures are in the first column and the "common-size" balance-sheet figures are in the second. The respective income statements begin with the item "Net Sales", and the respective Key Business Ratios begin with the item "Ratios." The latter are further broken down, or refined, into the median, and the upper quartile and lower quartile.

THE COMMON - SIZE FINANCIAL STATEMENT

The common-size balance-sheet and income statement present each item of the financial statement as a percentage of its respective aggregate total. Common-size percentages are computed for all statement items of all the individual companies used in the industry sample. An average for each statement item is then determined and presented as the industry norm.

This enables the analyst to examine the current composition of assets, liabilities and sales of a particular industry.

THE TYPICAL FINANCIAL STATEMENT

The typical balance-sheet figures are the result of translating the common-size percentages into dollar figures. They permit, for example, a quick check of the relative size of assets and liabilities between one's own company and that company's own line of business.

After the common-size percentages have been computed for the particular sample, the actual financial statements are then sequenced by both *total assets* and *total sales*, with the median, or mid-point figure in both these groups serving as the "typical" amount. We then compute the typical balance-sheet and income statement dollar figures by multiplying the common-size percentages for each statement item by their respective total amounts.

(For example, if the median total assets for an SIC category are $669,599, and the common-size figure for cash is 9.2 percent, then by multiplying the two we derive a cash figure of $61,603 for the typical balance sheet.)

KEY BUSINESS RATIOS

The Fourteen Key Business Ratios are broken down into median figures, with upper and lower quartiles, giving the analyst an even more refined set of figures to work with. These ratios cover all those critical areas of business performance with indicators of solvency, efficiency and profitability.

They provide a profound and well-documented insight into all aspects for everyone interested in the financial workings of business—business executives and managers, credit executives, bankers, lenders, investors, academicians and students.

In the ratio tables appearing in this book, the figures are broken down into the median—which is the midpoint of all companies in the sample—and the upper quartile and lower quartile—which are mid-points of the upper and lower halves.

Upper quartile figures are not always the highest numerical value, nor are lower quartile figures always the lowest numerical value. The quartile listings reflect *judgmental ranking*, thus the upper quartile represents the best condition in any given ratio and is not necessarily the highest numerical value. (For example, see the items Total Liabilities-to-Net Worth or Collection Period, where a lower numerical value represents a better condition.)

Each of the fourteen ratios is calculated individually for every concern in the sample. These individual figures are then sequenced for each ratio according to condition (best to worst), and the figure that falls in the middle of this series becomes the median (or mid-point) for that ratio in that line of business. The figure halfway between the median and the best condition of the series becomes the upper quartile; and the number halfway between the median and the least favorable condition of the series is the lower quartile.

In a statistical sense, each median is considered the *typical* ratio figure for a concern in a given category.

CALCULATIONS OF THE 14 KEY BUSINESS RATIOS

SOLVENCY RATIOS

Quick Ratio

Cash + Accounts Receivable
Current Liabilities

The Quick Ratio is computed by dividing cash plus accounts receivable by total current liabilities. Current liabilities are all the liabilities that fall due within one year. This ratio reveals the protection afforded short-term creditors in cash or near-cash assets. It shows the number of dollars of liquid assets available to cover each dollar of current debt. Any time this ratio is as much as 1 to 1 (1.0) the business is said to be in a liquid condition. The larger the ratio the greater the liquidity.

Current Ratio

Current Assets
Current Liabilities

Total current assets are divided by total current liabilities. Current assets include cash, accounts and notes receivable (less reserves for bad debts), advances on inventories, merchandise inventories and marketable securities. This ratio measures the degree to which current assets cover current liabilities. The higher the ratio the more assurance exists that the retirement of current liabilities can be made. The current ratio measures the margin of safety available to cover any possible shrinkage in the value of current assets. Normally a ratio of 2 to 1 (2.0) or better is considered good.

Current Liabilities to Net Worth

Current Liabilities
Net Worth

Current Liabilities to Net Worth is derived by dividing current liabilities by net worth. This contrasts the funds that creditors temporarily are risking with the funds permanently invested by the owners. The smaller the net worth and the larger the liabilities, the less security for the creditors. Care should be exercised when selling any firm with current liabilities exceeding two-thirds (66.6 percent) of net worth.

Current Liabilities to Inventory

Current Liabilities
Inventory

Dividing current liabilities by inventory yields another indication of the extent to which the business relies on funds from disposal of unsold inventories to meet its debts. This ratio combines with Net Sales to Inventory to indicate how management controls inventory. It is possible to have decreasing liquidity while maintaining consistent sales-to-inventory ratios. Large increases in sales with corresponding increases in inventory levels can cause an inappropriate rise in current liabilities if growth isn't made wisely.

Total Liabilities to Net Worth

Total Liabilities
Net Worth

Obtained by dividing total current plus long-term and deferred liabilities by net worth. The effect of long-term (funded) debt on a business can be determined by comparing this ratio with Current Liabilities to Net Worth. The difference will pinpoint the relative size of long-term debt, which, if sizable, can burden a firm with substantial interest charges. In general, total liabilities shouldn't exceed net worth (100 percent) since in such cases creditors have more at stake than owners.

Fixed Assets to Net Worth

Fixed Assets
Net Worth

Fixed assets are divided by net worth. The proportion of net worth that consists of fixed assets will vary greatly from industry to industry but generally a smaller proportion is desirable. A high ratio is unfavorable because heavy investment in fixed assets indicates that either the concern has a low net working capital and is overtrading or has utilized large funded debt to supplement working capital. Also, the larger the fixed assets, the bigger the annual depreciation charge that must be deducted from the income statement. Normally, fixed assets above 75 percent of net worth indicate possible over-investment and should be examined with care.

EFFICIENCY RATIOS

Collection Period

Accounts Receivable
Sales   x 365

Accounts receivable are divided by sales and then multiplied by 365 days to obtain this figure. The quality of the receivables of a company can be determined by this relationship when compared with selling terms and industry norms. In some industries where credit sales are not the normal way of doing business, the percentage of cash sales should be taken into consideration. Generally, where most sales are for credit, any collection period more than one-third over normal selling terms (40.0 for 30-day terms) is indicative of some slow-turning receivables. When comparing the collection period of one concern with that of another, allowances should be made for possible variations in selling terms.

Sales to Inventory

Annual Net Sales
Inventory

Obtained by dividing annual net sales by inventory. Inventory control is a prime management objective since poor controls allow inventory to become costly to store, obsolete or insufficient to meet demands. The sales-to-inventory relationship is a guide to the rapidity at which merchandise is being moved and the effect on the flow of funds into the business. This ratio varies widely between lines of business and a company's figure is only meaningful when compared with industry norms. Individual figures that are outside either the upper or lower quartiles for a given industry should be examined with care. Although low figures are usually the biggest problem, as they indicate excessively high inventories, extremely high turnovers might reflect insufficient merchandise to meet customer demand and result in lost sales.

Asset to Sales

Total Assets
Net Sales

Assets to sales is calculated by dividing total assets by annual net sales. This ratio ties in sales and the total investment that is used to generate those sales. While figures vary greatly from industry to industry, by comparing a company's ratio with industry norms it can be determined whether a firm is overtrading (handling an excessive volume of sales in relation to investment) or undertrading (not generating sufficient sales to warrant the assets invested). Abnormally low percentages (above the upper quartile) can indicate overtrading which may lead to financial difficulties if not corrected. Extremely high percentages (below the lower quartile) can be the result of overly conservative or poor sales management, indicating a more aggressive sales policy may need to be followed.

Sales to Net Working Capital

Sales
Net Working Capital

Net sales are divided by net working capital (net working capital is current assets minus current liabilities.). This relationship indicates whether a company is overtrading or conversely carrying more liquid assets than needed for its volume. Each industry can vary substantially and it is necessary to compare a company with its peers to see if it is either overtrading on its available funds or being overly conservative. Companies with substantial sales gains often reach a level where their working capital becomes strained. Even if they maintain an adequate total investment for the volume being generated (Assets to Sales), that investment may be so centered in fixed assets or other noncurrent items that it will be difficult to continue meeting all current obligations without additional investment or reducing sales.

Accounts Payable to Sales

Accounts Payable
Annual Net Sales

Computed by dividing accounts payable by annual net sales. This ratio measures how the company is paying its suppliers in relation to the volume being transacted. An increasing percentage, or one larger than the industry norm, indicates the firm may be using suppliers to help finance operations. This ratio is especially important to short-term creditors since a high percentage could indicate potential problems in paying vendors.

PROFITABILITY RATIOS

Return on Sales (Profit Margin)

Net Profit After Taxes
Annual Net Sales

Obtained by dividing net profit after taxes by annual net sales. This reveals the profits earned per dollar of sales and therefore measures the efficiency of the operation. Return must be adequate for the firm to be able to achieve satisfactory profits for its owners. This ratio is an indicator of the firm's ability to withstand adverse conditions such as falling prices, rising costs and declining sales.

Return on Assets

Net Profit After Taxes
Total Assets

Net profit after taxes divided by total assets. This ratio is the key indicator of profitability for a firm. It matches operating profits with the assets available to earn a return. Companies efficiently using their assets will have a relatively high return while less well-run businesses will be relatively low.

Return on Net Worth (Return on Equity)

Net Profit After Taxes
Net Worth

Obtained by dividing net profit after tax by net worth. This ratio is used to analyze the ability of the firm's management to realize an adequate return on the capital invested by the owners of the firm. Tendency is to look increasingly to this ratio as a final criterion of profitability. Generally, a relationship of at least 10 percent is regarded as a desirable objective for providing dividends plus funds for future growth.

Using Industry Norms for Financial Analysis

The principal purpose of financial analysis is to identify irregularities that require explanations to completely understand an industry's or company's current status and future potential. These irregularities can be identified by comparing the industry norms with the figures of specific companies (*comparative analysis*). D&B's Industry Norms are specifically formatted to accommodate this analysis.

Relative Position

Common-size and typical balance sheets provide an excellent picture of the makeup of the industry's assets and liabilities. Are assets concentrated in inventories or accounts receivable? Are payables to the trade or bank loans more important as a method for financing operations? The answers to these and other important questions are clearly shown by the Industry Norms, its common-size balance sheet approach and is then further crystallized by the typical balance sheets.

Financial Ratio Trends

Key Business Ratio changes indicate trends in the important *relationships* between key financial items, such as the relationship between Net Profits and Net Sales (a common indicator of profitability). Ratios that reflect short and long-term liquidity, efficiency in managing assets and controlling debt, and different measures of profitability are all included in the Key Business Ratios sections of the Industry Norms.

Comparative Analysis

Comparing a company with its peers is a reliable method for evaluating financial status. The key to this technique is the composition of the peer group and the timeliness of the data. The D&B Industry Norms are unique in scope of sample size and in level of detail.

Sample Size

The number of firms in the sample must be representative or they will be unduly influenced by irregular figures from relatively few companies. The more than one million companies used as a basis for the Industry Norms allow for more than adequate sample sizes in most cases.

Key Business Ratios Analysis

Valuable insights into an industry's performance can be obtained by equating two related statement items in the form of a financial ratio. For really effective ratio analysis, the items compared must be meaningful and the comparison should reflect the combined effort of two potentially diverse trends. While dozens of different ratios can be computed from financial statements, the fourteen included in the Industry Norms and Key Business Ratio books are those most commonly used and were rated as the most significant as shown in a survey of financial analysts. Many of the other ratios in existence are variations on these fourteen.

The fourteen Key Business Ratios are categorized into three major groups:

Solvency, or liquidity, measurements are significant in evaluating a company's ability to meet short and long-term obligations. These figures are of prime interest to credit managers of commercial companies and financial institutions.

Efficiency ratios indicate how effectively a company uses and controls its assets. This is critical information for evaluating how a company is managed. Studying these ratios is useful for credit, marketing and investment purposes.

Profitability ratios show how successfully a business is earning a return to its owners. Those interested in mergers and acquisitions consider this key data for selecting candidates.

Recent research efforts have revealed that the use of financial analysis (via Industry Norms) is very useful in several functional areas. To follow are only a few of the more widely used applications of this unique data.

Credit

Industry Norm data has proven to be an invaluable tool in determining minimum acceptable standards for risk. The credit worthiness of an existing or potential account is immediately visible by ranking its solvency status and comparing its solvency trends to that of the industry. Short term solvency gauges, such as the quick and current ratios, are ideal indicators when evaluating an account. Balance sheet comparisons supplement this qualification by allowing a comparison of the make-up of current assets and liability items. Moreover, leverage ratios such as current liability to net worth and total liability to net worth provide valuable benchmarks to spot potential problem accounts while profitability and collection period figures provide cash flow comparisons for an overall evaluation of accounts.

In addition to evaluating individual accounts against industry standards, internal credit polices also benefit from Industry Norm data. Are receivables growing at an excessive rate as compared to the industry? If so, how does your firm's collections stack up to the industry?

Finance

Here exists a unique opportunity for financial executives to rank their firm, or their firm's subsidiaries and divisions, against its peers. Determine the efficiency of management via ratio quartile breakdowns which provides you the opportunity to pinpoint your firm's profitability position versus the industry. For example, are returns on sales and gross profit margins comparatively low thereby indicating that pricing per unit may be too low or that the cost of goods is unnecessarily high?

In much the same way, matching the firm's growth and efficiency trends to that of the industry reveals conditions which prove to be vital in projecting budgets. If asset expansion exceeds the industry standard while asset utilization (as indicated by the asset to sales ratio) is sub par, should growth be slowed?

Investment executives have also utilized this diverse information when identifying optimal investment opportunities. By uncovering which industries exhibit the strongest sales growth while maintaining adequate returns, risk is minimized.

Corporate Planning

Corporate plans, competitive strategies and merger/acquisition decisions dictate a comprehensive analysis of the industry in question. Industry Norm data provides invaluable information in scrutinizing the performance of today's highly competitive, and sometimes unstable, markets. Does the liquidity of an industry provide a sufficient cushion to endure the recent record-high interest levels or is it too volatile to risk an entry? Are the profitability and equity statuses of an acquisition candidate among the best in the industry thereby qualifying it as an ideal acquisition target?

Industry Norm data provides these all-important benchmarks for setting strategic goals and measuring overall corporate performance.

Marketing and Sales

Attaining an in-depth knowledge of a potential or existing customer base is a key factor when developing successful marketing strategies and sales projections. Industry Norm data provides a competitive edge when determining market potential and market candidates. Identify those industries that meet or exceed your qualifications and take it one step further by focusing in on the specific region or size category that exhibits the greatest potential. For example, isolate the industries which have experienced the strongest growth trends in sales and inventory turnover and then fine tune marketing and sales strategies by identifying the particular *segment* which is the most attractive (such as firms with assets of $1 million or more).

You can also utilize this information from a different perspective by examining the industries of existing accounts. If an account's industry shows signs of faltering profitability and stagnating sales, should precautionary measures be taken? Will the next sale be profitable for your company or will it be written-off? Industry Norm data assist in answering these and many other important questions.

FINAL NOTE

The SIC categories in this directory reflect those appearing in the 1987 edition of the Standard Industrial Classification Manual

The Dun & Bradstreet Financial Information Base includes over one million U.S. companies and is the most extensive and complete source of financial information of its kind. This compilation of data should be regarded only as a source of financial information, to be used in conjunction with other sources of data, when performing financial analysis. When utilizing these figures, remember:

- Because of the size of this database, and in order to facilitate the many calculations and rankings, many of the very large group samples have been randomly reduced.

- On the other hand, some of the samples from our file are very small, and, therefore, may not present a true picture of an entire line of business. In these small groups there is a chance that a few extreme variations might have an undue influence on the overall figures in a particular category.

- The companies composing our database are organized by principal line of business without consideration for multiple-operation functions.

- Within the primary SIC numbers, no allowance has been made for differing accounting methods, terms of sale, or fiscal-year closing date, all of which might have had an effect on the composite data.

- Therefore, Dun & Bradstreet advises users that the Industry Norms and Key Business Ratios be used as yardsticks and not as absolutes.

SIC 01 AGRICULTURL CROPS (NO BREAKDOWN) — 1995 (1066 Establishments)

	$	%
Cash	119,713	9.6
Accounts Receivable	140,912	11.3
Notes Receivable	8,729	0.7
Inventory	157,123	12.6
Other Current	72,327	5.8
Total Current	**498,804**	**40.0**
Fixed Assets	554,919	44.5
Other Non-current	193,286	15.5
Total Assets	**1,247,009**	**100.0**
Accounts Payable	73,574	5.9
Bank Loans	3,741	0.3
Notes Payable	71,080	5.7
Other Current	140,912	11.3
Total Current	**289,306**	**23.2**
Other Long Term	233,191	18.7
Deferred Credits	4,988	0.4
Net Worth	719,524	57.7
Total Liab & Net Worth	**1,247,009**	**100.0**
Net Sales	1,986,752	100.0
Gross Profit	802,648	40.4
Net Profit After Tax	105,298	5.3
Working Capital	209,498	—

RATIOS	UQ	MED	LQ
SOLVENCY			
Quick Ratio (times)	2.2	0.8	0.4
Current Ratio (times)	4.7	1.9	1.0
Curr Liab To Nw (%)	8.3	27.8	71.3
Curr Liab To Inv (%)	43.9	105.7	219.3
Total Liab To Nw (%)	22.1	62.6	153.7
Fixed Assets To Nw (%)	41.6	80.2	129.6
EFFICIENCY			
Coll Period (days)	13.1	29.6	50.9
Sales To Inv (times)	28.7	9.2	3.6
Assets To Sales (%)	36.4	70.1	126.0
Sales To Nwc (times)	14.4	6.3	2.8
Acct Pay To Sales (%)	1.5	3.4	7.3
PROFITABILITY			
Return On Sales (%)	11.6	4.3	0.6
Return On Assets (%)	11.2	4.7	0.7
Return On Nw (%)	22.2	8.9	2.1

SIC 01 AGRICULTURL CROPS — NORTHEAST — 1995 (128 Establishments)

	$	%
Cash	64,680	8.5
Accounts Receivable	86,747	11.4
Notes Receivable	5,327	0.7
Inventory	92,835	12.2
Other Current	21,306	2.8
Total Current	**270,895**	**35.6**
Fixed Assets	386,558	50.8
Other Non-current	103,488	13.6
Total Assets	**760,940**	**100.0**
Accounts Payable	54,788	7.2
Bank Loans	2,283	0.3
Notes Payable	63,158	8.3
Other Current	89,791	11.8
Total Current	**210,019**	**27.6**
Other Long Term	172,733	22.7
Deferred Credits	3,044	0.4
Net Worth	375,143	49.3
Total Liab & Net Worth	**760,940**	**100.0**
Net Sales	1,265,956	100.0
Gross Profit	505,116	39.9
Net Profit After Tax	46,840	3.7
Working Capital	60,876	—

RATIOS	UQ	MED	LQ
SOLVENCY			
Quick Ratio (times)	1.5	0.7	0.3
Current Ratio (times)	2.9	1.4	0.7
Curr Liab To Nw (%)	11.5	44.6	101.7
Curr Liab To Inv (%)	80.3	151.6	217.5
Total Liab To Nw (%)	23.1	81.7	202.4
Fixed Assets To Nw (%)	62.5	95.3	176.4
EFFICIENCY			
Coll Period (days)	12.1	26.7	58.8
Sales To Inv (times)	23.6	9.6	4.6
Assets To Sales (%)	32.7	53.8	97.5
Sales To Nwc (times)	25.7	9.0	4.1
Acct Pay To Sales (%)	2.5	3.7	9.3
PROFITABILITY			
Return On Sales (%)	8.4	2.2	0.1
Return On Assets (%)	11.1	2.9	(0.2)
Return On Nw (%)	20.2	7.6	(0.2)

SIC 01 AGRICULTURL CROPS — CENTRAL — 1995 (361 Establishments)

	$	%
Cash	95,572	11.0
Accounts Receivable	75,588	8.7
Notes Receivable	6,951	0.8
Inventory	105,998	12.2
Other Current	32,147	3.7
Total Current	**316,255**	**36.4**
Fixed Assets	393,581	45.3
Other Non-current	158,996	18.3
Total Assets	**868,833**	**100.0**
Accounts Payable	42,573	4.9
Bank Loans	1,738	0.2
Notes Payable	46,917	5.4
Other Current	98,178	11.3
Total Current	**189,406**	**21.8**
Other Long Term	150,308	17.3
Deferred Credits	4,344	0.5
Net Worth	524,775	60.4
Total Liab & Net Worth	**868,833**	**100.0**
Net Sales	1,301,625	100.0
Gross Profit	580,525	44.6
Net Profit After Tax	75,494	5.8
Working Capital	126,849	—

RATIOS	UQ	MED	LQ
SOLVENCY			
Quick Ratio (times)	2.5	0.8	0.3
Current Ratio (times)	5.4	1.8	0.8
Curr Liab To Nw (%)	6.9	26.2	65.7
Curr Liab To Inv (%)	40.3	97.4	188.0
Total Liab To Nw (%)	17.7	58.8	143.5
Fixed Assets To Nw (%)	45.4	79.3	128.7
EFFICIENCY			
Coll Period (days)	10.2	21.2	35.4
Sales To Inv (times)	20.3	9.6	3.9
Assets To Sales (%)	40.8	75.5	138.4
Sales To Nwc (times)	14.0	6.2	3.1
Acct Pay To Sales (%)	1.4	3.0	5.3
PROFITABILITY			
Return On Sales (%)	10.2	3.6	1.2
Return On Assets (%)	10.5	4.5	1.5
Return On Nw (%)	23.1	8.3	2.9

SIC 01 AGRICULTURL CROPS — SOUTH — 1995 (264 Establishments)

	$	%
Cash	127,012	9.3
Accounts Receivable	150,229	11.0
Notes Receivable	12,291	0.9
Inventory	174,812	12.8
Other Current	83,309	6.1
Total Current	**547,654**	**40.1**
Fixed Assets	599,551	43.9
Other Non-current	218,515	16.0
Total Assets	**1,365,720**	**100.0**
Accounts Payable	75,115	5.5
Bank Loans	4,097	0.3
Notes Payable	80,577	5.9
Other Current	122,915	9.0
Total Current	**282,704**	**20.7**
Other Long Term	264,950	19.4
Deferred Credits	5,463	0.4
Net Worth	812,603	59.5
Total Liab & Net Worth	**1,365,720**	**100.0**
Net Sales	1,990,179	100.0
Gross Profit	752,288	37.8
Net Profit After Tax	115,430	5.8
Working Capital	264,950	—

RATIOS	UQ	MED	LQ
SOLVENCY			
Quick Ratio (times)	2.7	1.2	0.4
Current Ratio (times)	5.5	2.4	1.2
Curr Liab To Nw (%)	8.5	22.4	48.9
Curr Liab To Inv (%)	36.2	95.0	215.4
Total Liab To Nw (%)	21.9	52.0	130.4
Fixed Assets To Nw (%)	41.5	78.7	129.0
EFFICIENCY			
Coll Period (days)	13.1	28.3	45.3
Sales To Inv (times)	37.5	12.1	3.0
Assets To Sales (%)	36.0	67.2	137.8
Sales To Nwc (times)	17.1	5.7	2.3
Acct Pay To Sales (%)	1.5	3.6	7.1
PROFITABILITY			
Return On Sales (%)	13.2	5.2	1.6
Return On Assets (%)	12.1	5.2	2.1
Return On Nw (%)	17.6	9.5	3.6

	SIC 01 AGRICULTURL CROPS WEST 1995 (313 Establishments)		SIC 01 AGRICULTURL CROPS INDUSTRY ASSETS UNDER $100,000 1995 (44 Establishments)		SIC 01 AGRICULTURL CROPS INDUSTRY ASSETS $100,000 - $250,000 1995 (81 Establishments)		SIC 01 AGRICULTURL CROPS INDUSTRY ASSETS $250,000 - $500,000 1995 (148 Establishments)	
	$	%	$	%	$	%	$	%
Cash	186,725	8.8	17,528	30.9	29,881	17.0	42,996	11.7
Accounts Receivable	299,184	14.1	4,311	7.6	26,190	14.9	39,321	10.7
Notes Receivable	12,731	0.6	57	0.1	2,461	1.4	367	0.1
Inventory	277,966	13.1	5,559	9.8	22,323	12.7	27,562	7.5
Other Current	188,847	8.9	1,588	2.8	7,207	4.1	20,579	5.6
Total Current	**965,453**	**45.5**	**29,044**	**51.2**	**88,062**	**50.1**	**130,826**	**35.6**
Fixed Assets	882,700	41.6	21,442	37.8	65,915	37.5	182,642	49.7
Other Non-current	273,722	12.9	6,240	11.0	21,796	12.4	54,021	14.7
Total Assets	**2,121,875**	**100.0**	**56,726**	**100.0**	**175,773**	**100.0**	**367,489**	**100.0**
Accounts Payable	140,044	6.6	3,233	5.7	17,929	10.2	20,947	5.7
Bank Loans	6,366	0.3	—	—	—	—	367	0.1
Notes Payable	101,850	4.8	4,311	7.6	5,449	3.1	23,519	6.4
Other Current	277,966	13.1	11,062	19.5	32,694	18.6	41,526	11.3
Total Current	**526,225**	**24.8**	**18,606**	**32.8**	**56,072**	**31.9**	**86,360**	**23.5**
Other Long Term	371,328	17.5	11,175	19.7	33,221	18.9	59,901	16.3
Deferred Credits	8,488	0.4	—	—	176	0.1	735	0.2
Net Worth	1,215,834	57.3	26,945	47.5	86,305	49.1	220,493	60.0
Total Liab & Net Worth	**2,121,875**	**100.0**	**56,726**	**100.0**	**175,773**	**100.0**	**367,489**	**100.0**
Net Sales	3,941,333	100.0	248,670	100.0	526,453	100.0	840,918	100.0
Gross Profit	1,580,475	40.1	142,239	57.2	287,970	54.7	359,072	42.7
Net Profit After Tax	216,773	5.5	30,586	12.3	32,114	6.1	41,205	4.9
Working Capital	439,228	—	10,438	—	31,990	—	44,466	—

RATIOS	UQ	MED	LQ	UQ	MED	LQ	UQ	MED	LQ	UQ	MED	LQ
SOLVENCY												
Quick Ratio (times)	2.2	0.8	0.4	5.8	1.7	0.3	3.3	1.3	0.5	3.0	0.8	0.4
Current Ratio (times)	4.3	2.0	1.1	7.5	1.9	0.7	6.1	2.3	0.9	4.8	1.7	0.8
Curr Liab To Nw (%)	9.4	29.8	79.6	5.1	34.2	81.7	11.3	42.2	147.8	7.5	22.1	74.3
Curr Liab To Inv (%)	53.5	101.1	298.4	27.7	94.6	260.0	43.1	87.2	152.8	86.3	140.0	262.4
Total Liab To Nw (%)	25.1	74.7	158.0	12.2	81.2	166.2	24.9	88.3	255.4	18.1	55.1	138.0
Fixed Assets To Nw (%)	36.8	75.5	120.5	24.4	99.1	186.1	41.7	86.6	147.0	49.7	86.3	146.7
EFFICIENCY												
Coll Period (days)	20.0	37.1	62.6	16.2	19.0	27.8	5.5	16.4	29.2	8.2	19.6	31.4
Sales To Inv (times)	25.7	7.6	3.3	83.7	31.0	3.6	31.5	20.0	9.0	49.2	21.4	10.0
Assets To Sales (%)	41.1	74.9	131.2	13.5	16.3	33.2	24.7	30.3	59.1	24.2	38.7	76.5
Sales To Nwc (times)	10.7	5.5	2.4	40.0	17.0	6.3	11.4	7.3	5.2	38.1	16.7	7.0
Acct Pay To Sales (%)	1.2	3.5	7.2	0.3	0.8	1.6	0.8	2.2	3.1	1.0	2.7	4.1
PROFITABILITY												
Return On Sales (%)	12.1	4.9	0.3	20.4	10.1	4.1	10.7	2.9	0.6	11.7	5.3	0.4
Return On Assets (%)	11.2	5.4	0.2	101.4	20.0	11.8	17.4	8.7	1.6	17.1	10.4	0.8
Return On Nw (%)	25.5	9.2	0.3	172.3	57.1	37.0	48.3	17.4	1.6	41.0	13.3	1.2

SIC 01 AGRICULTURL CROPS — INDUSTRY ASSETS $500,000 - $1,000,000 — 1995 (213 Establishments)

	$	%
Cash	74,818	10.4
Accounts Receivable	71,221	9.9
Notes Receivable	7,913	1.1
Inventory	115,824	16.1
Other Current	28,057	3.9
Total Current	**297,834**	**41.4**
Fixed Assets	314,380	43.7
Other Non-current	107,191	14.9
Total Assets	**719,405**	**100.0**
Accounts Payable	41,725	5.8
Bank Loans	3,597	0.5
Notes Payable	41,006	5.7
Other Current	76,976	10.7
Total Current	**163,305**	**22.7**
Other Long Term	148,917	20.7
Deferred Credits	2,878	0.4
Net Worth	404,306	56.2
Total Liab & Net Worth	**719,405**	**100.0**
Net Sales	1,168,641	100.0
Gross Profit	451,095	38.6
Net Profit After Tax	58,432	5.0
Working Capital	134,529	—

RATIOS	UQ	MED	LQ
SOLVENCY			
Quick Ratio (times)	2.7	0.8	0.4
Current Ratio (times)	6.2	2.1	1.1
Curr Liab To Nw (%)	6.3	24.1	66.8
Curr Liab To Inv (%)	34.8	73.4	131.9
Total Liab To Nw (%)	17.9	66.8	172.7
Fixed Assets To Nw (%)	37.9	75.3	117.4
EFFICIENCY			
Coll Period (days)	10.4	20.8	37.6
Sales To Inv (times)	25.0	7.8	4.1
Assets To Sales (%)	34.5	52.9	91.2
Sales To Nwc (times)	17.3	7.8	3.4
Acct Pay To Sales (%)	1.4	3.0	6.8
PROFITABILITY			
Return On Sales (%)	9.2	2.1	(0.3)
Return On Assets (%)	10.5	3.3	(1.1)
Return On Nw (%)	29.0	8.8	(1.0)

SIC 01 AGRICULTURL CROPS — INDUSTRY ASSETS $1,000,000 - $5,000,000 — 1995 (402 Establishments)

	$	%
Cash	129,295	6.3
Accounts Receivable	246,276	12.0
Notes Receivable	14,366	0.7
Inventory	240,119	11.7
Other Current	133,400	6.5
Total Current	**763,457**	**37.2**
Fixed Assets	954,321	46.5
Other Non-current	334,525	16.3
Total Assets	**2,052,303**	**100.0**
Accounts Payable	112,877	5.5
Bank Loans	8,209	0.4
Notes Payable	133,400	6.5
Other Current	194,969	9.5
Total Current	**449,454**	**21.9**
Other Long Term	365,310	17.8
Deferred Credits	8,209	0.4
Net Worth	1,229,329	59.9
Total Liab & Net Worth	**2,052,303**	**100.0**
Net Sales	2,700,184	100.0
Gross Profit	1,088,174	40.3
Net Profit After Tax	153,910	5.7
Working Capital	314,003	—

RATIOS	UQ	MED	LQ
SOLVENCY			
Quick Ratio (times)	1.8	0.9	0.3
Current Ratio (times)	4.3	1.8	1.0
Curr Liab To Nw (%)	9.2	28.2	69.5
Curr Liab To Inv (%)	42.6	106.6	260.8
Total Liab To Nw (%)	24.0	57.3	136.7
Fixed Assets To Nw (%)	44.7	85.0	129.0
EFFICIENCY			
Coll Period (days)	15.2	32.5	63.4
Sales To Inv (times)	25.5	9.5	3.1
Assets To Sales (%)	45.5	76.8	134.8
Sales To Nwc (times)	10.7	5.3	2.6
Acct Pay To Sales (%)	1.7	4.4	8.1
PROFITABILITY			
Return On Sales (%)	13.0	3.8	1.0
Return On Assets (%)	8.8	3.7	1.1
Return On Nw (%)	16.9	7.7	2.7

SIC 01 AGRICULTURL CROPS — INDUSTRY ASSETS $5,000,000-$25,000,000 — 1995 (136 Establishments)

	$	%
Cash	522,343	6.5
Accounts Receivable	859,858	10.7
Notes Receivable	72,324	0.9
Inventory	1,325,949	16.5
Other Current	618,776	7.7
Total Current	**3,399,250**	**42.3**
Fixed Assets	3,166,205	39.4
Other Non-current	1,470,598	18.3
Total Assets	**8,036,053**	**100.0**
Accounts Payable	353,586	4.4
Bank Loans	24,108	0.3
Notes Payable	369,658	4.6
Other Current	948,254	11.8
Total Current	**1,695,607**	**21.1**
Other Long Term	1,510,778	18.8
Deferred Credits	80,361	1.0
Net Worth	4,749,307	59.1
Total Liab & Net Worth	**8,036,053**	**100.0**
Net Sales	6,991,290	100.0
Gross Profit	2,398,012	34.3
Net Profit After Tax	230,713	3.3
Working Capital	1,703,643	—

RATIOS	UQ	MED	LQ
SOLVENCY			
Quick Ratio (times)	2.2	0.7	0.3
Current Ratio (times)	4.7	2.1	1.3
Curr Liab To Nw (%)	8.8	28.2	77.0
Curr Liab To Inv (%)	49.2	127.3	258.9
Total Liab To Nw (%)	25.0	74.7	156.6
Fixed Assets To Nw (%)	38.1	63.1	117.1
EFFICIENCY			
Coll Period (days)	15.0	31.4	56.9
Sales To Inv (times)	22.1	6.0	2.7
Assets To Sales (%)	78.2	108.6	227.9
Sales To Nwc (times)	10.9	4.3	1.9
Acct Pay To Sales (%)	1.5	3.1	5.7
PROFITABILITY			
Return On Sales (%)	10.4	4.8	0.3
Return On Assets (%)	9.1	4.5	0.7
Return On Nw (%)	17.7	8.9	2.6

SIC 01 AGRICULTURL CROPS — INDUSTRY ASSETS $25,000,000-$50,000,000 — 1995 (18 Establishments)

	$	%
Cash	2,418,438	7.3
Accounts Receivable	4,273,678	12.9
Notes Receivable	496,939	1.5
Inventory	3,743,609	11.3
Other Current	4,306,807	13.0
Total Current	**15,239,472**	**46.0**
Fixed Assets	13,980,559	42.2
Other Non-current	3,909,256	11.8
Total Assets	**33,129,286**	**100.0**
Accounts Payable	2,981,636	9.0
Bank Loans	—	—
Notes Payable	1,060,137	3.2
Other Current	2,352,179	7.1
Total Current	**6,393,952**	**19.3**
Other Long Term	5,168,169	15.6
Deferred Credits	364,422	1.1
Net Worth	21,202,743	64.0
Total Liab & Net Worth	**33,129,286**	**100.0**
Net Sales	20,542,894	100.0
Gross Profit	9,408,645	45.8
Net Profit After Tax	1,027,145	5.0
Working Capital	8,845,520	—

RATIOS	UQ	MED	LQ
SOLVENCY			
Quick Ratio (times)	1.7	0.8	0.6
Current Ratio (times)	4.5	2.7	1.6
Curr Liab To Nw (%)	8.8	25.0	43.3
Curr Liab To Inv (%)	95.2	120.9	125.9
Total Liab To Nw (%)	23.0	28.9	121.9
Fixed Assets To Nw (%)	39.0	74.5	89.8
EFFICIENCY			
Coll Period (days)	35.9	51.1	99.5
Sales To Inv (times)	38.7	5.4	4.2
Assets To Sales (%)	113.9	137.4	211.3
Sales To Nwc (times)	4.1	3.2	2.4
Acct Pay To Sales (%)	3.0	5.9	8.6
PROFITABILITY			
Return On Sales (%)	11.8	7.7	2.6
Return On Assets (%)	10.9	7.2	2.7
Return On Nw (%)	14.7	10.6	4.5

	SIC 01 AGRICULTURL CROPS — INDUSTRY ASSETS OVER $50,000,000 — 1995 (24 Establishments) $	%	SIC 0111 WHEAT (NO BREAKDOWN) — 1995 (65 Establishments) $	%	SIC 0111 WHEAT — INDUSTRY ASSETS $1,000,000 - $5,000,000 — 1995 (25 Establishments) $	%	SIC 0115 CORN (NO BREAKDOWN) — 1995 (53 Establishments) $	%
Cash	10,498,584	6.2	75,207	7.9	74,295	4.4	133,963	9.5
Accounts Receivable	17,102,532	10.1	30,464	3.2	59,099	3.5	76,147	5.4
Notes Receivable	—	—	—	—	—	—	15,511	1.1
Inventory	20,489,172	12.1	105,671	11.1	180,673	10.7	289,077	20.5
Other Current	9,821,256	5.8	39,032	4.1	50,656	3.0	94,479	6.7
Total Current	**57,911,544**	**34.2**	**250,374**	**26.3**	**364,723**	**21.6**	**609,177**	**43.2**
Fixed Assets	89,576,628	52.9	362,709	38.1	457,592	27.1	637,380	45.2
Other Non-current	21,843,828	12.9	338,909	35.6	866,216	51.3	163,575	11.6
Total Assets	**169,332,000**	**100.0**	**951,992**	**100.0**	**1,688,531**	**100.0**	**1,410,132**	**100.0**
Accounts Payable	8,466,600	5.0	7,616	0.8	3,377	0.2	70,507	5.0
Bank Loans	—	—	—	—	—	—	—	—
Notes Payable	5,926,620	3.5	20,944	2.2	13,508	0.8	78,967	5.6
Other Current	22,521,156	13.3	116,143	12.2	238,083	14.1	159,345	11.3
Total Current	**36,914,376**	**21.8**	**144,703**	**15.2**	**254,968**	**15.1**	**308,819**	**21.9**
Other Long Term	43,856,988	25.9	196,110	20.6	422,133	25.0	188,958	13.4
Deferred Credits	2,878,644	1.7	1,904	0.2	—	—	2,820	0.2
Net Worth	85,681,992	50.6	609,275	64.0	1,011,430	59.9	909,535	64.5
Total Liab & Net Worth	**169,332,000**	**100.0**	**951,992**	**100.0**	**1,688,531**	**100.0**	**1,410,132**	**100.0**
Net Sales	63,271,319	100.0	855,182	100.0	1,871,369	100.0	827,519	100.0
Gross Profit	15,058,574	23.8	296,748	34.7	735,448	39.3	463,411	56.0
Net Profit After Tax	4,239,178	6.7	94,070	11.0	258,249	13.8	43,031	5.2
Working Capital	20,997,168	—	105,671	—	109,755	—	300,358	—

RATIOS	SIC 01 UQ	MED	LQ	Wheat NB UQ	MED	LQ	Wheat IA UQ	MED	LQ	Corn UQ	MED	LQ
SOLVENCY												
Quick Ratio (times)	1.4	1.0	0.4	1.3	0.5	0.3	0.9	0.6	0.2	4.1	0.5	0.3
Current Ratio (times)	3.0	2.0	1.3	4.9	1.4	0.7	3.0	1.5	1.0	9.4	2.5	1.3
Curr Liab To Nw (%)	19.6	34.7	63.0	5.4	14.1	33.4	6.3	14.1	31.7	3.9	19.0	43.9
Curr Liab To Inv (%)	68.5	179.6	230.0	34.8	77.9	132.0	26.6	59.2	128.7	29.1	73.1	105.9
Total Liab To Nw (%)	50.9	104.1	207.4	7.8	48.1	91.5	27.1	62.7	136.7	19.0	40.5	96.6
Fixed Assets To Nw (%)	65.2	107.8	167.4	31.1	52.7	97.4	29.8	46.0	83.8	52.8	66.5	94.8
EFFICIENCY												
Coll Period (days)	33.3	42.9	74.5	14.8	27.0	80.7	52.4	93.8	114.5	7.1	29.6	38.5
Sales To Inv (times)	10.0	6.1	3.0	5.3	3.7	2.5	3.8	2.2	1.9	4.0	2.9	2.2
Assets To Sales (%)	93.4	146.2	249.4	114.2	161.8	272.6	185.3	240.5	256.6	81.5	102.9	201.7
Sales To Nwc (times)	7.8	3.3	2.0	5.5	3.2	1.9	4.3	3.2	2.0	6.9	5.2	2.6
Acct Pay To Sales (%)	4.6	6.6	10.8	1.0	1.4	2.4	1.6	2.1	2.7	1.3	4.4	10.6
PROFITABILITY												
Return On Sales (%)	9.8	7.3	2.4	16.7	8.7	5.0	34.1	4.8	3.7	12.2	8.0	2.1
Return On Assets (%)	7.0	3.2	1.6	11.7	8.3	5.0	3.0	2.3	1.6	6.5	3.9	2.0
Return On Nw (%)	10.9	6.3	1.6	24.7	12.6	8.5	5.3	4.0	2.6	24.6	6.7	3.2

SIC 0115 — CORN
INDUSTRY ASSETS $1,000,000 - $5,000,000
1995 (22 Establishments)

	$	%
Cash	185,652	8.6
Accounts Receivable	94,985	4.4
Notes Receivable	56,127	2.6
Inventory	455,494	21.1
Other Current	56,127	2.6
Total Current	**848,385**	**39.3**
Fixed Assets	982,227	45.5
Other Non-current	328,128	15.2
Total Assets	**2,158,740**	**100.0**
Accounts Payable	41,016	1.9
Bank Loans	—	—
Notes Payable	161,906	7.5
Other Current	226,668	10.5
Total Current	**429,589**	**19.9**
Other Long Term	261,208	12.1
Deferred Credits	12,952	0.6
Net Worth	1,454,991	67.4
Total Liab & Net Worth	**2,158,740**	**100.0**
Net Sales	1,313,287	100.0
Gross Profit	814,238	62.0
Net Profit After Tax	73,544	5.6
Working Capital	418,796	—

RATIOS	UQ	MED	LQ
SOLVENCY			
Quick Ratio (times)	0.4	0.3	0.2
Current Ratio (times)	2.0	1.3	0.7
Curr Liab To Nw (%)	1.9	3.9	9.3
Curr Liab To Inv (%)	19.6	32.3	47.1
Total Liab To Nw (%)	4.7	19.0	21.3
Fixed Assets To Nw (%)	45.4	57.5	61.9
EFFICIENCY			
Coll Period (days)	12.4	29.6	31.4
Sales To Inv (times)	5.3	2.9	2.4
Assets To Sales (%)	72.5	96.9	132.0
Sales To Nwc (times)	4.7	3.3	1.7
Acct Pay To Sales (%)	1.9	3.4	4.5
PROFITABILITY			
Return On Sales (%)	10.7	5.7	3.0
Return On Assets (%)	5.8	3.7	1.9
Return On Nw (%)	8.4	3.7	2.3

SIC 0119 — CASH GRAINS, NEC
(NO BREAKDOWN)
1995 (17 Establishments)

	$	%
Cash	36,795	6.4
Accounts Receivable	60,367	10.5
Notes Receivable	575	0.1
Inventory	116,709	20.3
Other Current	15,523	2.7
Total Current	**229,969**	**40.0**
Fixed Assets	224,220	39.0
Other Non-current	120,734	21.0
Total Assets	**574,922**	**100.0**
Accounts Payable	11,498	2.0
Bank Loans	11,498	2.0
Notes Payable	60,942	10.6
Other Current	87,963	15.3
Total Current	**171,902**	**29.9**
Other Long Term	74,165	12.9
Deferred Credits		
Net Worth	328,855	57.2
Total Liab & Net Worth	**574,922**	**100.0**
Net Sales	574,328	100.0
Gross Profit	134,393	23.4
Net Profit After Tax	26,419	4.6
Working Capital	58,067	—

RATIOS	UQ	MED	LQ
SOLVENCY			
Quick Ratio (times)	0.9	0.4	0.3
Current Ratio (times)	2.3	1.5	0.7
Curr Liab To Nw (%)	28.6	38.6	47.8
Curr Liab To Inv (%)	63.6	97.3	137.8
Total Liab To Nw (%)	34.2	45.1	149.1
Fixed Assets To Nw (%)	37.7	78.1	98.9
EFFICIENCY			
Coll Period (days)	25.6	31.4	42.8
Sales To Inv (times)	5.6	3.0	2.1
Assets To Sales (%)	59.0	92.2	197.8
Sales To Nwc (times)	71.9	5.3	2.1
Acct Pay To Sales (%)	1.1	1.8	2.0
PROFITABILITY			
Return On Sales (%)	16.0	6.9	(2.6)
Return On Assets (%)	7.2	3.1	1.3
Return On Nw (%)	23.6	4.7	2.1

SIC 0131 — COTTON
(NO BREAKDOWN)
1995 (31 Establishments)

	$	%
Cash	171,712	11.7
Accounts Receivable	88,057	6.0
Notes Receivable	7,338	0.5
Inventory	114,475	7.8
Other Current	164,374	11.2
Total Current	**545,956**	**37.2**
Fixed Assets	766,100	52.2
Other Non-current	155,568	10.6
Total Assets	**1,467,624**	**100.0**
Accounts Payable	46,964	3.2
Bank Loans	—	—
Notes Payable	105,669	7.2
Other Current	114,475	7.8
Total Current	**267,108**	**18.2**
Other Long Term	308,201	21.0
Deferred Credits	2,935	0.2
Net Worth	889,380	60.6
Total Liab & Net Worth	**1,467,624**	**100.0**
Net Sales	1,086,648	100.0
Gross Profit	361,854	33.3
Net Profit After Tax	113,011	10.4
Working Capital	278,848	—

RATIOS	UQ	MED	LQ
SOLVENCY			
Quick Ratio (times)	3.1	1.4	0.5
Current Ratio (times)	6.7	2.5	1.1
Curr Liab To Nw (%)	4.2	30.0	54.5
Curr Liab To Inv (%)	33.1	41.7	138.1
Total Liab To Nw (%)	12.1	91.4	183.9
Fixed Assets To Nw (%)	76.5	116.8	144.9
EFFICIENCY			
Coll Period (days)	1.7	8.4	16.1
Sales To Inv (times)	17.1	12.9	8.7
Assets To Sales (%)	100.0	126.0	226.0
Sales To Nwc (times)	7.3	5.7	4.6
Acct Pay To Sales (%)	1.6	4.8	10.7
PROFITABILITY			
Return On Sales (%)	17.9	11.5	5.9
Return On Assets (%)	8.8	7.2	2.8
Return On Nw (%)	24.1	15.9	7.7

SIC 0134 — IRISH POTATOES
(NO BREAKDOWN)
1995 (40 Establishments)

	$	%
Cash	140,480	5.3
Accounts Receivable	180,238	6.8
Notes Receivable	34,457	1.3
Inventory	212,045	8.0
Other Current	111,324	4.2
Total Current	**678,543**	**25.6**
Fixed Assets	1,375,641	51.9
Other Non-current	596,376	22.5
Total Assets	**2,650,560**	**100.0**
Accounts Payable	90,119	3.4
Bank Loans	15,903	0.6
Notes Payable	201,443	7.6
Other Current	349,874	13.2
Total Current	**657,339**	**24.8**
Other Long Term	564,569	21.3
Deferred Credits	47,710	1.8
Net Worth	1,380,942	52.1
Total Liab & Net Worth	**2,650,560**	**100.0**
Net Sales	4,478,760	100.0
Gross Profit	998,763	22.3
Net Profit After Tax	111,969	2.5
Working Capital	21,204	—

RATIOS	UQ	MED	LQ
SOLVENCY			
Quick Ratio (times)	1.2	0.5	0.3
Current Ratio (times)	2.6	1.4	0.6
Curr Liab To Nw (%)	15.9	32.4	112.1
Curr Liab To Inv (%)	92.4	209.8	266.6
Total Liab To Nw (%)	53.0	93.3	158.3
Fixed Assets To Nw (%)	88.2	117.6	179.0
EFFICIENCY			
Coll Period (days)	17.1	31.6	48.7
Sales To Inv (times)	18.6	9.5	5.5
Assets To Sales (%)	53.6	80.4	110.2
Sales To Nwc (times)	9.6	3.8	2.8
Acct Pay To Sales (%)	1.6	4.2	6.1
PROFITABILITY			
Return On Sales (%)	5.3	0.5	(2.7)
Return On Assets (%)	8.3	1.9	(4.0)
Return On Nw (%)	15.2	2.6	(7.9)

SIC 0134 IRISH POTATOES — INDUSTRY ASSETS $1,000,000 - $5,000,000 — 1995 (18 Establishments)
SIC 0139 CROPS, EXC GRNS, NEC (NO BREAKDOWN) — 1995 (40 Establishments)
SIC 0139 CROPS, EXC GRNS, NEC — INDUSTRY ASSETS $1,000,000 - $5,000,000 — 1995 (21 Establishments)
SIC 0161 VEGETABLES, MELONS (NO BREAKDOWN) — 1995 (125 Establishments)

	SIC 0134 $	%	SIC 0139 (NB) $	%	SIC 0139 (IA) $	%	SIC 0161 $	%
Cash	73,278	3.8	100,354	6.9	76,207	4.1	151,029	7.9
Accounts Receivable	196,693	10.2	120,716	8.3	85,500	4.6	326,911	17.1
Notes Receivable	15,427	0.8	2,909	0.2	7,435	0.4	17,206	0.9
Inventory	140,770	7.3	202,162	13.9	321,555	17.3	149,117	7.8
Other Current	30,854	1.6	87,264	6.0	174,718	9.4	173,970	9.1
Total Current	**457,022**	**23.7**	**513,405**	**35.3**	**665,415**	**35.8**	**818,233**	**42.8**
Fixed Assets	1,052,885	54.6	753,381	51.8	916,339	49.3	890,880	46.6
Other Non-current	418,454	21.7	187,618	12.9	276,946	14.9	202,646	10.6
Total Assets	**1,928,361**	**100.0**	**1,454,404**	**100.0**	**1,858,700**	**100.0**	**1,911,759**	**100.0**
Accounts Payable	63,636	3.3	63,994	4.4	55,761	3.0	173,970	9.1
Bank Loans	—	—	1,454	0.1	1,859	0.1	11,471	0.6
Notes Payable	242,973	12.6	94,536	6.5	200,740	10.8	139,558	7.3
Other Current	225,618	11.7	110,535	7.6	96,652	5.2	250,440	13.1
Total Current	**532,228**	**27.6**	**270,519**	**18.6**	**355,012**	**19.1**	**575,439**	**30.1**
Other Long Term	300,824	15.6	216,706	14.9	355,012	19.1	315,440	16.5
Deferred Credits	11,570	0.6	1,454	0.1	3,717	0.2	7,647	0.4
Net Worth	1,083,739	56.2	965,724	66.4	1,144,959	61.6	1,013,232	53.0
Total Liab & Net Worth	**1,928,361**	**100.0**	**1,454,404**	**100.0**	**1,858,700**	**100.0**	**1,911,759**	**100.0**
Net Sales	2,217,316	100.0	1,496,751	100.0	1,496,751	100.0	4,200,522	100.0
Gross Profit	407,986	18.4	504,405	33.7	480,457	32.1	1,360,969	32.4
Net Profit After Tax	57,650	2.6	95,792	6.4	85,315	5.7	226,828	5.4
Working Capital	(75,206)	—	242,886	—	310,403	—	242,794	—

RATIOS	SIC 0134 UQ	MED	LQ	SIC 0139 (NB) UQ	MED	LQ	SIC 0139 (IA) UQ	MED	LQ	SIC 0161 UQ	MED	LQ
SOLVENCY												
Quick Ratio (times)	0.4	0.4	0.2	2.0	1.0	0.3	0.6	0.4	0.2	1.7	0.8	0.4
Current Ratio (times)	1.0	0.7	0.5	8.2	3.3	1.1	2.4	1.8	0.9	3.0	1.6	0.9
Curr Liab To Nw (%)	4.4	12.8	37.1	4.0	10.9	31.8	5.0	11.7	19.2	15.5	49.1	111.4
Curr Liab To Inv (%)	142.6	224.9	324.8	33.4	64.6	128.0	49.3	55.2	67.4	99.1	169.9	441.1
Total Liab To Nw (%)	14.4	42.8	74.6	18.2	36.9	98.4	13.8	46.5	59.1	36.3	85.7	169.2
Fixed Assets To Nw (%)	80.0	91.4	109.6	58.8	90.4	133.6	39.3	75.6	93.5	48.6	79.7	141.0
EFFICIENCY												
Coll Period (days)	4.6	19.2	30.0	5.1	16.8	42.3	5.1	5.1	7.7	14.0	31.2	50.1
Sales To Inv (times)	19.8	17.0	11.0	17.2	5.3	2.8	3.8	2.6	2.5	79.8	22.1	7.7
Assets To Sales (%)	47.1	53.4	93.1	60.3	105.7	177.9	56.8	71.9	81.5	29.1	47.6	87.8
Sales To Nwc (times)	5.8	4.3	2.7	6.4	2.5	1.7	2.6	2.2	1.9	25.5	8.7	4.1
Acct Pay To Sales (%)	1.5	3.0	5.7	0.4	0.8	3.1	1.1	1.5	2.3	1.7	5.0	10.3
PROFITABILITY												
Return On Sales (%)	3.8	1.8	(0.7)	13.9	4.2	(0.7)	(1.8)	(3.1)	(4.2)	11.2	3.5	0.4
Return On Assets (%)	5.8	2.6	(1.3)	9.4	7.0	(1.1)	(2.7)	(3.5)	(5.5)	11.8	4.7	0.8
Return On Nw (%)	13.6	4.9	(5.7)	14.4	8.0	(3.4)	(5.7)	(5.8)	(14.1)	28.7	8.8	2.2

SIC 0161 VEGETABLES, MELONS — INDUSTRY ASSETS $250,000 - $500,000 — 1995 (19 Establishments)

	$	%
Cash	29,444	9.7
Accounts Receivable	45,836	15.1
Notes Receivable	—	—
Inventory	4,553	1.5
Other Current	6,982	2.3
Total Current	**86,815**	**28.6**
Fixed Assets	170,595	56.2
Other Non-current	46,140	15.2
Total Assets	**303,550**	**100.0**
Accounts Payable	7,285	2.4
Bank Loans	—	—
Notes Payable	32,480	10.7
Other Current	67,388	22.2
Total Current	**107,153**	**35.3**
Other Long Term	37,033	12.2
Deferred Credits	—	—
Net Worth	159,364	52.5
Total Liab & Net Worth	**303,550**	**100.0**
Net Sales	853,020	100.0
Gross Profit	291,733	34.2
Net Profit After Tax	41,798	4.9
Working Capital	(20,338)	—

RATIOS	UQ	MED	LQ
SOLVENCY			
Quick Ratio (times)	1.2	0.6	0.4
Current Ratio (times)	1.5	0.7	0.4
Curr Liab To Nw (%)	15.5	74.3	166.5
Curr Liab To Inv (%)	215.9	291.7	367.6
Total Liab To Nw (%)	61.2	82.8	202.0
Fixed Assets To Nw (%)	79.0	162.0	203.7
EFFICIENCY			
Coll Period (days)	8.2	12.6	35.6
Sales To Inv (times)	8.5	8.5	8.5
Assets To Sales (%)	24.0	39.7	70.3
Sales To Nwc (times)	45.9	30.0	12.4
Acct Pay To Sales (%)	1.8	3.1	8.4
PROFITABILITY			
Return On Sales (%)	12.9	9.8	2.1
Return On Assets (%)	15.7	10.7	1.3
Return On Nw (%)	31.0	12.9	2.6

SIC 0161 VEGETABLES, MELONS — INDUSTRY ASSETS $500,000 - $1,000,000 — 1995 (19 Establishments)

	$	%
Cash	43,509	5.8
Accounts Receivable	83,267	11.1
Notes Receivable	750	0.1
Inventory	81,016	10.8
Other Current	58,512	7.8
Total Current	**267,054**	**35.6**
Fixed Assets	404,332	53.9
Other Non-current	78,766	10.5
Total Assets	**750,152**	**100.0**
Accounts Payable	80,266	10.7
Bank Loans	—	—
Notes Payable	70,514	9.4
Other Current	92,269	12.3
Total Current	**243,049**	**32.4**
Other Long Term	153,031	20.4
Deferred Credits	—	—
Net Worth	354,072	47.2
Total Liab & Net Worth	**750,152**	**100.0**
Net Sales	1,837,028	100.0
Gross Profit	597,034	32.5
Net Profit After Tax	71,644	3.9
Working Capital	24,005	—

RATIOS	UQ	MED	LQ
SOLVENCY			
Quick Ratio (times)	1.1	0.4	0.2
Current Ratio (times)	3.1	1.2	0.5
Curr Liab To Nw (%)	7.0	52.4	126.4
Curr Liab To Inv (%)	62.6	104.4	130.4
Total Liab To Nw (%)	39.5	140.3	176.5
Fixed Assets To Nw (%)	63.5	106.7	165.0
EFFICIENCY			
Coll Period (days)	2.4	11.0	23.9
Sales To Inv (times)	189.5	58.4	6.3
Assets To Sales (%)	30.9	43.0	54.8
Sales To Nwc (times)	7.8	6.5	6.3
Acct Pay To Sales (%)	4.9	10.1	11.6
PROFITABILITY			
Return On Sales (%)	10.1	1.5	(0.5)
Return On Assets (%)	10.7	0.1	(1.3)
Return On Nw (%)	46.3	1.6	(2.5)

SIC 0161 VEGETABLES, MELONS — INDUSTRY ASSETS $1,000,000 - $5,000,000 — 1995 (58 Establishments)

	$	%
Cash	135,257	6.1
Accounts Receivable	381,381	17.2
Notes Receivable	17,739	0.8
Inventory	161,865	7.3
Other Current	237,254	10.7
Total Current	**933,496**	**42.1**
Fixed Assets	1,093,143	49.3
Other Non-current	190,690	8.6
Total Assets	**2,217,329**	**100.0**
Accounts Payable	203,994	9.2
Bank Loans	31,043	1.4
Notes Payable	119,736	5.4
Other Current	232,820	10.5
Total Current	**587,592**	**26.5**
Other Long Term	396,902	17.9
Deferred Credits	8,869	0.4
Net Worth	1,223,966	55.2
Total Liab & Net Worth	**2,217,329**	**100.0**
Net Sales	5,407,598	100.0
Gross Profit	1,784,507	33.0
Net Profit After Tax	378,532	7.0
Working Capital	345,904	—

RATIOS	UQ	MED	LQ
SOLVENCY			
Quick Ratio (times)	1.6	1.1	0.5
Current Ratio (times)	2.7	1.8	1.1
Curr Liab To Nw (%)	17.0	44.4	93.8
Curr Liab To Inv (%)	73.1	184.5	374.1
Total Liab To Nw (%)	48.7	72.7	157.5
Fixed Assets To Nw (%)	52.7	79.4	122.5
EFFICIENCY			
Coll Period (days)	27.0	40.9	49.3
Sales To Inv (times)	79.8	17.5	6.8
Assets To Sales (%)	32.1	46.3	68.1
Sales To Nwc (times)	25.8	9.0	4.3
Acct Pay To Sales (%)	1.8	5.1	9.5
PROFITABILITY			
Return On Sales (%)	9.9	3.5	0.8
Return On Assets (%)	9.2	3.2	0.9
Return On Nw (%)	20.7	7.4	2.3

SIC 0161 VEGETABLES, MELONS — INDUSTRY ASSETS $5,000,000 - $25,000,000 — 1995 (19 Establishments)

	$	%
Cash	1,080,216	11.9
Accounts Receivable	1,897,185	20.9
Notes Receivable	190,626	2.1
Inventory	1,098,370	12.1
Other Current	1,043,906	11.5
Total Current	**5,310,304**	**58.5**
Fixed Assets	2,777,697	30.6
Other Non-current	989,441	10.9
Total Assets	**9,077,442**	**100.0**
Accounts Payable	971,286	10.7
Bank Loans	—	—
Notes Payable	571,879	6.3
Other Current	1,170,990	12.9
Total Current	**2,714,155**	**29.9**
Other Long Term	1,107,448	12.2
Deferred Credits	54,465	0.6
Net Worth	5,201,374	57.3
Total Liab & Net Worth	**9,077,442**	**100.0**
Net Sales	12,707,844	100.0
Gross Profit	3,532,781	27.8
Net Profit After Tax	660,808	5.2
Working Capital	2,596,149	—

RATIOS	UQ	MED	LQ
SOLVENCY			
Quick Ratio (times)	2.7	1.4	0.5
Current Ratio (times)	3.5	1.8	1.4
Curr Liab To Nw (%)	16.1	55.3	112.0
Curr Liab To Inv (%)	132.8	235.6	478.6
Total Liab To Nw (%)	37.6	100.3	128.0
Fixed Assets To Nw (%)	18.6	59.7	80.6
EFFICIENCY			
Coll Period (days)	17.1	27.0	33.6
Sales To Inv (times)	48.5	30.3	11.5
Assets To Sales (%)	28.8	51.7	122.3
Sales To Nwc (times)	24.7	10.7	3.9
Acct Pay To Sales (%)	1.6	3.5	9.5
PROFITABILITY			
Return On Sales (%)	5.2	3.0	0.8
Return On Assets (%)	13.1	8.6	2.1
Return On Nw (%)	27.6	14.8	2.9

	SIC 0171 BERRY CROPS (NO BREAKDOWN) 1995 (22 Establishments) $	%	SIC 0172 GRAPES (NO BREAKDOWN) 1995 (31 Establishments) $	%	SIC 0173 TREE NUTS (NO BREAKDOWN) 1995 (18 Establishments) $	%	SIC 0174 CITRUS FRUITS (NO BREAKDOWN) 1995 (39 Establishments) $	%
Cash	245,796	11.4	195,898	5.8	146,512	5.3	360,361	7.0
Accounts Receivable	127,210	5.9	273,582	8.1	511,410	18.5	555,985	10.8
Notes Receivable	17,249	0.8	16,888	0.5	2,764	0.1	87,516	1.7
Inventory	88,400	4.1	331,001	9.8	276,438	10.0	319,177	6.2
Other Current	86,244	4.0	243,184	7.2	315,139	11.4	375,805	7.3
Total Current	**564,899**	**26.2**	**1,060,554**	**31.4**	**1,252,264**	**45.3**	**1,698,844**	**33.0**
Fixed Assets	1,050,022	48.7	2,040,046	60.4	1,064,286	38.5	2,275,422	44.2
Other Non-current	541,182	25.1	276,960	8.2	447,830	16.2	1,173,747	22.8
Total Assets	**2,156,102**	**100.0**	**3,377,559**	**100.0**	**2,764,380**	**100.0**	**5,148,013**	**100.0**
Accounts Payable	25,873	1.2	114,837	3.4	77,403	2.8	185,328	3.6
Bank Loans	—	—	—	—	—	—	—	—
Notes Payable	75,464	3.5	128,347	3.8	140,983	5.1	154,440	3.0
Other Current	118,586	5.5	226,296	6.7	431,243	15.6	550,837	10.7
Total Current	**219,922**	**10.2**	**469,481**	**13.9**	**649,629**	**23.5**	**890,606**	**17.3**
Other Long Term	355,757	16.5	844,390	25.0	569,462	20.6	1,081,083	21.0
Deferred Credits	12,937	0.6	6,755	0.2	8,293	0.3	87,516	1.7
Net Worth	1,567,486	72.7	2,056,933	60.9	1,536,995	55.6	3,088,808	60.0
Total Liab & Net Worth	**2,156,102**	**100.0**	**3,377,559**	**100.0**	**2,764,380**	**100.0**	**5,148,013**	**100.0**
Net Sales	3,800,155	100.0	2,237,818	100.0	4,709,609	100.0	5,036,324	100.0
Gross Profit	1,793,673	47.2	935,408	41.8	1,229,208	26.1	1,264,117	25.1
Net Profit After Tax	273,611	7.2	118,604	5.3	475,671	10.1	236,707	4.7
Working Capital	344,977	—	591,073	—	602,635	—	808,238	—

RATIOS	UQ	MED	LQ	UQ	MED	LQ	UQ	MED	LQ	UQ	MED	LQ
SOLVENCY												
Quick Ratio (times)	6.1	2.8	0.3	2.8	1.1	0.5	1.3	0.8	0.5	3.7	1.4	0.5
Current Ratio (times)	7.0	3.8	0.7	4.9	2.5	1.1	3.2	1.7	1.1	6.2	2.9	1.4
Curr Liab To Nw (%)	4.5	6.1	30.5	4.8	18.1	55.5	11.5	27.8	69.0	6.8	10.7	35.6
Curr Liab To Inv (%)	11.3	13.2	15.2	32.7	61.0	254.8	94.0	111.1	134.9	57.9	132.1	232.5
Total Liab To Nw (%)	5.8	19.3	33.4	18.0	48.6	135.0	18.5	76.6	177.2	12.3	65.4	154.3
Fixed Assets To Nw (%)	39.5	48.9	109.7	72.4	95.9	125.8	38.9	59.4	99.4	43.3	75.8	116.2
EFFICIENCY												
Coll Period (days)	23.9	39.3	48.8	17.3	32.5	88.6	28.6	42.0	102.6	22.3	39.1	83.6
Sales To Inv (times)	24.2	22.8	14.2	23.4	4.1	2.3	11.7	7.3	4.3	52.0	25.6	4.1
Assets To Sales (%)	80.7	168.3	216.3	83.2	236.9	342.0	56.5	72.6	244.1	68.2	135.0	267.3
Sales To Nwc (times)	5.3	4.3	2.8	7.7	3.6	2.0	11.1	7.0	3.2	7.3	5.1	1.6
Acct Pay To Sales (%)	2.7	4.9	7.0	2.5	5.0	7.7	1.7	4.2	6.9	2.1	3.6	8.1
PROFITABILITY												
Return On Sales (%)	7.5	6.2	4.9	22.3	4.6	0.8	14.4	7.3	5.4	11.7	4.7	0.7
Return On Assets (%)	7.3	3.8	2.1	6.6	4.4	0.1	9.7	5.6	5.3	6.7	3.6	0.5
Return On Nw (%)	9.1	4.3	3.9	10.9	8.5	(2.6)	23.2	17.9	9.3	10.8	5.1	2.5

SIC 0175 DECID TREE FRUITS

	NO BREAKDOWN 1995 (78 Establishments) $	%	$250,000 - $500,000 1995 (14 Establishments) $	%	$500,000 - $1,000,000 1995 (20 Establishments) $	%	$1,000,000 - $5,000,000 1995 (29 Establishments) $	%
Cash	82,951	8.4	41,506	9.8	66,334	9.8	111,495	7.0
Accounts Receivable	80,976	8.2	29,647	7.0	31,813	4.7	235,732	14.8
Notes Receivable	—	—	—	—	—	—	1,593	0.1
Inventory	58,263	5.9	3,388	0.8	43,997	6.5	66,897	4.2
Other Current	44,438	4.5	26,259	6.2	17,599	2.6	87,603	5.5
Total Current	**266,629**	**27.0**	**100,801**	**23.8**	**159,742**	**23.6**	**503,319**	**31.6**
Fixed Assets	542,146	54.9	227,438	53.7	391,233	57.8	791,613	49.7
Other Non-current	178,740	18.1	95,295	22.5	125,899	18.6	297,850	18.7
Total Assets	**987,516**	**100.0**	**423,534**	**100.0**	**676,874**	**100.0**	**1,592,782**	**100.0**
Accounts Payable	39,501	4.0	27,953	6.6	12,861	1.9	92,381	5.8
Bank Loans	1,975	0.2	—	—	4,061	0.6	—	—
Notes Payable	79,989	8.1	42,353	10.0	71,749	10.6	68,490	4.3
Other Current	77,026	7.8	9,318	2.2	47,381	7.0	116,273	7.3
Total Current	**198,491**	**20.1**	**79,624**	**18.8**	**136,052**	**20.1**	**277,144**	**17.4**
Other Long Term	264,654	26.8	83,860	19.8	161,773	23.9	433,237	27.2
Deferred Credits	3,950	0.4	—	—	4,738	0.7	6,371	0.4
Net Worth	520,421	52.7	260,050	61.4	374,311	55.3	876,030	55.0
Total Liab & Net Worth	**987,516**	**100.0**	**423,534**	**100.0**	**676,874**	**100.0**	**1,592,782**	**100.0**
Net Sales	1,329,296	100.0	439,384	100.0	839,119	100.0	2,527,328	100.0
Gross Profit	497,157	37.4	235,070	53.5	299,565	35.7	758,198	30.0
Net Profit After Tax	(1,329)	(0.1)	33,393	7.6	(14,265)	(1.7)	(50,547)	(2.0)
Working Capital	68,138	—	21,177	—	23,690	—	226,175	—

RATIOS	UQ	MED	LQ	UQ	MED	LQ	UQ	MED	LQ	UQ	MED	LQ
SOLVENCY												
Quick Ratio (times)	2.7	0.8	0.3	3.6	2.6	0.6	2.6	0.9	0.3	2.8	1.3	0.6
Current Ratio (times)	4.0	1.5	0.7	5.9	3.1	0.7	5.0	1.7	0.7	4.5	2.5	1.2
Curr Liab To Nw (%)	8.1	23.6	72.9	2.2	14.0	39.8	3.4	17.2	23.1	10.5	39.8	72.9
Curr Liab To Inv (%)	63.3	130.2	248.3	187.8	286.0	384.2	28.3	62.9	167.3	122.5	170.4	232.9
Total Liab To Nw (%)	18.5	69.9	215.6	6.8	45.7	208.3	12.5	21.8	104.0	30.1	69.9	174.6
Fixed Assets To Nw (%)	67.8	101.2	159.9	50.6	98.0	228.9	74.3	94.8	102.0	64.3	93.6	146.3
EFFICIENCY												
Coll Period (days)	10.2	23.4	49.6	6.6	6.6	6.6	8.4	15.0	23.7	23.0	35.0	65.0
Sales To Inv (times)	17.2	10.7	5.5	16.2	16.2	16.2	13.3	9.7	7.5	28.3	17.8	11.6
Assets To Sales (%)	57.6	86.7	145.6	84.8	86.1	92.1	61.9	83.8	106.5	46.0	60.4	142.2
Sales To Nwc (times)	12.8	7.0	3.2	4.9	2.4	1.8	16.9	11.6	7.8	13.2	5.6	2.9
Acct Pay To Sales (%)	1.3	2.7	5.4	0.1	0.1	0.1	1.2	1.9	2.7	3.1	4.5	6.9
PROFITABILITY												
Return On Sales (%)	3.8	0.9	(2.5)	38.5	10.0	(4.7)	0.9	(1.8)	(4.1)	3.3	1.0	0.2
Return On Assets (%)	3.9	1.2	(2.3)	28.3	12.1	3.9	0.2	(2.0)	(10.1)	2.7	1.8	0.4
Return On Nw (%)	10.5	3.8	(4.0)	47.7	40.0	16.9	(0.5)	(4.0)	(11.4)	8.8	4.0	0.9

SIC 0179 FRTS,TREE NUTS,NEC (NO BREAKDOWN) — 1995 (12 Establishments)

	$	%
Cash	296,700	10.0
Accounts Receivable	341,205	11.5
Notes Receivable	—	—
Inventory	323,403	10.9
Other Current	471,753	15.9
Total Current	**1,433,060**	**48.3**
Fixed Assets	1,023,614	34.5
Other Non-current	510,324	17.2
Total Assets	**2,966,998**	**100.0**
Accounts Payable	341,205	11.5
Bank Loans	77,142	2.6
Notes Payable	44,505	1.5
Other Current	620,103	20.9
Total Current	**1,082,954**	**36.5**
Other Long Term	720,981	24.3
Deferred Credits	5,934	0.2
Net Worth	1,157,129	39.0
Total Liab & Net Worth	**2,966,998**	**100.0**
Net Sales	2,418,498	100.0
Gross Profit	948,051	39.2
Net Profit After Tax	108,832	4.5
Working Capital	350,106	—

RATIOS	UQ	MED	LQ
SOLVENCY			
Quick Ratio (times)	1.0	0.5	0.4
Current Ratio (times)	2.5	1.5	0.7
Curr Liab To Nw (%)	46.1	67.5	117.0
Curr Liab To Inv (%)	152.1	185.9	279.9
Total Liab To Nw (%)	123.9	272.9	356.8
Fixed Assets To Nw (%)	45.6	164.7	249.2
EFFICIENCY			
Coll Period (days)	10.3	31.0	45.7
Sales To Inv (times)	103.0	9.1	6.3
Assets To Sales (%)	27.5	73.3	111.5
Sales To Nwc (times)	15.0	6.0	4.8
Acct Pay To Sales (%)	0.6	4.4	6.2
PROFITABILITY			
Return On Sales (%)	6.3	1.4	(1.1)
Return On Assets (%)	14.2	1.8	(0.8)
Return On Nw (%)	26.9	6.3	(2.0)

SIC 0181 ORNMNTL NURS PRDCTS (NO BREAKDOWN) — 1995 (311 Establishments)

	$	%
Cash	96,569	12.2
Accounts Receivable	108,442	13.7
Notes Receivable	7,916	1.0
Inventory	153,561	19.4
Other Current	26,121	3.3
Total Current	**392,609**	**49.6**
Fixed Assets	309,496	39.1
Other Non-current	89,445	11.3
Total Assets	**791,551**	**100.0**
Accounts Payable	57,783	7.3
Bank Loans	2,375	0.3
Notes Payable	38,786	4.9
Other Current	96,569	12.2
Total Current	**195,513**	**24.7**
Other Long Term	136,147	17.2
Deferred Credits	3,166	0.4
Net Worth	456,725	57.7
Total Liab & Net Worth	**791,551**	**100.0**
Net Sales	1,640,311	100.0
Gross Profit	739,780	45.1
Net Profit After Tax	83,656	5.1
Working Capital	197,096	—

RATIOS	UQ	MED	LQ
SOLVENCY			
Quick Ratio (times)	2.7	1.0	0.4
Current Ratio (times)	5.5	2.5	1.2
Curr Liab To Nw (%)	10.7	29.3	71.2
Curr Liab To Inv (%)	38.5	86.9	186.4
Total Liab To Nw (%)	20.3	58.9	143.7
Fixed Assets To Nw (%)	37.8	65.9	127.5
EFFICIENCY			
Coll Period (days)	14.0	29.4	45.7
Sales To Inv (times)	29.0	8.2	3.4
Assets To Sales (%)	30.7	53.9	88.5
Sales To Nwc (times)	13.9	6.4	2.8
Acct Pay To Sales (%)	1.7	3.3	6.9
PROFITABILITY			
Return On Sales (%)	9.2	3.6	1.2
Return On Assets (%)	12.4	5.0	1.8
Return On Nw (%)	26.2	8.9	3.1

SIC 0181 ORNMNTL NURS PRDCTS — INDUSTRY ASSETS UNDER $100,000 — 1995 (23 Establishments)

	$	%
Cash	18,387	29.4
Accounts Receivable	2,877	4.6
Notes Receivable	63	0.1
Inventory	7,130	11.4
Other Current	2,001	3.2
Total Current	**30,457**	**48.7**
Fixed Assets	27,768	44.4
Other Non-current	4,315	6.9
Total Assets	**62,541**	**100.0**
Accounts Payable	2,314	3.7
Bank Loans	—	—
Notes Payable	2,689	4.3
Other Current	13,696	21.9
Total Current	**18,700**	**29.9**
Other Long Term	16,949	27.1
Deferred Credits	—	—
Net Worth	26,893	43.0
Total Liab & Net Worth	**62,541**	**100.0**
Net Sales	248,670	100.0
Gross Profit	148,456	59.7
Net Profit After Tax	31,332	12.6
Working Capital	11,757	—

RATIOS	UQ	MED	LQ
SOLVENCY			
Quick Ratio (times)	0.6	0.3	0.2
Current Ratio (times)	1.4	0.9	0.7
Curr Liab To Nw (%)	5.1	22.9	35.7
Curr Liab To Inv (%)	31.6	88.8	100.5
Total Liab To Nw (%)	12.6	67.1	110.1
Fixed Assets To Nw (%)	29.4	63.7	120.0
EFFICIENCY			
Coll Period (days)	9.2	13.9	15.7
Sales To Inv (times)	2.1	2.1	1.5
Assets To Sales (%)	13.8	27.4	33.2
Sales To Nwc (times)	9.6	5.2	2.9
Acct Pay To Sales (%)	0.5	0.6	0.9
PROFITABILITY			
Return On Sales (%)	3.9	2.8	(0.2)
Return On Assets (%)	3.9	2.7	(0.2)
Return On Nw (%)	7.2	2.1	(31.1)

SIC 0181 ORNMNTL NURS PRDCTS — INDUSTRY ASSETS $100,000 - $250,000 — 1995 (47 Establishments)

	$	%
Cash	27,772	15.8
Accounts Receivable	29,354	16.7
Notes Receivable	2,637	1.5
Inventory	24,432	13.9
Other Current	5,976	3.4
Total Current	**90,172**	**51.3**
Fixed Assets	65,915	37.5
Other Non-current	19,687	11.2
Total Assets	**175,773**	**100.0**
Accounts Payable	20,038	11.4
Bank Loans	—	—
Notes Payable	2,285	1.3
Other Current	29,706	16.9
Total Current	**52,029**	**29.6**
Other Long Term	32,518	18.5
Deferred Credits	176	0.1
Net Worth	91,050	51.8
Total Liab & Net Worth	**175,773**	**100.0**
Net Sales	455,468	100.0
Gross Profit	255,062	56.0
Net Profit After Tax	24,595	5.4
Working Capital	38,143	—

RATIOS	UQ	MED	LQ
SOLVENCY			
Quick Ratio (times)	4.3	1.6	0.5
Current Ratio (times)	6.7	3.1	0.9
Curr Liab To Nw (%)	11.2	40.5	140.5
Curr Liab To Inv (%)	44.1	102.5	160.6
Total Liab To Nw (%)	12.7	77.2	300.5
Fixed Assets To Nw (%)	39.6	79.5	142.3
EFFICIENCY			
Coll Period (days)	5.9	18.6	28.9
Sales To Inv (times)	31.2	20.0	9.5
Assets To Sales (%)	22.5	28.8	44.8
Sales To Nwc (times)	11.3	7.8	5.3
Acct Pay To Sales (%)	0.7	2.2	2.7
PROFITABILITY			
Return On Sales (%)	9.5	2.5	(0.1)
Return On Assets (%)	17.5	5.6	(0.2)
Return On Nw (%)	77.0	11.0	(0.2)

SIC 0181 ORNMNTL NURS PRDCTS — INDUSTRY ASSETS $250,000 - $500,000 — 1995 (41 Establishments)

	$	%
Cash	59,384	15.9
Accounts Receivable	43,698	11.7
Notes Receivable	747	0.2
Inventory	39,963	10.7
Other Current	5,229	1.4
Total Current	**149,021**	**39.9**
Fixed Assets	190,104	50.9
Other Non-current	34,361	9.2
Total Assets	**373,486**	**100.0**
Accounts Payable	25,397	6.8
Bank Loans	—	—
Notes Payable	19,048	5.1
Other Current	37,349	10.0
Total Current	**81,793**	**21.9**
Other Long Term	66,107	17.7
Deferred Credits	373	0.1
Net Worth	225,212	60.3
Total Liab & Net Worth	**373,486**	**100.0**
Net Sales	933,186	100.0
Gross Profit	458,194	49.1
Net Profit After Tax	36,394	3.9
Working Capital	67,228	—

RATIOS	UQ	MED	LQ
SOLVENCY			
Quick Ratio (times)	3.3	1.4	0.5
Current Ratio (times)	8.0	1.9	1.1
Curr Liab To Nw (%)	8.7	19.9	68.9
Curr Liab To Inv (%)	43.9	122.5	277.9
Total Liab To Nw (%)	16.3	70.0	124.3
Fixed Assets To Nw (%)	66.8	86.1	143.3
EFFICIENCY			
Coll Period (days)	18.3	19.6	24.2
Sales To Inv (times)	69.0	29.8	13.2
Assets To Sales (%)	24.9	38.0	51.0
Sales To Nwc (times)	23.7	11.5	7.8
Acct Pay To Sales (%)	1.6	3.2	6.7
PROFITABILITY			
Return On Sales (%)	7.5	3.0	0.7
Return On Assets (%)	12.4	6.8	1.3
Return On Nw (%)	18.2	9.6	1.4

SIC 0181 ORNMNTL NURS PRDCTS — INDUSTRY ASSETS $500,000 - $1,000,000 — 1995 (66 Establishments)

	$	%
Cash	97,272	13.3
Accounts Receivable	92,152	12.6
Notes Receivable	12,433	1.7
Inventory	182,842	25.0
Other Current	10,971	1.5
Total Current	**395,670**	**54.1**
Fixed Assets	271,338	37.1
Other Non-current	64,360	8.8
Total Assets	**731,368**	**100.0**
Accounts Payable	60,704	8.3
Bank Loans	3,657	0.5
Notes Payable	25,598	3.5
Other Current	77,525	10.6
Total Current	**167,483**	**22.9**
Other Long Term	135,303	18.5
Deferred Credits	5,120	0.7
Net Worth	423,462	57.9
Total Liab & Net Worth	**731,368**	**100.0**
Net Sales	1,541,220	100.0
Gross Profit	661,183	42.9
Net Profit After Tax	84,767	5.5
Working Capital	228,187	—

RATIOS	UQ	MED	LQ
SOLVENCY			
Quick Ratio (times)	3.2	1.0	0.4
Current Ratio (times)	5.8	2.9	1.5
Curr Liab To Nw (%)	12.3	28.1	59.7
Curr Liab To Inv (%)	39.9	74.5	148.4
Total Liab To Nw (%)	22.7	68.4	176.4
Fixed Assets To Nw (%)	30.6	64.1	97.5
EFFICIENCY			
Coll Period (days)	11.5	22.4	41.9
Sales To Inv (times)	31.0	7.6	3.4
Assets To Sales (%)	31.1	49.7	73.1
Sales To Nwc (times)	16.1	6.8	2.7
Acct Pay To Sales (%)	2.6	4.4	6.8
PROFITABILITY			
Return On Sales (%)	8.2	3.3	0.3
Return On Assets (%)	11.4	6.4	0.3
Return On Nw (%)	31.8	8.9	0.9

SIC 0181 ORNMNTL NURS PRDCTS — INDUSTRY ASSETS $1,000,000 - $5,000,000 — 1995 (101 Establishments)

	$	%
Cash	157,440	7.5
Accounts Receivable	363,161	17.3
Notes Receivable	12,595	0.6
Inventory	398,847	19.0
Other Current	96,563	4.6
Total Current	**1,028,606**	**49.0**
Fixed Assets	822,884	39.2
Other Non-current	247,705	11.8
Total Assets	**2,099,195**	**100.0**
Accounts Payable	144,844	6.9
Bank Loans	4,198	0.2
Notes Payable	151,142	7.2
Other Current	216,217	10.3
Total Current	**516,402**	**24.6**
Other Long Term	319,078	15.2
Deferred Credits	6,298	0.3
Net Worth	1,257,418	59.9
Total Liab & Net Worth	**2,099,195**	**100.0**
Net Sales	3,666,928	100.0
Gross Profit	1,492,440	40.7
Net Profit After Tax	165,012	4.5
Working Capital	512,204	—

RATIOS	UQ	MED	LQ
SOLVENCY			
Quick Ratio (times)	2.0	1.0	0.5
Current Ratio (times)	5.0	2.3	1.2
Curr Liab To Nw (%)	11.6	34.2	73.3
Curr Liab To Inv (%)	34.7	86.8	194.4
Total Liab To Nw (%)	25.4	49.1	116.6
Fixed Assets To Nw (%)	37.9	56.3	133.7
EFFICIENCY			
Coll Period (days)	20.1	37.2	66.3
Sales To Inv (times)	19.5	7.2	2.8
Assets To Sales (%)	44.3	60.2	94.0
Sales To Nwc (times)	10.2	5.4	2.6
Acct Pay To Sales (%)	2.3	4.3	7.4
PROFITABILITY			
Return On Sales (%)	8.7	3.1	1.6
Return On Assets (%)	11.7	4.4	2.4
Return On Nw (%)	19.4	8.9	4.1

SIC 0181 ORNMNTL NURS PRDCTS — INDUSTRY ASSETS $5,000,000-$25,000,000 — 1995 (27 Establishments)

	$	%
Cash	194,502	2.6
Accounts Receivable	605,948	8.1
Notes Receivable	89,770	1.2
Inventory	2,640,738	35.3
Other Current	329,157	4.4
Total Current	**3,860,115**	**51.6**
Fixed Assets	2,034,789	27.2
Other Non-current	1,585,939	21.2
Total Assets	**7,480,843**	**100.0**
Accounts Payable	239,387	3.2
Bank Loans	97,251	1.3
Notes Payable	508,697	6.8
Other Current	770,527	10.3
Total Current	**1,615,862**	**21.6**
Other Long Term	890,220	11.9
Deferred Credits	97,251	1.3
Net Worth	4,877,510	65.2
Total Liab & Net Worth	**7,480,843**	**100.0**
Net Sales	6,283,305	100.0
Gross Profit	2,274,556	36.2
Net Profit After Tax	232,482	3.7
Working Capital	2,244,253	—

RATIOS	UQ	MED	LQ
SOLVENCY			
Quick Ratio (times)	0.8	0.5	0.3
Current Ratio (times)	4.1	2.7	1.6
Curr Liab To Nw (%)	11.2	24.6	62.1
Curr Liab To Inv (%)	36.5	59.5	151.9
Total Liab To Nw (%)	17.8	38.2	116.6
Fixed Assets To Nw (%)	36.7	44.3	60.7
EFFICIENCY			
Coll Period (days)	14.1	35.4	45.6
Sales To Inv (times)	7.8	3.2	1.2
Assets To Sales (%)	92.4	125.6	248.7
Sales To Nwc (times)	10.5	2.8	1.5
Acct Pay To Sales (%)	2.2	3.3	8.0
PROFITABILITY			
Return On Sales (%)	9.5	4.4	(0.1)
Return On Assets (%)	8.5	3.7	0.6
Return On Nw (%)	12.3	7.9	1.0

SIC 0182 — CROPS, GRWN UNDR CVR (NO BREAKDOWN) — 1995 (19 Establishments)
SIC 0191 — GEN FARMS, PRIM CROP (NO BREAKDOWN) — 1995 (143 Establishments)
SIC 0191 — GEN FARMS, PRIM CROP — INDUSTRY ASSETS $250,000 - $500,000 — 1995 (28 Establishments)
SIC 0191 — GEN FARMS, PRIM CROP — INDUSTRY ASSETS $500,000 - $1,000,000 — 1995 (25 Establishments)

	SIC 0182 $	%	SIC 0191 (No Brkdn) $	%	SIC 0191 $250k–500k $	%	SIC 0191 $500k–1M $	%
Cash	93,261	8.3	130,156	11.2	58,734	16.2	46,860	7.3
Accounts Receivable	224,726	20.0	88,320	7.6	34,805	9.6	37,873	5.9
Notes Receivable	1,124	0.1	10,459	0.9	725	0.2	23,109	3.6
Inventory	105,621	9.4	101,103	8.7	29,729	8.2	31,454	4.9
Other Current	39,327	3.5	88,320	7.6	47,857	13.2	39,799	6.2
Total Current	**464,060**	**41.3**	**418,357**	**36.0**	**171,850**	**47.4**	**179,096**	**27.9**
Fixed Assets	524,736	46.7	518,298	44.6	140,308	38.7	246,498	38.4
Other Non-current	134,836	12.0	225,448	19.4	50,395	13.9	216,327	33.7
Total Assets	**1,123,631**	**100.0**	**1,162,104**	**100.0**	**362,553**	**100.0**	**641,921**	**100.0**
Accounts Payable	117,981	10.5	54,619	4.7	19,215	5.3	7,061	1.1
Bank Loans	4,495	0.4	—	—	—	—	—	—
Notes Payable	39,327	3.5	79,023	6.8	25,741	7.1	55,205	8.6
Other Current	104,498	9.3	119,697	10.3	48,945	13.5	71,895	11.2
Total Current	**266,301**	**23.7**	**253,339**	**21.8**	**93,901**	**25.9**	**134,161**	**20.9**
Other Long Term	284,279	25.3	206,855	17.8	65,622	18.1	142,506	22.2
Deferred Credits	—	—	5,811	0.5	—	—	—	—
Net Worth	573,052	51.0	696,100	59.9	203,030	56.0	365,253	56.9
Total Liab & Net Worth	**1,123,631**	**100.0**	**1,162,104**	**100.0**	**362,553**	**100.0**	**641,921**	**100.0**
Net Sales	9,612,860	100.0	1,564,234	100.0	733,461	100.0	1,274,016	100.0
Gross Profit	3,489,468	36.3	760,218	48.6	319,056	43.5	580,951	45.6
Net Profit After Tax	615,223	6.4	123,574	7.9	49,875	6.8	26,754	2.1
Working Capital	197,759	—	165,018	—	77,949	—	44,935	—

RATIOS

	SIC 0182 UQ	MED	LQ	SIC 0191 (NB) UQ	MED	LQ	SIC 0191 $250k–500k UQ	MED	LQ	SIC 0191 $500k–1M UQ	MED	LQ
SOLVENCY												
Quick Ratio (times)	1.7	1.1	0.7	1.5	0.8	0.3	1.5	0.4	0.2	1.1	0.8	0.3
Current Ratio (times)	2.3	1.7	1.2	4.3	1.6	0.9	2.4	1.6	1.0	2.2	1.5	1.0
Curr Liab To Nw (%)	28.7	53.4	72.3	7.2	26.7	78.6	7.5	20.9	68.1	10.8	39.7	90.6
Curr Liab To Inv (%)	93.0	206.0	290.8	40.7	118.7	196.8	118.1	126.1	232.0	24.5	174.0	190.5
Total Liab To Nw (%)	52.3	114.7	188.3	19.4	51.9	130.2	11.3	27.9	80.6	31.6	82.3	145.9
Fixed Assets To Nw (%)	75.2	97.9	141.3	41.1	86.6	124.0	28.2	52.8	76.5	38.3	94.5	138.7
EFFICIENCY												
Coll Period (days)	28.1	45.3	60.1	10.8	23.4	41.3	2.2	12.1	20.8	15.6	17.2	28.3
Sales To Inv (times)	31.5	22.7	10.7	20.3	9.2	3.3	36.2	21.4	16.5	19.0	17.6	16.7
Assets To Sales (%)	26.6	49.7	105.8	43.1	93.5	145.9	14.7	22.7	36.6	30.4	45.8	61.6
Sales To Nwc (times)	19.1	9.5	5.9	28.4	9.5	2.6	28.4	25.5	11.9	40.9	12.4	12.0
Acct Pay To Sales (%)	3.0	4.7	9.3	1.5	3.4	4.6	1.0	1.5	1.5	0.6	1.0	2.3
PROFITABILITY												
Return On Sales (%)	10.0	8.6	6.0	19.4	8.4	1.4	12.4	8.9	3.5	2.5	1.6	1.4
Return On Assets (%)	18.0	11.8	7.2	15.5	6.6	2.2	23.1	22.0	0.2	7.6	5.3	2.9
Return On Nw (%)	38.9	23.9	17.7	28.2	15.7	4.1	60.3	29.6	0.2	19.4	14.8	6.8

	SIC 0191 GEN FARMS, PRIM CROP — INDUSTRY ASSETS $1,000,000-$5,000,000 — 1995 (52 Establishments)		SIC 02 AGRICULTURAL PRD LVSK (NO BREAKDOWN) — 1995 (481 Establishments)		SIC 02 AGRICULTURAL PRD LVSK — NORTHEAST — 1995 (55 Establishments)		SIC 02 AGRICULTURAL PRD LVSK — CENTRAL — 1995 (191 Establishments)	
	$	%	$	%	$	%	$	%
Cash	114,929	5.6	130,241	6.5	67,226	5.0	134,310	6.8
Accounts Receivable	129,295	6.3	240,446	12.0	92,772	6.9	304,172	15.4
Notes Receivable	12,314	0.6	28,052	1.4	22,857	1.7	19,751	1.0
Inventory	192,916	9.4	354,658	17.7	211,090	15.7	422,681	21.4
Other Current	106,720	5.2	122,227	6.1	68,571	5.1	140,235	7.1
Total Current	**556,174**	**27.1**	**875,623**	**43.7**	**462,516**	**34.4**	**1,021,150**	**51.7**
Fixed Assets	1,073,354	52.3	783,453	39.1	716,631	53.3	624,146	31.6
Other Non-current	422,774	20.6	344,639	17.2	165,376	12.3	329,849	16.7
Total Assets	**2,052,303**	**100.0**	**2,003,715**	**100.0**	**1,344,524**	**100.0**	**1,975,145**	**100.0**
Accounts Payable	75,935	3.7	128,238	6.4	84,705	6.3	161,962	8.2
Bank Loans	—	—	6,011	0.3	1,345	0.1	3,950	0.2
Notes Payable	147,766	7.2	138,256	6.9	67,226	5.0	112,583	5.7
Other Current	184,707	9.0	292,542	14.6	162,687	12.1	391,079	19.8
Total Current	**408,408**	**19.9**	**565,048**	**28.2**	**315,963**	**23.5**	**669,574**	**33.9**
Other Long Term	379,676	18.5	380,706	19.0	340,165	25.3	343,675	17.4
Deferred Credits	14,366	0.7	6,011	0.3	1,345	0.1	3,950	0.2
Net Worth	1,249,853	60.9	1,051,950	52.5	687,052	51.1	957,945	48.5
Total Liab & Net Worth	**2,052,303**	**100.0**	**2,003,715**	**100.0**	**1,344,524**	**100.0**	**1,975,145**	**100.0**
Net Sales	2,094,452	100.0	2,778,467	100.0	1,213,904	100.0	2,688,392	100.0
Gross Profit	1,250,388	59.7	869,660	31.3	461,284	38.0	914,053	34.0
Net Profit After Tax	257,618	12.3	119,474	4.3	76,476	6.3	118,289	4.4
Working Capital	147,766	—	310,575	—	146,553	—	351,576	—

RATIOS	UQ	MED	LQ	UQ	MED	LQ	UQ	MED	LQ	UQ	MED	LQ
SOLVENCY												
Quick Ratio (times)	1.0	0.5	0.3	1.2	0.5	0.2	1.3	0.5	0.3	1.0	0.5	0.2
Current Ratio (times)	3.0	1.2	0.7	3.7	1.5	1.0	3.2	1.6	1.0	3.7	1.4	1.0
Curr Liab To Nw (%)	7.4	21.9	50.5	10.9	35.1	99.8	8.1	26.5	85.2	15.7	49.0	139.0
Curr Liab To Inv (%)	40.7	129.3	178.3	55.0	120.6	322.5	53.5	106.7	284.6	51.8	117.7	324.1
Total Liab To Nw (%)	25.8	48.6	112.3	24.1	76.1	148.3	33.1	69.3	160.4	29.8	92.4	209.9
Fixed Assets To Nw (%)	59.4	95.6	122.6	36.6	80.2	124.0	53.7	88.2	122.8	30.6	79.1	141.4
EFFICIENCY												
Coll Period (days)	6.1	23.0	50.0	12.8	23.4	35.4	11.5	23.6	35.8	13.5	24.5	31.3
Sales To Inv (times)	12.9	7.3	3.2	17.0	7.8	4.0	21.1	9.8	4.3	10.4	7.2	3.5
Assets To Sales (%)	95.8	126.2	205.9	44.1	72.7	120.4	53.3	82.2	165.0	51.8	76.8	95.6
Sales To Nwc (times)	38.0	4.4	2.4	14.5	7.2	3.5	14.1	8.0	6.3	17.3	7.8	3.9
Acct Pay To Sales (%)	1.8	6.2	8.7	1.9	4.0	6.8	1.3	4.4	9.1	2.8	4.8	6.9
PROFITABILITY												
Return On Sales (%)	26.1	15.7	2.8	8.2	2.5	—	10.6	3.1	(0.5)	7.9	4.6	1.1
Return On Assets (%)	13.0	6.6	4.2	8.8	4.3	(0.5)	12.2	4.7	0.7	9.6	6.5	1.4
Return On Nw (%)	20.2	11.1	8.7	18.5	8.4	(0.4)	23.1	9.3	(0.5)	23.3	9.8	3.7

	SIC 02 AGRICULTURAL PRD LVSK SOUTH 1995 (127 Establishments) $	%	SIC 02 AGRICULTURAL PRD LVSK WEST 1995 (108 Establishments) $	%	SIC 02 AGRICULTURAL PRD LVSK INDUSTRY ASSETS $100,000 - $250,000 1995 (27 Establishments) $	%	SIC 02 AGRICULTURAL PRD LVSK INDUSTRY ASSETS $250,000 - $500,000 1995 (55 Establishments) $	%
Cash	114,708	4.7	190,094	8.8	22,859	13.2	33,491	8.3
Accounts Receivable	290,431	11.9	203,055	9.4	13,681	7.9	37,527	9.3
Notes Receivable	46,371	1.9	25,922	1.2	520	0.3	807	0.2
Inventory	414,902	17.0	300,263	13.9	30,479	17.6	77,474	19.2
Other Current	139,114	5.7	118,809	5.5	6,408	3.7	15,737	3.9
Total Current	**1,005,527**	**41.2**	**838,143**	**38.8**	**73,947**	**42.7**	**165,036**	**40.9**
Fixed Assets	1,056,780	43.3	827,342	38.3	76,025	43.9	159,387	39.5
Other Non-current	378,293	15.5	494,677	22.9	23,206	13.4	79,088	19.6
Total Assets	**2,440,600**	**100.0**	**2,160,162**	**100.0**	**173,178**	**100.0**	**403,512**	**100.0**
Accounts Payable	148,877	6.1	88,567	4.1	6,927	4.0	24,211	6.0
Bank Loans	14,644	0.6		—		—		—
Notes Payable	229,416	9.4	146,891	6.8	12,988	7.5	14,123	3.5
Other Current	266,025	10.9	265,700	12.3	25,457	14.7	44,790	11.1
Total Current	**658,962**	**27.0**	**501,158**	**23.2**	**45,373**	**26.2**	**83,123**	**20.6**
Other Long Term	444,189	18.2	416,911	19.3	17,491	10.1	76,264	18.9
Deferred Credits	4,881	0.2	12,961	0.6		—		—
Net Worth	1,332,568	54.6	1,229,132	56.9	110,314	63.7	244,125	60.5
Total Liab & Net Worth	**2,440,600**	**100.0**	**2,160,162**	**100.0**	**173,178**	**100.0**	**403,512**	**100.0**
Net Sales	4,070,752	100.0	3,117,353	100.0	214,160	100.0	475,775	100.0
Gross Profit	1,152,023	28.3	894,680	28.7	92,517	43.2	251,685	52.9
Net Profit After Tax	142,476	3.5	127,811	4.1	13,920	6.5	34,256	7.2
Working Capital	346,565	—	336,985	—	28,574	—	81,913	—

RATIOS	UQ	MED	LQ	UQ	MED	LQ	UQ	MED	LQ	UQ	MED	LQ
SOLVENCY												
Quick Ratio (times)	1.1	0.6	0.2	1.8	0.7	0.2	6.2	0.9	0.2	1.7	0.5	0.2
Current Ratio (times)	3.1	1.5	0.8	4.9	1.8	1.1	6.2	4.6	0.4	6.9	2.5	1.0
Curr Liab To Nw (%)	12.3	34.3	86.0	6.7	24.1	76.2	9.2	27.7	85.6	5.7	13.4	52.4
Curr Liab To Inv (%)	64.8	123.4	312.6	56.2	122.9	321.1	22.8	187.0	436.3	16.8	65.8	272.6
Total Liab To Nw (%)	27.6	71.1	129.3	17.7	47.2	135.7	14.6	28.3	104.4	7.4	18.8	117.3
Fixed Assets To Nw (%)	47.8	80.2	117.5	27.1	79.1	114.9	31.5	113.6	166.4	21.0	61.7	119.1
EFFICIENCY												
Coll Period (days)	16.1	23.4	38.7	12.1	17.2	30.5	6.5	7.1	7.8	12.9	15.7	24.5
Sales To Inv (times)	21.8	9.7	4.4	17.3	5.6	3.4	5.4	5.4	5.4	6.2	3.6	2.3
Assets To Sales (%)	38.7	50.2	101.6	57.7	83.1	166.3	15.2	22.3	88.0	61.8	94.9	173.3
Sales To Nwc (times)	14.5	7.6	4.4	10.8	3.8	2.2	15.2	11.2	7.5	10.8	3.8	2.0
Acct Pay To Sales (%)	1.4	4.0	6.1	2.3	3.6	7.1	5.3	10.2	15.0	2.4	3.0	9.6
PROFITABILITY												
Return On Sales (%)	4.5	2.0	0.3	9.6	2.5	(0.4)	8.9	6.5	6.0	12.3	3.1	1.7
Return On Assets (%)	7.4	3.5	(0.8)	10.2	2.0	(0.9)	47.8	29.8	15.9	10.9	4.8	1.1
Return On Nw (%)	17.3	7.7	(0.8)	13.8	4.0	(1.0)	58.3	53.1	42.1	22.4	11.3	3.4

SIC 02 AGRICULTURAL PRD LVSK

Balance sheet figures ($) and percent (%) by industry asset size; 1995

	SIC 02 PRD LVSK $500,000–$1,000,000 (90 Establishments) $	%	SIC 02 PRD LVSK $1,000,000–$5,000,000 (176 Establishments) $	%	SIC 02 PRD LVSK $5,000,000–$25,000,000 (100 Establishments) $	%	SIC 0211 BEEF CATTLE, FEEDLOT (NO BREAKDOWN) (143 Establishments) $	%
Cash	57,502	7.4	112,267	5.0	371,955	4.8	176,981	6.3
Accounts Receivable	90,915	11.7	271,685	12.1	1,177,857	15.2	640,501	22.8
Notes Receivable	4,662	0.6	40,416	1.8	201,476	2.6	58,994	2.1
Inventory	100,240	12.9	413,141	18.4	1,534,314	19.8	654,548	23.3
Other Current	41,961	5.4	150,437	6.7	464,944	6.0	171,362	6.1
Total Current	**295,281**	**38.0**	**987,947**	**44.0**	**3,750,545**	**48.4**	**1,702,386**	**60.6**
Fixed Assets	369,878	47.6	844,245	37.6	2,572,688	33.2	792,199	28.2
Other Non-current	111,896	14.4	413,141	18.4	1,425,827	18.4	314,632	11.2
Total Assets	**777,054**	**100.0**	**2,245,333**	**100.0**	**7,749,059**	**100.0**	**2,809,217**	**100.0**
Accounts Payable	53,617	6.9	136,965	6.1	565,681	7.3	266,876	9.5
Bank Loans	777	0.1	4,491	0.2	61,992	0.8	14,046	0.5
Notes Payable	56,725	7.3	172,891	7.7	674,168	8.7	286,540	10.2
Other Current	99,463	12.8	287,403	12.8	1,425,827	18.4	634,883	22.6
Total Current	**210,582**	**27.1**	**601,749**	**26.8**	**2,727,669**	**35.2**	**1,202,345**	**42.8**
Other Long Term	166,290	21.4	426,613	19.0	1,232,100	15.9	325,869	11.6
Deferred Credits	—	—	4,491	0.2	23,247	0.3	5,618	0.2
Net Worth	400,183	51.5	1,212,480	54.0	3,766,043	48.6	1,275,385	45.4
Total Liab & Net Worth	**777,054**	**100.0**	**2,245,333**	**100.0**	**7,749,059**	**100.0**	**2,809,217**	**100.0**
Net Sales	1,181,657	100.0	2,846,622	100.0	9,348,431	100.0	7,162,299	100.0
Gross Profit	298,959	25.3	1,016,244	35.7	2,467,986	26.4	1,618,680	22.6
Net Profit After Tax	76,808	6.5	79,705	2.8	383,286	4.1	322,303	4.5
Working Capital	84,699	—	386,198	—	1,022,876	—	500,041	—

RATIOS (UQ / MED / LQ)

	$500,000–$1,000,000 UQ	MED	LQ	$1,000,000–$5,000,000 UQ	MED	LQ	$5,000,000–$25,000,000 UQ	MED	LQ	BEEF CATTLE, FEEDLOT UQ	MED	LQ
SOLVENCY												
Quick Ratio (times)	1.3	0.5	0.2	1.1	0.6	0.3	1.0	0.5	0.2	1.0	0.5	0.3
Current Ratio (times)	3.2	1.2	0.7	3.7	1.7	1.1	2.0	1.3	1.0	2.2	1.3	1.1
Curr Liab To Nw (%)	13.4	27.7	76.9	9.0	29.1	86.3	27.2	69.0	154.0	29.6	94.3	204.8
Curr Liab To Inv (%)	57.9	134.6	342.1	47.1	114.7	276.1	85.9	190.5	421.2	85.8	192.8	384.5
Total Liab To Nw (%)	16.0	48.1	124.5	28.0	71.4	132.1	52.9	105.8	217.1	39.2	111.8	213.0
Fixed Assets To Nw (%)	52.0	104.1	153.2	37.6	72.7	108.5	41.0	78.8	136.5	27.1	70.1	120.5
EFFICIENCY												
Coll Period (days)	11.7	22.9	30.7	12.3	23.4	37.7	16.8	24.8	45.7	15.3	27.6	45.1
Sales To Inv (times)	27.4	11.2	3.4	14.9	9.1	4.2	18.6	6.2	3.6	17.8	10.3	4.2
Assets To Sales (%)	39.8	70.2	96.3	39.7	66.8	154.7	49.3	78.2	132.6	36.3	50.3	75.2
Sales To Nwc (times)	15.7	5.5	1.9	14.7	7.3	3.7	11.1	6.8	4.1	15.5	8.4	4.5
Acct Pay To Sales (%)	1.6	3.5	6.2	2.8	4.3	8.8	1.5	4.1	6.2	2.1	3.5	6.0
PROFITABILITY												
Return On Sales (%)	11.2	2.1	(3.0)	8.4	2.5	(0.1)	7.2	2.0	0.1	6.8	2.5	0.5
Return On Assets (%)	8.9	3.1	(3.2)	7.8	4.3	(0.5)	7.4	3.6	(0.1)	7.1	3.6	0.3
Return On Nw (%)	12.5	4.3	(5.7)	19.8	7.6	(0.6)	16.5	8.2	(0.4)	18.5	8.4	0.1

Notes:
- SIC 02 AGRICULTURAL PRD LVSK INDUSTRY ASSETS $500,000–$1,000,000, 1995 (90 Establishments)
- SIC 02 AGRICULTURAL PRD LVSK INDUSTRY ASSETS $1,000,000–$5,000,000, 1995 (176 Establishments)
- SIC 02 AGRICULTURAL PRD LVSK INDUSTRY ASSETS $5,000,000–$25,000,000, 1995 (100 Establishments)
- SIC 0211 BEEF CATTLE, FEEDLOT (NO BREAKDOWN), 1995 (143 Establishments)

SIC 0211 BEEF CATTLE, FEEDLOT — INDUSTRY ASSETS $500,000 - $1,000,000 — 1995 (21 Establishments)
SIC 0211 BEEF CATTLE, FEEDLOT — INDUSTRY ASSETS $1,000,000 - $5,000,000 — 1995 (62 Establishments)
SIC 0211 BEEF CATTLE, FEEDLOT — INDUSTRY ASSETS $5,000,000 - $25,000,000 — 1995 (37 Establishments)
SIC 0212 BF CTTLE, EXC FDLOT — (NO BREAKDOWN) — 1995 (75 Establishments)

	SIC 0211 $500K-$1M $	%	SIC 0211 $1M-$5M $	%	SIC 0211 $5M-$25M $	%	SIC 0212 $	%
Cash	38,548	5.3	160,603	6.2	519,187	6.7	93,565	9.5
Accounts Receivable	210,196	28.9	536,207	20.7	2,022,504	26.1	55,154	5.6
Notes Receivable	—	—	51,807	2.0	340,959	4.4	17,728	1.8
Inventory	90,915	12.5	634,641	24.5	2,014,755	26.0	113,262	11.5
Other Current	42,912	5.9	152,832	5.9	317,711	4.1	91,595	9.3
Total Current	**382,571**	**52.6**	**1,536,091**	**59.3**	**5,215,117**	**67.3**	**371,304**	**37.7**
Fixed Assets	321,476	44.2	740,846	28.6	1,774,535	22.9	415,624	42.2
Other Non-current	23,274	3.2	313,435	12.1	759,408	9.8	197,963	20.1
Total Assets	**727,321**	**100.0**	**2,590,372**	**100.0**	**7,749,059**	**100.0**	**984,890**	**100.0**
Accounts Payable	129,463	17.8	191,688	7.4	790,404	10.2	50,229	5.1
Bank Loans	—	—	10,361	0.4	92,989	1.2	—	—
Notes Payable	62,550	8.6	313,435	12.1	1,061,621	13.7	58,109	5.9
Other Current	127,281	17.5	515,484	19.9	2,115,493	27.3	113,262	11.5
Total Current	**319,294**	**43.9**	**1,030,968**	**39.8**	**4,060,507**	**52.4**	**221,600**	**22.5**
Other Long Term	105,462	14.5	331,568	12.8	774,906	10.0	145,764	14.8
Deferred Credits	—	—	12,952	0.5	15,498	0.2	3,940	0.4
Net Worth	302,566	41.6	1,214,884	46.9	2,898,148	37.4	613,586	62.3
Total Liab & Net Worth	**727,321**	**100.0**	**2,590,372**	**100.0**	**7,749,059**	**100.0**	**984,890**	**100.0**
Net Sales	1,698,490	100.0	5,031,012	100.0	17,279,470	100.0	1,115,219	100.0
Gross Profit	242,884	14.3	1,323,156	26.3	3,438,615	19.9	517,462	46.4
Net Profit After Tax	142,673	8.4	266,644	5.3	483,825	2.8	74,720	6.7
Working Capital	63,277	—	505,123	—	1,154,610	—	149,704	—

RATIOS

	UQ	MED	LQ	UQ	MED	LQ	UQ	MED	LQ	UQ	MED	LQ
SOLVENCY												
Quick Ratio (times)	0.7	0.5	0.3	0.9	0.6	0.3	1.0	0.5	0.3	3.3	0.6	0.1
Current Ratio (times)	1.3	0.9	0.8	2.2	1.4	1.1	1.5	1.2	1.1	6.0	2.8	0.8
Curr Liab To Nw (%)	1.6	5.0	7.7	33.0	82.0	197.1	94.3	135.9	281.0	3.5	14.3	46.8
Curr Liab To Inv (%)	27.3	36.6	62.1	85.5	149.2	365.4	131.7	210.5	450.5	28.2	86.9	259.3
Total Liab To Nw (%)	2.6	5.8	11.2	45.7	103.2	212.0	101.6	179.8	380.8	12.9	31.5	80.2
Fixed Assets To Nw (%)	16.0	32.3	62.6	34.0	63.1	109.8	27.3	74.9	122.5	24.0	69.5	116.2
EFFICIENCY												
Coll Period (days)	12.0	14.1	15.9	18.6	26.5	33.6	26.9	38.5	70.7	7.5	26.7	67.6
Sales To Inv (times)	3.2	3.1	2.7	16.9	10.1	6.2	14.9	8.4	3.3	12.8	4.2	2.6
Assets To Sales (%)	24.3	35.7	51.2	31.9	43.9	64.6	44.5	55.0	69.0	46.6	99.6	202.2
Sales To Nwc (times)	1.1	1.0	0.7	21.1	13.0	4.5	12.2	8.7	6.8	4.3	1.7	0.5
Acct Pay To Sales (%)	1.1	1.8	2.3	2.6	4.6	10.7	1.8	3.9	5.5	4.6	9.9	17.1
PROFITABILITY												
Return On Sales (%)	1.8	(4.3)	(6.2)	4.6	1.8	0.2	6.4	1.5	0.8	33.0	10.1	(0.6)
Return On Assets (%)	(7.3)	(8.3)	(9.2)	7.1	2.2	(0.7)	6.4	3.6	2.1	13.2	8.8	(0.5)
Return On Nw (%)	(8.2)	(8.4)	(14.4)	18.5	7.6	(1.6)	24.6	13.1	3.9	26.5	12.8	0.3

SIC 0212 BF CTTLE, EXC FDLOT — INDUSTRY ASSETS $500,000 - $1,000,000 — 1995 (16 Establishments) | SIC 0212 BF CTTLE, EXC FDLOT — INDUSTRY ASSETS $1,000,000 - $5,000,000 — 1995 (22 Establishments) | SIC 0213 HOGS (NO BREAKDOWN) — 1995 (43 Establishments) | SIC 0213 HOGS — INDUSTRY ASSETS $1,000,000 - $5,000,000 — 1995 (17 Establishments)

	SIC 0212 $500K–$1M $	%	SIC 0212 $1M–$5M $	%	SIC 0213 No Brkdwn $	%	SIC 0213 $1M–$5M $	%
Cash	51,095	6.2	130,256	6.4	69,140	3.2	54,139	2.4
Accounts Receivable	5,769	0.7	162,820	8.0	60,497	2.8	65,418	2.9
Notes Receivable	8,241	1.0	50,881	2.5	45,373	2.1	103,766	4.6
Inventory	153,286	18.6	203,525	10.0	581,206	26.9	464,691	20.6
Other Current	105,487	12.8	183,173	9.0	71,300	3.3	128,579	5.7
Total Current	**323,878**	**39.3**	**730,656**	**35.9**	**827,517**	**38.3**	**816,592**	**36.2**
Fixed Assets	332,943	40.4	1,029,839	50.6	954,993	44.2	1,024,124	45.4
Other Non-current	167,296	20.3	274,759	13.5	378,108	17.5	415,064	18.4
Total Assets	**824,116**	**100.0**	**2,035,254**	**100.0**	**2,160,618**	**100.0**	**2,255,780**	**100.0**
Accounts Payable	19,779	2.4	61,058	3.0	82,103	3.8	117,301	5.2
Bank Loans	—	—	—	—	21,606	1.0	—	—
Notes Payable	51,919	6.3	156,715	7.7	123,155	5.7	103,766	4.6
Other Current	127,738	15.5	124,150	6.1	224,704	10.4	110,533	4.9
Total Current	**199,436**	**24.2**	**341,923**	**16.8**	**451,569**	**20.9**	**331,600**	**14.7**
Other Long Term	154,110	18.7	319,535	15.7	546,636	25.3	563,945	25.0
Deferred Credits	—	—	6,106	0.3	—	—	—	—
Net Worth	470,570	57.1	1,367,691	67.2	1,162,412	53.8	1,360,235	60.3
Total Liab & Net Worth	**824,116**	**100.0**	**2,035,254**	**100.0**	**2,160,618**	**100.0**	**2,255,780**	**100.0**
Net Sales	115,526	100.0	1,382,803	100.0	2,259,670	100.0	2,868,385	100.0
Gross Profit	—	—	645,769	46.7	1,089,161	48.2	2,013,606	70.2
Net Profit After Tax	40,781	35.3	(49,781)	(3.6)	42,934	1.9	(22,947)	(0.8)
Working Capital	124,442	—	388,733	—	375,948	—	484,992	—

RATIOS	SIC 0212 $500K–$1M UQ	MED	LQ	SIC 0212 $1M–$5M UQ	MED	LQ	SIC 0213 No Brkdwn UQ	MED	LQ	SIC 0213 $1M–$5M UQ	MED	LQ
SOLVENCY												
Quick Ratio (times)	0.2	0.1	0.1	2.6	0.8	0.2	0.5	0.3	0.1	0.5	0.3	0.2
Current Ratio (times)	1.1	0.8	0.5	5.0	3.2	1.8	3.1	2.1	1.2	3.9	2.8	1.6
Curr Liab To Nw (%)	2.1	8.8	12.9	5.4	8.2	15.9	17.0	29.0	66.9	15.5	19.3	33.2
Curr Liab To Inv (%)	18.6	57.0	74.0	27.2	31.2	48.0	43.3	63.4	139.0	38.0	62.0	123.5
Total Liab To Nw (%)	7.0	12.5	20.6	14.7	15.7	37.4	42.4	85.0	124.6	34.9	83.1	103.6
Fixed Assets To Nw (%)	13.2	18.5	31.3	58.0	69.5	77.6	58.8	88.8	144.8	69.2	89.5	110.5
EFFICIENCY												
Coll Period (days)	—	—	—	57.4	66.1	74.9	5.8	14.1	19.4	8.0	12.1	16.1
Sales To Inv (times)	2.2	2.2	2.2	36.9	14.6	8.0	4.0	3.4	3.1	4.5	4.4	4.3
Assets To Sales (%)	66.4	66.4	66.4	94.0	142.1	202.7	86.5	92.1	107.5	93.0	93.9	94.7
Sales To Nwc (times)	0.4	0.4	0.4	1.8	1.7	1.6	8.8	6.5	4.8	8.2	7.7	7.1
Acct Pay To Sales (%)	—	—	—	12.0	12.4	12.7	2.1	4.0	5.5	5.9	8.9	11.9
PROFITABILITY												
Return On Sales (%)	34.7	27.9	21.2	16.8	3.4	(17.6)	3.9	(4.5)	(4.8)	3.6	0.5	(2.6)
Return On Assets (%)	30.0	20.2	10.5	9.5	7.4	(9.9)	4.5	(4.0)	(5.7)	3.7	0.5	(2.8)
Return On Nw (%)	0.7	0.7	0.7	25.1	13.1	(9.2)	(6.3)	(7.2)	(8.6)	7.7	1.2	(5.3)

SIC 0241 DAIRY FARMS

	(NO BREAKDOWN) 1995 (85 Establishments)		$500,000 – $1,000,000 1995 (19 Establishments)		$1,000,000 – $5,000,000 1995 (30 Establishments)		$5,000,000 – $25,000,000 1995 (17 Establishments)	
	$	%	$	%	$	%	$	%
Cash	39,982	2.8	37,092	4.7	62,373	2.8	141,434	1.4
Accounts Receivable	68,541	4.8	59,978	7.6	80,194	3.6	414,200	4.1
Notes Receivable	8,568	0.6	12,627	1.6	8,910	0.4	20,205	0.2
Inventory	138,510	9.7	39,459	5.0	200,484	9.0	1,232,498	12.2
Other Current	79,965	5.6	17,362	2.2	155,932	7.0	1,020,347	10.1
Total Current	**335,566**	**23.5**	**166,518**	**21.1**	**507,893**	**22.8**	**2,828,683**	**28.0**
Fixed Assets	763,949	53.5	520,861	66.0	1,158,352	52.0	3,869,235	38.3
Other Non-current	328,427	23.0	101,805	12.9	561,355	25.2	3,404,523	33.7
Total Assets	**1,427,942**	**100.0**	**789,183**	**100.0**	**2,227,600**	**100.0**	**10,102,441**	**100.0**
Accounts Payable	49,978	3.5	15,784	2.0	95,787	4.3	333,381	3.3
Bank Loans	1,428	0.1	2,368	0.3	—	—	—	—
Notes Payable	78,537	5.5	26,043	3.3	126,973	5.7	495,020	4.9
Other Current	107,096	7.5	81,286	10.3	82,421	3.7	1,384,034	13.7
Total Current	**237,038**	**16.6**	**125,480**	**15.9**	**305,181**	**13.7**	**2,212,435**	**21.9**
Other Long Term	415,531	29.1	213,079	27.0	677,190	30.4	2,071,000	20.5
Deferred Credits	4,284	0.3	789	0.1	—	—	121,229	1.2
Net Worth	771,089	54.0	449,834	57.0	1,245,228	55.9	5,697,777	56.4
Total Liab & Net Worth	**1,427,942**	**100.0**	**789,183**	**100.0**	**2,227,600**	**100.0**	**10,102,441**	**100.0**
Net Sales	1,322,087	100.0	1,213,904	100.0	1,421,876	100.0	5,252,568	100.0
Gross Profit	576,430	43.6	387,235	31.9	662,594	46.6	2,037,996	38.8
Net Profit After Tax	70,071	5.3	61,909	5.1	78,203	5.5	346,669	6.6
Working Capital	98,528	—	41,038	—	202,712	—	616,248	—

RATIOS	UQ	MED	LQ	UQ	MED	LQ	UQ	MED	LQ	UQ	MED	LQ
SOLVENCY												
Quick Ratio (times)	1.1	0.5	0.2	0.5	0.3	0.2	1.1	0.5	0.3	0.7	0.2	0.1
Current Ratio (times)	7.3	1.6	0.8	1.5	0.9	0.7	8.5	2.0	1.1	5.8	1.4	0.4
Curr Liab To Nw (%)	7.0	15.0	35.2	7.0	11.8	18.7	5.1	8.5	24.6	11.7	32.9	67.8
Curr Liab To Inv (%)	39.6	92.9	294.9	21.4	41.0	60.6	47.7	92.9	253.4	18.0	129.1	547.4
Total Liab To Nw (%)	25.3	67.3	131.7	7.0	11.8	48.3	42.7	71.4	99.8	43.0	67.8	138.4
Fixed Assets To Nw (%)	72.6	99.8	135.5	54.1	92.1	123.7	75.9	87.9	104.0	44.3	92.8	120.0
EFFICIENCY												
Coll Period (days)	12.4	22.5	25.1	17.5	18.6	21.2	9.5	18.3	27.8	20.3	24.1	28.6
Sales To Inv (times)	26.2	11.6	4.1	14.3	11.2	6.7	10.5	5.5	3.7	126.8	22.0	12.6
Assets To Sales (%)	77.5	101.5	211.0	45.3	65.5	78.1	158.9	210.5	283.3	103.0	203.5	216.5
Sales To Nwc (times)	15.8	8.0	5.2	6.1	4.9	3.6	10.8	7.4	6.3	4.0	3.3	2.5
Acct Pay To Sales (%)	1.0	3.8	6.3	1.0	1.2	1.6	1.4	3.9	4.8	3.8	6.3	8.4
PROFITABILITY												
Return On Sales (%)	13.5	2.7	0.9	1.7	1.3	(2.1)	16.2	2.7	0.9	25.8	3.6	0.8
Return On Assets (%)	7.8	3.9	0.6	4.0	1.9	(0.4)	5.2	3.1	1.7	5.8	2.5	—
Return On Nw (%)	12.6	7.6	0.6	5.0	2.0	(5.5)	12.2	5.3	0.3	12.6	6.4	—

Balance Sheet

	SIC 0252 CHICKEN EGGS (NO BREAKDOWN) 1995 (37 Establishments) $	%	SIC 0252 CHICKEN EGGS INDUSTRY ASSETS $1,000,000 - $5,000,000 1995 (13 Establishments) $	%	SIC 0253 TURKEYS, TURKEY EGGS (NO BREAKDOWN) 1995 (16 Establishments) $	%	SIC 0291 GEN FRMS, PRIM ANMLS (NO BREAKDOWN) 1995 (15 Establishments) $	%
Cash	345,589	6.9	98,746	5.0	281,687	9.5	89,896	15.7
Accounts Receivable	596,016	11.9	310,063	15.7	329,129	11.1	16,032	2.8
Notes Receivable	70,120	1.4	82,947	4.2	5,930	0.2	1,145	0.2
Inventory	1,001,708	20.0	408,809	20.7	637,502	21.5	60,121	10.5
Other Current	240,410	4.8	122,445	6.2	320,233	10.8	28,629	5.0
Total Current	**2,253,843**	**45.0**	**1,023,011**	**51.8**	**1,574,481**	**53.1**	**195,824**	**34.2**
Fixed Assets	1,898,236	37.9	610,252	30.9	1,141,573	38.5	164,904	28.8
Other Non-current	856,460	17.1	341,662	17.3	249,070	8.4	211,856	37.0
Total Assets	**5,008,539**	**100.0**	**1,974,925**	**100.0**	**2,965,124**	**100.0**	**572,584**	**100.0**
Accounts Payable	315,538	6.3	98,746	5.0	323,199	10.9	2,863	0.5
Bank Loans	5,009	0.1	3,950	0.2	—	—	—	—
Notes Payable	295,504	5.9	161,944	8.2	166,047	5.6	573	0.1
Other Current	565,965	11.3	215,267	10.9	349,885	11.8	92,186	16.1
Total Current	**1,182,015**	**23.6**	**479,907**	**24.3**	**839,130**	**28.3**	**95,622**	**16.7**
Other Long Term	1,182,015	23.6	464,107	23.5	340,989	11.5	81,307	14.2
Deferred Credits	20,034	0.4						
Net Worth	2,624,474	52.4	1,030,911	52.2	1,785,005	60.2	395,656	69.1
Total Liab & Net Worth	**5,008,539**	**100.0**	**1,974,925**	**100.0**	**2,965,124**	**100.0**	**572,584**	**100.0**
Net Sales	7,244,583	100.0	3,607,528	100.0	3,214,425	100.0	275,255	100.0
Gross Profit	1,659,010	22.9	1,219,344	33.8	941,827	29.3	219,929	79.9
Net Profit After Tax	(36,223)	(0.5)	14,430	0.4	327,871	10.2	39,086	14.2
Working Capital	1,071,828	—	543,104	—	735,351	—	100,202	—

RATIOS

	UQ	MED	LQ	UQ	MED	LQ	UQ	MED	LQ	UQ	MED	LQ
SOLVENCY												
Quick Ratio (times)	1.1	0.6	0.2	3.1	0.9	0.2	1.5	0.6	0.3	0.5	0.3	0.2
Current Ratio (times)	2.6	1.6	1.3	4.7	1.9	1.1	3.3	1.8	1.4	1.4	1.1	0.9
Curr Liab To Nw (%)	27.4	36.4	54.9	15.5	31.4	52.1	19.0	35.8	97.4	4.9	7.7	17.3
Curr Liab To Inv (%)	85.3	112.8	206.7	51.4	105.4	169.2	68.0	104.3	228.3	29.5	39.4	48.4
Total Liab To Nw (%)	50.3	85.3	142.8	31.9	74.4	116.5	37.1	69.8	125.6	10.6	18.5	41.3
Fixed Assets To Nw (%)	40.7	94.2	109.2	35.1	52.5	122.0	39.5	68.4	104.4	16.5	30.5	37.4
EFFICIENCY												
Coll Period (days)	13.2	19.4	23.5	11.7	17.9	22.7	15.2	21.4	29.8	7.9	8.4	10.1
Sales To Inv (times)	13.2	7.7	4.6	11.7	9.6	5.7	7.7	6.2	4.1	5.2	4.1	3.1
Assets To Sales (%)	47.7	63.4	83.6	43.1	56.2	66.8	81.1	94.6	120.9	37.9	52.6	66.6
Sales To Nwc (times)	17.1	8.7	5.4	14.8	5.4	3.1	5.2	2.7	1.7	2.8	2.5	2.1
Acct Pay To Sales (%)	2.0	4.0	5.1	1.5	2.4	3.9	0.7	1.2	1.8	1.6	1.9	2.1
PROFITABILITY												
Return On Sales (%)	2.5	0.9	(3.3)	2.6	(0.4)	(2.5)	11.1	8.4	3.9	4.6	3.1	2.1
Return On Assets (%)	2.4	(0.3)	(4.7)	1.1	(0.3)	(3.3)	9.5	6.7	6.5	8.9	6.4	4.2
Return On Nw (%)	4.0	(1.0)	(12.7)	2.0	(1.5)	(11.8)	15.8	13.3	7.9	9.5	8.4	7.1

SIC 07 AGRICULTURAL SERVICES

	NO BREAKDOWN 1995 (2128 Establishments) $	%	NORTHEAST 1995 (398 Establishments) $	%	CENTRAL 1995 (582 Establishments) $	%	SOUTH 1995 (614 Establishments) $	%
Cash	49,591	14.2	43,393	15.0	38,959	13.2	49,454	13.5
Accounts Receivable	76,133	21.8	65,379	22.6	61,095	20.7	74,364	20.3
Notes Receivable	2,794	0.8	2,604	0.9	2,361	0.8	2,564	0.7
Inventory	25,494	7.3	23,143	8.0	27,153	9.2	25,276	6.9
Other Current	17,811	5.1	17,068	5.9	11,511	3.9	17,950	4.9
Total Current	**171,823**	**49.2**	**151,586**	**52.4**	**141,079**	**47.8**	**169,608**	**46.3**
Fixed Assets	145,631	41.7	117,161	40.5	131,634	44.6	156,786	42.8
Other Non-current	31,780	9.1	20,539	7.1	22,431	7.6	39,929	10.9
Total Assets	**349,234**	**100.0**	**289,286**	**100.0**	**295,144**	**100.0**	**366,323**	**100.0**
Accounts Payable	33,526	9.6	26,904	9.3	26,858	9.1	33,335	9.1
Bank Loans	698	0.2	579	0.2	1,181	0.4	1,099	0.3
Notes Payable	18,859	5.4	16,489	5.7	18,299	6.2	22,712	6.2
Other Current	56,227	16.1	51,204	17.7	47,223	16.0	49,454	13.5
Total Current	**109,310**	**31.3**	**95,175**	**32.9**	**93,561**	**31.7**	**106,600**	**29.1**
Other Long Term	66,704	19.1	52,361	18.1	60,209	20.4	75,463	20.6
Deferred Credits	1,397	0.4	1,446	0.5	1,476	0.5	366	0.1
Net Worth	171,823	49.2	140,304	48.5	139,898	47.4	183,894	50.2
Total Liab & Net Worth	**349,234**	**100.0**	**289,286**	**100.0**	**295,144**	**100.0**	**366,323**	**100.0**
Net Sales	1,088,030	100.0	879,980	100.0	954,264	100.0	1,159,291	100.0
Gross Profit	450,444	41.4	407,431	46.3	413,196	43.3	469,513	40.5
Net Profit After Tax	64,194	5.9	37,839	4.3	53,439	5.6	74,195	6.4
Working Capital	62,513	—	56,411	—	47,518	—	63,008	—

RATIOS	UQ	MED	LQ	UQ	MED	LQ	UQ	MED	LQ	UQ	MED	LQ
SOLVENCY												
Quick Ratio (times)	2.3	1.2	0.6	2.3	1.2	0.6	2.3	1.1	0.6	2.4	1.2	0.6
Current Ratio (times)	3.4	1.6	1.0	3.5	1.6	1.0	3.3	1.6	0.9	3.4	1.7	1.0
Curr Liab To Nw (%)	18.9	52.9	124.3	20.3	60.3	129.6	20.4	51.9	120.5	18.6	51.0	117.2
Curr Liab To Inv (%)	91.2	192.8	394.9	90.8	225.0	405.0	83.2	159.9	363.0	94.5	206.2	411.0
Total Liab To Nw (%)	33.6	90.5	196.9	29.2	102.3	198.6	39.6	96.8	209.6	32.5	83.8	183.2
Fixed Assets To Nw (%)	44.2	80.4	142.8	39.9	76.0	128.1	48.7	92.1	167.4	45.9	80.3	152.8
EFFICIENCY												
Coll Period (days)	15.7	32.1	55.1	16.6	36.5	64.5	13.9	28.5	47.3	15.0	30.3	48.7
Sales To Inv (times)	87.5	32.0	13.1	93.0	35.0	11.8	65.5	27.2	12.1	90.0	33.6	13.6
Assets To Sales (%)	23.5	35.6	57.6	23.0	35.3	53.7	26.3	36.6	54.1	23.2	34.6	60.4
Sales To Nwc (times)	23.8	11.0	5.7	24.7	10.0	5.2	24.3	10.8	6.0	22.4	11.3	6.1
Acct Pay To Sales (%)	1.3	3.3	7.0	1.1	3.2	7.8	1.3	3.0	5.8	1.3	3.2	7.1
PROFITABILITY												
Return On Sales (%)	9.6	4.0	1.1	7.3	2.6	0.6	8.2	3.7	1.5	10.6	5.1	1.4
Return On Assets (%)	22.2	8.4	2.2	19.7	7.1	1.6	19.6	8.9	3.6	25.6	9.0	1.8
Return On Nw (%)	45.6	17.9	5.2	38.7	12.8	3.6	39.5	18.8	8.5	51.5	22.0	5.2

SIC 07 AGRICULTURAL SERVICES

	WEST 1995 (534 Establishments) $	%	UNDER $100,000 1995 (468 Establishments) $	%	$100,000 - $250,000 1995 (420 Establishments) $	%	$250,000 - $500,000 1995 (439 Establishments) $	%
Cash	76,235	15.5	10,906	21.1	24,833	15.8	43,013	12.2
Accounts Receivable	119,025	24.2	7,547	14.6	30,334	19.3	86,026	24.4
Notes Receivable	4,918	1.0	207	0.4	1,886	1.2	3,173	0.9
Inventory	26,068	5.3	2,533	4.9	11,316	7.2	29,968	8.5
Other Current	29,510	6.0	1,706	3.3	7,859	5.0	16,218	4.6
Total Current	**255,757**	**52.0**	**22,898**	**44.3**	**76,228**	**48.5**	**178,397**	**50.6**
Fixed Assets	188,375	38.3	25,483	49.3	67,898	43.2	149,135	42.3
Other Non-current	47,708	9.7	3,308	6.4	13,045	8.3	25,032	7.1
Total Assets	**491,840**	**100.0**	**51,689**	**100.0**	**157,172**	**100.0**	**352,564**	**100.0**
Accounts Payable	53,611	10.9	3,463	6.7	12,417	7.9	35,962	10.2
Bank Loans	492	0.1	52	0.1	314	0.2	1,058	0.3
Notes Payable	17,214	3.5	2,895	5.6	8,016	5.1	20,449	5.8
Other Current	88,039	17.9	9,873	19.1	25,462	16.2	44,071	12.5
Total Current	**159,356**	**32.4**	**16,282**	**31.5**	**46,209**	**29.4**	**101,538**	**28.8**
Other Long Term	81,645	16.6	9,666	18.7	32,692	20.8	76,859	21.8
Deferred Credits	1,967	0.4	103	0.2	472	0.3	1,763	0.5
Net Worth	248,871	50.6	25,638	49.6	77,800	49.5	172,404	48.9
Total Liab & Net Worth	**491,840**	**100.0**	**51,689**	**100.0**	**157,172**	**100.0**	**352,564**	**100.0**
Net Sales	1,747,784	100.0	268,758	100.0	576,114	100.0	1,042,166	100.0
Gross Profit	616,968	35.3	145,398	54.1	286,329	49.7	447,089	42.9
Net Profit After Tax	125,840	7.2	20,694	7.7	36,295	6.3	65,656	6.3
Working Capital	96,401	—	6,616	—	30,019	—	76,859	—

RATIOS	WEST UQ	MED	LQ	UNDER $100,000 UQ	MED	LQ	$100,000-$250,000 UQ	MED	LQ	$250,000-$500,000 UQ	MED	LQ
SOLVENCY												
Quick Ratio (times)	2.5	1.2	0.7	2.7	1.3	0.5	2.7	1.3	0.6	2.8	1.3	0.7
Current Ratio (times)	3.3	1.6	1.0	3.5	1.6	0.7	3.9	1.8	1.0	3.9	1.8	1.1
Curr Liab To Nw (%)	17.7	50.3	126.0	15.6	41.0	124.9	15.1	45.5	104.1	18.3	50.8	121.2
Curr Liab To Inv (%)	106.0	215.4	416.1	71.1	154.2	322.6	75.4	167.7	361.5	83.3	160.4	372.1
Total Liab To Nw (%)	30.5	88.6	191.7	22.3	65.1	188.3	35.0	91.9	176.7	38.9	94.8	203.5
Fixed Assets To Nw (%)	40.7	76.1	122.1	48.9	90.7	183.4	43.9	88.2	143.3	44.6	84.7	149.7
EFFICIENCY												
Coll Period (days)	18.0	38.2	60.5	8.0	15.6	31.2	9.5	21.2	40.5	20.1	31.8	49.8
Sales To Inv (times)	106.9	33.5	13.8	146.4	50.8	20.6	89.7	33.8	14.5	69.6	27.6	11.4
Assets To Sales (%)	21.7	36.0	69.6	11.4	18.3	32.5	20.9	27.7	41.3	25.3	33.5	49.8
Sales To Nwc (times)	25.5	11.9	5.9	47.1	20.9	10.8	24.7	14.1	7.3	26.5	10.3	5.2
Acct Pay To Sales (%)	1.6	3.5	7.8	0.9	1.8	4.4	1.1	2.3	4.7	1.3	3.5	7.1
PROFITABILITY												
Return On Sales (%)	11.8	4.5	1.1	15.6	6.6	1.4	11.3	5.1	1.3	9.6	4.2	1.3
Return On Assets (%)	22.3	8.7	2.2	59.1	23.9	4.4	28.4	13.2	2.8	22.8	10.2	2.7
Return On Nw (%)	46.2	19.7	5.9	131.2	52.7	10.1	55.6	28.5	6.6	52.4	25.1	6.6

	SIC 07 AGRICULTURAL SERVICES $500,000-$1,000,000 1995 (319 Establishments)		SIC 07 AGRICULTURAL SERVICES $1,000,000-$5,000,000 1995 (383 Establishments)		SIC 07 AGRICULTURAL SERVICES $5,000,000-$25,000,000 1995 (81 Establishments)		SIC 0711 SOIL PREP SERVICES (NO BREAKDOWN) 1995 (61 Establishments)	
	$	%	$	%	$	%	$	%
Cash	67,190	9.9	208,022	11.8	904,620	11.0	39,501	10.1
Accounts Receivable	183,925	27.1	444,251	25.2	1,833,911	22.3	88,779	22.7
Notes Receivable	6,108	0.9	12,340	0.7	98,686	1.2	3,520	0.9
Inventory	51,581	7.6	144,558	8.2	682,577	8.3	25,030	6.4
Other Current	35,292	5.2	121,640	6.9	682,577	8.3	22,293	5.7
Total Current	**344,096**	**50.7**	**930,811**	**52.8**	**4,202,369**	**51.1**	**179,123**	**45.8**
Fixed Assets	269,440	39.7	611,726	34.7	2,919,454	35.5	178,732	45.7
Other Non-current	65,154	9.6	220,363	12.5	1,101,991	13.4	33,243	8.5
Total Assets	**678,691**	**100.0**	**1,762,900**	**100.0**	**8,223,815**	**100.0**	**391,098**	**100.0**
Accounts Payable	71,941	10.6	218,600	12.4	912,843	11.1	42,630	10.9
Bank Loans	3,393	0.5	1,763	0.1	16,448	0.2	5,866	1.5
Notes Payable	35,292	5.2	100,485	5.7	337,176	4.1	18,382	4.7
Other Current	105,876	15.6	275,012	15.6	1,751,673	21.3	67,660	17.3
Total Current	**216,502**	**31.9**	**595,860**	**33.8**	**3,018,140**	**36.7**	**134,538**	**34.4**
Other Long Term	118,771	17.5	299,693	17.0	1,192,453	14.5	81,739	20.9
Deferred Credits	2,036	0.3	7,052	0.4	49,343	0.6	3,911	1.0
Net Worth	341,382	50.3	860,295	48.8	3,963,879	48.2	170,910	43.7
Total Liab & Net Worth	**678,691**	**100.0**	**1,762,900**	**100.0**	**8,223,815**	**100.0**	**391,098**	**100.0**
Net Sales	1,750,076	100.0	3,568,606	100.0	11,229,430	100.0	1,350,554	100.0
Gross Profit	642,278	36.7	1,095,562	30.7	3,829,236	34.1	469,993	34.8
Net Profit After Tax	91,004	5.2	160,587	4.5	797,290	7.1	83,734	6.2
Working Capital	127,594	—	334,951	—	1,184,229	—	44,585	—

RATIOS	UQ	MED	LQ	UQ	MED	LQ	UQ	MED	LQ	UQ	MED	LQ
SOLVENCY												
Quick Ratio (times)	2.2	1.2	0.7	1.8	1.1	0.7	1.3	0.9	0.6	2.4	1.1	0.5
Current Ratio (times)	3.4	1.7	1.1	2.6	1.5	1.1	2.1	1.3	1.0	3.0	1.5	0.8
Curr Liab To Nw (%)	21.0	55.6	124.1	23.7	66.3	130.2	27.5	74.3	152.0	20.7	60.4	134.1
Curr Liab To Inv (%)	80.6	209.6	423.1	128.3	215.4	417.0	147.2	288.0	451.3	104.7	180.7	278.9
Total Liab To Nw (%)	38.3	92.7	185.6	41.4	95.5	213.6	47.0	116.7	225.8	38.1	109.0	258.9
Fixed Assets To Nw (%)	41.8	73.8	130.1	40.0	68.8	119.5	53.5	80.9	122.9	52.0	86.2	200.9
EFFICIENCY												
Coll Period (days)	20.1	37.2	63.9	19.7	40.4	64.4	19.4	49.6	110.6	15.7	43.8	88.0
Sales To Inv (times)	94.2	38.1	14.9	89.4	35.6	11.8	41.9	25.5	12.1	81.1	38.4	14.5
Assets To Sales (%)	29.9	38.5	55.6	33.7	51.1	83.7	52.3	66.6	121.5	33.4	48.0	70.6
Sales To Nwc (times)	17.7	9.5	6.2	16.4	9.2	4.0	18.8	9.5	4.4	16.6	7.5	3.6
Acct Pay To Sales (%)	1.3	3.1	7.5	1.5	4.2	9.4	2.7	4.8	10.1	2.4	4.2	11.6
PROFITABILITY												
Return On Sales (%)	7.5	3.6	1.2	7.3	2.8	0.8	8.3	3.6	0.4	8.5	4.4	1.4
Return On Assets (%)	14.7	7.2	2.3	11.6	5.1	1.5	10.3	4.5	0.6	11.9	7.4	1.2
Return On Nw (%)	35.5	13.9	4.9	27.3	11.9	4.3	25.6	9.7	1.8	50.1	17.5	5.2

Balance Sheet

	SIC 0711 SOIL PREP SERVICES $100,000-$250,000 1995 (14 Establishments) $	%	SIC 0711 SOIL PREP SERVICES $250,000-$500,000 1995 (15 Establishments) $	%	SIC 0711 SOIL PREP SERVICES $500,000-$1,000,000 1995 (10 Establishments) $	%	SIC 0721 CROP PLNTNG,PRTCTNG (NO BREAKDOWN) 1995 (80 Establishments) $	%
Cash	13,274	7.6	37,428	12.4	71,638	9.7	76,530	15.1
Accounts Receivable	32,138	18.4	63,688	21.1	168,386	22.8	75,516	14.9
Notes Receivable	—	—	9,659	3.2	2,216	0.3	3,548	0.7
Inventory	5,589	3.2	22,638	7.5	63,514	8.6	21,793	4.3
Other Current	8,034	4.6	14,186	4.7	39,142	5.3	26,355	5.2
Total Current	**59,036**	**33.8**	**147,600**	**48.9**	**344,896**	**46.7**	**203,741**	**40.2**
Fixed Assets	86,284	49.4	135,224	44.8	345,634	46.8	225,534	44.5
Other Non-current	29,343	16.8	19,016	6.3	48,005	6.5	77,543	15.3
Total Assets	**174,663**	**100.0**	**301,840**	**100.0**	**738,535**	**100.0**	**506,818**	**100.0**
Accounts Payable	15,545	8.9	33,504	11.1	89,363	12.1	38,011	7.5
Bank Loans	8,034	4.6	—	—	6,647	0.9	3,041	0.6
Notes Payable	1,397	0.8	14,186	4.7	14,032	1.9	26,861	5.3
Other Current	23,754	13.6	72,743	24.1	128,505	17.4	68,927	13.6
Total Current	**48,731**	**27.9**	**120,434**	**39.9**	**238,547**	**32.3**	**136,841**	**27.0**
Other Long Term	42,967	24.6	61,877	20.5	228,207	30.9	94,775	18.7
Deferred Credits	2,096	1.2	2,717	0.9	14,771	2.0	507	0.1
Net Worth	80,869	46.3	116,812	38.7	257,010	34.8	274,695	54.2
Total Liab & Net Worth	**174,663**	**100.0**	**301,840**	**100.0**	**738,535**	**100.0**	**506,818**	**100.0**
Net Sales	439,753	100.0	1,028,827	100.0	1,538,308	100.0	1,428,152	100.0
Gross Profit	176,781	40.2	205,765	20.0	559,944	36.4	541,270	37.9
Net Profit After Tax	29,463	6.7	69,960	6.8	23,075	1.5	112,824	7.9
Working Capital	10,305	—	27,166	—	106,349	—	66,900	—

Ratios

RATIOS	UQ	MED	LQ	UQ	MED	LQ	UQ	MED	LQ	UQ	MED	LQ
SOLVENCY												
Quick Ratio (times)	2.6	1.5	0.5	2.3	0.7	0.7	1.7	1.2	1.1	3.7	1.0	0.4
Current Ratio (times)	2.9	1.8	0.6	3.9	1.1	0.7	2.4	1.6	1.2	4.6	1.5	0.8
Curr Liab To Nw (%)	20.8	40.4	81.2	24.8	96.4	188.1	35.7	61.9	114.7	14.1	34.5	116.7
Curr Liab To Inv (%)	49.3	96.0	142.8	117.1	152.8	156.9	169.4	181.6	262.0	112.5	247.5	462.5
Total Liab To Nw (%)	81.2	103.6	146.9	50.2	191.5	405.7	67.3	100.9	275.9	20.9	63.8	151.8
Fixed Assets To Nw (%)	74.1	98.7	126.1	41.2	112.2	350.4	80.0	131.8	279.9	52.7	78.6	176.0
EFFICIENCY												
Coll Period (days)	34.1	58.6	82.5	13.9	17.9	47.5	17.3	31.6	47.6	17.4	30.7	39.7
Sales To Inv (times)	13.1	13.1	13.1	42.8	29.4	24.1	64.7	43.3	20.6	42.8	31.3	18.9
Assets To Sales (%)	28.0	48.5	58.7	31.8	33.4	39.7	39.3	48.2	55.1	34.2	42.7	60.1
Sales To Nwc (times)	15.4	9.2	7.7	40.4	20.0	4.4	17.8	9.6	7.3	22.4	11.1	4.4
Acct Pay To Sales (%)	4.8	10.0	14.3	1.3	4.0	4.2	3.5	7.8	10.0	0.8	3.1	6.5
PROFITABILITY												
Return On Sales (%)	15.7	6.3	5.1	8.5	4.4	2.9	4.7	2.1	(0.6)	9.4	5.8	2.1
Return On Assets (%)	20.4	11.8	2.1	16.6	13.3	9.6	8.1	7.0	(2.1)	21.7	8.8	2.6
Return On Nw (%)	45.4	40.7	40.1	59.4	52.9	51.2	14.3	10.8	(0.3)	42.8	22.7	5.6

Balance Sheet

	SIC 0721 CROP PLNTNG,PRTCTNG $250,000-$500,000 (21 Est.) $	%	SIC 0721 CROP PLNTNG,PRTCTNG $500,000-$1,000,000 (22 Est.) $	%	SIC 0721 CROP PLNTNG,PRTCTNG $1,000,000-$5,000,000 (16 Est.) $	%	SIC 0722 CROP HARVESTING (NO BREAKDOWN) (24 Est.) $	%
Cash	54,183	16.4	66,209	10.8	97,284	7.0	204,197	17.6
Accounts Receivable	46,254	14.0	127,513	20.8	257,108	18.5	87,016	7.5
Notes Receivable	2,643	0.8	5,517	0.9	13,898	1.0	2,320	0.2
Inventory	10,572	3.2	22,683	3.7	161,213	11.6	89,336	7.7
Other Current	13,876	4.2	30,652	5.0	132,028	9.5	106,739	9.2
Total Current	**127,528**	**38.6**	**252,574**	**41.2**	**661,531**	**47.6**	**489,609**	**42.2**
Fixed Assets	159,245	48.2	266,061	43.4	569,806	41.0	442,040	38.1
Other Non-current	43,611	13.2	94,409	15.4	158,434	11.4	228,561	19.7
Total Assets	**330,384**	**100.0**	**613,043**	**100.0**	**1,389,771**	**100.0**	**1,160,210**	**100.0**
Accounts Payable	25,440	7.7	50,883	8.3	158,434	11.4	60,331	5.2
Bank Loans	1,982	0.6	11,035	1.8	—	—	—	—
Notes Payable	11,894	3.6	55,787	9.1	112,571	8.1	110,220	9.5
Other Current	35,021	10.6	57,013	9.3	130,638	9.4	199,556	17.2
Total Current	**74,336**	**22.5**	**174,717**	**28.5**	**401,644**	**28.9**	**370,107**	**31.9**
Other Long Term	69,711	21.1	118,317	19.3	200,127	14.4	158,949	13.7
Deferred Credits	—	—	—	—	—	—	—	—
Net Worth	186,337	56.4	320,008	52.2	788,000	56.7	631,154	54.4
Total Liab & Net Worth	**330,384**	**100.0**	**613,043**	**100.0**	**1,389,771**	**100.0**	**1,160,210**	**100.0**
Net Sales	839,219	100.0	1,428,152	100.0	3,383,543	100.0	3,276,212	100.0
Gross Profit	276,942	33.0	742,639	52.0	697,010	20.6	1,493,953	45.6
Net Profit After Tax	68,816	8.2	122,821	8.6	148,876	4.4	160,534	4.9
Working Capital	53,192	—	77,857	—	259,887	—	119,502	—

RATIOS

	$250,000-$500,000 UQ	MED	LQ	$500,000-$1,000,000 UQ	MED	LQ	$1,000,000-$5,000,000 UQ	MED	LQ	CROP HARVESTING UQ	MED	LQ
SOLVENCY												
Quick Ratio (times)	1.5	0.4	0.3	3.7	1.0	0.6	1.5	1.0	0.6	1.5	0.7	0.5
Current Ratio (times)	1.8	1.0	0.4	4.5	1.5	0.9	2.6	1.5	1.2	2.2	1.6	0.9
Curr Liab To Nw (%)	10.1	19.4	46.4	8.5	38.2	126.4	22.0	26.2	63.5	25.7	65.4	118.4
Curr Liab To Inv (%)	147.2	247.4	260.9	247.5	364.2	422.2	105.3	161.9	311.7	114.0	180.5	362.1
Total Liab To Nw (%)	10.1	31.4	88.1	42.7	66.2	129.2	26.0	49.2	69.8	44.7	93.1	209.5
Fixed Assets To Nw (%)	42.4	68.1	109.9	56.1	77.2	131.5	67.7	90.8	128.1	66.4	92.7	127.9
EFFICIENCY												
Coll Period (days)	4.3	14.4	33.9	19.0	31.1	38.8	19.7	27.0	38.0	2.1	15.4	52.8
Sales To Inv (times)	35.5	26.1	18.2	103.9	41.6	31.5	37.8	31.3	13.6	8.2	5.6	5.4
Assets To Sales (%)	22.0	33.9	37.7	39.1	45.1	53.1	38.8	50.7	53.1	43.2	56.0	93.0
Sales To Nwc (times)	19.9	10.4	3.9	14.4	9.5	6.0	22.9	11.7	8.5	61.4	13.6	8.4
Acct Pay To Sales (%)	0.8	0.8	1.9	3.7	5.6	6.1	1.4	3.1	16.8	2.2	4.9	8.6
PROFITABILITY												
Return On Sales (%)	9.3	5.4	2.5	20.4	5.1	1.3	8.1	2.8	1.9	10.2	4.2	2.4
Return On Assets (%)	10.4	9.3	8.0	13.2	8.4	(0.9)	13.4	8.1	3.3	24.0	7.4	4.2
Return On Nw (%)	34.1	20.6	12.5	51.5	13.3	(1.3)	30.9	12.0	7.0	38.4	24.2	12.5

SIC 0723 CROP PREP SVCS,MRKT (NO BREAKDOWN) — 1995 (236 Establishments)

	$	%
Cash	271,732	13.7
Accounts Receivable	420,490	21.2
Notes Receivable	23,801	1.2
Inventory	251,897	12.7
Other Current	101,156	5.1
Total Current	**1,069,075**	**53.9**
Fixed Assets	692,221	34.9
Other Non-current	222,146	11.2
Total Assets	**1,983,442**	**100.0**
Accounts Payable	271,732	13.7
Bank Loans	1,983	0.1
Notes Payable	120,990	6.1
Other Current	323,301	16.3
Total Current	**718,006**	**36.2**
Other Long Term	313,384	15.8
Deferred Credits	7,934	0.4
Net Worth	944,118	47.6
Total Liab & Net Worth	**1,983,442**	**100.0**
Net Sales	4,179,192	100.0
Gross Profit	1,220,324	29.2
Net Profit After Tax	208,960	5.0
Working Capital	351,069	—

RATIOS	UQ	MED	LQ
SOLVENCY			
Quick Ratio (times)	1.5	1.0	0.5
Current Ratio (times)	2.4	1.4	1.1
Curr Liab To Nw (%)	27.0	72.8	149.5
Curr Liab To Inv (%)	108.1	204.2	375.5
Total Liab To Nw (%)	49.0	103.0	221.0
Fixed Assets To Nw (%)	39.8	77.9	125.8
EFFICIENCY			
Coll Period (days)	14.9	28.7	65.3
Sales To Inv (times)	42.3	20.5	8.7
Assets To Sales (%)	28.8	53.7	92.9
Sales To Nwc (times)	25.6	11.2	4.9
Acct Pay To Sales (%)	1.8	4.6	9.9
PROFITABILITY			
Return On Sales (%)	7.1	3.1	0.8
Return On Assets (%)	13.6	5.8	1.0
Return On Nw (%)	30.2	11.8	1.9

SIC 0723 CROP PREP SVCS,MRKT — INDUSTRY ASSETS $250,000 - $500,000 — 1995 (32 Establishments)

	$	%
Cash	64,284	15.3
Accounts Receivable	82,771	19.7
Notes Receivable	3,361	0.8
Inventory	63,444	15.1
Other Current	20,588	4.9
Total Current	**234,447**	**55.8**
Fixed Assets	167,222	39.8
Other Non-current	18,487	4.4
Total Assets	**420,156**	**100.0**
Accounts Payable	50,839	12.1
Bank Loans	—	—
Notes Payable	45,797	10.9
Other Current	25,209	6.0
Total Current	**121,845**	**29.0**
Other Long Term	78,569	18.7
Deferred Credits	4,622	1.1
Net Worth	215,120	51.2
Total Liab & Net Worth	**420,156**	**100.0**
Net Sales	1,047,510	100.0
Gross Profit	461,952	44.1
Net Profit After Tax	31,425	3.0
Working Capital	112,602	—

RATIOS	UQ	MED	LQ
Quick Ratio	3.1	1.8	0.4
Current Ratio	4.1	2.0	1.1
Curr Liab To Nw	12.8	57.5	137.5
Curr Liab To Inv	83.2	156.4	277.8
Total Liab To Nw	45.6	83.7	168.0
Fixed Assets To Nw	38.3	83.2	144.0
Coll Period	13.9	31.2	78.6
Sales To Inv	16.9	11.6	5.7
Assets To Sales	25.4	33.6	62.9
Sales To Nwc	22.0	8.3	3.9
Acct Pay To Sales	1.4	4.0	9.1
Return On Sales	6.2	1.2	(0.4)
Return On Assets	9.3	3.1	(1.8)
Return On Nw	31.1	6.1	(2.2)

SIC 0723 CROP PREP SVCS,MRKT — INDUSTRY ASSETS $500,000 - $1,000,000 — 1995 (32 Establishments)

	$	%
Cash	67,774	9.9
Accounts Receivable	153,348	22.4
Notes Receivable	13,692	2.0
Inventory	102,688	15.0
Other Current	37,652	5.5
Total Current	**375,154**	**54.8**
Fixed Assets	254,667	37.2
Other Non-current	54,767	8.0
Total Assets	**684,588**	**100.0**
Accounts Payable	94,473	13.8
Bank Loans	3,423	0.5
Notes Payable	43,129	6.3
Other Current	100,634	14.7
Total Current	**241,660**	**35.3**
Other Long Term	73,936	10.8
Deferred Credits	—	—
Net Worth	368,993	53.9
Total Liab & Net Worth	**684,588**	**100.0**
Net Sales	2,328,000	100.0
Gross Profit	558,720	24.0
Net Profit After Tax	72,168	3.1
Working Capital	133,494	—

RATIOS	UQ	MED	LQ
Quick Ratio	1.4	0.9	0.4
Current Ratio	2.7	1.4	1.0
Curr Liab To Nw	22.1	46.9	84.1
Curr Liab To Inv	56.8	152.9	297.8
Total Liab To Nw	25.9	77.7	163.5
Fixed Assets To Nw	30.3	61.5	83.8
Coll Period	19.1	26.5	49.4
Sales To Inv	89.1	21.0	7.4
Assets To Sales	16.7	33.9	37.7
Sales To Nwc	40.6	14.3	7.9
Acct Pay To Sales	2.2	4.0	5.9
Return On Sales	4.0	2.6	1.5
Return On Assets	24.4	7.7	2.1
Return On Nw	44.9	20.9	3.3

SIC 0723 CROP PREP SVCS,MRKT — INDUSTRY ASSETS $1,000,000 - $5,000,000 — 1995 (95 Establishments)

	$	%
Cash	286,666	13.0
Accounts Receivable	471,896	21.4
Notes Receivable	24,256	1.1
Inventory	269,025	12.2
Other Current	79,384	3.6
Total Current	**1,131,227**	**51.3**
Fixed Assets	734,305	33.3
Other Non-current	339,588	15.4
Total Assets	**2,205,120**	**100.0**
Accounts Payable	321,948	14.6
Bank Loans	2,205	0.1
Notes Payable	121,282	5.5
Other Current	374,870	17.0
Total Current	**820,305**	**37.2**
Other Long Term	359,435	16.3
Deferred Credits	6,615	0.3
Net Worth	1,018,765	46.2
Total Liab & Net Worth	**2,205,120**	**100.0**
Net Sales	4,170,025	100.0
Gross Profit	1,100,887	26.4
Net Profit After Tax	216,841	5.2
Working Capital	310,922	—

RATIOS	UQ	MED	LQ
Quick Ratio	1.3	1.0	0.6
Current Ratio	2.1	1.4	1.0
Curr Liab To Nw	27.4	70.2	145.4
Curr Liab To Inv	123.2	228.1	483.2
Total Liab To Nw	53.1	98.4	221.3
Fixed Assets To Nw	38.4	69.7	116.5
Coll Period	13.5	28.5	57.9
Sales To Inv	53.3	23.5	7.7
Assets To Sales	29.2	61.1	108.8
Sales To Nwc	18.0	10.4	3.5
Acct Pay To Sales	1.9	4.3	10.4
Return On Sales	8.5	4.1	1.0
Return On Assets	12.1	5.8	1.7
Return On Nw	30.4	15.6	5.8

	SIC 0723 CROP PREP SVCS,MRKT INDUSTRY ASSETS $5,000,000-$25,000,000 1995 (51 Establishments) $	%	SIC 0724 COTTON GINNING (NO BREAKDOWN) 1995 (93 Establishments) $	%	SIC 0724 COTTON GINNING INDUSTRY ASSETS $500,000 - $1,000,000 1995 (15 Establishments) $	%	SIC 0724 COTTON GINNING INDUSTRY ASSETS $1,000,000 - $5,000,000 1995 (59 Establishments) $	%
Cash	987,710	12.9	247,720	14.8	71,242	9.7	359,968	16.3
Accounts Receivable	1,699,780	22.2	202,528	12.1	58,022	7.9	278,258	12.6
Notes Receivable	107,193	1.4	21,759	1.3	26,440	3.6	13,250	0.6
Inventory	719,727	9.4	97,080	5.8	37,457	5.1	119,253	5.4
Other Current	627,847	8.2	53,561	3.2	19,096	2.6	75,085	3.4
Total Current	**4,142,256**	**54.1**	**622,648**	**37.2**	**212,257**	**28.9**	**845,815**	**38.3**
Fixed Assets	2,702,803	35.3	714,707	42.7	345,928	47.1	896,608	40.6
Other Non-current	811,607	10.6	336,431	20.1	176,269	24.0	465,971	21.1
Total Assets	**7,656,666**	**100.0**	**1,673,786**	**100.0**	**734,455**	**100.0**	**2,208,394**	**100.0**
Accounts Payable	1,041,307	13.6	117,165	7.0	24,237	3.3	161,213	7.3
Bank Loans	7,657	0.1	—	—	—	—	—	—
Notes Payable	398,147	5.2	103,775	6.2	66,835	9.1	110,420	5.0
Other Current	1,715,093	22.4	222,614	13.3	69,039	9.4	318,009	14.4
Total Current	**3,162,203**	**41.3**	**443,553**	**26.5**	**160,111**	**21.8**	**589,641**	**26.7**
Other Long Term	980,053	12.8	309,650	18.5	88,135	12.0	439,470	19.9
Deferred Credits	45,940	0.6	1,674	0.1	2,203	0.3	—	—
Net Worth	3,468,470	45.3	918,909	54.9	484,006	65.9	1,179,282	53.4
Total Liab & Net Worth	**7,656,666**	**100.0**	**1,673,786**	**100.0**	**734,455**	**100.0**	**2,208,394**	**100.0**
Net Sales	10,789,669	100.0	2,388,965	100.0	1,297,935	100.0	2,995,127	100.0
Gross Profit	3,129,004	29.0	843,305	35.3	765,782	59.0	886,558	29.6
Net Profit After Tax	755,277	7.0	191,117	8.0	170,029	13.1	203,669	6.8
Working Capital	980,053	—	179,095	—	52,146	—	256,174	—

RATIOS	UQ	MED	LQ	UQ	MED	LQ	UQ	MED	LQ	UQ	MED	LQ
SOLVENCY												
Quick Ratio (times)	1.0	0.9	0.7	1.8	1.1	0.6	0.9	0.7	0.3	1.5	1.1	0.7
Current Ratio (times)	1.5	1.2	1.0	2.8	1.5	0.9	1.7	1.1	0.6	2.4	1.4	1.1
Curr Liab To Nw (%)	47.6	99.2	151.3	21.0	45.5	80.4	5.6	22.8	32.3	21.6	46.1	78.4
Curr Liab To Inv (%)	151.4	276.1	437.2	119.5	212.2	381.8	53.1	70.9	146.2	119.5	186.4	256.5
Total Liab To Nw (%)	69.5	126.9	226.7	37.1	75.3	151.7	10.8	37.1	66.5	38.3	88.1	157.6
Fixed Assets To Nw (%)	59.9	88.3	134.5	50.6	88.8	159.5	39.1	51.6	70.9	50.3	85.8	154.6
EFFICIENCY												
Coll Period (days)	16.8	33.2	136.2	11.6	26.1	36.4	8.0	12.4	22.3	14.6	27.2	41.8
Sales To Inv (times)	41.4	25.2	12.3	132.6	52.5	14.3	22.5	18.8	13.6	186.4	53.9	12.6
Assets To Sales (%)	52.4	66.6	130.0	48.7	70.6	117.8	26.7	34.5	52.9	51.8	76.4	118.2
Sales To Nwc (times)	29.2	12.8	8.1	17.6	9.2	4.9	9.0	6.3	4.1	20.1	9.2	5.0
Acct Pay To Sales (%)	2.4	5.8	12.6	0.8	2.6	8.9	0.9	1.6	2.2	0.7	2.3	9.1
PROFITABILITY												
Return On Sales (%)	8.0	3.6	0.8	11.7	4.5	0.5	3.5	1.6	(0.1)	12.6	5.4	0.7
Return On Assets (%)	9.7	5.1	0.7	16.2	7.3	1.6	4.2	2.3	0.1	13.2	7.3	1.7
Return On Nw (%)	25.3	11.5	1.6	38.8	12.0	3.4	5.9	2.5	(0.4)	36.5	12.0	3.8

SIC 0741 VTRNRY SVCS,LVESTCK (NO BREAKDOWN) — 1995 (23 Establishments) | SIC 0742 VTRNRY SVCS,SPCLTES (NO BREAKDOWN) — 1995 (143 Establishments) | SIC 0742 VTRNRY SVCS,SPCLTES UNDER $100,000 — 1995 (59 Establishments) | SIC 0742 VTRNRY SVCS,SPCLTES INDUSTRY ASSETS $100,000 - $250,000 — 1995 (45 Establishments)

	SIC 0741 $	%	SIC 0742 (No Brkdwn) $	%	SIC 0742 Under $100,000 $	%	SIC 0742 $100,000-$250,000 $	%
Cash	17,356	10.6	32,367	24.7	18,136	37.7	29,578	19.4
Accounts Receivable	35,858	21.9	10,614	8.1	2,694	5.6	12,807	8.4
Notes Receivable	491	0.3	1,966	1.5	385	0.8	4,726	3.1
Inventory	28,981	17.7	9,435	7.2	3,656	7.6	10,672	7.0
Other Current	8,678	5.3	4,193	3.2	1,732	3.6	2,744	1.8
Total Current	**91,365**	**55.8**	**58,575**	**44.7**	**26,602**	**55.3**	**60,528**	**39.7**
Fixed Assets	53,050	32.4	52,154	39.8	16,692	34.7	65,712	43.1
Other Non-current	19,321	11.8	20,311	15.5	4,811	10.0	26,224	17.2
Total Assets	**163,736**	**100.0**	**131,040**	**100.0**	**48,105**	**100.0**	**152,464**	**100.0**
Accounts Payable	10,643	6.5	5,766	4.4	2,117	4.4	4,269	2.8
Bank Loans	—	—	—	—	—	—	—	—
Notes Payable	3,766	2.3	4,717	3.6	1,972	4.1	4,574	3.0
Other Current	26,525	16.2	20,442	15.6	8,178	17.0	22,717	14.9
Total Current	**40,934**	**25.0**	**30,925**	**23.6**	**12,267**	**25.5**	**31,560**	**20.7**
Other Long Term	24,397	14.9	22,670	17.3	3,704	7.7	24,699	16.2
Deferred Credits	1,965	1.2	524	0.4	289	0.6		0.6
Net Worth	96,441	58.9	76,920	58.7	31,846	66.2	96,205	63.1
Total Liab & Net Worth	**163,736**	**100.0**	**131,040**	**100.0**	**48,105**	**100.0**	**152,464**	**100.0**
Net Sales	852,125	100.0	615,508	100.0	406,648	100.0	662,226	100.0
Gross Profit	455,887	53.5	361,919	58.8	216,743	53.3	443,691	67.0
Net Profit After Tax	72,431	8.5	28,313	4.6	14,233	3.5	60,925	9.2
Working Capital	50,431	—	27,650	—	14,335	—	28,968	—

RATIOS	SIC 0741 UQ	MED	LQ	0742(NoBrk) UQ	MED	LQ	0742 Under$100K UQ	MED	LQ	0742 $100-250K UQ	MED	LQ
SOLVENCY												
Quick Ratio (times)	2.3	1.4	0.8	4.7	1.7	0.5	7.0	2.2	0.7	4.2	1.5	0.5
Current Ratio (times)	3.6	2.8	1.7	7.2	2.6	1.0	7.8	3.6	1.4	8.3	2.5	1.0
Curr Liab To Nw (%)	14.7	42.7	73.6	7.1	25.1	68.2	9.3	16.0	41.7	5.4	15.6	97.6
Curr Liab To Inv (%)	52.9	115.4	239.3	77.7	148.9	266.4	52.1	109.0	197.0	58.6	163.9	270.3
Total Liab To Nw (%)	31.8	58.9	105.1	13.0	45.5	155.7	10.1	25.1	83.3	11.1	40.1	134.3
Fixed Assets To Nw (%)	16.8	39.7	74.3	36.0	65.2	117.8	26.1	51.2	80.9	38.1	75.3	113.9
EFFICIENCY												
Coll Period (days)	26.8	33.1	35.8	6.3	11.7	21.0	1.8	7.7	11.0	13.2	15.7	26.5
Sales To Inv (times)	17.1	9.6	6.4	48.1	33.4	22.6	117.3	47.7	36.6	51.5	41.8	29.0
Assets To Sales (%)	16.5	32.2	38.7	12.3	21.1	38.1	6.8	10.2	15.0	18.7	22.5	32.4
Sales To Nwc (times)	13.2	5.2	4.7	31.8	23.2	10.9	53.4	25.5	13.7	27.5	24.3	11.7
Acct Pay To Sales (%)	1.2	3.6	4.9	1.1	2.9	6.0	1.2	1.2	1.3	0.6	1.1	5.4
PROFITABILITY												
Return On Sales (%)	16.1	13.2	4.2	10.7	4.6	0.7	5.7	2.7	1.9	18.2	5.9	1.0
Return On Assets (%)	41.3	18.3	5.1	36.1	16.3	3.2	46.2	25.0	10.4	41.2	15.0	0.9
Return On Nw (%)	62.6	24.7	6.2	72.4	33.7	4.5	76.4	58.4	20.7	97.5	21.1	1.0

	SIC 0742 VTRNRY SVCS,SPCLTES $250,000-$500,000 (22 Est.) $	%	SIC 0751 LVSTCK SVCS,EXC VET (NO BREAKDOWN) (27 Est.) $	%	SIC 0752 ANIMAL SPECLTY SVCS (NO BREAKDOWN) (50 Est.) $	%	SIC 0752 ANIMAL SPECLTY SVCS UNDER $100,000 (15 Est.) $	%
Cash	47,622	13.0	205,298	17.0	55,899	14.2	4,496	19.5
Accounts Receivable	30,038	8.2	194,429	16.1	9,448	2.4	392	1.7
Notes Receivable	4,396	1.2	2,415	0.2	1,968	0.5	—	—
Inventory	30,771	8.4	121,771	10.1	48,419	12.3	5,925	25.7
Other Current	10,990	3.0	101,441	8.4	29,524	7.5	1,037	4.5
Total Current	**123,817**	**33.8**	**625,555**	**51.8**	**145,258**	**36.9**	**11,850**	**51.4**
Fixed Assets	170,340	46.5	466,147	38.6	198,795	50.5	9,199	39.9
Other Non-current	72,166	19.7	115,933	9.6	49,600	12.6	2,006	8.7
Total Assets	**366,323**	**100.0**	**1,207,635**	**100.0**	**393,653**	**100.0**	**23,055**	**100.0**
Accounts Payable	34,068	9.3	66,420	5.5	17,321	4.4	784	3.4
Bank Loans	—	—	—	—	—	—	—	—
Notes Payable	13,188	3.6	6,038	0.5	5,117	1.3	646	2.8
Other Current	26,009	7.1	211,336	17.5	24,800	6.3	2,974	12.9
Total Current	**73,265**	**20.0**	**283,794**	**23.5**	**47,238**	**12.0**	**4,404**	**19.1**
Other Long Term	145,064	39.6	140,086	11.6	80,699	20.5	3,066	13.3
Deferred Credits	—	—	6,038	0.5	3,543	0.9	715	3.1
Net Worth	147,994	40.4	777,717	64.4	262,173	66.6	14,870	64.5
Total Liab & Net Worth	**366,323**	**100.0**	**1,207,635**	**100.0**	**393,653**	**100.0**	**23,055**	**100.0**
Net Sales	1,081,079	100.0	3,372,655	100.0	247,566	100.0	88,925	100.0
Gross Profit	795,674	73.6	1,662,719	49.3	136,161	55.0	47,842	53.8
Net Profit After Tax	62,703	5.8	84,316	2.5	29,708	12.0	11,738	13.2
Working Capital	50,552	—	341,761	—	98,020	—	7,446	—

RATIOS	0742 UQ	MED	LQ	0751 UQ	MED	LQ	0752 UQ	MED	LQ	0752U UQ	MED	LQ
SOLVENCY												
Quick Ratio (times)	2.7	0.9	0.9	2.9	2.1	0.9	4.3	1.6	0.6	1.0	0.7	0.5
Current Ratio (times)	4.0	1.6	1.0	4.6	3.4	1.7	8.6	3.3	1.6	1.6	1.6	0.5
Curr Liab To Nw (%)	29.1	52.8	65.0	13.9	21.3	45.6	1.7	6.2	22.1	8.6	16.1	23.3
Curr Liab To Inv (%)	139.7	160.4	321.2	101.8	159.9	290.9	41.6	101.0	324.5	16.3	82.5	99.6
Total Liab To Nw (%)	68.0	93.8	500.6	15.8	30.5	132.3	8.4	28.9	79.3	16.3	21.8	57.4
Fixed Assets To Nw (%)	57.4	101.5	260.4	34.1	54.3	126.9	35.6	78.4	118.0	27.3	48.9	83.1
EFFICIENCY												
Coll Period (days)	6.4	10.1	14.0	14.6	31.0	53.3	4.0	9.9	34.3	2.6	2.6	2.6
Sales To Inv (times)	34.1	22.1	17.9	43.8	21.8	10.7	58.2	23.0	8.3	13.5	8.0	4.1
Assets To Sales (%)	18.8	46.8	141.6	32.6	56.8	81.7	58.3	113.6	202.4	25.7	34.0	38.7
Sales To Nwc (times)	27.3	11.8	7.6	12.0	6.6	2.9	7.4	3.9	2.5	14.0	7.8	3.6
Acct Pay To Sales (%)	3.0	4.6	11.2	1.5	2.9	4.3	1.2	2.1	4.0	—	—	—
PROFITABILITY												
Return On Sales (%)	8.0	0.4	(39.4)	5.2	3.0	(0.1)	22.7	14.4	6.4	13.4	8.6	8.1
Return On Assets (%)	28.3	5.2	(3.7)	7.5	2.5	(0.1)	37.2	11.4	4.3	24.2	21.8	20.5
Return On Nw (%)	43.8	21.5	(9.7)	12.2	3.5	(0.2)	53.9	22.6	5.5	49.8	40.8	38.7

SIC 0762 FARM MNGMNT SVCS (NO BREAKDOWN) — 1995 (27 Establishments) | SIC 0781 LNDSCPE CNSLNG, PLNG (NO BREAKDOWN) — 1995 (223 Establishments) | SIC 0781 LNDSCPE CNSLNG, PLNG — INDUSTRY ASSETS UNDER $100,000 — 1995 (54 Establishments) | SIC 0781 LNDSCPE CNSLNG, PLNG — INDUSTRY ASSETS $100,000 - $250,000 — 1995 (55 Establishments)

	SIC 0762 $	%	SIC 0781 (No Brkdwn) $	%	SIC 0781 Under $100,000 $	%	SIC 0781 $100,000-$250,000 $	%
Cash	72,162	15.2	40,496	14.4	10,003	20.8	29,077	18.5
Accounts Receivable	64,566	13.6	79,586	28.3	7,262	15.1	36,935	23.5
Notes Receivable	5,697	1.2	1,969	0.7	—	—	2,043	1.3
Inventory	7,596	1.6	15,186	5.4	1,731	3.6	8,802	5.6
Other Current	38,929	8.2	17,155	6.1	1,683	3.5	13,360	8.5
Total Current	**188,950**	**39.8**	**154,392**	**54.9**	**20,680**	**43.0**	**90,217**	**57.4**
Fixed Assets	219,334	46.2	111,083	39.5	24,672	51.3	62,240	39.6
Other Non-current	66,465	14.0	15,749	5.6	2,741	5.7	4,715	3.0
Total Assets	**474,749**	**100.0**	**281,224**	**100.0**	**48,093**	**100.0**	**157,172**	**100.0**
Accounts Payable	50,323	10.6	29,247	10.4	2,886	6.0	14,460	9.2
Bank Loans	—	—	844	0.3	—	—	—	—
Notes Payable	29,434	6.2	16,030	5.7	2,789	5.8	7,544	4.8
Other Current	31,808	6.7	46,402	16.5	11,350	23.6	22,790	14.5
Total Current	**111,566**	**23.5**	**92,523**	**32.9**	**17,025**	**35.4**	**44,794**	**28.5**
Other Long Term	86,879	18.3	52,589	18.7	10,436	21.7	29,077	18.5
Deferred Credits	—	—	844	0.3	—	—	—	—
Net Worth	276,304	58.2	135,269	48.1	20,632	42.9	83,301	53.0
Total Liab & Net Worth	**474,749**	**100.0**	**281,224**	**100.0**	**48,093**	**100.0**	**157,172**	**100.0**
Net Sales	2,061,943	100.0	1,043,876	100.0	311,273	100.0	650,862	100.0
Gross Profit	540,229	26.2	450,954	43.2	188,943	60.7	317,621	48.8
Net Profit After Tax	191,761	9.3	57,413	5.5	36,108	11.6	31,241	4.8
Working Capital	77,384	—	61,869	—	3,655	—	45,423	—

RATIOS

	SIC 0762 UQ	MED	LQ	SIC 0781 (No Brkdwn) UQ	MED	LQ	SIC 0781 Under $100K UQ	MED	LQ	SIC 0781 $100-250K UQ	MED	LQ
SOLVENCY												
Quick Ratio (times)	1.6	1.1	0.6	2.5	1.2	0.8	1.7	0.9	0.5	3.4	1.8	0.7
Current Ratio (times)	5.3	1.5	0.9	3.5	1.7	1.1	2.2	1.2	0.6	4.5	2.3	1.1
Curr Liab To Nw (%)	8.1	17.5	61.1	22.2	54.4	137.5	8.2	31.2	77.9	15.1	40.8	61.9
Curr Liab To Inv (%)	227.4	349.8	398.7	83.9	205.6	487.3	32.1	65.3	185.2	79.2	172.4	477.9
Total Liab To Nw (%)	9.8	29.1	124.7	41.8	100.9	199.3	30.1	65.7	109.7	32.2	70.5	116.3
Fixed Assets To Nw (%)	37.0	81.7	122.6	40.5	72.9	134.9	56.2	96.5	120.0	34.0	56.2	113.9
EFFICIENCY												
Coll Period (days)	20.1	47.5	65.3	19.2	36.5	67.6	10.0	12.6	24.6	12.8	26.3	49.7
Sales To Inv (times)	75.5	70.7	25.4	89.6	42.4	18.0	50.0	31.0	17.2	99.5	40.9	13.5
Assets To Sales (%)	38.9	58.4	129.1	21.5	33.1	47.8	11.5	15.6	27.6	19.3	23.5	29.3
Sales To Nwc (times)	19.1	5.5	2.7	17.6	10.5	5.9	12.6	10.8	7.4	16.0	11.1	8.0
Acct Pay To Sales (%)	2.6	4.2	10.6	1.1	2.7	6.8	0.4	0.6	1.6	1.0	1.8	4.1
PROFITABILITY												
Return On Sales (%)	10.2	7.6	0.5	9.1	3.4	1.1	17.5	6.6	1.5	10.1	4.4	2.4
Return On Assets (%)	2.6	1.2	(1.2)	21.3	7.8	2.3	50.2	25.9	8.2	30.5	13.1	7.4
Return On Nw (%)	6.4	1.2	(2.0)	49.4	16.3	4.7	203.0	72.1	11.3	49.9	27.5	10.4

	SIC 0781 LNDSCPE CNSLNG, PLNG INDUSTRY ASSETS $250,000 - $500,000 1995 (40 Establishments)		SIC 0781 LNDSCPE CNSLNG, PLNG INDUSTRY ASSETS $500,000 - $1,000,000 1995 (38 Establishments)		SIC 0781 LNDSCPE CNSLNG, PLNG INDUSTRY ASSETS $1,000,000 - $5,000,000 1995 (34 Establishments)		SIC 0782 LAWN GARDEN SVCS (NO BREAKDOWN) 1995 (1008 Establishments)	
	$	%	$	%	$	%	$	%
Cash	41,592	12.0	75,275	10.8	102,452	6.4	36,793	13.1
Accounts Receivable	108,485	31.3	266,249	38.2	638,726	39.9	71,338	25.4
Notes Receivable	2,426	0.7	4,879	0.7	16,008	1.0	1,966	0.7
Inventory	13,517	3.9	50,880	7.3	128,065	8.0	19,941	7.1
Other Current	17,330	5.0	27,182	3.9	152,078	9.5	14,043	5.0
Total Current	**183,350**	**52.9**	**424,465**	**60.9**	**1,037,330**	**64.8**	**144,081**	**51.3**
Fixed Assets	142,452	41.1	232,794	33.4	430,620	26.9	117,680	41.9
Other Non-current	20,796	6.0	39,728	5.7	132,868	8.3	19,098	6.8
Total Assets	**346,598**	**100.0**	**696,987**	**100.0**	**1,600,818**	**100.0**	**280,859**	**100.0**
Accounts Payable	33,967	9.8	94,790	13.6	249,728	15.6	28,648	10.2
Bank Loans	5,199	1.5	697	0.1		—	562	0.2
Notes Payable	18,023	5.2	38,334	5.5	121,662	7.6	16,290	5.8
Other Current	53,723	15.5	84,335	12.1	244,925	15.3	46,903	16.7
Total Current	**110,911**	**32.0**	**218,157**	**31.3**	**616,315**	**38.5**	**92,403**	**32.9**
Other Long Term	75,905	21.9	105,942	15.2	252,929	15.8	54,768	19.5
Deferred Credits	2,080	0.6	2,788	0.4	12,807	0.8	843	0.3
Net Worth	157,702	45.5	370,100	53.1	718,767	44.9	132,846	47.3
Total Liab & Net Worth	**346,598**	**100.0**	**696,987**	**100.0**	**1,600,818**	**100.0**	**280,859**	**100.0**
Net Sales	1,090,290	100.0	1,851,166	100.0	3,309,665	100.0	903,993	100.0
Gross Profit	397,956	36.5	744,169	40.2	1,098,809	33.2	383,293	42.4
Net Profit After Tax	49,063	4.5	111,070	6.0	39,716	1.2	54,240	6.0
Working Capital	72,439	—	206,308	—	421,015	—	51,678	—

RATIOS	UQ	MED	LQ	UQ	MED	LQ	UQ	MED	LQ	UQ	MED	LQ
SOLVENCY												
Quick Ratio (times)	2.0	1.2	1.0	2.8	1.7	1.1	1.7	1.1	0.8	2.2	1.3	0.7
Current Ratio (times)	2.8	1.4	1.1	3.8	2.3	1.3	2.7	1.6	1.3	3.2	1.6	1.0
Curr Liab To Nw (%)	35.7	58.8	146.4	20.7	60.4	132.5	33.6	102.0	164.8	22.5	59.0	127.4
Curr Liab To Inv (%)	104.5	151.1	276.3	53.5	210.5	385.0	148.7	337.5	672.0	88.7	195.9	414.4
Total Liab To Nw (%)	49.3	114.5	232.4	34.9	109.9	196.4	73.8	152.9	189.4	38.2	94.8	200.3
Fixed Assets To Nw (%)	40.9	100.5	154.2	41.1	54.8	95.6	32.4	46.3	76.9	44.8	83.7	138.6
EFFICIENCY												
Coll Period (days)	28.2	36.7	50.2	23.7	56.2	80.3	40.0	60.6	108.6	17.3	35.0	54.9
Sales To Inv (times)	84.6	31.2	22.0	105.0	47.0	14.1	80.6	43.9	23.2	107.4	36.1	14.1
Assets To Sales (%)	23.2	31.6	37.2	32.2	37.3	54.1	33.7	47.3	70.6	23.1	31.8	46.8
Sales To Nwc (times)	31.3	15.0	6.5	10.9	7.1	5.4	16.4	9.1	3.2	25.2	11.6	6.2
Acct Pay To Sales (%)	1.1	2.8	4.8	1.2	2.7	8.1	2.2	6.9	11.7	1.5	3.4	6.6
PROFITABILITY												
Return On Sales (%)	7.7	3.4	1.1	12.5	5.3	1.4	3.4	1.5	0.4	9.4	4.1	1.2
Return On Assets (%)	15.7	5.9	2.8	18.4	8.3	2.8	7.3	2.8	0.6	23.1	9.6	2.7
Return On Nw (%)	39.7	17.2	4.4	38.5	12.5	4.7	11.9	5.6	1.4	52.4	22.6	7.3

SIC 0782 — LAWN GARDEN SVCS — INDUSTRY ASSETS — UNDER $100,000 — 1995 (270 Establishments)

	$	%
Cash	9,511	17.5
Accounts Receivable	10,164	18.7
Notes Receivable	217	0.4
Inventory	2,120	3.9
Other Current	1,848	3.4
Total Current	**23,860**	**43.9**
Fixed Assets	27,339	50.3
Other Non-current	3,152	5.8
Total Assets	**54,351**	**100.0**
Accounts Payable	4,402	8.1
Bank Loans	54	0.1
Notes Payable	3,207	5.9
Other Current	9,620	17.7
Total Current	**17,284**	**31.8**
Other Long Term	10,707	19.7
Deferred Credits	54	0.1
Net Worth	26,306	48.4
Total Liab & Net Worth	**54,351**	**100.0**
Net Sales	264,067	100.0
Gross Profit	136,259	51.6
Net Profit After Tax	20,333	7.7
Working Capital	6,576	—

RATIOS	UQ	MED	LQ
SOLVENCY			
Quick Ratio (times)	2.5	1.3	0.5
Current Ratio (times)	3.1	1.5	0.8
Curr Liab To Nw (%)	18.3	46.5	117.3
Curr Liab To Inv (%)	114.4	207.6	400.3
Total Liab To Nw (%)	26.0	66.3	168.3
Fixed Assets To Nw (%)	55.7	93.3	177.3
EFFICIENCY			
Coll Period (days)	8.8	19.4	35.8
Sales To Inv (times)	156.3	66.8	20.9
Assets To Sales (%)	12.3	19.2	31.6
Sales To Nwc (times)	43.2	21.2	10.5
Acct Pay To Sales (%)	1.0	2.3	4.5
PROFITABILITY			
Return On Sales (%)	14.6	6.8	1.2
Return On Assets (%)	58.0	23.1	3.9
Return On Nw (%)	117.6	40.5	9.1

SIC 0782 — LAWN GARDEN SVCS — INDUSTRY ASSETS — $100,000 - $250,000 — 1995 (221 Establishments)

	$	%
Cash	23,237	14.6
Accounts Receivable	32,945	20.7
Notes Receivable	1,273	0.8
Inventory	12,096	7.6
Other Current	8,117	5.1
Total Current	**77,669**	**48.8**
Fixed Assets	70,666	44.4
Other Non-current	10,823	6.8
Total Assets	**159,157**	**100.0**
Accounts Payable	13,051	8.2
Bank Loans	—	—
Notes Payable	9,231	5.8
Other Current	27,852	17.5
Total Current	**50,134**	**31.5**
Other Long Term	33,105	20.8
Deferred Credits	477	0.3
Net Worth	75,440	47.4
Total Liab & Net Worth	**159,157**	**100.0**
Net Sales	547,299	100.0
Gross Profit	275,291	50.3
Net Profit After Tax	34,480	6.3
Working Capital	27,535	—

RATIOS	UQ	MED	LQ
SOLVENCY			
Quick Ratio (times)	2.5	1.2	0.6
Current Ratio (times)	3.5	1.6	1.0
Curr Liab To Nw (%)	20.7	53.4	114.2
Curr Liab To Inv (%)	75.9	167.1	351.8
Total Liab To Nw (%)	42.3	104.2	183.0
Fixed Assets To Nw (%)	48.1	89.9	140.9
EFFICIENCY			
Coll Period (days)	9.1	19.0	39.1
Sales To Inv (times)	92.3	33.0	16.0
Assets To Sales (%)	22.1	28.6	43.1
Sales To Nwc (times)	25.3	13.3	7.0
Acct Pay To Sales (%)	1.1	2.5	4.8
PROFITABILITY			
Return On Sales (%)	10.4	5.1	1.5
Return On Assets (%)	28.0	15.4	3.7
Return On Nw (%)	60.6	29.1	9.3

SIC 0782 — LAWN GARDEN SVCS — INDUSTRY ASSETS — $250,000 - $500,000 — 1995 (248 Establishments)

	$	%
Cash	38,188	10.9
Accounts Receivable	94,944	27.1
Notes Receivable	3,153	0.9
Inventory	32,582	9.3
Other Current	15,065	4.3
Total Current	**183,932**	**52.5**
Fixed Assets	142,240	40.6
Other Non-current	24,174	6.9
Total Assets	**350,346**	**100.0**
Accounts Payable	37,487	10.7
Bank Loans	701	0.2
Notes Payable	21,371	6.1
Other Current	45,195	12.9
Total Current	**104,753**	**29.9**
Other Long Term	74,974	21.4
Deferred Credits	1,752	0.5
Net Worth	168,867	48.2
Total Liab & Net Worth	**350,346**	**100.0**
Net Sales	1,036,259	100.0
Gross Profit	460,099	44.4
Net Profit After Tax	71,502	6.9
Working Capital	79,179	—

RATIOS	UQ	MED	LQ
SOLVENCY			
Quick Ratio (times)	2.6	1.4	0.7
Current Ratio (times)	3.7	1.8	1.1
Curr Liab To Nw (%)	18.4	54.3	121.2
Curr Liab To Inv (%)	84.5	163.2	351.8
Total Liab To Nw (%)	41.9	105.2	192.1
Fixed Assets To Nw (%)	46.0	83.1	134.4
EFFICIENCY			
Coll Period (days)	21.2	35.4	56.4
Sales To Inv (times)	87.4	30.6	10.7
Assets To Sales (%)	27.5	34.3	49.8
Sales To Nwc (times)	25.5	9.6	5.3
Acct Pay To Sales (%)	1.5	3.7	8.0
PROFITABILITY			
Return On Sales (%)	10.5	4.2	1.7
Return On Assets (%)	23.0	11.9	3.4
Return On Nw (%)	54.7	28.8	8.9

SIC 0782 — LAWN GARDEN SVCS — INDUSTRY ASSETS — $500,000 - $1,000,000 — 1995 (157 Establishments)

	$	%
Cash	65,154	9.6
Accounts Receivable	216,502	31.9
Notes Receivable	4,072	0.6
Inventory	52,259	7.7
Other Current	33,935	5.0
Total Current	**371,923**	**54.8**
Fixed Assets	251,116	37.0
Other Non-current	55,653	8.2
Total Assets	**678,691**	**100.0**
Accounts Payable	80,086	11.8
Bank Loans	3,393	0.5
Notes Payable	35,971	5.3
Other Current	124,200	18.3
Total Current	**243,650**	**35.9**
Other Long Term	114,699	16.9
Deferred Credits	2,715	0.4
Net Worth	317,627	46.8
Total Liab & Net Worth	**678,691**	**100.0**
Net Sales	1,948,373	100.0
Gross Profit	662,447	34.0
Net Profit After Tax	93,522	4.8
Working Capital	128,273	—

RATIOS	UQ	MED	LQ
SOLVENCY			
Quick Ratio (times)	1.9	1.2	0.8
Current Ratio (times)	2.6	1.6	1.1
Curr Liab To Nw (%)	24.9	73.7	145.2
Curr Liab To Inv (%)	82.3	209.6	450.2
Total Liab To Nw (%)	55.3	104.9	209.3
Fixed Assets To Nw (%)	41.8	77.2	117.5
EFFICIENCY			
Coll Period (days)	24.5	40.2	65.3
Sales To Inv (times)	102.7	43.5	17.1
Assets To Sales (%)	28.1	37.4	52.2
Sales To Nwc (times)	18.3	10.2	6.5
Acct Pay To Sales (%)	1.7	3.4	7.6
PROFITABILITY			
Return On Sales (%)	6.5	3.2	1.5
Return On Assets (%)	12.3	7.2	2.7
Return On Nw (%)	34.8	15.1	6.9

	SIC 0782 LAWN GARDEN SVCS INDUSTRY ASSETS $1,000,000 - $5,000,000 1995 (109 Establishments) $	%	SIC 0783 ORNMNTL TREE SVCS (NO BREAKDOWN) 1995 (124 Establishments) $	%	SIC 0783 ORNMNTL TREE SVCS INDUSTRY ASSETS UNDER $100,000 1995 (34 Establishments) $	%	SIC 0783 ORNMNTL TREE SVCS INDUSTRY ASSETS $100,000 - $250,000 1995 (36 Establishments) $	%
Cash	167,455	10.9	32,130	13.9	7,857	15.2	20,836	15.1
Accounts Receivable	536,164	34.9	46,230	20.0	4,497	8.7	36,429	26.4
Notes Receivable	7,681	0.5	2,080	0.9	310	0.6	3,864	2.8
Inventory	116,758	7.6	7,166	3.1	52	0.1	4,692	3.4
Other Current	144,411	9.4	9,708	4.2	1,706	3.3	3,726	2.7
Total Current	**972,470**	**63.3**	**97,315**	**42.1**	**14,421**	**27.9**	**69,545**	**50.4**
Fixed Assets	451,668	29.4	123,435	53.4	36,027	69.7	60,024	43.5
Other Non-current	112,149	7.3	10,402	4.5	1,241	2.4	8,417	6.1
Total Assets	**1,536,287**	**100.0**	**231,151**	**100.0**	**51,689**	**100.0**	**137,987**	**100.0**
Accounts Payable	227,370	14.8	15,718	6.8	1,085	2.1	15,041	10.9
Bank Loans	—	—	1,618	0.7	310	0.6	—	—
Notes Payable	86,032	5.6	12,251	5.3	4,704	9.1	6,899	5.0
Other Current	290,358	18.9	42,994	18.6	13,853	26.8	25,114	18.2
Total Current	**603,761**	**39.3**	**72,581**	**31.4**	**19,952**	**38.6**	**47,054**	**34.1**
Other Long Term	258,096	16.8	61,024	26.4	13,594	26.3	39,740	28.8
Deferred Credits	7,681	0.5	231	0.1	—	—	—	—
Net Worth	666,749	43.4	97,315	42.1	18,143	35.1	51,193	37.1
Total Liab & Net Worth	**1,536,287**	**100.0**	**231,151**	**100.0**	**51,689**	**100.0**	**137,987**	**100.0**
Net Sales	3,927,680	100.0	794,942	100.0	237,716	100.0	478,524	100.0
Gross Profit	1,170,449	29.8	383,162	48.2	158,081	66.5	242,612	50.7
Net Profit After Tax	117,830	3.0	46,107	5.8	12,599	5.3	34,932	7.3
Working Capital	368,709	—	24,734	—	(5,531)	—	22,491	—

RATIOS	UQ	MED	LQ	UQ	MED	LQ	UQ	MED	LQ	UQ	MED	LQ
SOLVENCY												
Quick Ratio (times)	1.8	1.1	0.8	2.8	1.2	0.5	1.2	0.5	0.2	2.3	1.5	0.9
Current Ratio (times)	2.7	1.5	1.1	3.4	1.6	0.7	1.9	0.6	0.3	2.8	1.8	0.9
Curr Liab To Nw (%)	31.3	85.8	169.8	22.9	59.7	150.4	33.4	117.9	367.4	34.6	57.6	117.3
Curr Liab To Inv (%)	137.7	276.4	464.4	178.2	377.3	551.1	—	—	—	330.7	425.7	564.9
Total Liab To Nw (%)	47.4	124.3	236.1	45.0	109.7	250.5	37.3	188.5	444.4	74.0	116.6	273.2
Fixed Assets To Nw (%)	34.5	62.9	112.9	58.1	116.9	233.3	103.9	186.9	446.3	46.0	115.6	179.3
EFFICIENCY												
Coll Period (days)	36.9	48.4	70.8	22.3	31.8	48.6	19.5	27.1	48.4	19.7	28.8	44.9
Sales To Inv (times)	105.4	39.8	12.4	202.3	85.2	37.2	368.4	368.4	368.4	119.5	88.4	53.4
Assets To Sales (%)	30.7	37.8	53.2	23.3	35.4	50.2	11.9	29.9	33.0	20.2	31.7	39.5
Sales To Nwc (times)	15.1	7.9	4.4	26.9	15.5	6.7	55.5	16.1	8.4	22.3	17.4	12.3
Acct Pay To Sales (%)	2.6	4.6	9.6	1.0	2.2	3.9	0.9	1.0	1.4	1.3	3.0	5.3
PROFITABILITY												
Return On Sales (%)	4.5	2.0	0.7	11.2	5.1	1.9	12.0	7.1	1.5	12.9	5.4	3.1
Return On Assets (%)	11.1	4.8	1.4	21.5	8.3	3.1	45.3	17.0	(3.0)	13.5	8.2	3.4
Return On Nw (%)	23.4	11.9	5.2	53.2	17.9	6.1	132.8	98.6	(5.8)	26.8	14.0	6.9

	SIC 0783 ORNMNTL TREE SVCS INDUSTRY ASSETS $250,000 – $500,000 1995 (22 Establishments)		SIC 0783 ORNMNTL TREE SVCS INDUSTRY ASSETS $500,000 – $1,000,000 1995 (15 Establishments)		SIC 08 FORESTRY (NO BREAKDOWN) 1995 (88 Establishments)		SIC 08 FORESTRY CENTRAL 1995 (14 Establishments)	
	$	%	$	%	$	%	$	%
Cash	69,508	21.3	58,280	8.9	129,478	14.5	66,246	7.9
Accounts Receivable	67,224	20.6	132,277	20.2	125,014	14.0	213,831	25.5
Notes Receivable	—	—	—	—	8,037	0.9	4,193	0.5
Inventory	16,316	5.0	31,432	4.8	78,580	8.8	74,631	8.9
Other Current	14,685	4.5	30,777	4.7	76,794	8.6	39,412	4.7
Total Current	**167,733**	**51.4**	**252,767**	**38.6**	**417,903**	**46.8**	**398,313**	**47.5**
Fixed Assets	149,785	45.9	345,754	52.8	333,965	37.4	304,395	36.3
Other Non-current	8,811	2.7	56,316	8.6	141,087	15.8	135,846	16.2
Total Assets	**326,328**	**100.0**	**654,837**	**100.0**	**892,955**	**100.0**	**838,554**	**100.0**
Accounts Payable	22,190	6.8	41,910	6.4	57,149	6.4	54,506	6.5
Bank Loans	1,958	0.6	—	—	—	—	—	—
Notes Payable	14,685	4.5	8,513	1.3	70,543	7.9	76,308	9.1
Other Current	32,633	10.0	118,525	18.1	109,833	12.3	203,769	24.3
Total Current	**71,466**	**21.9**	**168,948**	**25.8**	**237,526**	**26.6**	**334,583**	**39.9**
Other Long Term	68,529	21.0	183,354	28.0	137,515	15.4	67,923	8.1
Deferred Credits	—	—	—	—	2,679	0.3	—	—
Net Worth	186,333	57.1	302,535	46.2	515,235	57.7	436,048	52.0
Total Liab & Net Worth	**326,328**	**100.0**	**654,837**	**100.0**	**892,955**	**100.0**	**838,554**	**100.0**
Net Sales	1,308,305	100.0	1,283,147	100.0	2,466,823	100.0	1,229,535	100.0
Gross Profit	553,413	42.3	583,832	45.5	912,725	37.0	458,617	37.3
Net Profit After Tax	61,490	4.7	65,440	5.1	103,607	4.2	(2,459)	(0.2)
Working Capital	96,267	—	83,819	—	180,377	—	63,730	—

RATIOS	UQ	MED	LQ	UQ	MED	LQ	UQ	MED	LQ	UQ	MED	LQ
SOLVENCY												
Quick Ratio (times)	5.1	2.9	0.9	2.9	1.2	0.7	2.3	1.1	0.5	1.3	0.9	0.7
Current Ratio (times)	5.9	2.9	1.9	3.4	1.7	1.0	4.4	2.1	1.1	2.4	1.1	0.9
Curr Liab To Nw (%)	12.7	23.9	82.3	17.8	42.0	110.5	8.5	34.8	91.8	34.5	57.9	84.3
Curr Liab To Inv (%)	65.1	524.1	632.0	167.8	218.4	271.7	74.8	119.8	248.4	99.7	155.6	193.3
Total Liab To Nw (%)	21.3	46.7	96.0	50.0	111.8	326.1	16.1	65.7	159.5	46.5	86.1	168.4
Fixed Assets To Nw (%)	28.3	65.2	124.6	57.6	90.7	377.4	36.7	63.4	118.9	39.4	78.0	103.5
EFFICIENCY												
Coll Period (days)	20.2	27.4	30.3	32.3	40.9	44.4	9.5	20.4	52.5	54.0	70.1	87.9
Sales To Inv (times)	327.1	94.3	38.8	197.4	51.1	28.6	44.0	18.0	7.8	113.6	83.9	54.2
Assets To Sales (%)	21.6	27.3	49.0	37.7	51.0	61.3	27.5	46.7	116.2	66.2	125.7	176.3
Sales To Nwc (times)	21.0	15.9	6.1	60.7	14.8	6.8	18.0	9.1	4.9	11.1	8.9	6.6
Acct Pay To Sales (%)	0.7	1.4	2.7	1.4	2.4	3.8	0.8	2.9	5.6	0.2	0.5	2.1
PROFITABILITY												
Return On Sales (%)	10.0	8.3	3.1	9.2	3.0	1.6	11.9	5.5	1.1	17.2	1.5	(8.1)
Return On Assets (%)	37.9	23.4	9.8	6.0	4.8	2.8	19.3	6.4	1.9	10.9	(1.6)	(7.6)
Return On Nw (%)	98.4	53.7	17.1	25.0	16.4	6.3	39.9	14.1	3.0	20.1	(1.8)	(9.9)

SIC 08 FORESTRY

	SOUTH 1995 (26 Establishments) $	%	WEST 1995 (42 Establishments) $	%	INDUSTRY ASSETS $250,000-$500,000 1995 (18 Establishments) $	%	INDUSTRY ASSETS $1,000,000-$5,000,000 1995 (21 Establishments) $	%
Cash	63,695	15.9	199,698	16.6	54,081	15.7	284,989	15.2
Accounts Receivable	47,671	11.9	153,984	12.8	64,415	18.7	296,239	15.8
Notes Receivable	2,804	0.7	10,827	0.9	7,234	2.1	1,875	0.1
Inventory	35,252	8.8	110,676	9.2	41,680	12.1	183,743	9.8
Other Current	34,852	8.7	87,819	7.3	36,513	10.6	193,118	10.3
Total Current	**184,274**	**46.0**	**563,004**	**46.8**	**203,924**	**59.2**	**959,963**	**51.2**
Fixed Assets	157,434	39.3	448,719	37.3	106,096	30.8	637,476	34.0
Other Non-current	58,888	14.7	191,277	15.9	34,447	10.0	277,489	14.8
Total Assets	**400,596**	**100.0**	**1,203,000**	**100.0**	**344,466**	**100.0**	**1,874,928**	**100.0**
Accounts Payable	38,057	9.5	56,541	4.7	26,179	7.6	123,745	6.6
Bank Loans	—	—	—	—	—	—	—	—
Notes Payable	49,273	12.3	63,759	5.3	25,490	7.4	67,497	3.6
Other Current	39,659	9.9	132,330	11.0	52,359	15.2	365,611	19.5
Total Current	**126,989**	**31.7**	**252,630**	**21.0**	**104,029**	**30.2**	**556,854**	**29.7**
Other Long Term	59,689	14.9	216,540	18.0	49,259	14.3	238,116	12.7
Deferred Credits	401	0.1	7,218	0.6	—	—	16,874	0.9
Net Worth	213,518	53.3	726,612	60.4	191,179	55.5	1,063,084	56.7
Total Liab & Net Worth	**400,596**	**100.0**	**1,203,000**	**100.0**	**344,466**	**100.0**	**1,874,928**	**100.0**
Net Sales	1,645,298	100.0	2,890,000	100.0	1,141,011	100.0	3,060,887	100.0
Gross Profit	640,021	38.9	1,014,390	35.1	439,289	38.5	838,683	27.4
Net Profit After Tax	64,167	3.9	144,500	5.0	66,179	5.8	(39,792)	(1.3)
Working Capital	57,285	—	310,374	—	99,895	—	403,109	—

RATIOS	UQ	MED	LQ	UQ	MED	LQ	UQ	MED	LQ	UQ	MED	LQ
SOLVENCY												
Quick Ratio (times)	2.5	0.9	0.4	2.9	1.6	0.7	2.9	1.0	0.4	1.3	0.9	0.6
Current Ratio (times)	3.8	1.5	0.7	5.1	2.2	1.3	4.9	2.2	1.2	1.7	1.2	0.9
Curr Liab To Nw (%)	14.8	42.5	152.7	7.9	29.0	58.2	6.6	37.1	118.3	11.1	18.2	34.7
Curr Liab To Inv (%)	38.5	150.2	248.4	77.4	114.3	394.8	74.8	82.2	155.6	66.6	114.3	194.6
Total Liab To Nw (%)	11.3	64.1	194.1	17.3	58.3	146.6	6.4	46.1	216.5	16.6	38.1	68.4
Fixed Assets To Nw (%)	37.0	63.8	121.5	32.7	61.7	122.0	37.4	56.8	112.8	19.5	41.2	61.1
EFFICIENCY												
Coll Period (days)	9.7	15.3	37.5	9.0	18.3	41.6	4.7	10.8	55.5	9.1	18.8	29.7
Sales To Inv (times)	37.5	15.4	6.5	41.6	17.5	7.3	208.6	22.0	13.3	18.2	14.8	2.6
Assets To Sales (%)	18.9	41.4	66.8	31.0	44.1	116.2	8.6	32.5	66.7	25.2	33.5	43.7
Sales To Nwc (times)	16.5	7.6	5.6	27.4	12.1	5.7	17.3	12.1	9.7	10.9	5.3	3.6
Acct Pay To Sales (%)	2.0	3.7	6.8	0.8	3.1	5.6	0.6	1.4	2.7	0.5	0.8	3.1
PROFITABILITY												
Return On Sales (%)	11.5	3.5	1.0	10.0	5.5	1.7	9.3	6.8	4.9	3.2	1.3	(3.6)
Return On Assets (%)	14.2	6.4	2.5	21.4	7.2	3.6	57.0	29.7	14.2	5.7	4.8	(4.6)
Return On Nw (%)	24.5	12.5	3.4	44.6	14.8	5.6	80.2	57.2	47.8	10.6	6.2	(17.9)

SIC 0811 TIMBER TRACTS (NO BREAKDOWN) — 1995 (44 Establishments)
SIC 0811 TIMBER TRACTS INDUSTRY ASSETS $1,000,000 - $5,000,000 — 1995 (11 Establishments)
SIC 0851 FORESTRY SERVICES (NO BREAKDOWN) — 1995 (39 Establishments)
SIC 09 FISHERIES (NO BREAKDOWN) — 1995 (38 Establishments)

	TIMBER TRACTS $	%	TIMBER TRACTS (IND. ASSETS) $	%	FORESTRY SERVICES $	%	FISHERIES $	%
Cash	193,118	10.3	184,343	8.1	84,298	18.7	283,583	20.9
Accounts Receivable	249,365	13.3	357,306	15.7	66,267	14.7	94,980	7.0
Notes Receivable	13,124	0.7	—	—	5,860	1.3	6,784	0.5
Inventory	232,491	12.4	250,342	11.0	22,540	5.0	103,121	7.6
Other Current	243,741	13.0	332,272	14.6	18,933	4.2	93,623	6.9
Total Current	**931,839**	**49.7**	**1,124,263**	**49.4**	**197,899**	**43.9**	**582,092**	**42.9**
Fixed Assets	571,853	30.5	671,372	29.5	190,686	42.3	538,672	39.7
Other Non-current	371,236	19.8	480,201	21.1	62,210	13.8	236,093	17.4
Total Assets	**1,874,928**	**100.0**	**2,275,836**	**100.0**	**450,794**	**100.0**	**1,356,857**	**100.0**
Accounts Payable	80,622	4.3	145,654	6.4	35,613	7.9	65,129	4.8
Bank Loans	—	—	—	—	—	—	—	—
Notes Payable	112,496	6.0	118,343	5.2	42,825	9.5	29,851	2.2
Other Current	224,991	12.0	512,063	22.5	58,603	13.0	151,968	11.2
Total Current	**418,109**	**22.3**	**776,060**	**34.1**	**137,041**	**30.4**	**246,948**	**18.2**
Other Long Term	268,115	14.3	161,584	7.1	78,889	17.5	328,359	24.2
Deferred Credits	5,625	0.3	20,483	0.9	1,352	0.3	5,427	0.4
Net Worth	1,183,080	63.1	1,317,709	57.9	233,511	51.8	776,122	57.2
Total Liab & Net Worth	**1,874,928**	**100.0**	**2,275,836**	**100.0**	**450,794**	**100.0**	**1,356,857**	**100.0**
Net Sales	2,890,000	100.0	2,890,000	100.0	2,051,738	100.0	1,655,496	100.0
Gross Profit	1,216,690	42.1	950,810	32.9	670,918	32.7	437,051	26.4
Net Profit After Tax	104,040	3.6	(63,580)	(2.2)	102,587	5.0	56,287	3.4
Working Capital	513,730	—	348,203	—	60,858	—	335,144	—

RATIOS	UQ	MED	LQ	UQ	MED	LQ	UQ	MED	LQ	UQ	MED	LQ
SOLVENCY												
Quick Ratio (times)	2.3	1.2	0.5	0.8	0.4	0.2	2.7	1.1	0.4	6.7	2.3	0.7
Current Ratio (times)	5.5	2.4	1.4	1.5	1.2	0.9	3.6	1.6	0.8	9.7	2.7	1.4
Curr Liab To Nw (%)	4.9	19.5	65.8	4.5	11.2	14.4	16.5	41.9	117.2	4.0	27.7	70.0
Curr Liab To Inv (%)	74.0	99.8	330.5	66.3	74.8	75.4	60.4	119.8	192.0	83.8	118.3	235.3
Total Liab To Nw (%)	9.0	47.5	177.9	4.5	13.1	37.8	36.7	86.0	153.4	17.2	69.7	116.4
Fixed Assets To Nw (%)	25.5	46.1	92.5	9.1	19.5	36.4	41.0	75.7	161.1	37.7	78.8	92.4
EFFICIENCY												
Coll Period (days)	8.1	15.2	47.2	9.9	13.1	17.2	10.8	21.5	47.3	6.9	20.4	46.7
Sales To Inv (times)	21.5	17.1	8.0	2.0	1.5	0.9	201.9	33.1	7.7	39.9	16.9	6.4
Assets To Sales (%)	43.7	99.5	205.8	26.4	46.7	68.9	27.4	34.7	66.2	36.0	55.8	88.9
Sales To Nwc (times)	15.8	7.6	4.5	10.4	5.0	4.5	25.4	10.2	6.8	14.1	9.2	4.5
Acct Pay To Sales (%)	0.5	2.0	6.4	0.2	0.3	0.6	0.9	1.8	4.4	2.0	2.9	5.2
PROFITABILITY												
Return On Sales (%)	16.0	6.0	2.1	5.5	4.3	(1.5)	9.2	4.8	1.4	8.9	2.4	0.5
Return On Assets (%)	23.0	6.4	3.5	7.7	6.3	4.3	19.1	9.8	3.2	6.2	4.3	(0.1)
Return On Nw (%)	40.9	16.6	6.8	18.5	11.2	7.5	46.1	16.9	4.5	17.2	5.5	0.2

	SIC 09 FISHERIES NORTHEAST 1995 (12 Establishments)		SIC 09 FISHERIES SOUTH 1995 (17 Establishments)		SIC 0912 FINFISH (NO BREAKDOWN) 1995 (13 Establishments)		SIC 0913 SHELLFISH (NO BREAKDOWN) 1995 (12 Establishments)	
	$	%	$	%	$	%	$	%
Cash	112,283	26.6	265,841	18.0	145,414	29.8	212,495	16.0
Accounts Receivable	6,332	1.5	147,690	10.0	40,989	8.4	132,810	10.0
Notes Receivable	—	—	13,292	0.9	976	0.2	15,937	1.2
Inventory	5,488	1.3	202,335	13.7	10,735	2.2	120,857	9.1
Other Current	31,659	7.5	72,368	4.9	22,934	4.7	87,654	6.6
Total Current	**155,761**	**36.9**	**701,525**	**47.5**	**221,050**	**45.3**	**569,753**	**42.9**
Fixed Assets	178,133	42.2	559,743	37.9	213,242	43.7	492,724	37.1
Other Non-current	88,222	20.9	215,627	14.6	53,676	11.0	265,619	20.0
Total Assets	**422,116**	**100.0**	**1,476,895**	**100.0**	**487,968**	**100.0**	**1,328,096**	**100.0**
Accounts Payable	1,688	0.4	82,706	5.6	15,127	3.1	49,140	3.7
Bank Loans	—	—	—	—	—	—	—	—
Notes Payable	—	—	67,937	4.6	—	—	42,499	3.2
Other Current	60,785	14.4	162,458	11.0	86,370	17.7	144,762	10.9
Total Current	**62,473**	**14.8**	**313,102**	**21.2**	**101,497**	**20.8**	**236,401**	**17.8**
Other Long Term	88,222	20.9	401,715	27.2	174,205	35.7	244,370	18.4
Deferred Credits	—	—	11,815	0.8	—	—	13,281	1.0
Net Worth	271,421	64.3	750,263	50.8	212,266	43.5	834,044	62.8
Total Liab & Net Worth	**422,116**	**100.0**	**1,476,895**	**100.0**	**487,968**	**100.0**	**1,328,096**	**100.0**
Net Sales	553,467	100.0	5,734,081	100.0	553,467	100.0	2,614,114	100.0
Gross Profit	182,091	32.9	1,370,445	23.9	158,292	28.6	658,757	25.2
Net Profit After Tax	(3,874)	(0.7)	149,086	2.6	35,975	6.5	57,511	2.2
Working Capital	93,288	—	388,423	—	119,553	—	333,352	—

RATIOS	UQ	MED	LQ	UQ	MED	LQ	UQ	MED	LQ	UQ	MED	LQ
SOLVENCY												
Quick Ratio (times)	13.6	2.5	1.4	5.1	1.6	0.6	3.0	2.5	1.7	5.9	1.6	0.6
Current Ratio (times)	18.1	2.7	1.6	6.5	2.3	1.4	6.3	2.6	1.7	7.0	2.7	1.4
Curr Liab To Nw (%)	2.2	4.3	53.9	15.3	42.0	85.6	12.8	37.3	90.1	9.9	22.9	65.4
Curr Liab To Inv (%)	90.3	109.4	140.2	108.8	143.1	196.0	165.3	246.7	247.2	108.4	117.9	290.2
Total Liab To Nw (%)	4.5	21.9	55.9	42.0	85.6	124.4	45.9	97.2	114.3	18.4	28.5	104.7
Fixed Assets To Nw (%)	36.8	56.2	89.9	52.4	83.3	99.4	46.4	86.0	128.0	32.6	78.8	111.0
EFFICIENCY												
Coll Period (days)	6.4	9.9	47.9	7.5	18.1	46.7	49.7	75.2	100.8	18.1	46.7	52.0
Sales To Inv (times)	36.2	16.4	12.6	27.6	11.0	5.3	31.9	27.1	22.2	34.8	10.9	5.2
Assets To Sales (%)	18.3	56.5	158.0	47.0	58.6	74.2	15.9	29.2	54.0	50.8	58.6	89.2
Sales To Nwc (times)	28.5	9.3	2.5	13.9	9.8	5.2	59.7	10.8	7.5	9.8	7.0	3.9
Acct Pay To Sales (%)	1.1	1.8	2.3	2.8	4.5	5.2	1.8	3.3	4.7	2.0	2.5	3.6
PROFITABILITY												
Return On Sales (%)	5.0	(1.1)	(1.9)	7.1	3.6	1.2	13.0	2.1	(1.2)	5.4	3.6	0.4
Return On Assets (%)	1.4	(0.5)	(11.7)	12.1	5.2	2.8	6.0	(0.1)	(10.9)	6.1	4.2	0.3
Return On Nw (%)	2.4	(0.2)	(11.3)	20.4	10.7	3.8	15.1	3.4	(5.6)	14.9	5.2	0.5

SIC 10 METAL MINING — Balance Sheet

	NO BREAKDOWN 1995 (110 Establishments) $	%	WEST 1995 (83 Establishments) $	%	INDUSTRY ASSETS $1,000,000-$5,000,000 1995 (15 Establishments) $	%	INDUSTRY ASSETS OVER $50,000,000 1995 (64 Establishments) $	%
Cash	6,663,359	9.2	5,775,126	9.3	377,691	13.3	47,134,560	8.0
Accounts Receivable	4,925,091	6.8	4,471,065	7.2	286,818	10.1	37,118,466	6.3
Notes Receivable	217,283	0.3	186,294	0.3	17,039	0.6	589,182	0.1
Inventory	4,707,808	6.5	4,346,869	7.0	241,381	8.5	43,010,286	7.3
Other Current	5,649,369	7.8	5,029,948	8.1	414,608	14.6	40,064,376	6.8
Total Current	**22,162,910**	**30.6**	**19,809,302**	**31.9**	**1,337,537**	**47.1**	**167,916,870**	**28.5**
Fixed Assets	36,503,617	50.4	31,794,241	51.2	1,127,393	39.7	328,763,556	55.8
Other Non-current	13,761,284	19.0	10,494,583	16.9	374,851	13.2	92,501,574	15.7
Total Assets	**72,427,811**	**100.0**	**62,098,126**	**100.0**	**2,839,782**	**100.0**	**589,182,000**	**100.0**
Accounts Payable	3,404,107	4.7	3,042,808	4.9	193,105	6.8	21,799,734	3.7
Bank Loans	—	—	—	—	—	—	—	—
Notes Payable	1,665,840	2.3	807,276	1.3	51,116	1.8	3,535,092	0.6
Other Current	7,967,059	11.0	7,141,284	11.5	391,890	13.8	61,274,928	10.4
Total Current	**13,037,006**	**18.0**	**10,991,368**	**17.7**	**636,111**	**22.4**	**86,609,754**	**14.7**
Other Long Term	16,513,541	22.8	14,282,569	23.0	247,061	8.7	168,506,052	28.6
Deferred Credits	1,086,417	1.5	931,472	1.5	22,718	0.8	11,783,640	2.0
Net Worth	41,790,847	57.7	35,892,717	57.8	1,933,892	68.1	322,282,554	54.7
Total Liab & Net Worth	**72,427,811**	**100.0**	**62,098,126**	**100.0**	**2,839,782**	**100.0**	**589,182,000**	**100.0**
Net Sales	51,245,000	100.0	28,691,292	100.0	1,206,279	100.0	108,880,000	100.0
Gross Profit	12,503,780	24.4	6,971,984	24.3	595,902	49.4	25,042,400	23.0
Net Profit After Tax	922,410	1.8	545,135	1.9	98,915	8.2	108,880	0.1
Working Capital	9,125,904	—	8,817,934	—	701,426	—	81,307,116	—

RATIOS

	NO BREAKDOWN UQ	MED	LQ	WEST UQ	MED	LQ	$1M-$5M UQ	MED	LQ	OVER $50M UQ	MED	LQ
SOLVENCY												
Quick Ratio (times)	1.6	0.9	0.4	1.6	0.9	0.4	1.1	0.6	0.3	1.5	0.9	0.5
Current Ratio (times)	3.0	1.9	1.4	3.5	2.1	1.5	2.1	1.6	1.4	2.7	2.1	1.6
Curr Liab To Nw (%)	11.6	23.9	39.8	11.6	22.5	38.4	4.3	6.2	23.1	14.7	21.2	31.6
Curr Liab To Inv (%)	119.6	158.2	252.6	118.1	149.0	227.2	33.9	63.6	89.2	118.6	143.0	221.5
Total Liab To Nw (%)	31.7	77.9	115.4	30.7	70.7	112.0	6.1	15.6	31.0	42.1	89.8	119.2
Fixed Assets To Nw (%)	71.9	107.7	142.8	82.2	105.2	138.8	31.4	48.1	60.6	85.6	114.1	149.3
EFFICIENCY												
Coll Period (days)	16.8	40.9	58.5	13.4	32.9	65.7	5.1	9.1	13.9	19.4	41.7	53.6
Sales To Inv (times)	11.9	6.5	3.8	10.4	6.4	2.9	5.3	4.0	2.4	10.9	6.9	3.8
Assets To Sales (%)	116.4	198.4	268.2	122.2	228.3	277.3	50.8	53.4	60.3	155.0	228.0	277.3
Sales To Nwc (times)	6.6	3.4	2.3	5.7	3.2	2.0	3.9	2.5	1.7	5.7	3.0	2.3
Acct Pay To Sales (%)	5.4	8.6	13.3	5.4	8.4	14.7	3.0	4.2	5.3	5.4	8.6	13.3
PROFITABILITY												
Return On Sales (%)	13.5	6.7	(4.0)	15.4	8.6	(8.1)	0.9	0.4	(1.1)	13.4	6.6	(6.0)
Return On Assets (%)	6.6	2.4	(2.9)	6.6	4.1	(2.6)	0.3	(0.8)	(2.7)	6.5	3.0	(2.8)
Return On Nw (%)	12.1	5.4	(8.3)	11.4	5.7	(6.1)	0.3	(0.8)	(2.9)	12.1	5.8	(8.3)

SIC 1041 GOLD ORES (NO BREAKDOWN) — 1995 (52 Establishments) · SIC 1041 GOLD ORES INDUSTRY ASSETS OVER $50,000,000 — 1995 (32 Establishments) · SIC 1081 METAL MINING SVCS (NO BREAKDOWN) — 1995 (18 Establishments) · SIC 12 BITUMINOUS & LIGNITE (NO BREAKDOWN) — 1995 (114 Establishments)

	SIC 1041 (No Breakdown) $	%	SIC 1041 Over $50,000,000 $	%	SIC 1081 $	%	SIC 12 $	%
Cash	9,040,544	9.4	42,120,000	9.0	138,416	10.5	1,059,117	8.3
Accounts Receivable	3,462,336	3.6	23,868,000	5.1	181,919	13.8	1,556,774	12.2
Notes Receivable	288,528	0.3	936,000	0.2	6,591	0.5	140,365	1.1
Inventory	5,193,504	5.4	22,932,000	4.9	63,276	4.8	446,616	3.5
Other Current	7,694,080	8.0	27,144,000	5.8	71,186	5.4	663,543	5.2
Total Current	**25,678,992**	**26.7**	**117,000,000**	**25.0**	**461,388**	**35.0**	**3,866,415**	**30.3**
Fixed Assets	51,550,336	53.6	281,736,000	60.2	639,352	48.5	6,584,390	51.6
Other Non-current	18,946,672	19.7	69,264,000	14.8	217,511	16.5	2,309,641	18.1
Total Assets	**96,176,000**	**100.0**	**468,000,000**	**100.0**	**1,318,251**	**100.0**	**12,760,446**	**100.0**
Accounts Payable	2,596,752	2.7	14,976,000	3.2	137,098	10.4	1,225,003	9.6
Bank Loans	—	—	468,000	0.1	—	—	—	—
Notes Payable	384,704	0.4	468,000	0.1	121,279	9.2	293,490	2.3
Other Current	9,136,720	9.5	40,716,000	8.7	100,187	7.6	1,811,983	14.2
Total Current	**12,118,176**	**12.6**	**56,628,000**	**12.1**	**358,564**	**27.2**	**3,330,476**	**26.1**
Other Long Term	19,619,904	20.4	126,360,000	27.0	341,427	25.9	3,828,134	30.0
Deferred Credits	1,923,520	2.0	13,104,000	2.8	9,228	0.7	204,167	1.6
Net Worth	62,514,400	65.0	271,908,000	58.1	609,032	46.2	5,397,669	42.3
Total Liab & Net Worth	**96,176,000**	**100.0**	**468,000,000**	**100.0**	**1,318,251**	**100.0**	**12,760,446**	**100.0**
Net Sales	79,806,000	100.0	97,455,756	100.0	1,172,910	100.0	14,936,261	100.0
Gross Profit	17,397,708	21.8	19,101,328	19.6	355,392	30.3	3,300,914	22.1
Net Profit After Tax	—	—	(1,851,659)	(1.9)	37,533	3.2	627,323	4.2
Working Capital	13,560,816	—	60,372,000	—	102,824	—	535,939	—

RATIOS	SIC 1041 (No Breakdown) UQ	MED	LQ	SIC 1041 Over $50M UQ	MED	LQ	SIC 1081 UQ	MED	LQ	SIC 12 UQ	MED	LQ
SOLVENCY												
Quick Ratio (times)	2.1	1.0	0.5	1.7	1.3	0.7	1.3	1.0	0.3	1.2	0.7	0.4
Current Ratio (times)	3.5	2.2	1.5	3.3	2.4	2.0	2.1	1.5	0.4	2.2	1.3	0.9
Curr Liab To Nw (%)	7.8	16.0	25.0	11.6	16.5	22.6	27.4	41.1	105.8	22.9	38.2	100.4
Curr Liab To Inv (%)	129.0	158.2	232.8	130.7	149.0	227.2	198.8	453.8	773.8	182.9	287.8	493.9
Total Liab To Nw (%)	20.6	62.7	101.7	34.3	81.0	107.8	33.7	112.3	281.3	44.1	91.3	233.9
Fixed Assets To Nw (%)	77.8	108.4	137.2	99.1	130.8	148.7	102.5	128.8	205.7	70.8	122.8	181.0
EFFICIENCY												
Coll Period (days)	11.1	24.7	57.6	16.8	29.6	57.6	35.6	65.0	69.6	17.7	34.5	45.6
Sales To Inv (times)	10.5	6.7	3.7	13.0	8.5	4.4	15.3	13.0	10.5	35.3	18.9	11.4
Assets To Sales (%)	215.4	266.5	312.8	221.7	263.5	312.8	35.9	40.9	94.9	53.4	89.1	155.3
Sales To Nwc (times)	4.7	2.8	2.3	4.3	2.8	2.4	16.3	12.2	7.4	18.3	10.3	5.1
Acct Pay To Sales (%)	5.4	7.1	12.7	5.4	6.9	11.2	5.1	8.2	12.5	3.4	5.5	9.9
PROFITABILITY												
Return On Sales (%)	14.3	5.7	(10.7)	14.3	4.6	(10.7)	3.1	2.7	(1.5)	10.6	4.1	0.3
Return On Assets (%)	4.9	0.3	(7.4)	5.0	(0.6)	(7.4)	6.8	3.2	(3.2)	9.6	3.8	0.4
Return On Nw (%)	11.0	0.5	(10.3)	11.1	(0.7)	(8.9)	23.3	7.9	(12.2)	26.4	11.1	1.4

SIC 12 — BITUMINOUS & LIGNITE

	NORTHEAST 1995 (20 Establishments) $	%	CENTRAL 1995 (26 Establishments) $	%	SOUTH 1995 (60 Establishments) $	%	INDUSTRY ASSETS $1,000,000 – $5,000,000 1995 (23 Establishments) $	%
Cash	630,471	10.4	1,503,008	3.2	899,348	10.2	306,817	11.0
Accounts Receivable	903,271	14.9	4,978,714	10.6	1,058,056	12.0	479,750	17.2
Notes Receivable	78,809	1.3	469,690	1.0	96,989	1.1	39,049	1.4
Inventory	218,240	3.6	1,549,977	3.3	255,697	2.9	72,520	2.6
Other Current	618,347	10.2	1,831,791	3.9	326,234	3.7	192,458	6.9
Total Current	**2,449,138**	**40.4**	**10,333,180**	**22.0**	**2,636,324**	**29.9**	**1,090,596**	**39.1**
Fixed Assets	2,424,889	40.0	24,376,911	51.9	4,884,694	55.4	1,322,103	47.4
Other Non-current	1,188,196	19.6	12,258,909	26.1	1,296,119	14.7	376,548	13.5
Total Assets	**6,062,223**	**100.0**	**46,969,000**	**100.0**	**8,817,137**	**100.0**	**2,789,247**	**100.0**
Accounts Payable	551,662	9.1	1,737,853	3.7	1,040,422	11.8	304,028	10.9
Bank Loans	—	—	—	—	—	—	—	—
Notes Payable	157,618	2.6	563,628	1.2	255,697	2.9	66,942	2.4
Other Current	885,085	14.6	6,481,722	13.8	1,296,119	14.7	354,234	12.7
Total Current	**1,594,365**	**26.3**	**8,783,203**	**18.7**	**2,592,238**	**29.4**	**725,204**	**26.0**
Other Long Term	2,024,782	33.4	16,251,274	34.6	2,556,970	29.0	577,374	20.7
Deferred Credits	103,058	1.7	798,473	1.7	52,903	0.6	11,157	0.4
Net Worth	2,340,018	38.6	21,136,050	45.0	3,615,026	41.0	1,475,512	52.9
Total Liab & Net Worth	**6,062,223**	**100.0**	**46,969,000**	**100.0**	**8,817,137**	**100.0**	**2,789,247**	**100.0**
Net Sales	9,540,661	100.0	25,796,810	100.0	14,303,069	100.0	5,375,942	100.0
Gross Profit	2,528,275	26.5	6,655,577	25.8	2,646,068	18.5	1,290,226	24.0
Net Profit After Tax	171,732	1.8	1,728,386	6.7	457,698	3.2	220,414	4.1
Working Capital	854,773	—	1,549,977	—	44,086	—	365,392	—

RATIOS	UQ	MED	LQ	UQ	MED	LQ	UQ	MED	LQ	UQ	MED	LQ
SOLVENCY												
Quick Ratio (times)	1.5	0.9	0.7	1.2	0.7	0.3	1.2	0.7	0.4	1.5	1.1	0.6
Current Ratio (times)	2.6	1.6	1.0	2.3	1.4	0.7	1.7	1.2	0.8	2.6	1.1	0.7
Curr Liab To Nw (%)	18.3	49.6	110.2	11.9	30.0	88.4	26.6	42.8	125.4	16.1	41.2	98.0
Curr Liab To Inv (%)	164.9	271.7	573.6	182.9	243.0	388.8	251.9	384.3	543.3	119.3	243.0	417.1
Total Liab To Nw (%)	41.1	135.7	307.2	44.1	84.7	169.5	44.0	86.4	243.7	24.5	52.0	122.6
Fixed Assets To Nw (%)	67.6	128.0	194.8	55.1	116.2	169.7	83.4	111.1	205.3	41.2	77.3	113.6
EFFICIENCY												
Coll Period (days)	27.4	46.0	52.6	6.6	29.6	40.2	16.5	35.1	44.4	14.2	20.8	43.8
Sales To Inv (times)	45.8	19.8	7.6	40.2	16.4	12.8	27.8	20.0	16.2	60.9	37.1	20.5
Assets To Sales (%)	53.4	69.1	165.9	70.4	108.7	175.3	48.0	77.4	138.1	44.8	56.3	68.4
Sales To Nwc (times)	13.0	6.5	3.8	18.4	11.3	5.3	18.9	11.1	6.8	48.7	7.6	5.2
Acct Pay To Sales (%)	4.0	6.4	9.2	2.6	3.3	4.7	3.9	6.0	12.4	2.1	4.4	7.8
PROFITABILITY												
Return On Sales (%)	5.0	2.3	(2.8)	13.2	3.7	2.6	9.0	4.4	(0.9)	4.1	2.7	0.3
Return On Assets (%)	7.1	3.3	0.5	10.3	3.3	2.3	9.4	4.7	(2.4)	7.4	5.4	1.2
Return On Nw (%)	11.6	7.4	1.2	24.4	13.1	7.1	33.4	8.7	0.3	17.9	7.4	2.4

SIC 12 BITUMINOUS & LIGNITE — INDUSTRY ASSETS $5,000,000-$25,000,000 — 1995 (19 Establishments) | SIC 12 BITUMINOUS & LIGNITE — INDUSTRY ASSETS OVER $50,000,000 — 1995 (46 Establishments) | SIC 1221 BIT COAL LGNTE-SRFC (NO BREAKDOWN) — 1995 (70 Establishments) | SIC 1221 BIT COAL LGNTE-SRFC — INDUSTRY ASSETS $1,000,000 - $5,000,000 — 1995 (15 Establishments)

	SIC 12 $5M-$25M $	%	SIC 12 Over $50M $	%	SIC 1221 No Breakdown $	%	SIC 1221 $1M-$5M $	%
Cash	848,160	9.8	9,094,160	3.8	2,974,802	7.6	375,954	13.1
Accounts Receivable	995,290	11.5	20,581,520	8.6	4,618,772	11.8	430,482	15.0
Notes Receivable	103,856	1.2	1,914,560	0.8	430,563	1.1	5,740	0.2
Inventory	294,260	3.4	10,290,760	4.3	1,369,975	3.5	63,137	2.2
Other Current	60,583	0.7	13,880,560	5.8	2,152,817	5.5	206,631	7.2
Total Current	**2,302,149**	**26.6**	**55,761,560**	**23.3**	**11,546,929**	**29.5**	**1,081,944**	**37.7**
Fixed Assets	4,439,859	51.3	123,249,800	51.5	20,862,757	53.3	1,538,255	53.6
Other Non-current	1,912,688	22.1	60,308,640	25.2	6,732,447	17.2	249,679	8.7
Total Assets	**8,654,696**	**100.0**	**239,320,000**	**100.0**	**39,142,133**	**100.0**	**2,869,878**	**100.0**
Accounts Payable	882,779	10.2	15,077,160	6.3	3,640,218	9.3	330,036	11.5
Bank Loans	—	—	—	—	—	—	—	—
Notes Payable	242,331	2.8	478,640	0.2	704,558	1.8	51,658	1.8
Other Current	1,332,823	15.4	28,957,720	12.1	6,223,599	15.9	364,475	12.7
Total Current	**2,457,934**	**28.4**	**44,513,520**	**18.6**	**10,568,376**	**27.0**	**746,168**	**26.0**
Other Long Term	2,596,409	30.0	97,163,920	40.6	11,312,076	28.9	820,785	28.6
Deferred Credits	—	—	6,461,640	2.7	587,132	1.5	2,870	0.1
Net Worth	3,600,354	41.6	91,180,920	38.1	16,674,549	42.6	1,300,055	45.3
Total Liab & Net Worth	**8,654,696**	**100.0**	**239,320,000**	**100.0**	**39,142,133**	**100.0**	**2,869,878**	**100.0**
Net Sales	10,542,175	100.0	179,352,000	100.0	21,185,906	100.0	6,630,916	100.0
Gross Profit	3,436,749	32.6	26,544,096	14.8	3,813,463	18.0	1,233,350	18.6
Net Profit After Tax	(42,169)	(0.4)	9,326,304	5.2	656,763	3.1	245,344	3.7
Working Capital	(155,785)	—	11,248,040	—	978,553	—	335,776	—

RATIOS

	SIC 12 $5M-$25M UQ	MED	LQ	SIC 12 Over $50M UQ	MED	LQ	SIC 1221 No Breakdown UQ	MED	LQ	SIC 1221 $1M-$5M UQ	MED	LQ
SOLVENCY												
Quick Ratio (times)	1.8	1.2	0.3	1.0	0.7	0.4	1.2	0.7	0.4	2.1	1.1	0.5
Current Ratio (times)	1.9	1.5	0.5	2.0	1.4	1.0	2.2	1.3	0.9	2.6	1.1	0.7
Curr Liab To Nw (%)	11.5	30.6	47.9	24.9	33.3	101.3	24.5	35.8	101.8	17.7	65.0	123.3
Curr Liab To Inv (%)	253.1	508.8	594.2	192.9	292.0	492.8	178.4	339.5	493.4	118.1	167.4	243.0
Total Liab To Nw (%)	39.6	73.3	90.7	85.2	117.4	266.8	41.0	88.1	158.4	25.0	63.7	186.6
Fixed Assets To Nw (%)	63.9	93.9	149.5	110.9	150.5	206.5	75.6	120.4	158.7	74.2	88.6	127.4
EFFICIENCY												
Coll Period (days)	27.4	34.0	41.3	32.5	39.8	46.7	24.1	35.0	44.5	12.9	18.7	28.1
Sales To Inv (times)	73.9	43.1	20.4	23.0	18.8	10.0	29.3	19.8	11.9	40.7	20.5	13.8
Assets To Sales (%)	50.5	68.8	98.0	112.7	148.9	180.0	59.8	103.2	150.3	47.1	56.4	70.0
Sales To Nwc (times)	15.8	13.0	9.6	12.9	7.5	4.4	19.3	7.9	5.3	36.2	7.7	6.3
Acct Pay To Sales (%)	2.9	4.1	9.0	4.5	6.2	11.5	3.0	5.2	11.2	2.4	5.0	11.3
PROFITABILITY												
Return On Sales (%)	13.5	9.1	(7.0)	7.3	4.7	(1.6)	9.8	4.1	(3.8)	3.9	2.2	0.3
Return On Assets (%)	13.2	9.7	(12.0)	7.5	2.9	0.5	8.7	3.8	(3.0)	6.0	2.6	0.7
Return On Nw (%)	34.7	16.8	5.2	18.1	7.7	1.9	25.0	8.6	(4.4)	7.4	5.5	0.9

SIC 1221 BIT COAL LGNTE-SRFC — INDUSTRY ASSETS $5,000,000-$25,000,000 — 1995 (12 Establishments); SIC 1221 BIT COAL LGNTE-SRFC — INDUSTRY ASSETS OVER $50,000,000 — 1995 (31 Establishments); SIC 1222 BIT COAL-UNDERGRND (NO BREAKDOWN) — 1995 (24 Establishments); SIC 1241 COAL MINING SVCS (NO BREAKDOWN) — 1995 (19 Establishments)

	SIC 1221 $5M-$25M $	%	SIC 1221 OVER $50M $	%	SIC 1222 $	%	SIC 1241 $	%
Cash	623,138	7.2	7,811,126	3.4	4,321,148	9.2	115,350	9.3
Accounts Receivable	986,635	11.4	21,825,205	9.5	3,945,396	8.4	262,949	21.2
Notes Receivable	138,475	1.6	2,067,651	0.9	657,566	1.4	2,481	0.2
Inventory	276,950	3.2	10,338,255	4.5	1,831,791	3.9	24,807	2.0
Other Current	69,238	0.8	13,554,601	5.9	2,254,512	4.8	33,489	2.7
Total Current	**2,094,436**	**24.2**	**55,596,838**	**24.2**	**13,010,413**	**27.7**	**439,075**	**35.4**
Fixed Assets	4,777,392	55.2	117,626,368	51.2	22,873,903	48.7	641,248	51.7
Other Non-current	1,782,867	20.6	56,515,794	24.6	11,084,684	23.6	160,002	12.9
Total Assets	**8,654,696**	**100.0**	**229,739,000**	**100.0**	**46,969,000**	**100.0**	**1,240,325**	**100.0**
Accounts Payable	943,362	10.9	16,081,730	7.0	3,522,675	7.5	188,529	15.2
Bank Loans	—	—	—	—	—	—	—	—
Notes Payable	276,950	3.2	459,478	0.2	1,503,008	3.2	40,931	3.3
Other Current	1,376,097	15.9	32,852,677	14.3	4,509,024	9.6	187,289	15.1
Total Current	**2,596,409**	**30.0**	**49,393,885**	**21.5**	**9,534,707**	**20.3**	**416,749**	**33.6**
Other Long Term	1,904,033	22.0	82,476,301	35.9	17,096,716	36.4	316,283	25.5
Deferred Credits	—	—	6,432,692	2.8	1,221,194	2.6	—	—
Net Worth	4,154,254	48.0	91,436,122	39.8	19,116,383	40.7	507,293	40.9
Total Liab & Net Worth	**8,654,696**	**100.0**	**229,739,000**	**100.0**	**46,969,000**	**100.0**	**1,240,325**	**100.0**
Net Sales	10,257,552	100.0	179,352,000	100.0	52,821,000	100.0	873,910	100.0
Gross Profit	2,523,358	24.6	27,440,856	15.3	13,469,355	25.5	334,708	38.3
Net Profit After Tax	(492,362)	(4.8)	11,837,232	6.6	3,274,902	6.2	52,435	6.0
Working Capital	(501,973)	—	6,202,953	—	3,475,706	—	22,326	—

RATIOS	UQ	MED	LQ	UQ	MED	LQ	UQ	MED	LQ	UQ	MED	LQ
SOLVENCY												
Quick Ratio (times)	1.9	1.0	0.2	0.9	0.7	0.5	1.5	0.7	0.4	1.2	0.9	0.7
Current Ratio (times)	2.3	1.2	0.4	1.7	1.3	1.0	2.1	1.5	0.9	1.6	1.1	0.9
Curr Liab To Nw (%)	10.9	30.6	50.8	25.7	33.3	101.3	15.2	36.1	77.5	31.3	69.1	137.8
Curr Liab To Inv (%)	214.8	348.7	497.1	241.9	384.3	504.5	193.5	287.8	563.2	136.9	271.7	449.9
Total Liab To Nw (%)	39.6	63.2	87.4	82.4	116.7	159.6	64.8	102.3	214.8	66.2	87.1	278.5
Fixed Assets To Nw (%)	70.0	84.8	142.1	88.3	134.7	170.4	111.0	169.4	222.3	49.1	107.6	212.4
EFFICIENCY												
Coll Period (days)	28.5	34.0	40.8	32.5	38.7	45.6	12.3	28.7	45.6	25.6	52.2	54.4
Sales To Inv (times)	71.1	26.9	13.7	25.8	19.8	11.6	39.4	18.9	12.9	40.0	7.9	7.2
Assets To Sales (%)	64.9	83.5	124.6	101.9	137.3	170.2	51.4	70.9	159.3	26.0	54.4	178.1
Sales To Nwc (times)	14.4	12.8	11.1	22.2	7.8	4.6	14.4	9.0	4.8	32.9	12.6	9.0
Acct Pay To Sales (%)	3.0	4.8	8.4	4.0	6.4	12.3	3.5	5.4	9.0	4.5	6.3	7.6
PROFITABILITY												
Return On Sales (%)	9.8	6.6	(18.9)	9.8	5.3	(3.8)	10.6	4.7	2.3	10.6	3.2	2.2
Return On Assets (%)	17.2	9.1	(13.2)	8.3	4.2	0.1	16.1	3.2	2.3	15.2	6.5	2.3
Return On Nw (%)	36.5	19.6	(1.4)	23.6	12.2	4.4	26.4	11.1	5.7	30.1	15.8	9.6

SIC 13 OIL, GAS EXTRACTION

Balance Sheet

	NO BREAKDOWN 1995 (1609 Establishments) $	%	NORTHEAST 1995 (50 Establishments) $	%	CENTRAL 1995 (361 Establishments) $	%	SOUTH 1995 (916 Establishments) $	%
Cash	205,853	14.0	4,343,324	12.3	91,473	19.6	286,404	12.3
Accounts Receivable	282,313	19.2	5,084,867	14.4	94,273	20.2	437,756	18.8
Notes Receivable	11,763	0.8	141,246	0.4	2,800	0.6	16,299	0.7
Inventory	32,348	2.2	459,050	1.3	14,934	3.2	48,898	2.1
Other Current	98,515	6.7	2,577,745	7.3	28,935	6.2	160,666	6.9
Total Current	**630,793**	**42.9**	**12,606,233**	**35.7**	**232,416**	**49.8**	**950,024**	**40.8**
Fixed Assets	596,974	40.6	13,418,399	38.0	149,810	32.1	1,003,579	43.1
Other Non-current	242,613	16.5	9,286,944	26.3	84,472	18.1	374,887	16.1
Total Assets	**1,470,380**	**100.0**	**35,311,576**	**100.0**	**466,698**	**100.0**	**2,328,489**	**100.0**
Accounts Payable	145,568	9.9	3,354,600	9.5	50,870	10.9	232,849	10.0
Bank Loans	2,941	0.2	211,869	0.6	—	—	4,657	0.2
Notes Payable	52,934	3.6	706,232	2.0	10,267	2.2	97,797	4.2
Other Current	166,153	11.3	3,283,977	9.3	62,538	13.4	246,820	10.6
Total Current	**367,595**	**25.0**	**7,556,677**	**21.4**	**123,675**	**26.5**	**582,122**	**25.0**
Other Long Term	263,198	17.9	7,486,054	21.2	67,671	14.5	461,041	19.8
Deferred Credits	14,704	1.0	1,341,840	3.8	467	0.1	30,270	1.3
Net Worth	824,883	56.1	18,927,005	53.6	274,885	58.9	1,255,056	53.9
Total Liab & Net Worth	**1,470,380**	**100.0**	**35,311,576**	**100.0**	**466,698**	**100.0**	**2,328,489**	**100.0**
Net Sales	2,356,668	100.0	3,862,205	100.0	791,192	100.0	3,234,613	100.0
Gross Profit	1,008,654	42.8	1,401,980	36.3	314,894	39.8	1,436,168	44.4
Net Profit After Tax	108,407	4.6	258,768	6.7	22,945	2.9	148,792	4.6
Working Capital	263,198	—	5,049,556	—	108,741	—	367,902	—

RATIOS

	UQ	MED	LQ	UQ	MED	LQ	UQ	MED	LQ	UQ	MED	LQ
SOLVENCY												
Quick Ratio (times)	2.9	1.2	0.7	2.3	0.9	0.5	5.2	1.6	0.7	2.3	1.1	0.6
Current Ratio (times)	4.2	1.7	1.0	3.3	1.5	1.1	7.6	2.2	1.0	3.3	1.5	0.9
Curr Liab To Nw (%)	10.7	29.0	75.7	14.8	41.8	73.8	6.6	23.4	76.0	12.4	30.4	81.9
Curr Liab To Inv (%)	151.9	331.9	543.7	170.0	335.0	648.1	82.5	258.4	408.1	158.3	342.5	580.6
Total Liab To Nw (%)	21.7	63.2	146.1	61.8	143.0	177.3	10.4	44.2	135.9	26.1	78.2	158.5
Fixed Assets To Nw (%)	30.0	78.2	142.6	52.3	100.3	199.2	16.7	39.8	97.5	41.1	92.0	158.8
EFFICIENCY												
Coll Period (days)	39.3	61.3	90.6	31.0	44.7	70.9	28.5	46.7	79.9	43.1	63.5	94.7
Sales To Inv (times)	75.7	30.5	14.2	37.7	22.4	11.6	68.4	26.1	9.8	71.7	28.6	14.1
Assets To Sales (%)	50.3	123.4	245.8	77.8	126.3	278.4	42.0	76.5	175.2	56.8	140.7	264.3
Sales To Nwc (times)	12.4	6.0	2.5	15.7	7.5	3.1	10.1	5.3	2.3	12.9	6.0	2.3
Acct Pay To Sales (%)	3.7	8.6	18.5	6.2	9.0	14.6	3.6	7.9	14.9	4.2	9.0	21.0
PROFITABILITY												
Return On Sales (%)	13.1	4.8	(0.2)	8.7	5.0	2.5	12.3	4.2	(2.7)	13.6	5.3	(0.4)
Return On Assets (%)	10.9	3.5	(0.6)	6.9	3.7	2.7	12.2	3.9	(3.8)	11.0	3.7	(0.4)
Return On Nw (%)	20.4	7.2	(0.5)	20.3	8.7	4.2	19.1	6.6	(4.0)	20.9	7.8	(0.4)

SIC 13 OIL, GAS EXTRACTION — WEST
1995 (282 Establishments)

	$	%
Cash	192,500	12.5
Accounts Receivable	308,000	20.0
Notes Receivable	21,560	1.4
Inventory	24,640	1.6
Other Current	95,480	6.2
Total Current	**642,180**	**41.7**
Fixed Assets	665,280	43.2
Other Non-current	232,540	15.1
Total Assets	**1,540,000**	**100.0**
Accounts Payable	133,980	8.7
Bank Loans	1,540	0.1
Notes Payable	55,440	3.6
Other Current	177,100	11.5
Total Current	**368,060**	**23.9**
Other Long Term	227,920	14.8
Deferred Credits	16,940	1.1
Net Worth	927,080	60.2
Total Liab & Net Worth	**1,540,000**	**100.0**
Net Sales	2,299,496	100.0
Gross Profit	926,697	40.3
Net Profit After Tax	119,574	5.2
Working Capital	274,120	—

RATIOS	UQ	MED	LQ
SOLVENCY			
Quick Ratio (times)	2.7	1.4	0.7
Current Ratio (times)	3.8	1.8	1.0
Curr Liab To Nw (%)	10.7	27.9	68.3
Curr Liab To Inv (%)	272.6	426.3	611.6
Total Liab To Nw (%)	23.8	53.3	108.2
Fixed Assets To Nw (%)	36.0	73.0	136.1
EFFICIENCY			
Coll Period (days)	40.2	63.2	87.6
Sales To Inv (times)	126.6	50.1	22.3
Assets To Sales (%)	43.8	97.3	240.6
Sales To Nwc (times)	11.0	5.9	3.0
Acct Pay To Sales (%)	3.1	7.3	14.7
PROFITABILITY			
Return On Sales (%)	12.5	4.4	(0.4)
Return On Assets (%)	10.8	3.3	(1.1)
Return On Nw (%)	16.6	5.7	(1.5)

SIC 13 OIL, GAS EXTRACTION — INDUSTRY ASSETS UNDER $100,000
1995 (116 Establishments)

	$	%
Cash	20,726	34.9
Accounts Receivable	10,333	17.4
Notes Receivable	772	1.3
Inventory	1,128	1.9
Other Current	2,613	4.4
Total Current	**35,573**	**59.9**
Fixed Assets	19,598	33.0
Other Non-current	4,216	7.1
Total Assets	**59,387**	**100.0**
Accounts Payable	6,236	10.5
Bank Loans	59	0.1
Notes Payable	1,247	2.1
Other Current	9,502	16.0
Total Current	**17,044**	**28.7**
Other Long Term	5,998	10.1
Deferred Credits	—	—
Net Worth	36,345	61.2
Total Liab & Net Worth	**59,387**	**100.0**
Net Sales	163,493	100.0
Gross Profit	69,648	42.6
Net Profit After Tax	15,041	9.2
Working Capital	18,529	—

RATIOS	UQ	MED	LQ
SOLVENCY			
Quick Ratio (times)	7.4	2.3	0.9
Current Ratio (times)	9.0	3.2	1.0
Curr Liab To Nw (%)	6.7	21.7	76.1
Curr Liab To Inv (%)	23.0	184.2	295.3
Total Liab To Nw (%)	7.1	26.8	81.6
Fixed Assets To Nw (%)	24.2	51.5	93.7
EFFICIENCY			
Coll Period (days)	27.5	39.4	73.4
Sales To Inv (times)	154.4	66.6	17.7
Assets To Sales (%)	19.6	35.3	57.4
Sales To Nwc (times)	16.9	7.7	4.4
Acct Pay To Sales (%)	1.3	2.6	5.7
PROFITABILITY			
Return On Sales (%)	19.8	7.5	3.3
Return On Assets (%)	37.2	23.5	7.7
Return On Nw (%)	57.5	25.8	7.6

SIC 13 OIL, GAS EXTRACTION — INDUSTRY ASSETS $100,000 - $250,000
1995 (149 Establishments)

	$	%
Cash	33,271	19.9
Accounts Receivable	40,962	24.5
Notes Receivable	1,170	0.7
Inventory	6,019	3.6
Other Current	10,199	6.1
Total Current	**91,621**	**54.8**
Fixed Assets	52,164	31.2
Other Non-current	23,407	14.0
Total Assets	**167,191**	**100.0**
Accounts Payable	19,729	11.8
Bank Loans	—	—
Notes Payable	7,524	4.5
Other Current	24,243	14.5
Total Current	**51,495**	**30.8**
Other Long Term	26,918	16.1
Deferred Credits	—	—
Net Worth	88,778	53.1
Total Liab & Net Worth	**167,191**	**100.0**
Net Sales	360,088	100.0
Gross Profit	167,081	46.4
Net Profit After Tax	12,603	3.5
Working Capital	40,126	—

RATIOS	UQ	MED	LQ
SOLVENCY			
Quick Ratio (times)	5.7	1.6	0.8
Current Ratio (times)	7.0	1.9	1.1
Curr Liab To Nw (%)	9.2	38.3	114.4
Curr Liab To Inv (%)	86.2	249.3	304.4
Total Liab To Nw (%)	13.5	56.5	171.6
Fixed Assets To Nw (%)	15.6	52.8	109.3
EFFICIENCY			
Coll Period (days)	38.3	59.9	98.6
Sales To Inv (times)	58.9	30.6	7.7
Assets To Sales (%)	30.2	47.5	70.2
Sales To Nwc (times)	14.4	7.7	3.6
Acct Pay To Sales (%)	2.7	5.5	10.2
PROFITABILITY			
Return On Sales (%)	16.6	7.2	(0.2)
Return On Assets (%)	20.8	11.1	(6.4)
Return On Nw (%)	36.3	18.2	(14.4)

SIC 13 OIL, GAS EXTRACTION — INDUSTRY ASSETS $250,000 - $500,000
1995 (229 Establishments)

	$	%
Cash	59,375	16.1
Accounts Receivable	102,892	27.9
Notes Receivable	2,950	0.8
Inventory	8,851	2.4
Other Current	24,340	6.6
Total Current	**198,407**	**53.8**
Fixed Assets	125,019	33.9
Other Non-current	45,361	12.3
Total Assets	**368,787**	**100.0**
Accounts Payable	43,517	11.8
Bank Loans	738	0.2
Notes Payable	24,340	6.6
Other Current	42,779	11.6
Total Current	**111,374**	**30.2**
Other Long Term	50,155	13.6
Deferred Credits	1,844	0.5
Net Worth	205,414	55.7
Total Liab & Net Worth	**368,787**	**100.0**
Net Sales	579,390	100.0
Gross Profit	292,592	50.5
Net Profit After Tax	29,549	5.1
Working Capital	87,033	—

RATIOS	UQ	MED	LQ
SOLVENCY			
Quick Ratio (times)	4.6	1.8	0.7
Current Ratio (times)	5.7	2.4	1.0
Curr Liab To Nw (%)	7.8	31.1	112.8
Curr Liab To Inv (%)	75.7	200.4	441.1
Total Liab To Nw (%)	18.6	47.6	146.9
Fixed Assets To Nw (%)	23.7	57.2	123.7
EFFICIENCY			
Coll Period (days)	31.0	55.2	89.1
Sales To Inv (times)	81.7	36.6	13.9
Assets To Sales (%)	31.1	60.3	108.6
Sales To Nwc (times)	12.3	5.9	3.9
Acct Pay To Sales (%)	1.5	5.9	16.2
PROFITABILITY			
Return On Sales (%)	14.3	5.1	0.6
Return On Assets (%)	16.5	6.2	0.2
Return On Nw (%)	31.6	12.8	0.2

SIC 13 OIL, GAS EXTRACTION
INDUSTRY ASSETS
$500,000 - $1,000,000
1995 (200 Establishments)

	$	%
Cash	103,174	14.6
Accounts Receivable	167,482	23.7
Notes Receivable	4,947	0.7
Inventory	16,254	2.3
Other Current	55,827	7.9
Total Current	**347,684**	**49.2**
Fixed Assets	258,643	36.6
Other Non-current	100,348	14.2
Total Assets	**706,674**	**100.0**
Accounts Payable	65,014	9.2
Bank Loans	707	0.1
Notes Payable	33,214	4.7
Other Current	78,441	11.1
Total Current	**177,375**	**25.1**
Other Long Term	88,334	12.5
Deferred Credits	3,533	0.5
Net Worth	437,431	61.9
Total Liab & Net Worth	**706,674**	**100.0**
Net Sales	1,168,477	100.0
Gross Profit	566,711	48.5
Net Profit After Tax	57,255	4.9
Working Capital	170,309	—

RATIOS	UQ	MED	LQ
SOLVENCY			
Quick Ratio (times)	3.8	1.6	0.8
Current Ratio (times)	5.7	2.1	1.1
Curr Liab To Nw (%)	9.2	30.3	69.7
Curr Liab To Inv (%)	116.6	349.1	567.2
Total Liab To Nw (%)	18.2	51.5	114.0
Fixed Assets To Nw (%)	29.5	61.8	109.2
EFFICIENCY			
Coll Period (days)	34.7	54.8	85.8
Sales To Inv (times)	203.6	54.2	21.6
Assets To Sales (%)	39.8	56.6	111.7
Sales To Nwc (times)	13.5	6.5	3.0
Acct Pay To Sales (%)	2.7	4.2	10.0
PROFITABILITY			
Return On Sales (%)	12.7	4.4	0.3
Return On Assets (%)	11.0	6.2	(1.5)
Return On Nw (%)	26.6	11.9	1.4

SIC 13 OIL, GAS EXTRACTION
INDUSTRY ASSETS
$1,000,000 - $5,000,000
1995 (368 Establishments)

	$	%
Cash	264,546	14.2
Accounts Receivable	421,038	22.6
Notes Receivable	26,082	1.4
Inventory	39,123	2.1
Other Current	147,177	7.9
Total Current	**897,966**	**48.2**
Fixed Assets	611,064	32.8
Other Non-current	353,970	19.0
Total Assets	**1,863,001**	**100.0**
Accounts Payable	217,971	11.7
Bank Loans	5,589	0.3
Notes Payable	87,561	4.7
Other Current	219,834	11.8
Total Current	**530,955**	**28.5**
Other Long Term	255,231	13.7
Deferred Credits	3,726	0.2
Net Worth	1,073,089	57.6
Total Liab & Net Worth	**1,863,001**	**100.0**
Net Sales	2,089,494	100.0
Gross Profit	827,440	39.6
Net Profit After Tax	104,475	5.0
Working Capital	367,011	—

RATIOS	UQ	MED	LQ
SOLVENCY			
Quick Ratio (times)	2.8	1.3	0.7
Current Ratio (times)	4.6	1.8	1.0
Curr Liab To Nw (%)	10.5	33.8	96.8
Curr Liab To Inv (%)	124.9	292.5	481.4
Total Liab To Nw (%)	16.9	55.2	129.3
Fixed Assets To Nw (%)	22.0	54.0	106.9
EFFICIENCY			
Coll Period (days)	41.5	62.6	90.6
Sales To Inv (times)	124.0	47.9	15.1
Assets To Sales (%)	45.3	87.1	210.6
Sales To Nwc (times)	10.9	5.6	2.3
Acct Pay To Sales (%)	3.1	7.0	14.7
PROFITABILITY			
Return On Sales (%)	12.5	4.7	(0.3)
Return On Assets (%)	12.1	4.1	(0.8)
Return On Nw (%)	22.1	8.6	(0.1)

SIC 13 OIL, GAS EXTRACTION
INDUSTRY ASSETS
$5,000,000-$25,000,000
1995 (186 Establishments)

	$	%
Cash	1,027,492	10.9
Accounts Receivable	1,178,316	12.5
Notes Receivable	65,986	0.7
Inventory	141,398	1.5
Other Current	678,710	7.2
Total Current	**3,091,902**	**32.8**
Fixed Assets	4,317,351	45.8
Other Non-current	2,017,278	21.4
Total Assets	**9,426,531**	**100.0**
Accounts Payable	980,359	10.4
Bank Loans	18,853	0.2
Notes Payable	197,957	2.1
Other Current	1,178,316	12.5
Total Current	**2,375,486**	**25.2**
Other Long Term	1,649,643	17.5
Deferred Credits	150,824	1.6
Net Worth	5,250,578	55.7
Total Liab & Net Worth	**9,426,531**	**100.0**
Net Sales	4,606,316	100.0
Gross Profit	1,902,409	41.3
Net Profit After Tax	221,103	4.8
Working Capital	716,416	—

RATIOS	UQ	MED	LQ
SOLVENCY			
Quick Ratio (times)	2.0	1.0	0.5
Current Ratio (times)	3.3	1.3	0.8
Curr Liab To Nw (%)	11.3	28.3	83.9
Curr Liab To Inv (%)	199.1	349.6	528.1
Total Liab To Nw (%)	27.2	75.9	149.0
Fixed Assets To Nw (%)	44.4	90.7	147.6
EFFICIENCY			
Coll Period (days)	38.6	58.6	88.3
Sales To Inv (times)	69.9	34.9	11.5
Assets To Sales (%)	130.3	198.2	262.8
Sales To Nwc (times)	8.4	3.6	1.4
Acct Pay To Sales (%)	5.7	11.3	23.6
PROFITABILITY			
Return On Sales (%)	15.9	6.1	(2.0)
Return On Assets (%)	10.2	3.0	(0.2)
Return On Nw (%)	20.8	7.4	0.2

SIC 13 OIL, GAS EXTRACTION
INDUSTRY ASSETS
$25,000,000-$50,000,000
1995 (76 Establishments)

	$	%
Cash	2,437,829	6.8
Accounts Receivable	2,975,585	8.3
Notes Receivable	143,402	0.4
Inventory	932,111	2.6
Other Current	1,900,072	5.3
Total Current	**8,388,999**	**23.4**
Fixed Assets	17,781,810	49.6
Other Non-current	9,679,614	27.0
Total Assets	**35,850,424**	**100.0**
Accounts Payable	2,509,530	7.0
Bank Loans	—	—
Notes Payable	466,056	1.3
Other Current	2,545,380	7.1
Total Current	**5,520,965**	**15.4**
Other Long Term	8,173,897	22.8
Deferred Credits	752,859	2.1
Net Worth	21,402,703	59.7
Total Liab & Net Worth	**35,850,424**	**100.0**
Net Sales	13,359,000	100.0
Gross Profit	3,606,930	27.0
Net Profit After Tax	400,770	3.0
Working Capital	2,868,034	—

RATIOS	UQ	MED	LQ
SOLVENCY			
Quick Ratio (times)	2.0	1.0	0.5
Current Ratio (times)	2.8	1.3	0.9
Curr Liab To Nw (%)	10.1	20.5	41.1
Curr Liab To Inv (%)	296.9	523.2	735.8
Total Liab To Nw (%)	28.6	55.5	118.7
Fixed Assets To Nw (%)	46.9	95.7	149.7
EFFICIENCY			
Coll Period (days)	40.8	60.3	96.2
Sales To Inv (times)	60.9	28.7	17.5
Assets To Sales (%)	150.1	229.8	471.9
Sales To Nwc (times)	7.2	4.6	2.8
Acct Pay To Sales (%)	7.6	13.2	22.8
PROFITABILITY			
Return On Sales (%)	13.0	5.0	(11.0)
Return On Assets (%)	7.8	2.4	(1.8)
Return On Nw (%)	17.3	4.8	(2.2)

	SIC 13 OIL,GAS EXTRACTION — INDUSTRY ASSETS OVER $50,000,000 — 1995 (285 Establishments) $	%	SIC 1311 CRUDE PTRLM,NAT GAS (NO BREAKDOWN) — 1995 (742 Establishments) $	%	SIC 1311 CRUDE PTRLM,NAT GAS — INDUSTRY ASSETS UNDER $100,000 — 1995 (38 Establishments) $	%	SIC 1311 CRUDE PTRLM,NAT GAS — INDUSTRY ASSETS $100,000 - $250,000 — 1995 (51 Establishments) $	%
Cash	11,207,300	5.0	502,165	14.3	22,112	42.4	36,068	23.0
Accounts Receivable	21,069,724	9.4	477,583	13.6	7,406	14.2	42,968	27.4
Notes Receivable	224,146	0.1	28,093	0.8	626	1.2	1,568	1.0
Inventory	4,258,774	1.9	59,698	1.7	1,304	2.5	4,077	2.6
Other Current	11,431,446	5.1	249,327	7.1	1,982	3.8	9,879	6.3
Total Current	**48,191,390**	**21.5**	**1,316,866**	**37.5**	**33,429**	**64.1**	**94,560**	**60.3**
Fixed Assets	137,625,644	61.4	1,481,913	42.2	14,655	28.1	39,047	24.9
Other Non-current	38,328,966	17.1	712,864	20.3	4,068	7.8	23,209	14.8
Total Assets	**224,146,000**	**100.0**	**3,511,643**	**100.0**	**52,152**	**100.0**	**156,816**	**100.0**
Accounts Payable	13,224,614	5.9	354,676	10.1	5,007	9.6	23,522	15.0
Bank Loans	224,146	0.1	3,512	0.1	—	—	—	—
Notes Payable	1,793,168	0.8	94,814	2.7	365	0.7	1,882	1.2
Other Current	17,707,534	7.9	389,792	11.1	6,623	12.7	25,404	16.2
Total Current	**32,949,462**	**14.7**	**842,794**	**24.0**	**11,995**	**23.0**	**50,808**	**32.4**
Other Long Term	73,968,180	33.0	607,514	17.3	4,381	8.4	8,468	5.4
Deferred Credits	7,620,964	3.4	49,163	1.4	—	—	—	—
Net Worth	109,607,394	48.9	2,012,171	57.3	35,776	68.6	97,540	62.2
Total Liab & Net Worth	**224,146,000**	**100.0**	**3,511,643**	**100.0**	**52,152**	**100.0**	**156,816**	**100.0**
Net Sales	87,958,000	100.0	2,688,694	100.0	51,043	100.0	122,133	100.0
Gross Profit	32,896,292	37.4	1,193,780	44.4	30,983	60.7	70,471	57.7
Net Profit After Tax	3,430,362	3.9	118,303	4.4	7,861	15.4	7,206	5.9
Working Capital	15,241,928	—	474,072	—	21,434	—	43,752	—

RATIOS	UQ	MED	LQ	UQ	MED	LQ	UQ	MED	LQ	UQ	MED	LQ
SOLVENCY												
Quick Ratio (times)	1.4	1.0	0.6	2.3	1.0	0.5	15.8	5.0	0.9	5.8	1.9	0.9
Current Ratio (times)	2.0	1.3	0.9	3.7	1.3	0.8	18.5	5.9	1.0	6.6	2.2	1.2
Curr Liab To Nw (%)	14.6	26.8	49.7	9.4	24.5	67.1	2.8	6.9	50.9	6.6	18.7	88.3
Curr Liab To Inv (%)	226.1	373.9	638.7	108.8	293.7	525.5	20.8	71.1	186.0	66.6	106.1	324.2
Total Liab To Nw (%)	56.1	106.6	171.4	19.6	61.7	153.7	2.8	9.6	50.9	8.4	29.6	89.5
Fixed Assets To Nw (%)	95.0	147.3	216.4	23.5	79.6	159.4	9.7	34.4	69.5	8.2	38.5	72.5
EFFICIENCY												
Coll Period (days)	51.8	67.9	86.9	38.6	61.2	104.5	76.3	100.4	126.7	93.6	104.8	185.8
Sales To Inv (times)	57.4	23.2	14.5	85.6	33.6	16.4	—	—	—	82.1	5.9	5.7
Assets To Sales (%)	146.0	228.9	345.6	127.3	208.7	326.0	40.4	90.6	144.4	48.2	101.6	172.8
Sales To Nwc (times)	15.5	6.1	2.7	12.5	4.6	1.6	2.1	1.7	1.3	4.7	2.5	1.2
Acct Pay To Sales (%)	7.3	12.3	20.7	6.1	13.3	25.8	2.4	3.9	18.4	5.6	16.2	40.0
PROFITABILITY												
Return On Sales (%)	9.7	3.9	(0.4)	17.1	5.5	(2.7)	12.4	5.4	2.9	40.0	20.6	(5.2)
Return On Assets (%)	4.2	2.2	(0.5)	8.7	2.7	(1.7)	16.0	8.3	7.7	18.1	12.2	(8.1)
Return On Nw (%)	9.4	4.7	(0.5)	16.2	5.9	(3.0)	22.0	8.9	8.1	26.7	18.2	(15.2)

SIC 1311 — CRUDE PTRLM, NAT GAS

	$250,000 - $500,000 (88 Establishments) $	%	$500,000 - $1,000,000 (66 Establishments) $	%	$1,000,000 - $5,000,000 (164 Establishments) $	%	$5,000,000 - $25,000,000 (114 Establishments) $	%
Cash	75,529	20.0	125,887	17.4	318,661	15.9	998,658	10.9
Accounts Receivable	96,299	25.5	113,587	15.7	286,595	14.3	723,798	7.9
Notes Receivable	3,399	0.9	6,511	0.9	28,058	1.4	73,296	0.8
Inventory	9,063	2.4	7,235	1.0	46,096	2.3	73,296	0.8
Other Current	34,366	9.1	51,368	7.1	162,337	8.1	778,770	8.5
Total Current	**218,655**	**57.9**	**304,588**	**42.1**	**841,747**	**42.0**	**2,647,818**	**28.9**
Fixed Assets	113,293	30.0	281,436	38.9	639,327	31.9	4,434,408	48.4
Other Non-current	45,695	12.1	137,462	19.0	523,086	26.1	2,079,774	22.7
Total Assets	**377,643**	**100.0**	**723,486**	**100.0**	**2,004,160**	**100.0**	**9,162,000**	**100.0**
Accounts Payable	47,961	12.7	76,690	10.6	248,516	12.4	925,362	10.1
Bank Loans	1,511	0.4	—	—	2,004	0.1	9,162	0.1
Notes Payable	29,456	7.8	30,386	4.2	64,133	3.2	109,944	1.2
Other Current	51,737	13.7	90,436	12.5	256,532	12.8	1,035,306	11.3
Total Current	**130,664**	**34.6**	**197,512**	**27.3**	**571,186**	**28.5**	**2,079,774**	**22.7**
Other Long Term	35,121	9.3	51,368	7.1	190,395	9.5	1,548,378	16.9
Deferred Credits	2,644	0.7	2,170	0.3	6,012	0.3	164,916	1.8
Net Worth	209,214	55.4	472,436	65.3	1,236,567	61.7	5,368,932	58.6
Total Liab & Net Worth	**377,643**	**100.0**	**723,486**	**100.0**	**2,004,160**	**100.0**	**9,162,000**	**100.0**
Net Sales	453,155	100.0	432,272	100.0	882,352	100.0	4,204,900	100.0
Gross Profit	202,560	44.7	218,297	50.5	401,470	45.5	1,841,746	43.8
Net Profit After Tax	19,939	4.4	9,078	2.1	47,647	5.4	218,655	5.2
Working Capital	87,991	—	107,076	—	270,561	—	568,044	—

RATIOS	UQ	MED	LQ	UQ	MED	LQ	UQ	MED	LQ	UQ	MED	LQ
SOLVENCY												
Quick Ratio (times)	4.4	1.4	0.6	2.5	0.9	0.4	2.6	1.1	0.5	2.0	0.8	0.5
Current Ratio (times)	6.0	2.0	0.9	4.2	1.3	0.6	4.1	1.6	0.8	3.3	1.2	0.8
Curr Liab To Nw (%)	9.6	34.6	146.6	7.6	28.5	60.5	6.7	23.8	75.9	7.9	21.6	67.1
Curr Liab To Inv (%)	22.5	81.9	316.9	179.6	461.4	536.8	73.0	172.3	384.2	237.1	374.3	488.7
Total Liab To Nw (%)	16.0	43.2	191.0	15.1	44.5	82.5	12.7	35.6	93.0	19.9	65.4	134.7
Fixed Assets To Nw (%)	18.1	40.8	95.2	16.5	54.5	109.6	15.9	41.0	94.1	42.0	92.9	146.6
EFFICIENCY												
Coll Period (days)	27.4	56.2	118.6	17.9	63.5	101.5	30.3	59.5	162.5	35.7	58.4	91.8
Sales To Inv (times)	76.6	30.2	20.6	244.6	24.2	20.7	87.9	21.9	6.4	135.3	45.3	12.6
Assets To Sales (%)	57.2	85.8	142.5	77.4	127.3	173.7	142.1	201.2	352.5	184.2	217.2	296.2
Sales To Nwc (times)	11.0	4.8	2.4	12.0	5.0	1.2	6.8	2.8	1.0	7.0	2.7	1.2
Acct Pay To Sales (%)	1.8	9.0	24.0	3.7	13.3	24.4	5.5	12.0	43.9	6.2	12.8	24.9
PROFITABILITY												
Return On Sales (%)	14.6	4.7	(1.5)	17.8	2.4	(22.8)	19.3	8.2	(2.6)	17.8	6.4	(3.6)
Return On Assets (%)	17.2	5.9	(0.4)	8.2	4.4	(4.9)	10.7	3.5	(2.2)	8.0	2.8	(1.4)
Return On Nw (%)	34.5	9.7	(0.8)	12.5	9.1	(3.9)	18.0	6.6	(2.8)	15.6	5.0	(2.6)

SIC 1311 CRUDE PTRLM,NAT GAS — INDUSTRY ASSETS $25,000,000-$50,000,000 — 1995 (47 Establishments)
SIC 1311 CRUDE PTRLM,NAT GAS — INDUSTRY ASSETS OVER $50,000,000 — 1995 (174 Establishments)
SIC 1381 DRILL OIL,GAS WELLS (NO BREAKDOWN) — 1995 (171 Establishments)
SIC 1381 DRILL OIL,GAS WELLS — INDUSTRY ASSETS $100,000 - $250,000 — 1995 (15 Establishments)

	SIC 1311 $25-50M $	%	SIC 1311 Over $50M $	%	SIC 1381 No Brkdwn $	%	SIC 1381 $100-250K $	%
Cash	2,276,888	6.2	12,426,762	5.1	351,308	13.0	21,637	11.7
Accounts Receivable	2,570,680	7.0	17,787,326	7.3	567,497	21.0	39,761	21.5
Notes Receivable	183,620	0.5	—	—	21,619	0.8	—	—
Inventory	881,376	2.4	2,436,620	1.0	56,750	2.1	6,843	3.7
Other Current	2,313,612	6.3	11,939,438	4.9	178,356	6.6	6,103	3.3
Total Current	**8,226,176**	**22.4**	**44,590,146**	**18.3**	**1,175,529**	**43.5**	**74,344**	**40.2**
Fixed Assets	18,435,448	50.2	151,557,764	62.2	1,175,529	43.5	57,330	31.0
Other Non-current	10,062,376	27.4	47,514,090	19.5	351,308	13.0	53,261	28.8
Total Assets	**36,724,000**	**100.0**	**243,662,000**	**100.0**	**2,702,366**	**100.0**	**184,935**	**100.0**
Accounts Payable	2,240,164	6.1	14,376,058	5.9	289,153	10.7	25,521	13.8
Bank Loans	—	—	487,324	0.2	5,405	0.2	—	—
Notes Payable	440,688	1.2	2,192,958	0.9	56,750	2.1	4,069	2.2
Other Current	2,350,336	6.4	16,569,016	6.8	367,522	13.6	34,213	18.5
Total Current	**5,031,188**	**13.7**	**33,625,356**	**13.8**	**718,829**	**26.6**	**63,803**	**34.5**
Other Long Term	9,511,516	25.9	91,129,588	37.4	440,486	16.3	33,288	18.0
Deferred Credits	661,032	1.8	9,259,156	3.8	29,726	1.1	—	1.1
Net Worth	21,520,264	58.6	109,647,900	45.0	1,513,325	56.0	87,844	47.5
Total Liab & Net Worth	**36,724,000**	**100.0**	**243,662,000**	**100.0**	**2,702,366**	**100.0**	**184,935**	**100.0**
Net Sales	12,252,000	100.0	76,116,000	100.0	5,701,350	100.0	384,478	100.0
Gross Profit	4,312,704	35.2	29,380,776	38.6	1,693,301	29.7	154,176	40.1
Net Profit After Tax	196,032	1.6	2,892,408	3.8	165,339	2.9	(4,614)	(1.2)
Working Capital	3,194,988	—	10,964,790	—	456,700	—	10,541	—

RATIOS	UQ	MED	LQ	UQ	MED	LQ	UQ	MED	LQ	UQ	MED	LQ
SOLVENCY												
Quick Ratio (times)	1.7	1.0	0.3	1.2	0.8	0.6	2.3	1.4	0.8	1.2	0.7	0.3
Current Ratio (times)	2.3	1.3	0.7	1.5	1.1	0.8	3.3	1.9	1.0	1.8	1.2	0.3
Curr Liab To Nw (%)	10.6	20.3	37.3	14.4	28.1	53.7	14.7	27.8	76.6	9.1	12.8	23.5
Curr Liab To Inv (%)	313.3	450.5	598.2	217.3	505.3	744.6	213.3	355.3	546.7	136.6	152.1	224.3
Total Liab To Nw (%)	24.9	55.5	129.7	72.0	146.8	210.3	26.1	56.6	113.1	9.7	15.5	24.3
Fixed Assets To Nw (%)	28.4	92.3	160.8	131.2	188.3	248.1	42.2	82.9	119.3	12.1	18.3	26.1
EFFICIENCY												
Coll Period (days)	38.7	65.7	98.0	47.1	60.2	80.9	44.3	66.6	79.5	24.1	35.0	50.8
Sales To Inv (times)	56.3	28.7	21.6	69.0	39.8	20.4	60.8	24.8	15.5	26.1	22.2	14.9
Assets To Sales (%)	179.7	267.6	471.9	178.1	276.8	399.2	52.7	114.2	188.1	30.9	43.1	52.8
Sales To Nwc (times)	8.5	4.7	3.0	19.1	12.1	2.7	9.8	5.5	2.8	7.6	7.2	6.5
Acct Pay To Sales (%)	8.9	13.9	28.0	8.3	15.1	23.5	4.3	6.9	11.0	2.3	3.5	4.9
PROFITABILITY												
Return On Sales (%)	19.1	3.8	(13.2)	11.7	4.3	(0.4)	8.4	4.3	0.2	1.9	(1.9)	(12.3)
Return On Assets (%)	6.2	2.0	(4.0)	4.1	2.1	(1.0)	10.7	4.1	0.5	(6.1)	(12.7)	(16.8)
Return On Nw (%)	13.4	2.9	(5.9)	9.6	4.6	(1.3)	20.8	7.2	1.7	(5.9)	(13.2)	(18.4)

SIC 1381 — DRILL OIL, GAS WELLS — INDUSTRY ASSETS — 1995

	$250,000–$500,000 (21 Establishments) $	%	$500,000–$1,000,000 (17 Establishments) $	%	$1,000,000–$5,000,000 (38 Establishments) $	%	$5,000,000–$25,000,000 (23 Establishments) $	%
Cash	70,074	18.5	108,121	15.3	336,240	14.5	1,099,355	9.8
Accounts Receivable	104,165	27.5	141,335	20.0	721,177	31.1	2,266,018	20.2
Notes Receivable	6,818	1.8	2,120	0.3	41,740	1.8	134,615	1.2
Inventory	1,136	0.3	34,627	4.9	32,465	1.4	201,922	1.8
Other Current	17,803	4.7	41,694	5.9	222,614	9.6	841,343	7.5
Total Current	**199,996**	**52.8**	**327,897**	**46.4**	**1,354,236**	**58.4**	**4,543,254**	**40.5**
Fixed Assets	126,513	33.4	317,297	44.9	721,177	31.1	5,014,406	44.7
Other Non-current	52,272	13.8	61,481	8.7	243,484	10.5	1,660,251	14.8
Total Assets	**378,780**	**100.0**	**706,674**	**100.0**	**2,318,897**	**100.0**	**11,217,910**	**100.0**
Accounts Payable	35,605	9.4	67,134	9.5	361,748	15.6	1,536,854	13.7
Bank Loans	—	—	—	—	13,913	0.6	33,654	0.3
Notes Payable	11,363	3.0	29,680	4.2	60,291	2.6	336,537	3.0
Other Current	85,226	22.5	87,628	12.4	289,862	12.5	1,570,507	14.0
Total Current	**132,194**	**34.9**	**184,442**	**26.1**	**725,815**	**31.3**	**3,477,552**	**31.0**
Other Long Term	50,757	13.4	125,788	17.8	303,776	13.1	919,869	8.2
Deferred Credits	9,470	2.5	7,067	1.0	2,319	0.1	325,319	2.9
Net Worth	186,360	49.2	389,377	55.1	1,286,988	55.5	6,495,170	57.9
Total Liab & Net Worth	**378,780**	**100.0**	**706,674**	**100.0**	**2,318,897**	**100.0**	**11,217,910**	**100.0**
Net Sales	987,200	100.0	1,198,547	100.0	4,415,266	100.0	12,758,044	100.0
Gross Profit	362,302	36.7	302,034	25.2	1,434,961	32.5	2,181,626	17.1
Net Profit After Tax	(3,949)	(0.4)	133,039	11.1	185,441	4.2	497,564	3.9
Working Capital	67,802	—	143,455	—	628,421	—	1,065,702	—

RATIOS

	UQ	MED	LQ	UQ	MED	LQ	UQ	MED	LQ	UQ	MED	LQ
SOLVENCY												
Quick Ratio (times)	2.9	1.7	0.6	5.6	1.3	0.8	2.2	1.4	1.0	1.7	1.1	0.6
Current Ratio (times)	4.6	2.1	0.7	7.3	2.4	0.8	3.4	1.8	1.1	3.8	1.5	0.7
Curr Liab To Nw (%)	16.4	26.0	239.5	7.9	21.5	58.3	26.7	56.2	108.8	14.2	62.3	121.9
Curr Liab To Inv (%)	—	—	—	99.9	116.6	415.3	324.4	448.5	706.0	188.4	230.0	395.9
Total Liab To Nw (%)	18.0	46.6	509.1	16.6	43.7	84.4	32.6	75.4	129.1	19.0	68.3	110.4
Fixed Assets To Nw (%)	48.0	97.7	338.1	53.0	70.0	96.3	29.4	50.4	97.2	58.2	82.6	107.6
EFFICIENCY												
Coll Period (days)	20.8	51.1	97.5	20.8	51.8	89.8	44.8	63.4	72.7	40.0	44.9	53.2
Sales To Inv (times)	—	—	—	60.0	41.1	37.4	243.7	151.5	47.9	44.4	20.6	15.8
Assets To Sales (%)	29.0	54.0	83.0	45.5	69.1	121.0	34.0	55.3	84.8	55.9	75.9	146.6
Sales To Nwc (times)	12.3	7.8	6.9	6.1	4.1	2.8	11.3	7.1	3.3	12.6	7.5	4.2
Acct Pay To Sales (%)	1.3	10.2	14.9	1.0	1.5	11.6	3.4	6.1	9.1	6.0	8.8	11.8
PROFITABILITY												
Return On Sales (%)	6.2	5.1	3.0	20.0	8.4	3.3	7.1	3.5	1.3	8.8	3.4	1.1
Return On Assets (%)	11.2	9.8	6.9	22.4	8.3	2.5	15.7	10.1	4.0	11.8	3.2	1.8
Return On Nw (%)	22.1	14.1	12.8	35.6	28.2	6.8	22.1	15.5	6.0	16.6	4.2	4.1

	SIC 1381 DRILL OIL,GAS WELLS — OVER $50,000,000 — 1995 (42 Establishments) $	%	SIC 1382 OIL GAS EXPLOR SVCS (NO BREAKDOWN) — 1995 (198 Establishments) $	%	SIC 1382 OIL GAS EXPLOR SVCS $250,000 - $500,000 — 1995 (27 Establishments) $	%	SIC 1382 OIL GAS EXPLOR SVCS $500,000 - $1,000,000 — 1995 (20 Establishments) $	%
Cash	15,241,928	6.8	676,894	15.8	62,438	17.0	116,579	15.1
Accounts Receivable	27,345,812	12.2	595,495	13.9	79,333	21.6	197,644	25.6
Notes Receivable	224,146	0.1	29,989	0.7	1,469	0.4	1,544	0.2
Inventory	5,155,358	2.3	64,262	1.5	4,775	1.3	12,353	1.6
Other Current	15,466,074	6.9	291,322	6.8	27,179	7.4	142,829	18.5
Total Current	**63,433,318**	**28.3**	**1,657,962**	**38.7**	**175,194**	**47.7**	**470,948**	**61.0**
Fixed Assets	142,556,856	63.6	1,799,339	42.0	136,997	37.3	158,269	20.5
Other Non-current	18,155,826	8.1	826,839	19.3	55,093	15.0	142,829	18.5
Total Assets	**224,146,000**	**100.0**	**4,284,140**	**100.0**	**367,284**	**100.0**	**772,046**	**100.0**
Accounts Payable	10,983,154	4.9	496,960	11.6	58,398	15.9	77,977	10.1
Bank Loans	—	—	4,284	0.1	—	—	—	—
Notes Payable	1,120,730	0.5	179,934	4.2	17,997	4.9	81,837	10.6
Other Current	19,948,994	8.9	419,846	9.8	27,914	7.6	131,248	17.0
Total Current	**32,052,878**	**14.3**	**1,101,024**	**25.7**	**104,309**	**28.4**	**291,061**	**37.7**
Other Long Term	53,795,040	24.0	882,533	20.6	70,519	19.2	56,359	7.3
Deferred Credits	2,017,314	0.9	72,830	1.7	—	—	10,037	1.3
Net Worth	136,280,768	60.8	2,227,753	52.0	192,457	52.4	414,589	53.7
Total Liab & Net Worth	**224,146,000**	**100.0**	**4,284,140**	**100.0**	**367,284**	**100.0**	**772,046**	**100.0**
Net Sales	152,424,000	100.0	2,968,140	100.0	296,204	100.0	449,739	100.0
Gross Profit	46,032,048	30.2	1,570,146	52.9	188,090	63.5	168,202	37.4
Net Profit After Tax	2,743,632	1.8	192,929	6.5	25,770	8.7	27,434	6.1
Working Capital	31,380,440	—	556,938	—	70,885	—	179,887	—

RATIOS	UQ	MED	LQ	UQ	MED	LQ	UQ	MED	LQ	UQ	MED	LQ
SOLVENCY												
Quick Ratio (times)	2.3	1.6	1.0	2.8	1.1	0.5	1.9	1.0	0.5	2.9	1.2	0.6
Current Ratio (times)	3.0	2.2	1.4	4.3	1.5	0.9	2.1	1.2	0.7	3.7	1.5	1.0
Curr Liab To Nw (%)	14.8	20.0	31.4	10.1	29.7	81.2	3.5	10.9	35.4	19.1	30.3	188.8
Curr Liab To Inv (%)	237.2	411.4	546.7	265.5	518.1	770.2	290.5	348.2	669.2	493.4	511.1	677.8
Total Liab To Nw (%)	35.6	58.3	91.9	30.3	86.6	144.0	10.3	48.3	74.5	29.5	100.2	188.8
Fixed Assets To Nw (%)	92.8	98.6	138.0	34.7	87.7	152.8	23.7	49.0	84.4	26.9	40.6	93.9
EFFICIENCY												
Coll Period (days)	67.7	75.2	84.7	36.9	66.4	111.7	21.9	74.5	92.9	38.9	67.5	139.3
Sales To Inv (times)	24.6	16.8	14.4	73.1	33.8	9.6	341.3	228.7	116.0	53.8	37.5	21.2
Assets To Sales (%)	146.2	191.3	237.7	111.4	205.4	335.2	37.3	62.0	114.0	64.4	175.2	216.9
Sales To Nwc (times)	6.1	3.7	2.2	8.2	4.6	1.7	5.2	4.6	2.7	5.1	1.9	1.2
Acct Pay To Sales (%)	4.9	7.2	10.5	6.3	15.8	28.8	1.8	4.6	19.5	6.8	15.3	38.9
PROFITABILITY												
Return On Sales (%)	8.5	4.0	(3.5)	17.4	6.8	(0.9)	10.2	6.4	(0.5)	23.2	0.5	(24.0)
Return On Assets (%)	4.1	2.9	0.3	7.8	2.8	(1.5)	14.0	(0.4)	(11.2)	11.8	(1.5)	(9.0)
Return On Nw (%)	7.6	4.8	0.6	16.4	5.1	(2.8)	20.3	3.0	(11.6)	21.5	(2.9)	(23.8)

Balance Sheet ($ and %)

	SIC 1382 OIL GAS EXPLOR SVCS $1,000,000 - $5,000,000 (38 Establishments)		SIC 1382 OIL GAS EXPLOR SVCS $5,000,000-$25,000,000 (34 Establishments)		SIC 1382 OIL GAS EXPLOR SVCS OVER $50,000,000 (44 Establishments)		SIC 1389 OIL GAS FLD SVC,NEC (NO BREAKDOWN) (489 Establishments)	
	$	%	$	%	$	%	$	%
Cash	444,741	19.1	1,707,020	15.4	5,909,100	3.0	83,374	13.1
Accounts Receivable	381,872	16.4	1,463,160	13.2	14,181,840	7.2	183,296	28.8
Notes Receivable	37,256	1.6	—	—	787,880	0.4	4,455	0.7
Inventory	13,971	0.6	376,875	3.4	3,348,490	1.7	21,003	3.3
Other Current	174,637	7.5	421,213	3.8	9,257,590	4.7	38,187	6.0
Total Current	**1,052,477**	**45.2**	**3,968,268**	**35.8**	**33,484,900**	**17.0**	**330,315**	**51.9**
Fixed Assets	707,861	30.4	4,999,131	45.1	129,803,230	65.9	233,575	36.7
Other Non-current	568,151	24.4	2,117,148	19.1	33,681,870	17.1	72,555	11.4
Total Assets	**2,328,489**	**100.0**	**11,084,547**	**100.0**	**196,970,000**	**100.0**	**636,445**	**100.0**
Accounts Payable	351,602	15.1	1,019,778	9.2	11,818,200	6.0	55,371	8.7
Bank Loans	9,314	0.4	—	—	—	—	1,273	0.2
Notes Payable	156,009	6.7	343,621	3.1	1,181,820	0.6	33,732	5.3
Other Current	249,148	10.7	1,440,991	13.0	14,181,840	7.2	73,191	11.5
Total Current	**766,073**	**32.9**	**2,804,390**	**25.3**	**27,181,860**	**13.8**	**163,566**	**25.7**
Other Long Term	435,427	18.7	3,037,166	27.4	59,091,000	30.0	112,651	17.7
Deferred Credits	4,657	0.2	66,507	0.6	10,439,410	5.3	1,909	0.3
Net Worth	1,122,332	48.2	5,176,483	46.7	100,257,730	50.9	358,319	56.3
Total Liab & Net Worth	**2,328,489**	**100.0**	**11,084,547**	**100.0**	**196,970,000**	**100.0**	**636,445**	**100.0**
Net Sales	1,416,536	100.0	6,768,292	100.0	78,235,999	100.0	1,623,455	100.0
Gross Profit	851,338	60.1	4,081,280	60.3	49,288,679	63.0	712,697	43.9
Net Profit After Tax	106,240	7.5	169,207	2.5	6,493,588	8.3	81,173	5.0
Working Capital	286,404	—	1,163,878	—	6,303,040	—	166,749	—

RATIOS

	UQ	MED	LQ	UQ	MED	LQ	UQ	MED	LQ	UQ	MED	LQ
SOLVENCY												
Quick Ratio (times)	3.2	1.0	0.6	2.0	1.2	0.8	1.1	0.8	0.4	4.3	1.7	1.0
Current Ratio (times)	4.7	1.3	1.0	3.4	1.6	0.9	1.7	1.1	0.8	5.6	2.2	1.3
Curr Liab To Nw (%)	19.7	57.0	106.3	24.3	51.4	83.4	12.1	19.1	47.8	11.5	36.8	87.0
Curr Liab To Inv (%)	169.5	338.4	507.4	151.7	342.6	526.7	264.5	469.3	745.1	166.3	301.1	528.3
Total Liab To Nw (%)	16.8	84.1	139.9	41.0	113.7	204.6	39.5	88.7	118.2	23.2	62.6	145.6
Fixed Assets To Nw (%)	13.3	48.1	121.7	53.1	126.0	169.4	90.7	135.8	176.7	35.8	71.2	125.5
EFFICIENCY												
Coll Period (days)	17.4	34.4	110.5	43.5	66.1	127.7	39.7	65.9	94.3	40.0	57.7	75.4
Sales To Inv (times)	781.6	285.9	152.6	31.9	11.1	8.0	76.5	25.0	11.1	75.4	32.4	14.2
Assets To Sales (%)	125.4	179.3	268.9	114.9	217.0	319.6	203.8	308.7	387.9	30.9	45.1	68.4
Sales To Nwc (times)	9.4	4.7	1.0	5.9	2.3	1.0	19.6	5.7	4.5	14.2	7.8	4.4
Acct Pay To Sales (%)	4.9	9.2	49.1	7.8	20.9	34.1	11.2	16.0	25.9	2.4	4.5	7.8
PROFITABILITY												
Return On Sales (%)	26.1	4.6	(3.5)	22.8	5.3	(4.1)	12.4	6.8	(0.5)	10.5	4.4	0.8
Return On Assets (%)	11.7	2.8	(1.6)	7.0	2.6	0.9	5.2	2.8	0.1	15.7	6.5	0.6
Return On Nw (%)	63.5	6.0	(7.4)	17.1	7.6	1.2	9.7	5.9	(0.1)	27.3	12.7	1.1

SIC 1389 OIL GAS FLD SVC, NEC — INDUSTRY ASSETS UNDER $100,000 — 1995 (55 Establishments)

	$	%
Cash	16,817	25.9
Accounts Receivable	14,284	22.0
Notes Receivable	1,169	1.8
Inventory	1,493	2.3
Other Current	3,052	4.7
Total Current	**36,815**	**56.7**
Fixed Assets	25,257	38.9
Other Non-current	2,857	4.4
Total Assets	**64,929**	**100.0**
Accounts Payable	5,454	8.4
Bank Loans	130	0.2
Notes Payable	2,402	3.7
Other Current	12,012	18.5
Total Current	**19,998**	**30.8**
Other Long Term	7,077	10.9
Deferred Credits	—	—
Net Worth	37,854	58.3
Total Liab & Net Worth	**64,929**	**100.0**
Net Sales	192,235	100.0
Gross Profit	83,814	43.6
Net Profit After Tax	16,917	8.8
Working Capital	16,817	—

RATIOS	UQ	MED	LQ
SOLVENCY			
Quick Ratio (times)	4.6	1.9	0.9
Current Ratio (times)	6.2	2.7	1.1
Curr Liab To Nw (%)	11.4	25.9	79.1
Curr Liab To Inv (%)	192.7	271.9	295.3
Total Liab To Nw (%)	13.4	35.4	96.2
Fixed Assets To Nw (%)	34.5	73.3	118.8
EFFICIENCY			
Coll Period (days)	27.4	35.0	45.6
Sales To Inv (times)	154.4	66.6	17.7
Assets To Sales (%)	17.6	29.4	52.5
Sales To Nwc (times)	17.3	8.0	5.3
Acct Pay To Sales (%)	1.4	2.4	4.1
PROFITABILITY			
Return On Sales (%)	17.5	9.8	4.3
Return On Assets (%)	35.0	22.0	4.3
Return On Nw (%)	55.3	24.2	(327.9)

SIC 1389 OIL GAS FLD SVC, NEC — INDUSTRY ASSETS $100,000 - $250,000 — 1995 (76 Establishments)

	$	%
Cash	31,930	18.5
Accounts Receivable	41,595	24.1
Notes Receivable	345	0.2
Inventory	7,594	4.4
Other Current	11,046	6.4
Total Current	**92,511**	**53.6**
Fixed Assets	60,408	35.0
Other Non-current	19,676	11.4
Total Assets	**172,595**	**100.0**
Accounts Payable	14,671	8.5
Bank Loans	—	—
Notes Payable	10,873	6.3
Other Current	23,473	13.6
Total Current	**49,017**	**28.4**
Other Long Term	38,834	22.5
Deferred Credits	—	—
Net Worth	84,744	49.1
Total Liab & Net Worth	**172,595**	**100.0**
Net Sales	441,831	100.0
Gross Profit	208,544	47.2
Net Profit After Tax	16,790	3.8
Working Capital	43,494	—

RATIOS	UQ	MED	LQ
SOLVENCY			
Quick Ratio (times)	6.4	1.6	0.9
Current Ratio (times)	9.2	2.1	1.1
Curr Liab To Nw (%)	8.5	40.5	126.9
Curr Liab To Inv (%)	86.3	273.9	343.6
Total Liab To Nw (%)	14.8	65.6	201.0
Fixed Assets To Nw (%)	30.2	85.3	163.5
EFFICIENCY			
Coll Period (days)	38.0	47.1	68.7
Sales To Inv (times)	78.5	37.9	12.4
Assets To Sales (%)	26.3	36.9	56.2
Sales To Nwc (times)	17.4	10.8	5.7
Acct Pay To Sales (%)	1.7	3.7	7.8
PROFITABILITY			
Return On Sales (%)	12.0	6.3	1.0
Return On Assets (%)	20.8	10.5	(2.9)
Return On Nw (%)	68.3	21.8	(12.2)

SIC 1389 OIL GAS FLD SVC, NEC — INDUSTRY ASSETS $250,000 - $500,000 — 1995 (92 Establishments)

	$	%
Cash	40,322	11.0
Accounts Receivable	118,766	32.4
Notes Receivable	1,833	0.5
Inventory	12,463	3.4
Other Current	15,029	4.1
Total Current	**188,413**	**51.4**
Fixed Assets	136,361	37.2
Other Non-current	41,788	11.4
Total Assets	**366,563**	**100.0**
Accounts Payable	35,190	9.6
Bank Loans	733	0.2
Notes Payable	25,293	6.9
Other Current	30,425	8.3
Total Current	**91,641**	**25.0**
Other Long Term	60,483	16.5
Deferred Credits	—	—
Net Worth	214,439	58.5
Total Liab & Net Worth	**366,563**	**100.0**
Net Sales	950,688	100.0
Gross Profit	530,484	55.8
Net Profit After Tax	60,844	6.4
Working Capital	96,772	—

RATIOS	UQ	MED	LQ
SOLVENCY			
Quick Ratio (times)	5.0	2.2	1.0
Current Ratio (times)	5.2	2.6	1.3
Curr Liab To Nw (%)	9.5	29.6	71.8
Curr Liab To Inv (%)	140.8	214.6	505.0
Total Liab To Nw (%)	24.9	47.1	125.4
Fixed Assets To Nw (%)	29.0	60.9	111.9
EFFICIENCY			
Coll Period (days)	36.1	48.4	71.8
Sales To Inv (times)	78.4	39.7	14.0
Assets To Sales (%)	27.4	35.1	45.6
Sales To Nwc (times)	15.9	7.9	4.9
Acct Pay To Sales (%)	1.2	4.6	7.8
PROFITABILITY			
Return On Sales (%)	13.4	4.6	1.5
Return On Assets (%)	15.8	9.5	1.1
Return On Nw (%)	28.6	15.7	1.9

SIC 1389 OIL GAS FLD SVC, NEC — INDUSTRY ASSETS $500,000 - $1,000,000 — 1995 (95 Establishments)

	$	%
Cash	82,014	12.0
Accounts Receivable	202,301	29.6
Notes Receivable	3,417	0.5
Inventory	19,137	2.8
Other Current	46,475	6.8
Total Current	**353,344**	**51.7**
Fixed Assets	248,776	36.4
Other Non-current	81,331	11.9
Total Assets	**683,451**	**100.0**
Accounts Payable	56,043	8.2
Bank Loans	683	0.1
Notes Payable	28,021	4.1
Other Current	62,877	9.2
Total Current	**147,625**	**21.6**
Other Long Term	111,403	16.3
Deferred Credits	2,050	0.3
Net Worth	422,373	61.8
Total Liab & Net Worth	**683,451**	**100.0**
Net Sales	1,580,095	100.0
Gross Profit	802,688	50.8
Net Profit After Tax	75,845	4.8
Working Capital	205,719	—

RATIOS	UQ	MED	LQ
SOLVENCY			
Quick Ratio (times)	4.6	1.9	1.2
Current Ratio (times)	6.0	2.1	1.5
Curr Liab To Nw (%)	10.9	36.7	71.9
Curr Liab To Inv (%)	151.4	322.0	783.4
Total Liab To Nw (%)	20.6	57.8	128.9
Fixed Assets To Nw (%)	35.1	68.2	122.9
EFFICIENCY			
Coll Period (days)	36.3	51.1	68.2
Sales To Inv (times)	203.6	72.8	37.9
Assets To Sales (%)	33.7	46.0	59.3
Sales To Nwc (times)	14.9	7.8	4.3
Acct Pay To Sales (%)	2.5	3.7	5.3
PROFITABILITY			
Return On Sales (%)	11.0	4.4	1.3
Return On Assets (%)	16.2	7.2	3.1
Return On Nw (%)	27.2	12.4	4.2

SIC 1389 OIL GAS FLD SVC,NEC — INDUSTRY ASSETS $1,000,000 - $5,000,000 — 1995 (128 Establishments)
SIC 1389 OIL GAS FLD SVC,NEC — INDUSTRY ASSETS $5,000,000-$25,000,000 — 1995 (13 Establishments)
SIC 1389 OIL GAS FLD SVC,NEC — INDUSTRY ASSETS OVER $50,000,000 — 1995 (23 Establishments)
SIC 14 NONMETALLIC MINERALS (NO BREAKDOWN) — 1995 (339 Establishments)

	$1M-$5M $	%	$5M-$25M $	%	OVER $50M $	%	NONMETALLIC $	%
Cash	162,551	10.7	286,769	4.6	10,161,228	4.9	225,391	11.6
Accounts Receivable	487,652	32.1	2,337,792	37.5	44,377,608	21.4	310,884	16.0
Notes Receivable	18,230	1.2	31,171	0.5	—		9,715	0.5
Inventory	37,979	2.5	130,916	2.1	14,308,668	6.9	163,214	8.4
Other Current	110,899	7.3	261,833	4.2	8,709,624	4.2	85,493	4.4
Total Current	**817,311**	**53.8**	**3,048,481**	**48.9**	**77,557,128**	**37.4**	**794,697**	**40.9**
Fixed Assets	531,708	35.0	2,088,428	33.5	92,280,540	44.5	872,418	44.9
Other Non-current	170,146	11.2	1,097,204	17.6	37,534,332	18.1	275,909	14.2
Total Assets	**1,519,165**	**100.0**	**6,234,113**	**100.0**	**207,372,000**	**100.0**	**1,943,024**	**100.0**
Accounts Payable	132,167	8.7	642,114	10.3	14,930,784	7.2	130,183	6.7
Bank Loans	4,557	0.3	87,278	1.4	—		1,943	0.1
Notes Payable	100,265	6.6	162,087	2.6	1,244,232	0.6	91,322	4.7
Other Current	161,031	10.6	1,028,629	16.5	27,373,104	13.2	190,416	9.8
Total Current	**398,021**	**26.2**	**1,920,107**	**30.8**	**43,548,120**	**21.0**	**413,864**	**21.3**
Other Long Term	268,892	17.7	804,201	12.9	55,575,696	26.8	394,434	20.3
Deferred Credits	3,038	0.2	24,936	0.4	3,525,324	1.7	11,658	0.6
Net Worth	849,213	55.9	3,484,869	55.9	104,722,860	50.5	1,123,068	57.8
Total Liab & Net Worth	**1,519,165**	**100.0**	**6,234,113**	**100.0**	**207,372,000**	**100.0**	**1,943,024**	**100.0**
Net Sales	3,476,212	100.0	19,224,157	100.0	182,336,000	100.0	2,347,437	100.0
Gross Profit	1,296,627	37.3	5,805,695	30.2	51,418,752	28.2	894,373	38.1
Net Profit After Tax	152,953	4.4	1,403,363	7.3	3,099,712	1.7	185,448	7.9
Working Capital	419,290	—	1,128,374	—	34,009,008	—	380,833	—

RATIOS	UQ	MED	LQ	UQ	MED	LQ	UQ	MED	LQ	UQ	MED	LQ
SOLVENCY												
Quick Ratio (times)	4.4	1.7	1.0	2.1	1.5	1.1	1.4	1.3	1.0	3.3	1.4	0.7
Current Ratio (times)	5.6	2.2	1.3	2.2	1.9	1.2	2.1	1.8	1.6	4.9	2.2	1.3
Curr Liab To Nw (%)	11.6	40.9	99.2	32.7	60.2	84.3	28.6	35.6	51.9	10.8	27.4	60.5
Curr Liab To Inv (%)	242.8	377.0	632.1	304.8	528.3	764.1	200.6	327.4	413.0	76.0	146.2	347.5
Total Liab To Nw (%)	20.0	88.7	159.1	60.2	84.3	112.3	57.9	89.8	146.2	19.4	53.1	129.2
Fixed Assets To Nw (%)	37.2	64.7	126.0	38.2	67.3	102.9	75.3	100.1	123.1	45.5	76.6	144.3
EFFICIENCY												
Coll Period (days)	52.0	63.2	76.7	52.9	74.1	77.0	71.0	79.2	100.4	30.3	44.2	61.0
Sales To Inv (times)	72.4	34.3	15.0	81.5	62.1	55.9	22.0	15.5	8.5	32.6	12.0	6.7
Assets To Sales (%)	37.8	49.8	69.0	31.2	47.3	69.4	94.4	104.9	165.0	60.2	84.3	124.6
Sales To Nwc (times)	12.9	7.2	4.4	16.4	11.1	7.8	8.7	5.3	3.8	10.2	5.2	2.6
Acct Pay To Sales (%)	2.5	4.6	9.0	3.2	4.5	7.3	7.0	7.8	10.0	2.6	4.8	7.8
PROFITABILITY												
Return On Sales (%)	8.9	3.5	0.5	10.5	6.8	4.0	5.5	3.4	0.4	14.2	7.2	2.3
Return On Assets (%)	13.7	4.7	0.2	18.6	14.0	10.8	3.1	1.2	—	14.4	7.7	3.1
Return On Nw (%)	22.4	10.3	1.1	34.6	25.1	19.8	6.7	3.8	(0.3)	23.9	13.1	5.9

SIC 14 — NONMETALLIC MINERALS

	NORTHEAST 1995 (39 Establishments)		CENTRAL 1995 (149 Establishments)		SOUTH 1995 (93 Establishments)		WEST 1995 (58 Establishments)	
	$	%	$	%	$	%	$	%
Cash	191,283	12.4	262,971	13.6	162,440	8.2	269,275	11.4
Accounts Receivable	174,315	11.3	305,511	15.8	354,595	17.9	392,102	16.6
Notes Receivable	27,767	1.8	3,867	0.2	11,886	0.6	4,724	0.2
Inventory	135,750	8.8	154,689	8.0	176,307	8.9	198,413	8.4
Other Current	18,511	1.2	102,481	5.3	93,106	4.7	92,120	3.9
Total Current	**547,626**	**35.5**	**829,520**	**42.9**	**798,333**	**40.3**	**956,635**	**40.5**
Fixed Assets	704,972	45.7	846,922	43.8	897,382	45.3	1,105,445	46.8
Other Non-current	290,010	18.8	257,170	13.3	285,260	14.4	299,982	12.7
Total Assets	**1,542,608**	**100.0**	**1,933,612**	**100.0**	**1,980,975**	**100.0**	**2,362,062**	**100.0**
Accounts Payable	89,471	5.8	116,017	6.0	150,554	7.6	184,241	7.8
Bank Loans	—	—	1,934	0.1	5,943	0.3	—	—
Notes Payable	70,960	4.6	87,013	4.5	120,839	6.1	82,672	3.5
Other Current	182,028	11.8	183,693	9.5	176,307	8.9	250,379	10.6
Total Current	**342,459**	**22.2**	**388,656**	**20.1**	**453,643**	**22.9**	**517,292**	**21.9**
Other Long Term	323,948	21.0	361,585	18.7	457,605	23.1	451,154	19.1
Deferred Credits	7,713	0.5	11,602	0.6	1,981	0.1	35,431	1.5
Net Worth	868,488	56.3	1,171,769	60.6	1,067,746	53.9	1,358,186	57.5
Total Liab & Net Worth	**1,542,608**	**100.0**	**1,933,612**	**100.0**	**1,980,975**	**100.0**	**2,362,062**	**100.0**
Net Sales	2,347,437	100.0	2,918,418	100.0	2,249,819	100.0	1,727,631	100.0
Gross Profit	957,754	40.8	1,164,449	39.9	848,182	37.7	583,939	33.8
Net Profit After Tax	86,855	3.7	306,434	10.5	148,488	6.6	133,028	7.7
Working Capital	205,167	—	440,864	—	344,690	—	439,343	—

RATIOS	UQ	MED	LQ	UQ	MED	LQ	UQ	MED	LQ	UQ	MED	LQ
SOLVENCY												
Quick Ratio (times)	1.7	1.0	0.5	4.2	1.7	0.8	2.5	1.2	0.7	2.8	1.5	0.8
Current Ratio (times)	3.0	1.6	0.9	5.7	2.6	1.5	3.9	1.9	1.3	4.5	2.1	1.2
Curr Liab To Nw (%)	13.2	44.8	66.4	9.3	25.3	55.8	11.4	28.4	47.9	10.8	34.1	62.7
Curr Liab To Inv (%)	80.4	115.1	452.3	66.9	127.6	273.6	93.5	199.1	353.5	72.8	142.0	412.3
Total Liab To Nw (%)	32.4	57.4	164.1	16.8	45.6	115.1	24.5	58.6	144.3	18.2	67.9	128.9
Fixed Assets To Nw (%)	45.6	77.3	166.6	43.4	75.3	141.4	46.9	70.9	146.4	50.0	76.6	145.2
EFFICIENCY												
Coll Period (days)	36.2	42.4	57.9	28.8	39.4	51.5	32.5	48.2	67.9	32.0	48.7	63.3
Sales To Inv (times)	18.2	11.9	7.6	55.8	10.9	6.8	31.7	11.1	6.4	30.0	13.6	7.4
Assets To Sales (%)	54.9	81.9	101.9	58.3	85.7	122.1	60.2	91.7	149.7	63.8	77.3	109.5
Sales To Nwc (times)	12.6	6.1	3.1	8.7	4.3	2.0	10.5	5.3	3.5	9.9	5.7	3.3
Acct Pay To Sales (%)	2.5	5.1	11.4	2.1	4.4	6.5	3.6	5.2	8.2	2.7	4.1	8.0
PROFITABILITY												
Return On Sales (%)	7.8	6.4	1.2	15.8	9.3	4.2	13.7	6.2	1.9	13.9	6.4	2.5
Return On Assets (%)	7.5	4.8	2.3	15.3	10.9	5.6	14.5	6.4	1.5	14.3	7.2	2.2
Return On Nw (%)	15.3	10.3	4.0	22.6	15.5	8.5	22.4	12.4	3.8	28.4	13.5	4.6

SIC 14 NONMETALLIC MINERALS

INDUSTRY ASSETS $100,000 - $250,000 — 1995 (18 Establishments)

	$	%
Cash	27,159	14.7
Accounts Receivable	35,289	19.1
Notes Receivable	1,478	0.8
Inventory	9,238	5.0
Other Current	8,314	4.5
Total Current	**81,478**	**44.1**
Fixed Assets	84,434	45.7
Other Non-current	18,845	10.2
Total Assets	**184,758**	**100.0**
Accounts Payable	14,781	8.0
Bank Loans	—	—
Notes Payable	28,453	15.4
Other Current	17,367	9.4
Total Current	**60,601**	**32.8**
Other Long Term	39,353	21.3
Deferred Credits	—	—
Net Worth	84,804	45.9
Total Liab & Net Worth	**184,758**	**100.0**
Net Sales	449,089	100.0
Gross Profit	305,830	68.1
Net Profit After Tax	35,927	8.0
Working Capital	20,877	—

RATIOS	UQ	MED	LQ
SOLVENCY			
Quick Ratio (times)	2.6	1.3	0.7
Current Ratio (times)	2.9	2.0	0.7
Curr Liab To Nw (%)	21.6	43.0	125.3
Curr Liab To Inv (%)	179.6	293.0	299.8
Total Liab To Nw (%)	25.2	91.0	138.7
Fixed Assets To Nw (%)	56.0	75.6	159.8
EFFICIENCY			
Coll Period (days)	38.1	43.8	50.9
Sales To Inv (times)	41.5	27.0	17.4
Assets To Sales (%)	37.7	50.6	64.3
Sales To Nwc (times)	9.4	6.8	5.6
Acct Pay To Sales (%)	1.0	4.4	7.2
PROFITABILITY			
Return On Sales (%)	18.6	7.2	2.2
Return On Assets (%)	38.7	21.0	4.3
Return On Nw (%)	54.3	27.7	11.8

INDUSTRY ASSETS $250,000 - $500,000 — 1995 (39 Establishments)

	$	%
Cash	55,196	15.6
Accounts Receivable	54,135	15.3
Notes Receivable	1,769	0.5
Inventory	31,844	9.0
Other Current	2,123	0.6
Total Current	**145,067**	**41.0**
Fixed Assets	197,786	55.9
Other Non-current	10,968	3.1
Total Assets	**353,821**	**100.0**
Accounts Payable	29,367	8.3
Bank Loans	—	—
Notes Payable	34,674	9.8
Other Current	33,259	9.4
Total Current	**97,301**	**27.5**
Other Long Term	88,455	25.0
Deferred Credits	3,892	1.1
Net Worth	164,173	46.4
Total Liab & Net Worth	**353,821**	**100.0**
Net Sales	681,342	100.0
Gross Profit	397,222	58.3
Net Profit After Tax	21,803	3.2
Working Capital	47,766	—

RATIOS	UQ	MED	LQ
SOLVENCY			
Quick Ratio (times)	3.1	1.3	0.4
Current Ratio (times)	3.2	1.9	0.6
Curr Liab To Nw (%)	19.0	39.0	85.3
Curr Liab To Inv (%)	95.0	115.1	288.6
Total Liab To Nw (%)	35.0	87.9	173.8
Fixed Assets To Nw (%)	55.6	96.0	232.9
EFFICIENCY			
Coll Period (days)	8.4	31.8	37.6
Sales To Inv (times)	50.7	16.2	7.2
Assets To Sales (%)	37.2	46.2	67.5
Sales To Nwc (times)	17.1	9.5	3.9
Acct Pay To Sales (%)	2.4	3.1	5.5
PROFITABILITY			
Return On Sales (%)	6.0	1.7	(1.0)
Return On Assets (%)	10.4	5.2	(1.1)
Return On Nw (%)	26.8	12.0	(1.6)

INDUSTRY ASSETS $500,000 - $1,000,000 — 1995 (63 Establishments)

	$	%
Cash	86,562	11.5
Accounts Receivable	127,209	16.9
Notes Receivable	753	0.1
Inventory	63,981	8.5
Other Current	24,840	3.3
Total Current	**303,344**	**40.3**
Fixed Assets	347,754	46.2
Other Non-current	101,617	13.5
Total Assets	**752,715**	**100.0**
Accounts Payable	57,959	7.7
Bank Loans	—	—
Notes Payable	39,141	5.2
Other Current	96,348	12.8
Total Current	**193,448**	**25.7**
Other Long Term	136,994	18.2
Deferred Credits	3,011	0.4
Net Worth	419,262	55.7
Total Liab & Net Worth	**752,715**	**100.0**
Net Sales	1,069,766	100.0
Gross Profit	369,069	34.5
Net Profit After Tax	80,232	7.5
Working Capital	109,896	—

RATIOS	UQ	MED	LQ
SOLVENCY			
Quick Ratio (times)	3.1	1.3	0.8
Current Ratio (times)	5.2	1.8	1.2
Curr Liab To Nw (%)	8.1	26.7	67.0
Curr Liab To Inv (%)	61.7	150.8	403.8
Total Liab To Nw (%)	19.2	46.1	135.9
Fixed Assets To Nw (%)	47.7	88.3	135.8
EFFICIENCY			
Coll Period (days)	28.1	42.0	52.6
Sales To Inv (times)	30.0	12.9	9.0
Assets To Sales (%)	53.6	73.6	89.6
Sales To Nwc (times)	18.8	6.6	3.7
Acct Pay To Sales (%)	2.6	5.2	11.6
PROFITABILITY			
Return On Sales (%)	17.1	8.5	1.4
Return On Assets (%)	16.0	11.1	1.4
Return On Nw (%)	36.6	16.6	2.4

INDUSTRY ASSETS $1,000,000 - $5,000,000 — 1995 (122 Establishments)

	$	%
Cash	270,646	11.3
Accounts Receivable	385,611	16.1
Notes Receivable	16,766	0.7
Inventory	189,213	7.9
Other Current	141,311	5.9
Total Current	**1,003,546**	**41.9**
Fixed Assets	1,032,288	43.1
Other Non-current	359,265	15.0
Total Assets	**2,395,099**	**100.0**
Accounts Payable	138,916	5.8
Bank Loans	7,185	0.3
Notes Payable	79,038	3.3
Other Current	222,744	9.3
Total Current	**447,884**	**18.7**
Other Long Term	464,649	19.4
Deferred Credits	2,395	0.1
Net Worth	1,480,171	61.8
Total Liab & Net Worth	**2,395,099**	**100.0**
Net Sales	2,427,694	100.0
Gross Profit	949,228	39.1
Net Profit After Tax	220,920	9.1
Working Capital	555,662	—

RATIOS	UQ	MED	LQ
SOLVENCY			
Quick Ratio (times)	4.0	1.6	0.8
Current Ratio (times)	5.3	2.4	1.3
Curr Liab To Nw (%)	8.9	26.5	54.6
Curr Liab To Inv (%)	68.1	146.1	423.7
Total Liab To Nw (%)	12.4	47.0	126.9
Fixed Assets To Nw (%)	43.2	68.1	138.0
EFFICIENCY			
Coll Period (days)	32.4	45.8	63.1
Sales To Inv (times)	53.5	15.4	6.9
Assets To Sales (%)	65.9	86.1	127.1
Sales To Nwc (times)	6.8	4.0	2.0
Acct Pay To Sales (%)	2.0	3.9	7.2
PROFITABILITY			
Return On Sales (%)	14.3	7.6	3.5
Return On Assets (%)	13.0	8.2	3.6
Return On Nw (%)	22.7	12.7	6.3

SIC 14 NONMETALLIC MINERALS — INDUSTRY ASSETS $5,000,000-$25,000,000 — 1995 (63 Establishments) | SIC 14 NONMETALLIC MINERALS — INDUSTRY ASSETS OVER $50,000,000 — 1995 (19 Establishments) | SIC 1411 DIMENSION STONE (NO BREAKDOWN) — 1995 (15 Establishments) | SIC 1422 CRUSHED BRKN LMSTNE (NO BREAKDOWN) — 1995 (79 Establishments)

	SIC 14 $5M-$25M $	%	SIC 14 OVER $50M $	%	SIC 1411 $	%	SIC 1422 $	%
Cash	1,074,143	12.7	11,747,964	2.2	93,300	8.1	418,632	13.5
Accounts Receivable	1,099,517	13.0	63,545,806	11.9	158,956	13.8	440,339	14.2
Notes Receivable	59,205	0.7	—	—	—	—	18,606	0.6
Inventory	761,204	9.0	51,263,843	9.6	169,323	14.7	319,401	10.3
Other Current	473,638	5.6	10,145,969	1.9	115,186	10.0	198,463	6.4
Total Current	**3,467,707**	**41.0**	**136,703,582**	**25.6**	**536,764**	**46.6**	**1,395,441**	**45.0**
Fixed Assets	3,416,960	40.4	281,951,138	52.8	475,716	41.3	1,234,190	39.8
Other Non-current	1,573,155	18.6	115,343,647	21.6	139,374	12.1	471,349	15.2
Total Assets	**8,457,822**	**100.0**	**533,998,367**	**100.0**	**1,151,855**	**100.0**	**3,100,980**	**100.0**
Accounts Payable	490,554	5.8	18,155,944	3.4	63,352	5.5	170,554	5.5
Bank Loans	—	—	—	—	—	—	—	—
Notes Payable	262,192	3.1	3,737,989	0.7	21,885	1.9	124,039	4.0
Other Current	761,204	9.0	40,049,878	7.5	85,237	7.4	254,280	8.2
Total Current	**1,513,950**	**17.9**	**61,943,811**	**11.6**	**170,475**	**14.8**	**548,873**	**17.7**
Other Long Term	1,412,456	16.7	189,035,422	35.4	237,282	20.6	564,378	18.2
Deferred Credits	152,241	1.8	4,271,987	0.8	5,759	0.5	6,202	0.2
Net Worth	5,379,175	63.6	278,747,148	52.2	738,339	64.1	1,981,526	63.9
Total Liab & Net Worth	**8,457,822**	**100.0**	**533,998,367**	**100.0**	**1,151,855**	**100.0**	**3,100,980**	**100.0**
Net Sales	7,980,855	100.0	324,820,000	100.0	1,617,098	100.0	3,926,513	100.0
Gross Profit	2,266,563	28.4	75,683,060	23.3	567,601	35.1	1,700,180	43.3
Net Profit After Tax	654,430	8.2	22,087,760	6.8	85,706	5.3	455,476	11.6
Working Capital	1,953,757	—	74,759,771	—	366,289	—	846,568	—

RATIOS

	SIC 14 $5M-$25M UQ	MED	LQ	SIC 14 OVER $50M UQ	MED	LQ	SIC 1411 UQ	MED	LQ	SIC 1422 UQ	MED	LQ
SOLVENCY												
Quick Ratio (times)	3.7	1.4	0.7	1.7	1.1	0.9	4.2	3.0	1.3	5.0	1.6	0.9
Current Ratio (times)	6.7	2.5	1.3	3.0	2.1	1.7	8.5	5.6	2.0	9.3	2.7	1.6
Curr Liab To Nw (%)	11.1	24.9	46.3	18.0	24.2	32.3	4.1	18.8	58.3	4.7	24.9	44.1
Curr Liab To Inv (%)	109.7	179.8	370.0	82.7	139.3	184.2	38.4	70.9	242.7	66.4	146.2	289.1
Total Liab To Nw (%)	22.9	45.9	115.5	55.6	93.4	185.1	8.9	51.3	128.2	12.7	48.1	102.2
Fixed Assets To Nw (%)	38.5	61.8	106.7	82.5	100.1	203.4	39.9	48.1	178.1	37.0	62.3	101.2
EFFICIENCY												
Coll Period (days)	33.2	45.6	61.0	39.3	52.2	69.3	24.5	42.7	45.6	29.9	39.8	54.5
Sales To Inv (times)	31.5	10.7	4.7	9.2	7.4	5.9	13.9	8.5	5.9	29.0	12.8	6.3
Assets To Sales (%)	75.7	107.4	139.9	95.2	151.6	182.7	54.0	85.9	97.8	74.5	93.9	130.0
Sales To Nwc (times)	10.8	5.5	2.0	8.8	4.9	4.2	8.6	4.7	2.5	10.2	3.9	2.0
Acct Pay To Sales (%)	3.7	4.9	10.7	3.4	5.1	6.7	1.2	1.7	6.0	2.4	4.7	7.3
PROFITABILITY												
Return On Sales (%)	14.4	7.4	2.5	12.7	8.5	5.6	8.6	6.5	4.2	19.7	11.6	4.7
Return On Assets (%)	13.7	7.0	3.2	8.1	6.6	2.6	6.7	4.9	1.6	20.8	10.4	5.6
Return On Nw (%)	19.5	11.9	6.9	13.5	13.4	10.8	16.6	6.4	2.9	31.3	14.3	8.3

	SIC 1422 CRUSHED BRKN LMSTNE $500,000-$1,000,000 (11 Est) $	%	SIC 1422 CRUSHED BRKN LMSTNE $1,000,000-$5,000,000 (30 Est) $	%	SIC 1422 CRUSHED BRKN LMSTNE $5,000,000-$25,000,000 (23 Est) $	%	SIC 1429 CRUSHD BRKN STN,NEC (NO BREAKDOWN) (18 Est) $	%
Cash	99,548	11.0	317,363	13.6	1,908,085	15.6	112,610	7.3
Accounts Receivable	121,267	13.4	387,369	16.6	1,210,900	9.9	206,709	13.4
Notes Receivable	—	—	4,667	0.2	48,925	0.4	1,543	0.1
Inventory	123,982	13.7	224,021	9.6	1,149,744	9.4	114,153	7.4
Other Current	5,430	0.6	261,357	11.2	599,335	4.9	138,835	9.0
Total Current	**350,226**	**38.7**	**1,194,777**	**51.2**	**4,916,989**	**40.2**	**573,850**	**37.2**
Fixed Assets	355,656	39.3	875,081	37.5	5,222,772	42.7	887,000	57.5
Other Non-current	199,095	22.0	263,691	11.3	2,091,555	17.1	81,758	5.3
Total Assets	**904,978**	**100.0**	**2,333,548**	**100.0**	**12,231,317**	**100.0**	**1,542,608**	**100.0**
Accounts Payable	56,109	6.2	142,346	6.1	611,566	5.0	103,355	6.7
Bank Loans	—	—	—	—	—	—	1,543	0.1
Notes Payable	76,923	8.5	74,674	3.2	305,783	2.5	18,511	1.2
Other Current	63,348	7.0	158,681	6.8	1,161,975	9.5	123,409	8.0
Total Current	**196,380**	**21.7**	**375,701**	**16.1**	**2,079,324**	**17.0**	**246,817**	**16.0**
Other Long Term	262,444	29.0	350,032	15.0	1,406,601	11.5	411,876	26.7
Deferred Credits	—	—	—	—	73,388	0.6	—	—
Net Worth	446,154	49.3	1,607,815	68.9	8,672,004	70.9	883,914	57.3
Total Liab & Net Worth	**904,978**	**100.0**	**2,333,548**	**100.0**	**12,231,317**	**100.0**	**1,542,608**	**100.0**
Net Sales	816,005	100.0	2,472,771	100.0	8,460,869	100.0	2,243,043	100.0
Gross Profit	354,962	43.5	1,147,366	46.4	2,783,626	32.9	637,024	28.4
Net Profit After Tax	124,033	15.2	294,260	11.9	922,235	10.9	172,714	7.7
Working Capital	153,846	—	819,076	—	2,837,665	—	327,033	—

RATIOS	UQ	MED	LQ	UQ	MED	LQ	UQ	MED	LQ	UQ	MED	LQ
SOLVENCY												
Quick Ratio (times)	2.0	1.2	0.6	7.5	2.5	1.2	4.6	1.4	0.8	2.2	1.4	0.6
Current Ratio (times)	2.7	1.9	1.2	15.4	4.3	1.8	7.5	2.6	1.3	5.5	2.8	1.4
Curr Liab To Nw (%)	3.3	29.5	58.5	2.8	11.4	40.0	7.7	19.5	40.0	8.9	28.3	31.3
Curr Liab To Inv (%)	67.7	176.0	220.0	37.8	146.2	373.1	103.3	158.9	452.2	86.0	184.2	270.2
Total Liab To Nw (%)	34.0	49.7	112.7	6.9	46.1	64.9	11.2	26.8	117.7	8.9	91.3	142.2
Fixed Assets To Nw (%)	44.6	59.7	110.9	38.8	60.3	93.0	36.8	62.9	136.1	74.7	101.3	194.3
EFFICIENCY												
Coll Period (days)	28.8	51.5	121.6	30.2	44.9	64.5	28.5	35.4	40.4	33.7	41.1	44.1
Sales To Inv (times)	11.0	9.6	7.0	27.1	15.2	7.4	35.8	13.1	4.5	39.4	18.0	7.7
Assets To Sales (%)	93.5	119.1	129.5	60.3	83.8	127.9	80.9	100.0	136.4	67.4	86.1	98.7
Sales To Nwc (times)	25.4	13.6	3.8	4.8	2.6	1.7	13.3	5.5	2.0	7.7	5.8	3.9
Acct Pay To Sales (%)	11.0	13.4	25.8	1.5	3.6	7.3	3.3	4.1	6.0	2.7	5.0	7.2
PROFITABILITY												
Return On Sales (%)	36.8	27.5	16.2	18.4	12.5	4.7	18.7	9.8	3.1	12.9	3.0	(0.6)
Return On Assets (%)	27.5	18.8	10.0	20.4	10.4	5.6	15.3	8.9	6.1	11.6	6.0	0.4
Return On Nw (%)	75.5	51.0	26.5	30.9	12.8	8.1	20.1	18.0	8.4	27.8	18.0	0.2

SIC 1442 CNSTR SAND,GRAVEL

	NO BREAKDOWN 1995 (149 Establishments) $	%	$250,000 - $500,000 INDUSTRY ASSETS 1995 (25 Establishments) $	%	$500,000 - $1,000,000 INDUSTRY ASSETS 1995 (32 Establishments) $	%	$1,000,000 - $5,000,000 INDUSTRY ASSETS 1995 (59 Establishments) $	%
Cash	154,170	13.3	61,695	17.4	98,286	13.9	277,766	11.9
Accounts Receivable	201,696	17.4	53,185	15.0	118,792	16.8	394,474	16.9
Notes Receivable	8,114	0.7	—	—	707	0.1	30,344	1.3
Inventory	74,187	6.4	26,238	7.4	48,789	6.9	147,052	6.3
Other Current	31,298	2.7	2,837	0.8	26,870	3.8	56,020	2.4
Total Current	**469,465**	**40.5**	**143,955**	**40.6**	**293,444**	**41.5**	**905,656**	**38.8**
Fixed Assets	548,288	47.3	199,268	56.2	336,577	47.6	1,048,040	44.9
Other Non-current	141,419	12.2	11,346	3.2	77,073	10.9	380,469	16.3
Total Assets	**1,159,172**	**100.0**	**354,569**	**100.0**	**707,094**	**100.0**	**2,334,164**	**100.0**
Accounts Payable	85,779	7.4	31,911	9.0	62,224	8.8	114,374	4.9
Bank Loans	3,478	0.3	—	—	—	—	16,339	0.7
Notes Payable	75,346	6.5	35,811	10.1	42,426	6.0	109,706	4.7
Other Current	128,668	11.1	31,911	9.0	125,156	17.7	256,758	11.0
Total Current	**293,271**	**25.3**	**99,634**	**28.1**	**229,806**	**32.5**	**497,177**	**21.3**
Other Long Term	257,336	22.2	97,152	27.4	121,620	17.2	539,192	23.1
Deferred Credits	6,955	0.6	5,673	1.6	4,950	0.7	2,334	0.1
Net Worth	601,610	51.9	152,110	42.9	350,719	49.6	1,295,461	55.5
Total Liab & Net Worth	**1,159,172**	**100.0**	**354,569**	**100.0**	**707,094**	**100.0**	**2,334,164**	**100.0**
Net Sales	1,805,517	100.0	736,909	100.0	1,104,817	100.0	2,427,694	100.0
Gross Profit	686,096	38.0	397,194	53.9	355,751	32.2	854,548	35.2
Net Profit After Tax	120,970	6.7	32,424	4.4	69,603	6.3	177,222	7.3
Working Capital	176,194	—	44,321	—	63,638	—	408,479	—

RATIOS	UQ	MED	LQ	UQ	MED	LQ	UQ	MED	LQ	UQ	MED	LQ
SOLVENCY												
Quick Ratio (times)	3.1	1.3	0.6	3.1	1.3	0.4	2.6	1.0	0.8	3.1	1.2	0.6
Current Ratio (times)	4.0	1.9	1.0	3.2	1.8	1.0	3.5	1.4	1.0	3.9	1.9	1.1
Curr Lib To Nw (%)	15.4	35.2	72.9	19.7	44.8	102.4	18.8	31.9	169.5	15.6	39.0	61.3
Curr Lib To Inv (%)	103.5	182.0	449.8	100.8	111.9	181.3	97.5	296.7	494.0	107.3	210.4	521.8
Total Liab To Nw (%)	24.8	64.0	153.2	37.6	96.1	274.4	23.5	60.4	261.7	24.2	57.1	147.5
Fixed Assets To Nw (%)	49.8	80.0	148.3	68.4	88.6	239.7	50.4	96.8	156.8	49.7	73.0	146.3
EFFICIENCY												
Coll Period (days)	30.1	42.4	62.3	21.0	30.3	35.5	26.2	32.1	50.4	34.2	48.0	66.0
Sales To Inv (times)	67.5	21.0	8.1	21.5	10.8	9.9	49.0	28.4	10.5	82.1	30.3	8.9
Assets To Sales (%)	55.0	75.9	111.2	36.5	42.8	58.5	47.3	73.5	80.2	66.0	85.7	126.9
Sales To Nwc (times)	11.6	6.2	2.9	29.8	11.6	5.3	21.2	10.7	4.1	8.0	5.0	2.5
Acct Pay To Sales (%)	2.6	4.8	8.7	2.9	3.1	3.6	2.2	4.8	9.5	2.3	4.5	7.8
PROFITABILITY												
Return On Sales (%)	10.9	5.6	1.7	4.8	2.1	1.1	11.4	5.6	0.9	9.2	6.4	2.5
Return On Assets (%)	13.7	7.2	1.9	16.7	6.0	3.8	14.6	11.1	1.1	12.2	7.1	1.8
Return On Nw (%)	24.9	13.3	5.2	46.6	13.5	10.6	28.3	14.2	2.4	22.8	12.5	5.2

	SIC 1442 CNSTR SAND, GRAVEL INDUSTRY ASSETS $5,000,000-$25,000,000 1995 (20 Establishments) $	%	SIC 1446 INDUSTRIAL SAND (NO BREAKDOWN) 1995 (19 Establishments) $	%	SIC 1499 MISC NONMET MNRLS (NO BREAKDOWN) 1995 (19 Establishments) $	%	SIC 15 GEN'L BLDG CONTRS (NO BREAKDOWN) 1995 (2241 Establishments) $	%
Cash	1,022,513	13.6	262,704	3.6	175,819	8.1	124,524	20.4
Accounts Receivable	1,405,956	18.7	1,539,737	21.1	286,520	13.2	199,604	32.7
Notes Receivable	120,296	1.6	21,892	0.3	—	—	4,883	0.8
Inventory	466,146	6.2	802,707	11.0	251,791	11.6	31,131	5.1
Other Current	368,405	4.9	145,947	2.0	80,312	3.7	89,730	14.7
Total Current	**3,383,316**	**45.0**	**2,772,986**	**38.0**	**794,443**	**36.6**	**449,872**	**73.7**
Fixed Assets	3,105,132	41.3	3,167,042	43.4	703,277	32.4	111,095	18.2
Other Non-current	1,030,032	13.7	1,357,304	18.6	672,888	31.0	49,443	8.1
Total Assets	**7,518,479**	**100.0**	**7,297,332**	**100.0**	**2,170,608**	**100.0**	**610,410**	**100.0**
Accounts Payable	556,367	7.4	758,923	10.4	97,677	4.5	133,069	21.8
Bank Loans	—	—	—	—	—	—	1,831	0.3
Notes Payable	368,405	4.9	58,379	0.8	34,730	1.6	25,637	4.2
Other Current	353,369	4.7	707,841	9.7	112,872	5.2	106,211	17.4
Total Current	**1,278,141**	**17.0**	**1,525,142**	**20.9**	**245,279**	**11.3**	**266,749**	**43.7**
Other Long Term	1,586,399	21.1	1,481,358	20.3	286,520	13.2	57,989	9.5
Deferred Credits	67,666	0.9	14,595	0.2	13,024	0.6	1,221	0.2
Net Worth	4,586,272	61.0	4,276,237	58.6	1,625,785	74.9	284,451	46.6
Total Liab & Net Worth	**7,518,479**	**100.0**	**7,297,332**	**100.0**	**2,170,608**	**100.0**	**610,410**	**100.0**
Net Sales	7,365,302	100.0	9,745,184	100.0	4,196,091	100.0	2,146,399	100.0
Gross Profit	1,436,234	19.5	3,673,934	37.7	1,988,947	47.4	407,816	19.0
Net Profit After Tax	545,032	7.4	711,398	7.3	331,491	7.9	88,002	4.1
Working Capital	2,105,175	—	1,247,844	—	549,164	—	183,123	—

RATIOS	SIC 1442 UQ	MED	LQ	SIC 1446 UQ	MED	LQ	SIC 1499 UQ	MED	LQ	SIC 15 UQ	MED	LQ
SOLVENCY												
Quick Ratio (times)	4.2	1.8	1.0	1.8	1.3	0.9	3.9	2.0	1.3	2.0	1.2	0.8
Current Ratio (times)	5.5	2.5	1.5	2.9	1.9	1.5	9.2	2.4	2.1	2.8	1.7	1.2
Curr Liab To Nw (%)	14.6	25.3	46.6	19.5	33.3	72.8	5.0	17.4	24.6	35.8	89.1	199.2
Curr Liab To Inv (%)	136.6	179.8	229.8	85.2	127.8	168.0	30.5	78.2	287.5	81.1	152.5	401.7
Total Liab To Nw (%)	25.2	39.2	81.8	38.0	70.3	121.6	10.9	24.3	47.8	47.4	109.2	231.2
Fixed Assets To Nw (%)	36.4	51.7	76.3	60.1	68.1	98.6	31.2	63.9	84.0	11.6	26.9	61.7
EFFICIENCY												
Coll Period (days)	45.3	59.7	82.1	31.2	42.9	68.1	41.1	74.8	77.7	22.6	42.7	65.6
Sales To Inv (times)	89.0	16.3	9.9	22.0	11.6	9.3	11.0	5.7	2.5	188.1	52.9	13.8
Assets To Sales (%)	70.0	85.7	129.7	72.2	120.0	177.4	104.0	139.0	196.3	20.5	29.4	43.6
Sales To Nwc (times)	10.8	7.7	2.3	10.9	7.7	4.7	6.8	4.3	2.5	22.4	11.4	6.2
Acct Pay To Sales (%)	7.7	9.5	11.3	5.0	7.5	12.9	2.1	4.7	5.1	3.3	6.7	11.2
PROFITABILITY												
Return On Sales (%)	10.5	4.5	2.9	10.9	4.3	2.8	13.8	8.2	7.0	6.9	2.6	0.8
Return On Assets (%)	12.0	4.4	3.6	11.7	5.7	3.7	10.6	7.1	5.6	18.0	6.9	2.0
Return On Nw (%)	14.2	8.0	7.2	19.6	11.2	8.3	12.6	10.7	7.9	41.7	18.2	5.1

	SIC 15 GEN'L BLDG CONTRS NORTHEAST 1995 (2133 Establishments)		SIC 15 GEN'L BLDG CONTRS CENTRAL 1995 (1442 Establishments)		SIC 15 GEN'L BLDG CONTRS SOUTH 1995 (2013 Establishments)		SIC 15 GEN'L BLDG CONTRS WEST 1995 (2163 Establishments)	
	$	%	$	%	$	%	$	%
Cash	107,559	20.2	123,610	18.3	122,917	19.7	129,728	22.2
Accounts Receivable	181,040	34.0	231,685	34.3	190,927	30.6	194,592	33.3
Notes Receivable	3,727	0.7	4,728	0.7	6,239	1.0	5,259	0.9
Inventory	29,286	5.5	52,011	7.7	29,949	4.8	25,127	4.3
Other Current	80,403	15.1	89,162	13.2	112,310	18.0	79,473	13.6
Total Current	**402,016**	**75.5**	**501,196**	**74.2**	**462,344**	**74.1**	**434,179**	**74.3**
Fixed Assets	88,390	16.6	123,610	18.3	111,686	17.9	108,107	18.5
Other Non-current	42,065	7.9	50,660	7.5	49,916	8.0	42,074	7.2
Total Assets	**532,472**	**100.0**	**675,466**	**100.0**	**623,946**	**100.0**	**584,360**	**100.0**
Accounts Payable	119,806	22.5	162,112	24.0	124,165	19.9	130,897	22.4
Bank Loans	1,065	0.2	675	0.1	624	0.1	1,169	0.2
Notes Payable	19,701	3.7	31,747	4.7	34,317	5.5	15,193	2.6
Other Current	97,975	18.4	112,803	16.7	106,071	17.0	99,926	17.1
Total Current	**238,547**	**44.8**	**307,337**	**45.5**	**265,177**	**42.5**	**247,184**	**42.3**
Other Long Term	45,260	8.5	68,898	10.2	60,523	9.7	53,177	9.1
Deferred Credits	1,065	0.2	1,351	0.2	1,248	0.2	1,169	0.2
Net Worth	247,599	46.5	297,881	44.1	296,998	47.6	282,830	48.4
Total Liab & Net Worth	**532,472**	**100.0**	**675,466**	**100.0**	**623,946**	**100.0**	**584,360**	**100.0**
Net Sales	1,626,271	100.0	2,400,000	100.0	2,253,788	100.0	2,263,712	100.0
Gross Profit	346,396	21.3	463,200	19.3	396,667	17.6	411,996	18.2
Net Profit After Tax	65,051	4.0	84,000	3.5	83,390	3.7	115,449	5.1
Working Capital	163,469	—	193,859	—	197,167	—	186,995	—

RATIOS	UQ	MED	LQ	UQ	MED	LQ	UQ	MED	LQ	UQ	MED	LQ
SOLVENCY												
Quick Ratio (times)	2.1	1.2	0.8	1.8	1.2	0.8	2.1	1.3	0.7	2.3	1.3	0.9
Current Ratio (times)	2.9	1.7	1.2	2.6	1.6	1.2	3.0	1.7	1.3	3.1	1.7	1.3
Curr Liab To Nw (%)	34.9	91.2	205.5	41.7	92.9	209.9	31.4	85.4	183.0	28.0	84.0	196.5
Curr Liab To Inv (%)	79.1	183.0	446.2	74.4	130.1	318.3	79.8	138.1	424.1	78.8	166.2	379.0
Total Liab To Nw (%)	45.5	110.1	234.0	54.8	116.9	243.2	43.6	110.2	220.7	40.3	106.7	232.6
Fixed Assets To Nw (%)	9.6	23.8	57.4	13.2	32.2	65.2	11.7	26.1	59.7	10.9	24.6	58.7
EFFICIENCY												
Coll Period (days)	23.0	44.5	73.4	24.5	44.2	68.0	22.3	42.3	63.9	24.5	43.8	64.2
Sales To Inv (times)	150.2	46.9	12.2	216.3	40.5	10.4	127.2	37.6	7.6	226.8	68.6	13.6
Assets To Sales (%)	20.1	30.7	45.5	20.8	28.8	40.7	21.3	30.4	45.6	19.9	27.8	41.5
Sales To Nwc (times)	20.7	10.0	5.2	20.3	11.3	6.5	20.5	11.4	5.9	21.0	11.7	6.5
Acct Pay To Sales (%)	3.2	7.1	13.0	3.5	7.1	11.7	2.9	6.6	10.9	3.3	6.7	11.2
PROFITABILITY												
Return On Sales (%)	6.2	2.5	0.6	5.3	2.3	0.9	6.8	2.6	0.8	8.1	3.1	0.9
Return On Assets (%)	17.4	6.3	1.6	17.3	7.6	2.5	16.6	6.8	2.0	19.4	7.5	2.3
Return On Nw (%)	42.3	16.0	4.3	38.2	18.8	7.2	42.5	17.5	4.9	45.0	19.3	6.2

SIC 15 GEN'L BLDG CONTRS — INDUSTRY ASSETS

	UNDER $100,000 (1547 Est.) $	%	$100,000–$250,000 (1767 Est.) $	%	$250,000–$500,000 (1810 Est.) $	%	$500,000–$1,000,000 (1970 Est.) $	%
Cash	16,722	32.7	37,565	22.3	69,841	19.7	126,708	18.3
Accounts Receivable	9,716	19.0	48,515	28.8	115,929	32.7	232,643	33.6
Notes Receivable	409	0.8	1,853	1.1	3,191	0.9	6,232	0.9
Inventory	1,585	3.1	10,444	6.2	21,271	6.0	43,621	6.3
Other Current	4,142	8.1	19,372	11.5	48,924	13.8	123,938	17.9
Total Current	**32,575**	**63.7**	**117,750**	**69.9**	**259,156**	**73.1**	**533,141**	**77.0**
Fixed Assets	15,393	30.1	39,082	23.2	67,359	19.0	105,243	15.2
Other Non-current	3,171	6.2	11,623	6.9	28,007	7.9	54,006	7.8
Total Assets	**51,138**	**100.0**	**168,455**	**100.0**	**354,523**	**100.0**	**692,391**	**100.0**
Accounts Payable	6,188	12.1	27,121	16.1	68,777	19.4	148,172	21.4
Bank Loans	102	0.2	337	0.2	709	0.2	692	0.1
Notes Payable	2,710	5.3	7,917	4.7	15,954	4.5	29,773	4.3
Other Current	9,000	17.6	25,605	15.2	54,242	15.3	119,091	17.2
Total Current	**18,001**	**35.2**	**60,981**	**36.2**	**139,682**	**39.4**	**297,728**	**43.0**
Other Long Term	4,807	9.4	18,699	11.1	35,452	10.0	63,700	9.2
Deferred Credits	—	—	337	0.2	709	0.2	1,385	0.2
Net Worth	28,330	55.4	88,439	52.5	178,680	50.4	329,578	47.6
Total Liab & Net Worth	**51,138**	**100.0**	**168,455**	**100.0**	**354,523**	**100.0**	**692,391**	**100.0**
Net Sales	375,311	100.0	738,769	100.0	1,249,078	100.0	2,162,124	100.0
Gross Profit	112,218	29.9	187,647	25.4	271,050	21.7	397,831	18.4
Net Profit After Tax	24,395	6.5	45,065	6.1	57,458	4.6	73,512	3.4
Working Capital	14,574	—	56,769	—	119,474	—	235,413	—

RATIOS

	UQ	MED	LQ	UQ	MED	LQ	UQ	MED	LQ	UQ	MED	LQ
SOLVENCY												
Quick Ratio (times)	4.1	1.5	0.7	3.2	1.5	0.8	2.6	1.4	0.9	2.0	1.3	0.8
Current Ratio (times)	5.3	2.0	1.0	4.5	2.1	1.2	3.6	1.9	1.3	2.9	1.8	1.3
Curr Liab To Nw (%)	12.9	42.5	119.7	17.6	52.8	140.1	25.6	68.2	152.7	37.7	81.9	167.0
Curr Liab To Inv (%)	83.2	224.9	416.3	73.5	167.7	400.7	79.9	148.6	366.9	86.3	176.0	466.6
Total Liab To Nw (%)	17.9	55.2	153.2	27.0	73.6	178.7	36.8	87.3	189.3	48.5	103.0	198.0
Fixed Assets To Nw (%)	21.2	54.9	106.9	15.7	36.9	82.0	13.2	29.7	67.3	11.1	24.5	50.2
EFFICIENCY												
Coll Period (days)	8.7	19.2	35.2	13.9	29.2	50.7	21.2	37.6	60.6	25.9	44.2	66.1
Sales To Inv (times)	187.8	77.0	33.2	128.8	42.4	13.3	139.8	44.0	14.8	188.5	45.7	10.9
Assets To Sales (%)	7.1	13.1	22.5	15.1	23.3	37.1	19.5	27.9	41.8	23.2	31.6	45.2
Sales To Nwc (times)	45.8	20.4	8.6	24.5	11.4	5.8	19.3	10.1	5.8	16.7	9.3	5.2
Acct Pay To Sales (%)	1.0	2.3	4.9	1.7	3.7	7.4	2.6	5.3	9.0	3.2	6.3	10.4
PROFITABILITY												
Return On Sales (%)	13.8	5.3	1.3	11.0	4.9	1.3	8.0	3.6	1.0	5.6	2.6	0.8
Return On Assets (%)	75.4	31.5	4.4	33.8	15.3	3.0	21.0	10.4	2.7	14.5	7.2	2.2
Return On Nw (%)	122.9	55.4	10.7	73.5	31.3	7.8	51.4	22.2	6.2	35.3	15.9	5.1

SIC 15 GEN'L BLDG CONTRS — INDUSTRY ASSETS $1,000,000–$5,000,000 — 1995 (1542 Establishments)

	$	%
Cash	298,398	16.2
Accounts Receivable	676,000	36.7
Notes Receivable	12,894	0.7
Inventory	97,624	5.3
Other Current	368,393	20.0
Total Current	**1,453,309**	**78.9**
Fixed Assets	239,455	13.0
Other Non-current	149,199	8.1
Total Assets	**1,841,963**	**100.0**
Accounts Payable	504,698	27.4
Bank Loans	5,526	0.3
Notes Payable	69,995	3.8
Other Current	331,553	18.0
Total Current	**911,772**	**49.5**
Other Long Term	158,409	8.6
Deferred Credits	5,526	0.3
Net Worth	766,257	41.6
Total Liab & Net Worth	**1,841,963**	**100.0**
Net Sales	5,418,648	100.0
Gross Profit	774,867	14.3
Net Profit After Tax	162,559	3.0
Working Capital	541,537	—

RATIOS	UQ	MED	LQ
SOLVENCY			
Quick Ratio (times)	1.5	1.2	0.7
Current Ratio (times)	2.2	1.5	1.3
Curr Liab To Nw (%)	60.2	124.3	225.7
Curr Liab To Inv (%)	82.7	146.6	373.1
Total Liab To Nw (%)	75.5	147.4	251.2
Fixed Assets To Nw (%)	10.1	21.2	43.2
EFFICIENCY			
Coll Period (days)	32.6	51.1	71.8
Sales To Inv (times)	187.9	51.5	11.8
Assets To Sales (%)	24.9	33.7	48.7
Sales To Nwc (times)	18.2	10.7	5.8
Acct Pay To Sales (%)	4.9	8.8	13.3
PROFITABILITY			
Return On Sales (%)	4.8	2.0	0.6
Return On Assets (%)	11.2	4.9	1.6
Return On Nw (%)	29.9	13.4	4.6

SIC 15 GEN'L BLDG CONTRS — INDUSTRY ASSETS $5,000,000–$25,000,000 — 1995 (788 Establishments)

	$	%
Cash	1,153,469	14.4
Accounts Receivable	3,196,070	39.9
Notes Receivable	56,071	0.7
Inventory	536,683	6.7
Other Current	1,561,989	19.5
Total Current	**6,504,282**	**81.2**
Fixed Assets	833,061	10.4
Other Non-current	672,857	8.4
Total Assets	**8,010,200**	**100.0**
Accounts Payable	2,595,305	32.4
Bank Loans	8,010	0.1
Notes Payable	368,469	4.6
Other Current	1,626,071	20.3
Total Current	**4,597,855**	**57.4**
Other Long Term	632,806	7.9
Deferred Credits	16,020	0.2
Net Worth	2,763,519	34.5
Total Liab & Net Worth	**8,010,200**	**100.0**
Net Sales	21,608,542	100.0
Gross Profit	2,247,288	10.4
Net Profit After Tax	518,605	2.4
Working Capital	1,906,427	—

RATIOS	UQ	MED	LQ
SOLVENCY			
Quick Ratio (times)	1.3	1.1	0.7
Current Ratio (times)	1.7	1.3	1.2
Curr Liab To Nw (%)	99.9	192.3	337.0
Curr Liab To Inv (%)	72.6	102.2	218.6
Total Liab To Nw (%)	115.3	221.1	371.7
Fixed Assets To Nw (%)	7.9	16.8	38.4
EFFICIENCY			
Coll Period (days)	40.0	58.4	74.5
Sales To Inv (times)	218.6	15.8	2.7
Assets To Sales (%)	26.8	34.3	52.8
Sales To Nwc (times)	22.8	14.0	7.0
Acct Pay To Sales (%)	7.2	11.8	16.4
PROFITABILITY			
Return On Sales (%)	3.4	1.4	0.6
Return On Assets (%)	8.0	3.7	1.5
Return On Nw (%)	27.1	13.3	5.1

SIC 15 GEN'L BLDG CONTRS — INDUSTRY ASSETS $25,000,000–$50,000,000 — 1995 (114 Establishments)

	$	%
Cash	5,460,500	16.3
Accounts Receivable	12,428,500	37.1
Notes Receivable	134,000	0.4
Inventory	2,445,500	7.3
Other Current	6,130,500	18.3
Total Current	**26,599,000**	**79.4**
Fixed Assets	3,350,000	10.0
Other Non-current	3,551,000	10.6
Total Assets	**33,500,000**	**100.0**
Accounts Payable	10,720,000	32.0
Bank Loans	33,500	0.1
Notes Payable	1,139,000	3.4
Other Current	7,504,000	22.4
Total Current	**19,396,500**	**57.9**
Other Long Term	3,249,500	9.7
Deferred Credits	67,000	0.2
Net Worth	10,787,000	32.2
Total Liab & Net Worth	**33,500,000**	**100.0**
Net Sales	78,329,214	100.0
Gross Profit	8,851,201	11.3
Net Profit After Tax	1,566,584	2.0
Working Capital	7,202,500	—

RATIOS	UQ	MED	LQ
SOLVENCY			
Quick Ratio (times)	1.2	1.0	0.5
Current Ratio (times)	1.6	1.3	1.1
Curr Liab To Nw (%)	96.2	220.7	377.4
Curr Liab To Inv (%)	63.5	105.1	193.3
Total Liab To Nw (%)	132.8	254.5	401.9
Fixed Assets To Nw (%)	6.0	14.4	34.8
EFFICIENCY			
Coll Period (days)	36.5	55.9	73.4
Sales To Inv (times)	173.2	9.0	3.0
Assets To Sales (%)	29.8	39.3	78.9
Sales To Nwc (times)	26.7	10.9	6.4
Acct Pay To Sales (%)	8.8	12.5	17.8
PROFITABILITY			
Return On Sales (%)	2.9	1.4	0.5
Return On Assets (%)	6.6	3.1	1.4
Return On Nw (%)	20.7	12.1	4.2

SIC 15 GEN'L BLDG CONTRS — INDUSTRY ASSETS OVER $50,000,000 — 1995 (127 Establishments)

	$	%
Cash	9,939,480	9.7
Accounts Receivable	27,564,124	26.9
Notes Receivable	307,407	0.3
Inventory	13,935,765	13.6
Other Current	21,108,586	20.6
Total Current	**72,855,361**	**71.1**
Fixed Assets	12,193,795	11.9
Other Non-current	17,419,707	17.0
Total Assets	**102,468,862**	**100.0**
Accounts Payable	23,670,307	23.1
Bank Loans	—	—
Notes Payable	5,943,194	5.8
Other Current	26,027,091	25.4
Total Current	**55,640,592**	**54.3**
Other Long Term	15,165,392	14.8
Deferred Credits	307,407	0.3
Net Worth	31,355,472	30.6
Total Liab & Net Worth	**102,468,862**	**100.0**
Net Sales	201,081,170	100.0
Gross Profit	24,732,984	12.3
Net Profit After Tax	7,238,922	3.6
Working Capital	17,214,769	—

RATIOS	UQ	MED	LQ
SOLVENCY			
Quick Ratio (times)	1.1	0.8	0.2
Current Ratio (times)	1.6	1.3	1.1
Curr Liab To Nw (%)	75.9	203.2	327.2
Curr Liab To Inv (%)	64.7	87.0	291.9
Total Liab To Nw (%)	119.4	260.2	349.6
Fixed Assets To Nw (%)	6.7	16.9	48.2
EFFICIENCY			
Coll Period (days)	8.1	43.7	66.5
Sales To Inv (times)	60.0	2.4	1.5
Assets To Sales (%)	33.7	58.7	99.6
Sales To Nwc (times)	24.0	11.7	4.2
Acct Pay To Sales (%)	6.5	9.6	14.8
PROFITABILITY			
Return On Sales (%)	3.2	2.2	0.6
Return On Assets (%)	4.7	3.4	1.0
Return On Nw (%)	17.0	11.5	3.0

SIC 1521 — SNGL-FAM HSNG CNSTR

	NO BREAKDOWN 1995 (2076 Establishments)		UNDER $100,000 1995 (1022 Establishments)		$100,000 - $250,000 1995 (871 Establishments)		$250,000 - $500,000 1995 (677 Establishments)	
	$	%	$	%	$	%	$	%
Cash	59,585	20.4	15,389	32.5	34,760	21.0	58,611	16.9
Accounts Receivable	59,585	20.4	7,765	16.4	40,719	24.6	87,397	25.2
Notes Receivable	2,629	0.9	331	0.7	1,986	1.2	2,428	0.7
Inventory	32,713	11.2	1,752	3.7	13,904	8.4	35,722	10.3
Other Current	45,273	15.5	3,646	7.7	19,863	12.0	53,756	15.5
Total Current	**199,785**	**68.4**	**28,884**	**61.0**	**111,231**	**67.2**	**237,914**	**68.6**
Fixed Assets	65,719	22.5	15,389	32.5	40,553	24.5	74,218	21.4
Other Non-current	26,580	9.1	3,078	6.5	13,738	8.3	34,681	10.0
Total Assets	**292,083**	**100.0**	**47,350**	**100.0**	**165,523**	**100.0**	**346,813**	**100.0**
Accounts Payable	40,015	13.7	5,682	12.0	24,166	14.6	51,328	14.8
Bank Loans	876	0.3	47	0.1	331	0.2	1,040	0.3
Notes Payable	19,570	6.7	2,604	5.5	9,269	5.6	23,236	6.7
Other Current	56,080	19.2	8,381	17.7	26,815	16.2	61,386	17.7
Total Current	**116,541**	**39.9**	**16,715**	**35.3**	**60,581**	**36.6**	**136,991**	**39.5**
Other Long Term	38,847	13.3	4,830	10.2	22,346	13.5	46,126	13.3
Deferred Credits	292	0.1	—	—	331	0.2	347	0.1
Net Worth	136,403	46.7	25,806	54.5	82,265	49.7	163,349	47.1
Total Liab & Net Worth	**292,083**	**100.0**	**47,350**	**100.0**	**165,523**	**100.0**	**346,813**	**100.0**
Net Sales	1,133,497	100.0	389,599	100.0	752,762	100.0	1,182,261	100.0
Gross Profit	259,571	22.9	120,386	30.9	200,987	26.7	279,014	23.6
Net Profit After Tax	54,408	4.8	25,714	6.6	47,424	6.3	56,749	4.8
Working Capital	83,244	—	12,169	—	50,650	—	100,923	—

RATIOS

	UQ	MED	LQ	UQ	MED	LQ	UQ	MED	LQ	UQ	MED	LQ
SOLVENCY												
Quick Ratio (times)	2.4	1.1	0.4	4.1	1.5	0.6	2.9	1.4	0.6	2.3	1.2	0.6
Current Ratio (times)	3.8	1.8	1.1	5.3	2.0	0.9	4.8	2.0	1.1	3.7	1.8	1.2
Curr Liab To Nw (%)	20.0	62.9	177.0	12.3	42.3	120.7	15.3	53.8	150.9	20.9	64.7	158.5
Curr Liab To Inv (%)	69.1	118.3	260.3	68.7	218.4	450.5	67.9	139.9	370.9	70.0	123.1	320.0
Total Liab To Nw (%)	34.0	89.0	230.8	16.7	55.0	165.7	25.6	78.0	212.6	35.9	91.2	206.3
Fixed Assets To Nw (%)	13.7	36.7	90.4	23.0	62.9	121.9	18.3	42.9	91.5	15.0	35.5	88.6
EFFICIENCY												
Coll Period (days)	9.5	25.4	45.3	7.0	15.7	27.5	11.7	23.9	44.2	12.8	30.7	50.9
Sales To Inv (times)	83.7	17.2	4.8	187.2	81.3	31.6	104.6	37.7	11.1	119.9	29.1	9.9
Assets To Sales (%)	17.2	28.6	50.0	6.3	11.5	19.8	14.6	22.8	35.3	19.3	29.5	46.5
Sales To Nwc (times)	23.7	11.1	5.7	55.5	22.3	10.9	30.2	11.7	5.7	25.9	10.5	6.0
Acct Pay To Sales (%)	1.9	4.1	7.1	1.0	2.3	4.6	1.7	3.4	5.9	2.2	4.6	8.1
PROFITABILITY												
Return On Sales (%)	8.9	3.5	1.0	12.6	5.3	1.5	13.0	5.0	1.2	8.6	3.8	0.9
Return On Assets (%)	25.8	8.5	2.0	78.0	32.0	6.4	33.8	15.9	4.1	22.2	10.7	2.3
Return On Nw (%)	59.4	24.0	6.3	128.9	58.8	12.8	81.0	34.2	9.3	59.2	24.7	5.4

SIC 1521 SNGL-FAM HSNG CNSTR

	$500,000 - $1,000,000 (608 Est.) $	%	$1,000,000 - $5,000,000 (775 Est.) $	%	$5,000,000-$25,000,000 (156 Est.) $	%	OVER $50,000,000 (26 Est.) $	%
Cash	99,481	14.5	181,532	10.8	566,149	6.7	5,759,093	6.8
Accounts Receivable	137,901	20.1	275,660	16.4	659,099	7.8	2,032,621	2.4
Notes Receivable	7,547	1.1	15,128	0.9	92,950	1.1	169,385	0.2
Inventory	97,423	14.2	304,235	18.1	2,425,146	28.7	19,902,749	23.5
Other Current	155,053	22.6	410,129	24.4	2,442,046	28.9	23,713,914	28.0
Total Current	**497,404**	**72.5**	**1,186,684**	**70.6**	**6,185,389**	**73.2**	**51,577,763**	**60.9**
Fixed Assets	116,633	17.0	285,745	17.0	1,267,498	15.0	15,752,814	18.6
Other Non-current	72,038	10.5	208,426	12.4	997,098	11.8	17,361,973	20.5
Total Assets	**686,074**	**100.0**	**1,680,855**	**100.0**	**8,449,985**	**100.0**	**84,692,550**	**100.0**
Accounts Payable	87,817	12.8	230,277	13.7	777,399	9.2	6,436,634	7.6
Bank Loans	2,058	0.3	13,447	0.8	25,350	0.3	—	—
Notes Payable	50,083	7.3	137,830	8.2	1,419,597	16.8	7,198,867	8.5
Other Current	152,308	22.2	398,363	23.7	2,095,596	24.8	22,358,833	26.4
Total Current	**292,268**	**42.6**	**779,917**	**46.4**	**4,317,942**	**51.1**	**35,994,334**	**42.5**
Other Long Term	98,795	14.4	267,256	15.9	1,385,798	16.4	13,550,808	16.0
Deferred Credits	2,744	0.4	3,362	0.2	16,900	0.2	—	—
Net Worth	292,268	42.6	630,321	37.5	2,729,345	32.3	35,147,408	41.5
Total Liab & Net Worth	**686,074**	**100.0**	**1,680,855**	**100.0**	**8,449,985**	**100.0**	**84,692,550**	**100.0**
Net Sales	1,824,362	100.0	4,170,540	100.0	13,542,612	100.0	114,791,057	100.0
Gross Profit	368,521	20.2	708,992	17.0	2,004,307	14.8	19,629,271	17.1
Net Profit After Tax	80,272	4.4	145,969	3.5	338,565	2.5	6,543,090	5.7
Working Capital	205,136	—	406,767	—	1,867,447	—	15,583,429	—

RATIOS

	UQ	MED	LQ	UQ	MED	LQ	UQ	MED	LQ	UQ	MED	LQ
SOLVENCY												
Quick Ratio (times)	2.0	0.9	0.3	1.2	0.5	0.2	0.4	0.2	0.1	0.5	0.2	0.1
Current Ratio (times)	3.4	1.7	1.2	2.6	1.5	1.1	2.1	1.4	1.1	2.2	1.3	1.1
Curr Liab To Nw (%)	27.9	75.3	194.1	37.6	106.1	252.6	51.0	157.0	293.7	33.9	72.2	164.7
Curr Liab To Inv (%)	70.5	120.8	269.7	61.1	99.1	141.9	66.6	89.3	112.3	36.4	68.7	116.0
Total Liab To Nw (%)	46.2	106.7	252.5	65.1	153.9	315.2	108.1	188.9	378.0	92.3	118.8	236.4
Fixed Assets To Nw (%)	11.4	25.5	70.8	9.1	27.3	74.4	5.1	23.0	80.5	4.4	14.3	60.8
EFFICIENCY												
Coll Period (days)	11.6	29.2	56.9	9.4	26.9	52.6	2.6	7.7	24.0	2.6	5.7	10.5
Sales To Inv (times)	35.8	10.8	4.8	32.8	6.7	2.9	5.6	3.2	2.1	2.7	2.1	1.8
Assets To Sales (%)	23.9	34.5	55.9	27.8	43.9	71.9	43.0	61.8	104.2	58.5	79.8	107.1
Sales To Nwc (times)	18.3	8.7	4.7	17.5	9.3	4.4	11.6	6.5	3.8	11.9	5.7	2.1
Acct Pay To Sales (%)	2.1	4.1	7.4	2.6	4.7	7.6	3.4	4.8	8.3	5.2	6.7	8.6
PROFITABILITY												
Return On Sales (%)	7.3	3.5	1.0	6.4	2.9	1.0	5.1	2.5	0.9	5.7	3.2	2.5
Return On Assets (%)	16.6	7.5	2.2	13.2	5.8	1.4	8.3	3.7	1.5	6.8	4.4	3.5
Return On Nw (%)	52.9	18.3	7.1	42.4	20.2	5.9	44.0	17.1	5.3	16.6	10.9	9.1

INDUSTRY ASSETS — 1995

SIC 1522 RSDNTL CNSTR, NEC

	No Breakdown (445 Est.) $	%	Under $100,000 (62 Est.) $	%	$100,000-$250,000 (64 Est.) $	%	$250,000-$500,000 (58 Est.) $	%
Cash	152,214	18.9	14,090	31.5	40,443	23.3	74,139	21.2
Accounts Receivable	243,221	30.2	10,959	24.5	42,873	24.7	105,963	30.3
Notes Receivable	10,470	1.3	581	1.3	1,909	1.1	2,448	0.7
Inventory	32,215	4.0	537	1.2	4,687	2.7	10,142	2.9
Other Current	141,745	17.6	3,713	8.3	18,573	10.7	58,052	16.6
Total Current	**579,864**	**72.0**	**29,879**	**66.8**	**108,485**	**62.5**	**250,744**	**71.7**
Fixed Assets	133,691	16.6	9,796	21.9	50,163	28.9	67,494	19.3
Other Non-current	91,812	11.4	5,054	11.3	14,928	8.6	31,474	9.0
Total Assets	**805,367**	**100.0**	**44,729**	**100.0**	**173,576**	**100.0**	**349,712**	**100.0**
Accounts Payable	143,355	17.8	4,473	10.0	22,044	12.7	45,812	13.1
Bank Loans	—	—	—	—	—	—	—	—
Notes Payable	36,242	4.5	2,639	5.9	2,951	1.7	12,939	3.7
Other Current	134,496	16.7	7,514	16.8	19,961	11.5	44,763	12.8
Total Current	**314,093**	**39.0**	**14,626**	**32.7**	**44,956**	**25.9**	**103,515**	**29.6**
Other Long Term	78,121	9.7	3,891	8.7	15,622	9.0	29,026	8.3
Deferred Credits	1,611	0.2	—	—	521	0.3	350	0.1
Net Worth	411,543	51.1	26,211	58.6	112,477	64.8	216,821	62.0
Total Liab & Net Worth	**805,367**	**100.0**	**44,729**	**100.0**	**173,576**	**100.0**	**349,712**	**100.0**
Net Sales	2,123,042	100.0	337,441	100.0	740,611	100.0	1,135,626	100.0
Gross Profit	401,255	18.9	108,656	32.2	182,190	24.6	266,872	23.5
Net Profit After Tax	114,644	5.4	17,884	5.3	31,846	4.3	112,427	9.9
Working Capital	265,771	—	15,253	—	63,529	—	147,229	—

RATIOS

	UQ	MED	LQ	UQ	MED	LQ	UQ	MED	LQ	UQ	MED	LQ
SOLVENCY												
Quick Ratio (times)	2.6	1.3	0.7	4.5	1.5	0.9	5.6	2.4	0.9	9.1	1.7	0.9
Current Ratio (times)	3.9	1.8	1.2	5.1	1.8	1.3	8.4	3.4	1.5	8.8	2.7	1.4
Curr Liab To Nw (%)	21.3	62.8	159.1	18.4	31.1	155.2	8.1	21.6	59.5	7.6	34.1	90.9
Curr Liab To Inv (%)	82.6	144.8	376.7	88.2	180.3	373.1	79.7	188.8	416.1	88.4	154.3	440.3
Total Liab To Nw (%)	32.0	84.5	190.2	21.3	54.2	158.9	13.1	28.4	91.7	16.9	51.2	135.5
Fixed Assets To Nw (%)	7.8	20.5	60.7	17.6	36.9	77.1	16.6	38.7	82.9	11.0	24.6	61.3
EFFICIENCY												
Coll Period (days)	21.5	40.5	75.8	24.5	35.0	78.8	9.5	29.6	40.9	17.2	34.0	74.1
Sales To Inv (times)	110.1	54.6	14.0	559.7	384.6	209.5	69.8	29.8	22.9	115.6	68.7	25.3
Assets To Sales (%)	22.3	33.9	60.5	12.0	22.4	36.8	13.3	22.6	38.4	19.1	30.3	49.7
Sales To Nwc (times)	16.2	9.1	4.8	34.6	10.9	6.5	17.3	12.4	8.7	14.2	8.5	4.5
Acct Pay To Sales (%)	2.6	6.2	11.0	0.5	1.6	2.9	1.2	2.8	5.3	1.8	4.0	7.3
PROFITABILITY												
Return On Sales (%)	9.7	4.3	1.2	7.4	4.5	(1.5)	6.9	5.2	2.3	18.3	8.9	4.3
Return On Assets (%)	21.8	7.1	1.4	31.4	9.0	(4.7)	34.4	15.4	(0.9)	43.5	30.1	20.8
Return On Nw (%)	45.2	19.0	4.5	83.0	21.3	(16.4)	80.7	29.3	(1.2)	102.8	49.0	26.4

	SIC 1522 RSDNTL CNSTR, NEC $500,000 - $1,000,000 1995 (64 Establishments)		SIC 1522 RSDNTL CNSTR, NEC $1,000,000 - $5,000,000 1995 (145 Establishments)		SIC 1522 RSDNTL CNSTR, NEC $5,000,000-$25,000,000 1995 (39 Establishments)		SIC 1531 OPERATIVE BUILDERS (NO BREAKDOWN) 1995 (322 Establishments)	
	$	%	$	%	$	%	$	%
Cash	101,157	15.8	317,351	15.1	1,346,826	14.7	194,923	12.4
Accounts Receivable	199,113	31.1	735,582	35.0	2,895,218	31.6	155,624	9.9
Notes Receivable	5,762	0.9	42,033	2.0	45,810	0.5	11,004	0.7
Inventory	51,219	8.0	67,253	3.2	531,401	5.8	353,691	22.5
Other Current	124,206	19.4	453,959	21.6	1,951,523	21.3	374,127	23.8
Total Current	**481,457**	**75.2**	**1,616,178**	**76.9**	**6,770,778**	**73.9**	**1,089,369**	**69.3**
Fixed Assets	101,797	15.9	205,963	9.8	1,181,908	12.9	275,093	17.5
Other Non-current	56,981	8.9	279,521	13.3	1,209,395	13.2	207,499	13.2
Total Assets	**640,235**	**100.0**	**2,101,662**	**100.0**	**9,162,081**	**100.0**	**1,571,961**	**100.0**
Accounts Payable	106,919	16.7	510,704	24.3	2,088,954	22.8	105,321	6.7
Bank Loans	—	—	—	—	—	—	1,572	0.1
Notes Payable	26,890	4.2	107,185	5.1	513,077	5.6	149,336	9.5
Other Current	116,523	18.2	371,994	17.7	1,924,037	21.0	369,411	23.5
Total Current	**250,332**	**39.1**	**989,883**	**47.1**	**4,526,068**	**49.4**	**625,640**	**39.8**
Other Long Term	70,426	11.0	187,048	8.9	1,062,801	11.6	304,960	19.4
Deferred Credits	—	—	2,102	0.1	82,459	0.9	1,572	0.1
Net Worth	319,477	49.9	922,630	43.9	3,490,753	38.1	639,788	40.7
Total Liab & Net Worth	**640,235**	**100.0**	**2,101,662**	**100.0**	**9,162,081**	**100.0**	**1,571,961**	**100.0**
Net Sales	1,606,074	100.0	5,050,587	100.0	19,266,280	100.0	2,733,049	100.0
Gross Profit	324,427	20.2	651,526	12.9	2,273,421	11.8	497,415	18.2
Net Profit After Tax	65,849	4.1	207,074	4.1	1,078,912	5.6	125,720	4.6
Working Capital	231,125	—	626,295	—	2,244,710	—	463,729	—

RATIOS	UQ	MED	LQ	UQ	MED	LQ	UQ	MED	LQ	UQ	MED	LQ
SOLVENCY												
Quick Ratio (times)	2.4	1.4	0.7	1.6	1.2	0.7	1.5	1.0	0.4	1.4	0.4	0.2
Current Ratio (times)	4.0	1.9	1.4	2.7	1.6	1.2	2.4	1.3	1.1	3.8	1.6	1.1
Curr Liab To Nw (%)	21.2	62.5	100.5	43.0	112.5	209.4	53.1	207.9	392.7	17.7	80.8	197.2
Curr Liab To Inv (%)	59.0	103.0	371.7	88.1	121.4	322.0	76.8	130.4	184.8	56.5	90.1	144.4
Total Liab To Nw (%)	40.1	99.4	131.6	58.0	128.0	238.7	66.5	150.4	347.7	53.7	140.9	298.9
Fixed Assets To Nw (%)	7.0	26.5	67.5	7.2	14.0	34.5	5.0	7.5	33.7	4.8	27.3	71.7
EFFICIENCY												
Coll Period (days)	25.0	38.2	72.4	25.7	48.8	78.1	37.0	54.8	95.5	3.3	10.6	49.1
Sales To Inv (times)	114.2	71.1	18.2	99.6	60.1	6.5	71.2	14.4	2.9	8.1	3.0	1.5
Assets To Sales (%)	22.8	38.0	62.8	23.6	34.6	66.7	28.5	45.2	78.9	34.5	58.3	132.9
Sales To Nwc (times)	13.6	8.0	3.3	16.3	9.7	4.7	14.4	8.7	2.9	15.5	6.6	3.0
Acct Pay To Sales (%)	2.2	5.3	8.0	4.6	8.4	13.2	5.6	12.3	17.3	1.6	4.4	9.7
PROFITABILITY												
Return On Sales (%)	9.8	4.2	0.9	6.4	2.5	1.0	7.4	2.3	1.3	7.7	3.6	1.5
Return On Assets (%)	17.3	4.6	1.7	13.3	5.3	1.6	9.5	4.0	1.4	12.0	4.8	1.5
Return On Nw (%)	35.2	12.1	3.1	31.1	14.8	4.0	60.7	13.3	6.0	54.5	17.8	5.8

SIC 1531 OPERATIVE BUILDERS — INDUSTRY ASSETS UNDER $100,000 — 1995 (19 Establishments)

	$	%
Cash	16,480	31.1
Accounts Receivable	7,207	13.6
Notes Receivable	—	—
Inventory	7,207	13.6
Other Current	10,333	19.5
Total Current	**41,227**	**77.8**
Fixed Assets	7,472	14.1
Other Non-current	4,292	8.1
Total Assets	**52,991**	**100.0**
Accounts Payable	2,809	5.3
Bank Loans	—	—
Notes Payable	2,491	4.7
Other Current	15,420	29.1
Total Current	**20,719**	**39.1**
Other Long Term	4,928	9.3
Deferred Credits	—	—
Net Worth	27,343	51.6
Total Liab & Net Worth	**52,991**	**100.0**
Net Sales	498,100	100.0
Gross Profit	126,019	25.3
Net Profit After Tax	26,897	5.4
Working Capital	20,508	—

RATIOS	UQ	MED	LQ
SOLVENCY			
Quick Ratio (times)	1.1	0.4	0.1
Current Ratio (times)	1.4	1.2	1.1
Curr Liab To Nw (%)	10.6	36.0	68.0
Curr Liab To Inv (%)	26.0	45.8	65.5
Total Liab To Nw (%)	36.0	96.2	154.4
Fixed Assets To Nw (%)	6.8	10.0	11.7
EFFICIENCY			
Coll Period (days)	13.1	14.1	15.1
Sales To Inv (times)	—	—	—
Assets To Sales (%)	10.1	12.3	20.7
Sales To Nwc (times)	24.4	15.1	8.0
Acct Pay To Sales (%)	1.6	2.6	3.5
PROFITABILITY			
Return On Sales (%)	2.8	1.1	0.1
Return On Assets (%)	3.5	2.1	(2.6)
Return On Nw (%)	40.1	12.9	(3.6)

SIC 1531 OPERATIVE BUILDERS — INDUSTRY ASSETS $100,000 - $250,000 — 1995 (36 Establishments)

	$	%
Cash	34,225	21.3
Accounts Receivable	19,282	12.0
Notes Receivable	—	—
Inventory	41,135	25.6
Other Current	25,870	16.1
Total Current	**120,512**	**75.0**
Fixed Assets	29,244	18.2
Other Non-current	10,926	6.8
Total Assets	**160,682**	**100.0**
Accounts Payable	6,588	4.1
Bank Loans	—	—
Notes Payable	11,408	7.1
Other Current	38,082	23.7
Total Current	**56,078**	**34.9**
Other Long Term	20,728	12.9
Deferred Credits	—	—
Net Worth	83,876	52.2
Total Liab & Net Worth	**160,682**	**100.0**
Net Sales	287,847	100.0
Gross Profit	58,721	20.4
Net Profit After Tax	18,998	6.6
Working Capital	64,434	—

RATIOS	UQ	MED	LQ
SOLVENCY			
Quick Ratio (times)	2.9	1.0	0.4
Current Ratio (times)	9.9	2.0	1.2
Curr Liab To Nw (%)	10.0	48.7	113.7
Curr Liab To Inv (%)	40.6	106.7	156.8
Total Liab To Nw (%)	13.4	78.0	211.6
Fixed Assets To Nw (%)	3.8	34.2	93.6
EFFICIENCY			
Coll Period (days)	1.8	6.9	29.6
Sales To Inv (times)	8.4	4.2	1.4
Assets To Sales (%)	27.4	48.9	102.1
Sales To Nwc (times)	21.2	7.5	3.1
Acct Pay To Sales (%)	1.0	2.5	6.9
PROFITABILITY			
Return On Sales (%)	14.5	5.5	2.1
Return On Assets (%)	13.0	3.7	1.0
Return On Nw (%)	48.7	10.1	5.5

SIC 1531 OPERATIVE BUILDERS — INDUSTRY ASSETS $250,000 - $500,000 — 1995 (22 Establishments)

	$	%
Cash	45,383	14.1
Accounts Receivable	73,063	22.7
Notes Receivable	—	—
Inventory	85,294	26.5
Other Current	32,186	10.0
Total Current	**235,926**	**73.3**
Fixed Assets	63,085	19.6
Other Non-current	22,852	7.1
Total Assets	**321,864**	**100.0**
Accounts Payable	38,946	12.1
Bank Loans	—	—
Notes Payable	33,796	10.5
Other Current	78,857	24.5
Total Current	**151,598**	**47.1**
Other Long Term	70,810	22.0
Deferred Credits	—	—
Net Worth	99,456	30.9
Total Liab & Net Worth	**321,864**	**100.0**
Net Sales	880,840	100.0
Gross Profit	171,764	19.5
Net Profit After Tax	22,902	2.6
Working Capital	84,328	—

RATIOS	UQ	MED	LQ
SOLVENCY			
Quick Ratio (times)	1.1	0.6	0.3
Current Ratio (times)	2.3	1.6	1.1
Curr Liab To Nw (%)	54.8	140.7	209.3
Curr Liab To Inv (%)	27.5	85.5	153.7
Total Liab To Nw (%)	73.2	276.1	535.8
Fixed Assets To Nw (%)	26.6	97.2	161.1
EFFICIENCY			
Coll Period (days)	25.5	49.0	75.1
Sales To Inv (times)	4.5	4.0	3.5
Assets To Sales (%)	31.2	36.0	44.3
Sales To Nwc (times)	23.2	12.5	5.7
Acct Pay To Sales (%)	1.2	2.5	7.2
PROFITABILITY			
Return On Sales (%)	5.9	2.6	1.1
Return On Assets (%)	7.5	5.8	1.3
Return On Nw (%)	143.8	82.2	18.9

SIC 1531 OPERATIVE BUILDERS — INDUSTRY ASSETS $500,000 - $1,000,000 — 1995 (49 Establishments)

	$	%
Cash	89,981	12.0
Accounts Receivable	62,237	8.3
Notes Receivable	10,498	1.4
Inventory	170,215	22.7
Other Current	173,964	23.2
Total Current	**506,895**	**67.6**
Fixed Assets	147,719	19.7
Other Non-current	95,230	12.7
Total Assets	**749,844**	**100.0**
Accounts Payable	36,742	4.9
Bank Loans	—	—
Notes Payable	74,984	10.0
Other Current	185,961	24.8
Total Current	**297,688**	**39.7**
Other Long Term	140,971	18.8
Deferred Credits	—	—
Net Worth	311,185	41.5
Total Liab & Net Worth	**749,844**	**100.0**
Net Sales	1,515,612	100.0
Gross Profit	224,311	14.8
Net Profit After Tax	122,765	8.1
Working Capital	209,207	—

RATIOS	UQ	MED	LQ
SOLVENCY			
Quick Ratio (times)	1.4	0.5	0.2
Current Ratio (times)	4.4	1.6	1.1
Curr Liab To Nw (%)	11.2	91.5	197.2
Curr Liab To Inv (%)	56.8	90.0	103.5
Total Liab To Nw (%)	44.7	141.2	259.7
Fixed Assets To Nw (%)	9.5	28.0	57.8
EFFICIENCY			
Coll Period (days)	5.9	30.5	52.1
Sales To Inv (times)	8.1	3.1	1.9
Assets To Sales (%)	37.4	61.1	125.0
Sales To Nwc (times)	15.0	5.7	3.1
Acct Pay To Sales (%)	0.8	1.7	3.6
PROFITABILITY			
Return On Sales (%)	28.9	8.8	3.0
Return On Assets (%)	37.3	9.3	4.5
Return On Nw (%)	124.1	43.5	28.4

SIC 1531 — OPERATIVE BUILDERS — INDUSTRY ASSETS — $1,000,000 - $5,000,000 — 1995 (105 Establishments)

	$	%
Cash	210,729	11.0
Accounts Receivable	143,679	7.5
Notes Receivable	15,326	0.8
Inventory	337,166	17.6
Other Current	603,451	31.5
Total Current	**1,310,351**	**68.4**
Fixed Assets	323,756	16.9
Other Non-current	281,611	14.7
Total Assets	**1,915,718**	**100.0**
Accounts Payable	130,269	6.8
Bank Loans	9,579	0.5
Notes Payable	159,005	8.3
Other Current	454,025	23.7
Total Current	**752,877**	**39.3**
Other Long Term	423,374	22.1
Deferred Credits	3,831	0.2
Net Worth	735,636	38.4
Total Liab & Net Worth	**1,915,718**	**100.0**
Net Sales	3,129,627	100.0
Gross Profit	547,685	17.5
Net Profit After Tax	140,833	4.5
Working Capital	557,474	—

RATIOS	UQ	MED	LQ
SOLVENCY			
Quick Ratio (times)	1.1	0.4	0.2
Current Ratio (times)	2.9	1.5	1.2
Curr Liab To Nw (%)	27.6	80.8	208.5
Curr Liab To Inv (%)	64.8	105.2	160.1
Total Liab To Nw (%)	59.8	127.9	329.0
Fixed Assets To Nw (%)	4.0	16.3	62.7
EFFICIENCY			
Coll Period (days)	4.4	12.3	41.0
Sales To Inv (times)	11.7	6.2	2.5
Assets To Sales (%)	33.4	47.2	141.8
Sales To Nwc (times)	18.0	8.5	3.5
Acct Pay To Sales (%)	1.3	3.7	6.5
PROFITABILITY			
Return On Sales (%)	9.0	5.1	1.6
Return On Assets (%)	17.8	7.4	2.7
Return On Nw (%)	74.6	20.0	5.3

SIC 1531 — OPERATIVE BUILDERS — INDUSTRY ASSETS — $5,000,000 - $25,000,000 — 1995 (48 Establishments)

	$	%
Cash	650,696	7.3
Accounts Receivable	713,092	8.0
Notes Receivable	106,964	1.2
Inventory	1,631,197	18.3
Other Current	1,675,766	18.8
Total Current	**4,777,715**	**53.6**
Fixed Assets	2,504,735	28.1
Other Non-current	1,631,197	18.3
Total Assets	**8,913,647**	**100.0**
Accounts Payable	677,437	7.6
Bank Loans	—	—
Notes Payable	846,796	9.5
Other Current	1,827,298	20.5
Total Current	**3,351,531**	**37.6**
Other Long Term	2,290,807	25.7
Deferred Credits	8,914	0.1
Net Worth	3,262,395	36.6
Total Liab & Net Worth	**8,913,647**	**100.0**
Net Sales	12,070,464	100.0
Gross Profit	2,100,261	17.4
Net Profit After Tax	241,409	2.0
Working Capital	1,426,184	—

RATIOS	UQ	MED	LQ
SOLVENCY			
Quick Ratio (times)	1.7	0.4	0.1
Current Ratio (times)	3.0	1.7	1.1
Curr Liab To Nw (%)	6.2	60.2	200.0
Curr Liab To Inv (%)	59.1	92.0	570.7
Total Liab To Nw (%)	83.3	153.7	416.4
Fixed Assets To Nw (%)	12.2	35.2	116.3
EFFICIENCY			
Coll Period (days)	3.3	6.6	54.8
Sales To Inv (times)	3.2	2.3	1.2
Assets To Sales (%)	50.1	75.2	237.6
Sales To Nwc (times)	10.0	6.4	1.4
Acct Pay To Sales (%)	4.2	5.3	11.5
PROFITABILITY			
Return On Sales (%)	4.9	2.9	1.0
Return On Assets (%)	7.5	3.3	1.2
Return On Nw (%)	30.2	16.3	8.6

SIC 1531 — OPERATIVE BUILDERS — INDUSTRY ASSETS — $25,000,000 - $50,000,000 — 1995 (13 Establishments)

	$	%
Cash	1,771,083	5.4
Accounts Receivable	6,231,587	19.0
Notes Receivable	32,798	0.1
Inventory	9,511,370	29.0
Other Current	11,315,251	34.5
Total Current	**28,862,089**	**88.0**
Fixed Assets	951,137	2.9
Other Non-current	2,984,602	9.1
Total Assets	**32,797,828**	**100.0**
Accounts Payable	2,722,220	8.3
Bank Loans	—	—
Notes Payable	4,034,133	12.3
Other Current	7,576,298	23.1
Total Current	**14,332,651**	**43.7**
Other Long Term	5,083,663	15.5
Deferred Credits	—	—
Net Worth	13,381,514	40.8
Total Liab & Net Worth	**32,797,828**	**100.0**
Net Sales	37,423,462	100.0
Gross Profit	10,441,146	27.9
Net Profit After Tax	3,293,265	8.8
Working Capital	14,529,438	—

RATIOS	UQ	MED	LQ
SOLVENCY			
Quick Ratio (times)	0.4	0.2	0.1
Current Ratio (times)	2.6	2.1	1.5
Curr Liab To Nw (%)	43.6	69.3	182.8
Curr Liab To Inv (%)	56.2	73.3	130.5
Total Liab To Nw (%)	70.7	111.2	304.9
Fixed Assets To Nw (%)	2.4	5.9	10.7
EFFICIENCY			
Coll Period (days)	1.5	2.9	13.2
Sales To Inv (times)	10.7	3.0	2.7
Assets To Sales (%)	57.0	90.0	137.2
Sales To Nwc (times)	7.1	4.2	2.0
Acct Pay To Sales (%)	3.8	7.7	11.8
PROFITABILITY			
Return On Sales (%)	12.0	5.5	2.1
Return On Assets (%)	9.3	6.2	3.8
Return On Nw (%)	20.1	14.7	9.2

SIC 1541 — INDL BLDNGS, WRHSES (NO BREAKDOWN) — 1995 (1126 Establishments)

	$	%
Cash	188,434	18.0
Accounts Receivable	434,446	41.5
Notes Receivable	8,375	0.8
Inventory	24,078	2.3
Other Current	140,279	13.4
Total Current	**795,611**	**76.0**
Fixed Assets	172,731	16.5
Other Non-current	78,514	7.5
Total Assets	**1,046,857**	**100.0**
Accounts Payable	269,042	25.7
Bank Loans	1,047	0.1
Notes Payable	38,734	3.7
Other Current	168,544	16.1
Total Current	**477,367**	**45.6**
Other Long Term	82,702	7.9
Deferred Credits	2,094	0.2
Net Worth	484,695	46.3
Total Liab & Net Worth	**1,046,857**	**100.0**
Net Sales	3,201,339	100.0
Gross Profit	582,644	18.2
Net Profit After Tax	105,644	3.3
Working Capital	318,244	—

RATIOS	UQ	MED	LQ
SOLVENCY			
Quick Ratio (times)	1.9	1.3	1.0
Current Ratio (times)	2.6	1.6	1.3
Curr Liab To Nw (%)	43.4	99.7	204.0
Curr Liab To Inv (%)	119.6	256.0	577.7
Total Liab To Nw (%)	52.6	119.4	233.2
Fixed Assets To Nw (%)	13.3	28.9	55.7
EFFICIENCY			
Coll Period (days)	35.0	54.4	71.5
Sales To Inv (times)	313.5	107.9	31.6
Assets To Sales (%)	23.2	31.3	43.0
Sales To Nwc (times)	21.0	10.8	6.1
Acct Pay To Sales (%)	4.2	8.1	12.5
PROFITABILITY			
Return On Sales (%)	5.0	2.1	0.6
Return On Assets (%)	13.2	5.5	1.5
Return On Nw (%)	29.6	13.5	3.6

SIC 1541 — INDL BLDNGS, WRHSES — INDUSTRY ASSETS

	UNDER $100,000 (77) $	%	$100,000–$250,000 (125) $	%	$250,000–$500,000 (149) $	%	$500,000–$1,000,000 (215) $	%
Cash	21,451	34.6	36,022	21.7	72,887	20.6	120,700	16.4
Accounts Receivable	10,788	17.4	61,420	37.0	131,974	37.3	301,013	40.9
Notes Receivable	1,054	1.7	2,490	1.5	1,769	0.5	5,152	0.7
Inventory	992	1.6	6,806	4.1	16,276	4.6	16,927	2.3
Other Current	8,246	13.3	16,268	9.8	33,613	9.5	105,980	14.4
Total Current	**42,531**	**68.6**	**123,005**	**74.1**	**256,519**	**72.5**	**549,773**	**74.7**
Fixed Assets	17,545	28.3	35,690	21.5	70,410	19.9	129,531	17.6
Other Non-current	1,922	3.1	7,304	4.4	26,890	7.6	56,670	7.7
Total Assets	**61,998**	**100.0**	**165,999**	**100.0**	**353,819**	**100.0**	**735,974**	**100.0**
Accounts Payable	6,200	10.0	34,196	20.6	74,302	21.0	170,010	23.1
Bank Loans	310	0.5	166	0.1	708	0.2	—	—
Notes Payable	3,410	5.5	10,624	6.4	17,337	4.9	33,855	4.6
Other Current	12,896	20.8	21,912	13.2	44,227	12.5	117,756	16.0
Total Current	**22,815**	**36.8**	**66,898**	**40.3**	**136,574**	**38.6**	**321,621**	**43.7**
Other Long Term	5,270	8.5	13,778	8.3	35,382	10.0	62,558	8.5
Deferred Credits	—	—	166	0.1	354	0.1	736	0.1
Net Worth	33,913	54.7	85,157	51.3	181,509	51.3	351,060	47.7
Total Liab & Net Worth	**61,998**	**100.0**	**165,999**	**100.0**	**353,819**	**100.0**	**735,974**	**100.0**
Net Sales	391,197	100.0	683,210	100.0	1,219,240	100.0	2,078,478	100.0
Gross Profit	103,276	26.4	176,268	25.8	297,495	24.4	480,128	23.1
Net Profit After Tax	20,342	5.2	43,725	6.4	58,524	4.8	51,962	2.5
Working Capital	19,716	—	56,107	—	119,945	—	228,152	—

RATIOS

	UQ	MED	LQ	UQ	MED	LQ	UQ	MED	LQ	UQ	MED	LQ
SOLVENCY												
Quick Ratio (times)	2.6	1.2	0.7	3.3	1.6	0.9	2.7	1.6	1.0	2.0	1.4	1.0
Current Ratio (times)	4.2	1.8	1.2	4.2	1.9	1.2	3.7	2.0	1.4	2.7	1.7	1.3
Curr Liab To Nw (%)	19.2	48.4	174.1	19.7	59.2	140.7	26.0	73.6	133.6	38.5	82.2	159.7
Curr Liab To Inv (%)	153.4	212.6	394.2	121.1	151.2	448.7	56.8	96.5	247.2	135.5	281.5	687.1
Total Liab To Nw (%)	26.7	66.0	186.5	28.8	74.9	155.9	39.5	84.3	185.9	49.6	96.6	188.7
Fixed Assets To Nw (%)	22.3	54.1	109.0	14.5	29.7	76.3	11.8	33.4	61.7	14.9	32.1	60.9
EFFICIENCY												
Coll Period (days)	2.9	7.3	26.7	20.8	37.6	70.1	27.4	42.7	62.8	33.9	53.1	71.0
Sales To Inv (times)	46.4	42.7	32.6	87.0	35.1	15.4	341.0	106.3	15.2	267.9	104.8	28.4
Assets To Sales (%)	8.2	13.7	18.9	16.3	26.9	40.8	21.9	27.3	39.8	24.3	33.2	43.7
Sales To Nwc (times)	35.3	27.3	10.0	23.5	9.7	5.7	16.9	8.6	5.6	16.8	10.0	6.0
Acct Pay To Sales (%)	0.5	1.9	4.2	2.2	4.5	8.6	2.7	6.1	9.7	3.7	7.4	11.2
PROFITABILITY												
Return On Sales (%)	10.7	3.6	0.5	10.9	4.4	1.7	8.6	2.7	0.9	5.0	2.2	0.3
Return On Assets (%)	68.2	30.9	0.6	29.9	13.0	2.0	15.6	8.2	2.3	12.0	5.8	0.6
Return On Nw (%)	103.3	56.1	1.6	52.1	25.9	4.7	37.0	19.2	4.6	23.8	13.4	1.0

1995 Establishment counts: UNDER $100,000 (77); $100,000–$250,000 (125); $250,000–$500,000 (149); $500,000–$1,000,000 (215).

SIC 1541 INDL BLDNGS, WRHSES — INDUSTRY ASSETS $1,000,000 - $5,000,000 — 1995 (397 Establishments)

	$	%
Cash	316,427	16.0
Accounts Receivable	909,727	46.0
Notes Receivable	11,866	0.6
Inventory	31,643	1.6
Other Current	290,717	14.7
Total Current	**1,560,379**	**78.9**
Fixed Assets	263,030	13.3
Other Non-current	154,258	7.8
Total Assets	**1,977,667**	**100.0**
Accounts Payable	583,412	29.5
Bank Loans	1,978	0.1
Notes Payable	55,375	2.8
Other Current	324,337	16.4
Total Current	**965,101**	**48.8**
Other Long Term	118,660	6.0
Deferred Credits	7,911	0.4
Net Worth	885,995	44.8
Total Liab & Net Worth	**1,977,667**	**100.0**
Net Sales	5,976,757	100.0
Gross Profit	818,816	13.7
Net Profit After Tax	149,419	2.5
Working Capital	595,278	—

RATIOS	UQ	MED	LQ
SOLVENCY			
Quick Ratio (times)	1.7	1.3	1.0
Current Ratio (times)	2.2	1.6	1.3
Curr Liab To Nw (%)	55.5	117.9	209.9
Curr Liab To Inv (%)	209.1	413.6	579.2
Total Liab To Nw (%)	65.9	126.3	238.1
Fixed Assets To Nw (%)	12.6	26.9	46.9
EFFICIENCY			
Coll Period (days)	39.8	59.1	75.4
Sales To Inv (times)	361.1	160.0	42.3
Assets To Sales (%)	24.7	32.4	43.1
Sales To Nwc (times)	18.7	10.8	5.9
Acct Pay To Sales (%)	5.5	8.7	13.7
PROFITABILITY			
Return On Sales (%)	4.2	1.9	0.6
Return On Assets (%)	9.6	4.9	1.7
Return On Nw (%)	26.2	12.3	4.2

SIC 1541 INDL BLDNGS, WRHSES — INDUSTRY ASSETS $5,000,000 - $25,000,000 — 1995 (118 Establishments)

	$	%
Cash	1,096,574	13.3
Accounts Receivable	3,949,314	47.9
Notes Receivable	74,204	0.9
Inventory	82,449	1.0
Other Current	1,310,941	15.9
Total Current	**6,513,482**	**79.0**
Fixed Assets	1,014,124	12.3
Other Non-current	717,308	8.7
Total Assets	**8,244,914**	**100.0**
Accounts Payable	2,836,250	34.4
Bank Loans	32,980	0.4
Notes Payable	123,674	1.5
Other Current	1,418,125	17.2
Total Current	**4,411,029**	**53.5**
Other Long Term	552,409	6.7
Deferred Credits	16,490	0.2
Net Worth	3,264,986	39.6
Total Liab & Net Worth	**8,244,914**	**100.0**
Net Sales	23,779,788	100.0
Gross Profit	2,520,658	10.6
Net Profit After Tax	594,495	2.5
Working Capital	2,102,453	—

RATIOS	UQ	MED	LQ
SOLVENCY			
Quick Ratio (times)	1.4	1.1	1.0
Current Ratio (times)	1.8	1.5	1.2
Curr Liab To Nw (%)	81.3	152.1	292.5
Curr Liab To Inv (%)	99.5	117.4	273.4
Total Liab To Nw (%)	83.8	174.2	317.6
Fixed Assets To Nw (%)	12.3	21.2	44.2
EFFICIENCY			
Coll Period (days)	45.3	59.5	74.5
Sales To Inv (times)	336.3	108.5	48.7
Assets To Sales (%)	26.6	32.2	47.9
Sales To Nwc (times)	24.9	14.1	6.8
Acct Pay To Sales (%)	7.9	11.0	15.2
PROFITABILITY			
Return On Sales (%)	3.2	1.3	0.5
Return On Assets (%)	8.5	3.1	1.8
Return On Nw (%)	23.4	10.3	3.8

SIC 1541 INDL BLDNGS, WRHSES — INDUSTRY ASSETS $25,000,000-$50,000,000 — 1995 (24 Establishments)

	$	%
Cash	5,876,083	16.7
Accounts Receivable	18,683,832	53.1
Notes Receivable	105,558	0.3
Inventory	457,420	1.3
Other Current	4,644,568	13.2
Total Current	**29,767,461**	**84.6**
Fixed Assets	2,885,262	8.2
Other Non-current	2,533,401	7.2
Total Assets	**35,186,124**	**100.0**
Accounts Payable	13,018,866	37.0
Bank Loans	—	—
Notes Payable	422,233	1.2
Other Current	9,218,764	26.2
Total Current	**22,659,864**	**64.4**
Other Long Term	1,583,376	4.5
Deferred Credits	70,372	0.2
Net Worth	10,872,512	30.9
Total Liab & Net Worth	**35,186,124**	**100.0**
Net Sales	101,469,482	100.0
Gross Profit	6,494,047	6.4
Net Profit After Tax	811,756	0.8
Working Capital	7,107,597	—

RATIOS	UQ	MED	LQ
SOLVENCY			
Quick Ratio (times)	1.3	1.0	0.9
Current Ratio (times)	1.4	1.2	1.1
Curr Liab To Nw (%)	115.7	273.2	360.6
Curr Liab To Inv (%)	214.2	214.2	214.2
Total Liab To Nw (%)	141.7	274.3	396.7
Fixed Assets To Nw (%)	10.7	25.8	38.1
EFFICIENCY			
Coll Period (days)	49.8	59.9	73.6
Sales To Inv (times)	230.1	200.0	132.2
Assets To Sales (%)	24.9	31.4	46.6
Sales To Nwc (times)	47.8	29.5	12.1
Acct Pay To Sales (%)	10.2	11.4	16.3
PROFITABILITY			
Return On Sales (%)	1.4	1.0	0.5
Return On Assets (%)	3.9	3.2	2.2
Return On Nw (%)	15.3	12.1	5.6

SIC 1541 INDL BLDNGS, WRHSES — INDUSTRY ASSETS OVER $50,000,000 — 1995 (21 Establishments)

	$	%
Cash	13,135,683	12.9
Accounts Receivable	42,156,378	41.4
Notes Receivable	1,018,270	1.0
Inventory	610,962	0.6
Other Current	14,663,088	14.4
Total Current	**71,584,381**	**70.3**
Fixed Assets	10,691,835	10.5
Other Non-current	19,550,784	19.2
Total Assets	**101,827,000**	**100.0**
Accounts Payable	30,242,619	29.7
Bank Loans	—	—
Notes Payable	—	—
Other Current	25,660,404	25.2
Total Current	**55,903,023**	**54.9**
Other Long Term	17,208,763	16.9
Deferred Credits	101,827	0.1
Net Worth	28,613,387	28.1
Total Liab & Net Worth	**101,827,000**	**100.0**
Net Sales	201,081,170	100.0
Gross Profit	16,086,494	8.0
Net Profit After Tax	(804,325)	(0.4)
Working Capital	15,681,358	—

RATIOS	UQ	MED	LQ
SOLVENCY			
Quick Ratio (times)	1.1	1.0	0.7
Current Ratio (times)	1.6	1.2	1.1
Curr Liab To Nw (%)	76.1	265.0	404.3
Curr Liab To Inv (%)	656.8	775.4	887.3
Total Liab To Nw (%)	117.5	324.4	398.6
Fixed Assets To Nw (%)	12.3	38.5	48.2
EFFICIENCY			
Coll Period (days)	34.4	73.4	84.9
Sales To Inv (times)	530.3	161.0	65.4
Assets To Sales (%)	32.3	55.8	85.0
Sales To Nwc (times)	47.2	35.8	21.3
Acct Pay To Sales (%)	7.0	14.9	17.7
PROFITABILITY			
Return On Sales (%)	1.4	0.3	(0.1)
Return On Assets (%)	0.9	0.1	(0.2)
Return On Nw (%)	7.8	1.4	(0.1)

SIC 1542 NONRESID CONSTR,NEC

	(NO BREAKDOWN) 1995 (1720 Establishments) $	%	UNDER $100,000 INDUSTRY ASSETS 1995 (367 Establishments) $	%	$100,000 - $250,000 INDUSTRY ASSETS 1995 (671 Establishments) $	%	$250,000 - $500,000 INDUSTRY ASSETS 1995 (904 Establishments) $	%
Cash	164,390	21.3	19,702	33.0	41,849	24.0	78,184	21.5
Accounts Receivable	314,888	40.8	15,403	25.8	58,239	33.4	136,004	37.4
Notes Receivable	5,402	0.7	537	0.9	1,744	1.0	3,636	1.0
Inventory	18,523	2.4	1,015	1.7	5,754	3.3	11,273	3.1
Other Current	113,452	14.7	4,597	7.7	19,181	11.0	48,365	13.3
Total Current	**616,655**	**79.9**	**41,254**	**69.1**	**126,766**	**72.7**	**277,462**	**76.3**
Fixed Assets	111,137	14.4	15,642	26.2	37,838	21.7	62,547	17.2
Other Non-current	43,992	5.7	2,806	4.7	9,765	5.6	23,637	6.5
Total Assets	**771,784**	**100.0**	**59,702**	**100.0**	**174,369**	**100.0**	**363,646**	**100.0**
Accounts Payable	216,100	28.0	8,060	13.5	31,212	17.9	82,548	22.7
Bank Loans	772	0.1	179	0.3	349	0.2	727	0.2
Notes Payable	20,066	2.6	2,746	4.6	6,103	3.5	10,909	3.0
Other Current	123,485	16.0	9,851	16.5	25,109	14.4	51,638	14.2
Total Current	**360,423**	**46.7**	**20,836**	**34.9**	**62,773**	**36.0**	**145,822**	**40.1**
Other Long Term	47,851	6.2	4,418	7.4	15,519	8.9	27,637	7.6
Deferred Credits	1,544	0.2	60	0.1	174	0.1	727	0.2
Net Worth	361,967	46.9	34,388	57.6	95,903	55.0	189,460	52.1
Total Liab & Net Worth	**771,784**	**100.0**	**59,702**	**100.0**	**174,369**	**100.0**	**363,646**	**100.0**
Net Sales	2,723,260	100.0	337,285	100.0	749,480	100.0	1,323,252	100.0
Gross Profit	446,615	16.4	95,114	28.2	181,374	24.2	267,297	20.2
Net Profit After Tax	95,314	3.5	22,935	6.8	43,470	5.8	56,900	4.3
Working Capital	256,232	—	20,418	—	63,993	—	131,640	—

RATIOS	UQ	MED	LQ	UQ	MED	LQ	UQ	MED	LQ	UQ	MED	LQ
SOLVENCY												
Quick Ratio (times)	2.0	1.3	1.0	4.4	1.8	1.0	3.2	1.6	1.0	2.6	1.5	1.0
Current Ratio (times)	2.6	1.6	1.3	5.5	2.2	1.2	3.9	2.1	1.4	3.3	2.0	1.4
Curr Liab To Nw (%)	43.8	106.8	211.0	14.3	41.7	96.8	22.5	54.5	136.1	30.8	70.4	147.8
Curr Liab To Inv (%)	116.4	244.1	488.3	119.7	235.7	410.0	89.5	250.3	507.8	110.9	239.8	436.4
Total Liab To Nw (%)	55.7	122.5	232.2	19.6	53.5	120.6	29.9	72.8	168.6	37.9	87.3	181.2
Fixed Assets To Nw (%)	10.2	21.0	45.0	17.6	41.8	83.9	14.1	33.3	72.2	12.5	26.4	54.9
EFFICIENCY												
Coll Period (days)	31.0	48.9	69.0	12.4	25.2	41.6	15.7	33.2	54.4	24.5	40.2	62.8
Sales To Inv (times)	282.7	84.1	27.3	151.7	72.0	39.3	200.6	68.4	19.0	142.3	46.5	17.9
Assets To Sales (%)	21.1	28.7	40.1	9.0	16.5	26.8	15.6	23.2	37.0	19.2	26.7	39.1
Sales To Nwc (times)	20.3	11.4	6.5	33.9	14.4	7.0	22.1	11.0	5.9	17.2	10.2	5.8
Acct Pay To Sales (%)	4.3	8.4	13.2	1.1	2.4	5.9	1.8	4.3	8.1	2.9	5.6	9.1
PROFITABILITY												
Return On Sales (%)	5.9	2.3	0.7	16.0	5.4	1.5	9.4	5.0	1.3	7.2	3.3	1.0
Return On Assets (%)	15.4	6.3	2.1	76.2	32.7	6.0	35.3	15.4	3.5	20.3	10.4	3.4
Return On Nw (%)	38.7	16.7	5.7	119.0	51.5	11.7	70.2	30.0	8.4	48.4	21.1	6.2

SIC 1542 NONRESID CONSTR,NEC — INDUSTRY ASSETS — $500,000 - $1,000,000 — 1995 (1034 Establishments)

	$	%
Cash	144,920	20.9
Accounts Receivable	275,972	39.8
Notes Receivable	5,547	0.8
Inventory	18,028	2.6
Other Current	110,250	15.9
Total Current	**554,718**	**80.0**
Fixed Assets	94,996	13.7
Other Non-current	43,684	6.3
Total Assets	**693,398**	**100.0**
Accounts Payable	180,977	26.1
Bank Loans	693	0.1
Notes Payable	18,028	2.6
Other Current	101,236	14.6
Total Current	**300,935**	**43.4**
Other Long Term	44,377	6.4
Deferred Credits	693	0.1
Net Worth	347,392	50.1
Total Liab & Net Worth	**693,398**	**100.0**
Net Sales	2,292,676	100.0
Gross Profit	380,584	16.6
Net Profit After Tax	71,073	3.1
Working Capital	253,783	—

RATIOS	UQ	MED	LQ
SOLVENCY			
Quick Ratio (times)	2.1	1.4	1.0
Current Ratio (times)	2.7	1.8	1.4
Curr Liab To Nw (%)	41.9	85.5	165.7
Curr Liab To Inv (%)	149.9	306.5	593.7
Total Liab To Nw (%)	49.7	102.5	181.4
Fixed Assets To Nw (%)	10.9	21.8	43.7
EFFICIENCY			
Coll Period (days)	29.9	46.0	66.8
Sales To Inv (times)	297.6	101.1	30.5
Assets To Sales (%)	22.7	30.2	40.4
Sales To Nwc (times)	16.2	9.5	5.5
Acct Pay To Sales (%)	4.1	7.0	11.2
PROFITABILITY			
Return On Sales (%)	4.9	2.3	0.8
Return On Assets (%)	14.2	7.2	2.4
Return On Nw (%)	32.3	16.2	5.4

SIC 1542 NONRESID CONSTR,NEC — INDUSTRY ASSETS — $1,000,000 - $5,000,000 — 1995 (1662 Establishments)

	$	%
Cash	341,376	19.0
Accounts Receivable	799,539	44.5
Notes Receivable	10,780	0.6
Inventory	28,747	1.6
Other Current	318,019	17.7
Total Current	**1,498,461**	**83.4**
Fixed Assets	192,249	10.7
Other Non-current	106,006	5.9
Total Assets	**1,796,716**	**100.0**
Accounts Payable	612,680	34.1
Bank Loans	1,797	0.1
Notes Payable	34,138	1.9
Other Current	300,052	16.7
Total Current	**948,666**	**52.8**
Other Long Term	95,226	5.3
Deferred Credits	5,390	0.3
Net Worth	747,434	41.6
Total Liab & Net Worth	**1,796,716**	**100.0**
Net Sales	6,186,617	100.0
Gross Profit	767,141	12.4
Net Profit After Tax	148,479	2.4
Working Capital	549,795	—

RATIOS	UQ	MED	LQ
SOLVENCY			
Quick Ratio (times)	1.6	1.2	1.0
Current Ratio (times)	2.0	1.5	1.3
Curr Liab To Nw (%)	75.3	141.1	232.7
Curr Liab To Inv (%)	136.5	352.4	581.9
Total Liab To Nw (%)	85.5	157.8	253.4
Fixed Assets To Nw (%)	9.6	19.2	37.6
EFFICIENCY			
Coll Period (days)	37.2	53.3	73.3
Sales To Inv (times)	311.2	108.2	36.3
Assets To Sales (%)	22.9	29.7	41.4
Sales To Nwc (times)	19.3	12.1	7.1
Acct Pay To Sales (%)	6.6	10.0	14.2
PROFITABILITY			
Return On Sales (%)	3.7	1.7	0.6
Return On Assets (%)	10.3	4.6	1.8
Return On Nw (%)	28.1	12.2	4.7

SIC 1542 NONRESID CONSTR,NEC — INDUSTRY ASSETS — $5,000,000-$25,000,000 — 1995 (427 Establishments)

	$	%
Cash	1,367,696	17.6
Accounts Receivable	3,916,584	50.4
Notes Receivable	38,855	0.5
Inventory	77,710	1.0
Other Current	1,383,238	17.8
Total Current	**6,784,083**	**87.3**
Fixed Assets	528,428	6.8
Other Non-current	458,489	5.9
Total Assets	**7,771,000**	**100.0**
Accounts Payable	3,224,965	41.5
Bank Loans		—
Notes Payable	116,565	1.5
Other Current	1,546,429	19.9
Total Current	**4,887,959**	**62.9**
Other Long Term	287,527	3.7
Deferred Credits	15,542	0.2
Net Worth	2,579,972	33.2
Total Liab & Net Worth	**7,771,000**	**100.0**
Net Sales	24,406,620	100.0
Gross Profit	2,025,749	8.3
Net Profit After Tax	536,946	2.2
Working Capital	1,896,124	—

RATIOS	UQ	MED	LQ
SOLVENCY			
Quick Ratio (times)	1.3	1.1	1.0
Current Ratio (times)	1.6	1.3	1.2
Curr Liab To Nw (%)	131.4	227.9	376.6
Curr Liab To Inv (%)	172.5	250.6	602.2
Total Liab To Nw (%)	140.7	240.2	392.8
Fixed Assets To Nw (%)	7.5	14.5	29.5
EFFICIENCY			
Coll Period (days)	48.9	62.1	76.3
Sales To Inv (times)	563.2	175.7	40.0
Assets To Sales (%)	25.4	31.4	41.1
Sales To Nwc (times)	23.8	16.5	9.9
Acct Pay To Sales (%)	9.6	13.4	17.7
PROFITABILITY			
Return On Sales (%)	2.5	1.2	0.6
Return On Assets (%)	7.8	3.8	1.6
Return On Nw (%)	26.2	13.3	5.3

SIC 1542 NONRESID CONSTR,NEC — INDUSTRY ASSETS — $25,000,000-$50,000,000 — 1995 (56 Establishments)

	$	%
Cash	7,228,642	20.7
Accounts Receivable	15,958,886	45.7
Notes Receivable	174,605	0.5
Inventory	139,684	0.4
Other Current	5,168,304	14.8
Total Current	**28,670,121**	**82.1**
Fixed Assets	3,492,098	10.0
Other Non-current	2,758,757	7.9
Total Assets	**34,920,976**	**100.0**
Accounts Payable	14,841,415	42.5
Bank Loans	34,921	0.1
Notes Payable	279,368	0.8
Other Current	6,879,432	19.7
Total Current	**22,035,136**	**63.1**
Other Long Term	2,514,310	7.2
Deferred Credits	—	—
Net Worth	10,371,530	29.7
Total Liab & Net Worth	**34,920,976**	**100.0**
Net Sales	98,009,375	100.0
Gross Profit	5,292,506	5.4
Net Profit After Tax	490,047	0.5
Working Capital	6,634,985	—

RATIOS	UQ	MED	LQ
SOLVENCY			
Quick Ratio (times)	1.2	1.1	0.9
Current Ratio (times)	1.5	1.3	1.1
Curr Liab To Nw (%)	158.3	257.2	428.2
Curr Liab To Inv (%)	341.4	341.4	341.4
Total Liab To Nw (%)	181.4	280.8	439.4
Fixed Assets To Nw (%)	8.4	14.0	31.3
EFFICIENCY			
Coll Period (days)	49.8	64.8	76.3
Sales To Inv (times)	295.0	242.6	129.8
Assets To Sales (%)	27.2	35.0	40.0
Sales To Nwc (times)	29.6	15.2	9.6
Acct Pay To Sales (%)	13.5	16.5	19.5
PROFITABILITY			
Return On Sales (%)	2.2	0.8	0.5
Return On Assets (%)	6.3	3.0	1.6
Return On Nw (%)	20.5	13.5	4.4

Balance Sheet

	SIC 1542 NONRESID CONSTR,NEC — INDUSTRY ASSETS OVER $50,000,000 1995 (40 Establishments)		SIC 16 HEAVY CONSTR CONTRS (NO BREAKDOWN) 1995 (2205 Establishments)		SIC 16 HEAVY CONSTR CONTRS NORTHEAST 1995 (630 Establishments)		SIC 16 HEAVY CONSTR CONTRS CENTRAL 1995 (1194 Establishments)	
	$	%	$	%	$	%	$	%
Cash	14,017,421	12.7	172,319	15.4	158,102	16.3	191,518	15.4
Accounts Receivable	50,992,506	46.2	336,806	30.1	316,204	32.6	350,703	28.2
Notes Receivable	—	—	6,714	0.6	4,850	0.5	6,218	0.5
Inventory	772,614	0.7	26,855	2.4	26,189	2.7	37,309	3.0
Other Current	18,101,236	16.4	123,085	11.0	116,394	12.0	105,708	8.5
Total Current	**83,883,776**	**76.0**	**665,779**	**59.5**	**621,738**	**64.1**	**691,456**	**55.6**
Fixed Assets	16,114,515	14.6	375,970	33.6	269,646	27.8	473,822	38.1
Other Non-current	10,375,099	9.4	77,208	6.9	78,566	8.1	78,348	6.3
Total Assets	**110,373,390**	**100.0**	**1,118,957**	**100.0**	**969,950**	**100.0**	**1,243,626**	**100.0**
Accounts Payable	41,058,901	37.2	170,081	15.2	166,831	17.2	174,108	14.0
Bank Loans	—	—	1,119	0.1	970	0.1	2,487	0.2
Notes Payable	1,655,601	1.5	44,758	4.0	35,888	3.7	47,258	3.8
Other Current	27,593,348	25.0	160,011	14.3	155,192	16.0	174,108	14.0
Total Current	**70,307,849**	**63.7**	**375,970**	**33.6**	**358,882**	**37.0**	**397,960**	**32.0**
Other Long Term	12,913,687	11.7	161,130	14.4	121,244	12.5	197,737	15.9
Deferred Credits	662,240	0.6	5,595	0.5	4,850	0.5	6,218	0.5
Net Worth	26,489,614	24.0	576,263	51.5	484,975	50.0	641,711	51.6
Total Liab & Net Worth	**110,373,390**	**100.0**	**1,118,957**	**100.0**	**969,950**	**100.0**	**1,243,626**	**100.0**
Net Sales	389,241,959	100.0	2,634,300	100.0	2,203,784	100.0	2,834,190	100.0
Gross Profit	16,737,404	4.3	634,866	24.1	546,538	24.8	668,869	23.6
Net Profit After Tax	3,113,936	0.8	115,909	4.4	81,540	3.7	127,539	4.5
Working Capital	13,575,927	—	289,809	—	262,856	—	293,496	—

RATIOS

	UQ	MED	LQ	UQ	MED	LQ	UQ	MED	LQ	UQ	MED	LQ
SOLVENCY												
Quick Ratio (times)	1.2	1.0	0.8	2.2	1.3	0.9	2.2	1.3	0.9	2.3	1.4	0.9
Current Ratio (times)	1.3	1.2	1.1	2.9	1.8	1.2	2.8	1.7	1.3	3.1	1.7	1.2
Curr Liab To Nw (%)	173.3	284.5	378.6	27.1	61.2	120.9	31.5	68.7	139.6	24.0	59.1	114.8
Curr Liab To Inv (%)	561.9	782.6	891.3	195.4	358.0	580.2	188.2	385.0	671.0	185.2	354.4	601.5
Total Liab To Nw (%)	240.7	325.4	394.3	42.3	90.6	177.9	46.4	95.7	192.9	38.2	92.1	188.2
Fixed Assets To Nw (%)	13.1	25.0	64.3	33.9	64.6	109.0	24.8	54.9	96.8	39.0	71.9	123.2
EFFICIENCY												
Coll Period (days)	52.5	55.9	66.5	31.0	50.7	71.9	34.0	57.3	88.3	24.1	46.0	66.4
Sales To Inv (times)	128.6	87.8	53.0	170.2	65.8	26.0	150.1	64.1	25.7	173.5	68.5	28.6
Assets To Sales (%)	26.4	31.1	40.9	32.3	43.0	58.3	32.5	44.5	63.5	32.1	42.2	57.5
Sales To Nwc (times)	30.3	21.7	14.4	16.7	8.9	5.2	14.6	7.9	4.6	18.0	10.0	5.6
Acct Pay To Sales (%)	10.7	13.2	15.6	3.0	5.8	10.0	3.6	6.8	11.7	2.3	4.8	8.5
PROFITABILITY												
Return On Sales (%)	1.6	0.5	0.4	7.9	3.4	1.1	6.9	2.8	0.8	7.0	3.0	1.2
Return On Assets (%)	3.7	1.4	1.0	14.9	6.9	2.4	12.6	5.5	1.8	14.6	7.1	2.9
Return On Nw (%)	21.3	12.7	3.8	31.7	14.1	5.0	27.1	11.0	3.2	30.2	13.4	6.2

SIC 16 HEAVY CONSTR CONTRS

	SOUTH 1995 (1667 Est.) $	%	WEST 1995 (920 Est.) $	%	INDUSTRY ASSETS UNDER $100,000 1995 (212 Est.) $	%	INDUSTRY ASSETS $100,000 - $250,000 1995 (441 Est.) $	%
Cash	176,178	15.7	161,569	14.5	15,663	26.4	35,903	19.9
Accounts Receivable	325,424	29.0	347,653	31.2	11,628	19.6	44,021	24.4
Notes Receivable	6,733	0.6	7,800	0.7	178	0.3	722	0.4
Inventory	22,443	2.0	23,400	2.1	1,365	2.3	4,330	2.4
Other Current	134,658	12.0	124,798	11.2	3,441	5.8	10,644	5.9
Total Current	**665,436**	**59.3**	**665,220**	**59.7**	**32,274**	**54.4**	**95,620**	**53.0**
Fixed Assets	371,432	33.1	377,738	33.9	22,960	38.7	76,135	42.2
Other Non-current	85,284	7.6	71,313	6.4	4,094	6.9	8,660	4.8
Total Assets	**1,122,152**	**100.0**	**1,114,271**	**100.0**	**59,328**	**100.0**	**180,415**	**100.0**
Accounts Payable	159,346	14.2	173,826	15.6	6,348	10.7	22,011	12.2
Bank Loans	1,122	0.1	1,114	0.1	—	—	361	0.2
Notes Payable	54,985	4.9	36,771	3.3	4,272	7.2	10,464	5.8
Other Current	150,368	13.4	179,398	16.1	9,848	16.6	23,274	12.9
Total Current	**365,822**	**32.6**	**391,109**	**35.1**	**20,468**	**34.5**	**56,109**	**31.1**
Other Long Term	150,368	13.4	157,112	14.1	5,873	9.9	29,588	16.4
Deferred Credits	4,489	0.4	5,571	0.5	—	—	541	0.3
Net Worth	601,473	53.6	560,478	50.3	32,986	55.6	94,177	52.2
Total Liab & Net Worth	**1,122,152**	**100.0**	**1,114,271**	**100.0**	**59,328**	**100.0**	**180,415**	**100.0**
Net Sales	2,481,212	100.0	2,847,896	100.0	237,493	100.0	517,156	100.0
Gross Profit	607,897	24.5	660,712	23.2	98,797	41.6	184,625	35.7
Net Profit After Tax	116,617	4.7	136,699	4.8	22,087	9.3	34,132	6.6
Working Capital	299,614	—	274,111	—	11,806	—	39,511	—

RATIOS	SOUTH UQ	MED	LQ	WEST UQ	MED	LQ	UNDER $100,000 UQ	MED	LQ	$100,000-$250,000 UQ	MED	LQ
SOLVENCY												
Quick Ratio (times)	2.3	1.4	0.9	2.2	1.3	0.9	3.5	1.5	0.7	3.6	1.6	0.8
Current Ratio (times)	3.1	1.8	1.3	2.8	1.7	1.2	4.4	1.7	0.9	4.1	1.9	1.0
Curr Liab To Nw (%)	27.1	57.8	119.1	25.6	68.5	135.2	12.1	44.7	123.7	14.0	46.4	110.7
Curr Liab To Inv (%)	206.6	387.8	633.2	175.4	329.7	465.4	86.7	280.7	423.8	95.0	326.2	492.2
Total Liab To Nw (%)	38.5	82.9	165.4	42.1	95.4	188.8	19.5	60.7	163.8	27.2	73.3	166.9
Fixed Assets To Nw (%)	33.9	65.7	108.1	36.6	65.3	106.8	34.4	78.1	119.7	42.2	80.6	130.0
EFFICIENCY												
Coll Period (days)	32.1	49.6	71.9	33.6	51.8	71.9	14.6	21.9	49.9	15.3	34.0	51.4
Sales To Inv (times)	183.6	72.4	28.1	178.3	67.4	22.6	196.1	50.4	17.6	149.6	65.9	22.8
Assets To Sales (%)	33.0	44.3	60.2	31.8	42.8	60.2	13.0	21.9	38.2	22.5	33.5	49.4
Sales To Nwc (times)	15.9	8.7	4.8	17.8	9.3	5.1	36.2	19.1	7.8	20.6	10.3	5.5
Acct Pay To Sales (%)	3.1	5.8	9.8	3.0	5.9	10.0	1.1	2.2	6.1	1.5	3.6	7.2
PROFITABILITY												
Return On Sales (%)	8.5	3.8	1.3	8.2	3.3	1.0	19.9	8.9	2.6	14.2	6.4	1.0
Return On Assets (%)	15.1	7.4	2.4	16.1	6.8	2.1	65.1	37.2	7.3	36.2	14.7	2.7
Return On Nw (%)	34.6	15.1	5.3	36.5	15.5	4.8	116.1	70.1	22.7	75.7	30.2	4.7

SIC 16 HEAVY CONSTR CONTRS — INDUSTRY ASSETS

	$250,000–$500,000 (604) $	%	$500,000–$1,000,000 (855) $	%	$1,000,000–$5,000,000 (1618) $	%	$5,000,000–$25,000,000 (514) $	%
Cash	61,724	16.4	107,724	15.0	284,311	14.0	1,172,101	13.8
Accounts Receivable	110,651	29.4	204,675	28.5	660,007	32.5	2,709,421	31.9
Notes Receivable	4,140	1.1	5,027	0.7	10,154	0.5	42,467	0.5
Inventory	10,162	2.7	16,518	2.3	42,647	2.1	212,337	2.5
Other Current	32,744	8.7	74,688	10.4	243,695	12.0	1,274,022	15.0
Total Current	**219,420**	**58.3**	**408,632**	**56.9**	**1,240,814**	**61.1**	**5,410,348**	**63.7**
Fixed Assets	136,620	36.3	264,282	36.8	645,792	31.8	2,327,214	27.4
Other Non-current	20,324	5.4	45,244	6.3	144,186	7.1	755,920	8.9
Total Assets	**376,364**	**100.0**	**718,158**	**100.0**	**2,030,792**	**100.0**	**8,493,482**	**100.0**
Accounts Payable	51,186	13.6	94,797	13.2	335,081	16.5	1,511,840	17.8
Bank Loans	—	—	718	0.1	2,031	0.1	16,987	0.2
Notes Payable	21,076	5.6	31,599	4.4	69,047	3.4	212,337	2.5
Other Current	50,433	13.4	95,515	13.3	302,588	14.9	1,316,490	15.5
Total Current	**122,695**	**32.6**	**222,629**	**31.0**	**708,746**	**34.9**	**3,057,654**	**36.0**
Other Long Term	60,971	16.2	99,106	13.8	278,219	13.7	1,078,672	12.7
Deferred Credits	1,505	0.4	2,154	0.3	10,154	0.5	50,961	0.6
Net Worth	191,193	50.8	394,269	54.9	1,033,673	50.9	4,306,195	50.7
Total Liab & Net Worth	**376,364**	**100.0**	**718,158**	**100.0**	**2,030,792**	**100.0**	**8,493,482**	**100.0**
Net Sales	967,350	100.0	1,652,975	100.0	4,451,848	100.0	17,181,364	100.0
Gross Profit	291,172	30.1	439,691	26.6	925,984	20.8	2,439,754	14.2
Net Profit After Tax	49,335	5.1	82,649	5.0	169,170	3.8	498,260	2.9
Working Capital	96,725	—	186,003	—	532,068	—	2,352,694	—

RATIOS

	UQ	MED	LQ	UQ	MED	LQ	UQ	MED	LQ	UQ	MED	LQ
SOLVENCY												
Quick Ratio (times)	2.7	1.4	0.9	2.5	1.5	0.9	2.0	1.3	1.0	1.7	1.2	0.9
Current Ratio (times)	3.7	1.8	1.2	3.2	1.9	1.2	2.6	1.7	1.3	2.6	1.7	1.3
Curr Liab To Nw (%)	24.1	51.1	126.0	23.1	51.4	98.6	32.2	68.6	129.8	33.8	74.5	126.1
Curr Liab To Inv (%)	147.4	292.6	553.8	144.6	334.6	575.9	221.1	379.1	621.0	270.4	402.0	602.2
Total Liab To Nw (%)	35.8	84.4	180.9	35.5	75.9	150.4	48.1	99.1	185.2	47.1	108.1	194.5
Fixed Assets To Nw (%)	33.4	67.7	126.8	37.7	67.8	113.6	35.0	64.8	105.7	32.5	59.3	96.6
EFFICIENCY												
Coll Period (days)	24.8	43.8	67.2	25.6	46.4	63.9	36.5	54.8	77.8	38.7	55.9	79.9
Sales To Inv (times)	139.2	52.5	23.7	197.0	89.8	31.0	179.0	73.4	27.2	199.7	66.4	28.6
Assets To Sales (%)	28.1	38.8	56.8	32.1	42.6	57.6	35.2	45.4	61.2	37.7	48.7	62.7
Sales To Nwc (times)	16.9	8.7	5.3	15.9	7.9	4.8	15.7	9.0	5.1	16.3	9.1	4.5
Acct Pay To Sales (%)	2.1	4.7	8.2	2.0	4.0	8.3	3.6	6.5	10.6	4.5	7.6	11.7
PROFITABILITY												
Return On Sales (%)	9.6	4.9	1.2	8.6	3.6	1.3	6.5	3.1	1.1	4.8	2.4	0.8
Return On Assets (%)	20.1	9.0	2.1	15.9	8.0	3.0	12.5	6.2	2.5	9.1	4.8	1.7
Return On Nw (%)	45.6	19.2	5.7	33.0	14.8	5.8	27.7	13.0	5.1	19.8	10.6	3.6

Note: All panels are for SIC 16 HEAVY CONSTR CONTRS, INDUSTRY ASSETS, 1995.

	SIC 16 HEAVY CONSTR CONTRS $25,000,000-$50,000,000 1995 (66 Establishments)		SIC 16 HEAVY CONSTR CONTRS OVER $50,000,000 1995 (101 Establishments)		SIC 1611 HIGHWAY,ST CONSTR (NO BREAKDOWN) 1995 (1414 Establishments)		SIC 1611 HIGHWAY,ST CONSTR UNDER $100,000 1995 (64 Establishments)	
	$	%	$	%	$	%	$	%
Cash	4,644,396	13.6	9,349,511	9.5	215,949	15.0	15,151	24.5
Accounts Receivable	10,723,090	31.4	25,883,382	26.3	417,501	29.0	11,564	18.7
Notes Receivable	102,450	0.3	295,248	0.3	8,638	0.6	247	0.4
Inventory	1,195,249	3.5	2,952,477	3.0	33,112	2.3	680	1.1
Other Current	4,849,296	14.2	16,927,535	17.2	149,724	10.4	2,968	4.8
Total Current	**21,514,480**	**63.0**	**55,408,152**	**56.3**	**824,924**	**57.3**	**30,611**	**49.5**
Fixed Assets	7,786,193	22.8	24,210,312	24.6	506,760	35.2	28,199	45.6
Other Non-current	4,849,296	14.2	18,797,437	19.1	107,974	7.5	3,030	4.9
Total Assets	**34,149,969**	**100.0**	**98,415,901**	**100.0**	**1,439,658**	**100.0**	**61,840**	**100.0**
Accounts Payable	5,293,245	15.5	13,384,563	13.6	223,147	15.5	5,071	8.2
Bank Loans	34,150	0.1	—	—	2,879	0.2	—	—
Notes Payable	922,049	2.7	1,377,823	1.4	53,267	3.7	3,710	6.0
Other Current	5,942,095	17.4	18,994,269	19.3	198,673	13.8	11,379	18.4
Total Current	**12,191,539**	**35.7**	**33,756,654**	**34.3**	**477,966**	**33.2**	**20,160**	**32.6**
Other Long Term	4,917,596	14.4	14,762,385	15.0	217,388	15.1	8,719	14.1
Deferred Credits	819,599	2.4	1,377,823	1.4	7,198	0.5	—	—
Net Worth	16,221,235	47.5	48,519,039	49.3	737,105	51.2	32,961	53.3
Total Liab & Net Worth	**34,149,969**	**100.0**	**98,415,901**	**100.0**	**1,439,658**	**100.0**	**61,840**	**100.0**
Net Sales	61,855,620	100.0	158,789,739	100.0	3,291,046	100.0	318,319	100.0
Gross Profit	11,381,434	18.4	19,848,717	12.5	737,194	22.4	139,105	43.7
Net Profit After Tax	1,608,246	2.6	5,716,431	3.6	141,515	4.3	28,649	9.0
Working Capital	9,322,941	—	21,651,498	—	346,958	—	10,451	—

RATIOS	UQ	MED	LQ	UQ	MED	LQ	UQ	MED	LQ	LQ	MED	UQ
SOLVENCY												
Quick Ratio (times)	1.7	1.3	1.0	1.5	1.0	0.9	2.2	1.3	0.9	0.7	1.4	2.9
Current Ratio (times)	2.4	1.7	1.3	2.2	1.6	1.3	2.8	1.7	1.2	0.9	1.6	3.4
Curr Liab To Nw (%)	33.7	62.6	135.9	33.2	66.4	117.2	26.8	61.7	119.3	126.0	60.0	13.3
Curr Liab To Inv (%)	179.4	352.5	471.3	296.4	419.2	747.7	230.2	389.0	609.8	328.4	272.7	173.4
Total Liab To Nw (%)	49.2	112.5	198.8	52.5	105.9	186.2	42.1	93.4	184.2	169.4	72.7	23.4
Fixed Assets To Nw (%)	25.1	44.1	89.0	23.0	55.4	85.7	38.9	70.1	114.3	133.3	80.5	47.8
EFFICIENCY												
Coll Period (days)	36.1	57.9	84.2	37.2	62.8	75.8	27.4	46.7	70.8	22.1	19.9	12.6
Sales To Inv (times)	82.6	38.9	11.4	86.5	34.3	19.8	172.7	76.8	28.2	18.8	53.7	161.7
Assets To Sales (%)	43.4	55.7	73.1	46.3	68.3	111.2	32.1	42.5	59.2	21.9	16.4	12.1
Sales To Nwc (times)	13.3	7.3	3.4	12.1	6.6	4.2	19.0	10.0	5.4	14.9	23.1	36.6
Acct Pay To Sales (%)	5.5	8.5	10.4	5.9	8.9	13.3	3.2	5.8	10.0	3.4	2.2	1.5
PROFITABILITY												
Return On Sales (%)	6.2	2.6	0.2	6.1	2.5	(0.1)	6.9	3.0	1.0	3.1	8.0	15.9
Return On Assets (%)	9.8	4.3	0.5	5.6	3.1	(1.2)	13.8	6.4	2.2	14.6	43.9	65.1
Return On Nw (%)	17.9	8.6	0.8	12.8	7.1	(0.8)	28.6	13.1	4.9	29.5	92.1	135.3

SIC 1611 HIGHWAY, ST CONSTR

INDUSTRY ASSETS — 1995

	$100,000 - $250,000 (125 Establishments)		$250,000 - $500,000 (165 Establishments)		$500,000 - $1,000,000 (237 Establishments)		$1,000,000 - $5,000,000 (539 Establishments)	
	$	%	$	%	$	%	$	%
Cash	31,043	17.0	58,203	15.4	115,577	16.2	301,967	14.3
Accounts Receivable	48,026	26.3	113,005	29.9	210,465	29.5	654,613	31.0
Notes Receivable	183	0.1	6,803	1.8	2,854	0.4	10,558	0.5
Inventory	4,930	2.7	7,559	2.0	10,702	1.5	50,680	2.4
Other Current	8,217	4.5	34,015	9.0	70,631	9.9	225,947	10.7
Total Current	**92,400**	**50.6**	**219,584**	**58.1**	**410,228**	**57.5**	**1,243,765**	**58.9**
Fixed Assets	81,078	44.4	134,547	35.6	260,406	36.5	711,628	33.7
Other Non-current	9,130	5.0	23,810	6.3	42,806	6.0	156,263	7.4
Total Assets	**182,608**	**100.0**	**377,942**	**100.0**	**713,440**	**100.0**	**2,111,656**	**100.0**
Accounts Payable	23,191	12.7	62,360	16.5	102,022	14.3	352,647	16.7
Bank Loans	913	0.5	378	0.1	—	—	4,223	0.2
Notes Payable	12,965	7.1	20,787	5.5	28,538	4.0	54,903	2.6
Other Current	23,374	12.8	46,487	12.3	87,753	12.3	306,190	14.5
Total Current	**60,443**	**33.1**	**130,012**	**34.4**	**218,313**	**30.6**	**717,963**	**34.0**
Other Long Term	27,209	14.9	69,541	18.4	99,168	13.9	306,190	14.5
Deferred Credits	183	0.1	756	0.2	2,854	0.4	12,670	0.6
Net Worth	94,774	51.9	177,633	47.0	393,105	55.1	1,074,833	50.9
Total Liab & Net Worth	**182,608**	**100.0**	**377,942**	**100.0**	**713,440**	**100.0**	**2,111,656**	**100.0**
Net Sales	533,696	100.0	977,237	100.0	1,672,993	100.0	4,588,243	100.0
Gross Profit	183,058	34.3	267,763	27.4	453,381	27.1	876,354	19.1
Net Profit After Tax	29,887	5.6	42,998	4.4	81,977	4.9	178,941	3.9
Working Capital	31,957	—	89,572	—	191,915	—	525,802	—

RATIOS

	UQ	MED	LQ	UQ	MED	LQ	UQ	MED	LQ	UQ	MED	LQ
SOLVENCY												
Quick Ratio (times)	3.2	1.3	0.7	2.3	1.4	0.8	2.9	1.5	0.9	2.0	1.3	1.0
Current Ratio (times)	3.4	1.6	0.9	3.1	1.7	1.2	3.6	1.9	1.3	2.6	1.7	1.3
Curr Liab To Nw (%)	14.3	48.4	117.8	24.3	52.0	141.4	19.8	50.0	98.3	31.8	67.1	130.6
Curr Liab To Inv (%)	101.9	303.5	527.0	152.2	336.2	537.7	286.5	511.0	711.9	232.3	385.7	608.1
Total Liab To Nw (%)	25.3	65.2	165.4	40.2	93.2	226.8	33.6	77.2	149.0	49.2	103.9	195.5
Fixed Assets To Nw (%)	45.5	87.5	152.9	32.5	63.1	117.6	39.5	63.3	111.7	39.2	72.0	114.2
EFFICIENCY												
Coll Period (days)	14.1	38.9	55.2	24.4	38.9	65.1	24.5	42.3	62.4	32.1	50.7	74.1
Sales To Inv (times)	141.6	64.8	16.1	127.7	55.8	33.7	197.5	101.8	49.0	170.7	83.6	34.0
Assets To Sales (%)	21.1	32.9	51.1	25.5	36.3	53.2	31.0	40.2	54.1	35.3	44.1	60.3
Sales To Nwc (times)	23.9	9.9	5.5	17.4	9.4	5.9	16.3	8.9	4.8	18.6	10.1	5.7
Acct Pay To Sales (%)	1.5	4.5	7.4	2.6	5.2	8.8	2.0	3.9	7.6	3.5	6.3	10.5
PROFITABILITY												
Return On Sales (%)	12.4	6.1	1.3	8.3	3.6	0.6	7.4	3.4	0.9	5.9	2.5	1.0
Return On Assets (%)	31.7	15.8	4.0	20.3	8.9	1.1	14.4	7.7	3.1	11.5	5.7	2.4
Return On Nw (%)	59.9	29.4	7.6	47.6	18.7	2.3	27.1	13.4	5.2	26.2	11.9	4.6

SIC 1611 HIGHWAY,ST CONSTR — INDUSTRY ASSETS $5,000,000-$25,000,000 — 1995 (219 Establishments)
SIC 1611 HIGHWAY,ST CONSTR — INDUSTRY ASSETS $25,000,000-$50,000,000 — 1995 (30 Establishments)
SIC 1611 HIGHWAY,ST CONSTR — INDUSTRY ASSETS OVER $50,000,000 — 1995 (35 Establishments)
SIC 1622 BRDGE,TNNEL,ELV HGY (NO BREAKDOWN) — 1995 (248 Establishments)

	$5,000,000-$25,000,000 $	%	$25,000,000-$50,000,000 $	%	OVER $50,000,000 $	%	SIC 1622 $	%
Cash	1,116,958	13.1	4,599,496	13.5	6,399,009	8.0	295,057	19.6
Accounts Receivable	2,370,339	27.8	9,062,712	26.6	21,676,642	27.1	459,145	30.5
Notes Receivable	51,158	0.6	102,211	0.3	559,913	0.7	7,527	0.5
Inventory	264,318	3.1	1,192,462	3.5	2,959,542	3.7	31,613	2.1
Other Current	1,210,749	14.2	5,553,466	16.3	12,798,018	16.0	216,777	14.4
Total Current	**5,013,523**	**58.8**	**20,510,347**	**60.2**	**44,393,124**	**55.5**	**1,010,120**	**67.1**
Fixed Assets	2,771,080	32.5	9,198,993	27.0	19,916,915	24.9	391,403	26.0
Other Non-current	741,797	8.7	4,361,004	12.8	15,677,572	19.6	103,872	6.9
Total Assets	**8,526,400**	**100.0**	**34,070,344**	**100.0**	**79,987,610**	**100.0**	**1,505,395**	**100.0**
Accounts Payable	1,432,435	16.8	4,769,848	14.0	10,638,352	13.3	243,874	16.2
Bank Loans	17,053	0.2	—	—	—	—	—	—
Notes Payable	230,213	2.7	885,829	2.6	1,039,839	1.3	55,700	3.7
Other Current	1,185,170	13.9	5,110,552	15.0	12,558,055	15.7	246,885	16.4
Total Current	**2,864,870**	**33.6**	**10,766,229**	**31.6**	**24,236,246**	**30.3**	**546,458**	**36.3**
Other Long Term	1,321,592	15.5	5,519,396	16.2	11,598,203	14.5	164,088	10.9
Deferred Credits	68,211	0.8	1,056,181	3.1	639,901	0.8	7,527	0.5
Net Worth	4,271,726	50.1	16,728,539	49.1	43,513,260	54.4	787,322	52.3
Total Liab & Net Worth	**8,526,400**	**100.0**	**34,070,344**	**100.0**	**79,987,610**	**100.0**	**1,505,395**	**100.0**
Net Sales	17,002,584	100.0	61,855,620	100.0	175,465,920	100.0	2,980,046	100.0
Gross Profit	2,346,357	13.8	9,835,044	15.9	20,529,513	11.7	560,249	18.8
Net Profit After Tax	527,080	3.1	1,793,813	2.9	4,386,648	2.5	104,302	3.5
Working Capital	2,148,653	—	9,744,118	—	20,156,878	—	463,662	—

RATIOS	UQ	MED	LQ	UQ	MED	LQ	UQ	MED	LQ	UQ	MED	LQ
SOLVENCY												
Quick Ratio (times)	1.6	1.2	0.9	1.8	1.2	0.8	1.5	1.1	0.9	2.2	1.4	1.0
Current Ratio (times)	2.3	1.7	1.3	2.4	1.7	1.5	2.3	1.8	1.5	3.0	1.9	1.4
Curr Liab To Nw (%)	33.3	68.7	112.8	32.0	61.1	84.9	31.7	66.3	92.8	33.7	67.6	127.1
Curr Liab To Inv (%)	279.5	401.4	636.1	251.1	352.5	403.1	196.5	336.9	737.6	268.0	453.6	652.0
Total Liab To Nw (%)	55.2	108.7	186.2	60.6	100.0	156.3	46.6	91.0	173.0	43.8	90.0	166.8
Fixed Assets To Nw (%)	40.5	72.3	116.2	34.0	68.3	107.3	23.7	67.4	94.3	29.7	52.5	87.9
EFFICIENCY												
Coll Period (days)	29.4	50.0	72.6	41.4	49.8	79.1	43.6	58.1	83.6	33.3	50.4	77.0
Sales To Inv (times)	180.9	78.6	30.1	92.8	20.0	15.4	73.3	34.6	21.7	138.7	62.5	26.4
Assets To Sales (%)	39.3	49.8	65.2	47.8	56.8	71.7	43.6	56.7	98.6	34.7	43.4	55.7
Sales To Nwc (times)	18.4	11.0	5.2	21.4	9.3	4.4	12.1	8.9	5.6	13.8	8.5	5.0
Acct Pay To Sales (%)	4.3	7.0	11.1	7.0	9.3	10.4	5.7	6.5	9.9	3.8	6.7	10.2
PROFITABILITY												
Return On Sales (%)	5.1	2.7	1.0	6.0	2.6	0.5	3.5	2.7	(0.3)	5.9	2.5	0.8
Return On Assets (%)	9.1	5.3	2.0	8.4	5.1	3.2	5.7	4.2	(0.5)	12.2	6.4	2.2
Return On Nw (%)	18.9	11.5	4.9	12.5	10.7	7.7	11.9	7.1	(0.6)	24.2	12.3	4.2

SIC 1622 — BRDGE, TNNEL, ELV HGY

INDUSTRY ASSETS $100,000 - $250,000 — 1995 (13 Establishments)

	$	%
Cash	33,527	17.6
Accounts Receivable	56,387	29.6
Notes Receivable	—	—
Inventory	4,191	2.2
Other Current	20,002	10.5
Total Current	**114,108**	**59.9**
Fixed Assets	68,769	36.1
Other Non-current	7,620	4.0
Total Assets	**190,497**	**100.0**
Accounts Payable	31,432	16.5
Bank Loans	—	—
Notes Payable	12,573	6.6
Other Current	34,670	18.2
Total Current	**78,675**	**41.3**
Other Long Term	15,240	8.0
Deferred Credits	—	—
Net Worth	96,582	50.7
Total Liab & Net Worth	**190,497**	**100.0**
Net Sales	411,224	100.0
Gross Profit	147,629	35.9
Net Profit After Tax	24,673	6.0
Working Capital	35,433	—

RATIOS	UQ	MED	LQ
SOLVENCY			
Quick Ratio (times)	2.3	1.4	0.7
Current Ratio (times)	2.4	1.5	1.1
Curr Liab To Nw (%)	30.2	105.2	119.6
Curr Liab To Inv (%)	383.2	383.2	383.2
Total Liab To Nw (%)	42.8	125.1	170.0
Fixed Assets To Nw (%)	49.8	67.7	91.0
EFFICIENCY			
Coll Period (days)	10.8	55.2	82.1
Sales To Inv (times)	77.8	76.7	43.2
Assets To Sales (%)	38.1	44.0	60.3
Sales To Nwc (times)	14.4	11.2	9.3
Acct Pay To Sales (%)	2.5	6.0	13.3
PROFITABILITY			
Return On Sales (%)	8.1	5.7	3.3
Return On Assets (%)	16.6	8.0	6.2
Return On Nw (%)	44.8	18.3	10.0

INDUSTRY ASSETS $250,000 - $500,000 — 1995 (27 Establishments)

	$	%
Cash	98,814	26.1
Accounts Receivable	109,036	28.8
Notes Receivable	1,136	0.3
Inventory	8,329	2.2
Other Current	24,609	6.5
Total Current	**241,923**	**63.9**
Fixed Assets	121,151	32.0
Other Non-current	15,522	4.1
Total Assets	**378,597**	**100.0**
Accounts Payable	49,218	13.0
Bank Loans	—	—
Notes Payable	20,823	5.5
Other Current	60,576	16.0
Total Current	**130,616**	**34.5**
Other Long Term	44,674	11.8
Deferred Credits	1,136	0.3
Net Worth	202,171	53.4
Total Liab & Net Worth	**378,597**	**100.0**
Net Sales	1,070,241	100.0
Gross Profit	185,152	17.3
Net Profit After Tax	25,686	2.4
Working Capital	111,307	—

RATIOS	UQ	MED	LQ
SOLVENCY			
Quick Ratio (times)	2.6	1.6	1.2
Current Ratio (times)	3.4	1.9	1.4
Curr Liab To Nw (%)	21.5	77.2	120.4
Curr Liab To Inv (%)	215.5	320.1	553.8
Total Liab To Nw (%)	36.0	91.0	157.2
Fixed Assets To Nw (%)	33.3	59.6	103.0
EFFICIENCY			
Coll Period (days)	31.3	43.6	52.3
Sales To Inv (times)	192.0	48.4	19.6
Assets To Sales (%)	31.6	37.3	44.5
Sales To Nwc (times)	17.1	9.2	5.5
Acct Pay To Sales (%)	2.1	5.4	7.0
PROFITABILITY			
Return On Sales (%)	6.3	2.4	0.9
Return On Assets (%)	15.4	5.8	2.3
Return On Nw (%)	22.9	9.0	2.5

INDUSTRY ASSETS $500,000 - $1,000,000 — 1995 (49 Establishments)

	$	%
Cash	148,041	20.9
Accounts Receivable	203,999	28.8
Notes Receivable	11,333	1.6
Inventory	16,292	2.3
Other Current	89,250	12.6
Total Current	**468,914**	**66.2**
Fixed Assets	199,041	28.1
Other Non-current	40,375	5.7
Total Assets	**708,330**	**100.0**
Accounts Payable	87,833	12.4
Bank Loans	—	—
Notes Payable	14,167	2.0
Other Current	94,916	13.4
Total Current	**196,916**	**27.8**
Other Long Term	85,708	12.1
Deferred Credits	708	0.1
Net Worth	424,998	60.0
Total Liab & Net Worth	**708,330**	**100.0**
Net Sales	1,731,628	100.0
Gross Profit	344,594	19.9
Net Profit After Tax	72,728	4.2
Working Capital	271,998	—

RATIOS	UQ	MED	LQ
SOLVENCY			
Quick Ratio (times)	3.4	2.2	1.2
Current Ratio (times)	3.9	2.5	1.6
Curr Liab To Nw (%)	26.4	42.6	72.8
Curr Liab To Inv (%)	184.6	408.5	518.2
Total Liab To Nw (%)	31.8	57.9	112.9
Fixed Assets To Nw (%)	25.9	46.3	100.9
EFFICIENCY			
Coll Period (days)	36.9	44.2	62.4
Sales To Inv (times)	100.0	49.1	31.0
Assets To Sales (%)	31.0	42.7	55.7
Sales To Nwc (times)	12.2	6.9	3.7
Acct Pay To Sales (%)	2.7	4.1	7.3
PROFITABILITY			
Return On Sales (%)	6.6	2.5	0.9
Return On Assets (%)	15.2	9.3	2.1
Return On Nw (%)	24.3	13.6	3.9

INDUSTRY ASSETS $1,000,000 - $5,000,000 — 1995 (103 Establishments)

	$	%
Cash	318,082	17.1
Accounts Receivable	606,401	32.6
Notes Receivable	3,720	0.2
Inventory	39,063	2.1
Other Current	273,439	14.7
Total Current	**1,240,705**	**66.7**
Fixed Assets	478,053	25.7
Other Non-current	141,370	7.6
Total Assets	**1,860,127**	**100.0**
Accounts Payable	314,361	16.9
Bank Loans	—	—
Notes Payable	66,965	3.6
Other Current	295,760	15.9
Total Current	**677,086**	**36.4**
Other Long Term	212,054	11.4
Deferred Credits	14,881	0.8
Net Worth	956,105	51.4
Total Liab & Net Worth	**1,860,127**	**100.0**
Net Sales	4,056,313	100.0
Gross Profit	758,531	18.7
Net Profit After Tax	121,689	3.0
Working Capital	563,619	—

RATIOS	UQ	MED	LQ
SOLVENCY			
Quick Ratio (times)	1.8	1.3	1.0
Current Ratio (times)	2.4	1.8	1.4
Curr Liab To Nw (%)	38.1	71.6	122.5
Curr Liab To Inv (%)	240.3	545.6	778.2
Total Liab To Nw (%)	52.4	91.5	172.5
Fixed Assets To Nw (%)	27.8	52.4	86.6
EFFICIENCY			
Coll Period (days)	32.9	51.5	78.8
Sales To Inv (times)	165.6	75.3	28.8
Assets To Sales (%)	37.2	44.2	56.6
Sales To Nwc (times)	12.1	8.3	6.0
Acct Pay To Sales (%)	4.7	7.3	10.5
PROFITABILITY			
Return On Sales (%)	4.5	2.5	1.5
Return On Assets (%)	10.0	6.3	3.4
Return On Nw (%)	22.8	11.5	4.6

SIC 1622 BRDGE,TNNEL,ELV HGY
INDUSTRY ASSETS
$5,000,000-$25,000,000
1995 (43 Establishments)

	$	%
Cash	1,618,829	19.4
Accounts Receivable	2,686,922	32.2
Notes Receivable	8,344	0.1
Inventory	100,134	1.2
Other Current	1,618,829	19.4
Total Current	**6,033,057**	**72.3**
Fixed Assets	1,677,240	20.1
Other Non-current	634,180	7.6
Total Assets	**8,344,477**	**100.0**
Accounts Payable	1,752,340	21.0
Bank Loans	16,689	0.2
Notes Payable	258,679	3.1
Other Current	1,335,116	16.0
Total Current	**3,362,824**	**40.3**
Other Long Term	867,826	10.4
Deferred Credits	25,033	0.3
Net Worth	4,088,794	49.0
Total Liab & Net Worth	**8,344,477**	**100.0**
Net Sales	18,807,381	100.0
Gross Profit	2,538,996	13.5
Net Profit After Tax	695,873	3.7
Working Capital	2,670,233	—

RATIOS	UQ	MED	LQ
SOLVENCY			
Quick Ratio (times)	1.6	1.2	1.0
Current Ratio (times)	2.5	1.8	1.4
Curr Liab To Nw (%)	43.1	81.0	150.5
Curr Liab To Inv (%)	463.3	571.6	652.5
Total Liab To Nw (%)	53.3	114.2	187.8
Fixed Assets To Nw (%)	34.8	45.8	65.6
EFFICIENCY			
Coll Period (days)	47.2	65.0	77.2
Sales To Inv (times)	146.3	68.0	50.9
Assets To Sales (%)	36.1	43.8	52.6
Sales To Nwc (times)	15.1	10.0	4.7
Acct Pay To Sales (%)	6.5	8.1	11.6
PROFITABILITY			
Return On Sales (%)	5.2	2.5	0.8
Return On Assets (%)	9.2	6.3	2.0
Return On Nw (%)	24.7	14.6	5.2

SIC 1623 WTER,SWER,UTIL LNES
(NO BREAKDOWN)
1995 (1668 Establishments)

	$	%
Cash	145,013	15.3
Accounts Receivable	294,765	31.1
Notes Receivable	5,687	0.6
Inventory	19,904	2.1
Other Current	96,675	10.2
Total Current	**562,044**	**59.3**
Fixed Assets	325,094	34.3
Other Non-current	60,659	6.4
Total Assets	**947,797**	**100.0**
Accounts Payable	136,483	14.4
Bank Loans	948	0.1
Notes Payable	40,755	4.3
Other Current	138,378	14.6
Total Current	**316,564**	**33.4**
Other Long Term	131,744	13.9
Deferred Credits	3,791	0.4
Net Worth	495,698	52.3
Total Liab & Net Worth	**947,797**	**100.0**
Net Sales	2,320,490	100.0
Gross Profit	573,161	24.7
Net Profit After Tax	109,063	4.7
Working Capital	245,480	—

RATIOS	UQ	MED	LQ
SOLVENCY			
Quick Ratio (times)	2.5	1.4	0.9
Current Ratio (times)	3.1	1.8	1.2
Curr Liab To Nw (%)	26.7	58.9	122.6
Curr Liab To Inv (%)	177.6	336.6	580.0
Total Liab To Nw (%)	38.9	87.2	174.5
Fixed Assets To Nw (%)	37.9	66.3	111.4
EFFICIENCY			
Coll Period (days)	34.3	52.8	73.5
Sales To Inv (times)	190.6	69.3	29.5
Assets To Sales (%)	32.7	42.9	58.1
Sales To Nwc (times)	16.0	8.5	4.8
Acct Pay To Sales (%)	2.5	5.5	9.5
PROFITABILITY			
Return On Sales (%)	8.6	3.8	1.1
Return On Assets (%)	16.2	7.3	2.3
Return On Nw (%)	36.2	15.6	5.0

SIC 1623 WTER,SWER,UTIL LNES
INDUSTRY ASSETS
UNDER $100,000
1995 (78 Establishments)

	$	%
Cash	14,440	22.1
Accounts Receivable	16,400	25.1
Notes Receivable	261	0.4
Inventory	1,764	2.7
Other Current	2,940	4.5
Total Current	**35,805**	**54.8**
Fixed Assets	23,260	35.6
Other Non-current	6,272	9.6
Total Assets	**65,338**	**100.0**
Accounts Payable	6,991	10.7
Bank Loans	—	—
Notes Payable	5,815	8.9
Other Current	10,977	16.8
Total Current	**23,783**	**36.4**
Other Long Term	6,860	10.5
Deferred Credits	—	—
Net Worth	34,694	53.1
Total Liab & Net Worth	**65,338**	**100.0**
Net Sales	168,410	100.0
Gross Profit	69,890	41.5
Net Profit After Tax	11,957	7.1
Working Capital	12,022	—

RATIOS	UQ	MED	LQ
SOLVENCY			
Quick Ratio (times)	4.2	1.5	0.6
Current Ratio (times)	4.8	1.6	0.9
Curr Liab To Nw (%)	12.9	53.0	145.6
Curr Liab To Inv (%)	137.5	320.2	389.9
Total Liab To Nw (%)	21.2	70.4	227.5
Fixed Assets To Nw (%)	31.1	67.7	115.8
EFFICIENCY			
Coll Period (days)	40.5	56.8	68.5
Sales To Inv (times)	165.0	68.2	46.7
Assets To Sales (%)	24.3	37.4	60.7
Sales To Nwc (times)	15.2	9.4	4.2
Acct Pay To Sales (%)	1.6	2.3	8.1
PROFITABILITY			
Return On Sales (%)	18.3	8.9	(0.2)
Return On Assets (%)	41.9	15.0	(1.8)
Return On Nw (%)	46.5	25.7	(4.2)

SIC 1623 WTER,SWER,UTIL LNES
INDUSTRY ASSETS
$100,000 - $250,000
1995 (178 Establishments)

	$	%
Cash	37,895	21.2
Accounts Receivable	43,973	24.6
Notes Receivable	536	0.3
Inventory	3,933	2.2
Other Current	9,474	5.3
Total Current	**95,811**	**53.6**
Fixed Assets	76,505	42.8
Other Non-current	6,435	3.6
Total Assets	**178,751**	**100.0**
Accounts Payable	20,556	11.5
Bank Loans	179	0.1
Notes Payable	9,295	5.2
Other Current	20,556	11.5
Total Current	**50,587**	**28.3**
Other Long Term	30,566	17.1
Deferred Credits	179	0.1
Net Worth	97,419	54.5
Total Liab & Net Worth	**178,751**	**100.0**
Net Sales	525,892	100.0
Gross Profit	185,640	35.3
Net Profit After Tax	39,442	7.5
Working Capital	45,224	—

RATIOS	UQ	MED	LQ
SOLVENCY			
Quick Ratio (times)	4.2	1.8	0.9
Current Ratio (times)	4.8	2.0	1.1
Curr Liab To Nw (%)	12.4	42.2	100.8
Curr Liab To Inv (%)	86.2	326.2	461.4
Total Liab To Nw (%)	27.1	71.9	150.9
Fixed Assets To Nw (%)	43.6	81.7	133.5
EFFICIENCY			
Coll Period (days)	19.3	34.3	50.5
Sales To Inv (times)	165.6	78.0	24.6
Assets To Sales (%)	24.2	33.8	49.3
Sales To Nwc (times)	17.9	10.0	5.4
Acct Pay To Sales (%)	1.3	3.4	6.8
PROFITABILITY			
Return On Sales (%)	16.7	7.7	0.9
Return On Assets (%)	41.6	15.7	2.2
Return On Nw (%)	90.6	39.9	4.9

SIC 1623 — WTER, SWER, UTIL LNES — INDUSTRY ASSETS

	$250,000 - $500,000 (260 Est.) $	%	$500,000 - $1,000,000 (367 Est.) $	%	$1,000,000 - $5,000,000 (623 Est.) $	%	$5,000,000 - $25,000,000 (137 Est.) $	%
Cash	58,293	15.2	107,630	14.6	278,261	13.9	1,127,788	14.1
Accounts Receivable	122,723	32.0	210,099	28.5	678,636	33.9	2,743,484	34.3
Notes Receivable	3,835	1.0	3,686	0.5	12,011	0.6	55,989	0.7
Inventory	8,437	2.2	16,955	2.3	36,034	1.8	127,976	1.6
Other Current	30,297	7.9	74,456	10.1	248,233	12.4	1,087,795	13.6
Total Current	**223,585**	**58.3**	**412,826**	**56.0**	**1,253,175**	**62.6**	**5,143,032**	**64.3**
Fixed Assets	137,296	35.8	279,395	37.9	618,580	30.9	2,175,591	27.2
Other Non-current	22,627	5.9	44,969	6.1	130,122	6.5	679,872	8.5
Total Assets	**383,508**	**100.0**	**737,190**	**100.0**	**2,001,877**	**100.0**	**7,998,495**	**100.0**
Accounts Payable	49,089	12.8	96,572	13.1	332,312	16.6	1,319,752	16.5
Bank Loans	384	0.1	1,474	0.2	4,004	0.2	7,998	0.1
Notes Payable	19,559	5.1	32,436	4.4	72,068	3.6	191,964	2.4
Other Current	54,075	14.1	102,469	13.9	312,293	15.6	1,215,771	15.2
Total Current	**123,106**	**32.1**	**232,952**	**31.6**	**720,676**	**36.0**	**2,735,485**	**34.2**
Other Long Term	60,594	15.8	105,418	14.3	254,238	12.7	895,831	11.2
Deferred Credits	1,918	0.5	2,212	0.3	8,008	0.4	47,991	0.6
Net Worth	197,890	51.6	396,608	53.8	1,018,955	50.9	4,319,187	54.0
Total Liab & Net Worth	**383,508**	**100.0**	**737,190**	**100.0**	**2,001,877**	**100.0**	**7,998,495**	**100.0**
Net Sales	948,088	100.0	1,707,024	100.0	4,684,088	100.0	15,957,000	100.0
Gross Profit	297,700	31.4	454,068	26.6	960,238	20.5	2,553,120	16.0
Net Profit After Tax	54,989	5.8	85,351	5.0	168,627	3.6	478,710	3.0
Working Capital	100,479	—	179,874	—	532,499	—	2,407,547	—

RATIOS

	UQ	MED	LQ	UQ	MED	LQ	UQ	MED	LQ	UQ	MED	LQ
SOLVENCY												
Quick Ratio (times)	2.9	1.5	0.9	2.5	1.5	0.9	2.1	1.4	1.0	2.1	1.3	1.0
Current Ratio (times)	3.7	1.9	1.2	3.1	1.9	1.2	2.6	1.7	1.3	3.1	1.8	1.3
Curr Liab To Nw (%)	25.0	50.2	117.1	24.6	54.8	105.2	34.2	67.5	131.9	26.2	72.0	125.2
Curr Liab To Inv (%)	149.4	231.1	434.8	185.2	308.3	555.8	232.2	380.4	653.2	265.0	399.4	597.4
Total Liab To Nw (%)	36.1	82.9	168.8	36.1	79.8	155.4	48.7	96.6	180.5	37.7	105.2	172.9
Fixed Assets To Nw (%)	35.1	69.6	135.6	42.3	70.8	117.3	37.4	63.3	101.3	32.7	57.3	86.9
EFFICIENCY												
Coll Period (days)	28.5	50.4	69.4	26.7	48.8	64.1	40.5	57.5	77.8	45.8	60.4	86.4
Sales To Inv (times)	159.9	46.8	23.2	162.7	78.5	31.2	210.1	72.9	32.0	295.5	83.6	37.9
Assets To Sales (%)	28.8	41.1	58.2	32.1	41.3	54.9	34.8	44.5	58.3	39.9	50.6	65.7
Sales To Nwc (times)	15.9	8.1	4.9	17.9	8.8	5.7	15.5	8.8	4.9	13.9	7.1	3.9
Acct Pay To Sales (%)	2.1	4.5	8.1	2.0	4.1	8.1	3.4	6.5	10.8	4.3	7.8	11.5
PROFITABILITY												
Return On Sales (%)	9.7	6.1	1.5	9.1	4.0	1.3	6.6	3.4	1.1	5.6	2.3	0.7
Return On Assets (%)	20.4	9.7	3.3	17.6	9.0	3.0	13.8	6.6	2.5	8.5	3.8	1.3
Return On Nw (%)	43.4	21.9	6.3	37.5	17.7	7.1	30.8	14.6	5.1	19.6	9.6	2.9

SIC 1629 HEAVY CONSTR,NEC

	(NO BREAKDOWN) 1995 (1081 Establishments)		UNDER $100,000 1995 (67 Establishments)		$100,000 - $250,000 1995 (125 Establishments)		$250,000 - $500,000 1995 (152 Establishments)	
	$	%	$	%	$	%	$	%
Cash	154,986	15.3	17,254	32.4	36,784	21.3	63,705	17.7
Accounts Receivable	288,699	28.5	8,148	15.3	37,302	21.6	87,819	24.4
Notes Receivable	6,078	0.6	—	—	1,554	0.9	1,800	0.5
Inventory	29,376	2.9	1,757	3.3	4,317	2.5	15,476	4.3
Other Current	119,532	11.8	4,420	8.3	13,297	7.7	36,711	10.2
Total Current	**598,671**	**59.1**	**31,580**	**59.3**	**93,254**	**54.0**	**205,511**	**57.1**
Fixed Assets	336,309	33.2	19,331	36.3	69,250	40.1	139,647	38.8
Other Non-current	77,999	7.7	2,343	4.4	10,189	5.9	14,756	4.1
Total Assets	**1,012,979**	**100.0**	**53,254**	**100.0**	**172,693**	**100.0**	**359,914**	**100.0**
Accounts Payable	147,895	14.6	6,976	13.1	21,069	12.2	43,550	12.1
Bank Loans	1,013	0.1	—	—	—	—	—	—
Notes Payable	45,584	4.5	3,355	6.3	9,325	5.4	24,114	6.7
Other Current	148,908	14.7	7,935	14.9	24,868	14.4	46,429	12.9
Total Current	**343,400**	**33.9**	**18,266**	**34.3**	**55,262**	**32.0**	**114,093**	**31.7**
Other Long Term	138,778	13.7	2,769	5.2	30,394	17.6	51,828	14.4
Deferred Credits	6,078	0.6	—	—	1,382	0.8	2,519	0.7
Net Worth	524,723	51.8	32,219	60.5	85,656	49.6	191,474	53.2
Total Liab & Net Worth	**1,012,979**	**100.0**	**53,254**	**100.0**	**172,693**	**100.0**	**359,914**	**100.0**
Net Sales	2,148,985	100.0	265,133	100.0	551,360	100.0	987,332	100.0
Gross Profit	571,630	26.6	103,402	39.0	208,965	37.9	327,794	33.2
Net Profit After Tax	103,151	4.8	31,286	11.8	34,736	6.3	52,329	5.3
Working Capital	255,271	—	13,314	—	37,992	—	91,418	—

RATIOS	UQ	MED	LQ	UQ	MED	LQ	UQ	MED	LQ	UQ	MED	LQ
SOLVENCY												
Quick Ratio (times)	2.1	1.3	0.9	3.9	1.5	0.7	3.4	1.5	0.9	2.8	1.3	0.7
Current Ratio (times)	3.0	1.7	1.2	6.0	2.2	0.9	3.8	1.8	1.0	3.8	1.8	1.1
Curr Liab To Nw (%)	24.7	60.5	126.5	8.4	37.2	107.2	16.1	46.7	104.2	22.4	49.4	114.6
Curr Liab To Inv (%)	157.6	329.5	555.3	85.0	270.7	801.1	211.0	356.1	629.4	78.3	292.6	590.0
Total Liab To Nw (%)	37.6	86.3	184.4	10.5	51.4	110.2	32.8	74.8	180.1	33.3	72.3	170.2
Fixed Assets To Nw (%)	28.6	62.8	105.2	34.0	79.5	118.5	33.0	71.3	118.9	34.8	73.3	114.4
EFFICIENCY												
Coll Period (days)	30.3	51.1	75.5	6.4	14.6	20.1	14.7	29.1	40.5	18.5	37.6	63.5
Sales To Inv (times)	168.7	57.8	20.0	162.9	28.5	13.5	139.8	64.0	56.7	118.3	53.2	25.7
Assets To Sales (%)	31.9	45.8	66.3	6.9	23.8	46.0	19.4	29.6	48.2	28.1	38.8	56.8
Sales To Nwc (times)	15.0	8.2	4.4	100.2	23.0	8.0	22.4	10.9	5.6	18.2	8.7	5.1
Acct Pay To Sales (%)	2.9	5.6	10.0	1.0	1.4	5.8	1.9	3.3	6.9	2.3	4.7	7.0
PROFITABILITY												
Return On Sales (%)	8.1	3.6	1.2	29.8	11.4	4.3	13.4	6.1	0.9	10.4	4.7	1.4
Return On Assets (%)	14.3	7.0	2.4	81.2	56.1	10.9	38.7	13.0	2.6	19.5	8.9	3.8
Return On Nw (%)	34.5	13.9	5.4	127.6	81.4	38.3	79.7	26.8	3.6	48.9	18.7	9.4

SIC 1629 HEAVY CONSTR, NEC — INDUSTRY ASSETS — 1995

	$500,000 - $1,000,000 (202 Establishments)		$1,000,000 - $5,000,000 (353 Establishments)		$5,000,000-$25,000,000 (115 Establishments)		$25,000,000-$50,000,000 (25 Establishments)	
	$	%	$	%	$	%	$	%
Cash	89,501	13.0	256,019	12.9	1,196,963	12.7	5,867,559	15.8
Accounts Receivable	187,951	27.3	637,071	32.1	3,477,791	36.9	13,851,896	37.3
Notes Receivable	7,573	1.1	7,939	0.4	18,850	0.2	37,136	0.1
Inventory	23,408	3.4	47,632	2.4	263,897	2.8	482,774	1.3
Other Current	74,354	10.8	246,096	12.4	1,555,110	16.5	5,793,286	15.6
Total Current	**382,788**	**55.6**	**1,194,757**	**60.2**	**6,512,611**	**69.1**	**26,032,651**	**70.1**
Fixed Assets	256,798	37.3	635,087	32.0	1,960,381	20.8	5,941,832	16.0
Other Non-current	48,881	7.1	154,802	7.8	951,916	10.1	5,161,967	13.9
Total Assets	**688,467**	**100.0**	**1,984,646**	**100.0**	**9,424,907**	**100.0**	**37,136,450**	**100.0**
Accounts Payable	83,993	12.2	315,559	15.9	1,884,981	20.0	7,501,563	20.2
Bank Loans	—	—	1,985	0.1	18,850	0.2	—	—
Notes Payable	38,554	5.6	77,401	3.9	207,348	2.2	631,320	1.7
Other Current	91,566	13.3	281,820	14.2	1,762,458	18.7	7,501,563	20.2
Total Current	**214,113**	**31.1**	**676,764**	**34.1**	**3,873,637**	**41.1**	**15,634,445**	**42.1**
Other Long Term	92,255	13.4	289,758	14.6	933,066	9.9	5,310,512	14.3
Deferred Credits	1,377	0.2	9,923	0.5	37,700	0.4	631,320	1.7
Net Worth	380,722	55.3	1,008,200	50.8	4,580,505	48.6	15,560,173	41.9
Total Liab & Net Worth	**688,467**	**100.0**	**1,984,646**	**100.0**	**9,424,907**	**100.0**	**37,136,450**	**100.0**
Net Sales	1,441,712	100.0	3,910,494	100.0	22,085,623	100.0	72,085,000	100.0
Gross Profit	396,471	27.5	961,982	24.6	2,871,131	13.0	15,714,530	21.8
Net Profit After Tax	74,969	5.2	168,151	4.3	441,712	2.0	1,730,040	2.4
Working Capital	168,675	—	517,993	—	2,638,974	—	10,398,206	—

RATIOS

	UQ	MED	LQ	UQ	MED	LQ	UQ	MED	LQ	UQ	MED	LQ
SOLVENCY												
Quick Ratio (times)	2.2	1.3	0.8	2.1	1.3	0.9	1.6	1.2	0.9	1.5	1.3	1.0
Current Ratio (times)	3.1	1.8	1.3	2.8	1.7	1.3	2.4	1.6	1.3	2.1	1.7	1.3
Curr Liab To Nw (%)	23.3	51.3	98.1	27.3	69.7	128.0	40.7	90.1	155.6	49.1	115.7	204.7
Curr Liab To Inv (%)	76.9	144.6	435.9	176.4	332.6	551.3	228.4	373.3	487.4	576.4	694.1	779.2
Total Liab To Nw (%)	37.9	72.1	153.2	42.9	100.8	184.1	55.3	107.1	211.1	84.1	156.4	266.4
Fixed Assets To Nw (%)	31.7	69.3	116.3	29.3	62.8	103.5	17.4	47.1	78.9	13.3	29.6	49.6
EFFICIENCY												
Coll Period (days)	23.9	49.0	63.4	37.1	56.2	81.1	43.3	55.9	81.0	33.8	61.7	82.2
Sales To Inv (times)	230.9	92.0	19.3	181.0	48.3	17.1	204.9	37.9	22.0	82.6	74.9	50.7
Assets To Sales (%)	34.9	46.9	66.2	36.2	49.0	70.8	33.4	44.2	61.8	41.0	53.7	70.8
Sales To Nwc (times)	14.1	7.5	4.3	13.6	8.3	4.4	13.7	9.0	4.2	12.5	7.3	5.0
Acct Pay To Sales (%)	2.0	4.4	9.3	3.6	6.2	10.4	4.6	7.4	12.4	5.1	8.5	11.8
PROFITABILITY												
Return On Sales (%)	9.1	3.4	1.5	7.5	3.9	1.3	3.6	2.1	0.7	6.4	4.3	0.8
Return On Assets (%)	14.0	7.0	3.3	12.6	6.4	2.7	9.1	4.7	1.3	13.9	7.5	2.0
Return On Nw (%)	36.2	12.9	5.9	30.1	12.7	5.7	20.2	9.8	1.9	32.4	18.0	4.2

SIC 1629 HEAVY CONSTR,NEC — INDUSTRY ASSETS OVER $50,000,000 — 1995 (42 Establishments)

	$	%
Cash	9,407,916	8.4
Accounts Receivable	28,895,742	25.8
Notes Receivable	111,999	0.1
Inventory	2,575,977	2.3
Other Current	20,271,819	18.1
Total Current	**61,263,453**	**54.7**
Fixed Assets	28,223,748	25.2
Other Non-current	22,511,799	20.1
Total Assets	**111,999,000**	**100.0**
Accounts Payable	15,791,859	14.1
Bank Loans	111,999	0.1
Notes Payable	335,997	0.3
Other Current	21,167,811	18.9
Total Current	**37,407,666**	**33.4**
Other Long Term	15,903,858	14.2
Deferred Credits	2,351,979	2.1
Net Worth	56,335,497	50.3
Total Liab & Net Worth	**111,999,000**	**100.0**
Net Sales	223,475,000	100.0
Gross Profit	31,063,025	13.9
Net Profit After Tax	6,033,825	2.7
Working Capital	23,855,787	—

RATIOS	UQ	MED	LQ
SOLVENCY			
Quick Ratio (times)	1.3	1.0	0.8
Current Ratio (times)	2.4	1.5	1.3
Curr Liab To Nw (%)	32.0	65.9	137.0
Curr Liab To Inv (%)	318.1	409.1	611.8
Total Liab To Nw (%)	49.6	110.1	165.7
Fixed Assets To Nw (%)	14.4	51.6	78.0
EFFICIENCY			
Coll Period (days)	45.9	66.4	72.4
Sales To Inv (times)	151.4	35.9	21.1
Assets To Sales (%)	45.0	68.3	137.9
Sales To Nwc (times)	15.8	6.5	3.8
Acct Pay To Sales (%)	6.1	9.4	13.8
PROFITABILITY			
Return On Sales (%)	6.2	2.5	(0.1)
Return On Assets (%)	4.4	0.4	(6.3)
Return On Nw (%)	11.6	0.5	(4.1)

SIC 17 SPECIAL TRADE CONTRS (NO BREAKDOWN) — 1995 (2312 Establishments)

	$	%
Cash	61,884	15.6
Accounts Receivable	147,570	37.2
Notes Receivable	2,777	0.7
Inventory	31,736	8.0
Other Current	31,736	8.0
Total Current	**275,702**	**69.5**
Fixed Assets	99,174	25.0
Other Non-current	21,818	5.5
Total Assets	**396,694**	**100.0**
Accounts Payable	63,471	16.0
Bank Loans	397	0.1
Notes Payable	18,645	4.7
Other Current	60,694	15.3
Total Current	**143,207**	**36.1**
Other Long Term	47,603	12.0
Deferred Credits	793	0.2
Net Worth	205,091	51.7
Total Liab & Net Worth	**396,694**	**100.0**
Net Sales	1,308,895	100.0
Gross Profit	417,538	31.9
Net Profit After Tax	65,445	5.0
Working Capital	132,495	—

RATIOS	UQ	MED	LQ
SOLVENCY			
Quick Ratio (times)	2.8	1.5	1.0
Current Ratio (times)	3.7	2.0	1.3
Curr Liab To Nw (%)	25.5	60.6	134.7
Curr Liab To Inv (%)	112.7	236.9	454.1
Total Liab To Nw (%)	35.0	79.4	175.9
Fixed Assets To Nw (%)	18.3	38.2	75.3
EFFICIENCY			
Coll Period (days)	28.8	47.5	69.7
Sales To Inv (times)	107.5	38.7	17.7
Assets To Sales (%)	22.8	31.7	43.7
Sales To Nwc (times)	16.4	8.7	5.0
Acct Pay To Sales (%)	2.7	4.9	8.0
PROFITABILITY			
Return On Sales (%)	8.2	3.5	1.2
Return On Assets (%)	20.1	9.0	2.9
Return On Nw (%)	43.6	18.9	6.1

SIC 17 SPECIAL TRADE CONTRS NORTHEAST — 1995 (2320 Establishments)

	$	%
Cash	63,853	16.0
Accounts Receivable	161,627	40.5
Notes Receivable	1,596	0.4
Inventory	27,137	6.8
Other Current	35,917	9.0
Total Current	**290,131**	**72.7**
Fixed Assets	86,999	21.8
Other Non-current	21,949	5.5
Total Assets	**399,080**	**100.0**
Accounts Payable	72,233	18.1
Bank Loans	798	0.2
Notes Payable	15,963	4.0
Other Current	71,435	17.9
Total Current	**160,430**	**40.2**
Other Long Term	42,702	10.7
Deferred Credits	1,197	0.3
Net Worth	194,751	48.8
Total Liab & Net Worth	**399,080**	**100.0**
Net Sales	1,246,463	100.0
Gross Profit	392,636	31.5
Net Profit After Tax	49,859	4.0
Working Capital	129,701	—

RATIOS	UQ	MED	LQ
SOLVENCY			
Quick Ratio (times)	2.5	1.4	0.9
Current Ratio (times)	3.2	1.8	1.3
Curr Liab To Nw (%)	29.9	74.1	156.6
Curr Liab To Inv (%)	134.1	296.1	548.9
Total Liab To Nw (%)	38.3	94.7	191.8
Fixed Assets To Nw (%)	15.4	33.8	74.0
EFFICIENCY			
Coll Period (days)	34.3	55.9	81.4
Sales To Inv (times)	104.2	41.9	18.9
Assets To Sales (%)	23.2	32.0	45.3
Sales To Nwc (times)	16.0	8.8	5.1
Acct Pay To Sales (%)	3.0	5.7	9.8
PROFITABILITY			
Return On Sales (%)	6.8	2.7	0.8
Return On Assets (%)	17.6	7.1	1.9
Return On Nw (%)	42.0	16.8	4.2

SIC 17 SPECIAL TRADE CONTRS CENTRAL — 1995 (2339 Establishments)

	$	%
Cash	58,727	14.8
Accounts Receivable	149,197	37.6
Notes Receivable	2,381	0.6
Inventory	37,299	9.4
Other Current	28,570	7.2
Total Current	**276,173**	**69.6**
Fixed Assets	99,200	25.0
Other Non-current	21,427	5.4
Total Assets	**396,801**	**100.0**
Accounts Payable	65,075	16.4
Bank Loans	1,190	0.3
Notes Payable	21,030	5.3
Other Current	62,695	15.8
Total Current	**149,991**	**37.8**
Other Long Term	51,584	13.0
Deferred Credits	1,190	0.3
Net Worth	194,036	48.9
Total Liab & Net Worth	**396,801**	**100.0**
Net Sales	1,435,944	100.0
Gross Profit	446,579	31.1
Net Profit After Tax	67,489	4.7
Working Capital	126,182	—

RATIOS	UQ	MED	LQ
SOLVENCY			
Quick Ratio (times)	2.5	1.4	0.9
Current Ratio (times)	3.3	1.9	1.3
Curr Liab To Nw (%)	27.8	66.9	150.3
Curr Liab To Inv (%)	112.2	226.3	460.0
Total Liab To Nw (%)	38.6	90.4	191.3
Fixed Assets To Nw (%)	19.0	39.3	84.9
EFFICIENCY			
Coll Period (days)	29.9	47.8	71.5
Sales To Inv (times)	84.5	34.4	15.2
Assets To Sales (%)	24.0	31.8	43.4
Sales To Nwc (times)	15.9	8.7	5.5
Acct Pay To Sales (%)	2.9	4.8	8.1
PROFITABILITY			
Return On Sales (%)	6.7	3.3	1.0
Return On Assets (%)	18.5	8.3	2.6
Return On Nw (%)	40.5	17.6	6.2

SIC 17 SPECIAL TRADE CONTRS

	SOUTH 1995 (2304 Establishments) $	%	WEST 1995 (2278 Establishments) $	%	INDUSTRY ASSETS UNDER $100,000 1995 (1980 Establishments) $	%	INDUSTRY ASSETS $100,000 - $250,000 1995 (2421 Establishments) $	%
Cash	67,777	17.2	61,644	15.8	13,518	25.7	29,098	17.1
Accounts Receivable	139,101	35.3	147,476	37.8	11,783	22.4	59,386	34.9
Notes Receivable	2,758	0.7	2,731	0.7	263	0.5	1,191	0.7
Inventory	27,978	7.1	28,091	7.2	3,314	6.3	14,804	8.7
Other Current	33,889	8.6	31,992	8.2	2,630	5.0	10,550	6.2
Total Current	**271,503**	**68.9**	**271,934**	**69.7**	**31,508**	**59.9**	**115,029**	**67.6**
Fixed Assets	99,301	25.2	95,977	24.6	18,358	34.9	46,454	27.3
Other Non-current	23,249	5.9	22,238	5.7	2,735	5.2	8,678	5.1
Total Assets	**394,053**	**100.0**	**390,149**	**100.0**	**52,601**	**100.0**	**170,161**	**100.0**
Accounts Payable	59,502	15.1	61,644	15.8	6,049	11.5	26,715	15.7
Bank Loans	394	0.1	390	0.1	53	0.1	510	0.3
Notes Payable	20,097	5.1	13,265	3.4	2,893	5.5	8,678	5.1
Other Current	57,532	14.6	62,814	16.1	9,205	17.5	23,652	13.9
Total Current	**137,524**	**34.9**	**138,113**	**35.4**	**18,200**	**34.6**	**59,556**	**35.0**
Other Long Term	46,104	11.7	45,257	11.6	7,101	13.5	22,631	13.3
Deferred Credits	788	0.2	1,170	0.3	—	—	340	0.2
Net Worth	209,636	53.2	205,609	52.7	27,300	51.9	87,633	51.5
Total Liab & Net Worth	**394,053**	**100.0**	**390,149**	**100.0**	**52,601**	**100.0**	**170,161**	**100.0**
Net Sales	1,356,345	100.0	1,419,223	100.0	318,584	100.0	636,426	100.0
Gross Profit	435,387	32.1	425,767	30.0	130,619	41.0	241,842	38.0
Net Profit After Tax	67,817	5.0	79,476	5.6	22,301	7.0	36,276	5.7
Working Capital	133,979	—	133,821	—	13,308	—	55,473	—

RATIOS	UQ	MED	LQ	UQ	MED	LQ	UQ	MED	LQ	UQ	MED	LQ
SOLVENCY												
Quick Ratio (times)	2.9	1.5	1.0	2.8	1.6	1.0	3.5	1.5	0.7	3.3	1.5	0.9
Current Ratio (times)	3.7	2.0	1.4	3.8	2.0	1.4	4.7	1.9	1.0	4.4	2.1	1.3
Curr Liab To Nw (%)	23.2	58.1	126.1	23.1	59.0	127.4	15.1	44.4	107.6	18.8	51.5	123.8
Curr Liab To Inv (%)	113.5	234.9	458.1	117.0	233.4	449.9	79.9	192.2	399.8	95.5	200.3	410.6
Total Liab To Nw (%)	32.6	78.0	166.4	33.0	81.1	167.5	21.7	61.0	160.4	28.8	70.8	170.8
Fixed Assets To Nw (%)	18.1	38.3	77.4	16.6	36.4	79.8	27.6	60.5	115.0	20.7	45.1	88.4
EFFICIENCY												
Coll Period (days)	28.1	46.4	66.1	29.9	48.9	71.5	13.5	25.9	41.3	22.6	35.8	55.5
Sales To Inv (times)	108.4	43.0	17.9	102.3	42.6	19.0	109.6	51.3	23.1	92.6	38.5	17.0
Assets To Sales (%)	21.6	30.3	41.7	22.9	31.5	42.3	10.1	16.1	25.0	19.0	25.9	36.6
Sales To Nwc (times)	16.4	9.0	5.4	15.4	8.8	5.4	36.7	16.3	8.6	19.6	9.8	5.6
Acct Pay To Sales (%)	2.8	4.7	7.8	2.8	4.9	8.1	1.4	3.1	5.5	2.1	4.1	7.0
PROFITABILITY												
Return On Sales (%)	8.5	3.8	1.3	9.5	4.0	1.3	14.6	6.2	1.3	10.8	4.5	1.2
Return On Assets (%)	21.3	9.1	3.2	22.5	9.4	3.3	68.1	25.2	4.6	29.7	13.3	2.9
Return On Nw (%)	43.4	19.1	6.6	50.2	21.0	7.7	119.8	50.9	10.0	68.1	26.4	6.5

SIC 17 — SPECIAL TRADE CONTRS — INDUSTRY ASSETS $250,000 - $500,000 — 1995 (2387 Establishments)

	$	%
Cash	53,105	14.9
Accounts Receivable	137,931	38.7
Notes Receivable	2,495	0.7
Inventory	31,364	8.8
Other Current	27,800	7.8
Total Current	**252,695**	**70.9**
Fixed Assets	84,113	23.6
Other Non-current	19,603	5.5
Total Assets	**356,411**	**100.0**
Accounts Payable	59,521	16.7
Bank Loans	356	0.1
Notes Payable	15,326	4.3
Other Current	48,115	13.5
Total Current	**123,318**	**34.6**
Other Long Term	43,126	12.1
Deferred Credits	713	0.2
Net Worth	189,254	53.1
Total Lia & Net Worth	**356,411**	**100.0**
Net Sales	1,148,497	100.0
Gross Profit	377,856	32.9
Net Profit After Tax	58,573	5.1
Working Capital	129,377	—

RATIOS	UQ	MED	LQ
SOLVENCY			
Quick Ratio (times)	3.0	1.6	1.0
Current Ratio (times)	4.0	2.2	1.4
Curr Liab To Nw (%)	22.4	53.2	120.5
Curr Liab To Inv (%)	109.2	223.6	443.7
Total Liab To Nw (%)	30.8	74.3	164.9
Fixed Assets To Nw (%)	18.0	35.9	73.1
EFFICIENCY			
Coll Period (days)	29.9	44.9	64.2
Sales To Inv (times)	84.8	34.4	15.3
Assets To Sales (%)	23.3	31.1	43.2
Sales To Nwc (times)	15.4	8.6	5.0
Acct Pay To Sales (%)	2.6	4.7	7.8
PROFITABILITY			
Return On Sales (%)	8.5	3.9	1.4
Return On Assets (%)	19.4	10.0	3.5
Return On Nw (%)	43.2	20.5	7.2

SIC 17 — SPECIAL TRADE CONTRS — INDUSTRY ASSETS $500,000 - $1,000,000 — 1995 (2167 Establishments)

	$	%
Cash	93,956	13.8
Accounts Receivable	281,188	41.3
Notes Receivable	3,404	0.5
Inventory	53,106	7.8
Other Current	63,999	9.4
Total Current	**495,653**	**72.8**
Fixed Assets	145,700	21.4
Other Non-current	39,489	5.8
Total Assets	**680,842**	**100.0**
Accounts Payable	115,062	16.9
Bank Loans	1,362	0.2
Notes Payable	26,553	3.9
Other Current	102,126	15.0
Total Current	**245,103**	**36.0**
Other Long Term	74,893	11.0
Deferred Credits	2,043	0.3
Net Worth	358,804	52.7
Total Lia & Net Worth	**680,842**	**100.0**
Net Sales	1,975,266	100.0
Gross Profit	576,778	29.2
Net Profit After Tax	82,961	4.2
Working Capital	250,550	—

RATIOS	UQ	MED	LQ
SOLVENCY			
Quick Ratio (times)	2.6	1.6	1.0
Current Ratio (times)	3.5	2.1	1.5
Curr Liab To Nw (%)	26.9	61.1	127.1
Curr Liab To Inv (%)	133.7	255.2	484.7
Total Liab To Nw (%)	36.6	80.8	167.3
Fixed Assets To Nw (%)	16.3	31.8	65.4
EFFICIENCY			
Coll Period (days)	35.8	52.2	73.7
Sales To Inv (times)	94.4	36.1	17.7
Assets To Sales (%)	27.2	34.5	46.3
Sales To Nwc (times)	12.6	7.8	4.9
Acct Pay To Sales (%)	2.9	5.0	8.5
PROFITABILITY			
Return On Sales (%)	6.9	3.1	1.2
Return On Assets (%)	15.9	7.9	2.7
Return On Nw (%)	33.7	16.1	5.3

SIC 17 — SPECIAL TRADE CONTRS — INDUSTRY ASSETS $1,000,000 - $5,000,000 — 1995 (2246 Establishments)

	$	%
Cash	196,223	11.9
Accounts Receivable	753,561	45.7
Notes Receivable	11,543	0.7
Inventory	100,585	6.1
Other Current	191,276	11.6
Total Current	**1,253,186**	**76.0**
Fixed Assets	293,509	17.8
Other Non-current	102,234	6.2
Total Assets	**1,648,929**	**100.0**
Accounts Payable	311,648	18.9
Bank Loans	3,298	0.2
Notes Payable	67,606	4.1
Other Current	308,350	18.7
Total Current	**690,901**	**41.9**
Other Long Term	154,999	9.4
Deferred Credits	6,596	0.4
Net Worth	796,433	48.3
Total Lia & Net Worth	**1,648,929**	**100.0**
Net Sales	4,563,410	100.0
Gross Profit	1,063,275	23.3
Net Profit After Tax	168,846	3.7
Working Capital	562,285	—

RATIOS	UQ	MED	LQ
SOLVENCY			
Quick Ratio (times)	2.1	1.4	1.0
Current Ratio (times)	2.7	1.8	1.4
Curr Liab To Nw (%)	41.1	88.0	161.3
Curr Liab To Inv (%)	189.3	353.7	586.1
Total Liab To Nw (%)	52.7	108.8	197.2
Fixed Assets To Nw (%)	13.8	29.1	61.1
EFFICIENCY			
Coll Period (days)	47.0	63.9	83.6
Sales To Inv (times)	124.9	47.7	21.8
Assets To Sales (%)	29.2	37.8	51.1
Sales To Nwc (times)	13.6	7.9	4.9
Acct Pay To Sales (%)	3.8	6.3	10.0
PROFITABILITY			
Return On Sales (%)	5.8	2.4	0.9
Return On Assets (%)	12.6	5.7	2.2
Return On Nw (%)	27.8	13.2	5.1

SIC 17 — SPECIAL TRADE CONTRS — INDUSTRY ASSETS $5,000,000 - $25,000,000 — 1995 (643 Establishments)

	$	%
Cash	711,142	9.1
Accounts Receivable	3,805,781	48.7
Notes Receivable	31,259	0.4
Inventory	359,478	4.6
Other Current	1,172,212	15.0
Total Current	**6,079,872**	**77.8**
Fixed Assets	1,094,064	14.0
Other Non-current	640,809	8.2
Total Assets	**7,814,745**	**100.0**
Accounts Payable	1,656,726	21.2
Bank Loans	15,629	0.2
Notes Payable	390,737	5.0
Other Current	1,625,467	20.8
Total Current	**3,688,560**	**47.2**
Other Long Term	703,327	9.0
Deferred Credits	23,444	0.3
Net Worth	3,399,414	43.5
Total Lia & Net Worth	**7,814,745**	**100.0**
Net Sales	19,083,409	100.0
Gross Profit	3,377,763	17.7
Net Profit After Tax	648,836	3.4
Working Capital	2,391,312	—

RATIOS	UQ	MED	LQ
SOLVENCY			
Quick Ratio (times)	1.6	1.2	0.9
Current Ratio (times)	2.1	1.6	1.3
Curr Liab To Nw (%)	61.0	118.7	212.8
Curr Liab To Inv (%)	213.8	396.1	640.3
Total Liab To Nw (%)	79.9	148.6	251.8
Fixed Assets To Nw (%)	11.5	25.4	52.2
EFFICIENCY			
Coll Period (days)	58.9	73.9	92.0
Sales To Inv (times)	175.7	74.9	24.9
Assets To Sales (%)	32.5	39.6	53.8
Sales To Nwc (times)	14.2	8.7	5.1
Acct Pay To Sales (%)	4.5	7.7	11.5
PROFITABILITY			
Return On Sales (%)	4.8	2.1	0.7
Return On Assets (%)	10.7	5.0	1.7
Return On Nw (%)	24.5	12.2	5.1

SIC 17 SPECIAL TRADE CONTRS — INDUSTRY ASSETS $25,000,000-$50,000,000 — 1995 (45 Establishments) / SIC 17 SPECIAL TRADE CONTRS — INDUSTRY ASSETS OVER $50,000,000 — 1995 (35 Establishments) / SIC 1711 PLBNG,HTNG,AIR-COND (NO BREAKDOWN) — 1995 (2099 Establishments) / SIC 1711 PLBNG,HTNG,AIR-COND — INDUSTRY ASSETS UNDER $100,000 — 1995 (1028 Establishments)

	SIC 17 $25M-$50M $	%	SIC 17 OVER $50M $	%	SIC 1711 NO BREAKDOWN $	%	SIC 1711 UNDER $100,000 $	%
Cash	3,595,019	10.9	3,501,332	4.6	62,687	16.7	13,409	24.6
Accounts Receivable	15,006,731	45.5	32,958,187	43.3	142,641	38.0	12,428	22.8
Notes Receivable	131,927	0.4	76,116	0.1	1,501	0.4	218	0.4
Inventory	1,121,382	3.4	4,414,722	5.8	36,411	9.7	4,851	8.9
Other Current	5,178,147	15.7	11,265,154	14.8	28,528	7.6	2,180	4.0
Total Current	**25,033,207**	**75.9**	**52,215,511**	**68.6**	**271,769**	**72.4**	**33,088**	**60.7**
Fixed Assets	4,617,456	14.0	14,918,717	19.6	83,708	22.3	18,642	34.2
Other Non-current	3,331,165	10.1	8,981,677	11.8	19,895	5.3	2,780	5.1
Total Assets	**32,981,827**	**100.0**	**76,115,905**	**100.0**	**375,372**	**100.0**	**54,510**	**100.0**
Accounts Payable	7,256,002	22.0	14,157,558	18.6	70,570	18.8	7,250	13.3
Bank Loans	—	—	152,232	0.2	375	0.1	55	0.1
Notes Payable	1,121,382	3.4	1,141,739	1.5	15,766	4.2	3,107	5.7
Other Current	6,431,456	19.5	16,364,920	21.5	57,057	15.2	9,321	17.1
Total Current	**14,808,840**	**44.9**	**31,816,448**	**41.8**	**143,767**	**38.3**	**19,733**	**36.2**
Other Long Term	3,430,110	10.4	16,288,804	21.4	42,042	11.2	7,577	13.9
Deferred Credits	65,964	0.2	304,464	0.4	751	0.2	—	—
Net Worth	14,676,913	44.5	27,706,189	36.4	188,812	50.3	27,200	49.9
Total Liab & Net Worth	**32,981,827**	**100.0**	**76,115,905**	**100.0**	**375,372**	**100.0**	**54,510**	**100.0**
Net Sales	76,156,000	100.0	179,285,000	100.0	1,373,030	100.0	332,494	100.0
Gross Profit	11,194,932	14.7	42,849,115	23.9	422,893	30.8	137,985	41.5
Net Profit After Tax	2,284,680	3.0	1,972,135	1.1	56,294	4.1	20,282	6.1
Working Capital	10,224,367	—	20,399,063	—	128,002	—	13,355	—

RATIOS	UQ	MED	LQ	UQ	MED	LQ	UQ	MED	LQ	UQ	MED	LQ
SOLVENCY												
Quick Ratio (times)	1.7	1.3	1.1	1.6	1.1	0.8	2.5	1.5	1.0	3.0	1.4	0.7
Current Ratio (times)	2.6	1.6	1.3	2.0	1.7	1.3	3.4	2.0	1.3	4.0	1.8	1.0
Curr Liab To Nw (%)	43.9	120.2	227.2	71.5	104.0	223.1	28.7	64.6	147.3	19.1	49.2	127.2
Curr Liab To Inv (%)	190.1	240.8	554.9	247.0	375.9	505.7	119.6	236.1	447.3	90.9	197.7	424.1
Total Liab To Nw (%)	58.1	149.3	269.1	105.2	195.6	339.7	37.5	84.4	182.7	27.6	70.5	166.6
Fixed Assets To Nw (%)	14.6	28.3	56.2	19.5	42.6	84.7	17.4	36.3	71.1	28.6	59.9	124.5
EFFICIENCY												
Coll Period (days)	69.4	85.1	97.1	72.3	79.9	97.5	29.2	46.0	67.9	13.5	23.4	35.9
Sales To Inv (times)	271.4	103.8	58.9	99.2	25.8	19.9	96.0	36.5	17.8	108.4	52.1	22.9
Assets To Sales (%)	35.2	40.1	63.2	36.1	46.4	78.0	22.6	30.1	39.5	11.1	16.4	25.3
Sales To Nwc (times)	12.6	7.2	3.3	13.6	8.0	6.0	16.3	9.4	5.7	35.3	16.8	9.8
Acct Pay To Sales (%)	6.5	10.5	13.3	7.0	8.5	13.4	3.2	5.4	9.0	1.9	3.7	5.9
PROFITABILITY												
Return On Sales (%)	2.1	1.4	0.5	3.2	2.3	1.0	6.7	2.8	0.9	12.8	5.1	1.0
Return On Assets (%)	4.6	2.2	1.2	6.9	3.6	1.5	17.1	7.4	2.4	54.1	21.3	2.4
Return On Nw (%)	10.1	5.4	2.4	16.6	10.5	4.4	37.2	16.0	5.3	92.7	42.8	7.4

SIC 1711 PLBNG, HTNG, AIR-COND — INDUSTRY ASSETS

Balance Sheet

	$100,000 – $250,000 1995 (1414 Establishments) $	%	$250,000 – $500,000 1995 (1343 Establishments) $	%	$500,000 – $1,000,000 1995 (1151 Establishments) $	%	$1,000,000 – $5,000,000 1995 (1173 Establishments) $	%
Cash	30,630	17.7	56,631	15.9	98,068	14.2	214,709	12.6
Accounts Receivable	60,049	34.7	136,058	38.2	291,442	42.2	824,755	48.4
Notes Receivable	692	0.4	2,137	0.6	3,453	0.5	8,520	0.5
Inventory	19,728	11.4	40,604	11.4	73,206	10.6	117,579	6.9
Other Current	9,172	5.3	24,220	6.8	62,156	9.0	213,005	12.5
Total Current	**120,271**	**69.5**	**259,649**	**72.9**	**528,325**	**76.5**	**1,378,568**	**80.9**
Fixed Assets	45,340	26.2	76,221	21.4	123,621	17.9	231,749	13.6
Other Non-current	7,441	4.3	20,302	5.7	38,675	5.6	93,722	5.5
Total Assets	**173,052**	**100.0**	**356,172**	**100.0**	**690,621**	**100.0**	**1,704,040**	**100.0**
Accounts Payable	30,976	17.9	65,892	18.5	138,124	20.0	397,041	23.3
Bank Loans	346	0.2	356	0.1	2,072	0.3	3,408	0.2
Notes Payable	8,133	4.7	14,247	4.0	25,553	3.7	57,937	3.4
Other Current	22,843	13.2	46,659	13.1	105,665	15.3	333,992	19.6
Total Current	**62,299**	**36.0**	**127,153**	**35.7**	**271,414**	**39.3**	**792,379**	**46.5**
Other Long Term	24,573	14.2	43,453	12.2	64,228	9.3	124,395	7.3
Deferred Credits	346	0.2	356	0.1	2,072	0.3	6,816	0.4
Net Worth	85,834	49.6	185,209	52.0	352,907	51.1	780,450	45.8
Total Liab & Net Worth	**173,052**	**100.0**	**356,172**	**100.0**	**690,621**	**100.0**	**1,704,040**	**100.0**
Net Sales	664,839	100.0	1,200,344	100.0	2,120,865	100.0	5,105,157	100.0
Gross Profit	251,309	37.8	397,314	33.1	602,326	28.4	1,097,609	21.5
Net Profit After Tax	34,572	5.2	52,815	4.4	74,230	3.5	137,839	2.7
Working Capital	57,972	—	132,496	—	256,911	—	586,189	—

RATIOS

	$100,000–$250,000 UQ	MED	LQ	$250,000–$500,000 UQ	MED	LQ	$500,000–$1,000,000 UQ	MED	LQ	$1,000,000–$5,000,000 UQ	MED	LQ
SOLVENCY												
Quick Ratio (times)	3.0	1.6	0.9	2.7	1.5	1.0	2.3	1.5	1.0	1.9	1.3	1.0
Current Ratio (times)	4.0	2.2	1.3	3.6	2.2	1.5	3.2	2.0	1.5	2.5	1.7	1.4
Curr Liab To Nw (%)	22.5	54.6	123.4	26.0	56.7	125.5	32.7	68.9	147.8	53.6	105.9	184.8
Curr Liab To Inv (%)	104.4	204.8	385.6	113.0	208.2	409.5	140.1	268.8	477.0	209.7	376.6	601.1
Total Liab To Nw (%)	34.1	76.5	167.1	35.0	74.9	169.4	41.6	88.9	182.7	62.9	126.0	216.6
Fixed Assets To Nw (%)	21.7	44.3	88.3	18.1	35.8	68.0	15.7	29.7	57.1	12.5	25.3	47.5
EFFICIENCY												
Coll Period (days)	21.9	33.2	49.6	28.5	40.9	59.0	34.6	50.0	70.9	45.6	61.0	81.0
Sales To Inv (times)	81.4	34.6	16.3	70.9	30.7	15.4	77.6	32.7	16.1	125.1	48.9	23.5
Assets To Sales (%)	19.1	24.7	33.4	23.0	29.6	38.9	26.3	32.6	42.4	27.7	33.7	43.1
Sales To Nwc (times)	19.9	10.6	6.2	15.2	8.9	5.5	13.6	8.4	5.0	14.7	9.0	5.7
Acct Pay To Sales (%)	2.6	4.3	6.9	3.1	5.0	8.1	3.6	5.8	9.3	4.7	7.4	11.2
PROFITABILITY												
Return On Sales (%)	9.7	4.1	1.1	6.9	3.2	1.1	5.8	2.7	1.1	4.4	1.8	0.7
Return On Assets (%)	29.9	13.8	3.3	17.6	9.0	3.0	13.3	7.1	2.7	10.2	4.9	1.9
Return On Nw (%)	71.5	29.0	9.2	41.4	18.5	6.7	30.3	14.3	5.3	25.0	12.1	4.4

	SIC 1711 PLBNG,HTNG,AIR-COND INDUSTRY ASSETS $5,000,000-$25,000,000 1995 (165 Establishments)		SIC 1711 PLBNG,HTNG,AIR-COND INDUSTRY ASSETS $25,000,000-$50,000,000 1995 (16 Establishments)		SIC 1721 PNTNG,PAPER HANGING (NO BREAKDOWN) INDUSTRY ASSETS 1995 (1012 Establishments)		SIC 1721 PNTNG,PAPER HANGING INDUSTRY ASSETS UNDER $100,000 1995 (241 Establishments)	
	$	%	$	%	$	%	$	%
Cash	814,282	10.2	4,222,082	14.2	54,530	17.5	13,977	26.8
Accounts Receivable	4,215,108	52.8	14,955,686	50.3	118,720	38.1	11,474	22.0
Notes Receivable	23,949	0.3	297,330	1.0	1,870	0.6	209	0.4
Inventory	343,276	4.3	386,529	1.3	9,660	3.1	1,252	2.4
Other Current	1,229,406	15.4	5,143,805	17.3	27,732	8.9	4,224	8.1
Total Current	**6,626,022**	**83.0**	**25,005,431**	**84.1**	**212,512**	**68.2**	**31,135**	**59.7**
Fixed Assets	782,350	9.8	2,289,439	7.7	78,835	25.3	17,628	33.8
Other Non-current	574,787	7.2	2,438,104	8.2	20,254	6.5	3,390	6.5
Total Assets	**7,983,159**	**100.0**	**29,732,974**	**100.0**	**311,601**	**100.0**	**52,153**	**100.0**
Accounts Payable	1,995,790	25.0	8,652,295	29.1	32,407	10.4	3,964	7.6
Bank Loans	7,983	0.1	—	—	935	0.3	209	0.4
Notes Payable	255,461	3.2	654,125	2.2	14,645	4.7	3,442	6.6
Other Current	1,860,076	23.3	5,887,129	19.8	48,298	15.5	7,719	14.8
Total Current	**4,119,310**	**51.6**	**15,193,550**	**51.1**	**96,285**	**30.9**	**15,333**	**29.4**
Other Long Term	550,838	6.9	2,794,900	9.4	33,030	10.6	5,737	11.0
Deferred Credits	23,949	0.3	—	—	935	0.3	52	0.1
Net Worth	3,289,062	41.2	11,744,525	39.5	181,352	58.2	31,031	59.5
Total Liab & Net Worth	**7,983,159**	**100.0**	**29,732,974**	**100.0**	**311,601**	**100.0**	**52,153**	**100.0**
Net Sales	21,842,842	100.0	77,498,400	100.0	986,681	100.0	302,921	100.0
Gross Profit	3,625,912	16.6	9,532,303	12.3	356,192	36.1	139,950	46.2
Net Profit After Tax	567,914	2.6	1,317,473	1.7	62,161	6.3	29,383	9.7
Working Capital	2,506,712	—	9,811,881	—	116,227	—	15,802	—

RATIOS	UQ	MED	LQ	UQ	MED	LQ	UQ	MED	LQ	UQ	MED	LQ
SOLVENCY												
Quick Ratio (times)	1.5	1.2	1.0	1.6	1.3	1.2	3.9	2.0	1.1	4.5	2.1	1.0
Current Ratio (times)	1.9	1.5	1.3	1.9	1.6	1.3	4.8	2.4	1.5	5.5	2.3	1.2
Curr Liab To Nw (%)	83.2	137.9	223.4	109.1	153.1	261.4	18.0	43.2	91.6	9.1	33.2	74.8
Curr Liab To Inv (%)	309.8	508.8	640.3	738.7	738.7	738.7	139.2	311.3	528.1	76.3	203.3	496.6
Total Liab To Nw (%)	97.4	163.2	250.6	137.4	183.9	278.7	24.1	58.8	122.6	12.3	43.2	90.2
Fixed Assets To Nw (%)	12.4	22.2	36.5	13.4	21.5	36.4	16.9	35.8	68.8	24.5	53.9	90.9
EFFICIENCY												
Coll Period (days)	61.8	76.0	90.2	86.5	95.6	97.1	33.6	56.9	80.3	9.7	25.2	46.2
Sales To Inv (times)	140.3	80.4	34.5	316.8	253.6	107.8	176.6	69.3	29.4	314.3	84.4	32.9
Assets To Sales (%)	31.2	35.6	45.0	32.5	39.0	46.8	23.5	33.1	48.0	9.0	16.9	23.6
Sales To Nwc (times)	14.8	9.9	6.6	13.1	9.6	6.7	13.6	7.2	4.3	41.3	16.4	7.0
Acct Pay To Sales (%)	5.4	8.0	12.0	7.9	12.1	14.3	1.7	3.2	6.0	0.7	1.6	3.4
PROFITABILITY												
Return On Sales (%)	3.3	1.8	0.6	2.1	1.3	(0.4)	11.5	4.9	1.2	25.5	8.4	1.8
Return On Assets (%)	9.3	3.8	1.7	4.3	1.9	(1.4)	24.3	10.7	2.6	81.2	41.1	3.2
Return On Nw (%)	22.5	11.0	5.1	11.1	3.5	(12.7)	45.8	20.4	5.4	145.7	61.7	7.9

SIC 1721 PNTNG, PAPER HANGING

	$100,000 - $250,000 (219 Establishments)		$250,000 - $500,000 (216 Establishments)		$500,000 - $1,000,000 (164 Establishments)		$1,000,000 - $5,000,000 (164 Establishments)	
	$	%	$	%	$	%	$	%
Cash	27,665	16.5	53,318	14.8	98,377	14.8	210,342	13.2
Accounts Receivable	64,719	38.6	160,313	44.5	289,812	43.6	720,263	45.2
Notes Receivable	1,677	1.0	3,242	0.9	3,988	0.6	3,187	0.2
Inventory	5,868	3.5	10,447	2.9	19,277	2.9	57,366	3.6
Other Current	9,725	5.8	31,342	8.7	62,482	9.4	216,716	13.6
Total Current	**109,654**	**65.4**	**258,663**	**71.8**	**473,936**	**71.3**	**1,207,875**	**75.8**
Fixed Assets	46,947	28.0	84,300	23.4	142,247	21.4	278,863	17.5
Other Non-current	11,066	6.6	17,292	4.8	48,524	7.3	106,765	6.7
Total Assets	**167,667**	**100.0**	**360,255**	**100.0**	**664,707**	**100.0**	**1,593,502**	**100.0**
Accounts Payable	16,264	9.7	43,591	12.1	70,459	10.6	194,407	12.2
Bank Loans	503	0.3	721	0.2	1,329	0.2	4,781	0.3
Notes Payable	8,551	5.1	14,050	3.9	20,606	3.1	73,301	4.6
Other Current	24,144	14.4	54,399	15.1	107,018	16.1	285,237	17.9
Total Current	**49,462**	**29.5**	**112,760**	**31.3**	**199,412**	**30.0**	**557,726**	**35.0**
Other Long Term	19,449	11.6	31,342	8.7	71,788	10.8	165,724	10.4
Deferred Credits	168	0.1	1,441	0.4	3,324	0.5	7,968	0.5
Net Worth	98,588	58.8	214,712	59.6	390,183	58.7	862,085	54.1
Total Liab & Net Worth	**167,667**	**100.0**	**360,255**	**100.0**	**664,707**	**100.0**	**1,593,502**	**100.0**
Net Sales	601,593	100.0	1,035,110	100.0	1,752,508	100.0	3,718,928	100.0
Gross Profit	254,474	42.3	350,902	33.9	552,040	31.5	1,056,176	28.4
Net Profit After Tax	33,088	5.5	61,071	5.9	91,130	5.2	223,136	6.0
Working Capital	60,192	—	145,903	—	274,524	—	650,149	—

RATIOS	UQ	MED	LQ	UQ	MED	LQ	UQ	MED	LQ	UQ	MED	LQ
SOLVENCY												
Quick Ratio (times)	4.3	2.2	1.2	3.9	2.2	1.2	3.6	1.9	1.3	3.1	1.7	1.1
Current Ratio (times)	5.2	2.5	1.4	4.7	2.7	1.6	4.6	2.3	1.6	3.9	2.4	1.5
Curr Liab To Nw (%)	18.0	37.5	77.0	20.6	40.1	94.8	21.3	49.4	91.8	25.2	57.5	127.8
Curr Liab To Inv (%)	122.5	228.7	489.7	142.5	379.6	575.3	167.7	350.3	613.2	206.8	315.7	489.7
Total Liab To Nw (%)	21.0	50.3	109.6	29.1	53.4	116.8	27.8	69.4	132.5	39.6	82.7	157.6
Fixed Assets To Nw (%)	19.7	38.6	70.9	19.6	32.8	57.6	11.8	27.0	53.4	14.3	31.1	62.3
EFFICIENCY												
Coll Period (days)	28.3	44.5	62.1	40.2	58.8	79.8	43.4	70.5	90.3	53.9	71.0	97.0
Sales To Inv (times)	199.7	65.6	24.9	181.3	86.8	35.0	118.1	58.6	30.2	205.2	65.9	23.1
Assets To Sales (%)	20.7	29.7	39.6	26.5	33.7	45.6	28.3	38.7	59.6	31.1	43.4	58.8
Sales To Nwc (times)	14.7	7.6	5.0	12.5	6.8	4.5	9.7	6.3	4.2	10.9	5.6	3.2
Acct Pay To Sales (%)	1.0	2.8	5.4	2.1	3.4	6.0	1.8	3.7	6.5	2.0	3.7	7.8
PROFITABILITY												
Return On Sales (%)	11.4	4.9	0.8	11.5	4.6	1.0	8.0	4.7	1.6	9.5	3.6	1.6
Return On Assets (%)	29.6	12.2	0.8	22.0	11.3	2.2	18.2	9.5	4.0	15.5	8.9	3.1
Return On Nw (%)	52.4	20.7	2.5	44.1	20.2	4.8	35.3	18.8	6.2	28.1	17.5	6.5

INDUSTRY ASSETS, 1995 (for all four panels)

	SIC 1731 ELECTRICAL WORK (NO BREAKDOWN) 1995 (2416 Establishments)		SIC 1731 ELECTRICAL WORK INDUSTRY ASSETS UNDER $100,000 1995 (855 Establishments)		SIC 1731 ELECTRICAL WORK INDUSTRY ASSETS $100,000 - $250,000 1995 (971 Establishments)		SIC 1731 ELECTRICAL WORK INDUSTRY ASSETS $250,000 - $500,000 1995 (975 Establishments)	
	$	%	$	%	$	%	$	%
Cash	67,375	16.7	13,729	26.1	28,875	17.3	55,271	15.6
Accounts Receivable	166,623	41.3	14,150	26.9	64,759	38.8	149,516	42.2
Notes Receivable	2,421	0.6	316	0.6	1,335	0.8	1,772	0.5
Inventory	31,065	7.7	3,629	6.9	16,357	9.8	32,950	9.3
Other Current	36,713	9.1	2,840	5.4	9,514	5.7	27,990	7.9
Total Current	**304,198**	**75.4**	**34,664**	**65.9**	**120,839**	**72.4**	**267,500**	**75.5**
Fixed Assets	77,865	19.3	15,517	29.5	38,388	23.0	68,381	19.3
Other Non-current	21,383	5.3	2,420	4.6	7,678	4.6	18,424	5.2
Total Assets	**403,445**	**100.0**	**52,601**	**100.0**	**166,905**	**100.0**	**354,304**	**100.0**
Accounts Payable	66,568	16.5	5,734	10.9	26,037	15.6	59,169	16.7
Bank Loans	807	0.2	105	0.2	501	0.3	709	0.2
Notes Payable	16,945	4.2	2,735	5.2	7,845	4.7	12,046	3.4
Other Current	63,744	15.8	9,100	17.3	22,866	13.7	49,603	14.0
Total Current	**148,064**	**36.7**	**17,674**	**33.6**	**57,248**	**34.3**	**121,526**	**34.3**
Other Long Term	38,731	9.6	5,628	10.7	20,196	12.1	37,911	10.7
Deferred Credits	1,210	0.3	—	—	167	0.1	1,063	0.3
Net Worth	215,440	53.4	29,299	55.7	89,294	53.5	193,804	54.7
Total Liab & Net Worth	**403,445**	**100.0**	**52,601**	**100.0**	**166,905**	**100.0**	**354,304**	**100.0**
Net Sales	1,314,559	100.0	287,275	100.0	584,306	100.0	1,114,927	100.0
Gross Profit	404,884	30.8	127,263	44.3	220,283	37.7	367,926	33.0
Net Profit After Tax	67,043	5.1	24,706	8.6	36,811	6.3	52,402	4.7
Working Capital	156,134	—	16,990	—	63,591	—	145,974	—

RATIOS	UQ	MED	LQ	UQ	MED	LQ	UQ	MED	LQ
SOLVENCY									
Quick Ratio (times)	3.0	1.6	1.1	4.6	1.7	0.8	3.7	1.8	1.0
Current Ratio (times)	4.0	2.1	1.4	6.0	2.1	1.2	4.9	2.4	1.4
Curr Liab To Nw (%)	23.2	59.1	131.5	13.7	40.3	109.7	17.7	46.8	117.7
Curr Liab To Inv (%)	117.0	240.4	461.9	72.3	191.9	377.4	89.0	190.8	415.8
Total Liab To Nw (%)	30.9	77.0	173.1	18.6	54.2	140.1	25.5	68.1	157.2
Fixed Assets To Nw (%)	13.6	29.1	59.1	20.4	50.0	96.3	16.3	39.5	70.8
EFFICIENCY									
Coll Period (days)	36.1	54.4	76.3	17.9	30.3	50.1	27.7	43.1	60.7
Sales To Inv (times)	116.3	41.5	17.7	109.6	46.5	18.9	92.1	34.8	15.2
Assets To Sales (%)	23.9	31.9	43.6	11.2	17.7	28.1	21.2	28.0	39.4
Sales To Nwc (times)	13.5	7.8	4.8	25.4	12.3	6.8	16.2	8.6	5.0
Acct Pay To Sales (%)	3.0	5.3	8.7	1.7	3.4	5.8	2.4	4.3	7.4
PROFITABILITY									
Return On Sales (%)	8.8	3.4	1.1	18.7	7.1	2.0	12.1	5.1	1.1
Return On Assets (%)	19.6	8.4	2.5	67.3	24.9	8.2	30.7	13.1	2.5
Return On Nw (%)	42.0	17.9	5.5	113.2	49.4	15.2	66.1	25.5	6.1

(SIC 1731 ELECTRICAL WORK, $250,000 - $500,000 panel, continued)

RATIOS	UQ	MED	LQ
SOLVENCY			
Quick Ratio (times)	3.3	1.7	1.1
Current Ratio (times)	4.2	2.3	1.5
Curr Liab To Nw (%)	21.4	51.8	120.4
Curr Liab To Inv (%)	111.6	223.3	447.4
Total Liab To Nw (%)	29.0	72.1	156.9
Fixed Assets To Nw (%)	15.9	31.5	59.6
EFFICIENCY			
Coll Period (days)	35.1	48.9	68.9
Sales To Inv (times)	94.2	35.3	14.1
Assets To Sales (%)	24.4	31.9	44.4
Sales To Nwc (times)	13.9	7.9	4.8
Acct Pay To Sales (%)	2.8	4.9	8.4
PROFITABILITY			
Return On Sales (%)	8.5	3.7	1.2
Return On Assets (%)	17.6	8.9	2.6
Return On Nw (%)	37.2	18.3	4.7

SIC 1731 ELECTRICAL WORK — INDUSTRY ASSETS

	$500,000–$1,000,000 (888 Est.) $	%	$1,000,000–$5,000,000 (941 Est.) $	%	$5,000,000–$25,000,000 (185 Est.) $	%	SIC 1741 MSNRY, OTHER STNWRK (No Breakdown) (514 Est.) $	%
Cash	95,352	14.1	225,363	12.9	732,251	10.0	81,720	18.4
Accounts Receivable	300,256	44.4	863,019	49.4	3,858,964	52.7	170,547	38.4
Notes Receivable	3,381	0.5	10,482	0.6	14,645	0.2	1,777	0.4
Inventory	53,424	7.9	103,073	5.9	292,900	4.0	11,992	2.7
Other Current	73,035	10.8	218,375	12.5	1,186,247	16.2	44,413	10.0
Total Current	**525,449**	**77.7**	**1,420,313**	**81.3**	**6,085,007**	**83.1**	**310,449**	**69.9**
Fixed Assets	110,229	16.3	227,110	13.0	798,154	10.9	106,592	24.0
Other Non-current	40,575	6.0	99,579	5.7	439,351	6.0	27,092	6.1
Total Assets	**676,253**	**100.0**	**1,747,002**	**100.0**	**7,322,512**	**100.0**	**444,133**	**100.0**
Accounts Payable	119,697	17.7	333,677	19.1	1,471,825	20.1	63,511	14.3
Bank Loans	2,029	0.3	3,494	0.2	29,290	0.4	444	0.1
Notes Payable	22,993	3.4	80,362	4.6	380,771	5.2	21,318	4.8
Other Current	100,762	14.9	328,436	18.8	1,669,533	22.8	75,058	16.9
Total Current	**245,480**	**36.3**	**745,970**	**42.7**	**3,551,418**	**48.5**	**160,332**	**36.1**
Other Long Term	64,920	9.6	134,519	7.7	439,351	6.0	52,852	11.9
Deferred Credits	2,705	0.4	6,988	0.4	21,968	0.3	444	0.1
Net Worth	363,148	53.7	859,525	49.2	3,309,775	45.2	230,505	51.9
Total Liab & Net Worth	**676,253**	**100.0**	**1,747,002**	**100.0**	**7,322,512**	**100.0**	**444,133**	**100.0**
Net Sales	1,995,629	100.0	4,919,021	100.0	20,278,963	100.0	1,418,386	100.0
Gross Profit	548,798	27.5	1,106,780	22.5	3,528,540	17.4	365,944	25.8
Net Profit After Tax	77,830	3.9	157,409	3.2	648,927	3.2	69,501	4.9
Working Capital	279,969	—	674,343	—	2,533,589	—	150,117	—

RATIOS

	UQ	MED	LQ	UQ	MED	LQ	UQ	MED	LQ	UQ	MED	LQ
SOLVENCY												
Quick Ratio (times)	2.9	1.7	1.1	2.2	1.5	1.1	1.7	1.3	1.0	3.2	1.6	1.0
Current Ratio (times)	3.9	2.2	1.5	2.8	1.9	1.4	2.2	1.7	1.4	3.9	2.0	1.3
Curr Liab To Nw (%)	26.0	62.0	126.8	44.5	86.9	161.7	67.8	113.5	206.5	20.5	64.9	142.2
Curr Liab To Inv (%)	125.5	240.3	462.2	200.1	368.9	599.4	184.7	466.5	701.6	117.1	242.9	533.2
Total Liab To Nw (%)	33.3	77.6	166.8	51.7	103.9	191.2	77.1	128.6	229.0	26.3	78.1	176.8
Fixed Assets To Nw (%)	12.5	25.1	51.4	11.5	22.1	40.9	9.0	21.7	35.7	17.7	36.0	70.5
EFFICIENCY												
Coll Period (days)	42.2	56.8	78.8	51.5	65.7	85.1	60.6	73.0	93.4	36.5	60.2	87.1
Sales To Inv (times)	101.3	37.5	17.7	141.1	51.7	23.0	234.1	88.5	28.8	191.4	61.3	22.1
Assets To Sales (%)	27.2	34.2	45.8	28.7	36.6	47.0	30.2	37.5	47.4	23.0	33.0	44.9
Sales To Nwc (times)	11.4	7.0	4.4	11.4	7.2	4.8	12.5	7.9	5.5	17.2	8.4	5.3
Acct Pay To Sales (%)	3.2	5.4	9.2	4.0	6.1	9.4	4.3	6.9	9.9	2.7	4.7	7.8
PROFITABILITY												
Return On Sales (%)	6.8	3.2	1.0	4.8	2.2	0.9	5.7	2.4	0.9	8.6	4.1	1.0
Return On Assets (%)	15.9	7.7	2.3	11.4	5.4	2.2	13.4	5.7	2.9	22.1	9.0	1.7
Return On Nw (%)	33.0	16.4	4.9	25.3	12.4	4.8	27.4	13.7	6.1	46.6	19.7	4.1

SIC 1741 MSNRY, OTHER STNWRK — INDUSTRY ASSETS — UNDER $100,000 — 1995 (85 Establishments)

	$	%
Cash	12,660	32.6
Accounts Receivable	5,514	14.2
Notes Receivable	78	0.2
Inventory	1,087	2.8
Other Current	2,718	7.0
Total Current	**22,058**	**56.8**
Fixed Assets	14,058	36.2
Other Non-current	2,718	7.0
Total Assets	**38,834**	**100.0**
Accounts Payable	3,184	8.2
Bank Loans	—	—
Notes Payable	1,903	4.9
Other Current	7,378	19.0
Total Current	**12,466**	**32.1**
Other Long Term	7,806	20.1
Deferred Credits	—	—
Net Worth	18,563	47.8
Total Liab & Net Worth	**38,834**	**100.0**
Net Sales	293,148	100.0
Gross Profit	109,931	37.5
Net Profit After Tax	19,055	6.5
Working Capital	9,592	—

RATIOS	UQ	MED	LQ
SOLVENCY			
Quick Ratio (times)	2.3	1.2	0.8
Current Ratio (times)	2.8	1.5	1.0
Curr Liab To Nw (%)	14.9	37.3	78.6
Curr Liab To Inv (%)	47.8	107.6	108.8
Total Liab To Nw (%)	16.8	57.5	129.5
Fixed Assets To Nw (%)	22.4	40.1	81.9
EFFICIENCY			
Coll Period (days)	10.9	14.8	24.7
Sales To Inv (times)	21.1	18.8	14.4
Assets To Sales (%)	8.4	13.6	21.2
Sales To Nwc (times)	26.1	16.2	7.6
Acct Pay To Sales (%)	1.4	2.9	3.4
PROFITABILITY			
Return On Sales (%)	5.2	1.6	0.2
Return On Assets (%)	6.0	1.8	(3.3)
Return On Nw (%)	13.7	3.8	(8.1)

SIC 1741 MSNRY, OTHER STNWRK — INDUSTRY ASSETS — $100,000 - $250,000 — 1995 (107 Establishments)

	$	%
Cash	29,789	17.9
Accounts Receivable	55,418	33.3
Notes Receivable	999	0.6
Inventory	4,826	2.9
Other Current	16,475	9.9
Total Current	**107,507**	**64.6**
Fixed Assets	49,426	29.7
Other Non-current	9,486	5.7
Total Assets	**166,419**	**100.0**
Accounts Payable	21,135	12.7
Bank Loans	—	—
Notes Payable	7,156	4.3
Other Current	20,969	12.6
Total Current	**49,260**	**29.6**
Other Long Term	23,299	14.0
Deferred Credits	—	—
Net Worth	93,860	56.4
Total Liab & Net Worth	**166,419**	**100.0**
Net Sales	625,373	100.0
Gross Profit	208,875	33.4
Net Profit After Tax	40,024	6.4
Working Capital	58,247	—

RATIOS	UQ	MED	LQ
SOLVENCY			
Quick Ratio (times)	3.6	2.0	1.0
Current Ratio (times)	4.5	2.5	1.5
Curr Liab To Nw (%)	15.1	35.9	96.5
Curr Liab To Inv (%)	69.0	226.4	333.4
Total Liab To Nw (%)	20.3	51.2	139.4
Fixed Assets To Nw (%)	17.4	40.5	87.8
EFFICIENCY			
Coll Period (days)	27.7	42.9	62.1
Sales To Inv (times)	197.0	47.5	17.0
Assets To Sales (%)	17.1	26.5	36.3
Sales To Nwc (times)	14.4	9.1	5.6
Acct Pay To Sales (%)	2.0	3.9	6.0
PROFITABILITY			
Return On Sales (%)	13.0	6.0	2.0
Return On Assets (%)	37.1	17.1	3.2
Return On Nw (%)	64.5	31.2	6.1

SIC 1741 MSNRY, OTHER STNWRK — INDUSTRY ASSETS — $250,000 - $500,000 — 1995 (97 Establishments)

	$	%
Cash	61,922	17.1
Accounts Receivable	156,072	43.1
Notes Receivable	1,448	0.4
Inventory	9,053	2.5
Other Current	26,072	7.2
Total Current	**254,568**	**70.3**
Fixed Assets	85,460	23.6
Other Non-current	22,089	6.1
Total Assets	**362,117**	**100.0**
Accounts Payable	55,766	15.4
Bank Loans	724	0.2
Notes Payable	21,003	5.8
Other Current	69,164	19.1
Total Current	**146,657**	**40.5**
Other Long Term	36,212	10.0
Deferred Credits	—	—
Net Worth	179,248	49.5
Total Liab & Net Worth	**362,117**	**100.0**
Net Sales	1,211,402	100.0
Gross Profit	293,159	24.2
Net Profit After Tax	60,570	5.0
Working Capital	107,911	—

RATIOS	UQ	MED	LQ
SOLVENCY			
Quick Ratio (times)	2.9	1.5	1.0
Current Ratio (times)	3.3	1.7	1.2
Curr Liab To Nw (%)	20.8	75.4	153.7
Curr Liab To Inv (%)	119.1	331.8	549.1
Total Liab To Nw (%)	26.4	83.9	178.2
Fixed Assets To Nw (%)	23.8	41.7	84.2
EFFICIENCY			
Coll Period (days)	31.8	55.3	73.7
Sales To Inv (times)	198.1	65.5	27.9
Assets To Sales (%)	24.2	31.5	40.8
Sales To Nwc (times)	19.2	10.6	6.4
Acct Pay To Sales (%)	2.0	4.4	7.4
PROFITABILITY			
Return On Sales (%)	8.9	4.9	1.0
Return On Assets (%)	25.2	13.3	1.7
Return On Nw (%)	72.3	32.6	8.4

SIC 1741 MSNRY, OTHER STNWRK — INDUSTRY ASSETS — $500,000 - $1,000,000 — 1995 (96 Establishments)

	$	%
Cash	118,638	16.6
Accounts Receivable	313,032	43.8
Notes Receivable	2,859	0.4
Inventory	18,582	2.6
Other Current	87,906	12.3
Total Current	**541,017**	**75.7**
Fixed Assets	139,364	19.5
Other Non-current	34,305	4.8
Total Assets	**714,685**	**100.0**
Accounts Payable	128,643	18.0
Bank Loans	—	—
Notes Payable	38,593	5.4
Other Current	112,206	15.7
Total Current	**279,442**	**39.1**
Other Long Term	62,892	8.8
Deferred Credits	1,429	0.2
Net Worth	370,922	51.9
Total Liab & Net Worth	**714,685**	**100.0**
Net Sales	1,979,922	100.0
Gross Profit	512,800	25.9
Net Profit After Tax	83,157	4.2
Working Capital	261,575	—

RATIOS	UQ	MED	LQ
SOLVENCY			
Quick Ratio (times)	2.8	1.6	1.1
Current Ratio (times)	3.6	2.0	1.4
Curr Liab To Nw (%)	26.6	68.7	127.4
Curr Liab To Inv (%)	137.7	223.0	500.0
Total Liab To Nw (%)	34.7	78.5	174.4
Fixed Assets To Nw (%)	17.2	37.6	54.2
EFFICIENCY			
Coll Period (days)	37.5	60.8	87.8
Sales To Inv (times)	99.0	56.2	26.8
Assets To Sales (%)	26.7	32.9	48.7
Sales To Nwc (times)	12.5	7.4	4.8
Acct Pay To Sales (%)	3.1	4.7	7.7
PROFITABILITY			
Return On Sales (%)	7.8	3.6	1.5
Return On Assets (%)	19.4	8.7	3.7
Return On Nw (%)	41.5	20.6	4.4

SIC 1741 MSNRY,OTHER STNWRK
INDUSTRY ASSETS $1,000,000 - $5,000,000
1995 (114 Establishments)

	$	%
Cash	214,096	13.3
Accounts Receivable	804,874	50.0
Notes Receivable	8,049	0.5
Inventory	41,853	2.6
Other Current	170,633	10.6
Total Current	**1,239,506**	**77.0**
Fixed Assets	272,047	16.9
Other Non-current	98,195	6.1
Total Assets	**1,609,748**	**100.0**
Accounts Payable	246,291	15.3
Bank Loans	8,049	0.5
Notes Payable	64,390	4.0
Other Current	296,194	18.4
Total Current	**614,924**	**38.2**
Other Long Term	140,048	8.7
Deferred Credits	3,219	0.2
Net Worth	851,557	52.9
Total Liab & Net Worth	**1,609,748**	**100.0**
Net Sales	4,029,889	100.0
Gross Profit	753,589	18.7
Net Profit After Tax	157,166	3.9
Working Capital	624,582	—

RATIOS	UQ	MED	LQ
SOLVENCY			
Quick Ratio (times)	3.1	1.6	1.2
Current Ratio (times)	4.0	2.0	1.5
Curr Liab To Nw (%)	24.3	80.2	152.4
Curr Liab To Inv (%)	123.5	348.4	645.5
Total Liab To Nw (%)	36.7	102.3	182.2
Fixed Assets To Nw (%)	11.5	26.1	48.3
EFFICIENCY			
Coll Period (days)	60.6	82.0	108.1
Sales To Inv (times)	239.4	58.0	15.7
Assets To Sales (%)	33.9	42.3	57.1
Sales To Nwc (times)	10.3	6.8	4.2
Acct Pay To Sales (%)	3.9	6.3	9.9
PROFITABILITY			
Return On Sales (%)	6.8	3.1	0.9
Return On Assets (%)	15.8	6.3	1.8
Return On Nw (%)	30.3	13.5	4.4

SIC 1741 MSNRY,OTHER STNWRK
INDUSTRY ASSETS $5,000,000 - $25,000,000
1995 (14 Establishments)

	$	%
Cash	629,400	9.1
Accounts Receivable	3,070,918	44.4
Notes Receivable	55,332	0.8
Inventory	207,494	3.0
Other Current	1,646,123	23.8
Total Current	**5,609,267**	**81.1**
Fixed Assets	663,982	9.6
Other Non-current	643,233	9.3
Total Assets	**6,916,482**	**100.0**
Accounts Payable	1,362,547	19.7
Bank Loans	—	—
Notes Payable	276,659	4.0
Other Current	1,466,294	21.2
Total Current	**3,105,500**	**44.9**
Other Long Term	414,989	6.0
Deferred Credits	82,998	1.2
Net Worth	3,312,995	47.9
Total Liab & Net Worth	**6,916,482**	**100.0**
Net Sales	18,423,325	100.0
Gross Profit	3,039,849	16.5
Net Profit After Tax	589,546	3.2
Working Capital	2,503,767	—

RATIOS	UQ	MED	LQ
SOLVENCY			
Quick Ratio (times)	1.4	1.2	1.0
Current Ratio (times)	2.0	1.7	1.4
Curr Liab To Nw (%)	72.8	107.9	155.7
Curr Liab To Inv (%)	345.7	360.3	374.8
Total Liab To Nw (%)	85.3	130.0	183.5
Fixed Assets To Nw (%)	12.3	24.0	38.9
EFFICIENCY			
Coll Period (days)	52.8	72.7	80.8
Sales To Inv (times)	572.9	157.7	117.3
Assets To Sales (%)	33.6	36.1	39.2
Sales To Nwc (times)	12.9	8.4	6.1
Acct Pay To Sales (%)	4.8	6.8	8.4
PROFITABILITY			
Return On Sales (%)	3.5	1.7	0.5
Return On Assets (%)	9.3	4.7	1.4
Return On Nw (%)	22.0	8.5	2.7

SIC 1742 PLSTRNG,DWALL,INSUL
(NO BREAKDOWN)
1995 (951 Establishments)

	$	%
Cash	73,172	14.0
Accounts Receivable	238,333	45.6
Notes Receivable	3,659	0.7
Inventory	32,405	6.2
Other Current	49,130	9.4
Total Current	**396,698**	**75.9**
Fixed Assets	94,079	18.0
Other Non-current	31,882	6.1
Total Assets	**522,659**	**100.0**
Accounts Payable	86,239	16.5
Bank Loans	1,045	0.2
Notes Payable	27,701	5.3
Other Current	90,943	17.4
Total Current	**205,928**	**39.4**
Other Long Term	54,879	10.5
Deferred Credits	1,045	0.2
Net Worth	260,807	49.9
Total Liab & Net Worth	**522,659**	**100.0**
Net Sales	1,896,288	100.0
Gross Profit	511,998	27.0
Net Profit After Tax	79,644	4.2
Working Capital	190,770	—

RATIOS	UQ	MED	LQ
SOLVENCY			
Quick Ratio (times)	2.9	1.5	1.0
Current Ratio (times)	3.6	2.0	1.4
Curr Liab To Nw (%)	27.9	72.6	149.8
Curr Liab To Inv (%)	148.6	281.8	572.0
Total Liab To Nw (%)	33.8	91.5	185.2
Fixed Assets To Nw (%)	12.4	27.7	59.3
EFFICIENCY			
Coll Period (days)	40.6	56.6	77.0
Sales To Inv (times)	100.7	41.9	21.4
Assets To Sales (%)	22.4	29.8	39.1
Sales To Nwc (times)	15.6	8.4	5.4
Acct Pay To Sales (%)	2.8	4.9	7.8
PROFITABILITY			
Return On Sales (%)	6.7	3.5	1.3
Return On Assets (%)	20.6	9.6	3.0
Return On Nw (%)	44.9	21.3	6.7

SIC 1742 PLSTRNG,DWALL,INSUL
INDUSTRY ASSETS UNDER $100,000
1995 (121 Establishments)

	$	%
Cash	12,742	23.9
Accounts Receivable	13,169	24.7
Notes Receivable	320	0.6
Inventory	1,919	3.6
Other Current	3,519	6.6
Total Current	**31,669**	**59.4**
Fixed Assets	19,620	36.8
Other Non-current	2,026	3.8
Total Assets	**53,315**	**100.0**
Accounts Payable	4,265	8.0
Bank Loans	107	0.2
Notes Payable	1,653	3.1
Other Current	11,569	21.7
Total Current	**17,594**	**33.0**
Other Long Term	8,104	15.2
Deferred Credits	—	—
Net Worth	27,617	51.8
Total Liab & Net Worth	**53,315**	**100.0**
Net Sales	463,431	100.0
Gross Profit	178,421	38.5
Net Profit After Tax	25,489	5.5
Working Capital	14,075	—

RATIOS	UQ	MED	LQ
SOLVENCY			
Quick Ratio (times)	4.1	1.9	0.7
Current Ratio (times)	5.7	2.2	1.0
Curr Liab To Nw (%)	13.0	35.6	92.9
Curr Liab To Inv (%)	90.5	206.7	315.2
Total Liab To Nw (%)	21.7	53.5	112.1
Fixed Assets To Nw (%)	25.5	55.2	127.3
EFFICIENCY			
Coll Period (days)	26.8	37.6	49.3
Sales To Inv (times)	159.5	58.8	35.5
Assets To Sales (%)	5.8	11.3	22.9
Sales To Nwc (times)	39.8	16.9	7.9
Acct Pay To Sales (%)	0.8	1.5	2.9
PROFITABILITY			
Return On Sales (%)	11.8	7.1	3.5
Return On Assets (%)	69.2	40.1	18.2
Return On Nw (%)	123.8	83.3	29.3

SIC 1742 PLSTRNG, DWALL, INSUL — INDUSTRY ASSETS

	$100,000 - $250,000 (164 Est.) $	%	$250,000 - $500,000 (197 Est.) $	%	$500,000 - $1,000,000 (231 Est.) $	%	$1,000,000 - $5,000,000 (201 Est.) $	%
Cash	22,407	13.3	53,284	14.2	88,536	12.7	190,950	12.2
Accounts Receivable	70,927	42.1	179,363	47.8	340,900	48.9	810,755	51.8
Notes Receivable	1,348	0.8	4,878	1.3	2,091	0.3	7,826	0.5
Inventory	12,130	7.2	22,889	6.1	46,708	6.7	97,040	6.2
Other Current	11,962	7.1	31,895	8.5	73,199	10.5	178,429	11.4
Total Current	**118,773**	**70.5**	**292,310**	**77.9**	**551,435**	**79.1**	**1,285,000**	**82.1**
Fixed Assets	39,423	23.4	63,040	16.8	106,662	15.3	159,647	10.2
Other Non-current	10,277	6.1	19,888	5.3	39,040	5.6	120,518	7.7
Total Assets	**168,473**	**100.0**	**375,237**	**100.0**	**697,137**	**100.0**	**1,565,165**	**100.0**
Accounts Payable	34,032	20.2	64,916	17.3	124,788	17.9	245,731	15.7
Bank Loans	168	0.1	—	—	2,091	0.3	1,565	0.1
Notes Payable	8,761	5.2	18,762	5.0	39,737	5.7	90,780	5.8
Other Current	25,271	15.0	54,785	14.6	109,451	15.7	313,033	20.0
Total Current	**68,232**	**40.5**	**138,462**	**36.9**	**276,066**	**39.6**	**651,109**	**41.6**
Other Long Term	27,630	16.4	33,021	8.8	59,954	8.6	123,648	7.9
Deferred Credits	—	—	—	—	2,789	0.4	7,826	0.5
Net Worth	72,612	43.1	203,754	54.3	358,328	51.4	782,583	50.0
Total Liab & Net Worth	**168,473**	**100.0**	**375,237**	**100.0**	**697,137**	**100.0**	**1,565,165**	**100.0**
Net Sales	756,411	100.0	1,403,009	100.0	2,265,184	100.0	4,596,908	100.0
Gross Profit	281,385	37.2	388,633	27.7	566,296	25.0	942,366	20.5
Net Profit After Tax	31,769	4.2	68,747	4.9	88,342	3.9	179,279	3.9
Working Capital	50,541	—	153,848	—	275,369	—	633,891	—

RATIOS	UQ	MED	LQ	UQ	MED	LQ	UQ	MED	LQ	UQ	MED	LQ
SOLVENCY												
Quick Ratio (times)	3.0	1.4	0.9	3.6	1.8	1.1	2.7	1.6	1.1	2.2	1.5	1.1
Current Ratio (times)	3.3	1.6	1.2	4.7	2.3	1.5	3.4	2.0	1.4	3.0	1.9	1.5
Curr Liab To Nw (%)	25.5	85.0	149.8	19.0	53.0	138.9	32.1	63.0	151.5	39.5	92.3	155.1
Curr Liab To Inv (%)	111.3	192.6	400.3	113.4	223.2	414.6	151.4	329.4	609.6	220.7	394.9	646.5
Total Liab To Nw (%)	39.2	117.8	221.7	21.4	63.9	149.3	37.2	88.9	183.2	48.2	100.3	173.1
Fixed Assets To Nw (%)	21.5	54.0	98.4	11.8	28.3	50.5	12.4	23.6	50.0	9.3	17.3	34.8
EFFICIENCY												
Coll Period (days)	30.3	44.2	58.4	38.0	52.2	68.3	39.7	55.2	78.8	54.4	71.2	86.1
Sales To Inv (times)	103.6	41.9	22.1	98.7	36.5	17.8	73.9	37.9	19.1	111.9	51.2	26.4
Assets To Sales (%)	16.8	22.1	30.7	21.3	28.8	38.9	25.3	31.3	39.0	28.1	34.5	47.9
Sales To Nwc (times)	21.8	14.1	7.3	13.7	8.0	5.1	14.3	8.1	5.5	11.5	7.1	4.9
Acct Pay To Sales (%)	2.4	4.6	7.6	2.9	4.5	7.4	2.9	5.3	8.2	3.0	4.7	8.0
PROFITABILITY												
Return On Sales (%)	6.3	3.7	1.7	7.8	4.0	1.8	6.4	3.2	1.1	5.5	2.6	0.8
Return On Assets (%)	34.3	17.1	5.8	26.3	12.8	4.3	15.3	8.2	2.5	13.2	5.5	2.4
Return On Nw (%)	98.7	42.4	17.0	44.7	25.0	8.1	36.2	19.9	6.3	32.2	12.3	5.1

SIC 1742 PLSTRNG,DWALL,INSUL
INDUSTRY ASSETS
$5,000,000-$25,000,000
1995 (31 Establishments)

	$	%
Cash	541,563	6.1
Accounts Receivable	4,510,070	50.8
Notes Receivable	17,756	0.2
Inventory	514,929	5.8
Other Current	1,296,201	14.6
Total Current	**6,880,520**	**77.5**
Fixed Assets	861,175	9.7
Other Non-current	1,136,396	12.8
Total Assets	**8,878,090**	**100.0**
Accounts Payable	1,606,934	18.1
Bank Loans	106,537	1.2
Notes Payable	932,199	10.5
Other Current	2,006,448	22.6
Total Current	**4,652,119**	**52.4**
Other Long Term	621,466	7.0
Deferred Credits	26,634	0.3
Net Worth	3,577,870	40.3
Total Liab & Net Worth	**8,878,090**	**100.0**
Net Sales	21,867,073	100.0
Gross Profit	3,542,466	16.2
Net Profit After Tax	437,341	2.0
Working Capital	2,228,401	—

RATIOS	UQ	MED	LQ
SOLVENCY			
Quick Ratio (times)	1.5	1.1	0.9
Current Ratio (times)	2.1	1.4	1.2
Curr Liab To Nw (%)	81.9	169.9	266.0
Curr Liab To Inv (%)	284.8	474.2	774.4
Total Liab To Nw (%)	90.0	192.8	303.2
Fixed Assets To Nw (%)	7.1	13.4	34.5
EFFICIENCY			
Coll Period (days)	55.9	74.1	81.4
Sales To Inv (times)	95.6	61.3	18.2
Assets To Sales (%)	27.2	34.0	49.5
Sales To Nwc (times)	16.6	10.1	5.0
Acct Pay To Sales (%)	4.1	6.3	7.7
PROFITABILITY			
Return On Sales (%)	3.8	1.5	0.7
Return On Assets (%)	6.7	3.0	1.1
Return On Nw (%)	14.8	7.7	3.3

SIC 1743 TRZ,TILE,MRBL,MSAIC (NO BREAKDOWN)
1995 (199 Establishments)

	$	%
Cash	69,049	16.7
Accounts Receivable	140,578	34.0
Notes Receivable	1,654	0.4
Inventory	35,971	8.7
Other Current	43,414	10.5
Total Current	**290,666**	**70.3**
Fixed Assets	94,270	22.8
Other Non-current	28,529	6.9
Total Assets	**413,465**	**100.0**
Accounts Payable	59,539	14.4
Bank Loans	1,240	0.3
Notes Payable	17,779	4.3
Other Current	72,770	17.6
Total Current	**151,328**	**36.6**
Other Long Term	37,625	9.1
Deferred Credits	—	—
Net Worth	224,511	54.3
Total Liab & Net Worth	**413,465**	**100.0**
Net Sales	1,386,553	100.0
Gross Profit	432,605	31.2
Net Profit After Tax	69,328	5.0
Working Capital	139,338	—

RATIOS	UQ	MED	LQ
SOLVENCY			
Quick Ratio (times)	2.6	1.3	0.9
Current Ratio (times)	4.0	2.0	1.3
Curr Liab To Nw (%)	23.2	59.3	130.3
Curr Liab To Inv (%)	97.8	233.4	419.3
Total Liab To Nw (%)	30.9	75.6	163.4
Fixed Assets To Nw (%)	15.0	33.4	72.3
EFFICIENCY			
Coll Period (days)	35.4	56.2	75.8
Sales To Inv (times)	102.1	30.5	17.9
Assets To Sales (%)	21.8	32.7	44.4
Sales To Nwc (times)	16.5	8.2	4.8
Acct Pay To Sales (%)	2.5	5.1	7.5
PROFITABILITY			
Return On Sales (%)	9.2	3.0	0.9
Return On Assets (%)	21.7	5.0	1.6
Return On Nw (%)	41.3	12.9	2.7

SIC 1743 TRZ,TILE,MRBL,MSAIC
INDUSTRY ASSETS
UNDER $100,000
1995 (46 Establishments)

	$	%
Cash	9,235	30.2
Accounts Receivable	3,731	12.2
Notes Receivable	367	1.2
Inventory	1,559	5.1
Other Current	1,407	4.6
Total Current	**16,298**	**53.3**
Fixed Assets	11,956	39.1
Other Non-current	2,324	7.6
Total Assets	**30,578**	**100.0**
Accounts Payable	1,835	6.0
Bank Loans	—	—
Notes Payable	1,712	5.6
Other Current	6,941	22.7
Total Current	**10,488**	**34.3**
Other Long Term	2,140	7.0
Deferred Credits	—	—
Net Worth	17,949	58.7
Total Liab & Net Worth	**30,578**	**100.0**
Net Sales	211,403	100.0
Gross Profit	87,521	41.4
Net Profit After Tax	24,100	11.4
Working Capital	5,810	—

RATIOS	UQ	MED	LQ
SOLVENCY			
Quick Ratio (times)	3.1	1.5	0.6
Current Ratio (times)	3.4	1.5	0.9
Curr Liab To Nw (%)	23.1	45.5	91.0
Curr Liab To Inv (%)	54.1	250.8	303.1
Total Liab To Nw (%)	25.1	57.2	107.1
Fixed Assets To Nw (%)	34.8	62.9	113.1
EFFICIENCY			
Coll Period (days)	12.4	13.9	29.6
Sales To Inv (times)	102.8	67.9	28.5
Assets To Sales (%)	8.1	11.4	18.2
Sales To Nwc (times)	59.9	27.3	19.9
Acct Pay To Sales (%)	0.8	1.0	1.4
PROFITABILITY			
Return On Sales (%)	24.6	11.4	5.1
Return On Assets (%)	138.4	63.2	29.9
Return On Nw (%)	274.2	106.8	51.2

SIC 1743 TRZ,TILE,MRBL,MSAIC
INDUSTRY ASSETS
$100,000 - $250,000
1995 (37 Establishments)

	$	%
Cash	28,808	17.6
Accounts Receivable	66,454	40.6
Notes Receivable	327	0.2
Inventory	14,240	8.7
Other Current	13,258	8.1
Total Current	**123,088**	**75.2**
Fixed Assets	34,046	20.8
Other Non-current	6,547	4.0
Total Assets	**163,681**	**100.0**
Accounts Payable	35,355	21.6
Bank Loans	655	0.4
Notes Payable	3,928	2.4
Other Current	30,281	18.5
Total Current	**70,219**	**42.9**
Other Long Term	17,678	10.8
Deferred Credits	—	—
Net Worth	75,784	46.3
Total Liab & Net Worth	**163,681**	**100.0**
Net Sales	729,702	100.0
Gross Profit	248,099	34.0
Net Profit After Tax	45,242	6.2
Working Capital	52,869	—

RATIOS	UQ	MED	LQ
SOLVENCY			
Quick Ratio (times)	2.1	1.2	0.9
Current Ratio (times)	3.6	1.8	1.3
Curr Liab To Nw (%)	27.4	69.6	159.7
Curr Liab To Inv (%)	110.0	205.9	298.8
Total Liab To Nw (%)	41.4	103.8	179.1
Fixed Assets To Nw (%)	23.8	42.5	81.3
EFFICIENCY			
Coll Period (days)	24.1	41.4	60.6
Sales To Inv (times)	125.1	31.1	19.2
Assets To Sales (%)	18.7	23.4	30.0
Sales To Nwc (times)	35.0	11.6	6.8
Acct Pay To Sales (%)	2.5	4.0	7.3
PROFITABILITY			
Return On Sales (%)	14.2	6.4	2.4
Return On Assets (%)	37.6	21.2	4.8
Return On Nw (%)	62.5	41.8	2.4

	SIC 1743 TRZ,TILE,MRBL,MSAIC INDUSTRY ASSETS $250,000 - $500,000 1995 (38 Establishments)		SIC 1743 TRZ,TILE,MRBL,MSAIC INDUSTRY ASSETS $500,000 - $1,000,000 1995 (36 Establishments)		SIC 1743 TRZ,TILE,MRBL,MSAIC INDUSTRY ASSETS $1,000,000 - $5,000,000 1995 (40 Establishments)		SIC 1751 CARPENTRY WORK (NO BREAKDOWN) 1995 (616 Establishments)	
	$	%	$	%	$	%	$	%
Cash	39,602	10.3	102,574	15.0	171,400	11.6	38,199	18.0
Accounts Receivable	150,333	39.1	271,479	39.7	554,094	37.5	73,214	34.5
Notes Receivable	1,153	0.3	684	0.1	4,433	0.3	1,273	0.6
Inventory	25,760	6.7	81,375	11.9	168,444	11.4	20,373	9.6
Other Current	51,905	13.5	78,640	11.5	205,384	13.9	15,067	7.1
Total Current	**268,754**	**69.9**	**534,753**	**78.2**	**1,103,755**	**74.7**	**148,126**	**69.8**
Fixed Assets	86,124	22.4	109,412	16.0	242,324	16.4	52,629	24.8
Other Non-current	29,605	7.7	39,662	5.8	131,505	8.9	11,460	5.4
Total Assets	**384,483**	**100.0**	**683,827**	**100.0**	**1,477,583**	**100.0**	**212,215**	**100.0**
Accounts Payable	66,516	17.3	96,420	14.1	190,608	12.9	36,713	17.3
Bank Loans	384	0.1	7,522	1.1	—	—	424	0.2
Notes Payable	14,610	3.8	33,508	4.9	70,924	4.8	7,852	3.7
Other Current	52,674	13.7	103,942	15.2	257,099	17.4	35,440	16.7
Total Current	**134,185**	**34.9**	**241,391**	**35.3**	**518,632**	**35.1**	**80,429**	**37.9**
Other Long Term	44,216	11.5	51,287	7.5	140,370	9.5	28,437	13.4
Deferred Credits	—	—	—	—	—	—	424	0.2
Net Worth	206,083	53.6	391,149	57.2	818,581	55.4	102,924	48.5
Total Liab & Net Worth	**384,483**	**100.0**	**683,827**	**100.0**	**1,477,583**	**100.0**	**212,215**	**100.0**
Net Sales	1,272,218	100.0	2,185,527	100.0	3,726,646	100.0	1,016,436	100.0
Gross Profit	386,754	30.4	708,111	32.4	831,042	22.3	319,161	31.4
Net Profit After Tax	57,250	4.5	50,267	2.3	100,619	2.7	55,904	5.5
Working Capital	134,569	—	293,362	—	585,123	—	67,697	—

RATIOS	UQ	MED	LQ	UQ	MED	LQ	UQ	MED	LQ	UQ	MED	LQ
SOLVENCY												
Quick Ratio (times)	3.7	1.7	1.0	2.3	1.7	0.9	2.0	1.3	0.9	3.0	1.4	0.9
Current Ratio (times)	4.6	3.0	1.2	3.3	2.3	1.5	3.5	2.2	1.6	4.1	1.9	1.2
Curr Liab To Nw (%)	14.0	40.3	148.6	32.9	59.2	127.2	29.2	60.8	133.2	21.7	63.0	157.6
Curr Liab To Inv (%)	62.7	285.7	449.4	98.6	222.0	363.2	109.8	250.0	484.6	95.8	206.3	370.2
Total Liab To Nw (%)	21.6	75.6	187.4	40.3	89.7	149.3	40.7	74.4	183.1	31.5	79.9	187.6
Fixed Assets To Nw (%)	22.8	37.0	71.6	9.2	24.7	36.9	11.1	24.0	42.9	16.9	41.5	88.3
EFFICIENCY												
Coll Period (days)	27.0	65.7	91.6	40.8	53.2	71.7	53.7	69.4	96.0	23.0	37.6	56.1
Sales To Inv (times)	122.6	56.4	23.6	31.7	18.8	9.5	85.2	35.7	15.3	59.2	28.5	13.8
Assets To Sales (%)	25.9	30.7	39.2	32.2	35.1	42.8	33.9	47.1	68.8	15.5	24.0	35.1
Sales To Nwc (times)	11.6	7.7	4.3	10.7	6.6	4.8	11.7	6.4	3.1	25.1	11.5	6.3
Acct Pay To Sales (%)	2.9	4.6	6.3	1.7	4.9	6.6	4.8	6.7	8.3	2.2	4.7	8.6
PROFITABILITY												
Return On Sales (%)	8.6	2.1	0.8	3.2	1.4	0.5	3.2	1.6	0.7	9.1	4.0	1.2
Return On Assets (%)	15.5	4.6	1.4	7.7	2.3	1.4	8.4	3.2	1.7	27.7	12.1	3.4
Return On Nw (%)	35.9	16.4	1.6	21.2	6.2	2.1	16.8	9.4	3.1	73.9	30.0	9.9

SIC 1751 CARPENTRY WORK — INDUSTRY ASSETS

	UNDER $100,000 1995 (203 Establishments) $	%	$100,000 - $500,000 1995 (148 Establishments) $	%	$250,000 - $500,000 1995 (123 Establishments) $	%	$500,000 - $1,000,000 1995 (75 Establishments) $	%
Cash	12,596	27.7	31,112	18.0	41,583	12.0	72,850	11.2
Accounts Receivable	8,867	19.5	62,916	36.4	138,610	40.0	282,945	43.5
Notes Receivable	364	0.8	346	0.2	2,426	0.7	4,553	0.7
Inventory	3,456	7.6	18,149	10.5	42,969	12.4	63,094	9.7
Other Current	2,365	5.2	11,926	6.9	25,296	7.3	53,987	8.3
Total Current	**27,648**	**60.8**	**124,450**	**72.0**	**250,884**	**72.4**	**477,430**	**73.4**
Fixed Assets	14,324	31.5	42,866	24.8	78,315	22.6	149,603	23.0
Other Non-current	3,501	7.7	5,531	3.2	17,326	5.0	23,416	3.6
Total Assets	**45,474**	**100.0**	**172,847**	**100.0**	**346,525**	**100.0**	**650,449**	**100.0**
Accounts Payable	6,366	14.0	28,001	16.2	67,226	19.4	115,129	17.7
Bank Loans	182	0.4	173	0.1	—	—	—	—
Notes Payable	1,955	4.3	6,741	3.9	8,663	2.5	26,668	4.1
Other Current	8,413	18.5	29,211	16.9	44,355	12.8	106,023	16.3
Total Current	**16,916**	**37.2**	**64,126**	**37.1**	**120,244**	**34.7**	**247,821**	**38.1**
Other Long Term	6,275	13.8	25,236	14.6	46,088	13.3	82,607	12.7
Deferred Credits	—	—	346	0.2	693	0.2	4,553	0.7
Net Worth	22,282	49.0	83,139	48.1	179,500	51.8	315,468	48.5
Total Liab & Net Worth	**45,474**	**100.0**	**172,847**	**100.0**	**346,525**	**100.0**	**650,449**	**100.0**
Net Sales	353,577	100.0	668,680	100.0	1,369,497	100.0	2,401,884	100.0
Gross Profit	133,652	37.8	244,737	36.6	443,717	32.4	629,294	26.2
Net Profit After Tax	24,750	7.0	42,796	6.4	71,214	5.2	115,290	4.8
Working Capital	10,732	—	60,324	—	130,640	—	229,609	—

RATIOS	UQ	MED	LQ	UQ	MED	LQ	UQ	MED	LQ	UQ	MED	LQ
SOLVENCY												
Quick Ratio (times)	4.2	1.2	0.6	2.9	1.5	0.9	3.2	1.8	1.0	2.7	1.4	1.1
Current Ratio (times)	4.8	1.7	0.9	4.0	2.0	1.1	4.4	2.3	1.5	4.0	2.0	1.4
Curr Liab To Nw (%)	15.6	49.8	128.0	23.3	48.4	156.0	17.0	53.1	132.6	28.6	69.4	180.3
Curr Liab To Inv (%)	70.6	193.4	394.4	122.4	236.0	374.6	89.1	174.3	340.1	97.6	180.2	311.0
Total Liab To Nw (%)	21.7	64.5	170.7	27.5	78.7	190.0	29.9	68.0	145.8	45.2	89.6	195.0
Fixed Assets To Nw (%)	32.4	64.2	123.7	21.1	46.7	96.7	14.6	29.4	65.4	16.2	30.1	72.6
EFFICIENCY												
Coll Period (days)	8.8	18.8	30.4	19.7	32.9	53.1	27.3	36.8	48.3	32.5	49.3	71.5
Sales To Inv (times)	67.9	32.6	19.3	81.1	31.8	14.5	46.9	27.9	13.9	43.9	20.7	10.9
Assets To Sales (%)	8.1	12.8	20.7	17.9	24.7	35.9	19.1	26.2	36.9	22.0	30.2	43.0
Sales To Nwc (times)	51.7	20.0	10.4	37.4	12.7	5.6	17.2	8.7	6.0	17.8	9.6	6.5
Acct Pay To Sales (%)	1.7	3.6	7.0	2.4	4.8	7.4	2.0	4.1	7.8	2.4	4.6	9.4
PROFITABILITY												
Return On Sales (%)	13.0	4.4	1.1	11.6	4.3	1.6	7.8	4.8	1.2	8.5	3.8	1.9
Return On Assets (%)	47.4	21.4	3.2	21.7	11.3	4.9	25.2	12.6	3.9	26.7	12.1	6.1
Return On Nw (%)	120.9	61.4	22.2	80.2	36.2	10.8	61.7	25.5	10.4	53.3	28.1	12.0

	SIC 1751 CARPENTRY WORK $1,000,000 - $5,000,000 (61)		SIC 1752 FLR LAYING WORK, NEC (NO BREAKDOWN) (661)		SIC 1752 FLR LAYING WORK, NEC UNDER $100,000 (176)		SIC 1752 FLR LAYING WORK, NEC $100,000 - $250,000 (154)	
	$	%	$	%	$	%	$	%
Cash	160,673	9.3	38,550	14.8	10,384	22.5	29,270	17.8
Accounts Receivable	922,574	53.4	110,700	42.5	13,753	29.8	62,981	38.3
Notes Receivable	13,821	0.8	1,302	0.5	323	0.7	493	0.3
Inventory	148,579	8.6	26,568	10.2	3,323	7.2	16,280	9.9
Other Current	198,682	11.5	17,712	6.8	1,708	3.7	9,538	5.8
Total Current	**1,444,329**	**83.6**	**194,832**	**74.8**	**29,491**	**63.9**	**118,562**	**72.1**
Fixed Assets	202,137	11.7	51,573	19.8	14,446	31.3	34,204	20.8
Other Non-current	81,200	4.7	14,065	5.4	2,215	4.8	11,675	7.1
Total Assets	**1,727,666**	**100.0**	**260,471**	**100.0**	**46,152**	**100.0**	**164,441**	**100.0**
Accounts Payable	437,099	25.3	44,280	17.0	6,092	13.2	27,133	16.5
Bank Loans	12,094	0.7	260	0.1	46	0.1		—
Notes Payable	58,741	3.4	13,024	5.0	2,677	5.8	6,907	4.2
Other Current	302,342	17.5	39,852	15.3	6,830	14.8	23,515	14.3
Total Current	**810,275**	**46.9**	**97,416**	**37.4**	**15,646**	**33.9**	**57,554**	**35.0**
Other Long Term	183,133	10.6	27,610	10.6	5,954	12.9	15,786	9.6
Deferred Credits	3,455	0.2	260	0.1		—		—
Net Worth	730,803	42.3	135,184	51.9	24,553	53.2	91,100	55.4
Total Liab & Net Worth	**1,727,666**	**100.0**	**260,471**	**100.0**	**46,152**	**100.0**	**164,441**	**100.0**
Net Sales	5,928,079	100.0	1,216,358	100.0	309,524	100.0	751,576	100.0
Gross Profit	1,043,342	17.6	372,206	30.6	118,238	38.2	261,548	34.8
Net Profit After Tax	148,202	2.5	60,818	5.0	24,762	8.0	44,343	5.9
Working Capital	634,054	—	97,416	—	13,845	—	61,008	—

RATIOS

	SIC 1751 UQ	MED	LQ	SIC 1752 (NO BD) UQ	MED	LQ	SIC 1752 <$100,000 UQ	MED	LQ	SIC 1752 $100-250K UQ	MED	LQ
SOLVENCY												
Quick Ratio (times)	1.9	1.3	1.1	3.0	1.6	1.0	3.6	1.7	0.9	4.1	1.8	1.0
Current Ratio (times)	2.5	1.6	1.4	4.2	2.0	1.4	4.4	2.0	1.1	5.4	2.3	1.4
Curr Liab To Nw (%)	58.5	128.6	197.9	22.9	64.9	144.0	17.8	45.9	125.9	14.7	42.0	133.0
Curr Liab To Inv (%)	156.3	356.7	479.6	133.8	241.0	457.0	74.2	145.8	333.4	132.6	229.8	428.3
Total Liab To Nw (%)	82.5	148.0	203.7	34.0	82.2	177.5	27.2	57.9	175.8	24.3	66.0	152.2
Fixed Assets To Nw (%)	9.8	19.3	51.7	12.5	26.7	62.2	23.5	60.6	106.0	14.5	32.5	59.5
EFFICIENCY												
Coll Period (days)	44.9	56.6	88.3	27.7	48.0	69.4	11.7	32.5	47.9	18.9	27.7	49.1
Sales To Inv (times)	46.7	30.9	12.3	70.5	33.8	17.0	87.6	45.4	26.0	68.8	39.7	20.9
Assets To Sales (%)	22.8	32.5	41.0	18.2	25.9	36.2	8.2	16.4	24.5	15.0	22.4	32.1
Sales To Nwc (times)	14.3	8.8	5.9	19.0	9.6	6.1	51.6	17.1	9.1	27.6	13.7	6.2
Acct Pay To Sales (%)	4.3	7.4	9.7	2.4	4.3	7.1	1.6	2.7	5.5	1.7	3.4	5.8
PROFITABILITY												
Return On Sales (%)	4.7	1.7	0.4	8.4	3.5	1.2	16.1	7.4	1.9	11.2	5.3	1.3
Return On Assets (%)	13.4	5.4	0.8	24.4	9.0	3.4	91.0	31.9	7.3	30.3	13.5	4.3
Return On Nw (%)	33.8	10.1	4.0	49.6	19.5	7.4	107.3	59.9	17.4	50.6	30.6	9.6

SIC 1752 — FLR LAYING WORK, NEC
INDUSTRY ASSETS — $250,000 - $500,000
1995 (133 Establishments)

	$	%
Cash	36,632	10.3
Accounts Receivable	181,738	51.1
Notes Receivable	2,134	0.6
Inventory	38,766	10.9
Other Current	21,695	6.1
Total Current	**280,965**	**79.0**
Fixed Assets	60,461	17.0
Other Non-current	14,226	4.0
Total Assets	**355,652**	**100.0**
Accounts Payable	70,063	19.7
Bank Loans	356	0.1
Notes Payable	17,427	4.9
Other Current	45,523	12.8
Total Current	**133,370**	**37.5**
Other Long Term	43,034	12.1
Deferred Credits	—	—
Net Worth	179,249	50.4
Total Liab & Net Worth	**355,652**	**100.0**
Net Sales	1,458,679	100.0
Gross Profit	417,182	28.6
Net Profit After Tax	64,182	4.4
Working Capital	147,595	—

RATIOS	UQ	MED	LQ
SOLVENCY			
Quick Ratio (times)	3.0	1.8	1.1
Current Ratio (times)	4.1	2.2	1.5
Curr Liab To Nw (%)	29.3	60.9	116.0
Curr Liab To Inv (%)	139.5	254.2	484.4
Total Liab To Nw (%)	34.1	79.6	151.6
Fixed Assets To Nw (%)	11.8	21.1	59.3
EFFICIENCY			
Coll Period (days)	34.5	51.5	66.5
Sales To Inv (times)	91.6	34.4	15.3
Assets To Sales (%)	20.6	25.6	33.9
Sales To Nwc (times)	15.6	8.5	5.7
Acct Pay To Sales (%)	2.8	4.6	7.3
PROFITABILITY			
Return On Sales (%)	7.1	3.2	1.4
Return On Assets (%)	19.2	10.4	4.7
Return On Nw (%)	41.0	21.8	9.2

SIC 1752 — FLR LAYING WORK, NEC
INDUSTRY ASSETS — $500,000 - $1,000,000
1995 (99 Establishments)

	$	%
Cash	70,266	10.9
Accounts Receivable	310,716	48.2
Notes Receivable	1,934	0.3
Inventory	73,489	11.4
Other Current	63,175	9.8
Total Current	**519,578**	**80.6**
Fixed Assets	88,960	13.8
Other Non-current	36,100	5.6
Total Assets	**644,638**	**100.0**
Accounts Payable	115,390	17.9
Bank Loans	1,289	0.2
Notes Payable	26,430	4.1
Other Current	111,522	17.3
Total Current	**254,632**	**39.5**
Other Long Term	63,175	9.8
Deferred Credits	1,289	0.2
Net Worth	325,542	50.5
Total Liab & Net Worth	**644,638**	**100.0**
Net Sales	2,416,801	100.0
Gross Profit	657,370	27.2
Net Profit After Tax	74,921	3.1
Working Capital	264,946	—

RATIOS	UQ	MED	LQ
SOLVENCY			
Quick Ratio (times)	2.5	1.5	1.1
Current Ratio (times)	3.8	2.1	1.5
Curr Liab To Nw (%)	29.1	85.1	168.7
Curr Liab To Inv (%)	145.9	245.3	506.1
Total Liab To Nw (%)	38.4	95.4	197.5
Fixed Assets To Nw (%)	10.4	21.0	42.4
EFFICIENCY			
Coll Period (days)	45.5	53.3	70.5
Sales To Inv (times)	56.3	29.0	18.2
Assets To Sales (%)	23.8	31.5	38.5
Sales To Nwc (times)	12.5	7.8	5.0
Acct Pay To Sales (%)	3.0	5.3	7.9
PROFITABILITY			
Return On Sales (%)	4.7	2.6	1.0
Return On Assets (%)	11.9	6.3	2.5
Return On Nw (%)	33.7	13.9	4.3

SIC 1752 — FLR LAYING WORK, NEC
INDUSTRY ASSETS — $1,000,000 - $5,000,000
1995 (94 Establishments)

	$	%
Cash	134,672	8.6
Accounts Receivable	806,466	51.5
Notes Receivable	10,962	0.7
Inventory	205,140	13.1
Other Current	161,293	10.3
Total Current	**1,318,533**	**84.2**
Fixed Assets	162,859	10.4
Other Non-current	84,562	5.4
Total Assets	**1,565,954**	**100.0**
Accounts Payable	292,833	18.7
Bank Loans	—	—
Notes Payable	93,957	6.0
Other Current	299,097	19.1
Total Current	**685,888**	**43.8**
Other Long Term	109,617	7.0
Deferred Credits	3,132	0.2
Net Worth	767,317	49.0
Total Liab & Net Worth	**1,565,954**	**100.0**
Net Sales	4,859,094	100.0
Gross Profit	1,098,155	22.6
Net Profit After Tax	145,773	3.0
Working Capital	632,645	—

RATIOS	UQ	MED	LQ
SOLVENCY			
Quick Ratio (times)	2.0	1.4	1.0
Current Ratio (times)	3.0	1.8	1.5
Curr Liab To Nw (%)	43.7	95.4	168.2
Curr Liab To Inv (%)	199.6	304.0	478.4
Total Liab To Nw (%)	49.3	108.3	184.3
Fixed Assets To Nw (%)	9.9	18.0	27.3
EFFICIENCY			
Coll Period (days)	44.5	61.7	83.2
Sales To Inv (times)	68.8	29.5	14.0
Assets To Sales (%)	27.4	31.1	39.5
Sales To Nwc (times)	12.9	8.0	5.9
Acct Pay To Sales (%)	3.1	5.8	7.6
PROFITABILITY			
Return On Sales (%)	4.4	2.3	1.1
Return On Assets (%)	11.0	4.9	2.8
Return On Nw (%)	24.0	14.4	6.9

SIC 1761 — RRNF, SDNG, SHT MTLWK
(NO BREAKDOWN)
1995 (1898 Establishments)

	$	%
Cash	70,703	17.1
Accounts Receivable	150,916	36.5
Notes Receivable	3,721	0.9
Inventory	31,010	7.5
Other Current	39,279	9.5
Total Current	**295,630**	**71.5**
Fixed Assets	92,203	22.3
Other Non-current	25,635	6.2
Total Assets	**413,468**	**100.0**
Accounts Payable	69,463	16.8
Bank Loans	413	0.1
Notes Payable	17,779	4.3
Other Current	60,780	14.7
Total Current	**148,435**	**35.9**
Other Long Term	42,587	10.3
Deferred Credits	827	0.2
Net Worth	221,619	53.6
Total Liab & Net Worth	**413,468**	**100.0**
Net Sales	1,480,725	100.0
Gross Profit	445,698	30.1
Net Profit After Tax	68,113	4.6
Working Capital	147,195	—

RATIOS	UQ	MED	LQ
SOLVENCY			
Quick Ratio (times)	2.8	1.5	1.0
Current Ratio (times)	3.7	2.1	1.4
Curr Liab To Nw (%)	25.0	58.1	126.3
Curr Liab To Inv (%)	150.7	286.7	527.0
Total Liab To Nw (%)	31.6	74.4	163.0
Fixed Assets To Nw (%)	17.5	35.1	69.1
EFFICIENCY			
Coll Period (days)	27.7	43.8	65.7
Sales To Inv (times)	92.4	46.1	23.4
Assets To Sales (%)	21.4	29.2	40.8
Sales To Nwc (times)	16.5	9.2	5.6
Acct Pay To Sales (%)	2.7	4.7	7.9
PROFITABILITY			
Return On Sales (%)	7.6	3.1	1.0
Return On Assets (%)	20.1	8.3	2.9
Return On Nw (%)	43.5	16.8	5.6

SIC 1761 — RRNF,SDNG,SHT MTLWK — INDUSTRY ASSETS

UNDER $100,000 — 1995 (299 Establishments)

	$	%
Cash	15,455	28.1
Accounts Receivable	11,935	21.7
Notes Receivable	715	1.3
Inventory	2,970	5.4
Other Current	2,750	5.0
Total Current	**33,825**	**61.5**
Fixed Assets	18,260	33.2
Other Non-current	2,915	5.3
Total Assets	**55,000**	**100.0**
Accounts Payable	6,875	12.5
Bank Loans	—	—
Notes Payable	2,475	4.5
Other Current	9,130	16.6
Total Current	**18,480**	**33.6**
Other Long Term	6,215	11.3
Deferred Credits	—	—
Net Worth	30,305	55.1
Total Liab & Net Worth	**55,000**	**100.0**
Net Sales	412,457	100.0
Gross Profit	155,909	37.8
Net Profit After Tax	26,810	6.5
Working Capital	15,345	—

RATIOS	UQ	MED	LQ
SOLVENCY			
Quick Ratio (times)	4.5	1.7	0.8
Current Ratio (times)	5.6	2.2	1.1
Curr Liab To Nw (%)	12.8	38.2	86.0
Curr Liab To Inv (%)	108.9	201.9	363.9
Total Liab To Nw (%)	19.5	56.1	119.1
Fixed Assets To Nw (%)	23.3	54.0	101.6
EFFICIENCY			
Coll Period (days)	8.8	20.6	31.7
Sales To Inv (times)	159.5	83.6	38.6
Assets To Sales (%)	9.0	12.8	17.9
Sales To Nwc (times)	31.4	14.9	9.3
Acct Pay To Sales (%)	1.0	2.1	3.6
PROFITABILITY			
Return On Sales (%)	13.3	4.6	0.9
Return On Assets (%)	65.9	29.9	5.7
Return On Nw (%)	110.0	45.2	9.4

$100,000 - $250,000 — 1995 (382 Establishments)

	$	%
Cash	31,689	19.0
Accounts Receivable	52,703	31.6
Notes Receivable	1,835	1.1
Inventory	12,342	7.4
Other Current	11,008	6.6
Total Current	**109,576**	**65.7**
Fixed Assets	46,699	28.0
Other Non-current	10,507	6.3
Total Assets	**166,782**	**100.0**
Accounts Payable	25,518	15.3
Bank Loans	334	0.2
Notes Payable	7,672	4.6
Other Current	21,682	13.0
Total Current	**55,205**	**33.1**
Other Long Term	18,846	11.3
Deferred Credits	167	0.1
Net Worth	92,564	55.5
Total Liab & Net Worth	**166,782**	**100.0**
Net Sales	723,785	100.0
Gross Profit	263,458	36.4
Net Profit After Tax	38,361	5.3
Working Capital	54,371	—

RATIOS	UQ	MED	LQ
SOLVENCY			
Quick Ratio (times)	3.3	1.6	0.9
Current Ratio (times)	4.2	2.1	1.3
Curr Liab To Nw (%)	18.3	47.5	113.5
Curr Liab To Inv (%)	116.4	240.4	434.7
Total Liab To Nw (%)	25.7	61.8	148.0
Fixed Assets To Nw (%)	21.2	44.6	79.9
EFFICIENCY			
Coll Period (days)	19.7	32.1	48.5
Sales To Inv (times)	90.7	47.6	24.0
Assets To Sales (%)	16.3	23.7	33.9
Sales To Nwc (times)	22.1	11.6	6.9
Acct Pay To Sales (%)	2.4	4.0	6.4
PROFITABILITY			
Return On Sales (%)	9.6	4.2	1.0
Return On Assets (%)	34.9	14.6	3.1
Return On Nw (%)	68.2	29.7	6.3

$250,000 - $500,000 — 1995 (389 Establishments)

	$	%
Cash	58,500	16.4
Accounts Receivable	133,766	37.5
Notes Receivable	4,281	1.2
Inventory	27,467	7.7
Other Current	33,887	9.5
Total Current	**257,901**	**72.3**
Fixed Assets	77,049	21.6
Other Non-current	21,759	6.1
Total Assets	**356,710**	**100.0**
Accounts Payable	58,144	16.3
Bank Loans	—	—
Notes Payable	16,409	4.6
Other Current	43,519	12.2
Total Current	**118,071**	**33.1**
Other Long Term	39,595	11.1
Deferred Credits	1,070	0.3
Net Worth	197,974	55.5
Total Liab & Net Worth	**356,710**	**100.0**
Net Sales	1,223,115	100.0
Gross Profit	395,066	32.3
Net Profit After Tax	61,156	5.0
Working Capital	139,830	—

RATIOS	UQ	MED	LQ
SOLVENCY			
Quick Ratio (times)	3.1	1.7	1.0
Current Ratio (times)	4.2	2.3	1.5
Curr Liab To Nw (%)	22.3	48.6	114.3
Curr Liab To Inv (%)	147.4	292.4	529.6
Total Liab To Nw (%)	28.7	62.7	148.9
Fixed Assets To Nw (%)	17.3	33.2	65.7
EFFICIENCY			
Coll Period (days)	25.1	39.4	56.3
Sales To Inv (times)	93.6	43.7	22.3
Assets To Sales (%)	22.3	28.8	39.3
Sales To Nwc (times)	15.5	8.4	4.7
Acct Pay To Sales (%)	2.2	4.1	6.6
PROFITABILITY			
Return On Sales (%)	8.9	3.4	1.1
Return On Assets (%)	23.3	10.0	3.0
Return On Nw (%)	48.0	18.9	4.9

$500,000 - $1,000,000 — 1995 (394 Establishments)

	$	%
Cash	101,945	14.9
Accounts Receivable	267,519	39.1
Notes Receivable	3,421	0.5
Inventory	56,104	8.2
Other Current	79,366	11.6
Total Current	**508,355**	**74.3**
Fixed Assets	133,417	19.5
Other Non-current	42,420	6.2
Total Assets	**684,192**	**100.0**
Accounts Payable	116,997	17.1
Bank Loans	2,053	0.3
Notes Payable	21,894	3.2
Other Current	93,734	13.7
Total Current	**234,678**	**34.3**
Other Long Term	66,367	9.7
Deferred Credits	1,368	0.2
Net Worth	381,779	55.8
Total Liab & Net Worth	**684,192**	**100.0**
Net Sales	2,160,519	100.0
Gross Profit	604,945	28.0
Net Profit After Tax	92,902	4.3
Working Capital	273,677	—

RATIOS	UQ	MED	LQ
SOLVENCY			
Quick Ratio (times)	2.7	1.6	1.1
Current Ratio (times)	3.7	2.2	1.6
Curr Liab To Nw (%)	25.7	54.6	105.8
Curr Liab To Inv (%)	151.6	275.1	536.0
Total Liab To Nw (%)	33.4	70.1	136.6
Fixed Assets To Nw (%)	16.2	33.7	62.5
EFFICIENCY			
Coll Period (days)	34.0	48.2	67.2
Sales To Inv (times)	90.0	47.1	22.3
Assets To Sales (%)	25.9	32.6	44.2
Sales To Nwc (times)	13.4	7.9	5.2
Acct Pay To Sales (%)	3.1	5.2	8.4
PROFITABILITY			
Return On Sales (%)	6.4	3.1	1.1
Return On Assets (%)	15.1	7.6	3.2
Return On Nw (%)	30.8	13.8	6.2

SIC 1761 RRNF,SDNG,SHT MTLWK
INDUSTRY ASSETS
$1,000,000 - $5,000,000
1995 (402 Establishments)

	$	%
Cash	186,382	11.9
Accounts Receivable	725,168	46.3
Notes Receivable	12,530	0.8
Inventory	125,299	8.0
Other Current	197,346	12.6
Total Current	**1,246,725**	**79.6**
Fixed Assets	222,406	14.2
Other Non-current	97,107	6.2
Total Assets	**1,566,238**	**100.0**
Accounts Payable	324,211	20.7
Bank Loans	3,132	0.2
Notes Payable	68,914	4.4
Other Current	288,188	18.4
Total Current	**684,446**	**43.7**
Other Long Term	126,865	8.1
Deferred Credits	4,699	0.3
Net Worth	750,228	47.9
Total Liab & Net Worth	**1,566,238**	**100.0**
Net Sales	4,776,020	100.0
Gross Profit	1,093,709	22.9
Net Profit After Tax	152,833	3.2
Working Capital	562,279	—

RATIOS	UQ	MED	LQ
SOLVENCY			
Quick Ratio (times)	2.0	1.3	1.0
Current Ratio (times)	2.5	1.8	1.4
Curr Lib To Nw (%)	47.9	100.7	172.6
Curr Lib To Inv (%)	204.5	337.1	570.6
Total Lib To Nw (%)	57.6	119.6	207.4
Fixed Assets To Nw (%)	16.2	29.1	54.4
EFFICIENCY			
Coll Period (days)	43.6	61.7	81.7
Sales To Inv (times)	80.3	42.2	22.6
Assets To Sales (%)	28.6	34.8	44.4
Sales To Nwc (times)	14.3	8.3	5.2
Acct Pay To Sales (%)	3.9	6.3	10.0
PROFITABILITY			
Return On Sales (%)	4.5	2.3	1.0
Return On Assets (%)	11.6	5.5	2.7
Return On Nw (%)	26.9	13.7	6.1

SIC 1761 RRNF,SDNG,SHT MTLWK
INDUSTRY ASSETS
$5,000,000-$25,000,000
1995 (27 Establishments)

	$	%
Cash	352,138	5.5
Accounts Receivable	3,156,433	49.3
Notes Receivable	6,403	0.1
Inventory	320,125	5.0
Other Current	992,388	15.5
Total Current	**4,827,486**	**75.4**
Fixed Assets	531,408	8.3
Other Non-current	1,043,608	16.3
Total Assets	**6,402,501**	**100.0**
Accounts Payable	1,414,953	22.1
Bank Loans	—	—
Notes Payable	332,930	5.2
Other Current	864,338	13.5
Total Current	**2,612,220**	**40.8**
Other Long Term	806,715	12.6
Deferred Credits	12,805	0.2
Net Worth	2,970,760	46.4
Total Liab & Net Worth	**6,402,501**	**100.0**
Net Sales	17,071,894	100.0
Gross Profit	2,543,712	14.9
Net Profit After Tax	307,294	1.8
Working Capital	2,215,266	—

RATIOS	UQ	MED	LQ
SOLVENCY			
Quick Ratio (times)	2.0	1.2	1.0
Current Ratio (times)	2.5	1.7	1.4
Curr Lib To Nw (%)	43.2	98.1	183.3
Curr Lib To Inv (%)	264.1	426.1	587.4
Total Lib To Nw (%)	49.8	136.7	230.0
Fixed Assets To Nw (%)	6.9	16.0	33.3
EFFICIENCY			
Coll Period (days)	57.3	65.2	84.3
Sales To Inv (times)	99.3	55.7	29.3
Assets To Sales (%)	32.8	42.0	51.0
Sales To Nwc (times)	12.2	8.9	6.3
Acct Pay To Sales (%)	5.3	9.5	14.5
PROFITABILITY			
Return On Sales (%)	2.6	1.4	0.6
Return On Assets (%)	5.6	3.7	1.2
Return On Nw (%)	13.7	8.4	4.6

SIC 1771 CONCRETE WORK
(NO BREAKDOWN)
1995 (1137 Establishments)

	$	%
Cash	69,068	16.9
Accounts Receivable	134,866	33.0
Notes Receivable	3,269	0.8
Inventory	7,765	1.9
Other Current	27,382	6.7
Total Current	**242,350**	**59.3**
Fixed Assets	142,222	34.8
Other Non-current	24,112	5.9
Total Assets	**408,684**	**100.0**
Accounts Payable	62,120	15.2
Bank Loans	817	0.2
Notes Payable	21,252	5.2
Other Current	62,120	15.2
Total Current	**146,309**	**35.8**
Other Long Term	58,442	14.3
Deferred Credits	1,226	0.3
Net Worth	202,707	49.6
Total Liab & Net Worth	**408,684**	**100.0**
Net Sales	1,458,710	100.0
Gross Profit	439,072	30.1
Net Profit After Tax	70,018	4.8
Working Capital	96,041	—

RATIOS	UQ	MED	LQ
SOLVENCY			
Quick Ratio (times)	2.6	1.4	0.9
Current Ratio (times)	3.1	1.7	1.1
Curr Lib To Nw (%)	25.5	63.6	135.7
Curr Lib To Inv (%)	153.4	350.6	640.5
Total Lib To Nw (%)	35.0	92.8	190.8
Fixed Assets To Nw (%)	30.3	62.1	119.9
EFFICIENCY			
Coll Period (days)	27.6	47.5	68.7
Sales To Inv (times)	229.3	103.3	35.2
Assets To Sales (%)	22.5	31.8	42.7
Sales To Nwc (times)	21.1	10.8	5.9
Acct Pay To Sales (%)	2.3	4.8	8.2
PROFITABILITY			
Return On Sales (%)	8.4	3.8	1.4
Return On Assets (%)	21.1	9.7	3.8
Return On Nw (%)	46.2	21.6	8.7

SIC 1771 CONCRETE WORK
INDUSTRY ASSETS
UNDER $100,000
1995 (161 Establishments)

	$	%
Cash	16,473	28.3
Accounts Receivable	9,430	16.2
Notes Receivable	175	0.3
Inventory	407	0.7
Other Current	2,212	3.8
Total Current	**28,698**	**49.3**
Fixed Assets	26,951	46.3
Other Non-current	2,561	4.4
Total Assets	**58,210**	**100.0**
Accounts Payable	6,345	10.9
Bank Loans	—	—
Notes Payable	4,249	7.3
Other Current	10,012	17.2
Total Current	**20,606**	**35.4**
Other Long Term	8,266	14.2
Deferred Credits	—	—
Net Worth	29,338	50.4
Total Liab & Net Worth	**58,210**	**100.0**
Net Sales	395,631	100.0
Gross Profit	152,318	38.5
Net Profit After Tax	27,694	7.0
Working Capital	8,092	—

RATIOS	UQ	MED	LQ
SOLVENCY			
Quick Ratio (times)	2.4	1.3	0.6
Current Ratio (times)	2.9	1.5	0.7
Curr Lib To Nw (%)	17.0	46.9	115.1
Curr Lib To Inv (%)	113.4	167.6	548.4
Total Lib To Nw (%)	26.4	71.7	179.7
Fixed Assets To Nw (%)	42.4	85.9	157.6
EFFICIENCY			
Coll Period (days)	5.5	17.9	31.0
Sales To Inv (times)	153.5	116.6	101.2
Assets To Sales (%)	10.0	14.4	22.9
Sales To Nwc (times)	56.5	22.0	9.1
Acct Pay To Sales (%)	0.9	2.3	3.8
PROFITABILITY			
Return On Sales (%)	13.2	6.2	1.8
Return On Assets (%)	66.1	28.6	8.6
Return On Nw (%)	127.7	49.2	19.1

SIC 1771 CONCRETE WORK — INDUSTRY ASSETS $100,000 - $250,000 — 1995 (250 Establishments)

	$	%
Cash	31,466	18.9
Accounts Receivable	42,953	25.8
Notes Receivable	1,498	0.9
Inventory	3,496	2.1
Other Current	10,489	6.3
Total Current	**89,902**	**54.0**
Fixed Assets	67,094	40.3
Other Non-current	9,490	5.7
Total Assets	**166,486**	**100.0**
Accounts Payable	18,813	11.3
Bank Loans	499	0.3
Notes Payable	9,989	6.0
Other Current	25,972	15.6
Total Current	**55,273**	**33.2**
Other Long Term	25,472	15.3
Deferred Credits	666	0.4
Net Worth	85,074	51.1
Total Liab & Net Worth	**166,486**	**100.0**
Net Sales	664,771	100.0
Gross Profit	230,676	34.7
Net Profit After Tax	30,579	4.6
Working Capital	34,629	—

RATIOS	UQ	MED	LQ
SOLVENCY			
Quick Ratio (times)	3.0	1.4	0.9
Current Ratio (times)	3.5	1.7	1.1
Curr Liab To Nw (%)	15.0	54.9	114.4
Curr Liab To Inv (%)	97.6	209.5	460.5
Total Liab To Nw (%)	28.9	76.1	178.8
Fixed Assets To Nw (%)	35.9	66.6	124.5
EFFICIENCY			
Coll Period (days)	20.7	35.0	52.8
Sales To Inv (times)	112.9	48.1	15.3
Assets To Sales (%)	18.4	24.5	34.7
Sales To Nwc (times)	26.1	11.8	6.8
Acct Pay To Sales (%)	1.2	3.0	6.1
PROFITABILITY			
Return On Sales (%)	10.3	4.5	1.0
Return On Assets (%)	35.4	13.4	2.3
Return On Nw (%)	68.9	32.8	7.3

SIC 1771 CONCRETE WORK — INDUSTRY ASSETS $250,000 - $500,000 — 1995 (240 Establishments)

	$	%
Cash	54,235	15.4
Accounts Receivable	119,739	34.0
Notes Receivable	2,465	0.7
Inventory	6,691	1.9
Other Current	20,074	5.7
Total Current	**203,204**	**57.7**
Fixed Assets	124,317	35.3
Other Non-current	24,652	7.0
Total Assets	**352,173**	**100.0**
Accounts Payable	56,700	16.1
Bank Loans	704	0.2
Notes Payable	19,017	5.4
Other Current	45,078	12.8
Total Current	**121,500**	**34.5**
Other Long Term	54,587	15.5
Deferred Credits	352	0.1
Net Worth	175,734	49.9
Total Liab & Net Worth	**352,173**	**100.0**
Net Sales	1,206,082	100.0
Gross Profit	420,923	34.9
Net Profit After Tax	66,335	5.5
Working Capital	81,704	—

RATIOS	UQ	MED	LQ
SOLVENCY			
Quick Ratio (times)	2.8	1.7	0.9
Current Ratio (times)	3.5	1.8	1.1
Curr Liab To Nw (%)	21.9	65.7	129.4
Curr Liab To Inv (%)	143.3	291.3	758.7
Total Liab To Nw (%)	34.1	89.9	184.5
Fixed Assets To Nw (%)	34.5	62.6	114.0
EFFICIENCY			
Coll Period (days)	24.1	43.3	55.9
Sales To Inv (times)	294.3	129.0	47.6
Assets To Sales (%)	23.6	29.9	38.6
Sales To Nwc (times)	21.2	11.9	6.3
Acct Pay To Sales (%)	1.9	4.7	7.1
PROFITABILITY			
Return On Sales (%)	9.1	3.8	2.0
Return On Assets (%)	18.6	10.3	5.1
Return On Nw (%)	42.1	20.8	11.4

SIC 1771 CONCRETE WORK — INDUSTRY ASSETS $500,000 - $1,000,000 — 1995 (202 Establishments)

	$	%
Cash	99,206	14.1
Accounts Receivable	261,735	37.2
Notes Receivable	9,147	1.3
Inventory	14,072	2.0
Other Current	59,101	8.4
Total Current	**443,261**	**63.0**
Fixed Assets	211,077	30.0
Other Non-current	49,251	7.0
Total Assets	**703,589**	**100.0**
Accounts Payable	109,760	15.6
Bank Loans	1,407	0.2
Notes Payable	28,144	4.0
Other Current	87,245	12.4
Total Current	**226,556**	**32.2**
Other Long Term	99,206	14.1
Deferred Credits	3,518	0.5
Net Worth	374,309	53.2
Total Liab & Net Worth	**703,589**	**100.0**
Net Sales	1,929,765	100.0
Gross Profit	588,578	30.5
Net Profit After Tax	79,120	4.1
Working Capital	216,705	—

RATIOS	UQ	MED	LQ
SOLVENCY			
Quick Ratio (times)	2.9	1.8	1.1
Current Ratio (times)	3.6	2.1	1.4
Curr Liab To Nw (%)	22.2	46.6	117.6
Curr Liab To Inv (%)	189.1	425.4	741.2
Total Liab To Nw (%)	28.0	62.6	162.0
Fixed Assets To Nw (%)	26.4	51.5	107.5
EFFICIENCY			
Coll Period (days)	27.0	49.5	69.4
Sales To Inv (times)	296.2	128.7	37.0
Assets To Sales (%)	27.7	34.6	48.1
Sales To Nwc (times)	13.5	8.3	5.3
Acct Pay To Sales (%)	2.5	4.7	9.3
PROFITABILITY			
Return On Sales (%)	7.5	4.1	1.5
Return On Assets (%)	16.8	10.3	4.2
Return On Nw (%)	39.3	20.7	10.0

SIC 1771 CONCRETE WORK — INDUSTRY ASSETS $1,000,000 - $5,000,000 — 1995 (251 Establishments)

	$	%
Cash	210,507	12.9
Accounts Receivable	698,427	42.8
Notes Receivable	13,055	0.8
Inventory	35,900	2.2
Other Current	120,756	7.4
Total Current	**1,078,645**	**66.1**
Fixed Assets	460,178	28.2
Other Non-current	93,015	5.7
Total Assets	**1,631,838**	**100.0**
Accounts Payable	308,417	18.9
Bank Loans	3,264	0.2
Notes Payable	65,274	4.0
Other Current	283,940	17.4
Total Current	**660,894**	**40.5**
Other Long Term	226,825	13.9
Deferred Credits	4,896	0.3
Net Worth	739,223	45.3
Total Liab & Net Worth	**1,631,838**	**100.0**
Net Sales	4,554,946	100.0
Gross Profit	974,758	21.4
Net Profit After Tax	191,308	4.2
Working Capital	417,751	—

RATIOS	UQ	MED	LQ
SOLVENCY			
Quick Ratio (times)	1.9	1.3	1.0
Current Ratio (times)	2.3	1.5	1.2
Curr Liab To Nw (%)	46.6	87.8	162.2
Curr Liab To Inv (%)	245.2	421.8	597.8
Total Liab To Nw (%)	70.6	123.6	236.3
Fixed Assets To Nw (%)	28.0	57.0	110.5
EFFICIENCY			
Coll Period (days)	41.2	58.6	82.3
Sales To Inv (times)	227.4	88.9	37.0
Assets To Sales (%)	29.3	37.8	48.0
Sales To Nwc (times)	17.4	10.4	5.8
Acct Pay To Sales (%)	3.7	5.9	9.4
PROFITABILITY			
Return On Sales (%)	7.0	2.9	1.4
Return On Assets (%)	15.3	6.5	3.0
Return On Nw (%)	36.2	18.8	7.4

SIC 1771 CONCRETE WORK
INDUSTRY ASSETS
$5,000,000-$25,000,000
1995 (31 Establishments)

SIC 1781 WATER WELL DRILLING (NO BREAKDOWN)
1995 (233 Establishments)

SIC 1781 WATER WELL DRILLING
INDUSTRY ASSETS
UNDER $100,000
1995 (34 Establishments)

SIC 1781 WATER WELL DRILLING
INDUSTRY ASSETS
$100,000 - $250,000
1995 (48 Establishments)

	SIC 1771 $	%	SIC 1781 (No Brk) $	%	SIC 1781 Under 100k $	%	SIC 1781 100-250k $	%
Cash	639,285	8.5	58,851	14.1	18,821	25.5	21,664	12.9
Accounts Receivable	3,948,525	52.5	102,258	24.5	14,909	20.2	32,748	19.5
Notes Receivable	45,126	0.6	3,339	0.8	1,033	1.4	504	0.3
Inventory	240,672	3.2	37,564	9.0	5,535	7.5	12,092	7.2
Other Current	879,957	11.7	23,791	5.7	3,764	5.1	8,061	4.8
Total Current	**5,753,565**	**76.5**	**225,803**	**54.1**	**44,062**	**59.7**	**75,070**	**44.7**
Fixed Assets	1,526,763	20.3	162,778	39.0	26,275	35.6	77,085	45.9
Other Non-current	240,672	3.2	28,799	6.9	3,469	4.7	15,786	9.4
Total Assets	**7,521,000**	**100.0**	**417,380**	**100.0**	**73,806**	**100.0**	**167,941**	**100.0**
Accounts Payable	1,722,309	22.9	37,982	9.1	7,159	9.7	15,954	9.5
Bank Loans	—	—	417	0.1	—	—	—	—
Notes Payable	330,924	4.4	17,113	4.1	4,724	6.4	8,061	4.8
Other Current	1,413,948	18.8	57,598	13.8	10,259	13.9	28,886	17.2
Total Current	**3,467,181**	**46.1**	**113,110**	**27.1**	**22,142**	**30.0**	**52,901**	**31.5**
Other Long Term	714,495	9.5	79,720	19.1	15,721	21.3	40,810	24.3
Deferred Credits	7,521	0.1	417	0.1	—	—	—	—
Net Worth	3,331,803	44.3	224,133	53.7	35,944	48.7	74,230	44.2
Total Liab & Net Worth	**7,521,000**	**100.0**	**417,380**	**100.0**	**73,806**	**100.0**	**167,941**	**100.0**
Net Sales	18,951,828	100.0	911,402	100.0	341,661	100.0	441,506	100.0
Gross Profit	2,937,533	15.5	380,966	41.8	188,597	55.2	207,066	46.9
Net Profit After Tax	606,458	3.2	61,975	6.8	36,899	10.8	28,698	6.5
Working Capital	2,286,384	—	112,693	—	21,920	—	22,169	—

RATIOS	1771 UQ	MED	LQ	NoBrk UQ	MED	LQ	U100k UQ	MED	LQ	100-250k UQ	MED	LQ
SOLVENCY												
Quick Ratio (times)	2.2	1.2	1.0	3.1	1.5	0.8	3.1	1.7	0.9	2.5	1.0	0.3
Current Ratio (times)	2.7	1.4	1.2	4.4	2.2	1.3	3.7	2.1	1.3	3.9	1.5	0.6
Curr Liab To Nw (%)	43.4	109.7	204.8	16.4	38.1	106.2	25.7	39.7	116.2	18.8	31.5	119.9
Curr Liab To Inv (%)	249.5	476.5	733.5	91.2	204.4	386.6	84.4	243.3	444.4	148.9	300.6	419.7
Total Liab To Nw (%)	50.2	131.2	263.4	26.2	66.1	158.3	32.3	43.6	173.3	21.8	58.9	160.0
Fixed Assets To Nw (%)	11.8	38.6	81.6	34.1	61.6	116.5	32.2	48.7	94.8	33.4	95.3	167.8
EFFICIENCY												
Coll Period (days)	61.0	83.2	108.0	31.0	50.9	72.5	18.3	35.8	40.7	25.2	37.3	49.1
Sales To Inv (times)	206.4	107.2	31.3	51.5	24.4	12.9	96.8	48.3	23.2	55.6	37.9	21.6
Assets To Sales (%)	34.2	37.1	69.9	35.2	46.5	66.1	18.3	20.7	31.9	26.9	36.1	47.2
Sales To Nwc (times)	19.7	6.8	4.2	11.1	6.4	3.6	15.4	9.4	7.1	22.4	7.9	4.7
Acct Pay To Sales (%)	5.7	8.3	13.8	2.3	3.9	6.4	3.2	5.7	8.0	2.1	3.9	6.8
PROFITABILITY												
Return On Sales (%)	3.9	2.1	1.2	10.8	4.7	1.1	15.9	4.4	0.7	9.1	3.9	0.1
Return On Assets (%)	9.0	5.7	2.5	15.7	7.3	1.6	20.1	6.1	(0.9)	19.0	9.7	0.7
Return On Nw (%)	22.2	13.6	7.7	33.1	13.4	2.7	30.3	4.9	(2.9)	61.3	22.6	2.1

	SIC 1781 WATER WELL DRILLING INDUSTRY ASSETS $250,000 - $500,000 1995 (53 Establishments)		SIC 1781 WATER WELL DRILLING INDUSTRY ASSETS $500,000 - $1,000,000 1995 (45 Establishments)		SIC 1781 WATER WELL DRILLING INDUSTRY ASSETS $1,000,000 - $5,000,000 1995 (45 Establishments)		SIC 1791 STRUCT STEEL ERCTN (NO BREAKDOWN) 1995 (356 Establishments)	
	$	%	$	%	$	%	$	%
Cash	49,079	14.1	103,129	14.2	168,489	9.7	99,974	14.8
Accounts Receivable	91,197	26.2	178,660	24.6	500,256	28.8	271,552	40.2
Notes Receivable	3,481	1.0	6,536	0.9	15,633	0.9	5,404	0.8
Inventory	40,029	11.5	63,911	8.8	163,278	9.4	26,345	3.9
Other Current	17,056	4.9	26,872	3.7	145,908	8.4	70,252	10.4
Total Current	**200,842**	**57.7**	**379,108**	**52.2**	**993,564**	**57.2**	**473,527**	**70.1**
Fixed Assets	127,745	36.7	309,387	42.6	611,424	35.2	158,743	23.5
Other Non-current	19,492	5.6	37,766	5.2	132,012	7.6	43,232	6.4
Total Assets	**348,080**	**100.0**	**726,260**	**100.0**	**1,737,000**	**100.0**	**675,502**	**100.0**
Accounts Payable	30,979	8.9	57,375	7.9	151,119	8.7	108,080	16.0
Bank Loans	—	—	—	—	8,685	0.5	1,351	0.2
Notes Payable	6,962	2.0	26,872	3.7	79,902	4.6	33,775	5.0
Other Current	38,637	11.1	83,520	11.5	255,339	14.7	124,292	18.4
Total Current	**76,578**	**22.0**	**167,766**	**23.1**	**495,045**	**28.5**	**267,499**	**39.6**
Other Long Term	63,002	18.1	134,358	18.5	250,128	14.4	81,060	12.0
Deferred Credits	348	0.1	2,179	0.3	1,737	0.1	4,053	0.6
Net Worth	208,152	59.8	421,957	58.1	990,090	57.0	322,890	47.8
Total Liab & Net Worth	**348,080**	**100.0**	**726,260**	**100.0**	**1,737,000**	**100.0**	**675,502**	**100.0**
Net Sales	736,814	100.0	1,174,470	100.0	3,535,009	100.0	2,151,594	100.0
Gross Profit	306,515	41.6	428,682	36.5	1,332,698	37.7	557,263	25.9
Net Profit After Tax	43,472	5.9	84,562	7.2	205,031	5.8	96,822	4.5
Working Capital	124,264	—	211,342	—	498,519	—	206,028	—

RATIOS	UQ	MED	LQ	UQ	MED	LQ	UQ	MED	LQ	UQ	MED	LQ
SOLVENCY												
Quick Ratio (times)	5.3	2.2	1.2	3.3	1.8	0.9	3.0	1.4	0.8	2.4	1.4	1.0
Current Ratio (times)	9.3	3.0	2.0	4.1	2.7	1.3	4.3	2.0	1.4	3.2	1.7	1.3
Curr Liab To Nw (%)	8.1	31.4	61.8	16.8	31.9	67.6	16.5	47.2	113.1	28.0	78.3	148.3
Curr Liab To Inv (%)	60.7	125.2	259.7	92.8	198.1	369.2	126.3	203.4	350.2	164.0	294.3	523.0
Total Liab To Nw (%)	12.6	62.2	107.0	24.2	56.5	138.7	32.8	95.1	151.5	44.2	104.3	204.4
Fixed Assets To Nw (%)	28.4	53.8	108.7	39.0	61.6	103.4	34.8	67.8	103.8	19.0	41.3	89.6
EFFICIENCY												
Coll Period (days)	29.9	51.5	70.0	35.1	56.4	73.9	46.4	52.2	75.6	40.9	60.2	80.7
Sales To Inv (times)	42.0	15.1	8.1	65.5	30.1	13.2	37.3	19.3	12.4	122.2	48.0	18.3
Assets To Sales (%)	38.2	48.9	69.8	43.0	58.4	68.7	46.6	55.4	66.2	28.1	34.8	52.1
Sales To Nwc (times)	8.9	5.8	3.2	7.0	5.5	3.5	10.4	6.0	3.7	15.3	8.5	5.2
Acct Pay To Sales (%)	2.1	3.7	5.3	1.8	3.2	6.3	2.5	4.4	6.4	3.0	5.7	9.5
PROFITABILITY												
Return On Sales (%)	10.4	5.1	1.8	13.8	6.4	1.6	8.8	3.4	(0.2)	9.0	3.7	1.0
Return On Assets (%)	13.7	9.0	3.1	17.7	11.2	2.8	8.6	4.9	(1.1)	18.9	7.5	1.0
Return On Nw (%)	28.8	16.3	5.4	34.0	17.5	5.0	17.5	7.5	(3.8)	46.9	19.8	2.5

SIC 1791 STRUCT STEEL ERCTN — INDUSTRY ASSETS UNDER $100,000 — 1995 (36 Establishments)

	$	%
Cash	15,887	33.0
Accounts Receivable	7,269	15.1
Notes Receivable	1,107	2.3
Inventory	867	1.8
Other Current	5,536	11.5
Total Current	**30,666**	**63.7**
Fixed Assets	15,694	32.6
Other Non-current	1,781	3.7
Total Assets	**48,141**	**100.0**
Accounts Payable	3,803	7.9
Bank Loans	—	—
Notes Payable	6,355	13.2
Other Current	8,617	17.9
Total Current	**18,775**	**39.0**
Other Long Term	6,788	14.1
Deferred Credits	48	0.1
Net Worth	22,530	46.8
Total Liab & Net Worth	**48,141**	**100.0**
Net Sales	269,959	100.0
Gross Profit	110,143	40.8
Net Profit After Tax	10,798	4.0
Working Capital	11,891	—

RATIOS	UQ	MED	LQ
SOLVENCY			
Quick Ratio (times)	3.6	1.3	0.6
Current Ratio (times)	3.8	1.7	1.1
Curr Liab To Nw (%)	18.3	60.0	137.5
Curr Liab To Inv (%)	273.1	517.1	718.3
Total Liab To Nw (%)	35.3	91.7	158.9
Fixed Assets To Nw (%)	29.3	73.5	96.7
EFFICIENCY			
Coll Period (days)	5.8	35.4	63.2
Sales To Inv (times)	190.9	56.5	52.7
Assets To Sales (%)	9.8	17.0	27.4
Sales To Nwc (times)	57.8	28.3	17.3
Acct Pay To Sales (%)	3.6	5.6	11.0
PROFITABILITY			
Return On Sales (%)	12.0	(0.4)	(3.2)
Return On Assets (%)	10.7	(7.5)	(17.2)
Return On Nw (%)	20.3	(37.9)	(55.1)

SIC 1791 STRUCT STEEL ERCTN — INDUSTRY ASSETS $100,000 - $250,000 — 1995 (44 Establishments)

	$	%
Cash	30,694	17.2
Accounts Receivable	61,566	34.5
Notes Receivable	178	0.1
Inventory	8,923	5.0
Other Current	9,636	5.4
Total Current	**110,997**	**62.2**
Fixed Assets	54,606	30.6
Other Non-current	12,849	7.2
Total Assets	**178,452**	**100.0**
Accounts Payable	28,374	15.9
Bank Loans	714	0.4
Notes Payable	9,458	5.3
Other Current	25,697	14.4
Total Current	**64,243**	**36.0**
Other Long Term	15,525	8.7
Deferred Credits	3,569	2.0
Net Worth	95,115	53.3
Total Liab & Net Worth	**178,452**	**100.0**
Net Sales	795,000	100.0
Gross Profit	277,455	34.9
Net Profit After Tax	25,440	3.2
Working Capital	46,754	—

RATIOS	UQ	MED	LQ
SOLVENCY			
Quick Ratio (times)	5.2	1.4	0.9
Current Ratio (times)	6.2	1.5	1.1
Curr Liab To Nw (%)	12.9	54.3	107.6
Curr Liab To Inv (%)	55.5	92.9	206.3
Total Liab To Nw (%)	20.4	81.3	162.2
Fixed Assets To Nw (%)	25.2	55.2	126.6
EFFICIENCY			
Coll Period (days)	15.9	44.2	85.3
Sales To Inv (times)	270.3	28.4	9.3
Assets To Sales (%)	16.5	24.7	53.8
Sales To Nwc (times)	19.7	9.2	5.3
Acct Pay To Sales (%)	2.0	4.6	9.5
PROFITABILITY			
Return On Sales (%)	8.0	3.4	0.4
Return On Assets (%)	22.7	5.4	(0.8)
Return On Nw (%)	55.6	16.2	(10.2)

SIC 1791 STRUCT STEEL ERCTN — INDUSTRY ASSETS $250,000 - $500,000 — 1995 (62 Establishments)

	$	%
Cash	53,001	14.4
Accounts Receivable	143,544	39.0
Notes Receivable	368	0.1
Inventory	6,625	1.8
Other Current	41,959	11.4
Total Current	**245,497**	**66.7**
Fixed Assets	98,641	26.8
Other Non-current	23,924	6.5
Total Assets	**368,062**	**100.0**
Accounts Payable	56,682	15.4
Bank Loans	—	—
Notes Payable	8,833	2.4
Other Current	66,619	18.1
Total Current	**132,134**	**35.9**
Other Long Term	51,529	14.0
Deferred Credits	4,417	1.2
Net Worth	179,982	48.9
Total Liab & Net Worth	**368,062**	**100.0**
Net Sales	1,204,432	100.0
Gross Profit	381,805	31.7
Net Profit After Tax	55,404	4.6
Working Capital	113,363	—

RATIOS	UQ	MED	LQ
SOLVENCY			
Quick Ratio (times)	3.7	1.5	1.0
Current Ratio (times)	3.7	1.7	1.2
Curr Liab To Nw (%)	17.1	69.6	135.0
Curr Liab To Inv (%)	135.6	260.0	351.8
Total Liab To Nw (%)	33.6	109.9	228.2
Fixed Assets To Nw (%)	21.6	47.1	104.1
EFFICIENCY			
Coll Period (days)	29.9	46.0	61.6
Sales To Inv (times)	77.3	53.4	29.1
Assets To Sales (%)	23.9	29.6	41.1
Sales To Nwc (times)	18.6	12.4	8.0
Acct Pay To Sales (%)	2.2	4.3	8.4
PROFITABILITY			
Return On Sales (%)	10.7	3.4	1.3
Return On Assets (%)	18.8	9.0	0.6
Return On Nw (%)	59.0	25.6	0.9

SIC 1791 STRUCT STEEL ERCTN — INDUSTRY ASSETS $500,000 - $1,000,000 — 1995 (86 Establishments)

	$	%
Cash	94,358	13.7
Accounts Receivable	323,021	46.9
Notes Receivable	1,377	0.2
Inventory	33,060	4.8
Other Current	55,788	8.1
Total Current	**507,605**	**73.7**
Fixed Assets	137,749	20.0
Other Non-current	43,391	6.3
Total Assets	**688,745**	**100.0**
Accounts Payable	132,239	19.2
Bank Loans	2,066	0.3
Notes Payable	30,305	4.4
Other Current	130,862	19.0
Total Current	**295,472**	**42.9**
Other Long Term	81,961	11.9
Deferred Credits	1,377	0.2
Net Worth	309,935	45.0
Total Liab & Net Worth	**688,745**	**100.0**
Net Sales	2,000,269	100.0
Gross Profit	468,063	23.4
Net Profit After Tax	104,014	5.2
Working Capital	212,133	—

RATIOS	UQ	MED	LQ
SOLVENCY			
Quick Ratio (times)	2.3	1.5	1.0
Current Ratio (times)	2.7	1.9	1.3
Curr Liab To Nw (%)	37.9	75.5	163.2
Curr Liab To Inv (%)	157.8	267.8	563.5
Total Liab To Nw (%)	57.7	101.0	204.0
Fixed Assets To Nw (%)	16.5	44.6	91.3
EFFICIENCY			
Coll Period (days)	41.7	57.3	75.7
Sales To Inv (times)	111.9	49.0	19.9
Assets To Sales (%)	29.8	34.5	43.4
Sales To Nwc (times)	15.4	7.6	5.5
Acct Pay To Sales (%)	3.3	5.7	9.6
PROFITABILITY			
Return On Sales (%)	10.0	5.6	2.4
Return On Assets (%)	22.8	12.3	6.4
Return On Nw (%)	66.1	36.1	16.6

SIC 1791 STRUCT STEEL ERCTN

	1791 $1,000,000-$5,000,000 (98 Est.) $	%	1791 $5,000,000-$25,000,000 (24 Est.) $	%	1793 No Breakdown (554 Est.) $	%	1793 Under $100,000 (111 Est.) $	%
Cash	181,063	10.7	709,087	8.5	41,710	15.8	13,157	23.8
Accounts Receivable	739,481	43.7	4,396,342	52.7	106,124	40.2	14,483	26.2
Notes Receivable	18,614	1.1	191,871	2.3	1,320	0.5	111	0.2
Inventory	72,764	4.3	433,795	5.2	38,279	14.5	6,910	12.5
Other Current	219,983	13.0	1,051,118	12.6	13,727	5.2	2,709	4.9
Total Current	**1,231,905**	**72.8**	**6,782,213**	**81.3**	**201,160**	**76.2**	**37,369**	**67.6**
Fixed Assets	336,743	19.9	1,284,700	15.4	48,046	18.2	14,373	26.0
Other Non-current	123,529	7.3	275,293	3.3	14,783	5.6	3,538	6.4
Total Assets	**1,692,177**	**100.0**	**8,342,205**	**100.0**	**263,990**	**100.0**	**55,280**	**100.0**
Accounts Payable	255,519	15.1	1,868,654	22.4	50,950	19.3	9,066	16.4
Bank Loans	3,384	0.2	—	—	264	0.1	—	—
Notes Payable	67,687	4.0	425,452	5.1	12,672	4.8	4,091	7.4
Other Current	348,588	20.6	1,318,068	15.8	37,751	14.3	10,172	18.4
Total Current	**675,179**	**39.9**	**3,612,175**	**43.3**	**101,636**	**38.5**	**23,328**	**42.2**
Other Long Term	196,293	11.6	767,483	9.2	26,399	10.0	7,242	13.1
Deferred Credits	5,077	0.3	16,684	0.2	264	0.1	—	—
Net Worth	815,629	48.2	3,945,863	47.3	135,691	51.4	24,710	44.7
Total Liab & Net Worth	**1,692,177**	**100.0**	**8,342,205**	**100.0**	**263,990**	**100.0**	**55,280**	**100.0**
Net Sales	4,581,762	100.0	16,257,342	100.0	933,182	100.0	311,782	100.0
Gross Profit	1,035,478	22.6	3,267,726	20.1	320,081	34.3	118,165	37.9
Net Profit After Tax	192,434	4.2	1,072,985	6.6	45,726	4.9	18,707	6.0
Working Capital	556,726	—	3,170,038	—	99,524	—	14,041	—

RATIOS (UQ / MED / LQ)

	UQ	MED	LQ	UQ	MED	LQ	UQ	MED	LQ	UQ	MED	LQ
SOLVENCY												
Quick Ratio (times)	2.1	1.4	1.0	1.9	1.5	1.1	2.8	1.5	1.0	2.6	1.1	0.7
Current Ratio (times)	2.9	1.7	1.4	2.7	2.0	1.3	3.8	2.1	1.4	3.2	1.6	1.1
Curr Liab To Nw (%)	31.7	87.5	173.4	50.5	83.6	169.9	27.6	62.2	141.0	24.2	58.2	156.3
Curr Liab To Inv (%)	213.4	334.7	495.6	294.7	437.8	560.7	105.3	202.4	404.4	105.8	213.5	454.0
Total Liab To Nw (%)	50.5	112.6	240.6	54.7	110.5	248.5	35.4	83.6	171.4	30.3	74.6	230.6
Fixed Assets To Nw (%)	15.0	33.3	71.4	10.8	23.7	42.3	12.0	27.3	58.5	17.3	40.6	104.4
EFFICIENCY												
Coll Period (days)	54.4	65.7	96.4	62.1	77.4	95.3	29.9	49.0	68.5	15.0	23.8	45.3
Sales To Inv (times)	126.6	59.9	21.4	129.9	43.1	16.6	52.0	25.2	12.8	58.2	37.1	22.0
Assets To Sales (%)	32.5	40.3	56.7	37.3	40.9	54.2	21.7	29.1	41.6	11.7	17.0	23.2
Sales To Nwc (times)	10.3	6.3	4.7	10.3	6.1	3.8	16.0	8.3	5.1	41.1	22.5	9.0
Acct Pay To Sales (%)	3.0	6.0	8.5	2.9	9.7	14.1	3.0	5.8	9.2	1.8	3.6	5.9
PROFITABILITY												
Return On Sales (%)	7.4	3.2	1.1	7.9	3.9	0.4	7.8	3.2	1.0	11.5	4.7	0.5
Return On Assets (%)	13.3	6.4	1.0	14.8	7.3	0.9	20.0	8.8	2.3	38.0	16.0	(0.3)
Return On Nw (%)	39.6	13.0	2.8	22.5	11.2	3.5	41.5	19.0	4.8	103.5	35.4	9.9

SIC 1793 — GLASS, GLAZING WORK — INDUSTRY ASSETS

	$100,000-$250,000 1995 (158 Establishments) $	%	$250,000-$500,000 1995 (145 Establishments) $	%	$500,000-$1,000,000 1995 (78 Establishments) $	%	$1,000,000-$5,000,000 1995 (59 Establishments) $	%
Cash	25,421	15.0	52,059	15.2	87,579	13.1	141,886	8.9
Accounts Receivable	66,943	39.5	149,670	43.7	300,174	44.9	817,837	51.3
Notes Receivable	678	0.4	2,397	0.7	2,006	0.3	9,565	0.6
Inventory	27,116	16.0	52,402	15.3	92,927	13.9	216,815	13.6
Other Current	6,779	4.0	15,755	4.6	40,781	6.1	145,074	9.1
Total Current	**126,938**	**74.9**	**272,284**	**79.5**	**523,466**	**78.3**	**1,331,178**	**83.5**
Fixed Assets	34,234	20.2	49,319	14.4	102,286	15.3	191,307	12.0
Other Non-current	8,304	4.9	20,892	6.1	42,786	6.4	71,740	4.5
Total Assets	**169,476**	**100.0**	**342,495**	**100.0**	**668,539**	**100.0**	**1,594,225**	**100.0**
Accounts Payable	32,370	19.1	71,581	20.9	132,371	19.8	328,410	20.6
Bank Loans	339	0.2	—	—	1,337	0.2	—	—
Notes Payable	7,287	4.3	13,015	3.8	21,393	3.2	89,277	5.6
Other Current	21,185	12.5	46,579	13.6	84,904	12.7	240,728	15.1
Total Current	**61,181**	**36.1**	**131,176**	**38.3**	**240,006**	**35.9**	**658,415**	**41.3**
Other Long Term	18,134	10.7	30,140	8.8	50,140	7.5	151,451	9.5
Deferred Credits	339	0.2	342	0.1	—	—	4,783	0.3
Net Worth	89,822	53.0	180,837	52.8	378,393	56.6	779,576	48.9
Total Liab & Net Worth	**169,476**	**100.0**	**342,495**	**100.0**	**668,539**	**100.0**	**1,594,225**	**100.0**
Net Sales	653,001	100.0	1,113,906	100.0	1,816,725	100.0	4,302,825	100.0
Gross Profit	238,345	36.5	408,804	36.7	534,117	29.4	1,067,101	24.8
Net Profit After Tax	37,874	5.8	50,126	4.5	61,769	3.4	163,507	3.8
Working Capital	65,757	—	141,108	—	283,460	—	672,763	—

RATIOS	UQ	MED	LQ	UQ	MED	LQ	UQ	MED	LQ	UQ	MED	LQ
SOLVENCY												
Quick Ratio (times)	3.0	1.6	1.0	2.8	1.6	1.0	3.4	1.6	1.1	2.0	1.3	1.1
Current Ratio (times)	4.5	2.2	1.4	3.7	2.2	1.4	4.4	2.5	1.5	2.7	2.0	1.5
Curr Liab To Nw (%)	23.0	57.5	137.6	29.1	63.9	135.0	25.8	56.5	119.1	46.5	92.4	151.7
Curr Liab To Inv (%)	85.4	178.6	373.4	106.1	204.2	410.3	110.3	199.7	388.4	154.2	300.2	412.8
Total Liab To Nw (%)	33.4	65.5	160.7	37.0	83.5	172.3	28.0	83.9	151.6	52.7	115.4	187.0
Fixed Assets To Nw (%)	12.8	37.2	70.0	11.1	22.7	43.5	10.9	19.0	36.8	9.2	19.0	31.8
EFFICIENCY												
Coll Period (days)	23.9	36.1	55.9	34.2	50.6	66.9	40.3	56.8	78.1	54.0	70.1	83.5
Sales To Inv (times)	65.5	27.5	12.5	51.9	26.9	13.8	48.7	19.9	11.1	32.9	21.6	10.9
Assets To Sales (%)	20.5	25.6	37.1	24.2	30.4	38.0	28.5	36.0	46.9	32.6	41.6	50.2
Sales To Nwc (times)	17.6	8.2	5.7	13.6	8.3	4.9	10.9	6.9	4.2	9.3	6.2	3.6
Acct Pay To Sales (%)	2.7	4.9	8.6	3.4	6.3	9.0	3.9	7.0	10.8	5.1	8.4	10.7
PROFITABILITY												
Return On Sales (%)	9.4	4.8	1.1	6.6	2.8	1.2	5.9	1.8	0.9	6.2	3.0	1.0
Return On Assets (%)	25.8	13.9	3.9	16.2	8.8	3.6	12.8	3.8	1.6	12.7	6.8	2.5
Return On Nw (%)	60.6	24.2	7.0	37.7	21.1	8.1	32.2	6.0	3.7	25.0	13.8	5.9

SIC 1794 EXCAVATION WORK

	NO BREAKDOWN 1995 (1380 Establishments) $	%	UNDER $100,000 1995 (121 Establishments) $	%	$100,000 - $250,000 1995 (235 Establishments) $	%	$250,000 - $500,000 1995 (255 Establishments) $	%
Cash	81,762	13.0	13,397	23.0	28,143	15.6	47,691	13.1
Accounts Receivable	154,719	24.6	8,388	14.4	37,704	20.9	77,907	21.4
Notes Receivable	3,145	0.5	58	0.1	541	0.3	1,820	0.5
Inventory	10,063	1.6	175	0.3	3,608	2.0	6,553	1.8
Other Current	37,736	6.0	2,388	4.1	5,773	3.2	20,023	5.5
Total Current	**287,425**	**45.7**	**24,405**	**41.9**	**75,769**	**42.0**	**153,994**	**42.3**
Fixed Assets	298,746	47.5	30,638	52.6	96,155	53.3	188,943	51.9
Other Non-current	42,768	6.8	3,204	5.5	8,479	4.7	21,115	5.8
Total Assets	**628,939**	**100.0**	**58,247**	**100.0**	**180,403**	**100.0**	**364,052**	**100.0**
Accounts Payable	65,410	10.4	3,728	6.4	12,989	7.2	32,401	8.9
Bank Loans	1,258	0.2	58	0.1	541	0.3	364	0.1
Notes Payable	29,560	4.7	4,136	7.1	11,546	6.4	23,299	6.4
Other Current	94,341	15.0	10,484	18.0	26,880	14.9	48,419	13.3
Total Current	**190,569**	**30.3**	**18,406**	**31.6**	**51,956**	**28.8**	**104,483**	**28.7**
Other Long Term	128,304	20.4	12,465	21.4	44,379	24.6	82,640	22.7
Deferred Credits	1,887	0.3	—	—	541	0.3	728	0.2
Net Worth	308,180	49.0	27,376	47.0	83,527	46.3	176,201	48.4
Total Liab & Net Worth	**628,939**	**100.0**	**58,247**	**100.0**	**180,403**	**100.0**	**364,052**	**100.0**
Net Sales	1,304,385	100.0	238,596	100.0	454,229	100.0	761,836	100.0
Gross Profit	430,447	33.0	125,263	52.5	212,579	46.8	299,402	39.3
Net Profit After Tax	82,176	6.3	18,849	7.9	29,979	6.6	53,329	7.0
Working Capital	96,856	—	5,999	—	23,813	—	49,511	—

RATIOS	UQ	MED	LQ	UQ	MED	LQ	UQ	MED	LQ	UQ	MED	LQ
SOLVENCY												
Quick Ratio (times)	2.3	1.3	0.8	6.2	1.4	0.4	3.2	1.3	0.6	2.4	1.2	0.6
Current Ratio (times)	2.9	1.6	1.0	6.3	1.6	0.6	4.1	1.6	0.8	3.2	1.7	0.8
Curr Liab To Nw (%)	20.4	51.7	109.0	8.9	27.3	107.2	14.6	39.9	91.6	14.5	46.1	91.4
Curr Liab To Inv (%)	170.6	393.7	598.7	48.9	74.3	99.6	58.5	156.8	441.6	144.9	352.2	628.5
Total Liab To Nw (%)	39.7	92.8	184.1	18.5	65.0	146.4	29.4	79.1	180.3	35.8	97.7	172.1
Fixed Assets To Nw (%)	53.5	95.9	160.1	52.0	82.3	180.8	58.2	112.1	182.3	56.7	101.1	172.6
EFFICIENCY												
Coll Period (days)	28.5	49.6	75.8	21.2	23.4	44.9	17.2	32.9	56.3	23.0	43.1	60.4
Sales To Inv (times)	172.1	70.5	27.9	144.9	144.9	144.9	165.6	43.5	12.8	90.9	56.8	26.1
Assets To Sales (%)	36.7	50.7	68.6	18.7	26.2	36.2	30.4	41.9	55.7	35.0	48.8	68.4
Sales To Nwc (times)	16.6	8.7	5.0	29.6	16.0	9.3	19.2	9.3	5.8	15.7	8.1	4.9
Acct Pay To Sales (%)	2.2	4.9	8.9	1.5	2.4	6.3	1.5	3.1	6.3	1.7	3.5	6.9
PROFITABILITY												
Return On Sales (%)	10.6	5.1	1.6	16.0	8.8	2.1	11.8	5.0	1.2	14.8	6.0	1.6
Return On Assets (%)	16.5	8.4	3.0	65.3	18.1	5.5	21.5	10.7	3.1	20.6	10.4	3.7
Return On Nw (%)	37.4	18.8	6.5	89.8	37.5	15.7	57.6	21.2	6.2	50.6	23.2	6.8

SIC 1794 EXCAVATION WORK
INDUSTRY ASSETS
$500,000 - $1,000,000
1995 (310 Establishments)

	$	%
Cash	79,832	11.5
Accounts Receivable	166,606	24.0
Notes Receivable	4,859	0.7
Inventory	9,024	1.3
Other Current	45,122	6.5
Total Current	**305,444**	**44.0**
Fixed Assets	329,740	47.5
Other Non-current	59,006	8.5
Total Assets	**694,190**	**100.0**
Accounts Payable	73,584	10.6
Bank Loans	1,388	0.2
Notes Payable	22,908	3.3
Other Current	101,352	14.6
Total Current	**199,233**	**28.7**
Other Long Term	136,061	19.6
Deferred Credits	694	0.1
Net Worth	358,202	51.6
Total Liab & Net Worth	**694,190**	**100.0**
Net Sales	1,357,993	100.0
Gross Profit	473,940	34.9
Net Profit After Tax	85,554	6.3
Working Capital	106,211	—

RATIOS	UQ	MED	LQ
SOLVENCY			
Quick Ratio (times)	2.1	1.3	0.8
Current Ratio (times)	2.7	1.5	1.0
Curr Liab To Nw (%)	19.9	50.2	104.9
Curr Liab To Inv (%)	300.5	424.0	593.3
Total Liab To Nw (%)	41.4	86.6	175.4
Fixed Assets To Nw (%)	53.9	99.7	163.2
EFFICIENCY			
Coll Period (days)	25.8	45.7	72.8
Sales To Inv (times)	169.0	93.1	31.6
Assets To Sales (%)	37.5	51.7	72.8
Sales To Nwc (times)	16.3	8.0	5.2
Acct Pay To Sales (%)	1.9	4.2	8.7
PROFITABILITY			
Return On Sales (%)	10.1	5.9	1.6
Return On Assets (%)	16.4	8.8	2.0
Return On Nw (%)	40.3	16.6	5.5

SIC 1794 EXCAVATION WORK
INDUSTRY ASSETS
$1,000,000-$5,000,000
1995 (399 Establishments)

	$	%
Cash	179,929	10.5
Accounts Receivable	510,656	29.8
Notes Receivable	11,995	0.7
Inventory	30,845	1.8
Other Current	119,953	7.0
Total Current	**853,378**	**49.8**
Fixed Assets	736,852	43.0
Other Non-current	123,380	7.2
Total Assets	**1,713,610**	**100.0**
Accounts Payable	215,915	12.6
Bank Loans	1,714	0.1
Notes Payable	59,976	3.5
Other Current	263,896	15.4
Total Current	**541,501**	**31.6**
Other Long Term	313,591	18.3
Deferred Credits	8,568	0.5
Net Worth	849,951	49.6
Total Liab & Net Worth	**1,713,610**	**100.0**
Net Sales	3,288,758	100.0
Gross Profit	766,281	23.3
Net Profit After Tax	184,170	5.6
Working Capital	311,877	—

RATIOS	UQ	MED	LQ
SOLVENCY			
Quick Ratio (times)	1.9	1.2	0.9
Current Ratio (times)	2.3	1.5	1.1
Curr Liab To Nw (%)	30.5	65.0	116.8
Curr Liab To Inv (%)	254.7	432.6	716.4
Total Liab To Nw (%)	51.5	108.2	182.8
Fixed Assets To Nw (%)	51.8	93.1	147.1
EFFICIENCY			
Coll Period (days)	38.7	62.1	84.3
Sales To Inv (times)	187.0	81.4	36.4
Assets To Sales (%)	42.5	56.6	76.4
Sales To Nwc (times)	18.2	8.8	5.1
Acct Pay To Sales (%)	3.1	6.1	9.6
PROFITABILITY			
Return On Sales (%)	8.4	4.6	1.9
Return On Assets (%)	14.3	7.1	3.3
Return On Nw (%)	29.5	17.3	6.6

SIC 1794 EXCAVATION WORK
INDUSTRY ASSETS
$5,000,000-$25,000,000
1995 (57 Establishments)

	$	%
Cash	832,745	10.2
Accounts Receivable	3,028,906	37.1
Notes Receivable	48,985	0.6
Inventory	122,463	1.5
Other Current	963,372	11.8
Total Current	**4,996,470**	**61.2**
Fixed Assets	2,416,593	29.6
Other Non-current	751,103	9.2
Total Assets	**8,164,167**	**100.0**
Accounts Payable	1,469,550	18.0
Bank Loans	24,493	0.3
Notes Payable	326,567	4.0
Other Current	1,363,416	16.7
Total Current	**3,184,025**	**39.0**
Other Long Term	1,142,983	14.0
Deferred Credits	57,149	0.7
Net Worth	3,780,009	46.3
Total Liab & Net Worth	**8,164,167**	**100.0**
Net Sales	14,210,400	100.0
Gross Profit	2,373,137	16.7
Net Profit After Tax	611,047	4.3
Working Capital	1,812,445	—

RATIOS	UQ	MED	LQ
SOLVENCY			
Quick Ratio (times)	1.6	1.2	0.9
Current Ratio (times)	2.1	1.5	1.2
Curr Liab To Nw (%)	44.1	97.1	158.8
Curr Liab To Inv (%)	416.3	434.4	610.7
Total Liab To Nw (%)	49.9	143.5	236.9
Fixed Assets To Nw (%)	34.0	72.1	112.5
EFFICIENCY			
Coll Period (days)	58.4	71.9	99.7
Sales To Inv (times)	228.4	98.4	16.2
Assets To Sales (%)	43.0	54.4	66.0
Sales To Nwc (times)	13.8	8.0	3.7
Acct Pay To Sales (%)	6.2	8.1	11.9
PROFITABILITY			
Return On Sales (%)	6.4	2.6	0.7
Return On Assets (%)	9.9	5.3	2.2
Return On Nw (%)	21.9	11.4	5.2

SIC 1795 WRCKNG, DMLTN WORK
(NO BREAKDOWN)
1995 (125 Establishments)

	$	%
Cash	92,157	13.8
Accounts Receivable	188,989	28.3
Notes Receivable	5,342	0.8
Inventory	17,363	2.6
Other Current	62,106	9.3
Total Current	**365,957**	**54.8**
Fixed Assets	264,450	39.6
Other Non-current	37,397	5.6
Total Assets	**667,804**	**100.0**
Accounts Payable	80,804	12.1
Bank Loans	—	—
Notes Payable	32,722	4.9
Other Current	107,516	16.1
Total Current	**221,043**	**33.1**
Other Long Term	114,862	17.2
Deferred Credits	1,336	0.2
Net Worth	330,563	49.5
Total Liab & Net Worth	**667,804**	**100.0**
Net Sales	1,803,936	100.0
Gross Profit	638,593	35.4
Net Profit After Tax	117,256	6.5
Working Capital	144,914	—

RATIOS	UQ	MED	LQ
SOLVENCY			
Quick Ratio (times)	2.5	1.4	0.9
Current Ratio (times)	2.9	1.8	1.0
Curr Liab To Nw (%)	24.7	53.8	125.7
Curr Liab To Inv (%)	112.4	300.1	672.6
Total Liab To Nw (%)	44.7	92.4	187.3
Fixed Assets To Nw (%)	40.2	70.3	130.5
EFFICIENCY			
Coll Period (days)	33.1	56.2	70.1
Sales To Inv (times)	125.6	52.1	28.6
Assets To Sales (%)	31.7	46.3	60.7
Sales To Nwc (times)	14.2	6.7	4.8
Acct Pay To Sales (%)	2.2	4.8	6.9
PROFITABILITY			
Return On Sales (%)	11.3	5.1	1.4
Return On Assets (%)	21.1	7.5	0.7
Return On Nw (%)	39.3	19.8	1.7

SIC 1795 WRCKNG, DMLTN WORK

	$100,000 - $250,000 (15 Establishments)		$250,000 - $500,000 (24 Establishments)		$500,000 - $1,000,000 (38 Establishments)		$1,000,000 - $5,000,000 (31 Establishments)	
	$	%	$	%	$	%	$	%
Cash	27,397	15.4	66,564	17.6	51,403	7.3	306,867	17.1
Accounts Receivable	48,211	27.1	88,879	23.5	235,889	33.5	579,638	32.3
Notes Receivable	1,067	0.6	3,404	0.9	4,225	0.6	12,562	0.7
Inventory	3,558	2.0	15,128	4.0	22,533	3.2	23,329	1.3
Other Current	8,717	4.9	31,391	8.3	51,403	7.3	181,249	10.1
Total Current	**88,951**	**50.0**	**205,366**	**54.3**	**365,451**	**51.9**	**1,103,646**	**61.5**
Fixed Assets	85,748	48.2	149,770	39.6	288,699	41.0	586,817	32.7
Other Non-current	3,202	1.8	23,071	6.1	49,994	7.1	104,084	5.8
Total Assets	**177,901**	**100.0**	**378,207**	**100.0**	**704,145**	**100.0**	**1,794,546**	**100.0**
Accounts Payable	9,785	5.5	65,052	17.2	90,131	12.8	195,606	10.9
Bank Loans		—		—		—		—
Notes Payable	4,981	2.8	12,103	3.2	57,740	8.2	69,987	3.9
Other Current	28,464	16.0	65,052	17.2	89,426	12.7	348,142	19.4
Total Current	**43,230**	**24.3**	**142,206**	**37.6**	**237,297**	**33.7**	**613,735**	**34.2**
Other Long Term	38,249	21.5	69,590	18.4	166,882	23.7	143,564	8.0
Deferred Credits	178	0.1	756	0.2	1,408	0.2	7,178	0.4
Net Worth	96,244	54.1	165,655	43.8	298,557	42.4	1,030,069	57.4
Total Liab & Net Worth	**177,901**	**100.0**	**378,207**	**100.0**	**704,145**	**100.0**	**1,794,546**	**100.0**
Net Sales	537,161	100.0	966,610	100.0	1,698,036	100.0	3,219,650	100.0
Gross Profit	347,006	64.6	317,048	32.8	572,238	33.7	1,059,265	32.9
Net Profit After Tax	95,077	17.7	54,130	5.6	91,694	5.4	115,907	3.6
Working Capital	45,721	—	63,160	—	128,154	—	489,911	—

RATIOS	UQ	MED	LQ	UQ	MED	LQ	UQ	MED	LQ	UQ	MED	LQ
SOLVENCY												
Quick Ratio (times)	4.2	1.9	0.8	2.5	1.2	0.7	2.0	1.2	0.9	2.2	1.4	1.0
Current Ratio (times)	4.6	2.0	1.4	3.3	1.6	0.9	2.7	1.8	1.0	2.8	1.9	1.4
Curr Liab To Nw (%)	9.4	20.1	56.6	23.9	59.7	314.4	39.0	65.1	109.3	27.9	50.5	110.8
Curr Liab To Inv (%)	116.0	163.7	211.4	75.8	79.1	341.1	128.4	186.9	868.7	277.9	611.4	877.3
Total Liab To Nw (%)	7.7	44.2	104.6	72.5	123.2	345.4	78.8	112.1	245.7	41.6	75.9	144.0
Fixed Assets To Nw (%)	59.5	91.5	101.1	43.2	101.7	135.4	52.8	97.3	231.6	36.1	56.1	67.6
EFFICIENCY												
Coll Period (days)	29.8	33.6	57.8	19.8	30.7	67.1	44.0	58.1	70.1	46.9	56.9	75.6
Sales To Inv (times)	90.9	48.3	32.1	69.8	34.1	25.2	129.4	75.3	48.8	78.4	52.1	25.3
Assets To Sales (%)	26.7	31.1	32.2	23.9	37.6	56.8	34.5	45.8	57.1	42.5	52.1	70.0
Sales To Nwc (times)	26.1	12.1	7.3	16.6	6.0	3.7	9.0	6.3	5.0	13.5	8.0	5.2
Acct Pay To Sales (%)	1.3	1.5	3.1	2.3	6.7	10.3	2.5	4.3	6.5	2.7	5.3	7.2
PROFITABILITY												
Return On Sales (%)	16.5	8.4	7.3	6.0	4.6	1.0	16.3	5.8	2.4	7.8	3.5	0.2
Return On Assets (%)	68.8	29.4	25.0	15.6	8.1	5.1	13.7	7.8	0.3	12.6	2.3	(0.3)
Return On Nw (%)	192.3	76.2	41.3	45.3	21.3	6.9	35.8	23.8	6.3	18.9	6.7	(0.5)

SIC 1796 INSTL BLDG EQPT, NEC

	(NO BREAKDOWN) 1995 (312 Establishments)		UNDER $100,000 1995 (36 Establishments)		$100,000 - $250,000 1995 (49 Establishments)		$250,000 - $500,000 1995 (57 Establishments)	
	$	%	$	%	$	%	$	%
Cash	76,238	13.1	15,039	24.8	23,955	13.3	53,399	14.0
Accounts Receivable	235,697	40.5	17,586	29.0	70,603	39.2	151,806	39.8
Notes Receivable	6,402	1.1	364	0.6	3,242	1.8	5,340	1.4
Inventory	32,590	5.6	3,093	5.1	9,006	5.0	24,030	6.3
Other Current	52,959	9.1	3,517	5.8	11,887	6.6	24,030	6.3
Total Current	**403,886**	**69.4**	**39,599**	**65.3**	**118,692**	**65.9**	**258,605**	**67.8**
Fixed Assets	143,746	24.7	17,707	29.2	53,493	29.7	104,510	27.4
Other Non-current	34,336	5.9	3,335	5.5	7,925	4.4	18,308	4.8
Total Assets	**581,968**	**100.0**	**60,642**	**100.0**	**180,110**	**100.0**	**381,423**	**100.0**
Accounts Payable	83,803	14.4	6,064	10.0	24,135	13.4	51,492	13.5
Bank Loans	1,746	0.3	—	—	901	0.5	—	—
Notes Payable	33,754	5.8	3,214	5.3	11,707	6.5	21,360	5.6
Other Current	99,517	17.1	10,430	17.2	30,979	17.2	54,925	14.4
Total Current	**218,820**	**37.6**	**19,709**	**32.5**	**67,721**	**37.6**	**127,777**	**33.5**
Other Long Term	61,107	10.5	4,973	8.2	30,258	16.8	24,030	6.3
Deferred Credits	2,910	0.5	—	—	540	0.3	6,866	1.8
Net Worth	299,132	51.4	35,961	59.3	81,590	45.3	222,751	58.4
Total Liab & Net Worth	**581,968**	**100.0**	**60,642**	**100.0**	**180,110**	**100.0**	**381,423**	**100.0**
Net Sales	1,781,328	100.0	324,402	100.0	640,558	100.0	1,185,774	100.0
Gross Profit	593,182	33.3	154,740	47.7	276,721	43.2	415,021	35.0
Net Profit After Tax	97,973	5.5	32,116	9.9	47,401	7.4	54,546	4.6
Working Capital	185,066	—	19,890	—	50,971	—	130,828	—

RATIOS	UQ	MED	LQ	UQ	MED	LQ	UQ	MED	LQ	UQ	MED	LQ
SOLVENCY												
Quick Ratio (times)	2.4	1.4	0.9	4.8	1.6	0.8	3.4	1.2	0.8	2.6	1.8	1.2
Current Ratio (times)	3.2	1.9	1.3	5.2	1.9	1.3	4.5	1.8	1.1	3.5	2.2	1.4
Curr Lib To Nw (%)	28.4	73.4	143.0	15.4	45.2	106.2	18.2	77.2	212.4	26.0	47.7	97.5
Curr Lib To Inv (%)	122.3	222.6	429.0	237.0	329.6	565.7	161.3	200.8	450.1	83.5	241.4	405.6
Total Lib To Nw (%)	40.9	93.6	177.1	19.8	72.3	147.7	37.2	127.8	256.4	29.4	55.6	105.5
Fixed Assets To Nw (%)	21.4	43.3	80.2	40.8	48.6	93.4	21.4	57.0	131.9	22.6	39.5	65.3
EFFICIENCY												
Coll Period (days)	34.7	53.3	72.5	12.1	34.7	43.3	24.7	38.0	52.2	31.2	48.7	73.7
Sales To Inv (times)	103.1	33.0	11.6	216.4	122.6	45.4	84.9	29.5	13.8	205.0	54.6	12.1
Assets To Sales (%)	23.2	34.7	44.6	9.0	14.6	20.0	18.9	24.0	37.3	23.3	30.3	40.3
Sales To Nwc (times)	16.3	8.2	5.3	59.2	15.5	7.9	18.7	11.9	5.9	17.0	7.9	5.4
Acct Pay To Sales (%)	2.0	4.3	8.2	0.8	2.0	2.5	1.8	3.8	6.0	1.7	3.9	5.8
PROFITABILITY												
Return On Sales (%)	8.5	3.6	1.2	12.6	6.8	0.9	18.8	3.8	0.6	8.6	4.1	1.9
Return On Assets (%)	19.4	6.9	2.7	72.5	63.0	7.6	22.9	5.2	0.2	20.6	11.7	2.7
Return On Nw (%)	35.8	15.9	6.9	100.6	87.0	18.2	109.2	13.5	0.2	36.5	20.3	3.3

	SIC 1796 INSTL BLDG EQPT,NEC $500,000-$1,000,000 1995 (67 Establishments)		SIC 1796 INSTL BLDG EQPT,NEC $1,000,000-$5,000,000 1995 (78 Establishments)		SIC 1796 INSTL BLDG EQPT,NEC $5,000,000-$25,000,000 1995 (23 Establishments)		SIC 1799 SPCL TRD CNTRS,NEC (NO BREAKDOWN) 1995 (2051 Establishments)	
	$	%	$	%	$	%	$	%
Cash	72,069	11.3	226,562	11.7	546,843	6.4	52,658	15.2
Accounts Receivable	275,521	43.2	832,664	43.0	3,973,159	46.5	119,519	34.5
Notes Receivable	4,464	0.7	23,237	1.2	17,089	0.2	2,771	0.8
Inventory	44,007	6.9	91,012	4.7	452,855	5.3	33,604	9.7
Other Current	45,282	7.1	261,418	13.5	1,204,764	14.1	27,022	7.8
Total Current	**441,343**	**69.2**	**1,434,892**	**74.1**	**6,194,711**	**72.5**	**235,574**	**68.0**
Fixed Assets	153,705	24.1	393,095	20.3	1,486,731	17.4	89,033	25.7
Other Non-current	42,731	6.7	108,440	5.6	862,987	10.1	21,825	6.3
Total Assets	**637,779**	**100.0**	**1,936,427**	**100.0**	**8,544,429**	**100.0**	**346,433**	**100.0**
Accounts Payable	97,580	15.3	280,782	14.5	1,871,230	21.9	53,351	15.4
Bank Loans	3,827	0.6	5,809	0.3	—	—	346	0.1
Notes Payable	34,440	5.4	112,313	5.8	649,377	7.6	18,361	5.3
Other Current	104,596	16.4	377,603	19.5	1,537,997	18.0	55,429	16.0
Total Current	**240,443**	**37.7**	**776,507**	**40.1**	**4,058,604**	**47.5**	**127,487**	**36.8**
Other Long Term	72,069	11.3	164,596	8.5	999,698	11.7	44,690	12.9
Deferred Credits	1,276	0.2	3,873	0.2	68,355	0.8	693	0.2
Net Worth	323,992	50.8	991,451	51.2	3,417,772	40.0	173,563	50.1
Total Liab & Net Worth	**637,779**	**100.0**	**1,936,427**	**100.0**	**8,544,429**	**100.0**	**346,433**	**100.0**
Net Sales	1,770,272	100.0	5,032,298	100.0	15,196,954	100.0	1,215,596	100.0
Gross Profit	623,136	35.2	1,227,881	24.4	3,373,724	22.2	415,734	34.2
Net Profit After Tax	56,649	3.2	241,550	4.8	1,443,711	9.5	63,211	5.2
Working Capital	200,900	—	658,385	—	2,136,107	—	108,087	—

RATIOS	UQ	MED	LQ	UQ	MED	LQ	UQ	MED	LQ	UQ	MED	LQ
SOLVENCY												
Quick Ratio (times)	2.4	1.4	1.0	2.0	1.5	1.0	1.5	1.1	0.9	2.7	1.4	0.8
Current Ratio (times)	3.0	2.0	1.3	2.5	1.9	1.5	2.1	1.3	1.2	3.6	1.9	1.2
Curr Liab To Nw (%)	28.4	66.3	121.9	46.9	85.9	131.8	48.8	145.7	253.3	24.3	61.7	138.5
Curr Liab To Inv (%)	127.3	218.3	328.5	117.8	239.7	529.4	153.5	172.4	187.5	91.6	185.4	393.8
Total Liab To Nw (%)	35.2	77.5	154.9	64.6	106.4	155.2	80.5	206.8	291.3	33.5	87.5	182.6
Fixed Assets To Nw (%)	19.8	42.6	86.2	12.8	34.7	60.6	16.9	28.0	91.3	19.7	40.9	92.6
EFFICIENCY												
Coll Period (days)	34.7	53.7	74.1	42.1	59.9	74.5	52.9	69.7	83.6	26.3	47.8	72.3
Sales To Inv (times)	47.1	20.4	10.9	101.6	34.6	13.7	113.1	52.2	10.7	88.8	31.2	14.0
Assets To Sales (%)	27.8	35.2	51.1	28.7	38.7	45.2	39.5	50.5	66.1	21.9	32.0	45.9
Sales To Nwc (times)	16.7	8.8	4.9	12.2	7.8	5.6	17.2	9.6	4.1	18.3	9.2	5.1
Acct Pay To Sales (%)	2.2	5.2	11.0	2.5	4.3	8.2	4.8	8.5	10.8	2.1	4.6	8.3
PROFITABILITY												
Return On Sales (%)	6.3	3.2	1.3	6.9	3.1	1.6	15.6	2.7	0.5	8.8	3.7	1.2
Return On Assets (%)	13.6	6.6	3.3	14.9	6.7	4.2	19.4	1.7	1.1	23.2	9.8	2.6
Return On Nw (%)	34.5	16.3	6.9	27.1	15.3	9.2	27.1	7.5	3.4	50.4	22.0	6.2

SIC 1799 SPCL TRD CNTRS,NEC — INDUSTRY ASSETS UNDER $100,000 — 1995 (399 Establishments)

	$	%
Cash	13,497	25.0
Accounts Receivable	9,934	18.4
Notes Receivable	432	0.8
Inventory	4,373	8.1
Other Current	2,267	4.2
Total Current	**30,503**	**56.5**
Fixed Assets	20,299	37.6
Other Non-current	3,185	5.9
Total Assets	**53,988**	**100.0**
Accounts Payable	5,291	9.8
Bank Loans	54	0.1
Notes Payable	2,645	4.9
Other Current	9,988	18.5
Total Current	**17,978**	**33.3**
Other Long Term	8,152	15.1
Deferred Credits	108	0.2
Net Worth	27,750	51.4
Total Liab & Net Worth	**53,988**	**100.0**
Net Sales	324,619	100.0
Gross Profit	145,754	44.9
Net Profit After Tax	24,022	7.4
Working Capital	12,525	—

RATIOS	UQ	MED	LQ
SOLVENCY			
Quick Ratio (times)	3.1	1.3	0.6
Current Ratio (times)	4.6	1.8	1.0
Curr Liab To Nw (%)	15.6	43.8	102.7
Curr Liab To Inv (%)	50.8	151.9	312.3
Total Liab To Nw (%)	20.9	71.3	157.9
Fixed Assets To Nw (%)	28.0	71.7	129.0
EFFICIENCY			
Coll Period (days)	8.7	20.3	32.5
Sales To Inv (times)	126.4	49.9	17.4
Assets To Sales (%)	9.3	15.6	26.8
Sales To Nwc (times)	51.0	19.4	9.0
Acct Pay To Sales (%)	0.9	2.1	5.0
PROFITABILITY			
Return On Sales (%)	14.1	5.8	2.2
Return On Assets (%)	62.9	29.3	4.9
Return On Nw (%)	129.0	66.9	18.2

SIC 1799 SPCL TRD CNTRS,NEC — INDUSTRY ASSETS $100,000 - $250,000 — 1995 (448 Establishments)

	$	%
Cash	26,669	15.6
Accounts Receivable	60,346	35.3
Notes Receivable	1,880	1.1
Inventory	16,070	9.4
Other Current	10,428	6.1
Total Current	**115,393**	**67.5**
Fixed Assets	45,303	26.5
Other Non-current	10,257	6.0
Total Assets	**170,953**	**100.0**
Accounts Payable	27,352	16.0
Bank Loans	513	0.3
Notes Payable	10,428	6.1
Other Current	26,156	15.3
Total Current	**64,449**	**37.7**
Other Long Term	22,566	13.2
Deferred Credits	171	0.1
Net Worth	83,767	49.0
Total Liab & Net Worth	**170,953**	**100.0**
Net Sales	675,780	100.0
Gross Profit	247,335	36.6
Net Profit After Tax	38,519	5.7
Working Capital	50,944	—

RATIOS	UQ	MED	LQ
SOLVENCY			
Quick Ratio (times)	2.9	1.4	0.7
Current Ratio (times)	4.0	1.9	1.1
Curr Liab To Nw (%)	20.0	60.2	153.3
Curr Liab To Inv (%)	93.6	198.9	410.5
Total Liab To Nw (%)	33.0	88.2	188.4
Fixed Assets To Nw (%)	20.8	45.4	108.1
EFFICIENCY			
Coll Period (days)	20.4	33.6	56.8
Sales To Inv (times)	89.6	39.9	17.6
Assets To Sales (%)	17.0	25.8	36.5
Sales To Nwc (times)	22.3	11.4	5.3
Acct Pay To Sales (%)	1.7	4.0	6.9
PROFITABILITY			
Return On Sales (%)	9.4	3.4	1.2
Return On Assets (%)	28.3	13.7	3.5
Return On Nw (%)	64.3	28.6	10.7

SIC 1799 SPCL TRD CNTRS,NEC — INDUSTRY ASSETS $250,000 - $500,000 — 1995 (428 Establishments)

	$	%
Cash	48,084	13.5
Accounts Receivable	131,785	37.0
Notes Receivable	1,781	0.5
Inventory	39,536	11.1
Other Current	27,069	7.6
Total Current	**248,255**	**69.7**
Fixed Assets	87,620	24.6
Other Non-current	20,302	5.7
Total Assets	**356,177**	**100.0**
Accounts Payable	56,276	15.8
Bank Loans	356	0.1
Notes Payable	17,809	5.0
Other Current	48,440	13.6
Total Current	**122,881**	**34.5**
Other Long Term	45,234	12.7
Deferred Credits	712	0.2
Net Worth	187,349	52.6
Total Liab & Net Worth	**356,177**	**100.0**
Net Sales	1,083,280	100.0
Gross Profit	383,481	35.4
Net Profit After Tax	66,080	6.1
Working Capital	125,374	—

RATIOS	UQ	MED	LQ
SOLVENCY			
Quick Ratio (times)	3.1	1.6	0.9
Current Ratio (times)	4.2	2.1	1.4
Curr Liab To Nw (%)	20.7	54.2	119.9
Curr Liab To Inv (%)	87.8	157.9	335.3
Total Liab To Nw (%)	27.7	72.9	165.3
Fixed Assets To Nw (%)	17.7	37.7	87.0
EFFICIENCY			
Coll Period (days)	27.6	47.5	68.8
Sales To Inv (times)	54.6	21.5	11.0
Assets To Sales (%)	23.9	32.3	45.9
Sales To Nwc (times)	14.1	8.0	4.8
Acct Pay To Sales (%)	2.1	4.5	7.9
PROFITABILITY			
Return On Sales (%)	10.3	4.8	1.5
Return On Assets (%)	23.8	10.8	3.3
Return On Nw (%)	56.0	24.4	8.3

SIC 1799 SPCL TRD CNTRS,NEC — INDUSTRY ASSETS $500,000 - $1,000,000 — 1995 (375 Establishments)

	$	%
Cash	92,534	13.5
Accounts Receivable	255,669	37.3
Notes Receivable	5,484	0.8
Inventory	76,769	11.2
Other Current	61,690	9.0
Total Current	**492,146**	**71.8**
Fixed Assets	150,797	22.0
Other Non-current	42,497	6.2
Total Assets	**685,440**	**100.0**
Accounts Payable	106,243	15.5
Bank Loans	685	0.1
Notes Payable	32,216	4.7
Other Current	105,558	15.4
Total Current	**244,702**	**35.7**
Other Long Term	82,938	12.1
Deferred Credits	2,742	0.4
Net Worth	355,058	51.8
Total Liab & Net Worth	**685,440**	**100.0**
Net Sales	1,992,198	100.0
Gross Profit	645,472	32.4
Net Profit After Tax	79,688	4.0
Working Capital	247,444	—

RATIOS	UQ	MED	LQ
SOLVENCY			
Quick Ratio (times)	2.7	1.5	1.0
Current Ratio (times)	3.6	2.0	1.4
Curr Liab To Nw (%)	28.1	63.7	125.1
Curr Liab To Inv (%)	90.0	189.1	372.8
Total Liab To Nw (%)	39.9	84.7	160.1
Fixed Assets To Nw (%)	18.7	36.2	69.4
EFFICIENCY			
Coll Period (days)	31.0	50.2	68.7
Sales To Inv (times)	75.0	26.5	12.3
Assets To Sales (%)	27.4	36.3	47.1
Sales To Nwc (times)	14.1	8.0	4.9
Acct Pay To Sales (%)	2.1	4.4	7.6
PROFITABILITY			
Return On Sales (%)	7.4	3.1	1.0
Return On Assets (%)	15.6	7.7	2.6
Return On Nw (%)	40.6	15.3	5.1

	SIC 1799 SPCL TRD CNTRS,NEC INDUSTRY ASSETS $1,000,000 - $5,000,000 1995 (341 Establishments)		SIC 1799 SPCL TRD CNTRS,NEC INDUSTRY ASSETS $5,000,000-$25,000,000 1995 (48 Establishments)		SIC 40 RAILROAD TRANSPORTAT (NO BREAKDOWN) 1995 (148 Establishments)		SIC 40 RAILROAD TRANSPORTAT NORTHEAST 1995 (17 Establishments)	
	$	%	$	%	$	%	$	%
Cash	156,149	9.9	442,780	5.2	2,871,444	11.4	11,121,795	17.7
Accounts Receivable	686,107	43.5	3,465,605	40.7	3,350,018	13.3	4,084,275	6.5
Notes Receivable	11,041	0.7	85,150	1.0	125,941	0.5	—	—
Inventory	129,335	8.2	945,165	11.1	377,822	1.5	1,068,195	1.7
Other Current	179,807	11.4	1,141,010	13.4	1,586,851	6.3	3,958,605	6.3
Total Current	**1,162,439**	**73.7**	**6,079,710**	**71.4**	**8,312,074**	**33.0**	**20,232,870**	**32.2**
Fixed Assets	294,947	18.7	1,379,430	16.2	14,709,853	58.4	37,135,485	59.1
Other Non-current	119,872	7.6	1,055,860	12.4	2,166,177	8.6	5,466,645	8.7
Total Assets	**1,577,258**	**100.0**	**8,515,000**	**100.0**	**25,188,104**	**100.0**	**62,835,000**	**100.0**
Accounts Payable	305,988	19.4	1,711,515	20.1	2,846,256	11.3	8,545,560	13.6
Bank Loans	3,155	0.2			25,188	0.1	62,835	0.1
Notes Payable	91,481	5.8	527,930	6.2	554,138	2.2	3,832,935	6.1
Other Current	271,288	17.2	1,609,335	18.9	3,047,761	12.1	2,890,410	4.6
Total Current	**671,912**	**42.6**	**3,848,780**	**45.2**	**6,473,343**	**25.7**	**15,331,740**	**24.4**
Other Long Term	170,344	10.8	1,226,160	14.4	5,566,571	22.1	7,100,355	11.3
Deferred Credits	4,732	0.3	25,545	0.3	528,950	2.1	2,324,895	3.7
Net Worth	730,270	46.3	3,414,515	40.1	12,619,240	50.1	38,078,010	60.6
Total Liab & Net Worth	**1,577,258**	**100.0**	**8,515,000**	**100.0**	**25,188,104**	**100.0**	**62,835,000**	**100.0**
Net Sales	4,017,115	100.0	19,624,273	100.0	3,982,000	100.0	2,595,460	100.0
Gross Profit	1,080,604	26.9	4,493,959	22.9	1,768,008	44.4	807,188	31.1
Net Profit After Tax	152,650	3.8	726,098	3.7	457,930	11.5	129,773	5.0
Working Capital	490,527	—	2,230,930	—	1,838,731	—	4,901,130	—

RATIOS	UQ	MED	LQ	UQ	MED	LQ	UQ	MED	LQ	UQ	MED	LQ
SOLVENCY												
Quick Ratio (times)	2.0	1.3	0.9	1.4	1.0	0.8	1.2	0.7	0.4	0.6	0.5	0.4
Current Ratio (times)	2.7	1.7	1.3	1.9	1.6	1.2	1.9	1.0	0.7	1.0	0.7	0.6
Curr Liab To Nw (%)	39.1	92.5	163.3	55.4	122.2	231.1	19.2	40.2	76.6	12.4	39.6	45.3
Curr Liab To Inv (%)	117.0	262.8	470.2	168.8	270.3	454.6	304.8	512.8	728.8	115.9	505.0	766.3
Total Liab To Nw (%)	50.5	120.7	206.1	66.9	154.3	298.1	53.8	109.7	192.5	37.7	106.8	185.0
Fixed Assets To Nw (%)	16.4	35.4	72.0	17.4	33.8	58.9	97.1	144.4	221.7	102.9	181.9	222.7
EFFICIENCY												
Coll Period (days)	48.6	66.8	84.0	46.4	70.5	92.0	30.3	52.9	72.4	27.8	52.9	66.8
Sales To Inv (times)	106.1	39.8	15.0	94.7	48.2	20.8	41.3	26.0	17.4	44.2	32.4	24.8
Assets To Sales (%)	31.7	40.4	55.9	36.6	49.1	63.7	129.7	190.9	242.8	193.1	233.3	280.0
Sales To Nwc (times)	14.5	7.6	4.3	14.4	8.2	5.5	13.2	5.9	2.9	3.5	2.9	2.8
Acct Pay To Sales (%)	3.5	6.6	10.5	3.5	6.4	14.4	4.5	9.9	18.1	2.8	8.1	19.3
PROFITABILITY												
Return On Sales (%)	6.3	2.9	0.8	5.1	2.0	0.9	18.3	10.7	5.9	10.3	8.6	5.8
Return On Assets (%)	13.2	6.0	1.8	10.2	4.5	1.7	12.3	5.7	2.9	4.5	3.5	2.9
Return On Nw (%)	30.7	14.1	4.4	29.9	15.0	4.4	26.1	12.9	6.2	10.5	6.0	3.4

SIC 40 RAILROAD TRANSPORTAT

	CENTRAL 1995 (55 Establishments) $	%	SOUTH 1995 (58 Establishments) $	%	WEST 1995 (18 Establishments) $	%	INDUSTRY ASSETS $1,000,000 - $5,000,000 1995 (29 Establishments) $	%
Cash	2,619,563	10.4	2,503,495	12.5	1,890,611	5.3	344,159	13.4
Accounts Receivable	3,375,206	13.4	2,904,054	14.5	5,350,786	15.0	398,094	15.5
Notes Receivable	100,752	0.4	180,252	0.9	35,672	0.1	30,820	1.2
Inventory	327,445	1.3	240,335	1.2	891,798	2.5	35,957	1.4
Other Current	1,360,158	5.4	1,161,622	5.8	3,995,254	11.2	259,403	10.1
Total Current	**7,783,124**	**30.9**	**6,989,757**	**34.9**	**12,164,120**	**34.1**	**1,068,434**	**41.6**
Fixed Assets	16,044,822	63.7	11,756,411	58.7	12,877,558	36.1	1,345,815	52.4
Other Non-current	1,360,158	5.4	1,281,789	6.4	10,630,228	29.8	154,101	6.0
Total Assets	**25,188,104**	**100.0**	**20,027,958**	**100.0**	**35,671,907**	**100.0**	**2,568,350**	**100.0**
Accounts Payable	2,518,810	10.0	2,563,579	12.8	3,032,112	8.5	423,778	16.5
Bank Loans	—	—	60,084	0.3	—	—	12,842	0.5
Notes Payable	629,703	2.5	280,391	1.4	142,688	0.4	41,094	1.6
Other Current	3,727,839	14.8	2,062,880	10.3	5,243,770	14.7	228,583	8.9
Total Current	**6,876,352**	**27.3**	**4,966,934**	**24.8**	**8,418,570**	**23.6**	**706,296**	**27.5**
Other Long Term	8,387,639	33.3	2,863,998	14.3	5,957,208	16.7	369,842	14.4
Deferred Credits	403,010	1.6	340,475	1.7	1,284,189	3.6	12,842	0.5
Net Worth	9,521,103	37.8	11,856,551	59.2	20,011,940	56.1	1,479,370	57.6
Total Liab & Net Worth	**25,188,104**	**100.0**	**20,027,958**	**100.0**	**35,671,907**	**100.0**	**2,568,350**	**100.0**
Net Sales	8,231,059	100.0	3,054,940	100.0	1,954,378	100.0	1,770,158	100.0
Gross Profit	3,613,435	43.9	1,585,514	51.9	957,645	49.0	736,386	41.6
Net Profit After Tax	1,078,269	13.1	378,813	12.4	183,712	9.4	251,362	14.2
Working Capital	906,772	—	2,022,823	—	3,745,550	—	362,138	—

RATIOS	UQ	MED	LQ	UQ	MED	LQ	UQ	MED	LQ	UQ	MED	LQ
SOLVENCY												
Quick Ratio (times)	0.9	0.6	0.5	1.3	0.8	0.5	1.1	0.6	0.2	4.3	1.1	0.6
Current Ratio (times)	1.8	0.8	0.7	1.9	1.2	0.8	1.3	1.0	0.6	6.7	1.6	0.9
Curr Lib To Nw (%)	25.4	49.6	95.6	16.3	30.3	61.8	36.7	48.7	80.5	6.5	41.4	104.1
Curr Lib To Inv (%)	427.4	605.6	779.5	286.4	378.5	513.7	307.3	505.4	761.8	126.5	309.8	326.5
Total Liab To Nw (%)	86.4	148.4	259.3	38.2	81.7	145.4	74.9	100.7	183.4	14.8	78.0	161.4
Fixed Assets To Nw (%)	114.3	181.9	288.5	94.5	115.4	188.1	44.0	109.5	175.7	71.7	104.0	165.4
EFFICIENCY												
Coll Period (days)	28.5	53.5	74.2	45.4	52.4	69.0	29.9	41.8	78.5	29.8	47.1	67.6
Sales To Inv (times)	36.2	23.1	15.7	58.7	26.0	17.4	31.0	23.5	19.0	192.2	36.2	27.3
Assets To Sales (%)	130.2	187.4	211.7	126.7	187.4	277.3	115.3	138.7	195.9	95.7	127.8	180.0
Sales To Nwc (times)	5.7	4.5	2.0	22.3	6.4	4.9	15.0	14.2	8.7	6.8	4.9	2.8
Acct Pay To Sales (%)	4.5	9.2	20.3	8.1	11.1	16.8	3.8	4.9	15.8	3.0	8.6	28.8
PROFITABILITY												
Return On Sales (%)	19.7	11.1	6.3	18.1	14.2	8.0	11.6	7.2	3.1	21.0	15.8	7.9
Return On Assets (%)	10.9	5.3	2.3	17.1	6.4	4.6	10.4	5.8	2.6	22.8	15.2	7.4
Return On Nw (%)	25.7	15.7	7.3	26.9	13.7	7.2	27.7	14.3	7.3	42.2	25.7	9.4

	SIC 40 RAILROAD TRANSPORTAT INDUSTRY ASSETS $5,000,000-$25,000,000 1995 (32 Establishments)		SIC 40 RAILROAD TRANSPORTAT INDUSTRY ASSETS $25,000,000-$50,000,000 1995 (12 Establishments)		SIC 4011 RR LINE-HAUL OPER (NO BREAKDOWN) 1995 (122 Establishments)		SIC 4011 RR LINE-HAUL OPER INDUSTRY ASSETS $1,000,000 - $5,000,000 1995 (21 Establishments)	
	$	%	$	%	$	%	$	%
Cash	1,450,725	11.5	1,567,175	4.9	3,082,020	9.9	374,804	14.5
Accounts Receivable	1,589,490	12.6	2,942,450	9.2	3,642,387	11.7	325,692	12.6
Notes Receivable	63,075	0.5	223,882	0.7	155,658	0.5	41,358	1.6
Inventory	163,995	1.3	575,697	1.8	466,973	1.5	31,018	1.2
Other Current	983,970	7.8	2,206,838	6.9	2,085,811	6.7	312,768	12.1
Total Current	**4,251,255**	**33.7**	**7,516,042**	**23.5**	**9,432,848**	**30.3**	**1,085,640**	**42.0**
Fixed Assets	7,417,620	58.8	19,477,742	60.9	18,616,644	59.8	1,320,862	51.1
Other Non-current	946,125	7.5	4,989,372	15.6	3,082,020	9.9	178,355	6.9
Total Assets	**12,615,000**	**100.0**	**31,983,156**	**100.0**	**31,131,512**	**100.0**	**2,584,857**	**100.0**
Accounts Payable	1,614,720	12.8	1,791,057	5.6	3,766,913	12.1	470,444	18.2
Bank Loans	—	—	—	—	62,263	0.2	18,094	0.7
Notes Payable	428,910	3.4	63,966	0.2	498,104	1.6	31,018	1.2
Other Current	1,917,480	15.2	4,669,541	14.6	3,580,124	11.5	178,355	6.9
Total Current	**3,961,110**	**31.4**	**6,524,564**	**20.4**	**7,907,404**	**25.4**	**697,911**	**27.0**
Other Long Term	3,393,435	26.9	6,076,800	19.0	7,191,379	23.1	390,313	15.1
Deferred Credits	176,610	1.4	831,562	2.6	716,025	2.3	15,509	0.6
Net Worth	5,083,845	40.3	18,550,230	58.0	15,316,704	49.2	1,481,123	57.3
Total Liab & Net Worth	**12,615,000**	**100.0**	**31,983,156**	**100.0**	**31,131,512**	**100.0**	**2,584,857**	**100.0**
Net Sales	5,423,991	100.0	15,341,186	100.0	3,982,000	100.0	1,770,158	100.0
Gross Profit	2,912,683	53.7	—	—	1,775,972	44.6	750,547	42.4
Net Profit After Tax	591,215	10.9	2,500,613	16.3	382,272	9.6	269,064	15.2
Working Capital	290,145	—	991,478	—	1,525,444	—	387,729	—

RATIOS	UQ	MED	LQ	UQ	MED	LQ	UQ	MED	LQ	UQ	MED	LQ
SOLVENCY												
Quick Ratio (times)	1.0	0.6	0.5	1.1	0.9	0.7	1.0	0.6	0.4	3.3	1.1	0.5
Current Ratio (times)	1.6	1.0	0.7	2.2	1.3	1.0	1.5	1.0	0.7	7.0	1.6	1.0
Curr Liab To Nw (%)	31.9	48.9	91.4	16.0	19.6	45.2	22.3	42.4	76.7	6.1	41.4	89.0
Curr Liab To Inv (%)	378.5	580.1	701.5	483.3	512.8	604.8	297.3	550.5	770.0	64.0	186.0	424.5
Total Liab To Nw (%)	57.4	128.1	291.7	35.1	51.7	122.1	59.2	123.1	209.4	26.6	78.0	151.9
Fixed Assets To Nw (%)	98.7	123.2	224.0	92.2	103.4	124.4	100.1	154.0	224.0	70.1	104.0	144.3
EFFICIENCY												
Coll Period (days)	47.5	58.8	97.5	52.8	73.0	87.2	29.6	51.5	71.8	32.0	61.0	74.7
Sales To Inv (times)	35.7	24.5	16.9	23.6	22.4	16.3	45.4	25.4	17.9	397.0	67.8	31.0
Assets To Sales (%)	130.2	187.4	239.3	161.1	208.2	303.5	133.2	201.3	247.8	92.9	120.6	180.0
Sales To Nwc (times)	8.7	2.2	1.0	11.0	6.0	4.5	15.0	6.0	4.5	8.1	5.1	3.2
Acct Pay To Sales (%)	7.5	12.8	17.3	6.2	11.5	20.0	5.6	10.9	18.7	4.4	9.9	28.8
PROFITABILITY												
Return On Sales (%)	19.8	10.6	3.5	25.1	18.5	7.5	16.9	10.0	4.8	21.3	15.8	9.9
Return On Assets (%)	9.0	3.4	1.3	16.7	6.1	3.8	10.5	5.1	2.9	23.3	21.7	12.2
Return On Nw (%)	24.6	10.7	3.1	25.1	14.9	5.8	24.7	13.0	6.4	44.5	27.0	19.8

SIC 4011 RR LINE-HAUL OPER
INDUSTRY ASSETS
$5,000,000-$25,000,000
1995 (25 Establishments)

	$	%
Cash	807,360	6.4
Accounts Receivable	1,551,645	12.3
Notes Receivable	25,230	0.2
Inventory	189,225	1.5
Other Current	1,009,200	8.0
Total Current	**3,582,660**	**28.4**
Fixed Assets	7,846,530	62.2
Other Non-current	1,185,810	9.4
Total Assets	**12,615,000**	**100.0**
Accounts Payable	1,753,485	13.9
Bank Loans	—	—
Notes Payable	75,690	0.6
Other Current	2,094,090	16.6
Total Current	**3,923,265**	**31.1**
Other Long Term	3,418,665	27.1
Deferred Credits	239,685	1.9
Net Worth	5,033,385	39.9
Total Liab & Net Worth	**12,615,000**	**100.0**
Net Sales	5,517,545	100.0
Gross Profit	2,962,922	53.7
Net Profit After Tax	446,921	8.1
Working Capital	(340,605)	—

RATIOS	UQ	MED	LQ
SOLVENCY			
Quick Ratio (times)	0.8	0.6	0.4
Current Ratio (times)	1.3	0.8	0.7
Curr Liab To Nw (%)	35.2	62.5	95.5
Curr Liab To Inv (%)	445.6	580.1	671.7
Total Liab To Nw (%)	75.0	146.5	302.0
Fixed Assets To Nw (%)	101.8	134.5	301.2
EFFICIENCY			
Coll Period (days)	47.0	58.4	97.8
Sales To Inv (times)	33.5	24.5	18.1
Assets To Sales (%)	133.6	175.8	246.6
Sales To Nwc (times)	9.8	5.4	2.3
Acct Pay To Sales (%)	9.7	13.9	22.0
PROFITABILITY			
Return On Sales (%)	12.3	8.1	3.1
Return On Assets (%)	6.9	3.1	1.2
Return On Nw (%)	20.1	10.7	3.7

SIC 4013 SWITCHING TERM SVCS
(NO BREAKDOWN)
1995 (26 Establishments)

	$	%
Cash	2,263,047	16.9
Accounts Receivable	2,624,599	19.6
Notes Receivable	93,736	0.7
Inventory	200,862	1.5
Other Current	615,977	4.6
Total Current	**5,798,222**	**43.3**
Fixed Assets	7,097,130	53.0
Other Non-current	495,460	3.7
Total Assets	**13,390,812**	**100.0**
Accounts Payable	1,084,656	8.1
Bank Loans	—	—
Notes Payable	615,977	4.6
Other Current	1,941,668	14.5
Total Current	**3,642,301**	**27.2**
Other Long Term	2,423,737	18.1
Deferred Credits	147,299	1.1
Net Worth	7,177,475	53.6
Total Liab & Net Worth	**13,390,812**	**100.0**
Net Sales	5,423,991	100.0
Gross Profit	2,326,892	42.9
Net Profit After Tax	998,014	18.4
Working Capital	2,155,921	—

RATIOS	UQ	MED	LQ
SOLVENCY			
Quick Ratio (times)	2.9	1.3	0.6
Current Ratio (times)	3.8	1.9	1.0
Curr Liab To Nw (%)	13.5	25.2	59.2
Curr Liab To Inv (%)	322.6	352.4	525.8
Total Liab To Nw (%)	32.8	70.9	119.6
Fixed Assets To Nw (%)	76.4	116.5	156.7
EFFICIENCY			
Coll Period (days)	45.3	54.8	71.8
Sales To Inv (times)	39.3	26.8	15.8
Assets To Sales (%)	124.4	159.3	217.7
Sales To Nwc (times)	7.4	5.0	2.0
Acct Pay To Sales (%)	1.3	4.5	8.4
PROFITABILITY			
Return On Sales (%)	28.5	19.0	12.5
Return On Assets (%)	19.6	10.1	3.2
Return On Nw (%)	33.5	12.2	3.6

SIC 41 LOCAL PASSENGER TRAN
(NO BREAKDOWN)
1995 (955 Establishments)

	$	%
Cash	83,959	12.1
Accounts Receivable	118,652	17.1
Notes Receivable	4,857	0.7
Inventory	6,939	1.0
Other Current	48,571	7.0
Total Current	**262,978**	**37.9**
Fixed Assets	355,957	51.3
Other Non-current	74,938	10.8
Total Assets	**693,874**	**100.0**
Accounts Payable	45,796	6.6
Bank Loans	1,388	0.2
Notes Payable	54,816	7.9
Other Current	113,795	16.4
Total Current	**215,795**	**31.1**
Other Long Term	162,367	23.4
Deferred Credits	3,469	0.5
Net Worth	312,243	45.0
Total Liab & Net Worth	**693,874**	**100.0**
Net Sales	1,319,695	100.0
Gross Profit	527,878	40.0
Net Profit After Tax	42,230	3.2
Working Capital	47,183	—

RATIOS	UQ	MED	LQ
SOLVENCY			
Quick Ratio (times)	2.0	0.9	0.4
Current Ratio (times)	2.7	1.2	0.6
Curr Liab To Nw (%)	15.7	50.0	138.0
Curr Liab To Inv (%)	237.1	436.6	721.2
Total Liab To Nw (%)	30.7	94.3	240.5
Fixed Assets To Nw (%)	57.2	105.1	217.8
EFFICIENCY			
Coll Period (days)	12.8	29.6	52.4
Sales To Inv (times)	175.5	65.4	28.0
Assets To Sales (%)	30.7	48.2	80.7
Sales To Nwc (times)	23.1	10.3	5.3
Acct Pay To Sales (%)	1.4	2.8	5.3
PROFITABILITY			
Return On Sales (%)	7.3	2.7	0.1
Return On Assets (%)	14.0	4.1	(0.3)
Return On Nw (%)	34.7	10.7	(0.5)

SIC 41 LOCAL PASSENGER TRAN
NORTHEAST
1995 (434 Establishments)

	$	%
Cash	74,958	11.5
Accounts Receivable	116,022	17.8
Notes Receivable	5,866	0.9
Inventory	5,866	0.9
Other Current	46,278	7.1
Total Current	**248,991**	**38.2**
Fixed Assets	331,119	50.8
Other Non-current	71,699	11.0
Total Assets	**651,809**	**100.0**
Accounts Payable	53,448	8.2
Bank Loans	1,955	0.3
Notes Payable	63,877	9.8
Other Current	110,808	17.0
Total Current	**230,089**	**35.3**
Other Long Term	135,576	20.8
Deferred Credits	2,607	0.4
Net Worth	283,537	43.5
Total Liab & Net Worth	**651,809**	**100.0**
Net Sales	1,391,275	100.0
Gross Profit	560,684	40.3
Net Profit After Tax	54,260	3.9
Working Capital	18,902	—

RATIOS	UQ	MED	LQ
SOLVENCY			
Quick Ratio (times)	1.6	0.8	0.4
Current Ratio (times)	2.2	1.1	0.6
Curr Liab To Nw (%)	20.5	56.9	159.9
Curr Liab To Inv (%)	363.2	542.7	718.1
Total Liab To Nw (%)	36.7	112.8	251.0
Fixed Assets To Nw (%)	63.3	105.9	220.8
EFFICIENCY			
Coll Period (days)	12.6	31.0	56.4
Sales To Inv (times)	175.2	82.7	37.6
Assets To Sales (%)	29.6	45.0	73.5
Sales To Nwc (times)	22.1	10.7	5.7
Acct Pay To Sales (%)	1.4	2.9	5.5
PROFITABILITY			
Return On Sales (%)	6.9	2.7	0.3
Return On Assets (%)	14.2	4.9	0.7
Return On Nw (%)	38.2	13.5	1.5

SIC 41 LOCAL PASSENGER TRAN

	CENTRAL 1995 (169 Establishments) $	%	SOUTH 1995 (217 Establishments) $	%	WEST 1995 (135 Establishments) $	%	INDUSTRY ASSETS UNDER $100,000 1995 (137 Establishments) $	%
Cash	116,021	15.2	68,549	12.6	86,982	9.5	12,275	21.0
Accounts Receivable	135,866	17.8	73,989	13.6	169,386	18.5	7,248	12.4
Notes Receivable	2,290	0.3	3,808	0.7	6,409	0.7	234	0.4
Inventory	12,976	1.7	4,896	0.9	7,325	0.8	351	0.6
Other Current	48,851	6.4	31,010	5.7	85,151	9.3	3,682	6.3
Total Current	**316,004**	**41.4**	**182,252**	**33.5**	**355,254**	**38.8**	**23,789**	**40.7**
Fixed Assets	388,517	50.9	288,883	53.1	462,379	50.5	28,173	48.2
Other Non-current	58,774	7.7	72,901	13.4	97,969	10.7	6,488	11.1
Total Assets	**763,294**	**100.0**	**544,036**	**100.0**	**915,602**	**100.0**	**58,450**	**100.0**
Accounts Payable	48,088	6.3	21,761	4.0	52,189	5.7	5,144	8.8
Bank Loans	763	0.1	1,088	0.2	—	—	—	—
Notes Payable	52,667	6.9	40,803	7.5	35,708	3.9	6,020	10.3
Other Current	93,122	12.2	93,574	17.2	170,302	18.6	12,391	21.2
Total Current	**194,640**	**25.5**	**157,226**	**28.9**	**258,200**	**28.2**	**23,555**	**40.3**
Other Long Term	176,321	23.1	136,553	25.1	265,525	29.0	10,404	17.8
Deferred Credits	1,527	0.2	1,632	0.3	11,903	1.3	—	—
Net Worth	390,807	51.2	248,624	45.7	379,975	41.5	24,491	41.9
Total Liab & Net Worth	**763,294**	**100.0**	**544,036**	**100.0**	**915,602**	**100.0**	**58,450**	**100.0**
Net Sales	1,331,832	100.0	786,895	100.0	1,803,204	100.0	218,500	100.0
Gross Profit	546,051	41.0	287,217	36.5	751,936	41.7	113,620	52.0
Net Profit After Tax	27,968	2.1	14,951	1.9	54,096	3.0	10,051	4.6
Working Capital	121,364	—	25,026	—	97,054	—	234	—

RATIOS	UQ	MED	LQ	UQ	MED	LQ	UQ	MED	LQ	UQ	MED	LQ
SOLVENCY												
Quick Ratio (times)	3.0	1.1	0.5	2.2	0.9	0.3	1.9	0.9	0.4	2.1	0.8	0.4
Current Ratio (times)	4.2	1.6	0.8	3.0	1.2	0.5	3.1	1.4	0.7	2.4	1.0	0.5
Curr Liab To Nw (%)	12.9	30.3	104.0	11.8	35.0	107.6	15.8	52.4	144.9	12.9	51.1	151.1
Curr Liab To Inv (%)	229.0	370.3	736.6	237.9	363.5	528.7	90.7	478.3	758.9	281.3	440.7	484.2
Total Liab To Nw (%)	22.2	70.6	207.5	24.3	81.6	237.2	49.7	106.5	272.1	22.9	82.3	178.5
Fixed Assets To Nw (%)	44.6	95.5	198.2	63.0	98.6	194.1	57.9	118.6	246.0	60.1	95.5	170.8
EFFICIENCY												
Coll Period (days)	12.4	26.7	52.2	13.9	23.4	49.3	15.3	31.8	50.6	7.3	15.3	23.4
Sales To Inv (times)	156.7	29.0	13.8	178.2	61.6	24.1	194.3	68.6	36.2	105.9	52.1	32.8
Assets To Sales (%)	30.2	55.7	102.5	34.5	50.0	88.0	32.6	50.9	89.0	9.7	18.2	37.9
Sales To Nwc (times)	17.7	8.9	4.1	27.2	8.7	5.8	24.8	10.4	5.1	81.4	19.9	10.2
Acct Pay To Sales (%)	1.4	2.1	4.6	1.4	2.6	4.7	1.4	2.7	6.1	0.7	1.6	2.4
PROFITABILITY												
Return On Sales (%)	7.9	2.8	(0.5)	8.1	3.8	(1.0)	7.2	2.0	(0.6)	11.2	2.7	(0.9)
Return On Assets (%)	10.6	2.9	(2.1)	15.9	5.4	(0.4)	8.0	2.5	(2.3)	44.0	9.3	(6.2)
Return On Nw (%)	23.4	7.9	(4.6)	34.8	11.1	(0.7)	23.0	6.1	(8.8)	108.4	43.1	(19.7)

SIC 41 LOCAL PASSENGER TRAN
INDUSTRY ASSETS $100,000 - $250,000
1995 (160 Establishments)

	$	%
Cash	22,439	13.3
Accounts Receivable	30,369	18.0
Notes Receivable	2,193	1.3
Inventory	1,012	0.6
Other Current	9,279	5.5
Total Current	**65,293**	**38.7**
Fixed Assets	88,070	52.2
Other Non-current	15,353	9.1
Total Assets	**168,716**	**100.0**
Accounts Payable	9,279	5.5
Bank Loans	—	—
Notes Payable	21,090	12.5
Other Current	29,188	17.3
Total Current	**59,557**	**35.3**
Other Long Term	38,299	22.7
Deferred Credits	337	0.2
Net Worth	70,523	41.8
Total Liab & Net Worth	**168,716**	**100.0**
Net Sales	504,434	100.0
Gross Profit	241,624	47.9
Net Profit After Tax	19,673	3.9
Working Capital	5,736	—

RATIOS	UQ	MED	LQ
SOLVENCY			
Quick Ratio (times)	2.4	0.7	0.2
Current Ratio (times)	2.8	1.0	0.4
Curr Liab To Nw (%)	13.7	59.3	166.8
Curr Liab To Inv (%)	50.1	77.7	210.0
Total Liab To Nw (%)	32.9	86.5	241.0
Fixed Assets To Nw (%)	58.3	123.9	222.2
EFFICIENCY			
Coll Period (days)	14.2	26.7	50.0
Sales To Inv (times)	89.0	66.0	26.2
Assets To Sales (%)	20.3	30.8	44.8
Sales To Nwc (times)	25.8	14.4	6.4
Acct Pay To Sales (%)	1.3	2.6	3.5
PROFITABILITY			
Return On Sales (%)	7.9	3.4	0.3
Return On Assets (%)	23.1	8.6	0.2
Return On Nw (%)	89.6	23.6	1.3

SIC 41 LOCAL PASSENGER TRAN
INDUSTRY ASSETS $250,000 - $500,000
1995 (147 Establishments)

	$	%
Cash	43,265	12.5
Accounts Receivable	61,956	17.9
Notes Receivable	1,731	0.5
Inventory	1,731	0.5
Other Current	20,075	5.8
Total Current	**128,757**	**37.2**
Fixed Assets	176,522	51.0
Other Non-current	40,842	11.8
Total Assets	**346,122**	**100.0**
Accounts Payable	23,536	6.8
Bank Loans	1,384	0.4
Notes Payable	24,229	7.0
Other Current	54,687	15.8
Total Current	**103,837**	**30.0**
Other Long Term	86,531	25.0
Deferred Credits	1,038	0.3
Net Worth	154,717	44.7
Total Liab & Net Worth	**346,122**	**100.0**
Net Sales	772,979	100.0
Gross Profit	346,295	44.8
Net Profit After Tax	28,600	3.7
Working Capital	24,920	—

RATIOS	UQ	MED	LQ
SOLVENCY			
Quick Ratio (times)	2.4	0.9	0.4
Current Ratio (times)	2.8	1.1	0.6
Curr Liab To Nw (%)	12.8	42.6	127.8
Curr Liab To Inv (%)	260.8	308.5	476.7
Total Liab To Nw (%)	32.1	98.4	232.9
Fixed Assets To Nw (%)	59.6	105.6	200.5
EFFICIENCY			
Coll Period (days)	14.1	30.7	48.0
Sales To Inv (times)	194.8	99.7	54.8
Assets To Sales (%)	31.9	41.3	57.4
Sales To Nwc (times)	25.0	9.4	5.6
Acct Pay To Sales (%)	1.0	2.4	4.7
PROFITABILITY			
Return On Sales (%)	6.5	2.4	0.5
Return On Assets (%)	13.4	5.4	0.9
Return On Nw (%)	33.6	12.9	1.2

SIC 41 LOCAL PASSENGER TRAN
INDUSTRY ASSETS $500,000 - $1,000,000
1995 (163 Establishments)

	$	%
Cash	91,745	12.8
Accounts Receivable	133,317	18.6
Notes Receivable	2,867	0.4
Inventory	7,168	1.0
Other Current	45,872	6.4
Total Current	**280,968**	**39.2**
Fixed Assets	384,898	53.7
Other Non-current	50,890	7.1
Total Assets	**716,756**	**100.0**
Accounts Payable	43,722	6.1
Bank Loans	3,584	0.5
Notes Payable	55,907	7.8
Other Current	119,698	16.7
Total Current	**222,911**	**31.1**
Other Long Term	172,021	24.0
Deferred Credits	717	0.1
Net Worth	321,107	44.8
Total Liab & Net Worth	**716,756**	**100.0**
Net Sales	1,423,456	100.0
Gross Profit	575,076	40.4
Net Profit After Tax	59,785	4.2
Working Capital	58,057	—

RATIOS	UQ	MED	LQ
SOLVENCY			
Quick Ratio (times)	2.3	1.1	0.4
Current Ratio (times)	2.8	1.3	0.7
Curr Liab To Nw (%)	17.4	63.9	143.3
Curr Liab To Inv (%)	240.4	592.5	813.9
Total Liab To Nw (%)	32.8	105.1	277.7
Fixed Assets To Nw (%)	55.0	105.1	240.0
EFFICIENCY			
Coll Period (days)	12.1	29.9	56.8
Sales To Inv (times)	169.0	66.2	38.9
Assets To Sales (%)	34.6	48.3	74.6
Sales To Nwc (times)	20.3	8.1	5.4
Acct Pay To Sales (%)	1.2	2.3	5.2
PROFITABILITY			
Return On Sales (%)	10.2	3.7	0.9
Return On Assets (%)	14.5	6.0	2.4
Return On Nw (%)	33.3	14.8	7.2

SIC 41 LOCAL PASSENGER TRAN
INDUSTRY ASSETS $1,000,000 - $5,000,000
1995 (238 Establishments)

	$	%
Cash	208,904	10.3
Accounts Receivable	381,301	18.8
Notes Receivable	14,197	0.7
Inventory	32,451	1.6
Other Current	148,058	7.3
Total Current	**784,912**	**38.7**
Fixed Assets	1,014,099	50.0
Other Non-current	229,186	11.3
Total Assets	**2,028,197**	**100.0**
Accounts Payable	131,833	6.5
Bank Loans	2,028	0.1
Notes Payable	141,974	7.0
Other Current	310,314	15.3
Total Current	**586,149**	**28.9**
Other Long Term	521,247	25.7
Deferred Credits	14,197	0.7
Net Worth	906,604	44.7
Total Liab & Net Worth	**2,028,197**	**100.0**
Net Sales	3,247,864	100.0
Gross Profit	1,091,282	33.6
Net Profit After Tax	107,180	3.3
Working Capital	198,763	—

RATIOS	UQ	MED	LQ
SOLVENCY			
Quick Ratio (times)	2.0	0.9	0.5
Current Ratio (times)	2.8	1.3	0.7
Curr Liab To Nw (%)	22.0	57.5	149.7
Curr Liab To Inv (%)	213.4	368.0	640.2
Total Liab To Nw (%)	34.6	110.5	272.2
Fixed Assets To Nw (%)	56.6	110.2	250.0
EFFICIENCY			
Coll Period (days)	16.1	31.8	54.8
Sales To Inv (times)	225.2	88.7	31.2
Assets To Sales (%)	42.5	61.3	94.6
Sales To Nwc (times)	19.9	10.5	5.1
Acct Pay To Sales (%)	1.6	2.8	4.9
PROFITABILITY			
Return On Sales (%)	6.9	2.8	0.4
Return On Assets (%)	8.5	3.4	0.2
Return On Nw (%)	27.4	9.3	0.9

	SIC 41 LOCAL PASSENGER TRAN INDUSTRY ASSETS $5,000,000-$25,000,000 1995 (70 Establishments) $	%	SIC 41 LOCAL PASSENGER TRAN INDUSTRY ASSETS $25,000,000-$50,000,000 1995 (14 Establishments) $	%	SIC 41 LOCAL PASSENGER TRAN INDUSTRY ASSETS OVER $50,000,000 1995 (26 Establishments) $	%	SIC 4111 LCL SUBURBAN TRANS (NO BREAKDOWN) 1995 (117 Establishments) $	%
Cash	578,289	6.6	1,398,998	4.0	5,300,400	2.4	122,475	9.5
Accounts Receivable	1,314,293	15.0	2,658,095	7.6	18,772,250	8.5	170,176	13.2
Notes Receivable	148,953	1.7	209,850	0.6	—	—	12,892	1.0
Inventory	131,429	1.5	629,549	1.8	1,545,950	0.7	14,181	1.1
Other Current	1,112,768	12.7	1,503,922	4.3	22,305,850	10.1	109,583	8.5
Total Current	**3,285,731**	**37.5**	**6,400,414**	**18.3**	**47,924,449**	**21.7**	**429,309**	**33.3**
Fixed Assets	4,416,023	50.4	22,733,710	65.0	112,633,498	51.0	688,441	53.4
Other Non-current	1,060,196	12.1	5,840,815	16.7	60,292,049	27.3	171,466	13.3
Total Assets	**8,761,950**	**100.0**	**34,974,939**	**100.0**	**220,849,997**	**100.0**	**1,289,215**	**100.0**
Accounts Payable	744,766	8.5	1,294,073	3.7	9,496,550	4.3	82,510	6.4
Bank Loans	—	—	—	—	—	—	—	—
Notes Payable	446,859	5.1	454,674	1.3	1,104,250	0.5	54,147	4.2
Other Current	1,472,008	16.8	2,728,045	7.8	18,772,250	8.5	208,853	16.2
Total Current	**2,663,633**	**30.4**	**4,476,792**	**12.8**	**29,373,050**	**13.3**	**345,510**	**26.8**
Other Long Term	1,664,771	19.0	9,128,459	26.1	44,611,699	20.2	233,348	18.1
Deferred Credits	184,001	2.1	—	—	3,975,300	1.8	24,495	1.9
Net Worth	4,249,546	48.5	21,369,688	61.1	142,889,948	64.7	685,862	53.2
Total Liab & Net Worth	**8,761,950**	**100.0**	**34,974,939**	**100.0**	**220,849,997**	**100.0**	**1,289,215**	**100.0**
Net Sales	13,259,337	100.0	16,763,830	100.0	98,896,000	100.0	2,272,035	100.0
Gross Profit	3,633,058	27.4	3,738,334	22.3	47,568,976	48.1	597,545	26.3
Net Profit After Tax	437,558	3.3	(3,118,072)	(18.6)	(7,516,096)	(7.6)	(111,330)	(4.9)
Working Capital	622,098	—	1,923,622	—	18,551,399	—	83,799	—

RATIOS	UQ	MED	LQ	UQ	MED	LQ	UQ	MED	LQ	UQ	MED	LQ
SOLVENCY												
Quick Ratio (times)	1.2	0.8	0.3	1.3	0.7	0.5	1.3	0.5	0.3	1.6	0.7	0.4
Current Ratio (times)	2.1	1.3	0.8	2.6	1.4	0.8	2.4	1.4	0.9	2.5	1.2	0.7
Curr Liab To Nw (%)	16.5	51.6	99.9	11.3	15.8	26.4	10.0	13.7	40.4	10.6	32.9	92.1
Curr Liab To Inv (%)	363.1	569.0	807.9	264.7	355.5	520.6	662.4	709.6	858.0	360.2	528.3	688.4
Total Liab To Nw (%)	30.9	101.9	205.6	16.5	40.3	92.8	19.0	40.4	103.7	18.6	57.9	195.5
Fixed Assets To Nw (%)	56.1	103.8	198.3	79.7	95.3	113.4	55.6	91.7	116.5	75.0	96.8	147.8
EFFICIENCY												
Coll Period (days)	11.3	26.5	52.2	17.9	20.4	34.3	19.7	66.4	112.3	13.1	23.4	37.6
Sales To Inv (times)	122.2	53.1	23.1	80.2	22.8	10.5	123.6	32.5	13.6	121.8	20.5	12.1
Assets To Sales (%)	45.7	65.0	106.5	109.9	212.8	305.9	133.2	241.4	473.2	31.9	54.0	232.6
Sales To Nwc (times)	20.7	9.1	3.4	10.0	2.3	0.9	11.7	5.1	2.2	25.6	12.2	3.4
Acct Pay To Sales (%)	3.1	4.8	6.3	4.2	5.0	16.1	3.2	11.0	19.8	2.4	4.3	6.6
PROFITABILITY												
Return On Sales (%)	5.4	2.1	(0.5)	(6.8)	(22.5)	(24.6)	4.3	(3.4)	(22.3)	5.0	(0.2)	(13.1)
Return On Assets (%)	6.4	2.5	(0.7)	(0.9)	(8.4)	(8.7)	1.1	(3.0)	(5.6)	8.7	0.9	(6.8)
Return On Nw (%)	16.8	6.6	(2.1)	(2.4)	(11.8)	(13.3)	2.3	(3.4)	(6.7)	19.6	0.9	(8.8)

SIC 4111 LCL SUBURBAN TRANS — INDUSTRY ASSETS $100,000 - $250,000 — 1995 (17 Establishments)

	$	%
Cash	15,772	12.8
Accounts Receivable	16,881	13.7
Notes Receivable	4,190	3.4
Inventory	986	0.8
Other Current	7,886	6.4
Total Current	**45,715**	**37.1**
Fixed Assets	66,663	54.1
Other Non-current	10,844	8.8
Total Assets	**123,222**	**100.0**
Accounts Payable	4,929	4.0
Bank Loans	—	—
Notes Payable	16,019	13.0
Other Current	8,256	6.7
Total Current	**29,204**	**23.7**
Other Long Term	31,545	25.6
Deferred Credits	—	—
Net Worth	62,474	50.7
Total Liab & Net Worth	**123,222**	**100.0**
Net Sales	537,217	100.0
Gross Profit	129,469	24.1
Net Profit After Tax	22,026	4.1
Working Capital	16,511	—

RATIOS	UQ	MED	LQ
SOLVENCY			
Quick Ratio (times)	1.2	0.6	0.2
Current Ratio (times)	3.5	0.8	0.2
Curr Liab To Nw (%)	4.0	22.1	41.2
Curr Liab To Inv (%)	47.6	47.6	47.6
Total Liab To Nw (%)	3.0	33.2	102.5
Fixed Assets To Nw (%)	75.5	87.4	142.7
EFFICIENCY			
Coll Period (days)	9.3	11.5	15.6
Sales To Inv (times)	—	—	—
Assets To Sales (%)	17.1	23.6	26.9
Sales To Nwc (times)	23.9	15.3	12.2
Acct Pay To Sales (%)	0.6	0.9	1.3
PROFITABILITY			
Return On Sales (%)	10.6	4.1	0.3
Return On Assets (%)	24.2	12.5	0.7
Return On Nw (%)	24.5	10.4	8.6

SIC 4111 LCL SUBURBAN TRANS — INDUSTRY ASSETS $500,000 - $1,000,000 — 1995 (19 Establishments)

	$	%
Cash	109,015	14.8
Accounts Receivable	123,747	16.8
Notes Receivable	—	—
Inventory	3,683	0.5
Other Current	67,766	9.2
Total Current	**304,211**	**41.3**
Fixed Assets	343,987	46.7
Other Non-current	88,391	12.0
Total Assets	**736,588**	**100.0**
Accounts Payable	79,552	10.8
Bank Loans	—	—
Notes Payable	16,942	2.3
Other Current	167,205	22.7
Total Current	**263,699**	**35.8**
Other Long Term	136,269	18.5
Deferred Credits	1,473	0.2
Net Worth	335,148	45.5
Total Liab & Net Worth	**736,588**	**100.0**
Net Sales	2,024,682	100.0
Gross Profit	714,713	35.3
Net Profit After Tax	(24,296)	(1.2)
Working Capital	40,512	—

RATIOS	UQ	MED	LQ
SOLVENCY			
Quick Ratio (times)	1.1	0.6	0.4
Current Ratio (times)	1.5	0.9	0.5
Curr Liab To Nw (%)	9.8	34.0	74.4
Curr Liab To Inv (%)	670.3	769.1	867.9
Total Liab To Nw (%)	16.1	54.6	128.3
Fixed Assets To Nw (%)	25.0	61.9	89.9
EFFICIENCY			
Coll Period (days)	13.1	22.6	31.8
Sales To Inv (times)	294.6	50.4	44.2
Assets To Sales (%)	28.3	32.1	44.2
Sales To Nwc (times)	17.0	12.8	9.9
Acct Pay To Sales (%)	1.8	2.6	3.5
PROFITABILITY			
Return On Sales (%)	1.8	0.1	(8.5)
Return On Assets (%)	3.9	—	(3.9)
Return On Nw (%)	12.0	0.2	(4.3)

SIC 4111 LCL SUBURBAN TRANS — INDUSTRY ASSETS $1,000,000 - $5,000,000 — 1995 (20 Establishments)

	$	%
Cash	133,715	6.6
Accounts Receivable	360,625	17.8
Notes Receivable	18,234	0.9
Inventory	48,624	2.4
Other Current	87,117	4.3
Total Current	**648,315**	**32.0**
Fixed Assets	1,138,604	56.2
Other Non-current	239,066	11.8
Total Assets	**2,025,985**	**100.0**
Accounts Payable	129,663	6.4
Bank Loans	—	—
Notes Payable	105,351	5.2
Other Current	437,613	21.6
Total Current	**672,627**	**33.2**
Other Long Term	478,132	23.6
Deferred Credits	93,195	4.6
Net Worth	782,030	38.6
Total Liab & Net Worth	**2,025,985**	**100.0**
Net Sales	4,042,019	100.0
Gross Profit	1,018,589	25.2
Net Profit After Tax	(64,672)	(1.6)
Working Capital	(24,312)	—

RATIOS	UQ	MED	LQ
SOLVENCY			
Quick Ratio (times)	1.0	0.7	0.4
Current Ratio (times)	1.4	0.9	0.7
Curr Liab To Nw (%)	40.6	72.4	127.4
Curr Liab To Inv (%)	350.0	367.6	396.9
Total Liab To Nw (%)	64.4	112.6	170.6
Fixed Assets To Nw (%)	95.9	120.1	172.7
EFFICIENCY			
Coll Period (days)	19.0	28.5	35.5
Sales To Inv (times)	91.7	29.9	19.8
Assets To Sales (%)	35.0	47.1	58.4
Sales To Nwc (times)	24.7	12.6	11.8
Acct Pay To Sales (%)	2.1	2.8	4.5
PROFITABILITY			
Return On Sales (%)	5.4	1.9	(1.6)
Return On Assets (%)	15.3	4.7	(2.5)
Return On Nw (%)	46.0	12.7	1.5

SIC 4111 LCL SUBURBAN TRANS — INDUSTRY ASSETS $5,000,000 - $25,000,000 — 1995 (12 Establishments)

	$	%
Cash	676,725	5.8
Accounts Receivable	1,750,151	15.0
Notes Receivable	268,356	2.3
Inventory	186,683	1.6
Other Current	1,563,468	13.4
Total Current	**4,445,382**	**38.1**
Fixed Assets	6,148,862	52.7
Other Non-current	1,073,426	9.2
Total Assets	**11,667,670**	**100.0**
Accounts Payable	828,405	7.1
Bank Loans	—	—
Notes Payable	373,365	3.2
Other Current	1,925,166	16.5
Total Current	**3,126,936**	**26.8**
Other Long Term	1,131,764	9.7
Deferred Credits	875,075	7.5
Net Worth	6,533,895	56.0
Total Liab & Net Worth	**11,667,670**	**100.0**
Net Sales	15,633,515	100.0
Gross Profit	1,407,016	9.0
Net Profit After Tax	(1,078,713)	(6.9)
Working Capital	1,318,446	—

RATIOS	UQ	MED	LQ
SOLVENCY			
Quick Ratio (times)	1.4	0.9	0.4
Current Ratio (times)	4.5	1.4	1.1
Curr Liab To Nw (%)	8.5	16.6	68.8
Curr Liab To Inv (%)	407.5	528.3	734.9
Total Liab To Nw (%)	10.2	22.7	75.1
Fixed Assets To Nw (%)	73.9	87.3	100.6
EFFICIENCY			
Coll Period (days)	16.5	27.8	39.7
Sales To Inv (times)	257.6	81.4	13.3
Assets To Sales (%)	41.9	55.0	403.8
Sales To Nwc (times)	50.8	8.6	3.0
Acct Pay To Sales (%)	4.1	5.1	5.8
PROFITABILITY			
Return On Sales (%)	(0.7)	(1.0)	(25.1)
Return On Assets (%)	(1.8)	(6.5)	(10.7)
Return On Nw (%)	(4.5)	(9.0)	(15.1)

SIC 4111 LCL SUBURBAN TRANS
INDUSTRY ASSETS
OVER $50,000,000
1995 (16 Establishments)

	$	%
Cash	12,738,654	2.7
Accounts Receivable	20,759,288	4.4
Notes Receivable	—	—
Inventory	4,246,218	0.9
Other Current	44,349,388	9.4
Total Current	**82,093,548**	**17.4**
Fixed Assets	289,686,428	61.4
Other Non-current	100,022,024	21.2
Total Assets	**471,802,000**	**100.0**
Accounts Payable	12,738,654	2.7
Bank Loans	—	—
Notes Payable	1,415,406	0.3
Other Current	46,708,398	9.9
Total Current	**60,862,458**	**12.9**
Other Long Term	70,770,300	15.0
Deferred Credits	3,774,416	0.8
Net Worth	336,394,826	71.3
Total Liab & Net Worth	**471,802,000**	**100.0**
Net Sales	48,667,530	100.0
Gross Profit	—	—
Net Profit After Tax	(7,835,472)	(16.1)
Working Capital	21,231,090	—

RATIOS	UQ	MED	LQ
SOLVENCY			
Quick Ratio (times)	0.6	0.4	0.3
Current Ratio (times)	2.4	1.1	0.8
Curr Liab To Nw (%)	9.9	11.6	24.3
Curr Liab To Inv (%)	653.8	688.4	793.4
Total Liab To Nw (%)	19.0	32.6	58.8
Fixed Assets To Nw (%)	86.8	98.6	133.1
EFFICIENCY			
Coll Period (days)	18.4	34.2	167.6
Sales To Inv (times)	44.3	15.9	11.6
Assets To Sales (%)	239.1	463.5	639.2
Sales To Nwc (times)	18.9	3.7	1.5
Acct Pay To Sales (%)	6.2	15.2	20.4
PROFITABILITY			
Return On Sales (%)	(4.7)	(11.2)	(35.9)
Return On Assets (%)	(2.6)	(3.6)	(6.0)
Return On Nw (%)	(3.1)	(5.0)	(7.7)

SIC 4119 LCL PASS TRANS NEC
(NO BREAKDOWN)
1995 (378 Establishments)

	$	%
Cash	55,346	13.0
Accounts Receivable	108,989	25.6
Notes Receivable	2,554	0.6
Inventory	2,980	0.7
Other Current	25,119	5.9
Total Current	**194,988**	**45.8**
Fixed Assets	180,939	42.5
Other Non-current	49,811	11.7
Total Assets	**425,739**	**100.0**
Accounts Payable	28,099	6.6
Bank Loans	426	0.1
Notes Payable	40,445	9.5
Other Current	71,950	16.9
Total Current	**140,920**	**33.1**
Other Long Term	83,445	19.6
Deferred Credits	1,277	0.3
Net Worth	200,097	47.0
Total Liab & Net Worth	**425,739**	**100.0**
Net Sales	977,968	100.0
Gross Profit	374,562	38.3
Net Profit After Tax	46,942	4.8
Working Capital	54,068	—

RATIOS	UQ	MED	LQ
SOLVENCY			
Quick Ratio (times)	3.0	1.2	0.5
Current Ratio (times)	3.7	1.5	0.7
Curr Liab To Nw (%)	14.8	45.8	146.1
Curr Liab To Inv (%)	197.1	441.8	737.7
Total Liab To Nw (%)	26.2	91.6	206.9
Fixed Assets To Nw (%)	44.6	83.7	177.3
EFFICIENCY			
Coll Period (days)	25.0	44.9	64.8
Sales To Inv (times)	222.1	135.9	49.2
Assets To Sales (%)	23.3	37.9	60.4
Sales To Nwc (times)	20.8	9.5	5.4
Acct Pay To Sales (%)	1.1	2.3	4.1
PROFITABILITY			
Return On Sales (%)	9.1	3.3	0.6
Return On Assets (%)	21.0	6.2	1.2
Return On Nw (%)	54.2	16.7	2.8

SIC 4119 LCL PASS TRANS NEC
INDUSTRY ASSETS
UNDER $100,000
1995 (70 Establishments)

	$	%
Cash	11,504	19.6
Accounts Receivable	8,452	14.4
Notes Receivable	176	0.3
Inventory	352	0.6
Other Current	2,583	4.4
Total Current	**23,067**	**39.3**
Fixed Assets	29,113	49.6
Other Non-current	6,515	11.1
Total Assets	**58,695**	**100.0**
Accounts Payable	5,165	8.8
Bank Loans	—	—
Notes Payable	9,215	15.7
Other Current	7,806	13.3
Total Current	**22,187**	**37.8**
Other Long Term	8,863	15.1
Deferred Credits	—	—
Net Worth	27,645	47.1
Total Liab & Net Worth	**58,695**	**100.0**
Net Sales	249,964	100.0
Gross Profit	133,481	53.4
Net Profit After Tax	12,498	5.0
Working Capital	880	—

RATIOS	UQ	MED	LQ
SOLVENCY			
Quick Ratio (times)	2.2	0.8	0.5
Current Ratio (times)	2.6	1.1	0.5
Curr Liab To Nw (%)	10.5	36.1	104.0
Curr Liab To Inv (%)	390.7	440.7	446.6
Total Liab To Nw (%)	20.2	86.7	152.6
Fixed Assets To Nw (%)	59.4	94.5	163.3
EFFICIENCY			
Coll Period (days)	9.7	16.4	31.6
Sales To Inv (times)	79.0	52.1	42.5
Assets To Sales (%)	9.6	14.9	32.1
Sales To Nwc (times)	75.8	17.5	11.2
Acct Pay To Sales (%)	0.6	1.7	3.5
PROFITABILITY			
Return On Sales (%)	12.7	3.3	0.1
Return On Assets (%)	51.0	18.5	1.2
Return On Nw (%)	118.2	62.1	2.4

SIC 4119 LCL PASS TRANS NEC
INDUSTRY ASSETS
$100,000 - $250,000
1995 (82 Establishments)

	$	%
Cash	22,609	13.7
Accounts Receivable	39,772	24.1
Notes Receivable	1,650	1.0
Inventory	330	0.2
Other Current	9,737	5.9
Total Current	**74,098**	**44.9**
Fixed Assets	74,263	45.0
Other Non-current	16,668	10.1
Total Assets	**165,028**	**100.0**
Accounts Payable	9,737	5.9
Bank Loans	—	—
Notes Payable	20,959	12.7
Other Current	33,171	20.1
Total Current	**63,866**	**38.7**
Other Long Term	31,850	19.3
Deferred Credits	825	0.5
Net Worth	68,487	41.5
Total Liab & Net Worth	**165,028**	**100.0**
Net Sales	517,503	100.0
Gross Profit	253,059	48.9
Net Profit After Tax	22,253	4.3
Working Capital	10,232	—

RATIOS	UQ	MED	LQ
SOLVENCY			
Quick Ratio (times)	3.2	0.9	0.3
Current Ratio (times)	3.3	1.3	0.4
Curr Liab To Nw (%)	12.8	68.7	171.0
Curr Liab To Inv (%)	85.2	85.2	85.2
Total Liab To Nw (%)	32.4	113.3	241.2
Fixed Assets To Nw (%)	50.7	107.2	214.0
EFFICIENCY			
Coll Period (days)	16.4	37.6	60.2
Sales To Inv (times)	—	—	—
Assets To Sales (%)	17.4	28.3	40.5
Sales To Nwc (times)	23.7	13.3	5.8
Acct Pay To Sales (%)	1.1	2.8	3.4
PROFITABILITY			
Return On Sales (%)	7.8	3.4	0.6
Return On Assets (%)	30.2	10.8	1.2
Return On Nw (%)	100.0	33.5	4.3

SIC 4119 — LCL PASS TRANS NEC — INDUSTRY ASSETS

$250,000 - $500,000 — 1995 (68 Establishments)

	$	%
Cash	32,413	9.3
Accounts Receivable	86,783	24.9
Notes Receivable	2,091	0.6
Inventory	2,091	0.6
Other Current	16,729	4.8
Total Current	**140,107**	**40.2**
Fixed Assets	170,429	48.9
Other Non-current	37,989	10.9
Total Assets	**348,526**	**100.0**
Accounts Payable	19,517	5.6
Bank Loans	1,046	0.3
Notes Payable	26,139	7.5
Other Current	63,780	18.3
Total Current	**110,483**	**31.7**
Other Long Term	80,858	23.2
Deferred Credits	349	0.1
Net Worth	156,837	45.0
Total Liab & Net Worth	**348,526**	**100.0**
Net Sales	786,895	100.0
Gross Profit	317,906	40.4
Net Profit After Tax	29,902	3.8
Working Capital	29,624	—

RATIOS	UQ	MED	LQ
SOLVENCY			
Quick Ratio (times)	2.6	1.0	0.4
Current Ratio (times)	2.8	1.1	0.6
Curr Liab To Nw (%)	18.0	47.5	131.4
Curr Liab To Inv (%)	313.3	476.7	531.5
Total Liab To Nw (%)	30.8	111.8	195.8
Fixed Assets To Nw (%)	54.4	107.5	184.4
EFFICIENCY			
Coll Period (days)	20.8	39.3	64.2
Sales To Inv (times)	187.5	118.1	44.6
Assets To Sales (%)	23.7	40.4	56.8
Sales To Nwc (times)	16.5	8.9	5.4
Acct Pay To Sales (%)	1.4	2.4	4.7
PROFITABILITY			
Return On Sales (%)	5.5	1.5	0.5
Return On Assets (%)	10.1	3.3	0.3
Return On Nw (%)	40.3	12.3	(0.4)

$500,000 - $1,000,000 — 1995 (60 Establishments)

	$	%
Cash	99,629	13.9
Accounts Receivable	225,061	31.4
Notes Receivable	6,451	0.9
Inventory	2,150	0.3
Other Current	29,387	4.1
Total Current	**362,679**	**50.6**
Fixed Assets	295,303	41.2
Other Non-current	58,774	8.2
Total Assets	**716,756**	**100.0**
Accounts Payable	36,555	5.1
Bank Loans	1,434	0.2
Notes Payable	63,791	8.9
Other Current	89,595	12.5
Total Current	**191,374**	**26.7**
Other Long Term	144,068	20.1
Deferred Credits	1,434	0.2
Net Worth	379,881	53.0
Total Liab & Net Worth	**716,756**	**100.0**
Net Sales	1,486,729	100.0
Gross Profit	481,700	32.4
Net Profit After Tax	86,230	5.8
Working Capital	171,305	—

RATIOS	UQ	MED	LQ
SOLVENCY			
Quick Ratio (times)	4.1	2.0	0.9
Current Ratio (times)	4.4	2.1	1.1
Curr Liab To Nw (%)	14.7	31.1	93.4
Curr Liab To Inv (%)	717.2	834.3	954.7
Total Liab To Nw (%)	20.1	80.2	145.6
Fixed Assets To Nw (%)	46.2	73.7	121.2
EFFICIENCY			
Coll Period (days)	30.8	58.4	85.8
Sales To Inv (times)	203.4	181.1	169.0
Assets To Sales (%)	34.6	46.4	61.1
Sales To Nwc (times)	11.1	6.6	4.4
Acct Pay To Sales (%)	0.8	1.8	3.1
PROFITABILITY			
Return On Sales (%)	12.0	4.6	1.4
Return On Assets (%)	17.7	7.3	3.5
Return On Nw (%)	28.2	18.0	8.6

$1,000,000 - $5,000,000 — 1995 (78 Establishments)

	$	%
Cash	254,694	12.8
Accounts Receivable	648,673	32.6
Notes Receivable	7,959	0.4
Inventory	31,837	1.6
Other Current	161,173	8.1
Total Current	**1,104,336**	**55.5**
Fixed Assets	654,642	32.9
Other Non-current	230,816	11.6
Total Assets	**1,989,794**	**100.0**
Accounts Payable	149,235	7.5
Bank Loans	3,980	0.2
Notes Payable	119,388	6.0
Other Current	374,081	18.8
Total Current	**646,683**	**32.5**
Other Long Term	360,153	18.1
Deferred Credits	5,969	0.3
Net Worth	976,989	49.1
Total Liab & Net Worth	**1,989,794**	**100.0**
Net Sales	3,712,208	100.0
Gross Profit	1,173,058	31.6
Net Profit After Tax	193,035	5.2
Working Capital	457,653	—

RATIOS	UQ	MED	LQ
SOLVENCY			
Quick Ratio (times)	3.6	1.4	0.9
Current Ratio (times)	4.2	1.6	1.1
Curr Liab To Nw (%)	19.6	63.1	175.8
Curr Liab To Inv (%)	107.6	508.7	794.0
Total Liab To Nw (%)	30.1	91.2	237.4
Fixed Assets To Nw (%)	33.5	72.5	145.0
EFFICIENCY			
Coll Period (days)	35.4	49.3	70.8
Sales To Inv (times)	372.9	161.4	70.4
Assets To Sales (%)	34.6	48.1	66.8
Sales To Nwc (times)	21.9	8.9	5.1
Acct Pay To Sales (%)	1.2	2.5	5.0
PROFITABILITY			
Return On Sales (%)	8.5	3.6	0.9
Return On Assets (%)	16.5	5.4	1.1
Return On Nw (%)	43.0	14.2	3.3

$5,000,000 - $25,000,000 — 1995 (13 Establishments)

	$	%
Cash	273,932	4.0
Accounts Receivable	1,253,238	18.3
Notes Receivable	41,090	0.6
Inventory	61,635	0.9
Other Current	814,947	11.9
Total Current	**2,444,842**	**35.7**
Fixed Assets	3,129,671	45.7
Other Non-current	1,273,783	18.6
Total Assets	**6,848,296**	**100.0**
Accounts Payable	410,898	6.0
Bank Loans	—	—
Notes Payable	438,291	6.4
Other Current	1,157,362	16.9
Total Current	**2,006,551**	**29.3**
Other Long Term	1,280,631	18.7
Deferred Credits	34,241	0.5
Net Worth	3,526,872	51.5
Total Liab & Net Worth	**6,848,296**	**100.0**
Net Sales	17,049,415	100.0
Gross Profit	2,898,401	17.0
Net Profit After Tax	1,210,508	7.1
Working Capital	438,291	—

RATIOS	UQ	MED	LQ
SOLVENCY			
Quick Ratio (times)	1.2	0.9	0.6
Current Ratio (times)	3.8	1.3	0.8
Curr Liab To Nw (%)	10.1	34.7	183.0
Curr Liab To Inv (%)	129.1	132.4	285.5
Total Liab To Nw (%)	10.4	93.1	386.3
Fixed Assets To Nw (%)	39.2	120.3	253.2
EFFICIENCY			
Coll Period (days)	7.0	39.8	56.2
Sales To Inv (times)	129.0	115.4	28.1
Assets To Sales (%)	45.0	62.0	74.4
Sales To Nwc (times)	18.4	6.5	2.9
Acct Pay To Sales (%)	2.1	3.8	5.6
PROFITABILITY			
Return On Sales (%)	15.9	3.0	0.3
Return On Assets (%)	5.9	2.0	0.5
Return On Nw (%)	10.2	4.3	3.0

	SIC 4121 TAXICABS (NO BREAKDOWN) 1995 (59 Establishments)		SIC 4131 INCTY RRL BUS TRAN (NO BREAKDOWN) 1995 (50 Establishments)		SIC 4131 INCTY RRL BUS TRAN INDUSTRY ASSETS $1,000,000 - $5,000,000 1995 (17 Establishments)		SIC 4131 INCTY RRL BUS TRAN INDUSTRY ASSETS $5,000,000-$25,000,000 1995 (17 Establishments)	
	$	%	$	%	$	%	$	%
Cash	44,254	11.6	677,774	14.2	299,639	8.9	806,099	9.2
Accounts Receivable	64,856	17.0	377,071	7.9	309,739	9.2	674,670	7.7
Notes Receivable	1,145	0.3	95,461	2.0	47,134	1.4	236,573	2.7
Inventory	3,815	1.0	100,234	2.1	80,801	2.4	210,287	2.4
Other Current	34,717	9.1	381,844	8.0	127,936	3.8	972,576	11.1
Total Current	**148,786**	**39.0**	**1,632,385**	**34.2**	**865,249**	**25.7**	**2,900,205**	**33.1**
Fixed Assets	170,913	44.8	2,544,039	53.3	1,935,868	57.5	4,897,930	55.9
Other Non-current	61,803	16.2	596,632	12.5	565,610	16.8	963,815	11.0
Total Assets	**381,503**	**100.0**	**4,773,056**	**100.0**	**3,366,727**	**100.0**	**8,761,950**	**100.0**
Accounts Payable	27,850	7.3	396,164	8.3	178,437	5.3	972,576	11.1
Bank Loans	—	—	—	—	—	—	—	—
Notes Payable	22,890	6.0	200,468	4.2	53,868	1.6	280,382	3.2
Other Current	67,145	17.6	548,901	11.5	262,605	7.8	1,182,863	13.5
Total Current	**117,884**	**30.9**	**1,145,533**	**24.0**	**494,909**	**14.7**	**2,435,822**	**27.8**
Other Long Term	80,879	21.2	1,064,391	22.3	976,351	29.0	1,647,247	18.8
Deferred Credits	1,526	0.4	42,958	0.9	33,667	1.0	105,143	1.2
Net Worth	181,214	47.5	2,520,174	52.8	1,861,800	55.3	4,573,738	52.2
Total Liab & Net Worth	**381,503**	**100.0**	**4,773,056**	**100.0**	**3,366,727**	**100.0**	**8,761,950**	**100.0**
Net Sales	629,307	100.0	4,619,431	100.0	3,621,644	100.0	17,065,924	100.0
Gross Profit	352,412	56.0	1,154,858	25.0	1,187,899	32.8	4,949,118	29.0
Net Profit After Tax	25,172	4.0	115,486	2.5	86,919	2.4	341,318	2.0
Working Capital	30,902	—	486,852	—	370,340	—	464,383	—

RATIOS	UQ	MED	LQ	UQ	MED	LQ	UQ	MED	LQ	UQ	MED	LQ
SOLVENCY												
Quick Ratio (times)	2.5	0.8	0.4	2.0	0.9	0.6	2.3	1.3	0.7	1.1	0.8	0.4
Current Ratio (times)	2.9	1.2	0.6	3.4	1.6	0.9	3.7	2.2	1.4	2.2	1.2	1.0
Curr Liab To Nw (%)	16.2	54.5	96.0	12.0	31.9	86.6	9.3	21.9	52.3	16.2	62.4	100.3
Curr Liab To Inv (%)	37.7	262.0	574.5	202.3	568.1	741.7	193.3	202.5	477.5	387.1	587.4	804.3
Total Liab To Nw (%)	32.2	67.9	180.3	22.7	76.6	183.3	15.8	45.9	271.9	39.6	108.6	177.0
Fixed Assets To Nw (%)	52.2	93.8	155.2	65.1	94.8	215.6	68.7	91.8	300.1	64.3	94.8	183.1
EFFICIENCY												
Coll Period (days)	11.7	23.4	32.6	7.4	15.0	26.7	11.3	17.9	43.9	6.4	9.7	17.0
Sales To Inv (times)	113.9	99.7	67.1	66.6	54.8	35.0	232.9	47.7	28.4	64.7	56.8	47.0
Assets To Sales (%)	26.4	43.9	69.6	43.9	63.8	108.3	52.8	82.8	114.6	41.1	60.7	105.4
Sales To Nwc (times)	23.7	8.9	7.8	19.4	9.6	5.8	16.0	7.9	5.0	20.3	11.5	8.0
Acct Pay To Sales (%)	1.3	2.4	5.0	3.5	4.2	6.1	1.9	3.4	4.5	4.4	5.7	9.1
PROFITABILITY												
Return On Sales (%)	4.0	2.2	(0.5)	4.7	2.2	(0.5)	5.0	1.3	(1.6)	4.6	2.2	0.1
Return On Assets (%)	7.5	2.8	(2.2)	7.6	3.8	(0.6)	7.1	2.7	(2.5)	7.3	6.2	0.9
Return On Nw (%)	13.9	7.8	(5.8)	18.2	10.6	(1.8)	17.3	6.1	(3.8)	21.5	16.5	2.1

SIC 4141 LCL BUS CHRTR SVCE

Balance Sheet

	NO BREAKDOWN 1995 (77 Establishments) $	%	$250,000 - $500,000 1995 (12 Establishments) $	%	$500,000 - $1,000,000 1995 (16 Establishments) $	%	$1,000,000 - $5,000,000 1995 (24 Establishments) $	%
Cash	89,654	11.1	21,683	6.3	76,374	10.8	174,859	8.8
Accounts Receivable	91,270	11.3	37,515	10.9	67,888	9.6	164,924	8.3
Notes Receivable	4,846	0.6	1,033	0.3	—	—	3,974	0.2
Inventory	8,885	1.1	—	—	4,243	0.6	41,728	2.1
Other Current	59,770	7.4	15,488	4.5	57,988	8.2	123,196	6.2
Total Current	**254,425**	**31.5**	**75,719**	**22.0**	**206,493**	**29.2**	**508,681**	**25.6**
Fixed Assets	487,041	60.3	265,361	77.1	425,008	60.1	1,283,624	64.6
Other Non-current	66,231	8.2	3,098	0.9	75,667	10.7	194,729	9.8
Total Assets	**807,697**	**100.0**	**344,178**	**100.0**	**707,168**	**100.0**	**1,987,034**	**100.0**
Accounts Payable	51,693	6.4	17,553	5.1	28,994	4.1	141,079	7.1
Bank Loans	808	0.1	—	—	—	—	3,974	0.2
Notes Payable	59,770	7.4	38,892	11.3	50,209	7.1	168,898	8.5
Other Current	165,578	20.5	64,361	18.7	154,870	21.9	345,744	17.4
Total Current	**277,848**	**34.4**	**120,806**	**35.1**	**234,073**	**33.1**	**659,695**	**33.2**
Other Long Term	253,617	31.4	143,178	41.6	271,553	38.4	623,929	31.4
Deferred Credits	808	0.1	—	—	—	—	7,948	0.4
Net Worth	275,425	34.1	80,193	23.3	201,543	28.5	695,462	35.0
Total Liab & Net Worth	**807,697**	**100.0**	**344,178**	**100.0**	**707,168**	**100.0**	**1,987,034**	**100.0**
Net Sales	1,145,129	100.0	967,738	100.0	754,780	100.0	2,587,494	100.0
Gross Profit	463,777	40.5	496,450	51.3	313,988	41.6	866,810	33.5
Net Profit After Tax	38,934	3.4	31,935	3.3	17,360	2.3	69,862	2.7
Working Capital	(23,423)	—	(45,087)	—	(27,580)	—	(151,014)	—

RATIOS

	UQ	MED	LQ	UQ	MED	LQ	UQ	MED	LQ	UQ	MED	LQ
SOLVENCY												
Quick Ratio (times)	1.2	0.5	0.2	0.3	0.1	0.1	1.3	0.6	0.2	1.1	0.4	0.2
Current Ratio (times)	1.8	0.9	0.3	0.4	0.3	0.2	1.8	1.0	0.4	1.5	0.8	0.4
Curr Liab To Nw (%)	30.2	69.1	163.7	10.1	57.0	115.7	48.6	82.0	177.2	35.8	58.0	125.0
Curr Liab To Inv (%)	240.6	406.0	733.2	—	—	—	189.3	261.5	333.8	296.2	366.8	642.2
Total Liab To Nw (%)	67.5	157.5	356.5	9.0	131.2	193.2	87.0	223.0	454.2	77.6	202.8	358.8
Fixed Assets To Nw (%)	77.3	181.4	360.6	51.8	99.0	257.8	44.3	183.7	313.9	98.5	202.9	366.9
EFFICIENCY												
Coll Period (days)	11.0	26.3	38.4	2.9	25.0	27.0	17.5	32.1	40.9	7.7	15.7	22.5
Sales To Inv (times)	92.1	56.3	34.5	—	—	—	54.4	54.4	54.4	90.8	58.1	36.1
Assets To Sales (%)	36.7	57.4	85.3	18.1	29.5	34.9	57.0	81.6	97.1	55.8	67.4	93.5
Sales To Nwc (times)	33.9	12.0	6.2	9.1	8.7	6.8	59.7	34.7	17.1	21.6	14.4	8.6
Acct Pay To Sales (%)	1.8	2.9	4.9	1.0	1.8	4.5	1.5	1.8	2.6	1.9	2.8	3.3
PROFITABILITY												
Return On Sales (%)	7.4	3.2	(1.0)	2.5	0.7	(1.3)	4.1	2.7	(3.8)	6.7	2.4	(2.0)
Return On Assets (%)	13.2	4.2	(1.2)	6.4	1.9	(4.2)	9.7	2.4	(5.2)	9.6	4.5	(1.4)
Return On Nw (%)	30.0	7.7	(3.9)	27.4	10.1	(40.0)	78.1	44.2	7.3	13.0	7.0	(9.9)

SIC 4142 — BS CHTR SVC, EXC LCL

	NO BREAKDOWN 1995 (137 Establishments) $	%	$100,000 - $250,000 1995 (17 Establishments) $	%	$250,000 - $500,000 1995 (21 Establishments) $	%	$500,000 - $1,000,000 1995 (26 Establishments) $	%
Cash	93,686	10.5	18,470	10.9	35,242	10.1	76,437	10.9
Accounts Receivable	72,272	8.1	7,456	4.4	34,893	10.0	53,296	7.6
Notes Receivable	5,353	0.6	2,033	1.2	349	0.1	4,909	0.7
Inventory	13,384	1.5	2,881	1.7	2,791	0.8	16,830	2.4
Other Current	66,026	7.4	8,981	5.3	37,335	10.7	37,868	5.4
Total Current	**250,721**	**28.1**	**39,821**	**23.5**	**110,610**	**31.7**	**189,340**	**27.0**
Fixed Assets	554,976	62.2	124,715	73.6	187,026	53.6	485,973	69.3
Other Non-current	86,548	9.7	4,914	2.9	51,293	14.7	25,947	3.7
Total Assets	**892,245**	**100.0**	**169,450**	**100.0**	**348,929**	**100.0**	**701,260**	**100.0**
Accounts Payable	49,073	5.5	5,253	3.1	19,889	5.7	46,984	6.7
Bank Loans	2,677	0.3	—	—	6,630	1.9	—	—
Notes Payable	70,487	7.9	26,604	15.7	18,493	5.3	51,192	7.3
Other Current	157,035	17.6	28,637	16.9	52,339	15.0	159,887	22.8
Total Current	**279,273**	**31.3**	**60,494**	**35.7**	**97,351**	**27.9**	**258,064**	**36.8**
Other Long Term	305,148	34.2	67,949	40.1	100,492	28.8	226,507	32.3
Deferred Credits	892	0.1	—	—	—	—	—	—
Net Worth	306,932	34.4	41,007	24.2	151,086	43.3	216,689	30.9
Total Liab & Net Worth	**892,245**	**100.0**	**169,450**	**100.0**	**348,929**	**100.0**	**701,260**	**100.0**
Net Sales	1,421,004	100.0	276,663	100.0	895,302	100.0	1,142,356	100.0
Gross Profit	645,136	45.4	146,908	53.1	472,719	52.8	590,598	51.7
Net Profit After Tax	52,577	3.7	9,130	3.3	38,498	4.3	47,979	4.2
Working Capital	(28,552)	—	(20,673)	—	13,259	—	(68,724)	—

RATIOS	UQ	MED	LQ	UQ	MED	LQ	UQ	MED	LQ	UQ	MED	LQ
SOLVENCY												
Quick Ratio (times)	1.1	0.5	0.2	0.2	0.2	0.1	0.9	0.6	0.4	0.9	0.3	0.3
Current Ratio (times)	1.8	0.8	0.4	0.4	0.2	0.1	2.2	0.9	0.5	1.1	0.6	0.4
Curr Liab To Nw (%)	22.8	69.3	188.1	21.0	32.0	68.9	11.3	47.5	111.3	34.8	102.3	326.2
Curr Liab To Inv (%)	263.1	365.6	623.7	70.3	89.7	109.0	272.7	284.7	296.6	315.5	434.6	710.6
Total Liab To Nw (%)	54.1	136.8	312.9	27.1	58.7	75.3	49.0	81.2	289.6	107.6	254.4	416.0
Fixed Assets To Nw (%)	85.2	154.5	274.5	53.2	87.1	109.4	79.8	139.4	194.4	114.2	260.5	421.9
EFFICIENCY												
Coll Period (days)	9.5	19.4	31.8	5.4	7.2	8.9	16.8	28.7	39.7	6.2	9.5	19.8
Sales To Inv (times)	254.6	53.1	22.5	11.2	10.7	10.3	332.0	155.7	98.6	174.0	27.8	15.7
Assets To Sales (%)	45.4	65.3	89.6	18.3	28.2	37.7	31.5	34.8	53.4	47.0	57.8	82.5
Sales To Nwc (times)	27.7	10.7	5.2	30.9	16.1	7.8	51.9	17.1	5.9	28.5	6.5	6.0
Acct Pay To Sales (%)	1.1	2.6	4.9	0.6	1.0	1.5	1.2	2.0	2.9	1.1	4.8	11.6
PROFITABILITY												
Return On Sales (%)	7.2	3.3	0.5	5.0	(1.9)	(6.0)	7.9	2.3	0.5	8.9	4.6	2.1
Return On Assets (%)	10.1	3.8	1.0	7.4	(12.2)	(35.7)	13.8	6.3	1.6	9.9	4.2	2.8
Return On Nw (%)	30.9	9.2	3.0	9.9	(55.3)	(95.9)	60.3	8.0	3.9	37.8	12.0	4.6

SIC 4142 — BS CHTR SVC, EXC LCL

	SIC 4142 BS CHTR SVC,EXC LCL $1,000,000 - $5,000,000 1995 (49 Establishments) $	%	SIC 4142 BS CHTR SVC,EXC LCL $5,000,000 - $25,000,000 1995 (12 Establishments) $	%	SIC 4151 SCHOOL BUSES (NO BREAKDOWN) 1995 (131 Establishments) $	%	SIC 4151 SCHOOL BUSES $100,000 - $250,000 1995 (17 Establishments) $	%
Cash	214,677	10.1	341,751	5.5	102,983	13.0	23,426	12.5
Accounts Receivable	174,293	8.2	907,194	14.6	95,854	12.1	14,993	8.0
Notes Receivable	10,628	0.5	6,214	0.1	6,337	0.8	4,873	2.6
Inventory	29,757	1.4	105,632	1.7	7,130	0.9	375	0.2
Other Current	136,033	6.4	484,665	7.8	55,453	7.0	13,681	7.3
Total Current	**565,388**	**26.6**	**1,845,456**	**29.7**	**267,757**	**33.8**	**57,348**	**30.6**
Fixed Assets	1,351,830	63.6	3,709,553	59.7	471,347	59.5	117,882	62.9
Other Non-current	208,301	9.8	658,648	10.6	53,076	6.7	12,182	6.5
Total Assets	**2,125,519**	**100.0**	**6,213,656**	**100.0**	**792,180**	**100.0**	**187,411**	**100.0**
Accounts Payable	112,653	5.3	646,220	10.4	56,245	7.1	11,057	5.9
Bank Loans	—	—	—	—	3,961	0.5	—	—
Notes Payable	176,418	8.3	155,341	2.5	74,465	9.4	26,612	14.2
Other Current	201,924	9.5	1,460,209	23.5	106,152	13.4	36,733	19.6
Total Current	**490,995**	**23.1**	**2,261,771**	**36.4**	**240,823**	**30.4**	**74,402**	**39.7**
Other Long Term	786,442	37.0	1,895,165	30.5	187,747	23.7	53,037	28.3
Deferred Credits	8,502	0.4	12,427	0.2	4,753	0.6	—	—
Net Worth	839,580	39.5	2,044,293	32.9	358,858	45.3	59,972	32.0
Total Liab & Net Worth	**2,125,519**	**100.0**	**6,213,656**	**100.0**	**792,180**	**100.0**	**187,411**	**100.0**
Net Sales	2,684,730	100.0	9,557,073	100.0	1,334,236	100.0	542,209	100.0
Gross Profit	910,123	33.9	8,954,977	93.7	585,730	43.9	295,504	54.5
Net Profit After Tax	85,911	3.2	277,155	2.9	58,706	4.4	16,266	3.0
Working Capital	74,393	—	(416,315)	—	26,934	—	(17,054)	—

RATIOS	UQ	MED	LQ	UQ	MED	LQ	UQ	MED	LQ	UQ	MED	LQ
SOLVENCY												
Quick Ratio (times)	1.4	0.6	0.4	0.8	0.6	0.3	1.5	0.9	0.5	0.4	0.2	0.1
Current Ratio (times)	2.0	1.0	0.5	1.5	0.8	0.6	2.5	1.2	0.7	0.8	0.3	0.1
Curr Liab To Nw (%)	21.9	56.0	140.3	43.1	90.1	124.8	19.4	56.2	149.7	54.6	103.2	126.1
Curr Liab To Inv (%)	359.7	369.1	425.5	502.7	684.7	831.5	179.9	482.9	766.6	601.9	601.9	601.9
Total Liab To Nw (%)	42.1	126.0	261.5	136.8	189.9	289.1	39.5	121.3	283.2	66.8	140.5	232.1
Fixed Assets To Nw (%)	86.2	150.8	264.4	123.8	193.1	272.8	80.7	144.0	248.6	73.0	167.3	205.7
EFFICIENCY												
Coll Period (days)	10.1	20.8	31.4	19.7	27.4	46.4	10.2	25.4	41.2	8.4	15.3	17.2
Sales To Inv (times)	288.4	96.7	28.4	45.4	37.7	27.0	147.8	80.1	38.7	110.3	110.3	110.3
Assets To Sales (%)	60.4	69.9	92.2	64.5	92.9	121.7	35.5	56.1	83.2	20.0	22.8	29.5
Sales To Nwc (times)	13.4	9.0	4.5	16.2	10.7	7.9	23.5	10.8	5.8	31.5	18.2	12.2
Acct Pay To Sales (%)	1.3	2.6	4.9	3.3	4.7	4.8	1.0	2.2	4.1	1.0	1.5	1.9
PROFITABILITY												
Return On Sales (%)	6.9	2.6	0.4	4.0	3.5	2.2	7.5	2.8	0.6	2.0	1.0	(0.1)
Return On Assets (%)	6.5	2.8	0.3	4.0	3.4	2.9	12.0	4.3	0.8	6.2	2.9	(1.1)
Return On Nw (%)	24.7	7.4	2.1	10.8	9.2	6.4	35.6	12.3	1.9	36.1	4.9	(1.2)

	SIC 4151 SCHOOL BUSES INDUSTRY ASSETS $250,000 - $500,000 1995 (23 Establishments) $	%	SIC 4151 SCHOOL BUSES INDUSTRY ASSETS $500,000 - $1,000,000 1995 (27 Establishments) $	%	SIC 4151 SCHOOL BUSES INDUSTRY ASSETS $1,000,000 - $5,000,000 1995 (44 Establishments) $	%	SIC 42 TRUCKING & WAREHSNG (NO BREAKDOWN) 1995 (2399 Establishments) $	%
Cash	74,380	22.4	110,548	14.7	154,823	8.5	89,541	11.6
Accounts Receivable	38,850	11.7	45,122	6.0	282,324	15.5	205,327	26.6
Notes Receivable	3,653	1.1	752	0.1	20,036	1.1	10,807	1.4
Inventory	1,992	0.6	10,528	1.4	20,036	1.1	10,807	1.4
Other Current	5,977	1.8	49,634	6.6	153,001	8.4	47,086	6.1
Total Current	**124,853**	**37.6**	**216,584**	**28.8**	**630,220**	**34.6**	**363,568**	**47.1**
Fixed Assets	190,268	57.3	503,107	66.9	1,029,116	56.5	335,007	43.4
Other Non-current	16,935	5.1	32,337	4.3	162,109	8.9	73,331	9.5
Total Assets	**332,055**	**100.0**	**752,028**	**100.0**	**1,821,444**	**100.0**	**771,906**	**100.0**
Accounts Payable	31,877	9.6	33,089	4.4	103,822	5.7	83,366	10.8
Bank Loans	—	—	18,801	2.5	—	—	1,544	0.2
Notes Payable	20,255	6.1	72,195	9.6	171,216	9.4	53,262	6.9
Other Current	26,896	8.1	56,402	7.5	275,038	15.1	117,330	15.2
Total Current	**79,029**	**23.8**	**180,487**	**24.0**	**550,076**	**30.2**	**255,501**	**33.1**
Other Long Term	67,407	20.3	160,182	21.3	438,968	24.1	174,451	22.6
Deferred Credits	4,649	1.4	—	—	7,286	0.4	3,088	0.4
Net Worth	180,970	54.5	411,359	54.7	825,114	45.3	338,867	43.9
Total Liab & Net Worth	**332,055**	**100.0**	**752,028**	**100.0**	**1,821,444**	**100.0**	**771,906**	**100.0**
Net Sales	719,968	100.0	1,626,207	100.0	2,770,702	100.0	2,483,931	100.0
Gross Profit	321,826	44.7	588,687	36.2	1,133,217	40.9	861,924	34.7
Net Profit After Tax	28,079	3.9	130,097	8.0	88,662	3.2	96,873	3.9
Working Capital	45,824	—	36,097	—	80,144	—	108,067	—

RATIOS	UQ	MED	LQ	UQ	MED	LQ	UQ	MED	LQ	UQ	MED	LQ
SOLVENCY												
Quick Ratio (times)	3.9	1.3	0.9	1.5	0.9	0.6	1.5	0.8	0.5	2.3	1.2	0.6
Current Ratio (times)	2.8	1.3	1.0	3.1	1.3	0.8	2.7	1.2	0.7	2.9	1.4	0.9
Curr Liab To Nw (%)	11.4	31.0	55.0	6.2	25.3	136.3	23.4	58.9	149.9	23.8	61.3	144.4
Curr Liab To Inv (%)	185.2	315.7	454.7	124.7	482.9	825.5	230.4	385.0	661.0	150.8	345.6	626.5
Total Liab To Nw (%)	38.3	62.5	207.7	19.0	40.4	174.4	49.2	149.5	329.2	44.4	112.2	243.0
Fixed Assets To Nw (%)	77.8	105.1	202.0	74.4	102.0	210.3	80.8	153.4	266.6	45.6	93.4	185.6
EFFICIENCY												
Coll Period (days)	7.3	21.5	30.3	8.6	10.6	26.0	22.3	34.7	50.0	23.7	34.0	45.3
Sales To Inv (times)	325.5	80.1	66.9	63.4	54.9	41.7	154.0	77.7	35.4	285.9	137.9	64.8
Assets To Sales (%)	39.6	53.4	61.5	35.5	42.8	60.8	55.3	76.3	129.0	22.8	34.1	53.7
Sales To Nwc (times)	43.4	11.6	6.3	28.1	6.6	4.0	16.8	10.4	4.5	27.1	13.9	7.4
Acct Pay To Sales (%)	0.4	1.2	2.6	0.8	1.7	3.5	1.6	2.6	4.0	1.6	3.0	5.3
PROFITABILITY												
Return On Sales (%)	8.1	3.9	0.1	14.4	6.2	2.1	5.5	2.1	0.5	6.7	2.8	0.8
Return On Assets (%)	14.9	7.3	—	28.2	11.9	3.7	6.8	2.9	0.7	15.3	7.0	1.9
Return On Nw (%)	24.0	11.7	(0.1)	85.4	14.8	9.2	21.2	7.3	1.6	39.4	17.7	5.0

SIC 42 TRUCKING & WAREHSNG — NORTHEAST — 1995 (1388 Establishments)

	$	%
Cash	82,075	12.8
Accounts Receivable	177,616	27.7
Notes Receivable	7,053	1.1
Inventory	7,695	1.2
Other Current	42,320	6.6
Total Current	**316,759**	**49.4**
Fixed Assets	260,332	40.6
Other Non-current	64,121	10.0
Total Assets	**641,212**	**100.0**
Accounts Payable	76,945	12.0
Bank Loans	641	0.1
Notes Payable	51,938	8.1
Other Current	105,800	16.5
Total Current	**235,325**	**36.7**
Other Long Term	120,548	18.8
Deferred Credits	2,565	0.4
Net Worth	282,774	44.1
Total Liab & Net Worth	**641,212**	**100.0**
Net Sales	1,698,591	100.0
Gross Profit	618,287	36.4
Net Profit After Tax	56,054	3.3
Working Capital	81,434	—

RATIOS	UQ	MED	LQ
SOLVENCY			
Quick Ratio (times)	2.2	1.1	0.6
Current Ratio (times)	2.7	1.4	0.8
Curr Liab To Nw (%)	26.2	68.0	159.9
Curr Liab To Inv (%)	157.7	342.7	614.4
Total Liab To Nw (%)	45.3	110.6	245.7
Fixed Assets To Nw (%)	39.6	84.2	167.7
EFFICIENCY			
Coll Period (days)	23.7	34.7	48.2
Sales To Inv (times)	275.1	113.4	50.0
Assets To Sales (%)	22.5	34.5	54.7
Sales To Nwc (times)	26.9	12.7	6.8
Acct Pay To Sales (%)	1.7	3.2	6.1
PROFITABILITY			
Return On Sales (%)	5.3	2.1	0.4
Return On Assets (%)	13.0	5.0	0.9
Return On Nw (%)	32.3	12.9	2.4

SIC 42 TRUCKING & WAREHSNG — CENTRAL — 1995 (2358 Establishments)

	$	%
Cash	92,752	10.6
Accounts Receivable	238,880	27.3
Notes Receivable	9,625	1.1
Inventory	15,750	1.8
Other Current	47,251	5.4
Total Current	**404,258**	**46.2**
Fixed Assets	399,883	45.7
Other Non-current	70,876	8.1
Total Assets	**875,018**	**100.0**
Accounts Payable	95,377	10.9
Bank Loans	3,500	0.4
Notes Payable	63,876	7.3
Other Current	139,128	15.9
Total Current	**301,881**	**34.5**
Other Long Term	193,379	22.1
Deferred Credits	3,500	0.4
Net Worth	376,258	43.0
Total Liab & Net Worth	**875,018**	**100.0**
Net Sales	3,082,730	100.0
Gross Profit	949,481	30.8
Net Profit After Tax	123,309	4.0
Working Capital	102,377	—

RATIOS	UQ	MED	LQ
SOLVENCY			
Quick Ratio (times)	2.1	1.1	0.6
Current Ratio (times)	2.5	1.3	0.8
Curr Liab To Nw (%)	26.7	67.6	150.6
Curr Liab To Inv (%)	127.1	347.6	607.1
Total Liab To Nw (%)	48.9	121.3	257.6
Fixed Assets To Nw (%)	49.1	103.0	196.0
EFFICIENCY			
Coll Period (days)	23.4	32.5	42.7
Sales To Inv (times)	301.5	129.9	52.1
Assets To Sales (%)	21.7	33.8	51.8
Sales To Nwc (times)	31.6	15.4	8.2
Acct Pay To Sales (%)	1.5	2.9	4.7
PROFITABILITY			
Return On Sales (%)	5.9	2.7	0.9
Return On Assets (%)	16.5	7.7	2.5
Return On Nw (%)	42.1	20.1	6.8

SIC 42 TRUCKING & WAREHSNG — SOUTH — 1995 (2153 Establishments)

	$	%
Cash	99,285	11.5
Accounts Receivable	207,204	24.0
Notes Receivable	10,360	1.2
Inventory	11,224	1.3
Other Current	54,391	6.3
Total Current	**382,463**	**44.3**
Fixed Assets	399,730	46.3
Other Non-current	81,155	9.4
Total Assets	**863,348**	**100.0**
Accounts Payable	75,111	8.7
Bank Loans	1,727	0.2
Notes Payable	62,161	7.2
Other Current	118,279	13.7
Total Current	**257,278**	**29.8**
Other Long Term	214,110	24.8
Deferred Credits	4,317	0.5
Net Worth	387,643	44.9
Total Liab & Net Worth	**863,348**	**100.0**
Net Sales	2,343,102	100.0
Gross Profit	904,437	38.6
Net Profit After Tax	107,783	4.6
Working Capital	125,185	—

RATIOS	UQ	MED	LQ
SOLVENCY			
Quick Ratio (times)	2.3	1.2	0.6
Current Ratio (times)	3.1	1.5	0.9
Curr Liab To Nw (%)	21.1	55.4	122.7
Curr Liab To Inv (%)	174.5	398.5	730.1
Total Liab To Nw (%)	43.1	109.5	246.8
Fixed Assets To Nw (%)	48.4	105.1	197.3
EFFICIENCY			
Coll Period (days)	23.4	33.6	45.3
Sales To Inv (times)	251.7	126.1	59.9
Assets To Sales (%)	23.8	38.5	60.7
Sales To Nwc (times)	26.1	13.8	7.1
Acct Pay To Sales (%)	1.5	2.9	5.2
PROFITABILITY			
Return On Sales (%)	7.8	3.5	1.2
Return On Assets (%)	14.8	7.0	2.3
Return On Nw (%)	40.6	17.8	6.1

SIC 42 TRUCKING & WAREHSNG — WEST — 1995 (1298 Establishments)

	$	%
Cash	80,935	11.6
Accounts Receivable	199,546	28.6
Notes Receivable	11,861	1.7
Inventory	7,675	1.1
Other Current	45,351	6.5
Total Current	**345,368**	**49.5**
Fixed Assets	286,063	41.0
Other Non-current	66,283	9.5
Total Assets	**697,714**	**100.0**
Accounts Payable	80,237	11.5
Bank Loans	698	0.1
Notes Payable	27,909	4.0
Other Current	103,959	14.9
Total Current	**212,803**	**30.5**
Other Long Term	150,009	21.5
Deferred Credits	3,489	0.5
Net Worth	331,414	47.5
Total Liab & Net Worth	**697,714**	**100.0**
Net Sales	2,233,000	100.0
Gross Profit	797,181	35.7
Net Profit After Tax	96,019	4.3
Working Capital	132,565	—

RATIOS	UQ	MED	LQ
SOLVENCY			
Quick Ratio (times)	2.7	1.4	0.7
Current Ratio (times)	3.3	1.6	1.0
Curr Liab To Nw (%)	19.6	52.2	123.4
Curr Liab To Inv (%)	156.4	355.1	662.2
Total Liab To Nw (%)	39.9	94.5	207.5
Fixed Assets To Nw (%)	39.8	79.3	148.0
EFFICIENCY			
Coll Period (days)	25.6	36.9	51.5
Sales To Inv (times)	255.1	136.4	55.3
Assets To Sales (%)	22.7	34.1	52.4
Sales To Nwc (times)	25.5	11.8	6.3
Acct Pay To Sales (%)	1.8	3.5	6.0
PROFITABILITY			
Return On Sales (%)	6.8	2.8	0.9
Return On Assets (%)	15.2	7.1	2.2
Return On Nw (%)	35.3	16.1	5.6

SIC 42 TRUCKING & WAREHSNG — INDUSTRY ASSETS UNDER $100,000 — 1995 (754 Establishments)

	$	%
Cash	12,415	22.2
Accounts Receivable	10,514	18.8
Notes Receivable	671	1.2
Inventory	671	1.2
Other Current	2,684	4.8
Total Current	**26,955**	**48.2**
Fixed Assets	24,942	44.6
Other Non-current	4,026	7.2
Total Assets	**55,923**	**100.0**
Accounts Payable	5,145	9.2
Bank Loans	112	0.2
Notes Payable	5,369	9.6
Other Current	9,954	17.8
Total Current	**20,580**	**36.8**
Other Long Term	10,290	18.4
Deferred Credits	112	0.2
Net Worth	24,942	44.6
Total Liab & Net Worth	**55,923**	**100.0**
Net Sales	266,341	100.0
Gross Profit	123,050	46.2
Net Profit After Tax	16,247	6.1
Working Capital	6,375	—

RATIOS	UQ	MED	LQ
SOLVENCY			
Quick Ratio (times)	3.2	1.1	0.5
Current Ratio (times)	3.9	1.3	0.6
Curr Liab To Nw (%)	14.8	55.3	158.4
Curr Liab To Inv (%)	127.1	232.8	411.9
Total Liab To Nw (%)	23.8	82.2	220.4
Fixed Assets To Nw (%)	40.7	87.1	180.9
EFFICIENCY			
Coll Period (days)	8.5	19.2	33.3
Sales To Inv (times)	122.5	73.8	36.1
Assets To Sales (%)	10.6	19.0	30.3
Sales To Nwc (times)	50.3	20.0	8.5
Acct Pay To Sales (%)	1.2	2.1	4.6
PROFITABILITY			
Return On Sales (%)	12.6	4.5	0.7
Return On Assets (%)	40.0	16.4	0.3
Return On Nw (%)	103.0	39.5	3.2

SIC 42 TRUCKING & WAREHSNG — INDUSTRY ASSETS $100,000 - $250,000 — 1995 (1041 Establishments)

	$	%
Cash	26,155	15.8
Accounts Receivable	43,370	26.2
Notes Receivable	1,655	1.0
Inventory	1,821	1.1
Other Current	9,601	5.8
Total Current	**82,602**	**49.9**
Fixed Assets	69,856	42.2
Other Non-current	13,077	7.9
Total Assets	**165,535**	**100.0**
Accounts Payable	18,043	10.9
Bank Loans	331	0.2
Notes Payable	13,905	8.4
Other Current	22,678	13.7
Total Current	**54,958**	**33.2**
Other Long Term	32,941	19.9
Deferred Credits	331	0.2
Net Worth	77,305	46.7
Total Liab & Net Worth	**165,535**	**100.0**
Net Sales	658,819	100.0
Gross Profit	274,728	41.7
Net Profit After Tax	32,282	4.9
Working Capital	27,644	—

RATIOS	UQ	MED	LQ
SOLVENCY			
Quick Ratio (times)	3.5	1.3	0.6
Current Ratio (times)	4.0	1.6	0.8
Curr Liab To Nw (%)	14.8	49.3	120.9
Curr Liab To Inv (%)	95.7	256.0	512.9
Total Liab To Nw (%)	28.9	82.0	212.2
Fixed Assets To Nw (%)	35.8	80.2	153.9
EFFICIENCY			
Coll Period (days)	16.1	29.6	42.7
Sales To Inv (times)	274.6	88.4	32.9
Assets To Sales (%)	16.7	25.8	40.6
Sales To Nwc (times)	27.2	13.3	6.8
Acct Pay To Sales (%)	1.0	2.4	4.4
PROFITABILITY			
Return On Sales (%)	9.4	3.6	0.6
Return On Assets (%)	26.2	10.4	0.8
Return On Nw (%)	57.3	22.9	1.8

SIC 42 TRUCKING & WAREHSNG — INDUSTRY ASSETS $250,000 - $500,000 — 1995 (1163 Establishments)

	$	%
Cash	44,894	12.4
Accounts Receivable	104,270	28.8
Notes Receivable	3,983	1.1
Inventory	5,069	1.4
Other Current	23,895	6.6
Total Current	**182,110**	**50.3**
Fixed Assets	152,422	42.1
Other Non-current	27,516	7.6
Total Assets	**362,047**	**100.0**
Accounts Payable	41,635	11.5
Bank Loans	724	0.2
Notes Payable	26,791	7.4
Other Current	52,497	14.5
Total Current	**121,648**	**33.6**
Other Long Term	77,116	21.3
Deferred Credits	362	0.1
Net Worth	162,921	45.0
Total Liab & Net Worth	**362,047**	**100.0**
Net Sales	1,172,269	100.0
Gross Profit	475,941	40.6
Net Profit After Tax	45,718	3.9
Working Capital	60,462	—

RATIOS	UQ	MED	LQ
SOLVENCY			
Quick Ratio (times)	2.9	1.3	0.7
Current Ratio (times)	3.7	1.6	0.9
Curr Liab To Nw (%)	18.6	56.9	130.8
Curr Liab To Inv (%)	95.9	236.1	565.3
Total Liab To Nw (%)	41.6	100.7	209.2
Fixed Assets To Nw (%)	39.7	80.9	164.0
EFFICIENCY			
Coll Period (days)	20.4	32.7	47.0
Sales To Inv (times)	335.1	137.0	37.9
Assets To Sales (%)	20.5	30.4	42.4
Sales To Nwc (times)	24.1	11.6	7.0
Acct Pay To Sales (%)	1.3	2.8	5.6
PROFITABILITY			
Return On Sales (%)	6.3	2.7	0.5
Return On Assets (%)	18.0	7.7	1.2
Return On Nw (%)	44.6	17.7	2.9

SIC 42 TRUCKING & WAREHSNG — INDUSTRY ASSETS $500,000 - $1,000,000 — 1995 (1293 Establishments)

	$	%
Cash	78,310	11.0
Accounts Receivable	205,031	28.8
Notes Receivable	9,255	1.3
Inventory	11,391	1.6
Other Current	42,003	5.9
Total Current	**345,989**	**48.6**
Fixed Assets	299,715	42.1
Other Non-current	66,208	9.3
Total Assets	**711,912**	**100.0**
Accounts Payable	79,734	11.2
Bank Loans	1,424	0.2
Notes Payable	45,562	6.4
Other Current	96,820	13.6
Total Current	**223,540**	**31.4**
Other Long Term	158,044	22.2
Deferred Credits	1,424	0.2
Net Worth	328,903	46.2
Total Liab & Net Worth	**711,912**	**100.0**
Net Sales	2,149,557	100.0
Gross Profit	752,345	35.0
Net Profit After Tax	68,786	3.2
Working Capital	122,449	—

RATIOS	UQ	MED	LQ
SOLVENCY			
Quick Ratio (times)	2.6	1.3	0.7
Current Ratio (times)	3.2	1.6	1.0
Curr Liab To Nw (%)	21.4	50.8	121.6
Curr Liab To Inv (%)	110.6	308.0	631.2
Total Liab To Nw (%)	41.7	98.6	208.5
Fixed Assets To Nw (%)	41.2	84.7	154.5
EFFICIENCY			
Coll Period (days)	23.0	33.6	48.6
Sales To Inv (times)	242.0	101.4	41.3
Assets To Sales (%)	23.8	32.3	51.9
Sales To Nwc (times)	23.7	12.8	6.3
Acct Pay To Sales (%)	1.6	3.0	5.3
PROFITABILITY			
Return On Sales (%)	5.6	2.3	0.7
Return On Assets (%)	13.8	6.3	1.7
Return On Nw (%)	38.0	14.0	3.5

SIC 42 TRUCKING & WAREHSNG — INDUSTRY ASSETS $1,000,000-$5,000,000 — 1995 (2063 Establishments)

	$	%
Cash	165,047	8.9
Accounts Receivable	517,393	27.9
Notes Receivable	27,817	1.5
Inventory	27,817	1.5
Other Current	118,685	6.4
Total Current	**856,759**	**46.2**
Fixed Assets	815,961	44.0
Other Non-current	181,737	9.8
Total Assets	**1,854,456**	**100.0**
Accounts Payable	198,427	10.7
Bank Loans	5,563	0.3
Notes Payable	118,685	6.4
Other Current	285,586	15.4
Total Current	**608,262**	**32.8**
Other Long Term	413,544	22.3
Deferred Credits	7,418	0.4
Net Worth	825,233	44.5
Total Liab & Net Worth	**1,854,456**	**100.0**
Net Sales	4,979,618	100.0
Gross Profit	1,503,845	30.2
Net Profit After Tax	194,205	3.9
Working Capital	248,497	—

RATIOS	UQ	MED	LQ
SOLVENCY			
Quick Ratio (times)	2.1	1.1	0.7
Current Ratio (times)	2.6	1.4	0.9
Curr Liab To Nw (%)	27.9	67.1	148.3
Curr Liab To Inv (%)	204.1	396.7	683.8
Total Liab To Nw (%)	50.2	122.9	256.7
Fixed Assets To Nw (%)	48.6	98.7	192.5
EFFICIENCY			
Coll Period (days)	25.9	34.7	47.3
Sales To Inv (times)	281.9	124.6	55.6
Assets To Sales (%)	27.1	39.2	59.2
Sales To Nwc (times)	28.4	13.1	7.0
Acct Pay To Sales (%)	1.7	3.2	5.4
PROFITABILITY			
Return On Sales (%)	5.7	2.7	1.0
Return On Assets (%)	12.9	6.4	2.2
Return On Nw (%)	33.0	16.3	6.0

SIC 42 TRUCKING & WAREHSNG — INDUSTRY ASSETS $5,000,000-$25,000,000 — 1995 (604 Establishments)

	$	%
Cash	498,144	5.6
Accounts Receivable	2,241,648	25.2
Notes Receivable	115,641	1.3
Inventory	133,431	1.5
Other Current	560,412	6.3
Total Current	**3,549,277**	**39.9**
Fixed Assets	4,394,342	49.4
Other Non-current	951,811	10.7
Total Assets	**8,895,430**	**100.0**
Accounts Payable	889,543	10.0
Bank Loans	8,895	0.1
Notes Payable	426,981	4.8
Other Current	1,592,282	17.9
Total Current	**2,917,701**	**32.8**
Other Long Term	2,392,871	26.9
Deferred Credits	88,954	1.0
Net Worth	3,495,904	39.3
Total Liab & Net Worth	**8,895,430**	**100.0**
Net Sales	18,957,193	100.0
Gross Profit	4,796,170	25.3
Net Profit After Tax	720,373	3.8
Working Capital	631,576	—

RATIOS	UQ	MED	LQ
SOLVENCY			
Quick Ratio (times)	1.4	0.9	0.6
Current Ratio (times)	1.8	1.2	0.8
Curr Liab To Nw (%)	38.8	86.8	176.2
Curr Liab To Inv (%)	293.8	507.8	755.3
Total Liab To Nw (%)	73.5	167.7	321.5
Fixed Assets To Nw (%)	67.4	134.2	257.9
EFFICIENCY			
Coll Period (days)	28.5	36.5	47.8
Sales To Inv (times)	263.2	142.0	71.8
Assets To Sales (%)	33.3	49.1	69.6
Sales To Nwc (times)	28.5	15.9	8.5
Acct Pay To Sales (%)	1.9	3.3	5.7
PROFITABILITY			
Return On Sales (%)	5.4	2.9	1.3
Return On Assets (%)	10.7	5.8	2.5
Return On Nw (%)	32.4	16.2	7.4

SIC 42 TRUCKING & WAREHSNG — INDUSTRY ASSETS $25,000,000-$50,000,000 — 1995 (97 Establishments)

	$	%
Cash	1,941,683	5.9
Accounts Receivable	6,384,517	19.4
Notes Receivable	296,189	0.9
Inventory	427,828	1.3
Other Current	2,073,323	6.3
Total Current	**11,123,541**	**33.8**
Fixed Assets	17,047,320	51.8
Other Non-current	4,739,023	14.4
Total Assets	**32,909,884**	**100.0**
Accounts Payable	2,237,872	6.8
Bank Loans		—
Notes Payable	855,657	2.6
Other Current	5,956,689	18.1
Total Current	**9,050,218**	**27.5**
Other Long Term	9,510,956	28.9
Deferred Credits	559,468	1.7
Net Worth	13,789,241	41.9
Total Liab & Net Worth	**32,909,884**	**100.0**
Net Sales	62,541,206	100.0
Gross Profit	17,636,620	28.2
Net Profit After Tax	2,689,272	4.3
Working Capital	2,073,323	—

RATIOS	UQ	MED	LQ
SOLVENCY			
Quick Ratio (times)	1.3	0.8	0.6
Current Ratio (times)	1.7	1.1	0.8
Curr Liab To Nw (%)	41.2	77.4	126.4
Curr Liab To Inv (%)	387.5	532.2	837.7
Total Liab To Nw (%)	83.0	164.5	292.0
Fixed Assets To Nw (%)	75.6	166.9	265.0
EFFICIENCY			
Coll Period (days)	31.8	36.5	42.9
Sales To Inv (times)	237.6	163.2	81.0
Assets To Sales (%)	42.8	59.1	76.1
Sales To Nwc (times)	74.5	21.6	10.2
Acct Pay To Sales (%)	1.9	3.1	4.9
PROFITABILITY			
Return On Sales (%)	5.7	3.2	1.9
Return On Assets (%)	10.2	6.4	4.0
Return On Nw (%)	24.3	18.7	13.4

SIC 42 TRUCKING & WAREHSNG — INDUSTRY ASSETS OVER $50,000,000 — 1995 (182 Establishments)

	$	%
Cash	4,098,541	3.1
Accounts Receivable	28,821,998	21.8
Notes Receivable	1,322,110	1.0
Inventory	1,322,110	1.0
Other Current	6,874,972	5.2
Total Current	**42,439,731**	**32.1**
Fixed Assets	70,732,885	53.5
Other Non-current	19,038,384	14.4
Total Assets	**132,211,000**	**100.0**
Accounts Payable	9,519,192	7.2
Bank Loans	132,211	0.1
Notes Payable	1,850,954	1.4
Other Current	23,269,136	17.6
Total Current	**34,771,493**	**26.3**
Other Long Term	39,531,089	29.9
Deferred Credits	5,817,284	4.4
Net Worth	52,091,134	39.4
Total Liab & Net Worth	**132,211,000**	**100.0**
Net Sales	189,843,868	100.0
Gross Profit	46,511,748	24.5
Net Profit After Tax	6,644,535	3.5
Working Capital	7,668,238	—

RATIOS	UQ	MED	LQ
SOLVENCY			
Quick Ratio (times)	1.3	0.9	0.7
Current Ratio (times)	1.6	1.2	0.9
Curr Liab To Nw (%)	38.5	63.0	114.6
Curr Liab To Inv (%)	446.9	629.0	823.7
Total Liab To Nw (%)	92.6	146.0	266.4
Fixed Assets To Nw (%)	96.3	143.9	190.4
EFFICIENCY			
Coll Period (days)	35.1	41.8	47.7
Sales To Inv (times)	289.6	144.2	84.2
Assets To Sales (%)	47.9	64.7	81.6
Sales To Nwc (times)	38.8	19.4	12.1
Acct Pay To Sales (%)	2.8	3.6	4.7
PROFITABILITY			
Return On Sales (%)	5.5	3.2	1.4
Return On Assets (%)	8.5	5.3	2.2
Return On Nw (%)	20.8	13.9	7.9

SIC 4212 — LCL TRCKG W/O STRGE

	NO BREAKDOWN (2134 Establishments)		UNDER $100,000 (377 Establishments)		$100,000 - $250,000 (408 Establishments)		$250,000 - $500,000 (403 Establishments)	
	$	%	$	%	$	%	$	%
Cash	60,948	13.2	11,514	21.7	27,624	16.3	46,213	12.7
Accounts Receivable	112,661	24.4	9,074	17.1	38,810	22.9	92,790	25.5
Notes Receivable	6,002	1.3	637	1.2	2,203	1.3	4,003	1.1
Inventory	5,079	1.1	478	0.9	2,034	1.2	4,003	1.1
Other Current	25,857	5.6	2,176	4.1	8,304	4.9	22,197	6.1
Total Current	**210,548**	**45.6**	**23,878**	**45.0**	**78,975**	**46.6**	**169,205**	**46.5**
Fixed Assets	209,162	45.3	25,523	48.1	74,738	44.1	167,385	46.0
Other Non-current	42,017	9.1	3,661	6.9	15,761	9.3	27,291	7.5
Total Assets	**461,727**	**100.0**	**53,062**	**100.0**	**169,474**	**100.0**	**363,881**	**100.0**
Accounts Payable	48,020	10.4	4,669	8.8	16,778	9.9	37,844	10.4
Bank Loans	923	0.2	159	0.3	339	0.2	728	0.2
Notes Payable	36,476	7.9	5,306	10.0	14,405	8.5	28,019	7.7
Other Current	66,950	14.5	9,870	18.6	21,184	12.5	50,579	13.9
Total Current	**152,370**	**33.0**	**20,004**	**37.7**	**52,706**	**31.1**	**117,170**	**32.2**
Other Long Term	94,192	20.4	9,763	18.4	34,573	20.4	76,779	21.1
Deferred Credits	1,385	0.3	53	0.1	169	0.1	—	—
Net Worth	213,780	46.3	23,241	43.8	82,025	48.4	169,932	46.7
Total Liab & Net Worth	**461,727**	**100.0**	**53,062**	**100.0**	**169,474**	**100.0**	**363,881**	**100.0**
Net Sales	1,348,825	100.0	250,026	100.0	632,350	100.0	1,100,909	100.0
Gross Profit	520,646	38.6	124,763	49.9	271,911	43.0	442,565	40.2
Net Profit After Tax	63,395	4.7	18,502	7.4	27,823	4.4	51,743	4.7
Working Capital	58,178	—	3,874	—	26,269	—	52,035	—

RATIOS	UQ	MED	LQ	UQ	MED	LQ	UQ	MED	LQ	UQ	MED	LQ
SOLVENCY												
Quick Ratio (times)	2.6	1.1	0.6	2.7	1.0	0.4	3.4	1.3	0.6	3.4	1.3	0.6
Current Ratio (times)	3.1	1.5	0.8	3.3	1.2	0.5	4.0	1.6	0.8	4.2	1.6	0.8
Curr Liab To Nw (%)	19.2	54.2	130.4	14.2	57.6	163.9	13.4	44.2	97.0	13.9	48.4	124.3
Curr Liab To Inv (%)	132.0	336.1	604.1	183.7	232.8	386.9	113.5	310.1	587.3	58.6	193.1	563.2
Total Liab To Nw (%)	36.3	96.1	217.3	22.9	93.5	236.2	23.4	70.7	160.8	34.1	98.3	214.7
Fixed Assets To Nw (%)	46.6	90.9	170.7	43.8	94.1	191.5	39.7	81.3	153.3	50.7	90.3	179.8
EFFICIENCY												
Coll Period (days)	20.8	32.9	47.8	7.5	17.9	28.9	15.3	30.1	41.6	19.0	33.6	49.3
Sales To Inv (times)	248.4	112.3	43.8	102.7	56.4	29.2	200.6	99.4	48.4	237.9	100.8	25.6
Assets To Sales (%)	21.9	33.7	52.5	12.0	19.6	33.0	18.0	28.1	42.2	23.1	33.5	47.6
Sales To Nwc (times)	25.0	12.7	6.7	48.9	20.3	9.0	24.1	12.3	6.4	23.5	11.8	6.7
Acct Pay To Sales (%)	1.6	3.1	5.8	1.2	2.5	4.9	1.1	2.7	4.9	1.4	2.7	6.0
PROFITABILITY												
Return On Sales (%)	7.8	2.9	0.8	12.7	5.5	0.7	8.4	3.2	0.5	7.8	3.3	0.6
Return On Assets (%)	18.2	7.5	1.7	43.3	16.4	0.9	24.3	9.9	0.9	20.1	8.3	1.0
Return On Nw (%)	42.5	17.0	3.8	103.3	35.9	3.7	54.0	19.5	1.1	50.1	23.2	2.7

Balance Sheet Data

	SIC 4212 LCL TRCKG W/O STRGE $500,000-$1,000,000 (395 Est.) $	%	SIC 4212 LCL TRCKG W/O STRGE $1,000,000-$5,000,000 (474 Est.) $	%	SIC 4212 LCL TRCKG W/O STRGE $5,000,000-$25,000,000 (67 Est.) $	%	SIC 4213 TRCKG, EXCEPT LOCAL (NO BREAKDOWN) (1822 Est.) $	%
Cash	62,520	9.0	175,270	10.4	615,317	7.7	111,267	9.7
Accounts Receivable	193,119	27.8	444,917	26.4	2,021,755	25.3	322,331	28.1
Notes Receivable	9,725	1.4	23,594	1.4	127,858	1.6	11,471	1.0
Inventory	6,947	1.0	18,538	1.1	119,867	1.5	17,206	1.5
Other Current	39,596	5.7	112,915	6.7	527,414	6.6	73,414	6.4
Total Current	**311,908**	**44.9**	**775,234**	**46.0**	**3,412,212**	**42.7**	**535,690**	**46.7**
Fixed Assets	313,297	45.1	743,214	44.1	3,635,963	45.5	515,042	44.9
Other Non-current	69,467	10.0	166,844	9.9	942,953	11.8	96,355	8.4
Total Assets	**694,672**	**100.0**	**1,685,292**	**100.0**	**7,991,128**	**100.0**	**1,147,087**	**100.0**
Accounts Payable	77,803	11.2	185,382	11.0	910,989	11.4	126,180	11.0
Bank Loans	1,389	0.2		—		—	3,441	0.3
Notes Payable	51,406	7.4	128,082	7.6	215,760	2.7	71,119	6.2
Other Current	91,697	13.2	246,053	14.6	1,390,456	17.4	180,093	15.7
Total Current	**222,295**	**32.0**	**559,517**	**33.2**	**2,517,205**	**31.5**	**380,833**	**33.2**
Other Long Term	154,217	22.2	332,003	19.7	1,710,101	21.4	271,860	23.7
Deferred Credits	1,389	0.2	10,112	0.6	55,938	0.7	6,883	0.6
Net Worth	316,770	45.6	783,661	46.5	3,707,883	46.4	487,512	42.5
Total Liab & Net Worth	**694,672**	**100.0**	**1,685,292**	**100.0**	**7,991,128**	**100.0**	**1,147,087**	**100.0**
Net Sales	1,907,978	100.0	4,456,360	100.0	18,420,465	100.0	3,715,360	100.0
Gross Profit	757,467	39.7	1,412,666	31.7	5,268,253	28.6	1,203,777	32.4
Net Profit After Tax	78,227	4.1	178,254	4.0	755,239	4.1	130,038	3.5
Working Capital	89,613	—	215,717	—	895,007	—	154,857	—

RATIOS

	UQ	MED	LQ	UQ	MED	LQ	UQ	MED	LQ	UQ	MED	LQ
SOLVENCY												
Quick Ratio (times)	2.4	1.2	0.6	2.1	1.1	0.7	2.0	1.1	0.6	2.0	1.1	0.6
Current Ratio (times)	2.9	1.5	0.8	2.5	1.4	0.9	2.3	1.4	1.0	2.5	1.4	0.9
Curr Liab To Nw (%)	21.2	48.2	125.4	26.7	65.1	150.8	28.8	74.3	129.2	29.0	67.6	151.2
Curr Liab To Inv (%)	117.0	304.0	604.4	255.5	445.5	667.6	242.8	531.0	745.8	193.7	399.0	686.8
Total Liab To Nw (%)	39.8	95.4	215.4	45.6	119.0	227.2	43.3	136.1	228.3	50.9	119.9	260.0
Fixed Assets To Nw (%)	48.4	90.5	166.0	48.8	94.5	164.7	56.2	111.9	193.6	47.8	103.3	199.4
EFFICIENCY												
Coll Period (days)	22.6	34.3	48.9	25.6	36.1	49.3	29.2	40.2	53.7	24.5	33.2	44.2
Sales To Inv (times)	245.6	107.8	34.5	284.5	130.3	46.7	194.5	135.4	62.0	256.2	122.9	58.5
Assets To Sales (%)	25.0	36.7	56.8	29.2	40.9	62.1	36.4	48.4	70.4	23.1	35.4	54.6
Sales To Nwc (times)	22.1	12.2	6.3	22.5	12.2	6.6	17.9	10.8	6.8	30.4	15.0	7.8
Acct Pay To Sales (%)	1.8	3.0	5.8	1.9	3.6	6.3	2.6	4.2	6.4	1.6	3.0	5.0
PROFITABILITY												
Return On Sales (%)	6.8	2.8	0.7	6.1	2.5	0.8	6.6	3.1	1.1	5.5	2.6	0.8
Return On Assets (%)	14.2	7.3	2.2	12.1	5.7	1.8	9.4	4.4	2.3	13.3	6.4	2.1
Return On Nw (%)	39.1	13.0	5.0	30.2	14.7	4.4	24.2	12.2	4.9	35.5	17.8	6.0

Column group headers:
- SIC 4212 LCL TRCKG W/O STRGE — INDUSTRY ASSETS $500,000 - $1,000,000 — 1995 (395 Establishments)
- SIC 4212 LCL TRCKG W/O STRGE — INDUSTRY ASSETS $1,000,000-$5,000,000 — 1995 (474 Establishments)
- SIC 4212 LCL TRCKG W/O STRGE — INDUSTRY ASSETS $5,000,000-$25,000,000 — 1995 (67 Establishments)
- SIC 4213 TRCKG, EXCEPT LOCAL (NO BREAKDOWN) — 1995 (1822 Establishments)

SIC 4213 TRCKG, EXCEPT LOCAL — INDUSTRY ASSETS

	UNDER $100,000 (206 Establishments)		$100,000 - $250,000 (403 Establishments)		$250,000 - $500,000 (491 Establishments)		$500,000 - $1,000,000 (663 Establishments)	
	$	%	$	%	$	%	$	%
Cash	15,305	22.7	25,745	15.7	42,198	11.5	78,087	10.7
Accounts Receivable	14,226	21.1	40,503	24.7	107,881	29.4	213,826	29.3
Notes Receivable	607	0.9	1,148	0.7	3,669	1.0	7,298	1.0
Inventory	944	1.4	1,312	0.8	5,871	1.6	13,136	1.8
Other Current	3,506	5.2	10,331	6.3	23,117	6.3	44,517	6.1
Total Current	**34,589**	**51.3**	**79,039**	**48.2**	**182,737**	**49.8**	**356,863**	**48.9**
Fixed Assets	28,453	42.2	74,611	45.5	158,885	43.3	310,887	42.6
Other Non-current	4,383	6.5	10,331	6.3	25,319	6.9	62,031	8.5
Total Assets	**67,424**	**100.0**	**163,981**	**100.0**	**366,941**	**100.0**	**729,782**	**100.0**
Accounts Payable	6,877	10.2	17,874	10.9	45,134	12.3	85,384	11.7
Bank Loans	—	—	492	0.3	734	0.2	1,460	0.2
Notes Payable	6,270	9.3	15,250	9.3	29,355	8.0	45,976	6.3
Other Current	12,541	18.6	22,957	14.0	52,840	14.4	101,440	13.9
Total Current	**25,689**	**38.1**	**56,573**	**34.5**	**128,062**	**34.9**	**234,260**	**32.1**
Other Long Term	13,889	20.6	36,240	22.1	85,497	23.3	168,580	23.1
Deferred Credits	405	0.6	164	0.1	367	0.1	1,460	0.2
Net Worth	27,442	40.7	71,004	43.3	153,014	41.7	325,483	44.6
Total Liab & Net Worth	**67,424**	**100.0**	**163,981**	**100.0**	**366,941**	**100.0**	**729,782**	**100.0**
Net Sales	330,608	100.0	667,728	100.0	1,300,731	100.0	2,353,178	100.0
Gross Profit	128,607	38.9	254,404	38.1	505,984	38.9	767,136	32.6
Net Profit After Tax	18,183	5.5	37,393	5.6	44,225	3.4	65,889	2.8
Working Capital	8,900	—	22,466	—	54,675	—	122,603	—

RATIOS	UQ	MED	LQ	UQ	MED	LQ	UQ	MED	LQ	UQ	MED	LQ
SOLVENCY												
Quick Ratio (times)	3.4	1.1	0.5	3.2	1.1	0.6	2.6	1.3	0.6	2.4	1.3	0.7
Current Ratio (times)	4.1	1.3	0.6	3.8	1.4	0.7	3.1	1.5	0.8	3.0	1.6	1.0
Curr Liab To Nw (%)	20.8	64.2	209.6	14.3	53.5	162.4	24.4	68.6	140.2	24.4	59.9	123.6
Curr Liab To Inv (%)	123.2	466.2	786.9	70.0	301.7	364.9	100.5	246.5	555.3	120.7	335.2	631.2
Total Liab To Nw (%)	30.4	90.0	233.6	28.7	99.7	267.5	53.5	107.7	214.9	48.0	106.4	212.8
Fixed Assets To Nw (%)	42.8	89.3	199.7	38.7	94.7	205.2	43.1	88.0	174.1	42.7	91.1	174.7
EFFICIENCY												
Coll Period (days)	13.7	22.1	33.6	14.8	28.3	38.5	19.7	28.8	41.5	22.4	32.5	43.4
Sales To Inv (times)	113.0	89.9	50.5	364.1	164.0	62.7	248.6	130.5	36.1	231.6	100.9	47.2
Assets To Sales (%)	10.1	18.7	28.3	15.6	23.6	39.5	19.0	28.4	39.3	23.1	30.1	46.9
Sales To Nwc (times)	69.8	17.3	7.4	32.6	16.1	8.3	27.6	12.7	7.6	28.3	14.4	7.6
Acct Pay To Sales (%)	0.8	2.1	5.1	0.9	2.0	3.8	1.3	2.7	5.6	1.5	3.0	5.1
PROFITABILITY												
Return On Sales (%)	12.0	4.0	0.6	10.5	3.7	0.8	5.6	2.5	0.5	4.7	2.0	0.5
Return On Assets (%)	29.9	14.1	(9.1)	26.3	10.6	0.8	18.1	6.9	1.2	12.9	5.4	1.3
Return On Nw (%)	114.3	41.7	(4.2)	66.1	24.6	2.5	50.2	18.4	2.5	37.6	14.6	2.7

SIC 4213 TRCKG, EXCEPT LOCAL — INDUSTRY ASSETS

	$1,000,000-$5,000,000 1995 (1198 Establishments) $	%	$5,000,000-$25,000,000 1995 (446 Establishments) $	%	$25,000,000-$50,000,000 1995 (78 Establishments) $	%	OVER $50,000,000 1995 (160 Establishments) $	%
Cash	151,746	8.0	425,063	4.8	2,040,413	6.2	4,008,809	3.1
Accounts Receivable	550,078	29.0	2,320,137	26.2	6,812,346	20.7	27,932,343	21.6
Notes Receivable	24,659	1.3	115,121	1.3	329,099	1.0	1,422,480	1.1
Inventory	22,762	1.2	115,121	1.3	362,009	1.1	1,293,164	1.0
Other Current	123,293	6.5	557,895	6.3	2,303,692	7.0	7,112,402	5.5
Total Current	**872,537**	**46.0**	**3,533,338**	**39.9**	**11,847,558**	**36.0**	**41,769,198**	**32.3**
Fixed Assets	847,879	44.7	4,480,874	50.6	16,652,401	50.6	70,736,073	54.7
Other Non-current	176,404	9.3	841,271	9.5	4,409,924	13.4	16,811,133	13.0
Total Assets	**1,896,820**	**100.0**	**8,855,483**	**100.0**	**32,909,884**	**100.0**	**129,316,404**	**100.0**
Accounts Payable	204,857	10.8	867,837	9.8	2,402,422	7.3	9,569,414	7.4
Bank Loans	7,587	0.4	8,855	0.1	—	—	—	—
Notes Payable	123,293	6.5	504,763	5.7	658,198	2.0	1,939,746	1.5
Other Current	294,007	15.5	1,647,120	18.6	6,450,337	19.6	23,018,320	17.8
Total Current	**629,744**	**33.2**	**3,028,575**	**34.2**	**9,510,956**	**28.9**	**34,527,480**	**26.7**
Other Long Term	438,165	23.1	2,461,824	27.8	10,103,334	30.7	39,441,503	30.5
Deferred Credits	7,587	0.4	106,266	1.2	658,198	2.0	6,077,871	4.7
Net Worth	821,323	43.3	3,258,818	36.8	12,637,395	38.4	49,269,550	38.1
Total Liab & Net Worth	**1,896,820**	**100.0**	**8,855,483**	**100.0**	**32,909,884**	**100.0**	**129,316,404**	**100.0**
Net Sales	5,366,884	100.0	20,049,910	100.0	62,766,107	100.0	214,838,000	100.0
Gross Profit	1,551,029	28.9	5,012,478	25.0	21,277,710	33.9	53,064,986	24.7
Net Profit After Tax	177,107	3.3	681,697	3.4	2,385,112	3.8	6,659,978	3.1
Working Capital	242,793	—	504,763	—	2,336,602	—	7,241,718	—

RATIOS	UQ	MED	LQ	UQ	MED	LQ	UQ	MED	LQ	UQ	MED	LQ
SOLVENCY												
Quick Ratio (times)	2.0	1.1	0.7	1.3	0.9	0.6	1.2	0.8	0.6	1.2	0.9	0.7
Current Ratio (times)	2.4	1.4	0.9	1.6	1.1	0.8	1.6	1.1	0.9	1.5	1.2	0.9
Curr Liab To Nw (%)	31.1	69.7	150.7	45.3	97.4	191.2	45.7	82.0	127.8	40.7	67.3	126.0
Curr Liab To Inv (%)	236.3	446.9	709.3	398.2	603.0	764.0	398.7	567.2	846.0	431.5	616.8	819.1
Total Liab To Nw (%)	54.8	126.1	273.7	87.0	180.7	352.3	94.6	183.0	294.5	95.5	152.2	274.9
Fixed Assets To Nw (%)	49.6	102.2	206.0	79.5	141.5	283.2	82.3	177.2	269.3	102.8	151.8	193.6
EFFICIENCY												
Coll Period (days)	25.7	33.2	43.8	28.1	35.8	46.4	31.6	36.3	42.7	36.1	42.0	47.5
Sales To Inv (times)	278.8	130.9	60.6	273.5	150.1	78.1	237.6	163.2	81.0	278.7	144.2	90.3
Assets To Sales (%)	25.9	37.9	54.6	32.6	48.0	64.9	42.8	59.0	74.5	48.0	64.0	80.3
Sales To Nwc (times)	31.0	14.8	7.4	32.0	17.3	10.0	92.4	22.6	10.1	38.7	19.7	12.3
Acct Pay To Sales (%)	1.7	3.0	5.0	1.8	3.2	5.2	2.1	3.1	4.9	2.8	3.6	4.6
PROFITABILITY												
Return On Sales (%)	5.3	2.7	1.0	5.1	2.7	1.3	5.7	3.3	1.9	5.5	3.2	1.4
Return On Assets (%)	13.1	6.5	2.3	10.8	5.9	2.6	10.0	6.4	4.5	8.5	5.3	2.7
Return On Nw (%)	35.4	17.4	6.1	34.3	18.1	8.7	28.3	19.2	13.8	21.0	15.1	8.3

SIC 4214 LCL TRCKG WTH STRGE

	NO BREAKDOWN (699 Establishments)		UNDER $100,000 (95 Establishments)		$100,000 - $250,000 (129 Establishments)		$250,000 - $500,000 (166 Establishments)	
	$	%	$	%	$	%	$	%
Cash	63,717	14.2	11,994	22.8	24,253	14.8	42,654	12.0
Accounts Receivable	139,548	31.1	9,048	17.2	50,800	31.0	120,497	33.9
Notes Receivable	9,872	2.2	684	1.3	2,786	1.7	4,976	1.4
Inventory	4,038	0.9	842	1.6	1,147	0.7	1,066	0.3
Other Current	28,717	6.4	2,630	5.0	11,307	6.9	29,502	8.3
Total Current	**245,893**	**54.8**	**25,197**	**47.9**	**90,292**	**55.1**	**198,695**	**55.9**
Fixed Assets	158,394	35.3	21,305	40.5	58,338	35.6	124,762	35.1
Other Non-current	44,422	9.9	6,102	11.6	15,240	9.3	31,990	9.0
Total Assets	**448,709**	**100.0**	**52,604**	**100.0**	**163,870**	**100.0**	**355,447**	**100.0**
Accounts Payable	53,845	12.0	4,840	9.2	21,139	12.9	44,431	12.5
Bank Loans	449	0.1	—	—	328	0.2	711	0.2
Notes Payable	26,923	6.0	5,050	9.6	9,504	5.8	23,815	6.7
Other Current	68,652	15.3	7,365	14.0	26,055	15.9	54,739	15.4
Total Current	**149,869**	**33.4**	**17,254**	**32.8**	**57,027**	**34.8**	**123,696**	**34.8**
Other Long Term	79,421	17.7	9,100	17.3	25,236	15.4	62,559	17.6
Deferred Credits	449	0.1	—	—	164	0.1	—	—
Net Worth	218,970	48.8	26,249	49.9	81,443	49.7	169,193	47.6
Total Liab & Net Worth	**448,709**	**100.0**	**52,604**	**100.0**	**163,870**	**100.0**	**355,447**	**100.0**
Net Sales	1,519,312	100.0	320,648	100.0	715,308	100.0	1,141,895	100.0
Gross Profit	606,205	39.9	148,781	46.4	326,180	45.6	517,278	45.3
Net Profit After Tax	53,176	3.5	12,505	3.9	26,466	3.7	43,392	3.8
Working Capital	96,024	—	7,943	—	33,265	—	74,999	—

RATIOS	UQ	MED	LQ	UQ	MED	LQ	UQ	MED	LQ	UQ	MED	LQ
SOLVENCY												
Quick Ratio (times)	2.9	1.4	0.8	4.4	1.4	0.5	4.2	1.6	0.8	2.7	1.4	0.8
Current Ratio (times)	3.6	1.7	1.0	4.8	1.6	0.7	5.0	1.8	1.0	3.4	1.8	1.1
Curr Liab To Nw (%)	20.0	54.8	126.5	13.1	44.1	122.1	15.6	49.1	111.1	21.8	63.4	129.9
Curr Liab To Inv (%)	155.6	347.6	777.1	42.4	139.6	300.8	166.5	301.4	590.7	204.9	339.4	808.7
Total Liab To Nw (%)	36.6	94.6	204.6	18.7	61.7	146.2	30.9	88.7	230.4	43.4	94.5	212.6
Fixed Assets To Nw (%)	31.9	65.7	128.7	24.3	65.4	120.0	35.6	63.6	98.8	32.7	64.8	131.8
EFFICIENCY												
Coll Period (days)	25.9	38.0	55.1	6.9	13.5	21.9	18.6	31.4	45.3	25.5	38.5	51.6
Sales To Inv (times)	414.2	204.1	97.8	160.1	107.4	31.7	357.1	156.8	54.9	553.5	386.0	149.6
Assets To Sales (%)	21.1	31.0	48.8	8.3	14.8	22.5	15.7	23.3	39.4	21.2	31.1	46.0
Sales To Nwc (times)	21.7	10.7	6.1	59.1	24.9	11.3	26.3	15.5	7.1	17.9	9.9	5.7
Acct Pay To Sales (%)	1.7	3.2	5.7	1.5	1.9	2.8	1.5	2.8	4.6	1.6	3.2	5.7
PROFITABILITY												
Return On Sales (%)	6.1	2.4	0.8	11.5	3.1	0.8	7.5	2.4	0.3	6.9	2.0	0.5
Return On Assets (%)	14.7	6.4	2.0	42.2	16.5	1.5	20.4	6.7	0.4	14.6	5.6	1.6
Return On Nw (%)	36.4	13.8	5.0	100.0	44.6	7.4	54.0	14.3	1.1	33.9	12.0	3.2

INDUSTRY ASSETS — 1995

SIC 4214 — LCL TRCKG WTH STRGE — INDUSTRY ASSETS $500,000 - $1,000,000 — 1995 (122 Establishments)

	$	%
Cash	120,572	17.3
Accounts Receivable	217,448	31.2
Notes Receivable	16,727	2.4
Inventory	6,273	0.9
Other Current	39,726	5.7
Total Current	**400,746**	**57.5**
Fixed Assets	226,509	32.5
Other Non-current	69,695	10.0
Total Assets	**696,950**	**100.0**
Accounts Payable	69,695	10.0
Bank Loans	—	—
Notes Payable	31,363	4.5
Other Current	96,876	13.9
Total Current	**197,934**	**28.4**
Other Long Term	126,845	18.2
Deferred Credits	1,394	0.2
Net Worth	370,777	53.2
Total Liab & Net Worth	**696,950**	**100.0**
Net Sales	1,864,577	100.0
Gross Profit	674,977	36.2
Net Profit After Tax	48,479	2.6
Working Capital	202,812	—

RATIOS	UQ	MED	LQ
SOLVENCY			
Quick Ratio (times)	4.9	1.8	0.9
Current Ratio (times)	5.2	2.1	1.3
Curr Liab To Nw (%)	17.2	47.0	105.2
Curr Liab To Inv (%)	221.5	615.3	903.9
Total Liab To Nw (%)	25.2	95.4	166.5
Fixed Assets To Nw (%)	29.2	52.7	107.6
EFFICIENCY			
Coll Period (days)	27.1	39.8	54.4
Sales To Inv (times)	401.4	162.0	65.5
Assets To Sales (%)	25.8	37.7	57.0
Sales To Nwc (times)	15.3	7.8	4.8
Acct Pay To Sales (%)	1.6	3.1	4.6
PROFITABILITY			
Return On Sales (%)	4.5	2.1	0.9
Return On Assets (%)	11.6	6.5	2.5
Return On Nw (%)	32.2	14.0	5.0

SIC 4214 — LCL TRCKG WTH STRGE — INDUSTRY ASSETS $1,000,000 - $5,000,000 — 1995 (163 Establishments)

	$	%
Cash	177,077	10.0
Accounts Receivable	603,832	34.1
Notes Receivable	65,518	3.7
Inventory	19,478	1.1
Other Current	99,163	5.6
Total Current	**965,069**	**54.5**
Fixed Assets	623,310	35.2
Other Non-current	182,389	10.3
Total Assets	**1,770,768**	**100.0**
Accounts Payable	235,512	13.3
Bank Loans	1,771	0.1
Notes Payable	95,621	5.4
Other Current	285,094	16.1
Total Current	**617,998**	**34.9**
Other Long Term	345,300	19.5
Deferred Credits	3,542	0.2
Net Worth	803,929	45.4
Total Liab & Net Worth	**1,770,768**	**100.0**
Net Sales	4,923,218	100.0
Gross Profit	1,531,121	31.1
Net Profit After Tax	182,159	3.7
Working Capital	347,071	—

RATIOS	UQ	MED	LQ
SOLVENCY			
Quick Ratio (times)	2.3	1.3	0.9
Current Ratio (times)	2.6	1.6	1.1
Curr Liab To Nw (%)	33.1	72.3	152.1
Curr Liab To Inv (%)	227.8	511.5	817.9
Total Liab To Nw (%)	51.4	117.5	251.8
Fixed Assets To Nw (%)	38.6	78.7	145.4
EFFICIENCY			
Coll Period (days)	32.5	43.3	59.0
Sales To Inv (times)	390.0	220.1	116.8
Assets To Sales (%)	26.5	34.4	51.4
Sales To Nwc (times)	21.8	10.8	6.7
Acct Pay To Sales (%)	2.2	3.8	6.3
PROFITABILITY			
Return On Sales (%)	5.3	2.7	1.0
Return On Assets (%)	12.3	6.2	2.2
Return On Nw (%)	28.6	13.4	7.0

SIC 4214 — LCL TRCKG WTH STRGE — INDUSTRY ASSETS $5,000,000-$25,000,000 — 1995 (22 Establishments)

	$	%
Cash	840,659	11.8
Accounts Receivable	2,486,356	34.9
Notes Receivable	192,354	2.7
Inventory	71,242	1.0
Other Current	391,833	5.5
Total Current	**3,982,444**	**55.9**
Fixed Assets	2,215,635	31.1
Other Non-current	926,150	13.0
Total Assets	**7,124,229**	**100.0**
Accounts Payable	1,090,007	15.3
Bank Loans	—	—
Notes Payable	284,969	4.0
Other Current	1,132,752	15.9
Total Current	**2,507,729**	**35.2**
Other Long Term	983,144	13.8
Deferred Credits	56,994	0.8
Net Worth	3,576,363	50.2
Total Liab & Net Worth	**7,124,229**	**100.0**
Net Sales	16,015,614	100.0
Gross Profit	5,637,496	35.2
Net Profit After Tax	560,546	3.5
Working Capital	1,474,715	—

RATIOS	UQ	MED	LQ
SOLVENCY			
Quick Ratio (times)	2.6	1.6	1.0
Current Ratio (times)	2.7	1.7	1.2
Curr Liab To Nw (%)	31.5	45.6	133.4
Curr Liab To Inv (%)	539.7	650.6	761.4
Total Liab To Nw (%)	40.9	81.8	177.8
Fixed Assets To Nw (%)	43.8	71.9	95.2
EFFICIENCY			
Coll Period (days)	32.4	46.0	70.5
Sales To Inv (times)	204.2	124.7	118.3
Assets To Sales (%)	31.0	40.1	59.1
Sales To Nwc (times)	26.5	9.0	6.7
Acct Pay To Sales (%)	2.1	5.9	8.6
PROFITABILITY			
Return On Sales (%)	4.6	3.3	1.8
Return On Assets (%)	10.9	7.7	4.9
Return On Nw (%)	21.7	14.9	7.8

SIC 4215 — COURIER SVC, EXC AIR (NO BREAKDOWN) — 1995 (143 Establishments)

	$	%
Cash	37,779	13.2
Accounts Receivable	108,757	38.0
Notes Receivable	3,148	1.1
Inventory	1,145	0.4
Other Current	15,741	5.5
Total Current	**166,570**	**58.2**
Fixed Assets	98,453	34.4
Other Non-current	21,179	7.4
Total Assets	**286,202**	**100.0**
Accounts Payable	26,617	9.3
Bank Loans	572	0.2
Notes Payable	22,038	7.7
Other Current	42,358	14.8
Total Current	**91,585**	**32.0**
Other Long Term	60,389	21.1
Deferred Credits	286	0.1
Net Worth	133,943	46.8
Total Liab & Net Worth	**286,202**	**100.0**
Net Sales	1,292,490	100.0
Gross Profit	482,099	37.3
Net Profit After Tax	51,700	4.0
Working Capital	74,985	—

RATIOS	UQ	MED	LQ
SOLVENCY			
Quick Ratio (times)	3.8	1.6	0.8
Current Ratio (times)	4.4	1.8	1.0
Curr Liab To Nw (%)	22.9	55.9	143.6
Curr Liab To Inv (%)	236.6	368.4	695.5
Total Liab To Nw (%)	49.8	108.3	201.2
Fixed Assets To Nw (%)	36.6	71.2	157.7
EFFICIENCY			
Coll Period (days)	26.7	34.0	43.1
Sales To Inv (times)	523.6	424.0	61.5
Assets To Sales (%)	16.1	22.8	34.0
Sales To Nwc (times)	29.3	13.3	7.8
Acct Pay To Sales (%)	1.1	2.1	4.3
PROFITABILITY			
Return On Sales (%)	5.8	3.7	0.9
Return On Assets (%)	24.0	13.1	4.8
Return On Nw (%)	47.4	31.1	8.3

SIC 4215 — COURIER SVC, EXC AIR

	UNDER $100,000 (34 Establishments)		$100,000 - $250,000 (32 Establishments)		$250,000 - $500,000 (23 Establishments)		$500,000 - $1,000,000 (23 Establishments)	
	$	%	$	%	$	%	$	%
Cash	11,351	22.1	16,208	10.7	51,765	17.6	54,325	7.3
Accounts Receivable	10,786	21.0	74,226	49.0	119,412	40.6	305,859	41.1
Notes Receivable	1,181	2.3	757	0.5	2,353	0.8	4,465	0.6
Inventory	411	0.8	1,060	0.7	—	—	—	—
Other Current	4,006	7.8	4,393	2.9	14,412	4.9	51,349	6.9
Total Current	**27,737**	**54.0**	**96,645**	**63.8**	**187,941**	**63.9**	**415,998**	**55.9**
Fixed Assets	22,446	43.7	46,959	31.0	86,471	29.4	234,417	31.5
Other Non-current	1,181	2.3	7,877	5.2	19,706	6.7	93,767	12.6
Total Assets	**51,364**	**100.0**	**151,481**	**100.0**	**294,118**	**100.0**	**744,182**	**100.0**
Accounts Payable	4,674	9.1	9,846	6.5	30,588	10.4	62,511	8.4
Bank Loans	—	—	—	—	—	—	—	—
Notes Payable	3,082	6.0	25,903	17.1	15,000	5.1	30,511	4.1
Other Current	6,677	13.0	23,631	15.6	31,471	10.7	107,906	14.5
Total Current	**14,433**	**28.1**	**59,381**	**39.2**	**77,059**	**26.2**	**200,929**	**27.0**
Other Long Term	11,043	21.5	27,267	18.0	76,177	25.9	137,674	18.5
Deferred Credits	—	—	757	0.5	—	—	—	—
Net Worth	25,887	50.4	64,076	42.3	140,883	47.9	405,579	54.5
Total Liab & Net Worth	**51,364**	**100.0**	**151,481**	**100.0**	**294,118**	**100.0**	**744,182**	**100.0**
Net Sales	204,716	100.0	822,856	100.0	1,294,000	100.0	3,208,397	100.0
Gross Profit	101,539	49.6	331,611	40.3	625,002	48.3	924,018	28.8
Net Profit After Tax	13,307	6.5	54,308	6.6	15,528	1.2	112,294	3.5
Working Capital	13,304	—	37,264	—	110,882	—	215,069	—

RATIOS	UQ	MED	LQ	UQ	MED	LQ	UQ	MED	LQ	UQ	MED	LQ
SOLVENCY												
Quick Ratio (times)	4.9	1.6	0.6	2.5	1.6	1.0	4.6	2.5	1.1	4.0	1.9	1.2
Current Ratio (times)	4.9	1.8	1.0	3.1	1.6	1.0	6.0	2.6	1.1	4.2	2.5	1.4
Curr Liab To Nw (%)	16.2	40.6	101.7	47.4	83.8	143.3	18.5	36.2	87.2	26.2	42.1	103.7
Curr Liab To Inv (%)	238.8	238.8	238.8	165.2	188.8	212.3	—	—	—	—	—	—
Total Liab To Nw (%)	35.6	74.4	228.7	73.2	136.2	187.5	39.1	71.1	149.4	31.6	92.1	177.5
Fixed Assets To Nw (%)	55.2	90.8	201.4	29.3	62.1	139.4	24.1	41.0	83.3	21.0	48.4	129.9
EFFICIENCY												
Coll Period (days)	12.6	31.8	51.7	29.9	38.0	50.7	30.2	40.0	50.8	24.5	31.2	38.3
Sales To Inv (times)	—	—	—	279.3	194.9	110.4	—	—	—	—	—	—
Assets To Sales (%)	10.3	16.3	31.6	14.1	16.9	29.0	17.6	25.0	34.4	16.7	22.5	26.7
Sales To Nwc (times)	57.2	8.9	7.8	36.0	15.5	7.6	15.6	10.3	5.7	27.5	20.0	10.9
Acct Pay To Sales (%)	2.1	2.9	4.5	0.4	0.8	2.6	1.5	3.0	4.3	0.4	1.2	3.5
PROFITABILITY												
Return On Sales (%)	16.9	7.0	1.4	7.7	3.8	2.0	4.1	2.1	—	5.7	3.9	2.2
Return On Assets (%)	75.3	38.2	0.6	31.6	19.8	11.5	10.5	7.1	0.4	30.2	19.8	7.0
Return On Nw (%)	122.8	75.6	(16.8)	67.8	41.0	22.5	29.9	10.9	3.0	46.5	36.4	14.6

SIC 4215 COURIER SVC, EXC AIR
INDUSTRY ASSETS
$1,000,000 - $5,000,000
1995 (23 Establishments)

	$	%
Cash	188,285	9.8
Accounts Receivable	806,937	42.0
Notes Receivable	34,583	1.8
Inventory	7,685	0.4
Other Current	107,592	5.6
Total Current	**1,145,082**	**59.6**
Fixed Assets	624,416	32.5
Other Non-current	151,781	7.9
Total Assets	**1,921,279**	**100.0**
Accounts Payable	259,373	13.5
Bank Loans	21,134	1.1
Notes Payable	113,355	5.9
Other Current	322,775	16.8
Total Current	**716,637**	**37.3**
Other Long Term	405,390	21.1
Deferred Credits	1,921	0.1
Net Worth	797,331	41.5
Total Liab & Net Worth	**1,921,279**	**100.0**
Net Sales	7,542,408	100.0
Gross Profit	2,051,535	27.2
Net Profit After Tax	203,645	2.7
Working Capital	428,445	—

RATIOS	UQ	MED	LQ
SOLVENCY			
Quick Ratio (times)	3.2	1.3	0.9
Current Ratio (times)	3.9	1.6	1.0
Curr Liab To Nw (%)	21.2	102.0	175.6
Curr Liab To Inv (%)	920.9	920.9	920.9
Total Liab To Nw (%)	80.7	183.6	303.8
Fixed Assets To Nw (%)	49.7	95.8	149.4
EFFICIENCY			
Coll Period (days)	25.6	32.9	39.8
Sales To Inv (times)	736.3	503.9	484.1
Assets To Sales (%)	18.1	22.5	32.8
Sales To Nwc (times)	21.5	15.7	9.9
Acct Pay To Sales (%)	1.6	2.1	4.7
PROFITABILITY			
Return On Sales (%)	5.6	3.4	1.0
Return On Assets (%)	17.2	12.7	7.9
Return On Nw (%)	42.6	31.1	19.2

SIC 4221 FRM PRDT WRHSG, STRG (NO BREAKDOWN)
1995 (72 Establishments)

	$	%
Cash	194,200	11.0
Accounts Receivable	248,930	14.1
Notes Receivable	21,186	1.2
Inventory	319,548	18.1
Other Current	93,569	5.3
Total Current	**877,433**	**49.7**
Fixed Assets	596,725	33.8
Other Non-current	291,301	16.5
Total Assets	**1,765,459**	**100.0**
Accounts Payable	210,090	11.9
Bank Loans	7,062	0.4
Notes Payable	93,569	5.3
Other Current	303,659	17.2
Total Current	**614,380**	**34.8**
Other Long Term	326,610	18.5
Deferred Credits	5,296	0.3
Net Worth	819,173	46.4
Total Liab & Net Worth	**1,765,459**	**100.0**
Net Sales	3,080,203	100.0
Gross Profit	616,041	20.0
Net Profit After Tax	141,689	4.6
Working Capital	263,053	—

RATIOS	UQ	MED	LQ
SOLVENCY			
Quick Ratio (times)	1.4	0.7	0.4
Current Ratio (times)	2.1	1.5	1.0
Curr Liab To Nw (%)	23.8	58.2	137.0
Curr Liab To Inv (%)	102.2	147.7	234.9
Total Liab To Nw (%)	42.3	91.2	188.2
Fixed Assets To Nw (%)	32.1	70.6	146.1
EFFICIENCY			
Coll Period (days)	8.8	19.4	52.6
Sales To Inv (times)	42.7	12.2	7.7
Assets To Sales (%)	27.9	56.5	161.9
Sales To Nwc (times)	22.8	10.8	4.6
Acct Pay To Sales (%)	2.6	3.8	9.5
PROFITABILITY			
Return On Sales (%)	7.7	2.3	0.4
Return On Assets (%)	7.6	3.1	0.9
Return On Nw (%)	19.3	6.1	1.5

SIC 4221 FRM PRDT WRHSG, STRG
INDUSTRY ASSETS
$500,000 - $1,000,000
1995 (15 Establishments)

	$	%
Cash	85,158	12.4
Accounts Receivable	100,954	14.7
Notes Receivable	687	0.1
Inventory	134,605	19.6
Other Current	14,422	2.1
Total Current	**335,826**	**48.9**
Fixed Assets	250,668	36.5
Other Non-current	100,267	14.6
Total Assets	**686,761**	**100.0**
Accounts Payable	89,279	13.0
Bank Loans	—	—
Notes Payable	26,784	3.9
Other Current	111,255	16.2
Total Current	**227,318**	**33.1**
Other Long Term	133,232	19.4
Deferred Credits	—	—
Net Worth	326,211	47.5
Total Liab & Net Worth	**686,761**	**100.0**
Net Sales	1,044,301	100.0
Gross Profit	210,949	20.2
Net Profit After Tax	26,108	2.5
Working Capital	108,508	—

RATIOS	UQ	MED	LQ
SOLVENCY			
Quick Ratio (times)	1.2	0.7	0.4
Current Ratio (times)	3.2	2.1	0.8
Curr Liab To Nw (%)	23.1	39.5	62.4
Curr Liab To Inv (%)	44.4	64.8	172.8
Total Liab To Nw (%)	37.1	68.8	93.4
Fixed Assets To Nw (%)	30.9	31.8	81.8
EFFICIENCY			
Coll Period (days)	17.0	31.0	67.0
Sales To Inv (times)	49.9	27.8	7.0
Assets To Sales (%)	29.3	81.6	114.6
Sales To Nwc (times)	12.8	4.6	2.9
Acct Pay To Sales (%)	1.2	2.6	5.3
PROFITABILITY			
Return On Sales (%)	8.0	1.8	(0.7)
Return On Assets (%)	2.1	1.7	(4.2)
Return On Nw (%)	4.8	3.2	0.1

SIC 4221 FRM PRDT WRHSG, STRG
INDUSTRY ASSETS
$1,000,000 - $5,000,000
1995 (37 Establishments)

	$	%
Cash	297,000	11.6
Accounts Receivable	371,250	14.5
Notes Receivable	20,483	0.8
Inventory	463,423	18.1
Other Current	89,612	3.5
Total Current	**1,241,769**	**48.5**
Fixed Assets	903,803	35.3
Other Non-current	414,776	16.2
Total Assets	**2,560,348**	**100.0**
Accounts Payable	227,871	8.9
Bank Loans	20,483	0.8
Notes Payable	145,940	5.7
Other Current	440,380	17.2
Total Current	**834,673**	**32.6**
Other Long Term	389,173	15.2
Deferred Credits	12,802	0.5
Net Worth	1,323,700	51.7
Total Liab & Net Worth	**2,560,348**	**100.0**
Net Sales	5,085,237	100.0
Gross Profit	874,661	17.2
Net Profit After Tax	203,409	4.0
Working Capital	407,096	—

RATIOS	UQ	MED	LQ
SOLVENCY			
Quick Ratio (times)	1.4	0.8	0.4
Current Ratio (times)	2.0	1.5	1.2
Curr Liab To Nw (%)	23.4	54.7	104.0
Curr Liab To Inv (%)	118.2	151.5	274.7
Total Liab To Nw (%)	42.5	89.7	174.7
Fixed Assets To Nw (%)	40.4	73.6	142.4
EFFICIENCY			
Coll Period (days)	9.9	17.8	25.4
Sales To Inv (times)	35.7	12.2	8.9
Assets To Sales (%)	25.9	40.3	129.0
Sales To Nwc (times)	30.4	11.5	5.0
Acct Pay To Sales (%)	2.2	3.4	7.5
PROFITABILITY			
Return On Sales (%)	6.1	2.3	0.4
Return On Assets (%)	7.1	3.5	1.1
Return On Nw (%)	17.6	7.5	2.0

	SIC 4222 RFRGT WRHSG,STORAGE (NO BREAKDOWN) 1995 (74 Establishments) $	%	SIC 4222 RFRGT WRHSG,STORAGE INDUSTRY ASSETS $1,000,000 - $5,000,000 1995 (26 Establishments) $	%	SIC 4222 RFRGT WRHSG,STORAGE INDUSTRY ASSETS $5,000,000-$25,000,000 1995 (18 Establishments) $	%	SIC 4225 GNRL WRHSG,STRGE (NO BREAKDOWN) 1995 (342 Establishments) $	%
Cash	176,130	7.6	152,800	7.3	642,595	6.3	120,782	13.3
Accounts Receivable	368,482	15.9	341,183	16.3	1,417,788	13.9	226,127	24.9
Notes Receivable	18,540	0.8	14,652	0.7	20,400	0.2	6,357	0.7
Inventory	60,255	2.6	81,633	3.9	214,198	2.1	14,530	1.6
Other Current	136,732	5.9	119,309	5.7	285,598	2.8	57,213	6.3
Total Current	**760,140**	**32.8**	**709,577**	**33.9**	**2,580,579**	**25.3**	**425,009**	**46.8**
Fixed Assets	1,244,497	53.7	1,247,516	59.6	5,191,757	50.9	385,959	42.5
Other Non-current	312,862	13.5	136,055	6.5	2,427,580	23.8	97,171	10.7
Total Assets	**2,317,499**	**100.0**	**2,093,147**	**100.0**	**10,199,916**	**100.0**	**908,139**	**100.0**
Accounts Payable	127,462	5.5	83,726	4.0	387,597	3.8	86,273	9.5
Bank Loans	—	—	—	—	—	—	1,816	0.2
Notes Payable	92,700	4.0	115,123	5.5	112,199	1.1	49,040	5.4
Other Current	340,672	14.7	203,035	9.7	1,111,791	10.9	135,313	14.9
Total Current	**560,835**	**24.2**	**401,884**	**19.2**	**1,611,587**	**15.8**	**272,442**	**30.0**
Other Long Term	641,947	27.7	632,130	30.2	3,926,968	38.5	196,158	21.6
Deferred Credits	9,270	0.4	2,093	0.1	—	—	2,724	0.3
Net Worth	1,105,447	47.7	1,057,039	50.5	4,661,362	45.7	436,815	48.1
Total Liab & Net Worth	**2,317,499**	**100.0**	**2,093,147**	**100.0**	**10,199,916**	**100.0**	**908,139**	**100.0**
Net Sales	2,021,536	100.0	2,427,216	100.0	8,668,420	100.0	1,675,892	100.0
Gross Profit	899,584	44.5	1,026,712	42.3	1,855,042	21.4	551,368	32.9
Net Profit After Tax	149,594	7.4	257,285	10.6	884,179	10.2	98,878	5.9
Working Capital	199,305	—	307,693	—	968,992	—	152,567	—

RATIOS	UQ	MED	LQ	UQ	MED	LQ	UQ	MED	LQ	UQ	MED	LQ
SOLVENCY												
Quick Ratio (times)	2.0	1.0	0.5	2.4	1.3	0.5	2.0	1.4	0.8	2.9	1.3	0.8
Current Ratio (times)	3.0	1.2	0.7	3.6	2.2	0.9	2.7	1.7	1.0	3.8	1.6	1.0
Curr Liab To Nw (%)	16.8	38.0	92.5	17.7	24.3	84.3	3.5	38.0	92.5	14.3	37.7	124.2
Curr Liab To Inv (%)	58.9	285.1	386.9	58.9	180.2	359.7	273.5	342.1	434.8	126.8	235.3	370.3
Total Liab To Nw (%)	25.7	90.2	356.6	23.4	73.1	374.2	33.2	145.2	291.7	30.9	86.3	235.9
Fixed Assets To Nw (%)	50.7	112.2	279.4	55.6	99.2	418.8	59.9	155.1	253.0	39.9	86.2	160.7
EFFICIENCY												
Coll Period (days)	24.8	37.1	52.6	29.2	36.9	66.4	26.7	40.5	46.4	26.3	37.6	52.2
Sales To Inv (times)	224.0	105.3	25.5	159.0	84.1	19.5	270.0	105.3	59.7	162.1	52.3	20.1
Assets To Sales (%)	39.9	100.2	163.3	61.2	103.6	182.4	106.0	151.8	257.6	26.9	41.2	84.2
Sales To Nwc (times)	25.1	7.5	4.7	18.6	6.3	3.9	9.2	7.7	5.4	24.9	9.7	5.1
Acct Pay To Sales (%)	1.3	2.4	4.4	2.0	3.7	4.8	1.3	1.7	3.0	1.4	2.8	5.5
PROFITABILITY												
Return On Sales (%)	14.7	4.7	1.6	17.9	10.4	3.7	27.0	4.0	0.2	10.9	4.3	1.3
Return On Assets (%)	13.7	7.9	2.0	14.3	9.9	4.3	3.2	2.0	1.6	16.2	8.0	2.1
Return On Nw (%)	31.6	15.3	5.9	37.8	21.9	12.2	11.3	6.0	4.0	34.6	15.8	6.0

SIC 4225 GNRL WRHSG,STRGE

Balance Sheet / Income

	UNDER $100,000 (30 Est.) $	%	$100,000 - $250,000 (45 Est.) $	%	$250,000 - $500,000 (55 Est.) $	%	$500,000 - $1,000,000 (53 Est.) $	%
Cash	12,357	25.0	37,444	20.3	53,663	14.8	115,082	15.1
Accounts Receivable	13,444	27.2	72,675	39.4	101,525	28.0	201,203	26.4
Notes Receivable	49	0.1	1,291	0.7	2,901	0.8	9,908	1.3
Inventory	1,483	3.0	4,611	2.5	9,790	2.7	12,194	1.6
Other Current	1,532	3.1	13,465	7.3	32,270	8.9	39,631	5.2
Total Current	**28,866**	**58.4**	**129,487**	**70.2**	**200,149**	**55.2**	**378,017**	**49.6**
Fixed Assets	18,190	36.8	47,589	25.8	125,093	34.5	315,523	41.4
Other Non-current	2,373	4.8	7,378	4.0	37,347	10.3	68,592	9.0
Total Assets	**49,428**	**100.0**	**184,455**	**100.0**	**362,588**	**100.0**	**762,132**	**100.0**
Accounts Payable	3,905	7.9	29,513	16.0	40,972	11.3	73,927	9.7
Bank Loans	445	0.9	—	—	—	—	4,573	0.6
Notes Payable	6,722	13.6	9,776	5.3	19,942	5.5	45,728	6.0
Other Current	7,562	15.3	18,814	10.2	64,178	17.7	98,315	12.9
Total Current	**18,634**	**37.7**	**58,103**	**31.5**	**125,093**	**34.5**	**222,543**	**29.2**
Other Long Term	4,745	9.6	17,154	9.3	49,312	13.6	168,431	22.1
Deferred Credits	49	0.1	—	—	363	0.1	762	0.1
Net Worth	25,999	52.6	109,197	59.2	187,821	51.8	370,396	48.6
Total Liab & Net Worth	**49,428**	**100.0**	**184,455**	**100.0**	**362,588**	**100.0**	**762,132**	**100.0**
Net Sales	149,707	100.0	560,082	100.0	1,141,038	100.0	1,672,000	100.0
Gross Profit	65,272	43.6	246,436	44.0	456,415	40.0	312,664	18.7
Net Profit After Tax	2,994	2.0	39,766	7.1	58,193	5.1	46,816	2.8
Working Capital	10,232	—	71,384	—	75,056	—	155,474	—

RATIOS

	UNDER $100,000 UQ	MED	LQ	$100,000-$250,000 UQ	MED	LQ	$250,000-$500,000 UQ	MED	LQ	$500,000-$1,000,000 UQ	MED	LQ
SOLVENCY												
Quick Ratio (times)	5.9	1.1	0.6	4.4	2.4	1.2	2.7	1.3	0.8	2.7	1.4	0.9
Current Ratio (times)	6.2	1.4	0.7	5.3	3.0	1.5	3.8	1.6	0.9	3.3	1.7	1.1
Curr Liab To Nw (%)	5.4	34.8	107.8	15.7	32.1	80.4	14.3	35.8	108.4	20.4	36.6	149.1
Curr Liab To Inv (%)	41.3	45.9	169.9	123.4	149.4	240.3	200.2	393.2	770.4	184.8	207.4	523.7
Total Liab To Nw (%)	5.4	64.9	132.4	19.8	41.9	104.9	31.6	79.1	174.7	26.3	57.0	247.3
Fixed Assets To Nw (%)	38.4	70.0	108.5	10.8	33.8	76.9	29.8	53.7	112.1	39.1	86.5	149.0
EFFICIENCY												
Coll Period (days)	26.3	34.7	104.8	23.3	39.3	57.2	18.2	27.0	43.7	29.4	38.0	55.4
Sales To Inv (times)	174.2	117.3	60.4	15.3	10.7	8.8	163.6	106.1	46.0	52.4	52.1	32.3
Assets To Sales (%)	13.5	21.0	40.7	20.4	26.2	38.7	21.9	34.9	52.6	26.8	43.0	78.0
Sales To Nwc (times)	27.0	8.6	3.8	10.1	6.3	3.8	17.0	10.8	6.7	28.4	7.9	5.3
Acct Pay To Sales (%)	1.4	1.8	2.7	1.1	3.3	5.4	0.8	1.5	3.9	1.6	2.4	4.7
PROFITABILITY												
Return On Sales (%)	10.6	4.7	(2.9)	12.5	9.1	3.2	7.8	3.5	1.5	7.7	5.0	1.2
Return On Assets (%)	34.1	23.6	(4.7)	42.5	23.1	8.4	17.3	11.5	3.4	14.2	7.7	1.8
Return On Nw (%)	51.9	36.0	(27.8)	58.6	29.6	12.8	34.1	18.2	5.8	35.1	13.9	4.7

SIC 4225 GNRL WRHSG,STRGE — INDUSTRY ASSETS $1,000,000 - $5,000,000 — 1995 (117 Establishments)
SIC 4225 GNRL WRHSG,STRGE — INDUSTRY ASSETS $5,000,000-$25,000,000 — 1995 (30 Establishments)
SIC 4226 SPCL WRHSG,STRG,NEC (NO BREAKDOWN) — 1995 (79 Establishments)
SIC 4226 SPCL WRHSG,STRG,NEC — INDUSTRY ASSETS $100,000 - $250,000 — 1995 (11 Establishments)

	SIC 4225 $1M-$5M $	%	SIC 4225 $5M-$25M $	%	SIC 4226 No Breakdown $	%	SIC 4226 $100K-$250K $	%
Cash	189,290	9.3	590,678	5.8	129,236	14.9	29,133	15.5
Accounts Receivable	417,251	20.5	1,690,563	16.6	199,492	23.0	61,462	32.7
Notes Receivable	10,177	0.5	10,184	0.1	13,010	1.5	—	—
Inventory	10,177	0.5	40,736	0.4	29,490	3.4	9,398	5.0
Other Current	130,264	6.4	611,047	6.0	50,307	5.8	4,323	2.3
Total Current	**757,158**	**37.2**	**2,943,208**	**28.9**	**421,536**	**48.6**	**104,316**	**55.5**
Fixed Assets	983,085	48.3	6,100,283	59.9	377,301	43.5	65,221	34.7
Other Non-current	295,129	14.5	1,140,621	11.2	68,521	7.9	18,420	9.8
Total Assets	**2,035,372**	**100.0**	**10,184,112**	**100.0**	**867,358**	**100.0**	**187,956**	**100.0**
Accounts Payable	158,759	7.8	672,151	6.6	69,389	8.0	28,569	15.2
Bank Loans	—	—	—	—	1,735	0.2	3,007	1.6
Notes Payable	83,450	4.1	132,393	1.3	30,358	3.5	2,819	1.5
Other Current	348,049	17.1	1,293,382	12.7	118,828	13.7	29,885	15.9
Total Current	**590,258**	**29.0**	**2,097,927**	**20.6**	**220,309**	**25.4**	**64,281**	**34.2**
Other Long Term	588,223	28.9	3,727,385	36.6	178,676	20.6	43,230	23.0
Deferred Credits	8,141	0.4	101,841	1.0	8,674	1.0	5,075	2.7
Net Worth	848,750	41.7	4,256,959	41.8	459,700	53.0	75,370	40.1
Total Liab & Net Worth	**2,035,372**	**100.0**	**10,184,112**	**100.0**	**867,358**	**100.0**	**187,956**	**100.0**
Net Sales	4,309,203	100.0	11,096,995	100.0	1,497,775	100.0	721,734	100.0
Gross Profit	1,495,293	34.7	1,875,392	16.9	741,399	49.5	285,807	39.6
Net Profit After Tax	288,717	6.7	699,111	6.3	161,760	10.8	61,347	8.5
Working Capital	166,900	—	845,281	—	201,227	—	40,035	—

RATIOS	C1 UQ	C1 MED	C1 LQ	C2 UQ	C2 MED	C2 LQ	C3 UQ	C3 MED	C3 LQ	C4 UQ	C4 MED	C4 LQ
SOLVENCY												
Quick Ratio (times)	2.4	1.2	0.7	1.4	1.1	0.9	2.9	1.8	0.8	2.2	1.9	1.3
Current Ratio (times)	3.7	1.4	0.9	2.6	1.3	1.0	3.3	2.0	1.0	2.2	2.1	1.7
Curr Liab To Nw (%)	13.7	43.9	150.8	11.1	35.3	90.7	13.6	32.2	68.5	44.7	54.2	83.6
Curr Liab To Inv (%)	152.0	300.6	398.4	230.1	247.9	265.6	99.6	439.2	736.3	37.4	63.1	88.9
Total Liab To Nw (%)	50.6	176.2	275.5	43.3	86.3	250.2	21.8	71.6	110.0	41.6	78.9	180.7
Fixed Assets To Nw (%)	56.5	115.5	218.4	73.2	123.1	353.5	39.0	78.1	120.6	42.8	104.4	137.8
EFFICIENCY												
Coll Period (days)	27.0	36.5	49.3	33.4	48.6	54.8	29.9	41.4	58.0	24.1	35.4	48.9
Sales To Inv (times)	247.0	108.6	21.7	379.2	161.0	156.5	144.4	72.6	20.9	8.6	8.6	8.6
Assets To Sales (%)	31.3	44.8	121.1	50.7	73.2	171.8	29.9	62.1	126.4	24.3	34.2	46.1
Sales To Nwc (times)	26.4	11.2	8.1	32.7	6.7	4.2	11.7	6.8	3.1	15.9	7.5	5.5
Acct Pay To Sales (%)	1.8	3.1	7.5	2.0	4.0	6.4	1.4	2.5	5.4	1.4	1.7	2.6
PROFITABILITY												
Return On Sales (%)	10.6	4.1	1.3	11.3	4.0	1.4	21.6	8.8	2.9	12.0	5.9	2.7
Return On Assets (%)	10.7	6.5	2.0	8.1	5.6	2.2	18.8	9.3	3.5	25.8	18.6	11.3
Return On Nw (%)	26.9	15.1	7.5	28.4	16.1	5.7	28.7	20.5	7.7	39.2	27.6	15.9

	SIC 4226 SPCL WRHSG,STRG,NEC $250,000-$500,000 1995 (11 Establishments) $	%	SIC 4226 SPCL WRHSG,STRG,NEC $500,000-$1,000,000 1995 (14 Establishments) $	%	SIC 4226 SPCL WRHSG,STRG,NEC $1,000,000-$5,000,000 1995 (25 Establishments) $	%	SIC 44 WATER TRANSPORTATION (NO BREAKDOWN) 1995 (464 Establishments) $	%
Cash	95,204	23.4	111,755	14.6	280,925	11.9	159,379	11.9
Accounts Receivable	81,371	20.0	205,140	26.8	467,421	19.8	199,559	14.9
Notes Receivable	—	—	28,322	3.7	44,854	1.9	6,697	0.5
Inventory	33,769	8.3	6,124	0.8	84,986	3.6	123,218	9.2
Other Current	21,970	5.4	46,692	6.1	129,839	5.5	81,699	6.1
Total Current	**232,314**	**57.1**	**398,033**	**52.0**	**1,008,024**	**42.7**	**570,552**	**42.6**
Fixed Assets	149,722	36.8	310,006	40.5	1,225,210	51.9	616,089	46.0
Other Non-current	24,818	6.1	57,409	7.5	127,479	5.4	152,683	11.4
Total Assets	**406,854**	**100.0**	**765,448**	**100.0**	**2,360,713**	**100.0**	**1,339,323**	**100.0**
Accounts Payable	25,632	6.3	73,483	9.6	92,068	3.9	101,789	7.6
Bank Loans	—	—	—	—	—	—	2,679	0.2
Notes Payable	5,696	1.4	88,027	11.5	80,264	3.4	48,216	3.6
Other Current	24,411	6.0	60,470	7.9	351,746	14.9	196,880	14.7
Total Current	**55,739**	**13.7**	**221,980**	**29.0**	**524,078**	**22.2**	**349,563**	**26.1**
Other Long Term	66,317	16.3	153,090	20.0	604,343	25.6	360,278	26.9
Deferred Credits	7,323	1.8	9,951	1.3	4,721	0.2	17,411	1.3
Net Worth	277,474	68.2	380,428	49.7	1,227,571	52.0	612,071	45.7
Total Liab & Net Worth	**406,854**	**100.0**	**765,448**	**100.0**	**2,360,713**	**100.0**	**1,339,323**	**100.0**
Net Sales	1,600,000	100.0	1,408,874	100.0	1,987,069	100.0	1,921,542	100.0
Gross Profit	761,600	47.6	835,462	59.3	794,828	40.0	849,322	44.2
Net Profit After Tax	139,200	8.7	92,986	6.6	290,112	14.6	88,391	4.6
Working Capital	176,575	—	176,053	—	483,946	—	220,989	—

RATIOS	UQ	MED	LQ	UQ	MED	LQ	UQ	MED	LQ	UQ	MED	LQ
SOLVENCY												
Quick Ratio (times)	4.8	2.2	1.3	4.4	2.0	0.7	3.1	1.8	0.8	2.3	1.1	0.4
Current Ratio (times)	6.5	3.7	1.7	4.4	2.1	1.0	3.5	2.2	1.0	3.3	1.7	1.0
Curr Liab To Nw (%)	10.0	17.0	53.8	10.0	17.8	70.0	15.9	23.8	33.7	13.4	39.4	101.5
Curr Liab To Inv (%)	193.2	375.5	557.7	721.3	721.3	721.3	158.3	562.2	735.1	88.1	150.2	346.9
Total Liab To Nw (%)	13.6	43.7	79.2	10.4	36.1	157.2	19.9	58.4	106.2	40.1	105.0	221.4
Fixed Assets To Nw (%)	33.6	51.6	120.0	30.6	60.4	148.1	44.7	78.1	105.6	43.8	96.2	169.0
EFFICIENCY												
Coll Period (days)	23.0	23.2	37.6	50.7	64.6	107.9	38.3	46.2	55.1	12.6	35.7	58.1
Sales To Inv (times)	—	—	—	291.8	279.1	149.4	69.7	65.7	21.9	51.7	20.2	7.7
Assets To Sales (%)	17.2	18.8	42.3	38.2	78.2	123.0	64.1	108.3	159.1	44.6	91.4	167.6
Sales To Nwc (times)	14.4	11.3	6.1	6.3	4.2	2.0	6.8	3.6	1.5	14.2	6.2	3.4
Acct Pay To Sales (%)	0.8	1.6	2.7	5.1	6.4	11.2	1.1	1.9	4.6	1.7	3.6	6.9
PROFITABILITY												
Return On Sales (%)	12.8	6.7	3.2	14.9	12.6	1.9	30.7	12.5	4.3	9.8	4.4	0.4
Return On Assets (%)	19.5	15.1	12.8	7.4	2.8	0.9	22.8	9.2	5.4	8.8	4.0	0.8
Return On Nw (%)	28.0	23.2	12.8	8.9	2.5	2.4	33.0	23.3	12.1	25.4	9.4	1.6

SIC 44 WATER TRANSPORTATION — NORTHEAST — 1995 (132 Establishments)

	$	%
Cash	94,846	14.2
Accounts Receivable	87,499	13.1
Notes Receivable	5,343	0.8
Inventory	104,197	15.6
Other Current	38,072	5.7
Total Current	**329,957**	**49.4**
Fixed Assets	271,179	40.6
Other Non-current	66,793	10.0
Total Assets	**667,929**	**100.0**
Accounts Payable	43,415	6.5
Bank Loans	1,336	0.2
Notes Payable	23,378	3.5
Other Current	138,929	20.8
Total Current	**207,058**	**31.0**
Other Long Term	158,967	23.8
Deferred Credits	5,343	0.8
Net Worth	296,560	44.4
Total Liab & Net Worth	**667,929**	**100.0**
Net Sales	1,059,575	100.0
Gross Profit	503,298	47.5
Net Profit After Tax	37,085	3.5
Working Capital	122,899	—

RATIOS	UQ	MED	LQ
SOLVENCY			
Quick Ratio (times)	2.0	0.9	0.5
Current Ratio (times)	3.0	1.6	1.0
Curr Liab To Nw (%)	18.1	48.2	116.9
Curr Liab To Inv (%)	71.2	115.6	238.2
Total Liab To Nw (%)	46.9	124.4	217.9
Fixed Assets To Nw (%)	34.1	85.1	160.8
EFFICIENCY			
Coll Period (days)	15.1	28.5	44.9
Sales To Inv (times)	29.4	11.2	4.0
Assets To Sales (%)	37.5	63.0	155.3
Sales To Nwc (times)	13.9	5.6	3.5
Acct Pay To Sales (%)	1.2	2.1	4.9
PROFITABILITY			
Return On Sales (%)	7.6	2.4	(0.5)
Return On Assets (%)	7.4	3.4	(0.3)
Return On Nw (%)	20.6	7.7	(0.2)

SIC 44 WATER TRANSPORTATION — CENTRAL — 1995 (90 Establishments)

	$	%
Cash	127,071	8.4
Accounts Receivable	199,684	13.2
Notes Receivable	9,077	0.6
Inventory	158,839	10.5
Other Current	69,587	4.6
Total Current	**564,258**	**37.3**
Fixed Assets	797,222	52.7
Other Non-current	151,276	10.0
Total Assets	**1,512,755**	**100.0**
Accounts Payable	105,893	7.0
Bank Loans	3,026	0.2
Notes Payable	75,638	5.0
Other Current	161,865	10.7
Total Current	**346,421**	**22.9**
Other Long Term	547,617	36.2
Deferred Credits	13,615	0.9
Net Worth	605,102	40.0
Total Liab & Net Worth	**1,512,755**	**100.0**
Net Sales	1,929,498	100.0
Gross Profit	814,248	42.2
Net Profit After Tax	92,616	4.8
Working Capital	217,837	—

RATIOS	UQ	MED	LQ
SOLVENCY			
Quick Ratio (times)	2.2	1.1	0.4
Current Ratio (times)	2.9	1.7	1.1
Curr Liab To Nw (%)	13.2	51.2	103.7
Curr Liab To Inv (%)	83.6	159.1	323.3
Total Liab To Nw (%)	46.3	127.0	297.5
Fixed Assets To Nw (%)	56.3	108.2	181.7
EFFICIENCY			
Coll Period (days)	10.3	38.3	62.5
Sales To Inv (times)	33.0	18.9	8.6
Assets To Sales (%)	72.7	120.2	152.2
Sales To Nwc (times)	12.9	7.0	4.3
Acct Pay To Sales (%)	1.8	3.3	8.7
PROFITABILITY			
Return On Sales (%)	8.9	5.7	2.1
Return On Assets (%)	13.1	4.5	2.0
Return On Nw (%)	27.5	12.2	4.4

SIC 44 WATER TRANSPORTATION — SOUTH — 1995 (180 Establishments)

	$	%
Cash	214,363	11.1
Accounts Receivable	370,790	19.2
Notes Receivable	5,794	0.3
Inventory	104,285	5.4
Other Current	144,840	7.5
Total Current	**840,072**	**43.5**
Fixed Assets	847,796	43.9
Other Non-current	243,331	12.6
Total Assets	**1,931,199**	**100.0**
Accounts Payable	171,877	8.9
Bank Loans	—	—
Notes Payable	63,730	3.3
Other Current	254,918	13.2
Total Current	**490,525**	**25.4**
Other Long Term	492,456	25.5
Deferred Credits	19,312	1.0
Net Worth	928,907	48.1
Total Liab & Net Worth	**1,931,199**	**100.0**
Net Sales	3,131,767	100.0
Gross Profit	1,374,846	43.9
Net Profit After Tax	184,774	5.9
Working Capital	349,547	—

RATIOS	UQ	MED	LQ
SOLVENCY			
Quick Ratio (times)	2.7	1.1	0.4
Current Ratio (times)	3.3	1.8	1.0
Curr Liab To Nw (%)	13.8	35.4	101.7
Curr Liab To Inv (%)	93.2	207.1	380.0
Total Liab To Nw (%)	41.6	91.4	222.0
Fixed Assets To Nw (%)	43.0	90.9	152.1
EFFICIENCY			
Coll Period (days)	14.1	43.8	66.6
Sales To Inv (times)	74.5	34.7	15.2
Assets To Sales (%)	49.5	98.4	173.0
Sales To Nwc (times)	15.2	7.4	3.6
Acct Pay To Sales (%)	2.5	4.4	9.5
PROFITABILITY			
Return On Sales (%)	11.7	5.5	1.3
Return On Assets (%)	15.8	4.7	1.4
Return On Nw (%)	30.1	11.3	4.0

SIC 44 WATER TRANSPORTATION — WEST — 1995 (62 Establishments)

	$	%
Cash	880,504	14.3
Accounts Receivable	523,377	8.5
Notes Receivable	—	—
Inventory	240,138	3.9
Other Current	338,656	5.5
Total Current	**1,982,674**	**32.2**
Fixed Assets	3,374,240	54.8
Other Non-current	800,458	13.0
Total Assets	**6,157,373**	**100.0**
Accounts Payable	443,331	7.2
Bank Loans	30,787	0.5
Notes Payable	147,777	2.4
Other Current	671,154	10.9
Total Current	**1,293,048**	**21.0**
Other Long Term	1,502,399	24.4
Deferred Credits	240,138	3.9
Net Worth	3,121,788	50.7
Total Liab & Net Worth	**6,157,373**	**100.0**
Net Sales	4,524,333	100.0
Gross Profit	1,655,906	36.6
Net Profit After Tax	158,352	3.5
Working Capital	689,626	—

RATIOS	UQ	MED	LQ
SOLVENCY			
Quick Ratio (times)	3.2	1.4	0.7
Current Ratio (times)	4.4	1.8	1.2
Curr Liab To Nw (%)	9.9	23.9	63.0
Curr Liab To Inv (%)	132.4	269.7	535.8
Total Liab To Nw (%)	25.7	91.6	200.0
Fixed Assets To Nw (%)	86.2	129.3	184.0
EFFICIENCY			
Coll Period (days)	9.7	36.5	52.8
Sales To Inv (times)	69.9	26.9	11.0
Assets To Sales (%)	55.6	92.9	198.8
Sales To Nwc (times)	11.5	6.8	2.6
Acct Pay To Sales (%)	1.8	4.0	8.9
PROFITABILITY			
Return On Sales (%)	8.7	4.4	(0.2)
Return On Assets (%)	5.5	2.3	(0.8)
Return On Nw (%)	16.3	7.7	0.8

SIC 44 WATER TRANSPORTATION — INDUSTRY ASSETS

	UNDER $100,000 (31 Establishments) $	%	$100,000 - $250,000 (43 Establishments) $	%	$250,000 - $500,000 (69 Establishments) $	%	$500,000 - $1,000,000 (71 Establishments) $	%
Cash	16,572	35.3	27,315	15.9	53,049	15.1	85,052	11.9
Accounts Receivable	7,276	15.5	27,658	16.1	44,618	12.7	124,362	17.4
Notes Receivable	—	—	2,405	1.4	3,865	1.1	6,433	0.9
Inventory	5,352	11.4	23,879	13.9	60,779	17.3	110,782	15.5
Other Current	2,394	5.1	11,166	6.5	18,269	5.2	45,028	6.3
Total Current	**31,594**	**67.3**	**92,423**	**53.8**	**180,579**	**51.4**	**371,656**	**52.0**
Fixed Assets	13,849	29.5	69,575	40.5	145,447	41.4	283,031	39.6
Other Non-current	1,502	3.2	9,792	5.7	25,295	7.2	60,037	8.4
Total Assets	**46,945**	**100.0**	**171,790**	**100.0**	**351,321**	**100.0**	**714,724**	**100.0**
Accounts Payable	3,615	7.7	14,430	8.4	27,403	7.8	71,472	10.0
Bank Loans	—	—	515	0.3	2,108	0.6	715	0.1
Notes Payable	2,113	4.5	7,902	4.6	12,999	3.7	50,745	7.1
Other Current	6,338	13.5	38,825	22.6	50,590	14.4	127,936	17.9
Total Current	**12,065**	**25.7**	**61,673**	**35.9**	**93,100**	**26.5**	**250,868**	**35.1**
Other Long Term	6,150	13.1	37,794	22.0	79,047	22.5	190,117	26.6
Deferred Credits	—	—	344	0.2	—	—	2,144	0.3
Net Worth	28,730	61.2	71,980	41.9	179,174	51.0	271,595	38.0
Total Liab & Net Worth	**46,945**	**100.0**	**171,790**	**100.0**	**351,321**	**100.0**	**714,724**	**100.0**
Net Sales	229,134	100.0	524,406	100.0	775,113	100.0	1,148,238	100.0
Gross Profit	107,693	47.0	283,704	54.1	354,227	45.7	538,524	46.9
Net Profit After Tax	12,373	5.4	8,915	1.7	31,005	4.0	55,115	4.8
Working Capital	19,529	—	30,750	—	87,479	—	120,788	—

RATIOS	UQ	MED	LQ	UQ	MED	LQ	UQ	MED	LQ	UQ	MED	LQ
SOLVENCY												
Quick Ratio (times)	6.8	2.5	1.1	2.4	1.1	0.4	6.0	1.2	0.3	1.5	0.8	0.3
Current Ratio (times)	7.0	3.5	1.3	4.0	1.6	1.0	8.3	2.3	1.0	2.5	1.5	1.2
Curr Liab To Nw (%)	9.5	27.9	51.5	16.1	71.5	102.4	9.4	28.3	171.5	29.1	69.0	160.8
Curr Liab To Inv (%)	45.8	93.0	339.7	19.6	100.6	171.8	36.6	93.2	207.1	101.3	124.8	267.9
Total Liab To Nw (%)	28.7	48.2	136.5	22.7	81.0	247.5	17.8	95.4	237.8	42.9	129.8	258.6
Fixed Assets To Nw (%)	32.3	46.9	76.2	29.1	71.0	147.5	34.4	61.9	136.6	45.3	88.5	140.8
EFFICIENCY												
Coll Period (days)	22.0	30.0	36.9	11.5	21.2	32.9	8.4	17.5	47.0	7.4	29.6	47.1
Sales To Inv (times)	47.6	27.8	27.0	28.3	13.2	4.7	18.1	11.3	6.0	12.9	9.9	3.6
Assets To Sales (%)	13.4	19.0	41.9	21.0	27.5	37.4	29.5	56.9	88.3	46.1	62.5	85.3
Sales To Nwc (times)	55.7	42.6	8.2	20.0	13.6	4.9	8.4	6.0	3.0	13.6	8.1	5.1
Acct Pay To Sales (%)	1.0	1.0	2.4	1.4	3.8	4.9	1.2	2.0	4.9	1.7	2.9	4.1
PROFITABILITY												
Return On Sales (%)	6.0	(0.1)	(1.4)	4.2	0.4	(1.5)	8.4	2.7	0.2	8.3	3.1	1.7
Return On Assets (%)	24.0	(0.2)	(6.4)	13.3	1.4	(5.0)	17.0	5.6	0.6	9.9	5.7	2.6
Return On Nw (%)	58.1	1.6	(3.1)	34.0	2.6	(14.3)	32.6	17.9	2.0	31.5	19.2	5.7

SIC 44 WATER TRANSPORTATION — INDUSTRY ASSETS — 1995

	$1,000,000–$5,000,000 (116 Establishments) $	%	$5,000,000–$25,000,000 (52 Establishments) $	%	$25,000,000–$50,000,000 (14 Establishments) $	%	OVER $50,000,000 (68 Establishments) $	%
Cash	183,563	8.9	1,026,859	9.9	5,187,807	12.7	19,427,148	5.4
Accounts Receivable	340,313	16.5	1,804,782	17.4	3,145,363	7.7	34,896,914	9.7
Notes Receivable	4,125	0.2						
Inventory	169,125	8.2	103,723	1.0	81,698	0.2	5,396,430	1.5
Other Current	144,375	7.0	653,456	6.3	2,532,630	6.2	18,707,624	5.2
Total Current	**841,500**	**40.8**	**3,588,820**	**34.6**	**10,947,499**	**26.8**	**78,428,116**	**21.8**
Fixed Assets	954,938	46.3	5,155,040	49.7	22,303,486	54.6	219,454,820	61.0
Other Non-current	266,063	12.9	1,628,453	15.7	7,597,891	18.6	61,879,064	17.2
Total Assets	**2,062,500**	**100.0**	**10,372,313**	**100.0**	**40,848,876**	**100.0**	**359,762,000**	**100.0**
Accounts Payable	171,188	8.3	715,690	6.9	2,573,479	6.3	14,750,242	4.1
Bank Loans	2,063	0.1		0.1			359,762	0.1
Notes Payable	63,938	3.1	290,425	2.8	1,797,351	4.4	359,762	0.1
Other Current	286,688	13.9	1,400,262	13.5	5,228,656	12.8	34,896,914	9.7
Total Current	**523,875**	**25.4**	**2,406,377**	**23.2**	**9,599,486**	**23.5**	**50,366,680**	**14.0**
Other Long Term	602,250	29.2	1,949,995	18.8	11,355,988	27.8	150,380,516	41.8
Deferred Credits	10,313	0.5	145,212	1.4	898,675	2.2	21,585,720	6.0
Net Worth	926,063	44.9	5,870,729	56.6	18,994,727	46.5	137,429,084	38.2
Total Liab & Net Worth	**2,062,500**	**100.0**	**10,372,313**	**100.0**	**40,848,876**	**100.0**	**359,762,000**	**100.0**
Net Sales	2,091,558	100.0	8,357,288	100.0	25,864,833	100.0	209,599,999	100.0
Gross Profit	939,110	44.9	3,067,125	36.7	3,258,969	12.6	51,352,000	24.5
Net Profit After Tax	92,029	4.4	534,866	6.4	1,448,431	5.6	10,899,200	5.2
Working Capital	317,625	—	1,182,443	—	1,348,013	—	28,061,436	—

RATIOS

	UQ	MED	LQ	UQ	MED	LQ	UQ	MED	LQ	UQ	MED	LQ
SOLVENCY												
Quick Ratio (times)	2.4	1.1	0.5	2.7	1.5	0.5	2.7	1.0	0.6	1.8	1.0	0.4
Current Ratio (times)	3.1	1.8	1.0	3.2	1.7	1.0	3.0	1.1	1.0	2.3	1.6	1.0
Curr Liab To Nw (%)	16.1	46.6	109.9	7.9	28.0	55.1	22.2	49.2	68.8	14.0	33.1	56.3
Curr Liab To Inv (%)	99.4	149.2	332.1	150.1	287.8	303.5	978.8	978.8	978.8	300.8	458.9	716.7
Total Liab To Nw (%)	43.0	105.0	230.5	30.0	73.1	125.0	78.3	139.0	159.2	85.1	173.6	232.0
Fixed Assets To Nw (%)	40.8	93.4	162.6	50.5	88.5	132.8	125.4	159.9	177.0	131.7	173.7	211.0
EFFICIENCY												
Coll Period (days)	12.1	40.5	79.8	22.1	40.9	59.9	31.4	38.3	50.7	30.3	46.0	55.9
Sales To Inv (times)	80.4	24.6	7.3	160.8	72.4	33.2	43.8	43.8	43.8	77.3	36.3	19.1
Assets To Sales (%)	61.7	98.4	150.6	95.8	135.9	227.3	88.5	185.7	522.4	144.2	176.3	256.8
Sales To Nwc (times)	12.0	5.1	3.6	15.5	6.7	1.6	37.0	5.8	1.8	11.5	5.2	2.9
Acct Pay To Sales (%)	1.0	2.6	6.8	2.2	4.5	10.0	3.3	4.2	6.4	3.5	4.9	10.0
PROFITABILITY												
Return On Sales (%)	10.4	4.4	1.2	14.4	8.5	2.8	7.8	4.6	1.2	10.3	5.6	0.9
Return On Assets (%)	10.8	4.2	0.8	8.0	4.7	2.5	6.2	1.8	0.5	4.6	2.6	1.0
Return On Nw (%)	26.2	8.3	1.6	18.8	9.4	4.4	10.6	4.6	1.5	11.6	7.5	3.5

	SIC 4412 DPSEA FRGN TRNS FRT (NO BREAKDOWN) 1995 (45 Establishments)		SIC 4424 DP SEA DOM TRNS FRT (NO BREAKDOWN) 1995 (16 Establishments)		SIC 4449 WTR TRANS FRHT,NEC (NO BREAKDOWN) 1995 (26 Establishments)		SIC 4482 FERRIES (NO BREAKDOWN) 1995 (15 Establishments)	
	$	%	$	%	$	%	$	%
Cash	4,082,176	19.4	43,430,067	17.1	603,747	11.9	586,275	14.3
Accounts Receivable	5,071,156	24.1	35,302,803	13.9	1,019,774	20.1	102,496	2.5
Notes Receivable	63,126	0.3	253,977	0.1	86,250	1.7	—	—
Inventory	147,295	0.7	3,301,701	1.3	81,176	1.6	49,198	1.2
Other Current	2,314,636	11.0	12,952,827	5.1	441,395	8.7	245,990	6.0
Total Current	**11,678,389**	**55.5**	**95,241,375**	**37.5**	**2,232,340**	**44.0**	**983,958**	**24.0**
Fixed Assets	7,259,539	34.5	135,369,741	53.3	2,551,971	50.3	2,414,798	58.9
Other Non-current	2,104,214	10.0	23,365,884	9.2	289,190	5.7	701,070	17.1
Total Assets	**21,042,142**	**100.0**	**253,977,000**	**100.0**	**5,073,500**	**100.0**	**4,099,826**	**100.0**
Accounts Payable	3,492,996	16.6	17,016,459	6.7	507,350	10.0	200,891	4.9
Bank Loans	21,042	0.1	—	—	25,368	0.5	—	—
Notes Payable	589,180	2.8	10,921,011	4.3	71,029	1.4	180,392	4.4
Other Current	2,861,731	13.6	27,175,539	10.7	451,542	8.9	569,876	13.9
Total Current	**6,964,949**	**33.1**	**55,113,009**	**21.7**	**1,055,288**	**20.8**	**951,160**	**23.2**
Other Long Term	3,998,007	19.0	69,589,698	27.4	1,410,433	27.8	1,033,156	25.2
Deferred Credits	715,433	3.4	22,603,953	8.9	136,985	2.7	36,898	0.9
Net Worth	9,363,753	44.5	106,670,340	42.0	2,470,795	48.7	2,078,612	50.7
Total Liab & Net Worth	**21,042,142**	**100.0**	**253,977,000**	**100.0**	**5,073,500**	**100.0**	**4,099,826**	**100.0**
Net Sales	25,864,833	100.0	124,846,000	100.0	18,627,379	100.0	2,212,243	100.0
Gross Profit	10,578,717	40.9	44,195,484	35.4	4,023,514	21.6	1,187,974	53.7
Net Profit After Tax	879,404	3.4	8,364,682	6.7	968,624	5.2	192,465	8.7
Working Capital	4,713,440	—	40,128,366	—	1,177,052	—	32,798	—

RATIOS	UQ	MED	LQ	UQ	MED	LQ	UQ	MED	LQ	UQ	MED	LQ
SOLVENCY												
Quick Ratio (times)	1.9	1.0	0.8	1.8	1.4	1.1	2.6	1.8	1.1	1.9	1.1	0.5
Current Ratio (times)	2.7	1.4	1.1	1.9	1.6	1.4	3.1	2.5	1.5	2.8	1.5	0.9
Curr Liab To Nw (%)	32.1	55.4	97.8	33.2	52.0	57.8	13.7	30.3	50.2	8.1	13.1	53.6
Curr Liab To Inv (%)	506.0	912.7	945.7	364.7	749.7	781.3	174.7	341.9	426.6	634.5	746.9	918.7
Total Liab To Nw (%)	58.7	156.3	246.9	123.3	180.6	205.5	49.2	133.5	200.6	14.6	60.8	113.1
Fixed Assets To Nw (%)	22.6	151.0	177.9	118.9	152.6	204.7	38.5	121.8	190.9	87.7	105.0	164.5
EFFICIENCY												
Coll Period (days)	28.5	41.6	53.7	47.5	51.7	54.5	42.5	60.5	96.9	3.7	5.8	11.3
Sales To Inv (times)	76.4	72.0	38.2	39.4	34.9	18.5	52.4	32.8	31.1	152.9	46.1	37.5
Assets To Sales (%)	25.6	101.1	198.0	97.4	139.4	198.3	43.3	117.4	139.4	91.3	164.9	181.6
Sales To Nwc (times)	32.7	16.9	4.1	10.7	7.8	4.6	11.2	6.0	4.7	9.3	5.1	4.6
Acct Pay To Sales (%)	2.3	4.4	12.5	1.7	3.1	6.5	1.7	3.7	8.9	1.0	1.1	1.2
PROFITABILITY												
Return On Sales (%)	6.7	3.2	0.4	7.2	5.4	2.2	9.3	6.1	4.1	13.7	6.3	3.5
Return On Assets (%)	13.2	6.2	2.8	5.3	2.6	2.2	16.7	4.9	3.9	8.6	5.0	2.1
Return On Nw (%)	34.1	15.1	6.6	12.6	8.0	5.7	32.7	20.0	10.8	11.5	8.2	2.9

	SIC 4489 WTR PASS TRANS, NEC (NO BREAKDOWN) 1995 (24 Establishments) $	%	SIC 4491 MARINE CARGO HNDLNG (NO BREAKDOWN) 1995 (50 Establishments) $	%	SIC 4491 MARINE CARGO HNDLNG INDUSTRY ASSETS $1,000,000 - $5,000,000 1995 (10 Establishments) $	%	SIC 4491 MARINE CARGO HNDLNG INDUSTRY ASSETS $5,000,000-$25,000,000 1995 (13 Establishments) $	%
Cash	307,244	18.5	568,825	9.4	250,619	6.8	526,403	6.4
Accounts Receivable	64,770	3.9	1,089,239	18.0	1,072,500	29.1	1,719,036	20.9
Notes Receivable	1,661	0.1	24,205	0.4	—	—	8,225	0.1
Inventory	41,519	2.5	90,770	1.5	228,505	6.2	16,450	0.2
Other Current	147,809	8.9	417,542	6.9	103,196	2.8	222,076	2.7
Total Current	**563,004**	**33.9**	**2,190,580**	**36.2**	**1,654,820**	**44.9**	**2,492,191**	**30.3**
Fixed Assets	815,442	49.1	2,668,635	44.1	1,326,804	36.0	3,890,451	47.3
Other Non-current	282,332	17.0	1,192,111	19.7	703,943	19.1	1,842,412	22.4
Total Assets	**1,660,778**	**100.0**	**6,051,327**	**100.0**	**3,685,567**	**100.0**	**8,225,054**	**100.0**
Accounts Payable	91,343	5.5	405,439	6.7	571,263	15.5	509,953	6.2
Bank Loans	—	—	6,051	0.1	—	—	—	—
Notes Payable	4,982	0.3	102,873	1.7	—	—	—	—
Other Current	390,283	23.5	508,311	8.4	416,469	11.3	756,705	9.2
Total Current	**486,608**	**29.3**	**1,022,674**	**16.9**	**987,732**	**26.8**	**1,266,658**	**15.4**
Other Long Term	335,477	20.2	1,597,550	26.4	692,887	18.8	2,089,164	25.4
Deferred Credits	39,859	2.4	48,411	0.8	—	—	24,675	0.3
Net Worth	798,834	48.1	3,382,692	55.9	2,004,948	54.4	4,844,557	58.9
Total Liab & Net Worth	**1,660,778**	**100.0**	**6,051,327**	**100.0**	**3,685,567**	**100.0**	**8,225,054**	**100.0**
Net Sales	1,322,321	100.0	3,496,719	100.0	3,001,696	100.0	6,011,589	100.0
Gross Profit	576,532	43.6	1,657,445	47.4	1,686,953	56.2	1,641,164	27.3
Net Profit After Tax	51,571	3.9	311,208	8.9	255,144	8.5	336,649	5.6
Working Capital	76,396	—	1,167,906	—	667,088	—	1,225,533	—

RATIOS	4489 UQ	MED	LQ	4491 (all) UQ	MED	LQ	4491 1–5M UQ	MED	LQ	4491 5–25M UQ	MED	LQ
SOLVENCY												
Quick Ratio (times)	2.6	0.7	0.2	2.8	1.6	0.9	1.3	1.1	0.5	1.9	1.7	1.4
Current Ratio (times)	3.2	1.4	0.4	3.9	2.1	1.6	1.8	1.5	1.0	2.5	1.8	1.6
Curr Liab To Nw (%)	13.9	36.8	104.7	6.5	21.4	60.9	7.6	25.7	30.8	6.8	23.0	48.8
Curr Liab To Inv (%)	126.7	587.3	881.3	125.4	353.3	536.1	115.1	170.2	242.8	—	—	—
Total Liab To Nw (%)	33.3	81.5	165.3	26.2	83.9	160.1	26.7	83.4	139.7	28.8	73.1	159.6
Fixed Assets To Nw (%)	24.2	83.2	142.2	45.6	85.8	132.2	33.8	77.9	106.2	45.3	72.4	132.2
EFFICIENCY												
Coll Period (days)	2.5	5.3	10.7	31.2	40.5	55.7	37.6	40.9	46.0	40.5	47.5	56.6
Sales To Inv (times)	135.9	72.4	33.6	158.0	85.1	25.3	16.8	11.4	11.0	235.7	145.6	130.8
Assets To Sales (%)	33.7	63.0	108.7	53.0	142.6	436.1	69.6	86.6	122.6	137.0	193.7	473.1
Sales To Nwc (times)	18.5	5.0	3.8	9.4	5.0	2.0	4.8	4.5	4.1	11.8	7.3	3.1
Acct Pay To Sales (%)	1.8	4.2	7.6	2.4	4.3	9.7	1.4	2.5	3.2	3.8	4.4	6.4
PROFITABILITY												
Return On Sales (%)	9.8	5.1	0.1	20.6	8.2	1.4	5.0	3.8	2.1	12.9	9.3	4.1
Return On Assets (%)	20.9	7.5	0.4	6.6	3.4	1.0	4.0	3.3	2.0	4.2	3.0	1.4
Return On Nw (%)	48.7	18.6	1.8	20.9	7.0	1.2	11.8	9.9	4.6	6.7	5.3	1.8

	SIC 4492 TOWING TUGBOAT SVCE (NO BREAKDOWN) 1995 (52 Establishments) $	%	SIC 4492 TOWING TUGBOAT SVCE INDUSTRY ASSETS $1,000,000 - $5,000,000 1995 (16 Establishments) $	%	SIC 4493 MARINAS (NO BREAKDOWN) 1995 (174 Establishments) $	%	SIC 4493 MARINAS INDUSTRY ASSETS UNDER $100,000 1995 (15 Establishments) $	%
Cash	245,769	10.5	195,751	7.4	68,081	10.7	19,866	29.8
Accounts Receivable	505,583	21.6	738,035	27.9	60,445	9.5	6,800	10.2
Notes Receivable	11,703	0.5	15,872	0.6	636	0.1	—	—
Inventory	39,791	1.7	23,808	0.9	145,069	22.8	14,533	21.8
Other Current	154,484	6.6	216,913	8.2	17,179	2.7	—	—
Total Current	**957,330**	**40.9**	**1,190,379**	**45.0**	**291,411**	**45.8**	**41,199**	**61.8**
Fixed Assets	1,032,231	44.1	1,007,854	38.1	292,047	45.9	24,266	36.4
Other Non-current	351,099	15.0	447,053	16.9	52,810	8.3	1,200	1.8
Total Assets	**2,340,660**	**100.0**	**2,645,286**	**100.0**	**636,268**	**100.0**	**66,665**	**100.0**
Accounts Payable	196,615	8.4	216,913	8.2	30,541	4.8	1,400	2.1
Bank Loans	—	—	—	—	1,273	0.2	—	—
Notes Payable	121,714	5.2	113,747	4.3	32,450	5.1	1,733	2.6
Other Current	339,396	14.5	314,789	11.9	112,619	17.7	13,066	19.6
Total Current	**657,725**	**28.1**	**645,450**	**24.4**	**176,883**	**27.8**	**16,200**	**24.3**
Other Long Term	575,802	24.6	775,069	29.3	192,153	30.2	10,200	15.3
Deferred Credits	9,363	0.4	—	—	1,909	0.3	—	—
Net Worth	1,097,770	46.9	1,224,767	46.3	265,324	41.7	40,266	60.4
Total Liab & Net Worth	**2,340,660**	**100.0**	**2,645,286**	**100.0**	**636,268**	**100.0**	**66,665**	**100.0**
Net Sales	4,140,073	100.0	4,633,535	100.0	891,507	100.0	194,165	100.0
Gross Profit	1,709,850	41.3	1,283,489	27.7	423,466	47.5	111,451	57.4
Net Profit After Tax	202,864	4.9	291,913	6.3	24,071	2.7	15,339	7.9
Working Capital	299,605	—	544,929	—	114,528	—	24,999	—

RATIOS	UQ	MED	LQ	UQ	MED	LQ	UQ	MED	LQ	UQ	MED	LQ
SOLVENCY												
Quick Ratio (times)	2.9	1.3	0.5	3.1	1.7	0.9	2.3	0.8	0.2	2.7	2.0	0.9
Current Ratio (times)	3.1	2.0	1.0	3.9	2.2	1.4	3.8	1.6	1.1	4.7	3.7	1.5
Curr Liab To Nw (%)	13.6	37.9	115.6	18.8	61.0	134.4	12.9	44.9	124.4	19.8	35.1	44.9
Curr Liab To Inv (%)	248.5	274.1	327.9	344.0	344.0	344.0	69.5	114.4	223.3	41.4	93.0	306.7
Total Liab To Nw (%)	49.5	88.6	185.3	54.8	100.5	191.7	38.9	110.8	263.0	35.4	54.3	136.5
Fixed Assets To Nw (%)	65.7	99.5	167.6	65.7	121.3	188.5	46.8	84.5	145.7	36.2	56.8	77.0
EFFICIENCY												
Coll Period (days)	31.8	58.4	86.2	47.9	69.4	85.2	8.0	17.9	36.1	17.8	31.8	42.0
Sales To Inv (times)	54.9	15.8	11.8	114.3	106.7	99.2	20.8	10.6	4.0	47.6	27.8	27.0
Assets To Sales (%)	49.3	63.8	132.3	52.1	58.5	96.8	39.2	66.3	122.4	16.5	20.9	41.9
Sales To Nwc (times)	14.3	6.1	3.5	9.3	4.5	3.5	14.2	7.0	4.4	45.4	29.3	10.0
Acct Pay To Sales (%)	3.0	4.5	9.2	1.3	3.2	7.8	1.1	2.0	3.4	1.0	1.0	1.7
PROFITABILITY												
Return On Sales (%)	9.3	6.0	0.3	10.6	7.3	5.1	6.4	2.0	(0.8)	11.9	2.8	(0.5)
Return On Assets (%)	18.2	4.7	1.1	24.6	18.2	5.1	7.3	2.5	(1.2)	24.0	1.0	(1.7)
Return On Nw (%)	29.2	7.3	3.7	60.4	30.8	8.3	24.3	7.5	(1.6)	55.0	3.3	(2.8)

SIC 4493 MARINAS — INDUSTRY ASSETS — 1995

	$100,000 - $250,000 (17 Establishments)		$250,000 - $500,000 (45 Establishments)		$500,000 - $1,000,000 (46 Establishments)		$1,000,000 - $5,000,000 (45 Establishments)	
	$	%	$	%	$	%	$	%
Cash	27,030	15.2	42,173	11.7	64,787	9.1	84,688	4.9
Accounts Receivable	21,161	11.9	45,417	12.6	58,380	8.2	120,982	7.0
Notes Receivable	—	—	721	0.2	1,424	0.2	1,728	0.1
Inventory	54,237	30.5	91,556	25.4	179,411	25.2	316,282	18.3
Other Current	7,291	4.1	6,128	1.7	18,511	2.6	65,676	3.8
Total Current	**109,719**	**61.7**	**185,995**	**51.6**	**322,512**	**45.3**	**589,357**	**34.1**
Fixed Assets	66,329	37.3	154,275	42.8	312,545	43.9	936,749	54.2
Other Non-current	1,778	1.0	20,185	5.6	76,890	10.8	202,213	11.7
Total Assets	**177,826**	**100.0**	**360,455**	**100.0**	**711,947**	**100.0**	**1,728,319**	**100.0**
Accounts Payable	10,136	5.7	23,069	6.4	50,548	7.1	32,838	1.9
Bank Loans	—	—	2,163	0.6	—	—	3,457	0.2
Notes Payable	3,734	2.1	19,825	5.5	53,396	7.5	81,231	4.7
Other Current	51,214	28.8	47,580	13.2	136,694	19.2	281,716	16.3
Total Current	**65,084**	**36.6**	**92,637**	**25.7**	**240,638**	**33.8**	**399,242**	**23.1**
Other Long Term	34,854	19.6	106,334	29.5	205,041	28.8	686,143	39.7
Deferred Credits	1,067	0.6	—	—	1,424	0.2	13,827	0.8
Net Worth	76,821	43.2	161,484	44.8	264,844	37.2	629,108	36.4
Total Liab & Net Worth	**177,826**	**100.0**	**360,455**	**100.0**	**711,947**	**100.0**	**1,728,319**	**100.0**
Net Sales	420,756	100.0	787,765	100.0	1,108,476	100.0	1,452,875	100.0
Gross Profit	243,197	57.8	345,829	43.9	506,574	45.7	678,493	46.7
Net Profit After Tax	8,415	2.0	22,845	2.9	36,580	3.3	14,529	1.0
Working Capital	44,635	—	93,358	—	81,874	—	190,115	—

RATIOS	UQ	MED	LQ	UQ	MED	LQ	UQ	MED	LQ	UQ	MED	LQ
SOLVENCY												
Quick Ratio (times)	4.5	1.2	0.4	5.4	1.2	0.3	1.1	0.5	0.2	1.9	0.5	0.2
Current Ratio (times)	12.3	1.4	1.1	8.3	2.1	1.2	2.3	1.4	0.9	3.0	1.6	1.0
Curr Liab To Nw (%)	2.6	11.7	79.3	11.0	55.2	172.7	29.9	72.5	185.2	16.7	44.9	103.7
Curr Liab To Inv (%)	17.9	88.2	148.4	45.2	93.5	213.6	101.0	119.0	245.1	95.8	122.4	223.2
Total Liab To Nw (%)	2.8	43.9	79.3	42.2	104.6	302.4	39.2	144.8	273.5	70.3	123.5	343.5
Fixed Assets To Nw (%)	46.8	69.6	87.6	34.9	65.7	137.0	57.7	94.9	155.4	78.2	109.3	174.0
EFFICIENCY												
Coll Period (days)	11.0	16.4	25.2	8.0	14.2	29.9	4.7	22.3	33.6	11.3	17.2	36.1
Sales To Inv (times)	28.5	8.2	4.3	15.3	8.4	5.1	12.9	9.9	3.6	24.6	9.9	3.5
Assets To Sales (%)	28.4	35.6	39.2	30.5	56.9	84.3	49.2	65.0	87.7	94.3	131.4	239.8
Sales To Nwc (times)	13.7	7.0	4.1	8.5	6.3	5.0	13.1	9.6	5.5	19.1	5.6	4.0
Acct Pay To Sales (%)	1.0	1.6	3.4	1.2	1.8	3.2	1.8	2.7	3.4	1.0	1.8	2.2
PROFITABILITY												
Return On Sales (%)	3.7	(0.9)	(1.5)	6.1	2.5	0.3	7.2	2.5	1.5	4.4	0.7	(1.9)
Return On Assets (%)	10.7	(2.5)	(5.0)	11.2	4.5	0.6	7.3	4.0	2.5	4.1	0.6	(1.6)
Return On Nw (%)	16.6	(1.0)	(10.9)	32.4	15.0	1.0	27.4	16.4	5.6	7.1	1.1	(3.3)

	SIC 4499 WTR TRANS SRVC,NEC (NO BREAKDOWN) 1995 (45 Establishments) $	%	SIC 4499 WTR TRANS SRVC,NEC INDUSTRY ASSETS $1,000,000 - $5,000,000 1995 (16 Establishments) $	%	SIC 45 TRANS BY AIR (NO BREAKDOWN) 1995 (536 Establishments) $	%	SIC 45 TRANS BY AIR NORTHEAST 1995 (67 Establishments) $	%
Cash	108,404	10.0	215,669	10.4	216,839	12.3	155,333	12.9
Accounts Receivable	222,229	20.5	375,347	18.1	405,472	23.0	297,421	24.7
Notes Receivable	23,849	2.2	4,147	0.2	10,578	0.6	4,817	0.4
Inventory	9,756	0.9	18,664	0.9	163,952	9.3	104,760	8.7
Other Current	115,993	10.7	132,719	6.4	111,064	6.3	85,494	7.1
Total Current	**480,231**	**44.3**	**746,546**	**36.0**	**907,905**	**51.5**	**647,824**	**53.8**
Fixed Assets	542,022	50.0	1,155,073	55.7	678,725	38.5	382,915	31.8
Other Non-current	61,791	5.7	172,120	8.3	176,292	10.0	173,395	14.4
Total Assets	**1,084,044**	**100.0**	**2,073,740**	**100.0**	**1,762,922**	**100.0**	**1,204,134**	**100.0**
Accounts Payable	91,060	8.4	120,277	5.8	216,839	12.3	164,966	13.7
Bank Loans	3,252	0.3	—	—	3,526	0.2	1,204	0.1
Notes Payable	29,269	2.7	68,433	3.3	61,702	3.5	48,165	4.0
Other Current	145,262	13.4	221,890	10.7	273,253	15.5	181,824	15.1
Total Current	**268,843**	**24.8**	**410,601**	**19.8**	**555,320**	**31.5**	**396,160**	**32.9**
Other Long Term	294,860	27.2	443,780	21.4	398,420	22.6	290,196	24.1
Deferred Credits	6,504	0.6	2,074	0.1	17,629	1.0	14,450	1.2
Net Worth	513,837	47.4	1,217,285	58.7	791,552	44.9	503,328	41.8
Total Liab & Net Worth	**1,084,044**	**100.0**	**2,073,740**	**100.0**	**1,762,922**	**100.0**	**1,204,134**	**100.0**
Net Sales	1,229,744	100.0	1,525,973	100.0	2,936,437	100.0	3,878,458	100.0
Gross Profit	429,181	34.9	437,954	28.7	1,013,071	34.5	1,105,361	28.5
Net Profit After Tax	60,257	4.9	112,922	7.4	111,585	3.8	104,718	2.7
Working Capital	211,388	—	335,945	—	352,585	—	251,664	—

RATIOS	UQ	MED	LQ	UQ	MED	LQ	UQ	MED	LQ	UQ	MED	LQ
SOLVENCY												
Quick Ratio (times)	2.7	1.2	0.6	13.4	1.2	0.8	2.1	1.0	0.5	2.5	0.9	0.6
Current Ratio (times)	3.8	2.2	0.9	15.9	2.0	0.8	3.2	1.6	1.0	3.4	1.5	1.0
Curr Liab To Nw (%)	14.5	45.0	117.2	2.5	18.6	66.4	20.7	56.3	155.9	17.8	78.2	170.4
Curr Liab To Inv (%)	104.0	285.4	410.5	151.9	285.4	349.9	96.7	181.1	387.3	110.4	176.2	465.7
Total Liab To Nw (%)	18.1	65.5	276.8	9.8	45.0	188.6	42.1	112.4	266.9	21.3	120.9	324.5
Fixed Assets To Nw (%)	39.4	100.0	165.4	50.1	105.0	141.9	35.8	86.6	170.2	20.8	81.0	145.6
EFFICIENCY												
Coll Period (days)	44.9	59.9	93.4	49.3	73.4	99.3	19.9	30.7	52.8	27.1	39.6	70.4
Sales To Inv (times)	118.5	61.8	26.1	187.2	87.6	34.2	57.1	26.8	10.2	31.5	18.9	5.0
Assets To Sales (%)	64.1	98.8	167.2	96.0	113.1	150.0	27.8	49.6	89.1	33.1	46.9	66.8
Sales To Nwc (times)	10.6	2.7	1.6	3.3	1.9	1.6	20.1	7.8	4.4	12.3	6.8	5.0
Acct Pay To Sales (%)	2.3	4.7	7.4	1.1	2.2	14.0	2.8	5.2	8.2	4.2	6.7	12.7
PROFITABILITY												
Return On Sales (%)	16.0	4.3	1.4	16.6	10.9	2.1	8.4	3.0	0.5	5.9	1.1	0.2
Return On Assets (%)	9.2	5.2	1.8	10.0	4.9	2.5	12.2	4.3	0.8	19.5	3.9	0.4
Return On Nw (%)	27.7	14.3	5.6	25.5	17.0	7.7	33.0	11.7	2.9	38.5	13.0	0.8

SIC 45 TRANS BY AIR

	CENTRAL 1995 (136 Establishments) $	%	SOUTH 1995 (192 Establishments) $	%	WEST 1995 (141 Establishments) $	%	INDUSTRY ASSETS UNDER $100,000 1995 (51 Establishments) $	%
Cash	180,349	11.7	270,537	12.7	283,880	12.2	15,939	28.5
Accounts Receivable	328,327	21.3	528,292	24.8	504,935	21.7	11,633	20.8
Notes Receivable	9,249	0.6	17,042	0.8	13,961	0.6	1,286	2.3
Inventory	171,100	11.1	204,500	9.6	181,497	7.8	3,412	6.1
Other Current	66,282	4.3	136,334	6.4	174,517	7.5	3,020	5.4
Total Current	**755,307**	**49.0**	**1,156,705**	**54.3**	**1,158,791**	**49.8**	**35,291**	**63.1**
Fixed Assets	681,318	44.2	720,011	33.8	979,620	42.1	17,394	31.1
Other Non-current	104,818	6.8	253,495	11.9	188,478	8.1	3,244	5.8
Total Assets	**1,541,443**	**100.0**	**2,130,211**	**100.0**	**2,326,889**	**100.0**	**55,928**	**100.0**
Accounts Payable	184,973	12.0	276,927	13.0	255,958	11.0	5,201	9.3
Bank Loans	6,166	0.4	2,130	0.1	—	—	—	—
Notes Payable	57,033	3.7	85,208	4.0	55,845	2.4	2,237	4.0
Other Current	211,178	13.7	317,401	14.9	416,513	17.9	8,837	15.8
Total Current	**459,350**	**29.8**	**681,668**	**32.0**	**728,316**	**31.3**	**16,275**	**29.1**
Other Long Term	366,863	23.8	487,818	22.9	493,300	21.2	6,040	10.8
Deferred Credits	7,707	0.5	17,042	0.8	32,576	1.4	224	0.4
Net Worth	707,522	45.9	943,683	44.3	1,072,696	46.1	33,389	59.7
Total Liab & Net Worth	**1,541,443**	**100.0**	**2,130,211**	**100.0**	**2,326,889**	**100.0**	**55,928**	**100.0**
Net Sales	2,071,928	100.0	3,210,053	100.0	2,977,831	100.0	235,270	100.0
Gross Profit	830,843	40.1	1,014,377	31.6	1,158,376	38.9	106,813	45.4
Net Profit After Tax	31,079	1.5	144,452	4.5	145,914	4.9	17,175	7.3
Working Capital	295,957	—	475,037	—	430,475	—	19,016	—

RATIOS	UQ	MED	LQ	UQ	MED	LQ	UQ	MED	LQ	UQ	MED	LQ
SOLVENCY												
Quick Ratio (times)	2.0	0.9	0.5	2.0	0.9	0.6	2.1	1.1	0.5	6.6	2.2	0.8
Current Ratio (times)	3.2	1.4	0.9	3.0	1.7	1.0	3.2	1.7	1.0	8.3	2.4	1.2
Curr Liab To Nw (%)	11.7	49.5	172.1	22.0	63.3	152.2	22.1	54.8	132.2	10.0	24.3	115.7
Curr Liab To Inv (%)	86.7	175.8	305.6	88.1	155.3	418.7	130.9	199.5	356.6	75.9	131.2	370.0
Total Liab To Nw (%)	33.3	114.6	284.5	46.2	111.5	267.2	48.6	107.3	229.1	17.3	67.5	140.3
Fixed Assets To Nw (%)	43.3	100.1	170.5	35.6	85.8	158.1	47.2	83.2	195.1	18.1	70.4	93.8
EFFICIENCY												
Coll Period (days)	16.6	25.6	39.3	20.6	32.1	56.4	19.4	28.8	52.2	12.4	19.4	33.6
Sales To Inv (times)	51.6	34.4	14.3	67.7	27.2	7.6	51.2	24.0	15.3	23.5	20.1	13.1
Assets To Sales (%)	24.0	46.2	86.3	29.4	50.3	97.7	27.9	51.0	97.5	17.3	23.9	40.2
Sales To Nwc (times)	26.2	8.2	5.0	19.0	7.4	3.9	19.1	8.6	5.3	41.7	14.1	4.2
Acct Pay To Sales (%)	1.8	4.5	6.2	3.3	5.6	9.6	2.7	5.1	7.9	0.9	3.1	5.6
PROFITABILITY												
Return On Sales (%)	4.9	2.4	0.4	12.1	3.2	0.5	10.8	3.4	1.0	14.5	7.9	3.2
Return On Assets (%)	6.7	3.8	0.4	12.1	4.7	0.5	14.2	5.4	1.4	30.9	17.3	7.9
Return On Nw (%)	21.3	8.4	2.2	33.1	13.9	2.9	40.7	11.6	6.2	81.0	37.6	9.1

	SIC 45 TRANS BY AIR $100,000 - $250,000 1995 (64 Establishments) $	%	SIC 45 TRANS BY AIR $250,000 - $500,000 1995 (46 Establishments) $	%	SIC 45 TRANS BY AIR $500,000 - $1,000,000 1995 (70 Establishments) $	%	SIC 45 TRANS BY AIR $1,000,000 - $5,000,000 1995 (111 Establishments) $	%
Cash	32,119	18.9	44,570	11.4	73,267	10.5	212,723	9.9
Accounts Receivable	43,506	25.6	137,621	35.2	212,127	30.4	597,345	27.8
Notes Receivable	1,869	1.1	1,955	0.5	1,396	0.2	8,595	0.4
Inventory	19,034	11.2	45,352	11.6	90,014	12.9	223,467	10.4
Other Current	8,837	5.2	39,097	10.0	35,587	5.1	131,072	6.1
Total Current	**105,365**	**62.0**	**268,596**	**68.7**	**412,391**	**59.1**	**1,173,202**	**54.6**
Fixed Assets	55,062	32.4	110,644	28.3	234,456	33.6	797,176	37.1
Other Non-current	9,517	5.6	11,729	3.0	50,938	7.3	178,344	8.3
Total Assets	**169,944**	**100.0**	**390,969**	**100.0**	**697,785**	**100.0**	**2,148,722**	**100.0**
Accounts Payable	19,544	11.5	65,292	16.7	109,552	15.7	360,985	16.8
Bank Loans	—	—	1,955	0.5	—	—	4,297	0.2
Notes Payable	8,667	5.1	22,676	5.8	30,703	4.4	79,503	3.7
Other Current	22,942	13.5	52,781	13.5	92,108	13.2	315,862	14.7
Total Current	**51,153**	**30.1**	**142,704**	**36.5**	**232,362**	**33.3**	**760,648**	**35.4**
Other Long Term	29,740	17.5	85,231	21.8	173,748	24.9	552,222	25.7
Deferred Credits	—	—	—	—	2,791	0.4	17,190	0.8
Net Worth	89,051	52.4	163,034	41.7	288,883	41.4	818,663	38.1
Total Liab & Net Worth	**169,944**	**100.0**	**390,969**	**100.0**	**697,785**	**100.0**	**2,148,722**	**100.0**
Net Sales	574,849	100.0	1,341,241	100.0	2,234,475	100.0	4,227,927	100.0
Gross Profit	220,742	38.4	524,425	39.1	822,287	36.8	1,492,458	35.3
Net Profit After Tax	34,491	6.0	60,356	4.5	118,427	5.3	71,875	1.7
Working Capital	54,212	—	125,892	—	180,029	—	412,554	—

RATIOS	UQ	MED	LQ	UQ	MED	LQ	UQ	MED	LQ	UQ	MED	LQ
SOLVENCY												
Quick Ratio (times)	3.9	1.9	0.7	1.9	1.3	0.7	2.8	1.1	0.7	1.6	1.0	0.6
Current Ratio (times)	5.4	2.3	1.2	3.2	1.9	1.3	4.4	1.9	1.1	2.8	1.5	1.0
Curr Liab To Nw (%)	15.6	43.0	95.8	37.8	88.9	169.9	23.6	58.7	184.1	31.1	78.6	182.2
Curr Liab To Inv (%)	65.3	145.9	242.9	103.4	187.1	317.8	65.5	131.0	227.4	112.0	171.7	330.0
Total Liab To Nw (%)	27.0	56.9	163.2	58.1	137.6	255.9	31.1	99.2	339.6	78.1	152.7	310.1
Fixed Assets To Nw (%)	19.6	46.9	84.0	19.1	71.5	136.0	25.6	60.8	244.3	32.9	97.3	188.6
EFFICIENCY												
Coll Period (days)	20.9	38.3	55.7	21.5	33.6	47.1	21.5	31.4	57.4	22.6	41.3	73.3
Sales To Inv (times)	43.8	19.1	9.3	70.6	29.0	16.7	26.5	11.4	7.5	36.5	17.2	7.2
Assets To Sales (%)	18.5	27.6	44.0	20.8	26.3	38.7	23.0	32.3	47.3	32.2	53.0	79.9
Sales To Nwc (times)	25.2	10.3	5.8	24.2	11.9	6.5	21.0	7.9	5.2	17.1	7.3	4.9
Acct Pay To Sales (%)	2.0	5.1	6.9	2.4	4.0	8.3	2.4	4.0	6.8	2.8	5.7	7.7
PROFITABILITY												
Return On Sales (%)	12.3	4.3	2.0	9.9	3.3	0.5	10.9	4.9	1.7	8.3	3.0	0.8
Return On Assets (%)	27.7	8.6	3.7	34.8	14.0	4.0	21.3	10.5	3.5	11.9	6.3	2.4
Return On Nw (%)	54.4	23.3	8.8	67.4	36.5	10.3	62.3	20.3	7.3	40.0	16.7	6.7

Balance Sheet (Dollar amounts and percentages)

	SIC 45 TRANS BY AIR $5,000,000-$25,000,000 1995 (70 Establishments) $	%	SIC 45 TRANS BY AIR $25,000,000-$50,000,000 1995 (27 Establishments) $	%	SIC 45 TRANS BY AIR OVER $50,000,000 1995 (97 Establishments) $	%	SIC 4512 AIR TRANS,SCHEDULED (NO BREAKDOWN) 1995 (100 Establishments) $	%
Cash	1,160,611	9.4	1,807,165	4.9	36,023,327	8.9	9,698,180	14.5
Accounts Receivable	2,136,019	17.3	4,831,400	13.1	41,285,162	10.2	13,443,684	20.1
Notes Receivable	—	—	295,047	0.8	2,023,782	0.5	267,536	0.4
Inventory	1,234,693	10.0	2,028,450	5.5	17,404,529	4.3	3,946,156	5.9
Other Current	864,285	7.0	2,065,331	5.6	25,904,415	6.4	4,882,532	7.3
Total Current	**5,395,608**	**43.7**	**11,027,394**	**29.9**	**122,641,216**	**30.3**	**32,238,088**	**48.2**
Fixed Assets	5,605,506	45.4	19,141,195	51.9	198,735,435	49.1	26,486,064	39.6
Other Non-current	1,345,815	10.9	6,712,327	18.2	83,379,836	20.6	8,159,848	12.2
Total Assets	**12,346,929**	**100.0**	**36,880,916**	**100.0**	**404,756,487**	**100.0**	**66,884,000**	**100.0**
Accounts Payable	1,271,734	10.3	2,876,711	7.8	22,666,363	5.6	8,895,572	13.3
Bank Loans	61,735	0.5	73,762	0.2	—	—	—	—
Notes Payable	283,979	2.3	368,809	1.0	5,261,834	1.3	1,003,260	1.5
Other Current	2,074,284	16.8	6,011,589	16.3	80,141,784	19.8	14,446,944	21.6
Total Current	**3,691,732**	**29.9**	**9,330,872**	**25.3**	**108,069,982**	**26.7**	**24,345,776**	**36.4**
Other Long Term	2,333,570	18.9	10,179,133	27.6	120,617,433	29.8	16,787,884	25.1
Deferred Credits	37,041	0.3	258,166	0.7	17,404,529	4.3	2,274,056	3.4
Net Worth	6,284,587	50.9	17,112,745	46.4	158,664,543	39.2	23,476,284	35.1
Total Liab & Net Worth	**12,346,929**	**100.0**	**36,880,916**	**100.0**	**404,756,487**	**100.0**	**66,884,000**	**100.0**
Net Sales	20,588,454	100.0	37,528,000	100.0	139,245,332	100.0	20,588,454	100.0
Gross Profit	4,611,814	22.4	5,516,616	14.7	14,899,251	10.7	7,082,428	34.4
Net Profit After Tax	679,419	3.3	(225,168)	(0.6)	5,569,813	4.0	555,888	2.7
Working Capital	1,703,876	—	1,696,522	—	14,571,234	—	7,892,312	—

RATIOS

	UQ	MED	LQ	UQ	MED	LQ	UQ	MED	LQ	UQ	MED	LQ
SOLVENCY												
Quick Ratio (times)	1.7	0.8	0.5	1.0	0.8	0.3	1.1	0.6	0.3	1.3	0.7	0.3
Current Ratio (times)	2.8	1.6	1.0	1.7	1.1	0.9	1.9	1.0	0.6	1.9	1.0	0.7
Curr Liab To Nw (%)	12.5	49.1	132.2	5.1	46.8	163.2	18.7	50.2	145.4	40.3	76.0	196.2
Curr Liab To Inv (%)	112.9	191.4	287.4	150.6	225.9	540.3	131.6	415.6	833.4	169.7	334.9	645.9
Total Liab To Nw (%)	23.8	66.9	236.9	20.0	123.6	241.3	83.3	142.1	353.8	75.2	144.0	334.3
Fixed Assets To Nw (%)	47.2	83.4	112.8	90.3	126.3	209.8	93.3	142.5	250.5	70.1	116.8	205.7
EFFICIENCY												
Coll Period (days)	15.4	31.4	54.3	28.9	31.0	44.6	16.9	25.5	35.4	17.7	24.5	34.0
Sales To Inv (times)	68.7	19.6	6.5	79.1	40.0	14.8	68.4	40.0	27.1	46.6	32.5	21.3
Assets To Sales (%)	40.0	57.4	101.3	33.2	74.0	91.3	80.3	96.6	127.1	43.7	83.5	104.9
Sales To Nwc (times)	11.7	7.2	4.0	25.1	12.0	3.1	10.1	5.0	2.9	20.6	7.3	4.9
Acct Pay To Sales (%)	2.6	5.8	10.8	4.6	9.3	11.5	4.3	5.5	6.7	4.2	5.2	6.5
PROFITABILITY												
Return On Sales (%)	7.1	1.7	0.6	1.5	0.3	(4.7)	6.1	2.6	(0.5)	5.5	2.2	0.3
Return On Assets (%)	6.5	2.4	0.6	1.1	0.4	(1.6)	5.7	3.3	(0.1)	8.1	3.8	0.9
Return On Nw (%)	20.5	8.6	1.1	7.0	1.3	(1.5)	13.5	8.3	1.5	22.1	11.8	6.8

SIC 4512 AIR TRANS, SCHEDULED — INDUSTRY ASSETS $1,000,000 - $5,000,000 — 1995 (15 Establishments)

	$	%
Cash	308,325	18.1
Accounts Receivable	379,870	22.3
Notes Receivable	1,703	0.1
Inventory	103,911	6.1
Other Current	131,166	7.7
Total Current	**924,976**	**54.3**
Fixed Assets	642,202	37.7
Other Non-current	136,276	8.0
Total Assets	**1,703,454**	**100.0**
Accounts Payable	352,615	20.7
Bank Loans	1,703	0.1
Notes Payable	25,552	1.5
Other Current	270,849	15.9
Total Current	**650,719**	**38.2**
Other Long Term	553,623	32.5
Deferred Credits	10,221	0.6
Net Worth	488,891	28.7
Total Liab & Net Worth	**1,703,454**	**100.0**
Net Sales	4,550,651	100.0
Gross Profit	1,874,868	41.2
Net Profit After Tax	209,330	4.6
Working Capital	274,257	—

RATIOS	UQ	MED	LQ
SOLVENCY			
Quick Ratio (times)	1.5	1.1	0.7
Current Ratio (times)	2.2	1.4	1.0
Curr Liab To Nw (%)	47.7	126.1	352.1
Curr Liab To Inv (%)	182.1	197.6	373.5
Total Liab To Nw (%)	109.9	197.9	318.8
Fixed Assets To Nw (%)	19.4	123.3	175.1
EFFICIENCY			
Coll Period (days)	24.8	34.7	148.0
Sales To Inv (times)	28.9	18.8	17.8
Assets To Sales (%)	39.1	53.0	90.2
Sales To Nwc (times)	21.2	8.6	7.2
Acct Pay To Sales (%)	3.6	4.8	7.7
PROFITABILITY			
Return On Sales (%)	14.1	3.0	0.8
Return On Assets (%)	10.4	4.4	2.5
Return On Nw (%)	31.7	17.5	8.1

SIC 4512 AIR TRANS, SCHEDULED — INDUSTRY ASSETS $5,000,000-$25,000,000 — 1995 (11 Establishments)

	$	%
Cash	1,665,634	11.2
Accounts Receivable	3,004,089	20.2
Notes Receivable	—	—
Inventory	2,409,220	16.2
Other Current	1,427,686	9.6
Total Current	**8,506,628**	**57.2**
Fixed Assets	4,907,670	33.0
Other Non-current	1,457,429	9.8
Total Assets	**14,871,728**	**100.0**
Accounts Payable	2,959,474	19.9
Bank Loans	—	0.1
Notes Payable	163,589	1.1
Other Current	3,688,189	24.8
Total Current	**6,811,251**	**45.8**
Other Long Term	2,557,937	17.2
Deferred Credits	104,102	0.7
Net Worth	5,398,437	36.3
Total Liab & Net Worth	**14,871,728**	**100.0**
Net Sales	23,992,454	100.0
Gross Profit	4,702,521	19.6
Net Profit After Tax	(23,992)	(0.1)
Working Capital	1,695,377	—

RATIOS	UQ	MED	LQ
SOLVENCY			
Quick Ratio (times)	0.9	0.6	0.4
Current Ratio (times)	1.4	1.3	1.0
Curr Liab To Nw (%)	64.6	115.9	222.8
Curr Liab To Inv (%)	130.7	185.8	246.0
Total Liab To Nw (%)	69.1	71.6	181.6
Fixed Assets To Nw (%)	47.3	86.7	113.6
EFFICIENCY			
Coll Period (days)	31.0	34.0	58.0
Sales To Inv (times)	20.1	10.3	6.8
Assets To Sales (%)	36.5	56.8	94.1
Sales To Nwc (times)	16.2	9.5	4.8
Acct Pay To Sales (%)	5.2	6.5	11.8
PROFITABILITY			
Return On Sales (%)	1.3	0.5	(1.5)
Return On Assets (%)	3.3	0.8	(4.8)
Return On Nw (%)	15.5	6.9	(6.8)

SIC 4513 AIR COURIER SVCS (NO BREAKDOWN) — 1995 (67 Establishments)

	$	%
Cash	87,464	17.7
Accounts Receivable	191,234	38.7
Notes Receivable	5,930	1.2
Inventory	2,965	0.6
Other Current	19,272	3.9
Total Current	**306,864**	**62.1**
Fixed Assets	152,197	30.8
Other Non-current	35,084	7.1
Total Assets	**494,145**	**100.0**
Accounts Payable	78,075	15.8
Bank Loans	494	0.1
Notes Payable	18,283	3.7
Other Current	72,639	14.7
Total Current	**169,492**	**34.3**
Other Long Term	83,016	16.8
Deferred Credits	2,471	0.5
Net Worth	239,166	48.4
Total Liab & Net Worth	**494,145**	**100.0**
Net Sales	1,641,351	100.0
Gross Profit	503,895	30.7
Net Profit After Tax	103,405	6.3
Working Capital	137,372	—

RATIOS	UQ	MED	LQ
SOLVENCY			
Quick Ratio (times)	3.0	1.8	1.0
Current Ratio (times)	3.9	2.0	1.2
Curr Liab To Nw (%)	26.6	68.9	145.1
Curr Liab To Inv (%)	61.1	324.1	728.7
Total Liab To Nw (%)	44.9	89.7	209.9
Fixed Assets To Nw (%)	20.1	52.2	134.3
EFFICIENCY			
Coll Period (days)	37.2	51.1	68.3
Sales To Inv (times)	193.9	119.7	70.2
Assets To Sales (%)	19.4	30.8	44.2
Sales To Nwc (times)	25.4	12.7	6.4
Acct Pay To Sales (%)	2.1	4.5	7.0
PROFITABILITY			
Return On Sales (%)	9.8	5.0	2.6
Return On Assets (%)	25.5	14.6	8.1
Return On Nw (%)	62.5	36.6	20.2

SIC 4522 AIR TRANS, NONSCHED (NO BREAKDOWN) — 1995 (138 Establishments)

	$	%
Cash	290,364	12.3
Accounts Receivable	502,825	21.3
Notes Receivable	7,082	0.3
Inventory	129,837	5.5
Other Current	177,051	7.5
Total Current	**1,107,159**	**46.9**
Fixed Assets	1,050,503	44.5
Other Non-current	203,019	8.6
Total Assets	**2,360,681**	**100.0**
Accounts Payable	318,692	13.5
Bank Loans	—	—
Notes Payable	101,509	4.3
Other Current	337,577	14.3
Total Current	**757,779**	**32.1**
Other Long Term	632,663	26.8
Deferred Credits	21,246	0.9
Net Worth	948,994	40.2
Total Liab & Net Worth	**2,360,681**	**100.0**
Net Sales	4,035,920	100.0
Gross Profit	1,537,686	38.1
Net Profit After Tax	96,862	2.4
Working Capital	349,380	—

RATIOS	UQ	MED	LQ
SOLVENCY			
Quick Ratio (times)	2.2	1.0	0.5
Current Ratio (times)	3.6	1.4	0.9
Curr Liab To Nw (%)	24.6	51.6	159.4
Curr Liab To Inv (%)	115.0	204.9	485.1
Total Liab To Nw (%)	41.6	127.6	314.0
Fixed Assets To Nw (%)	46.6	104.6	226.2
EFFICIENCY			
Coll Period (days)	20.4	32.5	59.9
Sales To Inv (times)	55.6	23.9	12.6
Assets To Sales (%)	27.4	54.9	89.1
Sales To Nwc (times)	17.0	7.7	5.1
Acct Pay To Sales (%)	2.1	5.2	8.2
PROFITABILITY			
Return On Sales (%)	8.2	3.0	0.6
Return On Assets (%)	17.9	5.0	1.0
Return On Nw (%)	49.8	10.5	4.7

SIC 4522 AIR TRANS, NONSCHED

INDUSTRY ASSETS

	$100,000 - $250,000 (16 Establishments)		$250,000 - $500,000 (10 Establishments)		$500,000 - $1,000,000 (16 Establishments)		$1,000,000 - $5,000,000 (48 Establishments)	
	$	%	$	%	$	%	$	%
Cash	43,206	24.3	43,247	10.9	83,833	13.2	228,524	9.3
Accounts Receivable	35,560	20.0	126,568	31.9	175,288	27.6	624,139	25.4
Notes Receivable	—	—	397	0.1	2,540	0.4	14,743	0.6
Inventory	14,402	8.1	17,458	4.4	59,064	9.3	108,119	4.4
Other Current	9,424	5.3	67,053	16.9	37,471	5.9	167,092	6.8
Total Current	**102,592**	**57.7**	**254,723**	**64.2**	**358,197**	**56.4**	**1,142,618**	**46.5**
Fixed Assets	65,431	36.8	133,710	33.7	188,625	29.7	1,142,618	46.5
Other Non-current	9,779	5.5	8,332	2.1	88,279	13.9	172,007	7.0
Total Assets	**177,802**	**100.0**	**396,765**	**100.0**	**635,101**	**100.0**	**2,457,242**	**100.0**
Accounts Payable	18,491	10.4	81,734	20.6	105,427	16.6	402,988	16.4
Bank Loans	—	—	—	—	—	—	—	—
Notes Payable	11,557	6.5	9,126	2.3	59,064	9.3	110,576	4.5
Other Current	24,359	13.7	51,976	13.1	45,727	7.2	304,698	12.4
Total Current	**54,407**	**30.6**	**142,835**	**36.0**	**210,218**	**33.1**	**818,262**	**33.3**
Other Long Term	27,026	15.2	129,742	32.7	125,115	19.7	751,916	30.6
Deferred Credits	—	—	—	—	—	—	24,572	1.0
Net Worth	96,369	54.2	124,187	31.3	299,768	47.2	862,492	35.1
Total Liab & Net Worth	**177,802**	**100.0**	**396,765**	**100.0**	**635,101**	**100.0**	**2,457,242**	**100.0**
Net Sales	447,299	100.0	1,290,743	100.0	3,099,267	100.0	3,988,689	100.0
Gross Profit	177,578	39.7	363,990	28.2	1,871,957	60.4	1,447,894	36.3
Net Profit After Tax	42,046	9.4	5,163	0.4	179,757	5.8	(31,910)	(0.8)
Working Capital	48,185	—	111,888	—	147,979	—	324,356	—

RATIOS	UQ	MED	LQ	UQ	MED	LQ	UQ	MED	LQ	UQ	MED	LQ
SOLVENCY												
Quick Ratio (times)	4.1	1.9	0.4	2.0	1.3	0.8	2.6	1.1	0.8	1.7	1.0	0.7
Current Ratio (times)	4.3	3.1	0.4	3.3	2.0	1.3	3.6	1.8	1.1	3.4	1.3	1.0
Curr Liab To Nw (%)	19.7	31.6	56.7	24.6	64.4	175.7	31.3	51.6	179.6	24.9	68.4	183.9
Curr Liab To Inv (%)	134.6	200.0	381.1	399.0	789.5	812.6	78.7	122.7	233.8	167.2	295.8	412.0
Total Liab To Nw (%)	26.4	42.9	101.7	65.6	169.9	238.0	35.8	77.3	305.5	68.2	212.0	446.8
Fixed Assets To Nw (%)	30.9	41.4	89.0	22.5	95.8	259.3	12.8	45.8	153.8	60.7	105.0	286.4
EFFICIENCY												
Coll Period (days)	28.9	45.5	58.8	27.2	35.3	46.7	28.0	32.1	39.8	19.0	43.3	81.8
Sales To Inv (times)	64.7	43.8	28.8	66.4	46.2	25.9	53.5	39.5	22.0	63.2	21.7	17.7
Assets To Sales (%)	21.8	30.0	46.7	21.3	24.9	42.1	17.1	19.3	61.5	38.6	66.2	91.7
Sales To Nwc (times)	8.4	6.0	5.2	19.0	12.1	11.6	62.1	8.5	7.2	19.1	7.2	4.6
Acct Pay To Sales (%)	3.0	4.1	5.4	3.2	7.4	12.9	4.1	5.2	5.7	2.1	6.0	8.5
PROFITABILITY												
Return On Sales (%)	18.7	6.2	3.3	6.4	0.2	(6.0)	7.8	4.9	1.8	12.0	2.9	0.7
Return On Assets (%)	41.8	16.3	4.7	38.2	21.5	2.9	26.5	13.9	5.2	15.7	5.7	2.3
Return On Nw (%)	63.6	30.2	5.4	66.1	38.0	(7.1)	82.8	32.8	6.4	51.2	19.7	8.4

SIC 4522 AIR TRANS, NONSCHED — INDUSTRY ASSETS $5,000,000-$25,000,000 — 1995 (21 Establishments)

	$	%
Cash	947,329	11.9
Accounts Receivable	1,042,859	13.1
Notes Receivable	7,961	0.1
Inventory	318,430	4.0
Other Current	971,212	12.2
Total Current	**3,287,791**	**41.3**
Fixed Assets	3,956,494	49.7
Other Non-current	716,468	9.0
Total Assets	**7,960,752**	**100.0**
Accounts Payable	549,292	6.9
Bank Loans	7,961	0.1
Notes Payable	111,451	1.4
Other Current	1,202,074	15.1
Total Current	**1,870,777**	**23.5**
Other Long Term	2,515,598	31.6
Deferred Credits	15,922	0.2
Net Worth	3,558,456	44.7
Total Liab & Net Worth	**7,960,752**	**100.0**
Net Sales	11,584,323	100.0
Gross Profit	4,367,290	37.7
Net Profit After Tax	405,451	3.5
Working Capital	1,417,014	—

RATIOS	UQ	MED	LQ
SOLVENCY			
Quick Ratio (times)	1.7	0.7	0.6
Current Ratio (times)	3.5	1.6	1.0
Curr Liab To Nw (%)	12.8	44.9	136.6
Curr Liab To Inv (%)	116.9	221.2	551.0
Total Liab To Nw (%)	44.7	84.1	328.0
Fixed Assets To Nw (%)	47.1	96.9	226.1
EFFICIENCY			
Coll Period (days)	7.7	14.6	27.0
Sales To Inv (times)	34.1	22.0	17.4
Assets To Sales (%)	36.3	66.0	88.7
Sales To Nwc (times)	18.8	7.8	6.6
Acct Pay To Sales (%)	1.3	3.7	7.9
PROFITABILITY			
Return On Sales (%)	7.4	2.1	1.1
Return On Assets (%)	6.4	1.8	1.2
Return On Nw (%)	28.9	8.6	2.8

SIC 4522 AIR TRANS, NONSCHED — INDUSTRY ASSETS OVER $50,000,000 — 1995 (13 Establishments)

	$	%
Cash	21,166,848	9.6
Accounts Receivable	24,694,656	11.2
Notes Receivable	881,952	0.4
Inventory	13,670,256	6.2
Other Current	7,276,104	3.3
Total Current	**67,689,816**	**30.7**
Fixed Assets	129,426,456	58.7
Other Non-current	23,371,728	10.6
Total Assets	**220,488,000**	**100.0**
Accounts Payable	16,316,112	7.4
Bank Loans	—	—
Notes Payable	7,055,616	3.2
Other Current	56,003,952	25.4
Total Current	**79,375,680**	**36.0**
Other Long Term	52,476,144	23.8
Deferred Credits	9,701,472	4.4
Net Worth	78,934,704	35.8
Total Liab & Net Worth	**220,488,000**	**100.0**
Net Sales	203,008,000	100.0
Gross Profit	—	—
Net Profit After Tax	4,669,184	2.3
Working Capital	(11,685,864)	—

RATIOS	UQ	MED	LQ
SOLVENCY			
Quick Ratio (times)	1.1	0.7	0.4
Current Ratio (times)	1.9	1.0	0.6
Curr Liab To Nw (%)	15.6	40.7	169.0
Curr Liab To Inv (%)	120.8	142.2	409.6
Total Liab To Nw (%)	24.0	99.4	317.0
Fixed Assets To Nw (%)	70.1	115.4	253.7
EFFICIENCY			
Coll Period (days)	18.4	33.4	54.6
Sales To Inv (times)	39.4	16.2	7.1
Assets To Sales (%)	65.3	84.1	142.9
Sales To Nwc (times)	6.6	6.1	4.4
Acct Pay To Sales (%)	2.1	3.6	8.6
PROFITABILITY			
Return On Sales (%)	4.4	2.8	(2.4)
Return On Assets (%)	4.7	1.0	(2.8)
Return On Nw (%)	13.0	6.8	4.8

SIC 4581 ARPTS, FLY FLDS, SVCS (NO BREAKDOWN) — 1995 (231 Establishments)

	$	%
Cash	101,487	10.0
Accounts Receivable	208,048	20.5
Notes Receivable	7,104	0.7
Inventory	156,290	15.4
Other Current	59,877	5.9
Total Current	**532,807**	**52.5**
Fixed Assets	372,457	36.7
Other Non-current	109,606	10.8
Total Assets	**1,014,870**	**100.0**
Accounts Payable	103,517	10.2
Bank Loans	3,045	0.3
Notes Payable	36,535	3.6
Other Current	144,112	14.2
Total Current	**287,208**	**28.3**
Other Long Term	215,152	21.2
Deferred Credits	3,045	0.3
Net Worth	509,465	50.2
Total Liab & Net Worth	**1,014,870**	**100.0**
Net Sales	2,646,281	100.0
Gross Profit	902,382	34.1
Net Profit After Tax	111,144	4.2
Working Capital	245,599	—

RATIOS	UQ	MED	LQ
SOLVENCY			
Quick Ratio (times)	2.3	0.9	0.5
Current Ratio (times)	3.3	1.9	1.2
Curr Liab To Nw (%)	8.8	53.5	131.8
Curr Liab To Inv (%)	88.4	143.9	234.2
Total Liab To Nw (%)	23.4	96.6	220.8
Fixed Assets To Nw (%)	29.5	78.3	133.4
EFFICIENCY			
Coll Period (days)	17.5	30.3	47.5
Sales To Inv (times)	46.2	15.6	6.1
Assets To Sales (%)	32.0	46.3	87.3
Sales To Nwc (times)	15.2	6.9	3.6
Acct Pay To Sales (%)	2.7	5.7	9.6
PROFITABILITY			
Return On Sales (%)	10.3	2.7	0.2
Return On Assets (%)	8.0	3.2	(0.1)
Return On Nw (%)	19.7	7.3	(0.1)

SIC 4581 ARPTS, FLY FLDS, SVCS — INDUSTRY ASSETS UNDER $100,000 — 1995 (26 Establishments)

	$	%
Cash	15,646	26.5
Accounts Receivable	11,277	19.1
Notes Receivable	768	1.3
Inventory	6,553	11.1
Other Current	4,723	8.0
Total Current	**38,966**	**66.0**
Fixed Assets	16,236	27.5
Other Non-current	3,838	6.5
Total Assets	**59,040**	**100.0**
Accounts Payable	3,542	6.0
Bank Loans	—	—
Notes Payable	4,310	7.3
Other Current	8,207	13.9
Total Current	**16,059**	**27.2**
Other Long Term	4,664	7.9
Deferred Credits	413	0.7
Net Worth	37,904	64.2
Total Liab & Net Worth	**59,040**	**100.0**
Net Sales	204,722	100.0
Gross Profit	98,881	48.3
Net Profit After Tax	13,307	6.5
Working Capital	22,907	—

RATIOS	UQ	MED	LQ
SOLVENCY			
Quick Ratio (times)	7.8	2.3	1.0
Current Ratio (times)	11.1	2.5	1.6
Curr Liab To Nw (%)	6.2	21.4	105.9
Curr Liab To Inv (%)	75.9	131.2	370.0
Total Liab To Nw (%)	10.5	28.1	137.2
Fixed Assets To Nw (%)	9.4	65.2	80.1
EFFICIENCY			
Coll Period (days)	11.9	15.9	25.4
Sales To Inv (times)	23.5	20.1	13.1
Assets To Sales (%)	19.7	27.3	62.8
Sales To Nwc (times)	43.1	11.8	4.2
Acct Pay To Sales (%)	2.3	4.9	5.8
PROFITABILITY			
Return On Sales (%)	12.6	7.9	0.9
Return On Assets (%)	18.4	12.1	5.3
Return On Nw (%)	75.1	15.4	6.7

SIC 4581 ARPTS,FLY FLDS,SVCS — INDUSTRY ASSETS $100,000 - $250,000 — 1995 (32 Establishments)

	$	%
Cash	21,762	14.1
Accounts Receivable	38,739	25.1
Notes Receivable	3,395	2.2
Inventory	28,553	18.5
Other Current	10,186	6.6
Total Current	**102,635**	**66.5**
Fixed Assets	45,684	29.6
Other Non-current	6,019	3.9
Total Assets	**154,338**	**100.0**
Accounts Payable	18,829	12.2
Bank Loans	—	—
Notes Payable	6,328	4.1
Other Current	23,151	15.0
Total Current	**48,308**	**31.3**
Other Long Term	23,459	15.2
Deferred Credits	—	—
Net Worth	82,571	53.5
Total Liab & Net Worth	**154,338**	**100.0**
Net Sales	574,849	100.0
Gross Profit	233,964	40.7
Net Profit After Tax	19,545	3.4
Working Capital	54,327	—

RATIOS	UQ	MED	LQ
SOLVENCY			
Quick Ratio (times)	4.0	1.4	0.6
Current Ratio (times)	6.7	2.1	1.2
Curr Liab To Nw (%)	12.5	44.5	73.0
Curr Liab To Inv (%)	67.5	137.3	235.8
Total Liab To Nw (%)	28.1	57.9	152.7
Fixed Assets To Nw (%)	17.5	46.9	83.5
EFFICIENCY			
Coll Period (days)	15.0	31.0	42.0
Sales To Inv (times)	34.0	14.3	6.2
Assets To Sales (%)	16.1	33.4	43.5
Sales To Nwc (times)	27.0	9.6	4.9
Acct Pay To Sales (%)	1.9	5.6	9.4
PROFITABILITY			
Return On Sales (%)	6.5	2.6	0.4
Return On Assets (%)	14.2	6.3	1.1
Return On Nw (%)	27.3	14.5	7.6

SIC 4581 ARPTS,FLY FLDS,SVCS — INDUSTRY ASSETS $250,000 - $500,000 — 1995 (24 Establishments)

	$	%
Cash	37,878	9.9
Accounts Receivable	117,077	30.6
Notes Receivable	3,443	0.9
Inventory	76,138	19.9
Other Current	33,669	8.8
Total Current	**268,206**	**70.1**
Fixed Assets	106,747	27.9
Other Non-current	7,652	2.0
Total Assets	**382,605**	**100.0**
Accounts Payable	51,652	13.5
Bank Loans	3,826	1.0
Notes Payable	28,695	7.5
Other Current	61,217	16.0
Total Current	**145,390**	**38.0**
Other Long Term	72,312	18.9
Deferred Credits	—	—
Net Worth	164,903	43.1
Total Liab & Net Worth	**382,605**	**100.0**
Net Sales	1,310,592	100.0
Gross Profit	567,486	43.3
Net Profit After Tax	73,393	5.6
Working Capital	122,816	—

RATIOS	UQ	MED	LQ
SOLVENCY			
Quick Ratio (times)	1.8	0.8	0.6
Current Ratio (times)	2.9	1.7	1.1
Curr Liab To Nw (%)	47.3	88.1	167.6
Curr Liab To Inv (%)	103.4	187.1	301.8
Total Liab To Nw (%)	67.0	137.6	265.9
Fixed Assets To Nw (%)	11.1	71.8	103.6
EFFICIENCY			
Coll Period (days)	15.0	19.4	37.1
Sales To Inv (times)	40.1	23.7	16.7
Assets To Sales (%)	24.4	26.9	34.2
Sales To Nwc (times)	21.3	9.1	6.6
Acct Pay To Sales (%)	2.4	2.4	7.9
PROFITABILITY			
Return On Sales (%)	10.6	2.7	0.1
Return On Assets (%)	33.2	7.7	(0.2)
Return On Nw (%)	80.9	10.7	(0.2)

SIC 4581 ARPTS,FLY FLDS,SVCS — INDUSTRY ASSETS $500,000 - $1,000,000 — 1995 (35 Establishments)

	$	%
Cash	60,653	7.9
Accounts Receivable	204,224	26.6
Notes Receivable	2,303	0.3
Inventory	155,855	20.3
Other Current	42,227	5.5
Total Current	**465,263**	**60.6**
Fixed Assets	272,555	35.5
Other Non-current	29,943	3.9
Total Assets	**767,760**	**100.0**
Accounts Payable	114,396	14.9
Bank Loans	—	—
Notes Payable	21,497	2.8
Other Current	86,757	11.3
Total Current	**222,650**	**29.0**
Other Long Term	192,708	25.1
Deferred Credits	(768)	(0.1)
Net Worth	353,170	46.0
Total Liab & Net Worth	**767,760**	**100.0**
Net Sales	1,868,623	100.0
Gross Profit	687,653	36.8
Net Profit After Tax	104,643	5.6
Working Capital	242,613	—

RATIOS	UQ	MED	LQ
SOLVENCY			
Quick Ratio (times)	3.0	1.0	0.7
Current Ratio (times)	5.7	2.0	1.6
Curr Liab To Nw (%)	15.9	61.1	156.9
Curr Liab To Inv (%)	104.1	146.3	230.8
Total Liab To Nw (%)	19.0	99.2	248.5
Fixed Assets To Nw (%)	29.9	73.1	165.4
EFFICIENCY			
Coll Period (days)	17.8	33.6	64.5
Sales To Inv (times)	20.1	10.3	6.2
Assets To Sales (%)	29.7	35.5	49.0
Sales To Nwc (times)	16.1	7.3	3.5
Acct Pay To Sales (%)	2.8	4.0	7.1
PROFITABILITY			
Return On Sales (%)	12.4	4.5	1.5
Return On Assets (%)	15.2	5.0	3.1
Return On Nw (%)	26.9	16.8	7.5

SIC 4581 ARPTS,FLY FLDS,SVCS — INDUSTRY ASSETS $1,000,000 - $5,000,000 — 1995 (38 Establishments)

	$	%
Cash	185,462	8.0
Accounts Receivable	556,387	24.0
Notes Receivable	4,637	0.2
Inventory	519,295	22.4
Other Current	127,505	5.5
Total Current	**1,393,287**	**60.1**
Fixed Assets	723,304	31.2
Other Non-current	201,690	8.7
Total Assets	**2,318,281**	**100.0**
Accounts Payable	292,103	12.6
Bank Loans	9,273	0.4
Notes Payable	74,185	3.2
Other Current	424,245	18.3
Total Current	**799,807**	**34.5**
Other Long Term	521,613	22.5
Deferred Credits	20,865	0.9
Net Worth	975,996	42.1
Total Liab & Net Worth	**2,318,281**	**100.0**
Net Sales	4,071,183	100.0
Gross Profit	1,371,989	33.7
Net Profit After Tax	105,851	2.6
Working Capital	593,480	—

RATIOS	UQ	MED	LQ
SOLVENCY			
Quick Ratio (times)	1.6	0.9	0.5
Current Ratio (times)	2.8	2.1	1.3
Curr Liab To Nw (%)	33.2	72.1	155.1
Curr Liab To Inv (%)	93.8	123.6	170.0
Total Liab To Nw (%)	84.1	132.3	224.1
Fixed Assets To Nw (%)	26.3	56.9	143.5
EFFICIENCY			
Coll Period (days)	22.6	30.7	60.6
Sales To Inv (times)	16.4	7.8	4.3
Assets To Sales (%)	41.8	49.0	77.2
Sales To Nwc (times)	7.9	6.9	4.3
Acct Pay To Sales (%)	2.5	4.8	6.2
PROFITABILITY			
Return On Sales (%)	5.6	2.9	0.6
Return On Assets (%)	7.4	4.0	1.6
Return On Nw (%)	26.9	10.6	3.1

	SIC 4581 ARPTS,FLY FLDS,SVCS INDUSTRY ASSETS $5,000,000-$25,000,000 1995 (33 Establishments) $	%	SIC 4581 ARPTS,FLY FLDS,SVCS INDUSTRY ASSETS $25,000,000-$50,000,000 1995 (15 Establishments) $	%	SIC 4581 ARPTS,FLY FLDS,SVCS INDUSTRY ASSETS OVER $50,000,000 1995 (28 Establishments) $	%	SIC 46 PIPE LINES EX NAT GAS (NO BREAKDOWN) 1995 (52 Establishments) $	%
Cash	701,796	5.3	2,126,331	6.7	7,418,587	3.4	3,672,754	2.3
Accounts Receivable	2,052,423	15.5	2,538,903	8.0	17,455,500	8.0	12,295,743	7.7
Notes Receivable	—	—	412,572	1.3	218,194	0.1	—	—
Inventory	1,787,594	13.5	793,407	2.5	11,782,462	5.4	2,075,905	1.3
Other Current	423,726	3.2	1,872,441	5.9	10,036,912	4.6	14,531,333	9.1
Total Current	**4,965,540**	**37.5**	**7,743,653**	**24.4**	**46,911,656**	**21.5**	**32,575,735**	**20.4**
Fixed Assets	6,580,996	49.7	17,835,790	56.2	94,696,087	43.4	105,072,714	65.8
Other Non-current	1,694,904	12.8	6,156,839	19.4	76,586,006	35.1	22,036,527	13.8
Total Assets	**13,241,440**	**100.0**	**31,736,282**	**100.0**	**218,193,749**	**100.0**	**159,684,976**	**100.0**
Accounts Payable	1,257,937	9.5	1,523,342	4.8	6,109,425	2.8	6,866,454	4.3
Bank Loans	132,414	1.0	126,945	0.4	—	—	—	—
Notes Payable	450,209	3.4	—	—	436,387	0.2	4,630,864	2.9
Other Current	2,105,389	15.9	2,983,211	9.4	23,128,537	10.6	13,253,853	8.3
Total Current	**3,945,949**	**29.8**	**4,633,497**	**14.6**	**29,674,350**	**13.6**	**24,751,171**	**15.5**
Other Long Term	1,721,387	13.0	8,346,642	26.3	93,386,925	42.8	56,688,166	35.5
Deferred Credits	26,483	0.2	63,473	0.2	872,775	0.4	7,664,879	4.8
Net Worth	7,547,621	57.0	18,692,670	58.9	94,259,700	43.2	70,580,759	44.2
Total Liab & Net Worth	**13,241,440**	**100.0**	**31,736,282**	**100.0**	**218,193,749**	**100.0**	**159,684,976**	**100.0**
Net Sales	12,565,859	100.0	32,098,256	100.0	43,866,711	100.0	52,568,496	100.0
Gross Profit	2,387,513	19.0	4,461,658	13.9	4,693,738	10.7	24,549,488	46.7
Net Profit After Tax	515,200	4.1	64,197	0.2	2,412,669	5.5	13,089,556	24.9
Working Capital	1,019,591	—	3,110,156	—	17,237,306	—	7,824,564	—

RATIOS	UQ	MED	LQ	UQ	MED	LQ	UQ	MED	LQ	UQ	MED	LQ
SOLVENCY												
Quick Ratio (times)	1.6	0.8	0.5	2.2	0.8	0.3	1.8	0.8	0.4	1.1	0.7	0.3
Current Ratio (times)	2.8	1.7	1.1	2.8	1.4	1.0	2.8	1.7	1.2	2.6	1.3	0.9
Curr Liab To Nw (%)	4.2	49.1	106.3	2.7	5.7	167.1	5.4	10.5	53.8	10.9	19.1	60.8
Curr Liab To Inv (%)	113.4	187.3	220.3	291.9	481.1	613.7	45.9	68.4	291.1	306.4	594.4	824.7
Total Liab To Nw (%)	18.8	42.9	158.2	11.9	20.5	123.6	73.7	130.2	241.6	46.8	135.3	182.8
Fixed Assets To Nw (%)	60.1	93.6	105.3	81.7	106.2	133.2	96.7	140.6	196.5	100.9	192.5	253.3
EFFICIENCY												
Coll Period (days)	23.7	31.8	54.0	29.4	31.0	40.9	24.5	30.3	38.7	18.3	34.0	45.6
Sales To Inv (times)	67.1	22.0	4.3	61.7	25.9	22.6	164.7	125.8	61.6	129.9	89.5	52.8
Assets To Sales (%)	50.1	64.2	494.5	50.8	76.1	91.3	104.6	612.6	854.4	103.1	223.6	302.3
Sales To Nwc (times)	11.1	4.2	3.6	15.2	12.0	1.8	10.7	4.6	2.6	21.8	6.4	3.6
Acct Pay To Sales (%)	4.8	9.9	13.0	5.3	9.6	11.6	3.7	6.9	9.4	2.1	4.7	8.7
PROFITABILITY												
Return On Sales (%)	12.5	2.2	0.6	0.8	(3.2)	(4.7)	23.6	3.7	(1.2)	33.1	24.6	21.0
Return On Assets (%)	4.9	1.9	0.3	0.8	(0.1)	(1.9)	3.3	1.1	(0.9)	29.8	15.3	8.3
Return On Nw (%)	15.9	5.2	0.4	1.6	(0.1)	(2.4)	8.5	2.2	(1.5)	67.0	32.0	17.2

	SIC 46 PIPE LINES EX NAT GAS — SOUTH 1995 (30 Establishments) $	%	SIC 46 PIPE LINES EX NAT GAS — INDUSTRY ASSETS OVER $50,000,000 1995 (29 Establishments) $	%	SIC 4612 CRD PTRLEUM PPLNS (NO BREAKDOWN) 1995 (28 Establishments) $	%	SIC 4612 CRD PTRLEUM PPLNS — INDUSTRY ASSETS OVER $50,000,000 1995 (16 Establishments) $	%
Cash	2,554,960	1.6	9,237,664	1.7	1,755,248	1.0	2,586,185	0.5
Accounts Receivable	15,170,073	9.5	38,037,440	7.0	16,674,860	9.5	50,689,226	9.8
Notes Receivable	—	—	—	—	—	—	—	—
Inventory	3,513,069	2.2	8,694,272	1.6	3,686,022	2.1	12,413,688	2.4
Other Current	17,086,292	10.7	44,558,144	8.2	25,977,676	14.8	81,206,209	15.7
Total Current	**38,324,394**	**24.0**	**100,527,520**	**18.5**	**48,093,806**	**27.4**	**146,895,308**	**28.4**
Fixed Assets	94,214,136	59.0	370,049,952	68.1	92,677,116	52.8	235,342,835	45.5
Other Non-current	27,146,446	17.0	72,814,528	13.4	34,753,918	19.8	134,998,857	26.1
Total Assets	**159,684,976**	**100.0**	**543,392,000**	**100.0**	**175,524,840**	**100.0**	**517,237,000**	**100.0**
Accounts Payable	10,060,153	6.3	23,909,248	4.4	10,707,015	6.1	34,654,879	6.7
Bank Loans	—	—	—	—	—	—	—	—
Notes Payable	6,866,454	4.3	7,607,488	1.4	—	—	—	—
Other Current	11,657,003	7.3	40,754,400	7.5	14,744,087	8.4	43,447,908	8.4
Total Current	**28,583,611**	**17.9**	**72,271,136**	**13.3**	**25,451,102**	**14.5**	**78,102,787**	**15.1**
Other Long Term	58,923,756	36.9	236,918,912	43.6	53,710,601	30.6	161,895,181	31.3
Deferred Credits	8,942,359	5.6	22,279,072	4.1	6,318,894	3.6	25,861,850	5.0
Net Worth	63,235,250	39.6	211,922,880	39.0	90,044,243	51.3	251,377,182	48.6
Total Liab & Net Worth	**159,684,976**	**100.0**	**543,392,000**	**100.0**	**175,524,840**	**100.0**	**517,237,000**	**100.0**
Net Sales	47,663,778	100.0	180,490,000	100.0	42,717,829	100.0	130,224,657	100.0
Gross Profit	19,971,123	41.9	116,055,070	64.3	16,275,493	38.1	66,023,901	50.7
Net Profit After Tax	11,343,979	23.8	48,732,300	27.0	10,465,868	24.5	41,281,216	31.7
Working Capital	9,740,783	—	28,256,384	—	22,642,704	—	68,792,521	—

RATIOS	UQ	MED	LQ	UQ	MED	LQ	UQ	MED	LQ	UQ	MED	LQ
SOLVENCY												
Quick Ratio (times)	1.0	0.6	0.3	0.7	0.3	0.2	0.9	0.4	0.2	0.5	0.2	0.2
Current Ratio (times)	2.5	1.2	0.9	1.4	1.2	0.6	2.8	1.8	1.1	2.6	2.0	0.6
Curr Liab To Nw (%)	15.5	47.8	82.4	10.8	15.9	24.3	16.1	24.3	55.4	15.9	24.3	61.8
Curr Liab To Inv (%)	315.3	594.4	827.6	200.8	425.3	725.1	390.9	759.2	824.7	328.4	514.9	701.3
Total Liab To Nw (%)	58.8	144.3	183.7	47.0	117.4	147.9	45.6	65.7	263.6	47.9	100.0	263.6
Fixed Assets To Nw (%)	118.3	192.5	534.3	103.9	161.4	206.3	92.8	113.3	213.9	78.1	100.9	167.5
EFFICIENCY												
Coll Period (days)	17.5	33.2	42.0	16.1	22.6	33.8	17.2	29.2	42.0	16.4	21.2	40.2
Sales To Inv (times)	95.4	65.3	31.8	90.9	81.7	51.9	90.2	84.4	41.8	90.9	88.1	55.3
Assets To Sales (%)	75.2	165.8	285.6	104.4	170.5	244.4	75.2	204.5	304.4	180.9	301.6	308.0
Sales To Nwc (times)	26.0	5.3	2.9	11.0	4.1	3.1	8.9	4.5	2.9	4.6	4.1	2.8
Acct Pay To Sales (%)	4.4	6.6	10.6	1.6	3.0	4.8	4.3	6.8	10.3	6.5	10.0	10.3
PROFITABILITY												
Return On Sales (%)	27.8	23.8	20.2	25.7	24.1	20.5	30.4	25.2	23.4	38.2	29.5	24.9
Return On Assets (%)	30.3	15.7	7.7	11.6	9.5	6.8	29.8	13.2	8.3	14.4	11.0	9.4
Return On Nw (%)	141.9	62.0	19.5	26.9	18.6	15.8	59.3	36.9	16.5	31.5	22.7	15.2

	SIC 4613 RFND PTRLM PPLNS (NO BREAKDOWN) 1995 (24 Establishments)		SIC 47 TRANSPORTATION SVS (NO BREAKDOWN) 1995 (1998 Establishments)		SIC 47 TRANSPORTATION SVS NORTHEAST 1995 (435 Establishments)		SIC 47 TRANSPORTATION SVS CENTRAL 1995 (418 Establishments)	
	$	%	$	%	$	%	$	%
Cash	5,338,702	3.4	84,527	23.9	116,200	27.5	86,258	21.1
Accounts Receivable	9,892,300	6.3	138,638	39.2	165,638	39.2	168,019	41.1
Notes Receivable	—	—	3,183	0.9	2,535	0.6	4,497	1.1
Inventory	785,103	0.5	5,305	1.5	5,916	1.4	6,950	1.7
Other Current	6,751,887	4.3	25,818	7.3	33,804	8.0	30,252	7.4
Total Current	**22,767,993**	**14.5**	**257,471**	**72.8**	**324,093**	**76.7**	**295,976**	**72.4**
Fixed Assets	120,120,788	76.5	64,368	18.2	59,156	14.0	73,176	17.9
Other Non-current	14,131,857	9.0	31,830	9.0	39,297	9.3	39,654	9.7
Total Assets	**157,020,638**	**100.0**	**353,669**	**100.0**	**422,546**	**100.0**	**408,806**	**100.0**
Accounts Payable	4,553,599	2.9	88,771	25.1	114,510	27.1	110,378	27.0
Bank Loans	—	—	354	0.1	1,690	0.4	409	0.1
Notes Payable	8,322,094	5.3	10,964	3.1	8,873	2.1	15,535	3.8
Other Current	12,875,692	8.2	54,111	15.3	80,284	19.0	55,189	13.5
Total Current	**25,751,385**	**16.4**	**154,200**	**43.6**	**205,357**	**48.6**	**181,510**	**44.4**
Other Long Term	61,866,131	39.4	29,001	8.2	24,085	5.7	37,610	9.2
Deferred Credits	9,107,197	5.8	1,061	0.3	423	0.1	2,862	0.7
Net Worth	60,295,925	38.4	169,407	47.9	192,681	45.6	186,824	45.7
Total Liab & Net Worth	**157,020,638**	**100.0**	**353,669**	**100.0**	**422,546**	**100.0**	**408,806**	**100.0**
Net Sales	64,575,805	100.0	2,000,000	100.0	2,118,562	100.0	2,784,656	100.0
Gross Profit	35,774,996	55.4	472,000	23.6	523,285	24.7	634,902	22.8
Net Profit After Tax	16,273,103	25.2	78,000	3.9	74,150	3.5	100,248	3.6
Working Capital	(2,983,392)	—	103,271	—	118,736	—	114,466	—

RATIOS	UQ	MED	LQ	UQ	MED	LQ	UQ	MED	LQ	UQ	MED	LQ
SOLVENCY												
Quick Ratio (times)	1.1	0.9	0.4	2.8	1.4	1.0	2.2	1.3	0.9	2.5	1.4	0.9
Current Ratio (times)	2.2	1.2	0.9	3.4	1.6	1.1	2.8	1.6	1.1	3.0	1.6	1.1
Curr Liab To Nw (%)	10.4	15.0	105.6	23.9	80.1	199.7	30.5	101.7	244.1	27.5	82.3	199.2
Curr Liab To Inv (%)	315.3	425.3	587.8	99.7	204.8	431.9	133.2	202.4	367.2	111.4	170.5	381.3
Total Liab To Nw (%)	116.0	146.8	172.8	33.4	96.6	237.0	37.2	106.0	281.5	38.0	103.5	252.9
Fixed Assets To Nw (%)	189.5	208.1	253.3	10.8	30.3	71.5	10.0	24.0	62.8	10.1	33.1	79.4
EFFICIENCY												
Coll Period (days)	26.7	34.4	51.2	21.9	38.7	62.4	18.8	40.2	73.0	24.5	37.2	49.6
Sales To Inv (times)	144.9	129.5	69.4	153.2	45.3	16.6	97.9	20.2	12.5	73.0	30.1	12.9
Assets To Sales (%)	135.2	242.7	300.7	11.8	20.5	45.3	12.1	21.1	50.7	11.5	17.9	40.5
Sales To Nwc (times)	33.8	17.3	4.1	39.2	16.2	6.8	36.2	15.1	7.1	46.4	18.5	8.0
Acct Pay To Sales (%)	1.5	3.0	6.4	2.4	5.7	10.8	2.4	6.2	13.3	2.7	5.8	8.4
PROFITABILITY												
Return On Sales (%)	33.4	24.6	20.6	6.5	2.5	0.7	5.5	1.9	0.3	5.6	2.4	0.8
Return On Assets (%)	25.6	15.5	8.2	21.3	7.7	2.0	18.6	5.4	1.1	18.7	8.6	2.9
Return On Nw (%)	178.2	27.1	18.0	56.0	22.4	5.9	47.0	17.9	3.5	62.2	23.5	7.9

	SIC 47 TRANSPORTATION SVS SOUTH 1995 (632 Establishments) $	%	SIC 47 TRANSPORTATION SVS WEST 1995 (513 Establishments) $	%	SIC 47 TRANSPORTATION SVS INDUSTRY ASSETS UNDER $100,000 1995 (465 Establishments) $	%	SIC 47 TRANSPORTATION SVS INDUSTRY ASSETS $100,000 - $250,000 1995 (392 Establishments) $	%
Cash	71,645	23.5	85,104	23.5	21,330	39.3	46,475	28.1
Accounts Receivable	116,767	38.3	140,512	38.8	12,157	22.4	63,676	38.5
Notes Receivable	3,354	1.1	3,259	0.9	488	0.9	2,150	1.3
Inventory	4,268	1.4	5,794	1.6	651	1.2	1,654	1.0
Other Current	21,341	7.0	25,350	7.0	3,365	6.2	11,247	6.8
Total Current	**217,375**	**71.3**	**260,019**	**71.8**	**37,992**	**70.0**	**125,201**	**75.7**
Fixed Assets	62,499	20.5	69,894	19.3	11,723	21.6	26,628	16.1
Other Non-current	25,000	8.2	32,231	8.9	4,559	8.4	13,562	8.2
Total Assets	**304,874**	**100.0**	**362,144**	**100.0**	**54,274**	**100.0**	**165,391**	**100.0**
Accounts Payable	68,902	22.6	90,174	24.9	8,033	14.8	39,198	23.7
Bank Loans	—	—	362	0.1	109	0.2	—	—
Notes Payable	11,585	3.8	9,778	2.7	1,954	3.6	4,796	2.9
Other Current	42,073	13.8	56,132	15.5	9,118	16.8	20,508	12.4
Total Current	**122,559**	**40.2**	**156,446**	**43.2**	**19,213**	**35.4**	**64,502**	**39.0**
Other Long Term	29,268	9.6	26,437	7.3	3,691	6.8	12,074	7.3
Deferred Credits	915	0.3	1,086	0.3	109	0.2	662	0.4
Net Worth	152,132	49.9	178,175	49.2	31,262	57.6	88,153	53.3
Total Liab & Net Worth	**304,874**	**100.0**	**362,144**	**100.0**	**54,274**	**100.0**	**165,391**	**100.0**
Net Sales	1,536,260	100.0	2,398,479	100.0	368,626	100.0	1,127,467	100.0
Gross Profit	373,311	24.3	532,462	22.2	93,262	25.3	263,827	23.4
Net Profit After Tax	64,523	4.2	105,533	4.4	16,220	4.4	55,246	4.9
Working Capital	94,816	—	103,573	—	18,779	—	60,699	—

RATIOS	UQ	MED	LQ	UQ	MED	LQ	UQ	MED	LQ	UQ	MED	LQ
SOLVENCY												
Quick Ratio (times)	3.2	1.5	1.0	2.9	1.4	1.0	5.1	1.9	1.0	4.2	1.8	1.1
Current Ratio (times)	3.9	1.8	1.2	3.4	1.6	1.1	6.2	2.4	1.1	4.6	2.1	1.3
Curr Liab To Nw (%)	21.8	63.6	185.4	21.9	81.3	185.6	11.1	36.6	113.0	17.7	57.4	137.1
Curr Liab To Inv (%)	74.1	157.0	366.9	81.6	268.4	510.6	117.3	210.6	669.6	52.5	128.0	304.7
Total Liab To Nw (%)	31.3	85.4	228.3	30.7	98.0	216.4	13.4	45.0	119.6	24.1	71.5	175.1
Fixed Assets To Nw (%)	11.3	33.8	74.7	12.4	31.8	71.3	11.0	28.6	73.7	8.7	23.5	59.0
EFFICIENCY												
Coll Period (days)	23.2	40.9	64.8	20.4	36.5	56.0	6.9	19.7	42.0	17.3	31.8	45.3
Sales To Inv (times)	206.0	66.8	25.4	188.7	47.0	24.3	169.2	96.2	41.7	163.9	42.3	17.5
Assets To Sales (%)	11.4	21.6	45.5	12.5	20.0	44.2	4.1	12.6	27.4	9.3	14.7	27.3
Sales To Nwc (times)	37.3	15.3	6.6	38.6	16.6	6.7	62.6	21.1	8.0	34.2	16.0	7.5
Acct Pay To Sales (%)	2.1	5.3	11.5	2.6	5.7	10.3	0.8	2.3	7.0	1.7	5.0	9.8
PROFITABILITY												
Return On Sales (%)	8.2	3.3	0.8	6.9	2.6	0.8	10.1	2.6	0.6	8.6	3.4	1.1
Return On Assets (%)	26.0	10.6	2.1	20.4	7.8	2.5	50.3	19.9	0.7	35.6	15.8	5.3
Return On Nw (%)	66.5	26.8	6.3	48.7	21.1	7.2	89.6	38.2	2.1	78.0	41.2	11.3

SIC 47 TRANSPORTATION SVS — INDUSTRY ASSETS

	$250,000-$500,000 (330 Est.) $	%	$500,000-$1,000,000 (262 Est.) $	%	$1,000,000-$5,000,000 (358 Est.) $	%	$5,000,000-$25,000,000 (112 Est.) $	%
Cash	67,548	19.2	131,476	19.3	291,703	16.3	908,182	10.4
Accounts Receivable	170,628	48.5	309,956	45.5	826,789	46.2	3,920,901	44.9
Notes Receivable	3,518	1.0	6,131	0.9	14,317	0.8	17,465	0.2
Inventory	7,388	2.1	6,812	1.0	26,844	1.5	209,580	2.4
Other Current	22,516	6.4	53,817	7.9	139,588	7.8	899,450	10.3
Total Current	**271,598**	**77.2**	**508,192**	**74.6**	**1,299,240**	**72.6**	**5,955,579**	**68.2**
Fixed Assets	53,123	15.1	108,314	15.9	334,653	18.7	1,842,562	21.1
Other Non-current	27,089	7.7	64,716	9.5	155,694	8.7	934,380	10.7
Total Assets	**351,811**	**100.0**	**681,222**	**100.0**	**1,789,587**	**100.0**	**8,732,520**	**100.0**
Accounts Payable	109,765	31.2	190,742	28.0	551,193	30.8	2,392,710	27.4
Bank Loans	1,055	0.3	681	0.1	1,790	0.1	17,465	0.2
Notes Payable	10,203	2.9	13,624	2.0	59,056	3.3	497,754	5.7
Other Current	46,087	13.1	103,546	15.2	291,703	16.3	1,632,981	18.7
Total Current	**167,110**	**47.5**	**308,594**	**45.3**	**903,741**	**50.5**	**4,540,910**	**52.0**
Other Long Term	22,164	6.3	58,585	8.6	143,167	8.0	1,091,565	12.5
Deferred Credits	352	0.1	1,362	0.2	5,369	0.3	61,128	0.7
Net Worth	162,185	46.1	312,681	45.9	737,310	41.2	3,038,917	34.8
Total Liab & Net Worth	**351,811**	**100.0**	**681,222**	**100.0**	**1,789,587**	**100.0**	**8,732,520**	**100.0**
Net Sales	1,728,099	100.0	3,232,462	100.0	6,161,535	100.0	27,365,819	100.0
Gross Profit	409,559	23.7	840,440	26.0	1,349,376	21.9	5,911,017	21.6
Net Profit After Tax	57,027	3.3	106,671	3.3	234,138	3.8	684,145	2.5
Working Capital	104,488	—	199,598	—	395,499	—	1,414,669	—

RATIOS

	UQ	MED	LQ	UQ	MED	LQ	UQ	MED	LQ	UQ	MED	LQ
SOLVENCY												
Quick Ratio (times)	2.3	1.4	1.0	2.3	1.4	1.0	1.8	1.2	0.9	1.4	1.0	0.8
Current Ratio (times)	2.9	1.6	1.2	2.9	1.6	1.2	2.2	1.4	1.1	1.8	1.2	1.0
Curr Liab To Nw (%)	32.0	92.5	231.7	35.1	93.2	211.3	47.6	123.6	280.7	75.4	153.2	341.0
Curr Liab To Inv (%)	105.7	310.4	537.0	58.9	168.2	553.6	109.7	189.5	367.0	95.9	236.7	351.6
Total Liab To Nw (%)	41.2	104.6	266.2	44.6	126.4	240.5	60.3	144.5	320.6	93.7	185.1	377.6
Fixed Assets To Nw (%)	9.2	26.3	63.4	10.9	29.4	61.8	12.5	38.0	79.4	19.3	46.9	110.0
EFFICIENCY												
Coll Period (days)	25.2	37.6	56.8	24.8	38.0	59.9	27.4	45.3	85.3	36.7	45.3	66.3
Sales To Inv (times)	136.1	31.5	12.5	145.3	53.3	16.2	102.4	30.3	12.6	201.6	81.6	22.9
Assets To Sales (%)	12.8	20.3	36.7	13.0	20.0	39.7	16.9	29.5	74.3	18.5	29.2	59.7
Sales To Nwc (times)	40.9	16.3	7.4	32.0	17.9	7.8	30.7	11.8	4.9	40.3	20.8	9.5
Acct Pay To Sales (%)	2.6	6.4	12.2	2.7	5.1	8.0	3.1	7.3	15.3	3.6	6.9	11.8
PROFITABILITY												
Return On Sales (%)	5.8	2.6	0.7	4.5	2.2	0.8	5.7	2.3	0.5	4.0	1.5	0.4
Return On Assets (%)	22.2	11.1	2.2	18.0	8.6	2.8	11.2	4.7	1.5	8.1	3.5	1.4
Return On Nw (%)	63.9	26.4	6.8	45.1	22.3	6.9	33.2	16.7	5.0	31.9	13.1	5.7

	SIC 47 TRANSPORTATION SVS INDUSTRY ASSETS $25,000,000-$50,000,000 1995 (35 Establishments) $	%	SIC 47 TRANSPORTATION SVS INDUSTRY ASSETS OVER $50,000,000 1995 (44 Establishments) $	%	SIC 4724 TRAVEL AGENCIES (NO BREAKDOWN) 1995 (465 Establishments) $	%	SIC 4724 TRAVEL AGENCIES INDUSTRY ASSETS UNDER $100,000 1995 (161 Establishments) $	%
Cash	4,548,853	14.0	20,123,148	6.2	64,432	36.9	25,305	46.1
Accounts Receivable	10,494,854	32.3	93,150,703	28.7	40,685	23.3	9,551	17.4
Notes Receivable	682,328	2.1	324,567	0.1	1,746	1.0	329	0.6
Inventory	1,169,705	3.6	12,008,976	3.7	2,270	1.3	439	0.8
Other Current	4,093,968	12.6	30,184,723	9.3	15,890	9.1	3,403	6.2
Total Current	**20,989,707**	**64.6**	**155,792,117**	**48.0**	**125,023**	**71.6**	**39,028**	**71.1**
Fixed Assets	7,765,542	23.9	91,203,302	28.1	28,811	16.5	9,716	17.7
Other Non-current	3,736,558	11.5	77,571,491	23.9	20,779	11.9	6,148	11.2
Total Assets	**32,491,807**	**100.0**	**324,566,910**	**100.0**	**174,613**	**100.0**	**54,891**	**100.0**
Accounts Payable	8,577,837	26.4	49,658,737	15.3	27,240	15.6	6,752	12.3
Bank Loans	—	—	—	—	349	0.2	165	0.3
Notes Payable	422,393	1.3	3,570,236	1.1	4,016	2.3	1,427	2.6
Other Current	7,830,525	24.1	67,185,350	20.7	35,097	20.1	10,320	18.8
Total Current	**16,830,756**	**51.8**	**120,414,324**	**37.1**	**66,702**	**38.2**	**18,663**	**34.0**
Other Long Term	4,711,312	14.5	80,168,027	24.7	13,794	7.9	4,391	8.0
Deferred Credits	974,754	3.0	2,596,535	0.8	1,048	0.6	165	0.3
Net Worth	9,974,985	30.7	121,388,024	37.4	93,069	53.3	31,672	57.7
Total Liab & Net Worth	**32,491,807**	**100.0**	**324,566,910**	**100.0**	**174,613**	**100.0**	**54,891**	**100.0**
Net Sales	80,168,106	100.0	343,674,000	100.0	2,011,077	100.0	264,356	100.0
Gross Profit	13,227,737	16.5	82,138,086	23.9	349,927	17.4	60,538	22.9
Net Profit After Tax	1,763,698	2.2	30,243,312	8.8	74,410	3.7	8,195	3.1
Working Capital	4,158,951	—	35,377,793	—	58,321	—	20,365	—

RATIOS	UQ	MED	LQ	UQ	MED	LQ	UQ	MED	LQ	UQ	MED	LQ
SOLVENCY												
Quick Ratio (times)	1.4	1.0	0.7	1.2	0.9	0.6	3.7	1.6	0.9	4.9	2.1	1.1
Current Ratio (times)	1.8	1.2	1.0	1.6	1.3	1.0	4.6	2.0	1.2	5.8	2.5	1.2
Curr Liab To Nw (%)	54.1	225.9	502.1	42.9	89.9	165.9	19.1	55.7	143.1	16.1	36.2	87.1
Curr Liab To Inv (%)	145.4	202.4	264.1	138.3	155.5	344.8	79.5	263.3	535.1	130.2	227.6	392.5
Total Liab To Nw (%)	95.1	229.8	645.9	105.7	189.6	292.2	22.2	74.4	178.4	17.1	42.5	96.1
Fixed Assets To Nw (%)	27.7	64.0	126.8	38.8	71.3	149.1	8.9	24.8	59.1	8.6	20.4	51.7
EFFICIENCY												
Coll Period (days)	23.9	42.4	66.0	16.2	53.0	80.8	4.8	15.3	43.1	3.2	9.5	28.5
Sales To Inv (times)	16.1	13.0	10.3	113.3	45.4	29.9	184.6	72.3	20.2	174.5	122.5	76.4
Assets To Sales (%)	20.2	39.3	81.8	39.4	69.3	204.8	6.3	18.1	42.9	3.6	15.4	38.6
Sales To Nwc (times)	36.9	15.4	4.9	27.8	7.1	4.8	54.3	18.7	5.5	66.8	20.3	7.6
Acct Pay To Sales (%)	5.0	8.0	10.4	4.3	10.8	15.5	0.7	2.1	6.9	0.4	1.2	4.8
PROFITABILITY												
Return On Sales (%)	3.8	1.1	0.4	9.1	4.4	2.2	7.3	1.8	0.4	8.0	2.2	(0.1)
Return On Assets (%)	3.9	2.1	0.8	8.5	4.7	2.0	21.1	9.0	1.4	35.0	15.9	(3.3)
Return On Nw (%)	17.1	11.5	4.2	24.8	12.3	5.6	41.8	20.0	4.6	60.5	27.0	(0.4)

SIC 4724 TRAVEL AGENCIES — INDUSTRY ASSETS $100,000 - $250,000 — 1995 (123 Establishments)

	$	%
Cash	58,037	37.9
Accounts Receivable	35,067	22.9
Notes Receivable	2,909	1.9
Inventory	1,378	0.9
Other Current	14,088	9.2
Total Current	**111,479**	**72.8**
Fixed Assets	25,420	16.6
Other Non-current	16,232	10.6
Total Assets	**153,131**	**100.0**
Accounts Payable	22,663	14.8
Bank Loans	153	0.1
Notes Payable	2,603	1.7
Other Current	25,573	16.7
Total Current	**50,993**	**33.3**
Other Long Term	11,944	7.8
Deferred Credits	1,225	0.8
Net Worth	88,969	58.1
Total Liab & Net Worth	**153,131**	**100.0**
Net Sales	1,421,167	100.0
Gross Profit	196,121	13.8
Net Profit After Tax	89,534	6.3
Working Capital	60,486	—

RATIOS	UQ	MED	LQ
SOLVENCY			
Quick Ratio (times)	4.6	2.1	1.2
Current Ratio (times)	5.4	2.5	1.4
Curr Liab To Nw (%)	11.5	48.1	99.6
Curr Liab To Inv (%)	64.6	195.0	334.5
Total Liab To Nw (%)	15.6	62.6	141.1
Fixed Assets To Nw (%)	6.2	17.9	56.1
EFFICIENCY			
Coll Period (days)	4.6	11.0	44.4
Sales To Inv (times)	142.3	95.8	49.4
Assets To Sales (%)	4.8	13.0	41.6
Sales To Nwc (times)	52.7	12.9	4.7
Acct Pay To Sales (%)	0.5	1.4	5.9
PROFITABILITY			
Return On Sales (%)	11.4	3.7	1.2
Return On Assets (%)	38.6	15.4	6.5
Return On Nw (%)	63.5	27.1	10.6

SIC 4724 TRAVEL AGENCIES — INDUSTRY ASSETS $250,000 - $500,000 — 1995 (56 Establishments)

	$	%
Cash	99,751	29.3
Accounts Receivable	96,687	28.4
Notes Receivable	2,043	0.6
Inventory	11,235	3.3
Other Current	36,428	10.7
Total Current	**246,144**	**72.3**
Fixed Assets	48,344	14.2
Other Non-current	45,960	13.5
Total Assets	**340,448**	**100.0**
Accounts Payable	60,940	17.9
Bank Loans	3,064	0.9
Notes Payable	11,916	3.5
Other Current	67,068	19.7
Total Current	**142,988**	**42.0**
Other Long Term	23,491	6.9
Deferred Credits	340	0.1
Net Worth	173,628	51.0
Total Liab & Net Worth	**340,448**	**100.0**
Net Sales	2,145,532	100.0
Gross Profit	236,009	11.0
Net Profit After Tax	51,493	2.4
Working Capital	103,156	—

RATIOS	UQ	MED	LQ
SOLVENCY			
Quick Ratio (times)	2.8	1.3	0.9
Current Ratio (times)	4.0	1.6	1.1
Curr Liab To Nw (%)	21.5	75.3	224.4
Curr Liab To Inv (%)	56.2	292.0	660.9
Total Liab To Nw (%)	24.8	101.1	207.7
Fixed Assets To Nw (%)	7.1	24.9	46.6
EFFICIENCY			
Coll Period (days)	4.0	11.7	29.2
Sales To Inv (times)	33.0	25.4	7.2
Assets To Sales (%)	7.3	14.0	42.1
Sales To Nwc (times)	88.8	27.6	6.6
Acct Pay To Sales (%)	0.7	2.1	4.5
PROFITABILITY			
Return On Sales (%)	5.9	1.2	0.4
Return On Assets (%)	14.6	5.9	1.4
Return On Nw (%)	41.5	9.3	2.8

SIC 4724 TRAVEL AGENCIES — INDUSTRY ASSETS $500,000 - $1,000,000 — 1995 (52 Establishments)

	$	%
Cash	209,945	30.9
Accounts Receivable	201,792	29.7
Notes Receivable	12,230	1.8
Inventory	8,153	1.2
Other Current	69,302	10.2
Total Current	**501,422**	**73.8**
Fixed Assets	93,762	13.8
Other Non-current	84,250	12.4
Total Assets	**679,434**	**100.0**
Accounts Payable	125,016	18.4
Bank Loans	—	—
Notes Payable	7,474	1.1
Other Current	152,193	22.4
Total Current	**284,683**	**41.9**
Other Long Term	55,034	8.1
Deferred Credits	—	—
Net Worth	339,717	50.0
Total Liab & Net Worth	**679,434**	**100.0**
Net Sales	5,269,831	100.0
Gross Profit	932,760	17.7
Net Profit After Tax	189,714	3.6
Working Capital	216,739	—

RATIOS	UQ	MED	LQ
SOLVENCY			
Quick Ratio (times)	2.6	1.5	1.0
Current Ratio (times)	3.4	1.8	1.2
Curr Liab To Nw (%)	26.0	71.8	195.9
Curr Liab To Inv (%)	395.0	553.6	681.1
Total Liab To Nw (%)	28.2	96.1	227.7
Fixed Assets To Nw (%)	9.6	21.7	50.6
EFFICIENCY			
Coll Period (days)	5.1	19.7	59.9
Sales To Inv (times)	283.6	162.3	98.6
Assets To Sales (%)	7.0	12.5	38.0
Sales To Nwc (times)	35.8	21.6	7.6
Acct Pay To Sales (%)	0.9	2.3	4.5
PROFITABILITY			
Return On Sales (%)	3.2	1.3	0.5
Return On Assets (%)	16.0	9.3	3.7
Return On Nw (%)	32.2	22.9	6.8

SIC 4724 TRAVEL AGENCIES — INDUSTRY ASSETS $1,000,000 - $5,000,000 — 1995 (47 Establishments)

	$	%
Cash	451,671	29.8
Accounts Receivable	406,201	26.8
Notes Receivable	3,031	0.2
Inventory	7,578	0.5
Other Current	162,177	10.7
Total Current	**1,030,659**	**68.0**
Fixed Assets	286,463	18.9
Other Non-current	198,553	13.1
Total Assets	**1,515,675**	**100.0**
Accounts Payable	298,588	19.7
Bank Loans	—	—
Notes Payable	31,829	2.1
Other Current	409,232	27.0
Total Current	**739,649**	**48.8**
Other Long Term	134,895	8.9
Deferred Credits	1,516	0.1
Net Worth	639,615	42.2
Total Liab & Net Worth	**1,515,675**	**100.0**
Net Sales	6,246,344	100.0
Gross Profit	1,174,313	18.8
Net Profit After Tax	187,390	3.0
Working Capital	291,010	—

RATIOS	UQ	MED	LQ
SOLVENCY			
Quick Ratio (times)	1.8	1.0	0.8
Current Ratio (times)	2.1	1.3	1.0
Curr Liab To Nw (%)	58.8	112.0	219.6
Curr Liab To Inv (%)	369.4	369.4	369.4
Total Liab To Nw (%)	80.1	143.1	278.7
Fixed Assets To Nw (%)	19.1	38.3	76.4
EFFICIENCY			
Coll Period (days)	10.1	24.6	55.2
Sales To Inv (times)	684.7	576.5	293.5
Assets To Sales (%)	15.1	26.3	48.1
Sales To Nwc (times)	27.9	11.6	3.6
Acct Pay To Sales (%)	1.3	6.1	12.1
PROFITABILITY			
Return On Sales (%)	4.5	1.2	0.3
Return On Assets (%)	9.7	3.7	0.8
Return On Nw (%)	26.3	12.2	4.7

SIC 4724 TRAVEL AGENCIES — INDUSTRY ASSETS $5,000,000-$25,000,000 — 1995 (16 Establishments)
SIC 4725 TOUR OPERATORS (NO BREAKDOWN) — 1995 (127 Establishments)
SIC 4725 TOUR OPERATORS — INDUSTRY ASSETS UNDER $100,000 — 1995 (41 Establishments)
SIC 4725 TOUR OPERATORS — INDUSTRY ASSETS $100,000 - $250,000 — 1995 (24 Establishments)

	Travel Agencies $	%	Tour Op. (No Brkdn) $	%	Tour Op. Under $100,000 $	%	Tour Op. $100,000-$250,000 $	%
Cash	1,397,750	20.2	77,089	30.9	18,054	35.8	59,900	34.5
Accounts Receivable	2,297,291	33.2	40,166	16.1	8,069	16.0	22,224	12.8
Notes Receivable	13,839	0.2	1,996	0.8	656	1.3	347	0.2
Inventory	429,012	6.2	748	0.3	101	0.2	868	0.5
Other Current	774,990	11.2	35,426	14.2	4,791	9.5	16,841	9.7
Total Current	**4,912,882**	**71.0**	**155,426**	**62.3**	**31,669**	**62.8**	**100,180**	**57.7**
Fixed Assets	830,346	12.0	64,865	26.0	16,238	32.2	41,843	24.1
Other Non-current	1,176,324	17.0	29,189	11.7	2,521	5.0	31,599	18.2
Total Assets	**6,919,552**	**100.0**	**249,480**	**100.0**	**50,429**	**100.0**	**173,623**	**100.0**
Accounts Payable	1,287,037	18.6	35,177	14.1	5,598	11.1	11,980	6.9
Bank Loans	—	—	—	—	—	—	—	—
Notes Payable	311,380	4.5	7,983	3.2	2,168	4.3	7,119	4.1
Other Current	1,487,704	21.5	58,628	23.5	11,599	23.0	33,336	19.2
Total Current	**3,086,120**	**44.6**	**101,788**	**40.8**	**19,365**	**38.4**	**52,434**	**30.2**
Other Long Term	442,851	6.4	27,193	10.9	3,328	6.6	14,411	8.3
Deferred Credits	179,908	2.6	1,996	0.8	—	—	—	—
Net Worth	3,210,672	46.4	118,503	47.5	27,736	55.0	106,778	61.5
Total Liab & Net Worth	**6,919,552**	**100.0**	**249,480**	**100.0**	**50,429**	**100.0**	**173,623**	**100.0**
Net Sales	23,648,700	100.0	1,944,287	100.0	603,820	100.0	1,233,358	100.0
Gross Profit	2,719,601	11.5	476,350	24.5	164,239	27.2	345,340	28.0
Net Profit After Tax	472,974	2.0	66,106	3.4	21,134	3.5	53,034	4.3
Working Capital	1,826,762	—	53,638	—	12,304	—	47,746	—

RATIOS	TA UQ	TA MED	TA LQ	TO(NB) UQ	TO(NB) MED	TO(NB) LQ	TO<$100K UQ	TO<$100K MED	TO<$100K LQ	TO$100-250K UQ	TO$100-250K MED	TO$100-250K LQ
SOLVENCY												
Quick Ratio (times)	1.8	1.1	0.9	3.5	1.3	0.6	4.6	1.5	0.7	7.6	2.0	0.9
Current Ratio (times)	2.3	1.3	1.2	4.0	1.5	1.0	6.5	1.8	0.9	8.3	2.3	1.4
Curr Liab To Nw (%)	43.7	138.8	253.4	16.3	76.1	184.5	10.0	49.5	150.1	6.9	27.4	63.1
Curr Liab To Inv (%)	4.1	4.1	4.1	60.1	126.3	356.1	101.0	101.0	101.0	348.6	356.1	363.5
Total Liab To Nw (%)	58.6	155.8	275.7	31.6	104.7	231.6	14.4	75.7	162.8	15.2	47.9	63.9
Fixed Assets To Nw (%)	15.7	25.5	44.2	20.4	40.5	106.7	28.9	46.1	113.1	24.0	53.6	84.1
EFFICIENCY												
Coll Period (days)	25.9	27.0	82.9	3.3	14.6	33.6	10.8	19.0	33.8	1.5	2.9	18.3
Sales To Inv (times)	—	—	—	301.2	102.4	46.9	63.4	63.4	63.4	529.6	529.6	529.6
Assets To Sales (%)	18.6	30.4	85.0	10.2	19.0	40.8	3.9	8.3	28.9	7.6	14.0	20.9
Sales To Nwc (times)	38.3	23.2	4.4	69.4	29.5	9.5	89.0	38.6	15.1	37.0	18.0	4.6
Acct Pay To Sales (%)	1.2	4.2	10.4	1.2	2.7	6.8	1.5	4.0	8.2	0.5	1.7	2.3
PROFITABILITY												
Return On Sales (%)	3.2	1.0	0.3	5.9	1.8	0.3	8.4	2.3	1.5	5.7	1.9	0.6
Return On Assets (%)	5.9	2.8	1.4	22.8	7.2	1.2	91.6	52.6	12.5	25.6	6.6	3.6
Return On Nw (%)	13.3	10.0	5.2	51.7	22.0	4.2	168.7	77.8	21.0	35.3	8.8	6.7

SIC 4725 TOUR OPERATORS — INDUSTRY ASSETS

	$250,000 - $500,000 1995 (16 Est.) $	%	$500,000 - $1,000,000 1995 (13 Est.) $	%	$1,000,000 - $5,000,000 1995 (22 Est.) $	%	SIC 4729 PSSGR TRNS ARGT,NEC (NO BREAKDOWN) 1995 (12 Est.) $	%
Cash	94,389	26.6	236,935	31.3	521,460	28.0	410,469	20.0
Accounts Receivable	62,098	17.5	74,184	9.8	385,508	20.7	621,861	30.3
Notes Receivable	2,484	0.7	8,327	1.1	18,624	1.0	—	—
Inventory	2,129	0.6	757	0.1	7,449	0.4	—	—
Other Current	53,582	15.1	164,265	21.7	396,682	21.3	96,460	4.7
Total Current	**214,682**	**60.5**	**484,468**	**64.0**	**1,329,722**	**71.4**	**1,128,791**	**55.0**
Fixed Assets	85,163	24.0	224,066	29.6	307,289	16.5	701,903	34.2
Other Non-current	55,001	15.5	48,447	6.4	225,345	12.1	221,653	10.8
Total Assets	**354,846**	**100.0**	**756,981**	**100.0**	**1,862,356**	**100.0**	**2,052,347**	**100.0**
Accounts Payable	46,130	13.0	139,285	18.4	484,213	26.0	34,890	1.7
Bank Loans	—	—	2,271	0.3	—	—	—	—
Notes Payable	14,549	4.1	10,598	1.4	22,348	1.2	28,733	1.4
Other Current	70,260	19.8	168,050	22.2	493,524	26.5	679,327	33.1
Total Current	**130,938**	**36.9**	**320,203**	**42.3**	**1,000,085**	**53.7**	**742,950**	**36.2**
Other Long Term	48,259	13.6	194,544	25.7	171,337	9.2	215,496	10.5
Deferred Credits	—	—	—	—	80,081	4.3	—	—
Net Worth	175,649	49.5	242,234	32.0	610,853	32.8	1,093,901	53.3
Total Liab & Net Worth	**354,846**	**100.0**	**756,981**	**100.0**	**1,862,356**	**100.0**	**2,052,347**	**100.0**
Net Sales	1,600,452	100.0	3,377,032	100.0	8,016,665	100.0	2,936,399	100.0
Gross Profit	380,908	23.8	928,684	27.5	1,579,283	19.7	1,209,796	41.2
Net Profit After Tax	46,413	2.9	155,343	4.6	216,450	2.7	23,491	0.8
Working Capital	83,744	—	164,265	—	329,637	—	385,841	—

RATIOS

	UQ	MED	LQ	UQ	MED	LQ	UQ	MED	LQ	UQ	MED	LQ
SOLVENCY												
Quick Ratio (times)	2.8	1.4	0.9	1.7	1.3	0.8	1.8	0.9	0.5	7.4	3.2	0.7
Current Ratio (times)	3.9	1.7	1.2	2.2	1.5	1.2	2.0	1.4	0.9	7.4	2.2	0.9
Curr Liab To Nw (%)	17.5	63.5	194.8	71.2	146.6	193.1	68.3	143.6	241.8	11.2	89.6	419.5
Curr Liab To Inv (%)	11.6	11.6	11.6	19.1	19.1	19.1	187.9	249.4	311.0			
Total Liab To Nw (%)	46.1	98.4	295.7	126.9	219.0	382.9	77.4	177.3	376.2	11.5	20.7	388.7
Fixed Assets To Nw (%)	18.7	37.0	72.5	25.8	34.7	140.1	24.1	37.4	59.9	46.9	82.7	155.8
EFFICIENCY												
Coll Period (days)	22.6	28.1	33.6	2.6	3.3	12.4	3.7	11.7	34.0	24.0	62.8	88.7
Sales To Inv (times)	491.9	334.9	177.8	517.5	359.5	201.6	91.3	80.2	63.6	102.8	102.8	102.8
Assets To Sales (%)	11.5	22.2	31.1	13.7	19.4	96.4	11.8	24.4	44.7	13.8	37.8	65.8
Sales To Nwc (times)	51.3	27.9	12.1	36.8	27.4	14.8	56.0	21.7	9.3	98.8	9.7	3.5
Acct Pay To Sales (%)	0.8	1.2	2.1	1.5	3.4	5.3	1.4	3.9	11.1	0.2	0.4	0.8
PROFITABILITY												
Return On Sales (%)	6.9	2.1	(0.2)	9.5	2.5	0.7	3.3	1.4	0.2	5.5	0.1	(1.9)
Return On Assets (%)	17.8	10.8	1.6	21.4	8.9	2.6	11.9	2.9	1.0	7.6	2.3	(3.6)
Return On Nw (%)	39.1	14.4	1.9	70.3	27.1	19.6	43.3	10.8	3.9	22.0	2.5	(10.7)

SIC 4731 FRGT TRANS ARNGMNT (NO BREAKDOWN)
1995 (1225 Establishments)

	$	%
Cash	81,489	19.6
Accounts Receivable	205,386	49.4
Notes Receivable	4,158	1.0
Inventory	3,326	0.8
Other Current	25,777	6.2
Total Current	**320,137**	**77.0**
Fixed Assets	66,106	15.9
Other Non-current	29,519	7.1
Total Assets	**415,762**	**100.0**
Accounts Payable	132,628	31.9
Bank Loans	416	0.1
Notes Payable	12,889	3.1
Other Current	53,633	12.9
Total Current	**199,566**	**48.0**
Other Long Term	27,440	6.6
Deferred Credits	832	0.2
Net Worth	187,924	45.2
Total Liab & Net Worth	**415,762**	**100.0**
Net Sales	2,068,709	100.0
Gross Profit	482,009	23.3
Net Profit After Tax	76,542	3.7
Working Capital	120,571	—

RATIOS	UQ	MED	LQ
SOLVENCY			
Quick Ratio (times)	2.3	1.4	1.0
Current Ratio (times)	2.8	1.5	1.1
Curr Liab To Nw (%)	32.2	100.9	235.5
Curr Liab To Inv (%)	82.2	189.5	510.6
Total Liab To Nw (%)	39.6	111.1	264.8
Fixed Assets To Nw (%)	10.2	27.9	67.7
EFFICIENCY			
Coll Period (days)	27.4	41.6	66.0
Sales To Inv (times)	189.1	61.1	22.2
Assets To Sales (%)	12.3	19.2	38.7
Sales To Nwc (times)	37.5	16.7	7.8
Acct Pay To Sales (%)	3.3	6.9	12.3
PROFITABILITY			
Return On Sales (%)	5.8	2.5	0.7
Return On Assets (%)	21.7	7.5	2.2
Return On Nw (%)	60.4	24.1	6.7

SIC 4731 FRGT TRANS ARNGMNT
INDUSTRY ASSETS UNDER $100,000
1995 (233 Establishments)

	$	%
Cash	19,102	36.6
Accounts Receivable	14,405	27.6
Notes Receivable	522	1.0
Inventory	835	1.6
Other Current	3,027	5.8
Total Current	**37,891**	**72.6**
Fixed Assets	10,856	20.8
Other Non-current	3,445	6.6
Total Assets	**52,191**	**100.0**
Accounts Payable	9,655	18.5
Bank Loans	157	0.3
Notes Payable	2,035	3.9
Other Current	6,680	12.8
Total Current	**18,528**	**35.5**
Other Long Term	2,871	5.5
Deferred Credits	52	0.1
Net Worth	30,740	58.9
Total Liab & Net Worth	**52,191**	**100.0**
Net Sales	407,546	100.0
Gross Profit	92,920	22.8
Net Profit After Tax	20,785	5.1
Working Capital	19,363	—

RATIOS	UQ	MED	LQ
Quick Ratio (times)	6.2	2.0	1.1
Current Ratio (times)	7.5	2.4	1.2
Curr Liab To Nw (%)	9.4	34.8	114.9
Curr Liab To Inv (%)	83.9	193.3	479.9
Total Liab To Nw (%)	11.1	45.4	122.0
Fixed Assets To Nw (%)	10.7	27.1	70.0
Coll Period (days)	12.4	24.5	46.4
Sales To Inv (times)	220.2	45.6	34.8
Assets To Sales (%)	4.3	11.8	22.2
Sales To Nwc (times)	57.7	18.4	8.4
Acct Pay To Sales (%)	1.1	2.6	7.6
Return On Sales (%)	11.6	2.8	0.7
Return On Assets (%)	56.7	21.0	1.2
Return On Nw (%)	97.7	41.5	1.9

SIC 4731 FRGT TRANS ARNGMNT
INDUSTRY ASSETS $100,000 - $250,000
1995 (226 Establishments)

	$	%
Cash	38,382	22.2
Accounts Receivable	86,619	50.1
Notes Receivable	1,902	1.1
Inventory	864	0.5
Other Current	9,336	5.4
Total Current	**137,104**	**79.3**
Fixed Assets	24,724	14.3
Other Non-current	11,065	6.4
Total Assets	**172,893**	**100.0**
Accounts Payable	53,943	31.2
Bank Loans	—	—
Notes Payable	5,878	3.4
Other Current	16,252	9.4
Total Current	**76,073**	**44.0**
Other Long Term	10,892	6.3
Deferred Credits	346	0.2
Net Worth	85,582	49.5
Total Liab & Net Worth	**172,893**	**100.0**
Net Sales	1,187,782	100.0
Gross Profit	291,007	24.5
Net Profit After Tax	51,075	4.3
Working Capital	61,031	—

RATIOS	UQ	MED	LQ
Quick Ratio (times)	3.6	1.6	1.1
Current Ratio (times)	3.8	1.9	1.2
Curr Liab To Nw (%)	23.2	70.9	178.0
Curr Liab To Inv (%)	35.1	40.4	64.9
Total Liab To Nw (%)	32.3	88.8	197.5
Fixed Assets To Nw (%)	8.5	22.4	52.6
Coll Period (days)	23.4	35.8	45.3
Sales To Inv (times)	226.3	115.3	48.4
Assets To Sales (%)	10.2	14.1	23.6
Sales To Nwc (times)	31.9	17.6	9.3
Acct Pay To Sales (%)	3.0	5.6	10.5
Return On Sales (%)	6.5	3.3	1.1
Return On Assets (%)	36.3	16.1	5.5
Return On Nw (%)	88.0	49.0	16.7

SIC 4731 FRGT TRANS ARNGMNT
INDUSTRY ASSETS $250,000 - $500,000
1995 (228 Establishments)

	$	%
Cash	61,605	17.5
Accounts Receivable	200,304	56.9
Notes Receivable	3,520	1.0
Inventory	2,464	0.7
Other Current	17,601	5.0
Total Current	**285,495**	**81.1**
Fixed Assets	47,876	13.6
Other Non-current	18,657	5.3
Total Assets	**352,028**	**100.0**
Accounts Payable	133,771	38.0
Bank Loans	704	0.2
Notes Payable	8,097	2.3
Other Current	37,667	10.7
Total Current	**180,238**	**51.2**
Other Long Term	16,545	4.7
Deferred Credits	352	0.1
Net Worth	154,892	44.0
Total Liab & Net Worth	**352,028**	**100.0**
Net Sales	1,876,203	100.0
Gross Profit	444,660	23.7
Net Profit After Tax	60,038	3.2
Working Capital	105,257	—

RATIOS	UQ	MED	LQ
Quick Ratio (times)	2.2	1.4	1.1
Current Ratio (times)	2.5	1.5	1.2
Curr Liab To Nw (%)	37.9	106.1	239.6
Curr Liab To Inv (%)	77.0	310.4	517.2
Total Liab To Nw (%)	57.1	116.3	278.4
Fixed Assets To Nw (%)	9.3	25.1	58.4
Coll Period (days)	27.1	41.1	65.0
Sales To Inv (times)	115.9	38.6	17.7
Assets To Sales (%)	13.2	19.1	33.5
Sales To Nwc (times)	37.3	16.3	7.9
Acct Pay To Sales (%)	4.2	8.1	13.7
Return On Sales (%)	5.5	2.8	0.8
Return On Assets (%)	23.8	11.3	2.5
Return On Nw (%)	72.2	30.2	9.6

SIC 4731 FRGT TRANS ARNGMNT

Balance sheet / composition data by INDUSTRY ASSETS size class:

	$500,000 - $1,000,000 (179 Est.) $	%	$1,000,000 - $5,000,000 (250 Est.) $	%	$5,000,000 - $25,000,000 (71 Est.) $	%	OVER $50,000,000 (19 Est.) $	%
Cash	101,693	14.7	246,301	13.6	681,482	7.8	13,355,372	7.4
Accounts Receivable	378,407	54.7	990,639	54.7	4,962,586	56.8	85,185,616	47.2
Notes Receivable	4,843	0.7	18,110	1.0	17,474	0.2	180,478	0.1
Inventory	4,151	0.6	10,866	0.6	43,685	0.5	9,926,290	5.5
Other Current	46,350	6.7	119,529	6.6	830,010	9.5	13,174,894	7.3
Total Current	**535,443**	**77.4**	**1,385,446**	**76.5**	**6,535,236**	**74.8**	**121,822,650**	**67.5**
Fixed Assets	94,083	13.6	286,144	15.8	1,633,809	18.7	28,515,524	15.8
Other Non-current	62,261	9.0	139,450	7.7	567,902	6.5	30,139,826	16.7
Total Assets	**691,787**	**100.0**	**1,811,040**	**100.0**	**8,736,947**	**100.0**	**180,478,000**	**100.0**
Accounts Payable	230,365	33.3	659,219	36.4	3,075,405	35.2	43,495,198	24.1
Bank Loans	692	0.1	1,811	0.1	17,474	0.2	—	—
Notes Payable	15,911	2.3	54,331	3.0	576,639	6.6	2,346,214	1.3
Other Current	89,932	13.0	264,412	14.6	1,598,861	18.3	43,134,242	23.9
Total Current	**336,900**	**48.7**	**979,773**	**54.1**	**5,268,379**	**60.3**	**88,975,654**	**49.3**
Other Long Term	44,274	6.4	121,340	6.7	1,065,908	12.2	28,876,480	16.0
Deferred Credits	2,075	0.3	1,811	0.1	26,211	0.3	1,082,868	0.6
Net Worth	308,537	44.6	708,117	39.1	2,376,450	27.2	61,542,998	34.1
Total Liab & Net Worth	**691,787**	**100.0**	**1,811,040**	**100.0**	**8,736,947**	**100.0**	**180,478,000**	**100.0**
Net Sales	3,261,889	100.0	6,665,553	100.0	36,262,930	100.0	426,050,000	100.0
Gross Profit	851,353	26.1	1,419,763	21.3	8,014,108	22.1	106,512,500	25.0
Net Profit After Tax	84,809	2.6	266,622	4.0	688,996	1.9	15,337,800	3.6
Working Capital	198,543	—	405,673	—	1,266,857	—	32,846,996	—

RATIOS

	$500,000-$1,000,000 UQ	MED	LQ	$1,000,000-$5,000,000 UQ	MED	LQ	$5,000,000-$25,000,000 UQ	MED	LQ	OVER $50,000,000 UQ	MED	LQ
SOLVENCY												
Quick Ratio (times)	2.0	1.4	1.1	1.7	1.2	1.0	1.3	1.1	0.9	1.3	1.2	0.8
Current Ratio (times)	2.4	1.5	1.2	2.0	1.4	1.1	1.5	1.2	1.0	1.3	1.3	1.0
Curr Liab To Nw (%)	40.1	120.5	235.5	56.2	137.1	319.9	116.9	225.7	463.4	89.9	163.0	207.3
Curr Liab To Inv (%)	101.1	168.2	510.6	141.4	367.0	604.5	224.4	383.1	541.7	91.9	176.2	260.5
Total Liab To Nw (%)	50.3	127.7	251.7	70.6	155.3	362.7	140.9	262.6	518.4	111.7	239.7	339.0
Fixed Assets To Nw (%)	11.1	26.3	56.0	10.0	30.0	73.5	22.2	57.8	150.8	23.2	42.7	70.2
EFFICIENCY												
Coll Period (days)	30.5	40.9	60.5	34.5	50.7	116.5	38.6	47.7	63.1	50.0	76.3	104.4
Sales To Inv (times)	109.7	53.3	16.2	176.5	78.5	37.8	543.8	168.4	96.3	56.9	33.5	14.3
Assets To Sales (%)	14.3	19.6	36.6	16.6	28.8	83.5	16.8	24.1	47.1	36.6	41.5	67.3
Sales To Nwc (times)	30.2	17.5	8.7	33.4	12.7	4.9	41.3	22.9	11.8	16.8	11.0	6.1
Acct Pay To Sales (%)	4.1	6.3	8.8	4.7	8.7	18.6	4.5	8.4	12.6	8.5	10.8	17.2
PROFITABILITY												
Return On Sales (%)	4.4	2.2	0.8	5.2	2.4	0.7	3.4	1.1	0.5	4.5	2.8	2.1
Return On Assets (%)	17.7	7.9	2.8	11.3	4.9	1.9	6.6	3.4	1.7	8.4	5.1	1.5
Return On Nw (%)	51.4	22.2	6.1	34.9	17.5	5.8	42.0	15.6	7.5	24.2	13.8	6.0

	SIC 4741 RENTL RAILRD CARS (NO BREAKDOWN) 1995 (16 Establishments) $	%	SIC 4783 PACKING AND CRATING (NO BREAKDOWN) 1995 (79 Establishments) $	%	SIC 4783 PACKING AND CRATING INDUSTRY ASSETS UNDER $100,000 1995 (21 Establishments) $	%	SIC 4783 PACKING AND CRATING INDUSTRY ASSETS $100,000 - $250,000 1995 (11 Establishments) $	%
Cash	317,592	4.8	64,059	18.0	19,235	28.5	42,732	29.8
Accounts Receivable	337,441	5.1	117,442	33.0	14,510	21.5	47,751	33.3
Notes Receivable	6,616	0.1	2,491	0.7	—	—	—	—
Inventory	39,699	0.6	38,436	10.8	2,430	3.6	10,898	7.6
Other Current	178,645	2.7	13,880	3.9	2,902	4.3	9,607	6.7
Total Current	**879,994**	**13.3**	**236,308**	**66.4**	**39,077**	**57.9**	**110,988**	**77.4**
Fixed Assets	4,201,476	63.5	88,972	25.0	18,830	27.9	26,958	18.8
Other Non-current	1,535,027	23.2	30,606	8.6	9,584	14.2	5,449	3.8
Total Assets	**6,616,497**	**100.0**	**355,886**	**100.0**	**67,490**	**100.0**	**143,395**	**100.0**
Accounts Payable	291,126	4.4	56,942	16.0	6,074	9.0	23,230	16.2
Bank Loans	—	—	—	—	—	—	—	—
Notes Payable	463,155	7.0	19,930	5.6	1,350	2.0	7,170	5.0
Other Current	297,742	4.5	45,553	12.8	15,118	22.4	19,215	13.4
Total Current	**1,052,023**	**15.9**	**122,425**	**34.4**	**22,542**	**33.4**	**49,615**	**34.6**
Other Long Term	2,229,759	33.7	45,553	12.8	5,332	7.9	15,343	10.7
Deferred Credits	33,082	0.5	—	—	—	—	—	—
Net Worth	3,301,632	49.9	187,908	52.8	39,617	58.7	78,437	54.7
Total Liab & Net Worth	**6,616,497**	**100.0**	**355,886**	**100.0**	**67,490**	**100.0**	**143,395**	**100.0**
Net Sales	2,746,493	100.0	1,034,018	100.0	304,574	100.0	823,541	100.0
Gross Profit	722,328	26.3	377,417	36.5	151,069	49.6	304,710	37.0
Net Profit After Tax	216,973	7.9	47,565	4.6	10,660	3.5	46,942	5.7
Working Capital	(172,029)	—	113,883	—	16,535	—	61,373	—

RATIOS	UQ	MED	LQ	UQ	MED	LQ	UQ	MED	LQ	UQ	MED	LQ
SOLVENCY												
Quick Ratio (times)	2.8	0.6	0.4	3.2	1.7	0.9	5.0	1.9	0.9	2.7	1.8	1.5
Current Ratio (times)	3.6	0.7	0.5	3.7	2.3	1.4	5.4	2.7	0.9	3.1	2.4	1.8
Curr Liab To Nw (%)	9.7	34.3	71.2	24.4	52.6	130.2	13.1	30.7	54.5	40.0	57.1	98.8
Curr Liab To Inv (%)	167.1	167.1	167.1	130.4	237.4	409.0	138.6	697.7	843.8	197.7	240.2	268.4
Total Liab To Nw (%)	58.6	118.3	194.0	35.5	88.8	169.3	17.5	41.4	98.8	41.0	69.3	182.6
Fixed Assets To Nw (%)	83.1	170.8	252.4	15.6	53.7	74.7	32.0	51.6	65.2	16.4	26.6	47.3
EFFICIENCY												
Coll Period (days)	45.3	47.8	78.9	29.8	40.8	59.4	16.4	41.1	83.8	32.8	45.3	60.2
Sales To Inv (times)	27.7	25.1	23.0	118.9	33.4	17.1	126.1	109.1	63.4	92.4	38.7	23.1
Assets To Sales (%)	157.4	222.8	240.9	21.3	29.9	47.5	16.0	21.8	37.2	22.3	26.7	39.5
Sales To Nwc (times)	29.3	15.5	4.8	17.5	9.7	6.0	14.4	11.5	6.2	13.5	9.9	6.5
Acct Pay To Sales (%)	4.6	6.3	15.5	2.6	5.3	7.9	3.2	4.8	21.0	3.2	5.3	7.0
PROFITABILITY												
Return On Sales (%)	20.6	9.2	7.5	10.2	2.9	1.2	9.3	2.7	1.3	13.6	6.6	2.5
Return On Assets (%)	10.5	7.3	0.2	19.9	11.6	4.8	21.4	16.7	3.2	19.7	14.1	6.7
Return On Nw (%)	40.2	11.6	1.5	46.9	21.8	14.1	77.4	37.2	15.2	52.4	34.5	17.5

Balance Sheet Composite

	SIC 4783 PACKING AND CRATING $	%	SIC 4785 INSPCTN FXD FCLTS $	%	SIC 4789 TRANS SRVCS, NEC (NO BREAKDOWN) $	%	SIC 4789 TRANS SRVCS, NEC (INDUSTRY ASSETS) $	%
	INDUSTRY ASSETS $250,000 - $500,000 1995 (18 Establishments)		(NO BREAKDOWN) 1995 (24 Establishments)		1995 (50 Establishments)		$1,000,000 - $5,000,000 1995 (19 Establishments)	
Cash	46,847	12.7	997,312	8.4	142,798	12.3	222,808	11.0
Accounts Receivable	151,238	41.0	2,445,788	20.6	299,528	25.8	496,254	24.5
Notes Receivable	9,222	2.5	23,746	0.2	10,449	0.9	28,357	1.4
Inventory	38,363	10.4	35,618	0.3	109,131	9.4	160,016	7.9
Other Current	14,755	4.0	1,032,930	8.7	75,463	6.5	105,327	5.2
Total Current	**260,424**	**70.6**	**4,535,393**	**38.2**	**637,369**	**54.9**	**1,012,763**	**50.0**
Fixed Assets	67,135	18.2	4,274,193	36.0	442,327	38.1	870,976	43.0
Other Non-current	41,314	11.2	3,063,171	25.8	81,267	7.0	141,787	7.0
Total Assets	**368,873**	**100.0**	**11,872,757**	**100.0**	**1,160,963**	**100.0**	**2,025,525**	**100.0**
Accounts Payable	57,544	15.6	747,984	6.3	102,165	8.8	127,608	6.3
Bank Loans	—	—	—	—	—	—	—	—
Notes Payable	21,026	5.7	35,618	0.3	67,336	5.8	113,429	5.6
Other Current	55,700	15.1	1,519,713	12.8	154,408	13.3	188,374	9.3
Total Current	**134,270**	**36.4**	**2,303,315**	**19.4**	**323,909**	**27.9**	**429,411**	**21.2**
Other Long Term	44,634	12.1	2,469,533	20.8	229,871	19.8	423,335	20.9
Deferred Credits	—	—	—	—	5,805	0.5	—	—
Net Worth	189,970	51.5	7,099,909	59.8	601,379	51.8	1,172,779	57.9
Total Liab & Net Worth	**368,873**	**100.0**	**11,872,757**	**100.0**	**1,160,963**	**100.0**	**2,025,525**	**100.0**
Net Sales	1,034,018	100.0	9,521,851	100.0	1,850,482	100.0	2,139,112	100.0
Gross Profit	408,437	39.5	3,056,514	32.1	780,903	42.2	776,498	36.3
Net Profit After Tax	63,075	6.1	1,628,237	17.1	109,178	5.9	104,816	4.9
Working Capital	126,154	—	2,232,078	—	313,460	—	583,352	—

RATIOS

	4783 UQ	MED	LQ	4785 UQ	MED	LQ	4789(50) UQ	MED	LQ	4789(19) UQ	MED	LQ
SOLVENCY												
Quick Ratio (times)	2.9	1.5	0.9	2.5	1.3	0.5	3.2	1.4	0.7	1.0	0.7	0.3
Current Ratio (times)	4.0	2.1	1.5	8.9	2.7	1.4	4.6	2.5	1.3	2.2	1.6	1.1
Curr Liab To Nw (%)	27.2	70.3	143.2	7.2	17.7	46.1	15.1	36.8	88.4	4.6	10.4	15.4
Curr Liab To Inv (%)	139.3	266.7	611.2	155.5	155.5	155.5	78.3	134.3	344.4	49.2	91.7	102.1
Total Liab To Nw (%)	44.2	90.1	149.2	22.8	61.0	135.5	22.5	75.6	231.2	13.9	24.7	80.1
Fixed Assets To Nw (%)	11.4	32.3	65.4	57.7	65.4	97.4	36.6	70.1	139.3	15.8	52.5	64.9
EFFICIENCY												
Coll Period (days)	30.6	40.5	47.3	8.4	31.8	69.7	38.7	48.9	62.4	8.4	25.9	38.4
Sales To Inv (times)	209.3	123.5	13.8	132.7	45.4	30.8	22.1	12.2	9.4	12.5	8.4	6.5
Assets To Sales (%)	22.2	38.9	49.0	85.9	211.2	624.7	26.6	51.3	75.4	36.8	51.6	72.4
Sales To Nwc (times)	20.7	9.7	4.9	8.2	1.9	1.0	12.2	5.7	4.3	4.8	3.0	1.2
Acct Pay To Sales (%)	2.2	4.5	5.2	2.8	5.0	9.6	2.2	3.5	7.3	1.8	2.5	3.0
PROFITABILITY												
Return On Sales (%)	7.9	3.1	1.6	25.6	14.9	3.4	8.6	4.8	1.7	6.4	4.1	0.4
Return On Assets (%)	22.1	16.0	4.9	10.1	4.6	2.1	18.0	10.9	4.1	4.1	2.4	—
Return On Nw (%)	44.3	26.4	17.7	13.0	8.4	4.3	37.2	25.3	7.5	7.5	4.2	0.7

SIC 48 COMMUNICATION

	NO BREAKDOWN 1995 (1725 Establishments)		NORTHEAST 1995 (307 Establishments)		CENTRAL 1995 (530 Establishments)		SOUTH 1995 (578 Establishments)	
	$	%	$	%	$	%	$	%
Cash	726,935	12.6	1,009,560	11.1	619,105	13.0	929,068	12.4
Accounts Receivable	790,398	13.7	1,464,316	16.1	557,194	11.7	1,063,933	14.2
Notes Receivable	34,616	0.6	18,190	0.2	23,812	0.5	52,447	0.7
Inventory	138,464	2.4	218,283	2.4	100,009	2.1	202,297	2.7
Other Current	375,006	6.5	627,564	6.9	352,413	7.4	382,117	5.1
Total Current	**2,065,419**	**35.8**	**3,337,913**	**36.7**	**1,652,533**	**34.7**	**2,629,863**	**35.1**
Fixed Assets	2,492,350	43.2	3,638,052	40.0	2,152,579	45.2	3,191,799	42.6
Other Non-current	1,211,559	21.0	2,119,166	23.3	957,231	20.1	1,670,824	22.3
Total Assets	**5,769,328**	**100.0**	**9,095,131**	**100.0**	**4,762,343**	**100.0**	**7,492,486**	**100.0**
Accounts Payable	478,854	8.3	827,657	9.1	319,077	6.7	681,816	9.1
Bank Loans	—	—	9,095	0.1	4,762	0.1	—	—
Notes Payable	126,925	2.2	136,427	1.5	66,673	1.4	209,790	2.8
Other Current	617,318	10.7	1,136,891	12.5	428,611	9.0	764,234	10.2
Total Current	**1,223,098**	**21.2**	**2,110,070**	**23.2**	**819,123**	**17.2**	**1,655,839**	**22.1**
Other Long Term	1,603,873	27.8	2,583,017	28.4	1,362,030	28.6	2,180,313	29.1
Deferred Credits	109,617	1.9	245,569	2.7	80,960	1.7	164,835	2.2
Net Worth	2,832,740	49.1	4,156,475	45.7	2,500,230	52.5	3,491,498	46.6
Total Liab & Net Worth	**5,769,328**	**100.0**	**9,095,131**	**100.0**	**4,762,343**	**100.0**	**7,492,486**	**100.0**
Net Sales	3,639,368	100.0	4,637,900	100.0	2,751,317	100.0	4,526,885	100.0
Gross Profit	1,688,667	46.4	1,971,108	42.5	1,331,637	48.4	2,218,174	49.0
Net Profit After Tax	389,412	10.7	296,826	6.4	415,449	15.1	511,538	11.3
Working Capital	842,321	—	1,227,843	—	833,410	—	974,024	—

RATIOS	UQ	MED	LQ	UQ	MED	LQ	UQ	MED	LQ	UQ	MED	LQ
SOLVENCY												
Quick Ratio (times)	2.7	1.2	0.7	2.1	1.1	0.6	3.1	1.5	0.7	2.5	1.2	0.7
Current Ratio (times)	4.0	1.8	1.0	2.9	1.6	0.9	5.1	2.4	1.1	3.6	1.7	1.0
Curr Liab To Nw (%)	11.4	23.6	60.9	15.6	30.6	75.1	9.2	18.5	45.0	12.4	26.5	61.7
Curr Liab To Inv (%)	176.9	381.1	613.3	246.5	439.2	679.8	215.1	389.1	563.0	160.5	352.7	610.9
Total Liab To Nw (%)	36.4	91.2	185.4	45.4	91.1	180.9	30.5	83.3	173.8	42.3	99.2	188.3
Fixed Assets To Nw (%)	47.2	96.0	167.8	31.9	95.3	167.9	47.6	91.5	155.8	55.3	98.5	169.4
EFFICIENCY												
Coll Period (days)	32.5	53.3	73.2	41.7	61.6	84.3	35.2	51.8	67.0	29.8	49.5	69.0
Sales To Inv (times)	66.5	30.9	17.2	75.0	33.8	19.6	61.2	31.8	17.7	73.1	30.0	16.3
Assets To Sales (%)	67.5	195.0	308.0	64.9	179.6	254.7	126.0	221.6	321.9	60.0	193.1	305.9
Sales To Nwc (times)	11.9	4.4	1.8	13.6	5.7	3.1	8.0	3.0	1.3	13.3	5.0	2.1
Acct Pay To Sales (%)	4.0	8.2	14.2	4.0	8.4	14.5	3.9	8.3	13.5	4.2	8.1	13.8
PROFITABILITY												
Return On Sales (%)	20.9	11.5	3.0	14.6	7.8	0.8	25.1	16.3	7.4	22.3	11.8	3.6
Return On Assets (%)	10.7	6.2	2.6	8.4	5.1	1.3	11.5	7.6	4.5	10.7	6.4	2.6
Return On Nw (%)	21.4	13.4	6.7	18.9	12.1	4.4	20.3	13.8	8.8	24.1	14.4	7.8

SIC 48 COMMUNICATION

	WEST 1995 (310 Establishments) $	%	UNDER $100,000 1995 (115 Establishments) $	%	$100,000-$250,000 1995 (113 Establishments) $	%	$250,000-$500,000 1995 (124 Establishments) $	%
Cash	518,934	13.6	13,798	25.2	29,709	17.9	52,206	14.4
Accounts Receivable	549,459	14.4	8,816	16.1	33,361	20.1	76,496	21.1
Notes Receivable	45,788	1.2	55	0.1	996	0.6	4,350	1.2
Inventory	99,208	2.6	4,161	7.6	13,942	8.4	17,039	4.7
Other Current	286,177	7.5	3,778	6.9	6,473	3.9	25,015	6.9
Total Current	**1,499,565**	**39.3**	**30,608**	**55.9**	**84,480**	**50.9**	**175,107**	**48.3**
Fixed Assets	1,675,087	43.9	20,369	37.2	66,223	39.9	146,104	40.3
Other Non-current	641,036	16.8	3,778	6.9	15,270	9.2	41,330	11.4
Total Assets	**3,815,688**	**100.0**	**54,755**	**100.0**	**165,973**	**100.0**	**362,541**	**100.0**
Accounts Payable	331,965	8.7	4,818	8.8	16,099	9.7	42,417	11.7
Bank Loans	3,816	0.1	—	—	166	0.1	363	0.1
Notes Payable	114,471	3.0	2,300	4.2	10,290	6.2	18,127	5.0
Other Current	499,855	13.1	10,239	18.7	26,722	16.1	45,318	12.5
Total Current	**950,106**	**24.9**	**17,357**	**31.7**	**53,277**	**32.1**	**106,225**	**29.3**
Other Long Term	885,240	23.2	6,297	11.5	25,726	15.5	64,170	17.7
Deferred Credits	38,157	1.0	55	0.1	498	0.3	725	0.2
Net Worth	1,942,185	50.9	31,046	56.7	86,472	52.1	191,422	52.8
Total Liab & Net Worth	**3,815,688**	**100.0**	**54,755**	**100.0**	**165,973**	**100.0**	**362,541**	**100.0**
Net Sales	3,013,213	100.0	240,639	100.0	490,329	100.0	859,729	100.0
Gross Profit	1,328,827	44.1	126,095	52.4	233,887	47.7	398,914	46.4
Net Profit After Tax	241,057	8.0	20,695	8.6	32,362	6.6	67,919	7.9
Working Capital	549,459	—	13,251	—	31,203	—	68,882	—

RATIOS	WEST UQ	MED	LQ	UQ	MED	LQ	UQ	MED	LQ	UQ	MED	LQ
SOLVENCY												
Quick Ratio (times)	3.1	1.2	0.6	6.5	1.5	0.5	3.4	1.1	0.6	4.7	1.4	0.7
Current Ratio (times)	4.5	1.8	0.8	7.7	2.1	1.0	4.0	1.6	0.8	6.1	1.9	0.9
Curr Liab To Nw (%)	10.0	26.4	77.5	8.2	31.0	121.2	10.7	41.9	125.4	8.3	31.1	110.3
Curr Liab To Inv (%)	117.0	374.5	620.6	51.0	111.3	290.0	35.0	116.9	260.7	91.3	159.9	458.3
Total Liab To Nw (%)	30.6	87.9	194.2	13.0	41.4	187.1	18.4	66.5	158.2	15.8	67.9	187.9
Fixed Assets To Nw (%)	44.2	97.2	192.0	31.5	73.4	169.1	31.5	64.7	149.1	31.2	72.5	109.6
EFFICIENCY												
Coll Period (days)	25.9	52.6	73.0	8.8	17.9	39.5	14.1	27.4	41.8	14.6	33.6	50.6
Sales To Inv (times)	66.8	29.9	17.7	95.2	23.5	10.8	33.0	21.3	12.6	80.3	36.4	17.5
Assets To Sales (%)	43.1	180.3	324.0	13.2	20.4	33.6	22.2	32.7	51.5	22.9	40.7	78.8
Sales To Nwc (times)	13.0	4.3	1.6	28.1	13.7	7.1	18.9	9.3	5.0	14.8	6.8	3.4
Acct Pay To Sales (%)	3.9	8.4	15.5	0.9	2.4	3.9	1.0	3.3	4.9	1.4	3.1	6.2
PROFITABILITY												
Return On Sales (%)	18.9	9.7	2.0	14.7	6.8	2.3	17.3	6.3	0.7	16.5	8.1	2.0
Return On Assets (%)	12.0	5.6	1.3	55.0	25.4	(0.3)	25.2	6.2	(0.7)	22.3	11.2	3.3
Return On Nw (%)	24.7	12.9	3.1	118.0	49.5	0.9	45.5	13.5	(1.1)	59.8	24.5	4.3

SIC 48 COMMUNICATION — INDUSTRY ASSETS

	$500,000 - $1,000,000 (105 Establishments)		$1,000,000 - $5,000,000 (378 Establishments)		$5,000,000-$25,000,000 (423 Establishments)		$25,000,000-$50,000,000 (127 Establishments)	
	$	%	$	%	$	%	$	%
Cash	124,522	17.4	329,770	13.0	1,215,833	11.7	2,982,232	8.8
Accounts Receivable	162,451	22.7	370,357	14.6	1,101,523	10.6	3,355,011	9.9
Notes Receivable	10,735	1.5	17,757	0.7	62,350	0.6	135,556	0.4
Inventory	22,901	3.2	38,050	1.5	103,917	1.0	372,779	1.1
Other Current	25,048	3.5	200,398	7.9	748,205	7.2	1,999,451	5.9
Total Current	**345,657**	**48.3**	**956,332**	**37.7**	**3,231,828**	**31.1**	**8,845,029**	**26.1**
Fixed Assets	296,993	41.5	1,108,533	43.7	4,697,062	45.2	16,368,387	48.3
Other Non-current	72,996	10.2	471,824	18.6	2,462,840	23.7	8,675,584	25.6
Total Assets	**715,645**	**100.0**	**2,536,689**	**100.0**	**10,391,731**	**100.0**	**33,889,000**	**100.0**
Accounts Payable	72,996	10.2	243,522	9.6	758,596	7.3	2,440,008	7.2
Bank Loans	1,431	0.2	—	—	10,392	0.1	—	—
Notes Payable	21,469	3.0	38,050	1.5	124,701	1.2	542,224	1.6
Other Current	107,347	15.0	251,132	9.9	841,730	8.1	2,812,787	8.3
Total Current	**203,243**	**28.4**	**532,705**	**21.0**	**1,735,419**	**16.7**	**5,795,019**	**17.1**
Other Long Term	166,030	23.2	641,782	25.3	3,283,787	31.6	11,420,593	33.7
Deferred Credits	1,431	0.2	32,977	1.3	290,968	2.8	982,781	2.9
Net Worth	344,941	48.2	1,329,225	52.4	5,081,556	48.9	15,690,607	46.3
Total Liab & Net Worth	**715,645**	**100.0**	**2,536,689**	**100.0**	**10,391,731**	**100.0**	**33,889,000**	**100.0**
Net Sales	878,966	100.0	1,655,798	100.0	4,451,924	100.0	12,700,654	100.0
Gross Profit	391,140	44.5	667,287	40.3	1,900,972	42.7	6,121,715	48.2
Net Profit After Tax	54,496	6.2	185,449	11.2	632,173	14.2	1,955,901	15.4
Working Capital	142,414	—	423,627	—	1,496,409	—	3,050,010	—

RATIOS	UQ	MED	LQ	UQ	MED	LQ	UQ	MED	LQ	UQ	MED	LQ
SOLVENCY												
Quick Ratio (times)	3.4	1.7	0.8	3.5	1.5	0.8	3.0	1.6	0.8	2.2	1.2	0.8
Current Ratio (times)	4.4	2.0	1.1	5.1	2.2	1.1	4.9	2.4	1.3	2.9	1.9	1.1
Curr Liab To Nw (%)	8.1	30.2	69.1	7.3	19.0	67.2	10.0	18.2	38.7	13.4	20.4	40.1
Curr Liab To Inv (%)	115.1	282.7	325.6	156.4	361.4	527.8	315.6	449.3	633.7	325.5	444.8	710.3
Total Liab To Nw (%)	24.9	55.4	193.2	22.2	68.9	152.5	47.1	91.9	176.4	62.7	103.3	179.1
Fixed Assets To Nw (%)	40.1	70.3	135.1	44.0	80.8	130.1	58.2	105.5	164.7	82.3	108.6	169.7
EFFICIENCY												
Coll Period (days)	19.2	40.2	61.4	32.4	50.9	64.7	38.4	55.3	72.9	29.6	51.5	69.9
Sales To Inv (times)	95.0	13.6	10.0	91.3	31.0	16.2	61.3	29.8	18.3	52.3	28.3	17.5
Assets To Sales (%)	27.5	77.5	159.7	65.0	167.6	308.2	173.5	263.8	343.1	158.6	254.7	335.9
Sales To Nwc (times)	23.6	7.5	3.4	10.9	4.1	1.4	5.4	2.6	1.3	6.2	3.2	1.5
Acct Pay To Sales (%)	2.7	5.0	9.0	3.6	7.0	13.5	5.0	9.5	15.6	6.4	10.6	14.6
PROFITABILITY												
Return On Sales (%)	15.4	3.6	0.2	23.6	11.3	1.7	25.3	15.5	6.7	25.4	17.0	7.8
Return On Assets (%)	13.1	5.1	0.2	12.3	7.5	2.5	9.6	6.1	3.8	9.3	6.6	4.0
Return On Nw (%)	39.1	10.4	0.3	24.3	12.7	7.1	18.8	13.4	8.5	17.9	13.7	8.8

All SIC 48 COMMUNICATION, 1995.

	SIC 48 COMMUNICATION INDUSTRY ASSETS OVER $50,000,000 1995 (340 Establishments) $	%	SIC 4812 RDIO TELPHON COMM (NO BREAKDOWN) 1995 (185 Establishments) $	%	SIC 4812 RDIO TELPHON COMM INDUSTRY ASSETS UNDER $100,000 1995 (31 Establishments) $	%	SIC 4812 RDIO TELPHON COMM INDUSTRY ASSETS $100,000 - $250,000 1995 (22 Establishments) $	%
Cash	11,924,712	5.4	149,131	14.7	11,874	27.3	31,896	18.5
Accounts Receivable	19,653,692	8.9	149,131	14.7	5,437	12.5	33,276	19.3
Notes Receivable	441,656	0.2	14,203	1.4	—	—	172	0.1
Inventory	2,208,280	1.0	82,174	8.1	6,655	15.3	27,241	15.8
Other Current	12,366,368	5.6	31,449	3.1	913	2.1	5,000	2.9
Total Current	**46,594,708**	**21.1**	**426,089**	**42.0**	**24,879**	**57.2**	**97,585**	**56.6**
Fixed Assets	93,410,244	42.3	383,480	37.8	16,224	37.3	65,172	37.8
Other Non-current	80,823,048	36.6	204,929	20.2	2,392	5.5	9,655	5.6
Total Assets	**220,828,000**	**100.0**	**1,014,498**	**100.0**	**43,495**	**100.0**	**172,412**	**100.0**
Accounts Payable	11,041,400	5.0	94,348	9.3	2,827	6.5	20,862	12.1
Bank Loans	—	—	—	—	—	—	—	—
Notes Payable	2,208,280	1.0	23,333	2.3	261	0.6	5,517	3.2
Other Current	21,861,972	9.9	130,870	12.9	9,177	21.1	24,655	14.3
Total Current	**35,111,652**	**15.9**	**248,552**	**24.5**	**12,266**	**28.2**	**51,034**	**29.6**
Other Long Term	89,214,512	40.4	252,610	24.9	3,610	8.3	13,621	7.9
Deferred Credits	8,833,120	4.0	6,087	0.6	87	0.2	1,034	0.6
Net Worth	87,668,716	39.7	507,249	50.0	27,532	63.3	106,723	61.9
Total Liab & Net Worth	**220,828,000**	**100.0**	**1,014,498**	**100.0**	**43,495**	**100.0**	**172,412**	**100.0**
Net Sales	89,055,491	100.0	1,841,911	100.0	218,863	100.0	584,368	100.0
Gross Profit	47,377,521	53.2	979,897	53.2	106,149	48.5	313,806	53.7
Net Profit After Tax	7,035,384	7.9	127,092	6.9	23,856	10.9	52,593	9.0
Working Capital	11,483,056	—	177,537	—	12,613	—	46,551	—

RATIOS	UQ	MED	LQ	UQ	MED	LQ	UQ	MED	LQ	UQ	MED	LQ
SOLVENCY												
Quick Ratio (times)	1.2	0.8	0.5	3.0	1.2	0.7	6.7	2.3	0.7	2.0	1.4	0.9
Current Ratio (times)	1.9	1.2	0.7	3.9	1.8	1.0	10.6	2.6	1.6	3.1	1.7	1.4
Curr Liab To Nw (%)	18.3	35.9	64.4	11.0	37.3	88.5	7.9	20.4	99.2	12.9	46.3	72.1
Curr Liab To Inv (%)	324.3	568.8	755.0	86.1	174.1	402.0	44.4	91.3	144.7	36.6	132.4	250.2
Total Liab To Nw (%)	78.4	149.0	228.6	20.0	67.9	176.7	8.1	29.3	116.8	23.1	56.6	91.1
Fixed Assets To Nw (%)	71.2	142.0	207.0	36.8	66.1	125.9	30.4	45.7	98.1	37.4	53.0	72.0
EFFICIENCY												
Coll Period (days)	50.8	66.4	92.0	25.9	41.3	55.9	17.5	22.1	36.9	22.3	27.7	31.8
Sales To Inv (times)	67.1	40.6	23.0	39.0	18.7	11.5	90.0	19.2	8.7	30.1	18.5	13.2
Assets To Sales (%)	184.1	231.9	339.3	36.0	76.7	227.1	12.8	17.0	30.2	21.4	25.9	39.9
Sales To Nwc (times)	15.9	5.8	3.0	14.8	7.9	4.0	22.7	14.5	7.8	16.5	13.3	6.8
Acct Pay To Sales (%)	6.5	11.1	16.4	3.7	6.5	12.9	0.7	1.0	3.6	3.4	4.7	7.2
PROFITABILITY												
Return On Sales (%)	16.1	10.6	3.6	16.8	8.3	0.2	19.2	8.1	2.7	21.2	10.2	2.7
Return On Assets (%)	8.3	5.5	1.5	19.7	5.6	(1.3)	56.1	5.3	3.2	29.1	18.5	5.4
Return On Nw (%)	18.5	13.1	5.2	48.2	15.1	(0.1)	103.1	58.3	3.8	60.0	33.3	8.8

SIC 4812 — RDIO TELPHON COMM — INDUSTRY ASSETS — 1995

	$250,000–$500,000 (28 Establishments)		$500,000–$1,000,000 (11 Establishments)		$1,000,000–$5,000,000 (32 Establishments)		$5,000,000–$25,000,000 (21 Establishments)	
	$	%	$	%	$	%	$	%
Cash	46,304	11.9	81,712	12.2	393,261	12.6	1,751,438	17.8
Accounts Receivable	71,207	18.3	117,210	17.5	514,984	16.5	1,613,684	16.4
Notes Receivable	7,004	1.8	78,363	11.7	62,422	2.0	—	—
Inventory	38,522	9.9	58,270	8.7	124,845	4.0	344,384	3.5
Other Current	23,347	6.0	10,716	1.6	46,817	1.5	393,582	4.0
Total Current	**186,384**	**47.9**	**346,271**	**51.7**	**1,142,329**	**36.6**	**4,103,088**	**41.7**
Fixed Assets	149,418	38.4	232,410	34.7	1,276,537	40.9	3,827,581	38.9
Other Non-current	53,308	13.7	91,089	13.6	702,251	22.5	1,908,871	19.4
Total Assets	**389,110**	**100.0**	**669,769**	**100.0**	**3,121,117**	**100.0**	**9,839,539**	**100.0**
Accounts Payable	36,576	9.4	81,042	12.1	330,838	10.6	1,357,856	13.8
Bank Loans	—	—	—	—	6,242	0.2	—	—
Notes Payable	17,899	4.6	32,819	4.9	31,211	1.0	147,593	1.5
Other Current	45,526	11.7	65,637	9.8	340,202	10.9	1,210,263	12.3
Total Current	**100,001**	**25.7**	**179,498**	**26.8**	**708,494**	**22.7**	**2,715,713**	**27.6**
Other Long Term	82,102	21.1	264,559	39.5	827,096	26.5	2,026,945	20.6
Deferred Credits	2,724	0.7	—	—	24,969	0.8	—	—
Net Worth	204,283	52.5	225,712	33.7	1,560,559	50.0	5,096,881	51.8
Total Liab & Net Worth	**389,110**	**100.0**	**669,769**	**100.0**	**3,121,117**	**100.0**	**9,839,539**	**100.0**
Net Sales	880,144	100.0	1,015,740	100.0	2,457,626	100.0	5,818,461	100.0
Gross Profit	433,911	49.3	521,075	51.3	909,322	37.0	2,723,040	46.8
Net Profit After Tax	62,490	7.1	109,700	10.8	280,169	11.4	541,117	9.3
Working Capital	86,383	—	166,773	—	433,835	—	1,387,375	—

RATIOS

	UQ	MED	LQ	UQ	MED	LQ	UQ	MED	LQ	UQ	MED	LQ
SOLVENCY												
Quick Ratio (times)	3.0	1.3	0.8	6.5	1.7	1.1	3.4	1.4	0.7	4.7	1.0	0.5
Current Ratio (times)	4.2	2.5	1.6	22.0	2.5	1.5	3.7	1.7	1.1	5.3	1.4	0.7
Curr Liab To Nw (%)	20.8	36.7	90.3	2.2	23.7	57.7	13.5	45.9	88.8	8.3	26.8	177.5
Curr Liab To Inv (%)	82.3	151.1	551.4	98.1	115.1	184.2	119.7	186.4	653.0	326.3	364.0	485.6
Total Liab To Nw (%)	33.3	116.4	242.1	59.8	96.8	168.2	27.6	64.5	189.0	8.7	92.4	261.7
Fixed Assets To Nw (%)	45.8	71.4	97.2	18.9	103.2	144.5	46.7	69.4	162.0	48.8	75.2	160.5
EFFICIENCY												
Coll Period (days)	17.9	31.4	36.4	23.4	39.8	58.8	45.9	52.4	59.5	45.3	54.2	114.8
Sales To Inv (times)	82.8	19.2	16.2	13.1	11.4	10.4	37.8	26.3	17.8	16.8	10.8	7.9
Assets To Sales (%)	29.5	42.9	75.5	40.8	72.2	83.8	58.4	101.6	136.5	80.6	123.4	252.5
Sales To Nwc (times)	14.8	11.4	4.8	17.9	7.5	3.5	12.5	7.2	4.6	4.7	3.6	2.1
Acct Pay To Sales (%)	1.4	3.4	6.2	3.8	6.1	8.0	4.2	6.0	10.7	5.1	9.7	19.7
PROFITABILITY												
Return On Sales (%)	16.8	8.3	1.2	19.4	11.3	2.0	24.9	12.3	4.6	12.1	10.5	(16.6)
Return On Assets (%)	20.2	10.3	4.3	23.7	8.8	3.4	25.7	8.9	2.2	14.5	5.5	(3.0)
Return On Nw (%)	60.3	24.8	6.1	130.7	53.8	21.9	42.4	23.8	5.0	27.6	14.7	1.5

SIC 4812 RDIO TELPHON COMM — INDUSTRY ASSETS OVER $50,000,000 — 1995 (35 Establishments)

	$	%
Cash	8,734,337	3.1
Accounts Receivable	16,059,911	5.7
Notes Receivable	—	—
Inventory	5,916,809	2.1
Other Current	8,452,585	3.0
Total Current	**39,163,642**	**13.9**
Fixed Assets	96,641,218	34.3
Other Non-current	145,947,961	51.8
Total Assets	**281,752,821**	**100.0**
Accounts Payable	12,115,371	4.3
Bank Loans	—	—
Notes Payable	5,916,809	2.1
Other Current	24,794,248	8.8
Total Current	**42,826,429**	**15.2**
Other Long Term	154,964,052	55.0
Deferred Credits	1,972,270	0.7
Net Worth	81,990,071	29.1
Total Liab & Net Worth	**281,752,821**	**100.0**
Net Sales	148,009,906	100.0
Gross Profit	106,123,103	71.7
Net Profit After Tax	(5,328,357)	(3.6)
Working Capital	(3,662,787)	—

RATIOS	UQ	MED	LQ
SOLVENCY			
Quick Ratio (times)	1.1	0.8	0.4
Current Ratio (times)	1.6	1.1	0.6
Curr Liab To Nw (%)	12.5	23.4	78.9
Curr Liab To Inv (%)	256.4	348.5	464.9
Total Liab To Nw (%)	36.6	90.1	185.1
Fixed Assets To Nw (%)	39.7	103.5	146.1
EFFICIENCY			
Coll Period (days)	38.5	53.7	57.7
Sales To Inv (times)	39.3	19.3	10.6
Assets To Sales (%)	208.7	356.3	425.6
Sales To Nwc (times)	7.9	4.2	2.4
Acct Pay To Sales (%)	8.1	12.9	17.0
PROFITABILITY			
Return On Sales (%)	8.1	(3.7)	(13.0)
Return On Assets (%)	1.6	(2.5)	(7.1)
Return On Nw (%)	2.5	(8.1)	(56.5)

SIC 4813 TEL COMM, EXC RDIO (NO BREAKDOWN) — 1995 (924 Establishments)

	$	%
Cash	1,188,930	12.6
Accounts Receivable	1,226,674	13.0
Notes Receivable	56,616	0.6
Inventory	169,847	1.8
Other Current	632,209	6.7
Total Current	**3,274,276**	**34.7**
Fixed Assets	4,482,079	47.5
Other Non-current	1,679,600	17.8
Total Assets	**9,435,955**	**100.0**
Accounts Payable	811,492	8.6
Bank Loans	—	—
Notes Payable	160,411	1.7
Other Current	811,492	8.6
Total Current	**1,783,395**	**18.9**
Other Long Term	2,698,683	28.6
Deferred Credits	283,079	3.0
Net Worth	4,670,798	49.5
Total Liab & Net Worth	**9,435,955**	**100.0**
Net Sales	4,118,879	100.0
Gross Profit	1,729,929	42.0
Net Profit After Tax	597,237	14.5
Working Capital	1,490,881	—

RATIOS	UQ	MED	LQ
Quick Ratio (times)	2.8	1.4	0.7
Current Ratio (times)	4.3	2.1	1.1
Curr Liab To Nw (%)	11.6	20.6	47.8
Curr Liab To Inv (%)	282.8	445.9	644.2
Total Liab To Nw (%)	51.5	107.0	186.7
Fixed Assets To Nw (%)	68.0	113.5	188.7
Coll Period (days)	39.4	55.3	73.4
Sales To Inv (times)	67.9	33.7	19.7
Assets To Sales (%)	154.4	244.1	331.3
Sales To Nwc (times)	8.7	3.0	1.4
Acct Pay To Sales (%)	5.7	9.5	15.3
Return On Sales (%)	23.8	14.8	7.4
Return On Assets (%)	9.8	6.5	4.0
Return On Nw (%)	19.3	14.0	9.4

SIC 4813 TEL COMM, EXC RDIO — INDUSTRY ASSETS UNDER $100,000 — 1995 (45 Establishments)

	$	%
Cash	15,660	28.6
Accounts Receivable	11,334	20.7
Notes Receivable	—	—
Inventory	3,121	5.7
Other Current	5,695	10.4
Total Current	**35,810**	**65.4**
Fixed Assets	15,222	27.8
Other Non-current	3,723	6.8
Total Assets	**54,755**	**100.0**
Accounts Payable	5,366	9.8
Bank Loans	—	—
Notes Payable	2,409	4.4
Other Current	11,991	21.9
Total Current	**19,767**	**36.1**
Other Long Term	7,282	13.3
Deferred Credits	—	—
Net Worth	27,706	50.6
Total Liab & Net Worth	**54,755**	**100.0**
Net Sales	250,570	100.0
Gross Profit	133,804	53.4
Net Profit After Tax	19,795	7.9
Working Capital	16,043	—

RATIOS	UQ	MED	LQ
Quick Ratio (times)	6.5	1.4	0.5
Current Ratio (times)	8.6	1.8	0.9
Curr Liab To Nw (%)	11.4	38.6	173.5
Curr Liab To Inv (%)	99.9	274.5	419.2
Total Liab To Nw (%)	19.6	53.4	340.9
Fixed Assets To Nw (%)	24.0	79.5	302.3
Coll Period (days)	13.7	31.4	46.0
Sales To Inv (times)	103.4	27.4	11.4
Assets To Sales (%)	13.5	15.7	31.3
Sales To Nwc (times)	22.2	13.7	5.8
Acct Pay To Sales (%)	0.9	2.2	3.7
Return On Sales (%)	12.3	6.6	1.6
Return On Assets (%)	30.4	5.6	(16.4)
Return On Nw (%)	52.0	18.6	(49.4)

SIC 4813 TEL COMM, EXC RDIO — INDUSTRY ASSETS $100,000 - $250,000 — 1995 (30 Establishments)

	$	%
Cash	33,636	21.6
Accounts Receivable	37,062	23.8
Notes Receivable	2,336	1.5
Inventory	15,417	9.9
Other Current	6,385	4.1
Total Current	**94,836**	**60.9**
Fixed Assets	47,496	30.5
Other Non-current	13,392	8.6
Total Assets	**155,724**	**100.0**
Accounts Payable	17,441	11.2
Bank Loans	—	—
Notes Payable	11,368	7.3
Other Current	19,154	12.3
Total Current	**47,963**	**30.8**
Other Long Term	18,220	11.7
Deferred Credits	—	—
Net Worth	89,541	57.5
Total Liab & Net Worth	**155,724**	**100.0**
Net Sales	655,976	100.0
Gross Profit	284,694	43.4
Net Profit After Tax	26,239	4.0
Working Capital	46,873	—

RATIOS	UQ	MED	LQ
Quick Ratio (times)	6.0	1.6	0.7
Current Ratio (times)	9.9	2.1	0.9
Curr Liab To Nw (%)	9.1	29.8	98.5
Curr Liab To Inv (%)	21.9	52.9	256.9
Total Liab To Nw (%)	10.3	30.4	97.3
Fixed Assets To Nw (%)	9.4	28.6	92.1
Coll Period (days)	19.3	32.4	64.4
Sales To Inv (times)	21.2	15.5	12.1
Assets To Sales (%)	15.7	24.7	36.1
Sales To Nwc (times)	30.7	8.7	3.8
Acct Pay To Sales (%)	0.7	2.9	4.5
Return On Sales (%)	10.5	3.5	(0.1)
Return On Assets (%)	11.8	0.3	(3.8)
Return On Nw (%)	26.4	0.6	(27.1)

SIC 4813 — TEL COMM, EXC RDIO

Balance Sheet / Income Data

Item	$250,000–$500,000 (29 Est.) $	%	$500,000–$1,000,000 (32 Est.) $	%	$1,000,000–$5,000,000 (204 Est.) $	%	$5,000,000–$25,000,000 (306 Est.) $	%
Cash	60,560	17.7	131,427	18.9	376,930	14.0	1,253,304	11.7
Accounts Receivable	89,301	26.1	267,026	38.4	390,391	14.5	1,006,928	9.4
Notes Receivable	5,132	1.5	695	0.1	18,846	0.7	53,560	0.5
Inventory	19,502	5.7	29,901	4.3	35,001	1.3	107,120	1.0
Other Current	31,478	9.2	25,034	3.6	269,235	10.0	642,720	6.0
Total Current	**205,973**	**60.2**	**454,082**	**65.3**	**1,090,403**	**40.5**	**3,063,632**	**28.6**
Fixed Assets	111,540	32.6	206,528	29.7	1,214,252	45.1	5,313,152	49.6
Other Non-current	24,635	7.2	34,769	5.0	387,699	14.4	2,335,216	21.8
Total Assets	**342,148**	**100.0**	**695,379**	**100.0**	**2,692,354**	**100.0**	**10,712,000**	**100.0**
Accounts Payable	55,770	16.3	125,864	18.1	298,851	11.1	696,280	6.5
Bank Loans	—	—	—	—	—	—	10,712	0.1
Notes Payable	15,055	4.4	34,074	4.9	40,385	1.5	96,408	0.9
Other Current	54,059	15.8	154,374	22.2	220,773	8.2	642,720	6.0
Total Current	**124,884**	**36.5**	**314,311**	**45.2**	**560,010**	**20.8**	**1,446,120**	**13.5**
Other Long Term	62,613	18.3	81,359	11.7	619,241	23.0	3,770,624	35.2
Deferred Credits	—	—	2,086	0.3	51,155	1.9	364,208	3.4
Net Worth	154,651	45.2	297,622	42.8	1,461,948	54.3	5,131,048	47.9
Total Liab & Net Worth	**342,148**	**100.0**	**695,379**	**100.0**	**2,692,354**	**100.0**	**10,712,000**	**100.0**
Net Sales	1,583,827	100.0	2,565,354	100.0	1,284,610	100.0	3,937,000	100.0
Gross Profit	560,675	35.4	1,005,619	39.2	461,175	35.9	1,468,501	37.3
Net Profit After Tax	80,775	5.1	138,529	5.4	204,253	15.9	700,786	17.8
Working Capital	81,089	—	139,771	—	530,393	—	1,617,512	—

RATIOS

	$250,000–$500,000 UQ	MED	LQ	$500,000–$1,000,000 UQ	MED	LQ	$1,000,000–$5,000,000 UQ	MED	LQ	$5,000,000–$25,000,000 UQ	MED	LQ
SOLVENCY												
Quick Ratio (times)	4.8	0.9	0.7	2.4	1.3	0.9	3.3	1.7	0.9	3.3	1.8	1.0
Current Ratio (times)	5.8	1.6	0.8	2.9	1.6	1.1	5.6	3.1	1.4	5.1	2.9	1.6
Curr Liab To Nw (%)	8.6	60.9	193.7	24.0	61.1	188.2	6.9	16.0	38.9	9.5	17.0	29.0
Curr Liab To Inv (%)	144.4	193.6	445.2	150.5	286.8	328.7	211.7	396.3	528.9	330.7	476.5	637.1
Total Liab To Nw (%)	16.9	159.6	256.5	38.9	81.4	283.2	25.2	77.7	149.4	63.6	105.2	177.2
Fixed Assets To Nw (%)	20.8	69.7	208.0	40.4	57.1	103.0	47.1	88.3	135.0	73.0	116.0	172.3
EFFICIENCY												
Coll Period (days)	12.2	33.6	46.9	29.8	38.0	67.9	35.8	49.7	65.3	40.2	55.5	73.0
Sales To Inv (times)	91.0	63.8	44.2	165.7	23.2	11.3	93.5	32.9	19.6	62.1	30.7	19.7
Assets To Sales (%)	17.0	19.4	56.2	18.9	23.9	55.6	121.6	251.1	333.6	231.5	281.4	354.7
Sales To Nwc (times)	27.8	14.3	4.3	62.5	13.5	5.2	5.7	2.3	0.9	4.6	2.2	1.2
Acct Pay To Sales (%)	2.6	4.2	6.3	2.8	7.3	8.3	4.8	8.9	14.1	5.5	9.6	15.5
PROFITABILITY												
Return On Sales (%)	12.5	5.2	2.1	8.5	1.7	(0.1)	26.9	16.5	6.1	26.7	18.7	11.0
Return On Assets (%)	14.7	11.1	0.7	15.6	5.5	(2.0)	11.2	7.8	4.7	9.6	6.9	4.3
Return On Nw (%)	39.8	22.2	5.7	40.0	10.4	(11.9)	21.7	13.2	9.3	18.6	13.9	10.5

INDUSTRY ASSETS — 1995

SIC 4813 — TEL COMM, EXC RDIO — INDUSTRY ASSETS $25,000,000-$50,000,000 — 1995 (88 Establishments)

	$	%
Cash	3,338,210	9.9
Accounts Receivable	3,169,614	9.4
Notes Receivable	134,877	0.4
Inventory	337,193	1.0
Other Current	1,348,772	4.0
Total Current	**8,328,666**	**24.7**
Fixed Assets	17,095,683	50.7
Other Non-current	8,294,947	24.6
Total Assets	**33,719,295**	**100.0**
Accounts Payable	2,528,947	7.5
Bank Loans	—	—
Notes Payable	337,193	1.0
Other Current	2,056,877	6.1
Total Current	**4,923,017**	**14.6**
Other Long Term	11,228,525	33.3
Deferred Credits	1,112,737	3.3
Net Worth	16,455,016	48.8
Total Liab & Net Worth	**33,719,295**	**100.0**
Net Sales	12,130,000	100.0
Gross Profit	4,027,160	33.2
Net Profit After Tax	2,231,920	18.4
Working Capital	3,405,649	—

RATIOS	UQ	MED	LQ
SOLVENCY			
Quick Ratio (times)	2.5	1.5	0.8
Current Ratio (times)	3.4	2.1	1.2
Curr Liab To Nw (%)	12.7	18.3	35.1
Curr Liab To Inv (%)	313.9	444.8	710.1
Total Liab To Nw (%)	70.8	109.6	182.0
Fixed Assets To Nw (%)	91.5	125.0	175.3
EFFICIENCY			
Coll Period (days)	34.0	51.8	68.6
Sales To Inv (times)	53.3	27.9	19.0
Assets To Sales (%)	193.7	288.7	369.8
Sales To Nwc (times)	5.6	2.7	1.3
Acct Pay To Sales (%)	7.2	11.0	15.3
PROFITABILITY			
Return On Sales (%)	26.3	20.1	13.5
Return On Assets (%)	9.1	7.1	4.8
Return On Nw (%)	18.1	14.4	11.1

SIC 4813 — TEL COMM, EXC RDIO — INDUSTRY ASSETS OVER $50,000,000 — 1995 (190 Establishments)

	$	%
Cash	13,821,248	5.6
Accounts Receivable	21,965,912	8.9
Notes Receivable	987,232	0.4
Inventory	3,208,504	1.3
Other Current	12,093,592	4.9
Total Current	**52,076,488**	**21.1**
Fixed Assets	148,578,416	60.2
Other Non-current	46,153,096	18.7
Total Assets	**246,808,000**	**100.0**
Accounts Payable	14,808,480	6.0
Bank Loans	—	—
Notes Payable	2,221,272	0.9
Other Current	21,225,488	8.6
Total Current	**38,255,240**	**15.5**
Other Long Term	78,238,136	31.7
Deferred Credits	16,042,520	6.5
Net Worth	114,272,104	46.3
Total Liab & Net Worth	**246,808,000**	**100.0**
Net Sales	79,210,000	100.0
Gross Profit	43,644,710	55.1
Net Profit After Tax	8,950,730	11.3
Working Capital	13,821,248	—

RATIOS	UQ	MED	LQ
SOLVENCY			
Quick Ratio (times)	1.1	0.7	0.5
Current Ratio (times)	1.6	1.1	0.7
Curr Liab To Nw (%)	20.5	37.8	60.8
Curr Liab To Inv (%)	434.6	629.5	899.6
Total Liab To Nw (%)	89.5	149.5	212.6
Fixed Assets To Nw (%)	119.1	192.8	222.2
EFFICIENCY			
Coll Period (days)	51.9	65.7	83.8
Sales To Inv (times)	68.0	43.6	29.5
Assets To Sales (%)	184.0	217.7	303.7
Sales To Nwc (times)	17.7	7.3	3.4
Acct Pay To Sales (%)	8.4	12.1	17.7
PROFITABILITY			
Return On Sales (%)	17.6	12.4	9.2
Return On Assets (%)	8.4	5.9	4.0
Return On Nw (%)	18.6	14.6	10.3

SIC 4822 — TLGRPH, OTHER COMM (NO BREAKDOWN) — 1995 (20 Establishments)

	$	%
Cash	96,313	28.6
Accounts Receivable	64,321	19.1
Notes Receivable	—	—
Inventory	20,879	6.2
Other Current	21,889	6.5
Total Current	**203,403**	**60.4**
Fixed Assets	100,691	29.9
Other Non-current	32,666	9.7
Total Assets	**336,760**	**100.0**
Accounts Payable	55,902	16.6
Bank Loans	—	—
Notes Payable	7,409	2.2
Other Current	69,373	20.6
Total Current	**132,683**	**39.4**
Other Long Term	46,136	13.7
Deferred Credits	—	—
Net Worth	157,940	46.9
Total Liab & Net Worth	**336,760**	**100.0**
Net Sales	2,086,798	100.0
Gross Profit	657,341	31.5
Net Profit After Tax	100,166	4.8
Working Capital	70,720	—

RATIOS	UQ	MED	LQ
SOLVENCY			
Quick Ratio (times)	2.3	1.1	0.7
Current Ratio (times)	3.2	1.2	1.1
Curr Liab To Nw (%)	13.3	73.9	124.5
Curr Liab To Inv (%)	13.2	25.2	49.1
Total Liab To Nw (%)	18.0	94.8	181.7
Fixed Assets To Nw (%)	25.2	47.4	67.8
EFFICIENCY			
Coll Period (days)	15.1	46.2	78.7
Sales To Inv (times)	220.5	91.3	59.3
Assets To Sales (%)	29.8	43.1	59.3
Sales To Nwc (times)	17.8	15.4	8.9
Acct Pay To Sales (%)	3.4	5.4	15.6
PROFITABILITY			
Return On Sales (%)	8.8	5.8	1.1
Return On Assets (%)	18.0	11.0	5.4
Return On Nw (%)	26.6	17.6	8.5

SIC 4832 — RAD BRDCSTG STNS (NO BREAKDOWN) — 1995 (204 Establishments)

	$	%
Cash	100,302	9.9
Accounts Receivable	166,157	16.4
Notes Receivable	5,066	0.5
Inventory	6,079	0.6
Other Current	56,737	5.6
Total Current	**334,340**	**33.0**
Fixed Assets	376,893	37.2
Other Non-current	301,920	29.8
Total Assets	**1,013,153**	**100.0**
Accounts Payable	60,789	6.0
Bank Loans	1,013	0.1
Notes Payable	21,276	2.1
Other Current	126,644	12.5
Total Current	**209,723**	**20.7**
Other Long Term	323,196	31.9
Deferred Credits	3,039	0.3
Net Worth	477,195	47.1
Total Liab & Net Worth	**1,013,153**	**100.0**
Net Sales	1,668,004	100.0
Gross Profit	999,134	59.9
Net Profit After Tax	125,100	7.5
Working Capital	124,617	—

RATIOS	UQ	MED	LQ
SOLVENCY			
Quick Ratio (times)	3.6	1.6	0.8
Current Ratio (times)	4.4	1.8	1.1
Curr Liab To Nw (%)	7.1	25.2	63.0
Curr Liab To Inv (%)	59.3	367.3	425.7
Total Liab To Nw (%)	15.9	64.0	187.4
Fixed Assets To Nw (%)	32.8	65.7	109.8
EFFICIENCY			
Coll Period (days)	46.4	68.3	89.8
Sales To Inv (times)	45.7	30.0	17.9
Assets To Sales (%)	66.8	113.8	232.4
Sales To Nwc (times)	10.0	5.7	3.8
Acct Pay To Sales (%)	1.6	3.3	6.8
PROFITABILITY			
Return On Sales (%)	13.6	7.2	(2.3)
Return On Assets (%)	16.3	5.8	(0.9)
Return On Nw (%)	36.7	9.2	(1.3)

SIC 4832 — RAD BRDCSTG STNS — INDUSTRY ASSETS UNDER $100,000 — 1995 (14 Establishments)

	$	%
Cash	15,673	22.4
Accounts Receivable	10,985	15.7
Notes Receivable	—	—
Inventory	1,329	1.9
Other Current	8,816	12.6
Total Current	**36,804**	**52.6**
Fixed Assets	25,259	36.1
Other Non-current	7,907	11.3
Total Assets	**69,970**	**100.0**
Accounts Payable	6,017	8.6
Bank Loans	—	—
Notes Payable	5,108	7.3
Other Current	12,874	18.4
Total Current	**24,000**	**34.3**
Other Long Term	8,816	12.6
Deferred Credits	—	—
Net Worth	37,154	53.1
Total Liab & Net Worth	**69,970**	**100.0**
Net Sales	209,859	100.0
Gross Profit	198,317	94.5
Net Profit After Tax	18,887	9.0
Working Capital	12,804	—

RATIOS	UQ	MED	LQ
SOLVENCY			
Quick Ratio (times)	3.1	1.1	0.4
Current Ratio (times)	3.1	1.9	1.2
Curr Liab To Nw (%)	9.8	39.9	128.4
Curr Liab To Inv (%)	150.5	242.3	334.0
Total Liab To Nw (%)	21.3	47.4	206.2
Fixed Assets To Nw (%)	62.0	72.4	138.1
EFFICIENCY			
Coll Period (days)	4.1	4.4	33.8
Sales To Inv (times)	—	—	—
Assets To Sales (%)	28.9	42.1	54.3
Sales To Nwc (times)	34.1	17.3	4.2
Acct Pay To Sales (%)	1.5	1.9	2.2
PROFITABILITY			
Return On Sales (%)	10.7	8.5	7.0
Return On Assets (%)	39.6	25.4	16.9
Return On Nw (%)	100.4	77.9	43.5

SIC 4832 — RAD BRDCSTG STNS — INDUSTRY ASSETS $100,000 - $250,000 — 1995 (30 Establishments)

	$	%
Cash	21,576	13.0
Accounts Receivable	40,165	24.2
Notes Receivable	996	0.6
Inventory	1,992	1.2
Other Current	7,137	4.3
Total Current	**71,866**	**43.3**
Fixed Assets	71,866	43.3
Other Non-current	22,240	13.4
Total Assets	**165,973**	**100.0**
Accounts Payable	17,427	10.5
Bank Loans	—	—
Notes Payable	2,656	1.6
Other Current	33,361	20.1
Total Current	**53,443**	**32.2**
Other Long Term	43,651	26.3
Deferred Credits	1,328	0.8
Net Worth	67,551	40.7
Total Liab & Net Worth	**165,973**	**100.0**
Net Sales	298,204	100.0
Gross Profit	110,335	37.0
Net Profit After Tax	28,926	9.7
Working Capital	18,423	—

RATIOS	UQ	MED	LQ
SOLVENCY			
Quick Ratio (times)	2.4	1.0	0.5
Current Ratio (times)	2.4	1.4	1.0
Curr Liab To Nw (%)	15.2	52.0	309.4
Curr Liab To Inv (%)	236.4	236.4	236.4
Total Liab To Nw (%)	32.3	72.4	205.6
Fixed Assets To Nw (%)	49.9	107.6	190.1
EFFICIENCY			
Coll Period (days)	20.5	32.1	53.1
Sales To Inv (times)	208.5	208.5	208.5
Assets To Sales (%)	45.4	48.2	65.7
Sales To Nwc (times)	12.4	8.5	7.0
Acct Pay To Sales (%)	1.1	2.2	3.9
PROFITABILITY			
Return On Sales (%)	16.3	6.5	0.1
Return On Assets (%)	11.5	2.7	(2.7)
Return On Nw (%)	15.0	3.2	(3.6)

SIC 4832 — RAD BRDCSTG STNS — INDUSTRY ASSETS $250,000 - $500,000 — 1995 (33 Establishments)

	$	%
Cash	25,941	7.3
Accounts Receivable	76,758	21.6
Notes Receivable	355	0.1
Inventory	—	—
Other Current	21,322	6.0
Total Current	**124,377**	**35.0**
Fixed Assets	174,127	49.0
Other Non-current	56,858	16.0
Total Assets	**355,362**	**100.0**
Accounts Payable	22,388	6.3
Bank Loans	—	—
Notes Payable	13,504	3.8
Other Current	38,379	10.8
Total Current	**74,271**	**20.9**
Other Long Term	87,774	24.7
Deferred Credits	—	—
Net Worth	193,317	54.4
Total Liab & Net Worth	**355,362**	**100.0**
Net Sales	491,938	100.0
Gross Profit	330,582	67.2
Net Profit After Tax	53,129	10.8
Working Capital	50,106	—

RATIOS	UQ	MED	LQ
SOLVENCY			
Quick Ratio (times)	7.4	2.0	0.8
Current Ratio (times)	9.2	2.0	1.0
Curr Liab To Nw (%)	4.7	19.4	62.2
Curr Liab To Inv (%)	—	—	—
Total Liab To Nw (%)	5.3	28.0	127.6
Fixed Assets To Nw (%)	51.9	80.6	108.5
EFFICIENCY			
Coll Period (days)	55.1	65.7	91.3
Sales To Inv (times)	208.5	208.5	208.5
Assets To Sales (%)	51.1	69.6	94.2
Sales To Nwc (times)	4.8	4.0	3.2
Acct Pay To Sales (%)	1.2	1.7	2.8
PROFITABILITY			
Return On Sales (%)	17.6	10.6	2.9
Return On Assets (%)	30.4	15.8	4.9
Return On Nw (%)	62.2	29.2	5.1

SIC 4832 — RAD BRDCSTG STNS — INDUSTRY ASSETS $500,000 - $1,000,000 — 1995 (28 Establishments)

	$	%
Cash	118,227	15.3
Accounts Receivable	144,499	18.7
Notes Receivable	—	—
Inventory	6,182	0.8
Other Current	17,000	2.2
Total Current	**285,908**	**37.0**
Fixed Assets	378,634	49.0
Other Non-current	108,181	14.0
Total Assets	**772,723**	**100.0**
Accounts Payable	50,227	6.5
Bank Loans	4,636	0.6
Notes Payable	5,409	0.7
Other Current	84,227	10.9
Total Current	**144,499**	**18.7**
Other Long Term	205,544	26.6
Deferred Credits	1,545	0.2
Net Worth	421,134	54.5
Total Liab & Net Worth	**772,723**	**100.0**
Net Sales	874,134	100.0
Gross Profit	506,998	58.0
Net Profit After Tax	35,839	4.1
Working Capital	141,409	—

RATIOS	UQ	MED	LQ
SOLVENCY			
Quick Ratio (times)	3.5	2.1	1.1
Current Ratio (times)	5.2	2.3	1.2
Curr Liab To Nw (%)	6.5	29.1	57.2
Curr Liab To Inv (%)	180.3	314.9	362.8
Total Liab To Nw (%)	32.1	49.7	123.2
Fixed Assets To Nw (%)	47.4	80.4	127.8
EFFICIENCY			
Coll Period (days)	30.2	55.7	75.7
Sales To Inv (times)	337.5	21.1	15.5
Assets To Sales (%)	61.7	91.6	130.6
Sales To Nwc (times)	7.3	5.2	3.1
Acct Pay To Sales (%)	1.8	3.3	6.2
PROFITABILITY			
Return On Sales (%)	12.7	2.1	(4.2)
Return On Assets (%)	16.2	4.0	0.1
Return On Nw (%)	25.4	9.0	(0.6)

	SIC 4832 RAD BRDCSTG STNS $1,000,000-$5,000,000 1995 (57 Establishments) $	%	SIC 4832 RAD BRDCSTG STNS $5,000,000-$25,000,000 1995 (14 Establishments) $	%	SIC 4833 TEL BRDCSTG STNS (NO BREAKDOWN) 1995 (116 Establishments) $	%	SIC 4833 TEL BRDCSTG STNS $1,000,000 - $5,000,000 1995 (27 Establishments) $	%
Cash	134,798	8.2	567,146	5.6	998,648	8.7	405,931	12.0
Accounts Receivable	231,788	14.1	1,144,420	11.3	1,411,882	12.3	534,475	15.8
Notes Receivable	8,219	0.5	303,828	3.0	22,957	0.2	16,914	0.5
Inventory	8,219	0.5	10,128	0.1	34,436	0.3	16,914	0.5
Other Current	115,072	7.0	759,571	7.5	1,090,478	9.5	236,793	7.0
Total Current	**498,097**	**30.3**	**2,785,093**	**27.5**	**3,558,401**	**31.0**	**1,211,026**	**35.8**
Fixed Assets	627,963	38.2	2,329,350	23.0	4,281,560	37.3	1,576,364	46.6
Other Non-current	517,823	31.5	5,013,167	49.5	3,638,752	31.7	595,365	17.6
Total Assets	**1,643,883**	**100.0**	**10,127,610**	**100.0**	**11,478,714**	**100.0**	**3,382,755**	**100.0**
Accounts Payable	72,331	4.4	729,188	7.2	573,936	5.0	307,831	9.1
Bank Loans	—	—	—	—	—	—	—	—
Notes Payable	21,370	1.3	202,552	2.0	195,138	1.7	84,569	2.5
Other Current	215,349	13.1	1,245,696	12.3	1,377,446	12.0	392,400	11.6
Total Current	**309,050**	**18.8**	**2,177,436**	**21.5**	**2,146,520**	**18.7**	**784,799**	**23.2**
Other Long Term	511,248	31.1	3,402,877	33.6	3,719,103	32.4	882,899	26.1
Deferred Credits	1,644	0.1	20,255	0.2	114,787	1.0	—	—
Net Worth	821,942	50.0	4,527,042	44.7	5,498,304	47.9	1,715,057	50.7
Total Liab & Net Worth	**1,643,883**	**100.0**	**10,127,610**	**100.0**	**11,478,714**	**100.0**	**3,382,755**	**100.0**
Net Sales	1,998,747	100.0	7,144,701	100.0	7,217,193	100.0	3,885,173	100.0
Gross Profit	1,255,213	62.8	3,908,151	54.7	4,344,750	60.2	2,424,348	62.4
Net Profit After Tax	173,891	8.7	750,194	10.5	570,158	7.9	155,407	4.0
Working Capital	189,047	—	607,657	—	1,411,881	—	426,227	—

RATIOS	UQ	MED	LQ	UQ	MED	LQ	UQ	MED	LQ	UQ	MED	LQ
SOLVENCY												
Quick Ratio (times)	4.6	1.4	0.7	3.0	1.4	0.6	1.7	1.1	0.7	2.4	1.1	0.6
Current Ratio (times)	4.8	1.7	1.1	3.2	1.9	1.0	2.8	1.6	1.1	2.7	1.5	0.9
Curr Liab To Nw (%)	5.6	20.9	46.0	3.6	23.0	108.8	14.0	34.4	102.5	13.9	41.2	106.4
Curr Liab To Inv (%)	41.5	59.3	213.3	—	—	—	178.8	242.6	527.4	314.7	527.4	655.0
Total Liab To Nw (%)	11.3	63.7	135.1	3.6	44.5	226.8	28.1	64.9	229.6	26.2	62.7	119.4
Fixed Assets To Nw (%)	37.5	62.4	107.3	19.6	34.2	71.3	30.1	84.8	130.1	51.9	97.6	129.4
EFFICIENCY												
Coll Period (days)	24.8	55.5	69.0	39.8	68.3	73.6	28.2	61.2	83.2	24.9	55.9	65.0
Sales To Inv (times)	27.2	23.1	18.9	59.9	59.9	59.9	106.3	42.9	28.3	169.5	42.9	30.0
Assets To Sales (%)	73.3	109.0	177.4	115.3	141.1	166.9	88.8	144.1	236.5	60.1	90.1	135.2
Sales To Nwc (times)	17.4	7.9	5.8	7.3	6.2	4.8	14.4	5.9	3.3	13.5	6.4	3.5
Acct Pay To Sales (%)	0.7	2.5	5.2	1.6	4.1	8.3	2.2	3.8	7.1	2.7	4.3	8.8
PROFITABILITY												
Return On Sales (%)	13.7	5.5	(2.6)	13.5	10.5	8.2	16.1	6.1	1.8	12.1	3.7	(1.7)
Return On Assets (%)	16.2	7.0	(1.1)	22.3	7.6	1.0	11.5	4.4	0.7	15.3	3.7	(2.5)
Return On Nw (%)	27.4	10.2	0.7	52.9	5.7	(20.6)	38.7	9.7	2.0	36.2	5.1	(4.5)

	SIC 4833 TEL BRDCSTG STNS INDUSTRY ASSETS $5,000,000-$25,000,000 1995 (34 Establishments)		SIC 4833 TEL BRDCSTG STNS INDUSTRY ASSETS $25,000,000-$50,000,000 1995 (10 Establishments)		SIC 4833 TEL BRDCSTG STNS INDUSTRY ASSETS OVER $50,000,000 1995 (36 Establishments)		SIC 4841 CABLE,PAY TV SVCS (NO BREAKDOWN) 1995 (222 Establishments)	
	$	%	$	%	$	%	$	%
Cash	756,293	9.0	807,619	2.3	16,170,128	5.2	360,537	13.2
Accounts Receivable	957,971	11.4	4,705,260	13.4	34,827,968	11.2	316,835	11.6
Notes Receivable	—	—	—	—	310,964	0.1	19,119	0.7
Inventory	33,613	0.4	70,228	0.2	932,892	0.3	71,015	2.6
Other Current	823,519	9.8	4,389,235	12.5	32,651,220	10.5	207,582	7.6
Total Current	**2,571,396**	**30.6**	**9,972,342**	**28.4**	**84,893,172**	**27.3**	**975,088**	**35.7**
Fixed Assets	3,436,931	40.9	15,379,879	43.8	42,913,032	13.8	1,166,281	42.7
Other Non-current	2,394,928	28.5	9,761,658	27.8	183,157,796	58.9	589,969	21.6
Total Assets	**8,403,255**	**100.0**	**35,113,879**	**100.0**	**310,964,000**	**100.0**	**2,731,338**	**100.0**
Accounts Payable	310,920	3.7	1,509,897	4.3	7,152,172	2.3	232,164	8.5
Bank Loans	—	—	—	—			2,731	0.1
Notes Payable	159,662	1.9	596,936	1.7	4,042,532	1.3	122,910	4.5
Other Current	1,008,391	12.0	4,810,601	13.7	41,358,212	13.3	368,731	13.5
Total Current	**1,478,973**	**17.6**	**6,917,434**	**19.7**	**52,552,916**	**16.9**	**726,536**	**26.6**
Other Long Term	1,714,264	20.4	16,924,890	48.2	152,061,396	48.9	663,715	24.3
Deferred Credits	67,226	0.8	596,936	1.7	6,530,244	2.1	19,119	0.7
Net Worth	5,142,792	61.2	10,674,619	30.4	99,819,444	32.1	1,321,968	48.4
Total Liab & Net Worth	**8,403,255**	**100.0**	**35,113,879**	**100.0**	**310,964,000**	**100.0**	**2,731,338**	**100.0**
Net Sales	7,594,713	100.0	28,202,000	100.0	65,931,000	100.0	2,409,552	100.0
Gross Profit	5,346,678	70.4	23,999,902	85.1	30,591,984	46.4	1,127,670	46.8
Net Profit After Tax	782,255	10.3	1,579,312	5.6	5,999,721	9.1	55,420	2.3
Working Capital	1,092,423	—	3,054,908	—	32,340,256	—	248,552	—

RATIOS	UQ	MED	LQ	UQ	MED	LQ	UQ	MED	LQ	UQ	MED	LQ
SOLVENCY												
Quick Ratio (times)	2.1	1.3	0.6	1.2	0.9	0.6	1.3	1.0	0.7	2.3	0.7	0.3
Current Ratio (times)	3.4	2.0	1.1	1.8	1.5	1.3	2.3	1.3	1.1	3.7	1.2	0.6
Curr Liab To Nw (%)	12.1	30.8	45.2	17.1	19.7	57.4	20.2	44.4	142.8	11.4	26.5	80.4
Curr Liab To Inv (%)	242.6	242.6	242.6	—	—	—	178.8	178.8	178.8	102.4	250.7	489.5
Total Liab To Nw (%)	18.7	41.5	72.8	56.4	59.6	129.6	60.0	170.9	692.1	18.7	62.3	173.7
Fixed Assets To Nw (%)	27.0	88.4	105.0	24.9	46.0	129.1	15.3	65.1	137.3	32.0	74.5	155.9
EFFICIENCY												
Coll Period (days)	23.4	58.8	70.5	42.0	63.8	71.5	60.2	83.6	98.9	11.3	27.2	54.8
Sales To Inv (times)	106.3	72.8	44.9	—	—	—	39.5	39.5	39.5	65.6	29.0	14.0
Assets To Sales (%)	85.6	107.6	134.2	82.3	114.5	282.1	196.5	254.4	373.2	45.5	126.8	225.3
Sales To Nwc (times)	12.2	5.2	3.5	9.8	7.2	5.1	15.6	6.9	2.5	16.1	5.9	2.7
Acct Pay To Sales (%)	1.6	3.1	4.4	2.0	4.4	6.1	2.1	4.0	8.1	3.0	6.7	16.5
PROFITABILITY												
Return On Sales (%)	16.0	4.1	1.8	17.2	6.0	5.8	17.4	9.2	4.3	15.2	5.1	(6.3)
Return On Assets (%)	17.7	5.0	1.2	10.7	6.2	0.5	11.5	6.7	2.9	12.9	4.5	(1.9)
Return On Nw (%)	34.8	8.3	2.5	0.6	(6.9)	(14.4)	64.4	15.9	6.2	25.1	8.4	(2.5)

SIC 4841 CABLE, PAY TV SVCS — INDUSTRY ASSETS — 1995

	UNDER $100,000 (16 Establishments) $	%	$100,000 - $250,000 (20 Establishments) $	%	$250,000 - $500,000 (22 Establishments) $	%	$500,000 - $1,000,000 (20 Establishments) $	%
Cash	14,390	21.3	30,312	16.8	66,340	19.2	133,460	16.6
Accounts Receivable	6,756	10.0	19,486	10.8	84,307	24.4	73,966	9.2
Notes Receivable	270	0.4	180	0.1	7,947	2.3	2,412	0.3
Inventory	3,446	5.1	9,924	5.5	19,349	5.6	30,551	3.8
Other Current	3,919	5.8	5,052	2.8	13,821	4.0	31,355	3.9
Total Current	**28,781**	**42.6**	**64,955**	**36.0**	**191,764**	**55.5**	**271,744**	**33.8**
Fixed Assets	34,726	51.4	106,454	59.0	133,026	38.5	405,204	50.4
Other Non-current	4,054	6.0	9,022	5.0	20,731	6.0	127,028	15.8
Total Assets	**67,561**	**100.0**	**180,430**	**100.0**	**345,521**	**100.0**	**803,976**	**100.0**
Accounts Payable	4,594	6.8	7,939	4.4	54,247	15.7	39,395	4.9
Bank Loans	—	—	1,083	0.6	2,073	0.6	—	—
Notes Payable	3,243	4.8	30,493	16.9	30,751	8.9	10,452	1.3
Other Current	8,310	12.3	26,343	14.6	35,934	10.4	101,301	12.6
Total Current	**16,147**	**23.9**	**65,857**	**36.5**	**123,005**	**35.6**	**151,147**	**18.8**
Other Long Term	10,202	15.1	30,132	16.7	34,552	10.0	238,781	29.7
Deferred Credits	—	—	—	—	—	—	4,020	0.5
Net Worth	41,212	61.0	84,441	46.8	187,963	54.4	410,028	51.0
Total Liab & Net Worth	**67,561**	**100.0**	**180,430**	**100.0**	**345,521**	**100.0**	**803,976**	**100.0**
Net Sales	240,889	100.0	458,897	100.0	1,263,310	100.0	466,706	100.0
Gross Profit	109,123	45.3	224,860	49.0	591,229	46.8	322,494	69.1
Net Profit After Tax	15,176	6.3	12,849	2.8	132,648	10.5	24,735	5.3
Working Capital	12,634	—	(902)	—	68,759	—	120,597	—

RATIOS

	UQ	MED	LQ	UQ	MED	LQ	UQ	MED	LQ	UQ	MED	LQ
SOLVENCY												
Quick Ratio (times)	6.8	2.3	0.6	3.3	0.7	0.2	4.3	0.8	0.5	7.9	1.2	0.5
Current Ratio (times)	7.3	2.6	1.4	4.2	0.9	0.4	5.4	1.2	0.7	7.9	1.3	0.5
Curr Liab To Nw (%)	6.7	23.9	34.0	12.3	73.3	179.3	15.8	31.0	96.7	4.2	11.6	20.3
Curr Liab To Inv (%)	67.6	134.4	225.8	87.0	217.3	386.2	92.3	108.5	194.4	238.6	318.7	334.4
Total Liab To Nw (%)	14.9	27.4	124.7	57.8	122.7	213.6	21.7	35.7	115.7	6.4	13.6	128.7
Fixed Assets To Nw (%)	54.1	81.0	214.1	65.9	143.6	264.9	19.2	55.4	104.9	32.6	83.9	141.1
EFFICIENCY												
Coll Period (days)	3.7	9.9	17.5	13.1	15.7	29.2	10.3	25.9	45.6	10.6	26.7	77.8
Sales To Inv (times)	40.5	33.8	27.0	79.7	27.4	18.4	52.2	29.0	22.2	59.5	14.0	9.9
Assets To Sales (%)	10.3	22.0	30.0	31.7	44.9	52.1	20.7	26.7	69.4	109.9	185.6	325.2
Sales To Nwc (times)	24.0	13.9	11.4	22.4	10.4	6.2	7.6	7.0	5.9	11.5	4.3	1.1
Acct Pay To Sales (%)	5.3	6.7	8.1	1.0	2.3	3.9	1.4	3.2	7.7	1.3	4.3	17.5
PROFITABILITY												
Return On Sales (%)	15.2	5.1	2.2	9.7	4.8	0.5	18.4	10.5	3.6	15.0	6.1	(4.9)
Return On Assets (%)	106.5	72.9	36.0	18.8	5.7	1.4	28.9	20.4	3.9	5.5	3.3	(2.1)
Return On Nw (%)	166.8	125.1	73.5	59.7	19.9	1.1	96.7	44.8	9.5	9.3	5.5	0.2

Balance Sheet

	SIC 4841 CABLE,PAY TV SVCS $1,000,000-$5,000,000 (40 Est.) $	%	SIC 4841 CABLE,PAY TV SVCS $5,000,000-$25,000,000 (39 Est.) $	%	SIC 4841 CABLE,PAY TV SVCS OVER $50,000,000 (45 Est.) $	%	SIC 4899 COMMNCTN SVCS,NEC (NO BREAKDOWN) (54 Est.) $	%
Cash	238,868	9.8	1,333,409	11.8	12,654,570	9.0	303,212	15.9
Accounts Receivable	194,994	8.0	1,582,010	14.0	10,826,688	7.7	411,910	21.6
Notes Receivable	—	—	169,501	1.5	140,606	0.1	—	—
Inventory	51,186	2.1	33,900	0.3	140,606	0.1	47,675	2.5
Other Current	85,310	3.5	1,785,412	15.8	10,404,869	7.4	175,443	9.2
Total Current	**570,358**	**23.4**	**4,904,232**	**43.4**	**34,167,339**	**24.3**	**938,240**	**49.2**
Fixed Assets	1,394,208	57.2	3,062,320	27.1	41,338,262	29.4	646,470	33.9
Other Non-current	472,861	19.4	3,333,522	29.5	65,100,733	46.3	322,282	16.9
Total Assets	**2,437,426**	**100.0**	**11,300,073**	**100.0**	**140,606,335**	**100.0**	**1,906,992**	**100.0**
Accounts Payable	207,181	8.5	1,322,109	11.7	6,467,891	4.6	186,885	9.8
Bank Loans	—	—	—	—	—	—	—	—
Notes Payable	51,186	2.1	327,702	2.9	421,819	0.3	64,838	3.4
Other Current	216,931	8.9	1,762,811	15.6	23,200,045	16.5	289,863	15.2
Total Current	**475,298**	**19.5**	**3,412,622**	**30.2**	**30,089,756**	**21.4**	**541,586**	**28.4**
Other Long Term	787,289	32.3	2,124,414	18.8	53,430,407	38.0	329,910	17.3
Deferred Credits	24,374	1.0	101,701	0.9	2,390,308	1.7	34,326	1.8
Net Worth	1,150,465	47.2	5,661,337	50.1	54,695,864	38.9	1,001,171	52.5
Total Liab & Net Worth	**2,437,426**	**100.0**	**11,300,073**	**100.0**	**140,606,335**	**100.0**	**1,906,992**	**100.0**
Net Sales	1,231,957	100.0	6,440,941	100.0	99,369,000	100.0	2,985,854	100.0
Gross Profit	620,906	50.4	2,376,707	36.9	41,635,611	41.9	991,304	33.2
Net Profit After Tax	24,639	2.0	(334,929)	(5.2)	2,682,963	2.7	68,675	2.3
Working Capital	95,060	—	1,491,610	—	4,077,583	—	396,654	—

RATIOS

	UQ	MED	LQ	UQ	MED	LQ	UQ	MED	LQ	UQ	MED	LQ
SOLVENCY												
Quick Ratio (times)	2.1	0.7	0.2	1.4	0.6	0.3	0.7	0.5	0.1	2.2	1.0	0.6
Current Ratio (times)	3.0	1.1	0.6	2.7	1.3	0.6	1.1	0.8	0.2	3.5	1.5	1.0
Curr Liab To Nw (%)	6.9	20.6	55.1	13.8	42.9	95.1	14.2	21.3	33.6	20.1	40.8	95.6
Curr Liab To Inv (%)	53.4	250.7	489.5	291.8	437.6	583.3	49.8	68.9	88.0	93.9	169.7	210.3
Total Liab To Nw (%)	13.3	53.2	179.2	17.9	53.5	156.2	35.6	60.1	82.3	18.7	69.9	180.2
Fixed Assets To Nw (%)	54.9	84.6	136.5	13.8	30.3	82.9	26.5	50.3	81.3	32.7	64.1	153.1
EFFICIENCY												
Coll Period (days)	11.0	24.1	38.0	20.7	44.6	66.1	9.9	20.4	54.0	31.6	55.1	71.7
Sales To Inv (times)	58.8	36.1	6.9	16.1	13.9	11.6	54.5	37.0	12.2	79.9	20.8	10.0
Assets To Sales (%)	79.5	175.5	280.5	72.7	147.4	399.7	126.8	151.2	176.4	30.9	59.6	102.8
Sales To Nwc (times)	17.8	11.4	4.9	5.4	4.2	1.0	3.4	2.7	2.0	10.9	6.3	3.3
Acct Pay To Sales (%)	3.0	5.2	24.6	8.3	16.1	20.1	3.5	5.7	8.1	3.1	9.0	17.7
PROFITABILITY												
Return On Sales (%)	17.0	6.5	(15.9)	6.3	(3.5)	(19.7)	5.2	1.8	(11.5)	8.7	2.5	(3.2)
Return On Assets (%)	12.8	6.7	(1.6)	5.8	(1.9)	(5.0)	2.4	0.8	(4.8)	11.2	3.9	(1.7)
Return On Nw (%)	19.4	13.0	4.6	13.0	(3.0)	(16.0)	3.2	0.6	(10.0)	30.2	9.6	(1.5)

	SIC 4899 COMMNCTN SVCS,NEC INDUSTRY ASSETS $1,000,000 - $5,000,000 1995 (17 Establishments) $	%	SIC 49 ELEC,GAS,SANITARY SV (NO BREAKDOWN) 1995 (1568 Establishments) $	%	SIC 49 ELEC,GAS,SANITARY SV NORTHEAST 1995 (663 Establishments) $	%	SIC 49 ELEC,GAS,SANITARY SV CENTRAL 1995 (721 Establishments) $	%
Cash	493,911	25.9	1,266,539	6.0	2,154,620	6.5	1,099,019	5.6
Accounts Receivable	453,864	23.8	2,364,207	11.2	4,839,608	14.6	2,099,911	10.7
Notes Receivable	—	—	63,327	0.3	66,296	0.2	58,876	0.3
Inventory	72,466	3.8	379,962	1.8	497,220	1.5	510,259	2.6
Other Current	162,094	8.5	1,224,321	5.8	1,988,880	6.0	1,197,146	6.1
Total Current	**1,182,335**	**62.0**	**5,298,356**	**25.1**	**9,546,623**	**28.8**	**4,965,211**	**25.3**
Fixed Assets	398,561	20.9	11,926,579	56.5	17,866,770	53.9	11,696,703	59.6
Other Non-current	326,096	17.1	3,884,054	18.4	5,734,603	17.3	2,963,426	15.1
Total Assets	**1,906,992**	**100.0**	**21,108,989**	**100.0**	**33,147,997**	**100.0**	**19,625,341**	**100.0**
Accounts Payable	179,257	9.4	1,456,520	6.9	2,585,544	7.8	1,354,149	6.9
Bank Loans	—	—	21,109	0.1	66,296	0.2	39,251	0.2
Notes Payable	11,442	0.6	506,616	2.4	795,552	2.4	569,135	2.9
Other Current	312,747	16.4	1,920,918	9.1	3,944,612	11.9	1,746,655	8.9
Total Current	**503,446**	**26.4**	**3,905,163**	**18.5**	**7,392,003**	**22.3**	**3,709,189**	**18.9**
Other Long Term	335,631	17.6	7,240,383	34.3	11,038,283	33.3	6,397,861	32.6
Deferred Credits	15,256	0.8	569,943	2.7	1,524,808	4.6	686,887	3.5
Net Worth	1,052,660	55.2	9,393,500	44.5	13,192,903	39.8	8,831,403	45.0
Total Liab & Net Worth	**1,906,992**	**100.0**	**21,108,989**	**100.0**	**33,147,997**	**100.0**	**19,625,341**	**100.0**
Net Sales	2,209,228	100.0	9,888,953	100.0	8,183,772	100.0	10,555,286	100.0
Gross Profit	620,793	28.1	3,461,134	35.0	2,757,931	33.7	4,095,451	38.8
Net Profit After Tax	(110,461)	(5.0)	652,671	6.6	499,210	6.1	791,646	7.5
Working Capital	678,889	—	1,393,193	—	2,154,620	—	1,256,022	—

RATIOS	UQ	MED	LQ	UQ	MED	LQ	UQ	MED	LQ	UQ	MED	LQ
SOLVENCY												
Quick Ratio (times)	4.0	1.8	1.0	1.5	0.8	0.4	1.5	0.7	0.4	1.2	0.7	0.4
Current Ratio (times)	6.6	3.4	1.4	2.6	1.3	0.9	2.4	1.2	0.8	2.3	1.3	0.8
Curr Liab To Nw (%)	10.1	43.5	146.4	10.9	25.5	57.8	16.2	35.4	70.8	13.1	27.5	56.2
Curr Liab To Inv (%)	90.4	93.9	195.0	252.3	387.3	564.2	294.3	444.9	621.7	215.5	345.2	518.5
Total Liab To Nw (%)	12.4	52.7	261.5	63.6	142.0	216.7	76.9	174.3	253.0	70.5	144.5	211.7
Fixed Assets To Nw (%)	10.3	40.2	71.7	88.8	157.5	226.9	100.7	177.7	240.0	104.2	169.4	223.6
EFFICIENCY												
Coll Period (days)	33.4	62.4	95.8	25.6	35.4	51.5	29.2	41.1	59.8	25.9	34.0	47.1
Sales To Inv (times)	237.3	11.0	6.8	49.3	26.5	14.1	57.5	29.9	15.2	37.5	18.9	12.4
Assets To Sales (%)	42.6	59.6	119.6	92.0	209.9	310.4	58.1	181.1	346.1	111.6	207.3	290.3
Sales To Nwc (times)	9.0	3.4	0.8	18.9	8.1	3.2	18.8	8.8	3.0	20.1	8.5	3.8
Acct Pay To Sales (%)	2.9	4.8	15.4	4.3	6.6	9.7	4.0	6.5	9.9	4.4	6.3	8.7
PROFITABILITY												
Return On Sales (%)	5.7	(3.2)	(18.3)	11.5	6.5	2.6	10.9	6.1	2.1	11.3	7.4	3.8
Return On Assets (%)	9.9	(1.2)	(7.8)	5.4	3.3	1.2	5.0	3.0	1.2	5.2	3.6	2.1
Return On Nw (%)	20.2	(1.4)	(22.3)	13.3	8.7	3.0	14.0	9.5	3.2	13.5	9.1	5.0

SIC 49 ELEC, GAS, SANITARY SV

	SOUTH 1995 (1245 Establishments) $	%	WEST 1995 (507 Establishments) $	%	INDUSTRY ASSETS UNDER $100,000 1995 (130 Establishments) $	%	INDUSTRY ASSETS $100,000 - $250,000 1995 (140 Establishments) $	%
Cash	1,298,105	6.3	1,529,197	7.8	11,090	24.6	22,243	13.5
Accounts Receivable	1,978,065	9.6	2,509,452	12.8	8,701	19.3	41,851	25.4
Notes Receivable	82,419	0.4	58,815	0.3	406	0.9	1,153	0.7
Inventory	309,073	1.5	450,917	2.3	1,488	3.3	6,261	3.8
Other Current	1,174,476	5.7	1,078,280	5.5	2,615	5.8	6,920	4.2
Total Current	**4,842,139**	**23.5**	**5,626,661**	**28.7**	**24,299**	**53.9**	**78,429**	**47.6**
Fixed Assets	11,270,850	54.7	10,527,934	53.7	17,762	39.4	69,696	42.3
Other Non-current	4,491,856	21.8	3,450,496	17.6	3,020	6.7	16,641	10.1
Total Assets	**20,604,845**	**100.0**	**19,605,092**	**100.0**	**45,082**	**100.0**	**164,766**	**100.0**
Accounts Payable	1,339,315	6.5	1,352,751	6.9	4,824	10.7	17,959	10.9
Bank Loans	—	—	19,605	0.1	—	—	494	0.3
Notes Payable	494,516	2.4	333,287	1.7	3,201	7.1	10,215	6.2
Other Current	1,565,968	7.6	1,803,668	9.2	8,746	19.4	24,550	14.9
Total Current	**3,399,799**	**16.5**	**3,509,311**	**17.9**	**16,771**	**37.2**	**53,219**	**32.3**
Other Long Term	7,252,905	35.2	6,410,865	32.7	6,988	15.5	32,788	19.9
Deferred Credits	329,678	1.6	411,707	2.1	—	—	—	—
Net Worth	9,622,463	46.7	9,273,209	47.3	21,324	47.3	78,758	47.8
Total Liab & Net Worth	**20,604,845**	**100.0**	**19,605,092**	**100.0**	**45,082**	**100.0**	**164,766**	**100.0**
Net Sales	11,702,987	100.0	10,271,922	100.0	126,246	100.0	434,637	100.0
Gross Profit	4,037,531	34.5	3,874,108	37.9	55,548	44.0	179,070	41.2
Net Profit After Tax	702,179	6.0	858,641	8.4	7,196	5.7	25,644	5.9
Working Capital	1,442,340	—	2,117,350	—	7,528	—	25,210	—

RATIOS	South UQ	South MED	South LQ	West UQ	West MED	West LQ	Under UQ	Under MED	Under LQ	$100-250k UQ	$100-250k MED	$100-250k LQ
SOLVENCY												
Quick Ratio (times)	1.7	0.9	0.5	1.9	0.9	0.5	3.5	1.3	0.4	2.5	1.3	0.6
Current Ratio (times)	3.2	1.5	0.9	3.6	1.6	1.0	3.6	1.6	0.7	3.3	1.6	1.0
Curr Liab To Nw (%)	9.0	20.2	48.5	9.1	21.7	54.2	14.9	49.4	113.6	16.5	44.4	112.9
Curr Liab To Inv (%)	261.0	414.2	594.3	198.4	378.4	570.9	72.1	257.6	435.3	96.9	203.1	438.8
Total Liab To Nw (%)	62.1	117.8	188.2	48.4	132.3	213.8	15.4	58.2	140.9	37.8	87.2	188.9
Fixed Assets To Nw (%)	84.6	135.7	219.6	78.4	133.0	220.7	32.9	78.2	141.4	44.2	85.0	157.4
EFFICIENCY												
Coll Period (days)	23.4	33.6	47.5	29.5	40.2	55.2	17.5	27.6	47.3	20.5	36.3	65.1
Sales To Inv (times)	56.1	31.3	15.5	48.1	24.8	15.5	55.0	27.8	18.9	113.0	36.3	19.4
Assets To Sales (%)	104.6	205.7	306.9	93.7	232.6	332.6	12.6	32.7	69.9	23.1	34.5	70.0
Sales To Nwc (times)	19.6	7.9	3.2	13.9	6.2	2.6	29.2	11.6	5.0	33.9	16.0	6.7
Acct Pay To Sales (%)	4.4	6.7	9.8	4.1	6.6	9.8	2.0	3.7	8.5	1.4	3.1	7.1
PROFITABILITY												
Return On Sales (%)	11.9	6.0	2.2	14.9	8.3	3.8	17.5	4.2	(0.9)	15.5	4.0	1.0
Return On Assets (%)	5.2	3.2	1.1	6.4	3.4	1.4	39.1	6.7	(4.5)	22.5	9.0	3.0
Return On Nw (%)	12.8	7.5	3.0	14.9	9.2	3.3	92.0	35.4	0.5	48.8	19.6	6.8

SIC 49 ELEC, GAS, SANITARY SV — INDUSTRY ASSETS $5,000,000-$25,000,000
1995 (693 Establishments)

	$	%
Cash	693,676	5.3
Accounts Receivable	1,047,058	8.0
Notes Receivable	26,176	0.2
Inventory	196,323	1.5
Other Current	811,470	6.2
Total Current	**2,774,704**	**21.2**
Fixed Assets	7,303,230	55.8
Other Non-current	3,010,292	23.0
Total Assets	**13,088,225**	**100.0**
Accounts Payable	680,588	5.2
Bank Loans	—	—
Notes Payable	209,412	1.6
Other Current	850,735	6.5
Total Current	**1,740,734**	**13.3**
Other Long Term	4,620,143	35.3
Deferred Credits	130,882	1.0
Net Worth	6,596,465	50.4
Total Liab & Net Worth	**13,088,225**	**100.0**
Net Sales	6,127,979	100.0
Gross Profit	1,887,418	30.8
Net Profit After Tax	527,006	8.6
Working Capital	1,033,970	—

RATIOS	UQ	MED	LQ
SOLVENCY			
Quick Ratio (times)	2.0	1.1	0.7
Current Ratio (times)	4.3	2.0	1.1
Curr Liab To Nw (%)	6.5	13.2	29.2
Curr Liab To Inv (%)	187.2	321.2	485.0
Total Liab To Nw (%)	55.0	97.8	171.1
Fixed Assets To Nw (%)	84.6	110.2	186.7
EFFICIENCY			
Coll Period (days)	27.0	36.9	54.0
Sales To Inv (times)	61.5	31.4	17.3
Assets To Sales (%)	116.1	222.6	326.0
Sales To Nwc (times)	14.1	6.0	2.2
Acct Pay To Sales (%)	3.9	6.4	9.0
PROFITABILITY			
Return On Sales (%)	12.8	6.5	2.8
Return On Assets (%)	5.2	3.2	1.3
Return On Nw (%)	11.1	7.0	2.7

SIC 49 ELEC, GAS, SANITARY SV — INDUSTRY ASSETS $1,000,000-$5,000,000
1995 (389 Establishments)

	$	%
Cash	221,815	9.1
Accounts Receivable	443,631	18.2
Notes Receivable	9,750	0.4
Inventory	43,876	1.8
Other Current	160,877	6.6
Total Current	**879,949**	**36.1**
Fixed Assets	1,206,578	49.5
Other Non-current	351,005	14.4
Total Assets	**2,437,532**	**100.0**
Accounts Payable	268,129	11.0
Bank Loans	4,875	0.2
Notes Payable	70,688	2.9
Other Current	299,816	12.3
Total Current	**643,508**	**26.4**
Other Long Term	665,446	27.3
Deferred Credits	29,250	1.2
Net Worth	1,099,327	45.1
Total Liab & Net Worth	**2,437,532**	**100.0**
Net Sales	2,278,202	100.0
Gross Profit	856,604	37.6
Net Profit After Tax	84,293	3.7
Working Capital	236,441	—

RATIOS	UQ	MED	LQ
SOLVENCY			
Quick Ratio (times)	2.4	1.1	0.6
Current Ratio (times)	3.5	1.5	0.9
Curr Liab To Nw (%)	9.2	36.2	101.4
Curr Liab To Inv (%)	170.2	297.4	545.9
Total Liab To Nw (%)	44.2	102.4	212.8
Fixed Assets To Nw (%)	68.7	102.1	182.8
EFFICIENCY			
Coll Period (days)	28.4	43.1	62.4
Sales To Inv (times)	75.3	39.6	19.3
Assets To Sales (%)	43.2	76.6	236.7
Sales To Nwc (times)	19.4	8.5	3.3
Acct Pay To Sales (%)	3.2	6.6	10.1
PROFITABILITY			
Return On Sales (%)	9.8	3.8	0.6
Return On Assets (%)	9.9	3.7	0.5
Return On Nw (%)	29.6	10.1	1.2

SIC 49 ELEC, GAS, SANITARY SV — INDUSTRY ASSETS $500,000 - $1,000,000
1995 (199 Establishments)

	$	%
Cash	65,795	9.3
Accounts Receivable	172,622	24.4
Notes Receivable	6,367	0.9
Inventory	14,149	2.0
Other Current	36,081	5.1
Total Current	**295,014**	**41.7**
Fixed Assets	359,394	50.8
Other Non-current	53,060	7.5
Total Assets	**707,468**	**100.0**
Accounts Payable	87,726	12.4
Bank Loans	707	0.1
Notes Payable	29,006	4.1
Other Current	94,093	13.3
Total Current	**211,533**	**29.9**
Other Long Term	178,989	25.3
Deferred Credits	3,537	0.5
Net Worth	313,408	44.3
Total Liab & Net Worth	**707,468**	**100.0**
Net Sales	1,218,827	100.0
Gross Profit	507,032	41.6
Net Profit After Tax	51,191	4.2
Working Capital	83,481	—

RATIOS	UQ	MED	LQ
SOLVENCY			
Quick Ratio (times)	2.5	1.1	0.7
Current Ratio (times)	3.0	1.4	0.9
Curr Liab To Nw (%)	15.2	42.0	128.5
Curr Liab To Inv (%)	143.7	254.2	462.1
Total Liab To Nw (%)	35.3	100.6	252.1
Fixed Assets To Nw (%)	63.6	104.4	183.5
EFFICIENCY			
Coll Period (days)	32.8	46.0	67.7
Sales To Inv (times)	131.5	62.6	16.3
Assets To Sales (%)	35.7	55.0	129.9
Sales To Nwc (times)	22.1	11.1	6.0
Acct Pay To Sales (%)	2.3	5.6	8.9
PROFITABILITY			
Return On Sales (%)	10.3	4.2	0.4
Return On Assets (%)	12.5	5.8	0.4
Return On Nw (%)	32.7	13.1	2.4

SIC 49 ELEC, GAS, SANITARY SV — INDUSTRY ASSETS $250,000 - $500,000
1995 (135 Establishments)

	$	%
Cash	38,744	11.2
Accounts Receivable	78,180	22.6
Notes Receivable	692	0.2
Inventory	6,919	2.0
Other Current	18,334	5.3
Total Current	**142,869**	**41.3**
Fixed Assets	174,694	50.5
Other Non-current	28,366	8.2
Total Assets	**345,929**	**100.0**
Accounts Payable	47,046	13.6
Bank Loans	—	—
Notes Payable	19,372	5.6
Other Current	42,203	12.2
Total Current	**108,622**	**31.4**
Other Long Term	77,488	22.4
Deferred Credits	346	0.1
Net Worth	159,473	46.1
Total Liab & Net Worth	**345,929**	**100.0**
Net Sales	649,192	100.0
Gross Profit	279,802	43.1
Net Profit After Tax	40,250	6.2
Working Capital	34,247	—

RATIOS	UQ	MED	LQ
SOLVENCY			
Quick Ratio (times)	2.5	1.1	0.4
Current Ratio (times)	3.1	1.4	0.7
Curr Liab To Nw (%)	12.1	45.4	109.7
Curr Liab To Inv (%)	166.6	277.5	342.3
Total Liab To Nw (%)	40.2	84.3	216.9
Fixed Assets To Nw (%)	55.4	116.8	186.5
EFFICIENCY			
Coll Period (days)	28.6	42.2	71.7
Sales To Inv (times)	94.0	36.1	14.2
Assets To Sales (%)	28.8	45.2	119.8
Sales To Nwc (times)	15.2	9.5	3.7
Acct Pay To Sales (%)	2.3	4.4	10.0
PROFITABILITY			
Return On Sales (%)	16.5	7.8	(0.1)
Return On Assets (%)	16.5	6.8	(0.7)
Return On Nw (%)	43.2	14.3	(0.1)

	SIC 49 ELEC,GAS,SANITARY SV INDUSTRY ASSETS $25,000,000-$50,000,000 1995 (305 Establishments) $	%	SIC 49 ELEC,GAS,SANITARY SV INDUSTRY ASSETS OVER $50,000,000 1995 (1145 Establishments) $	%	SIC 4911 ELECTRIC SERVICES (NO BREAKDOWN) 1995 (1038 Establishments) $	%	SIC 4911 ELECTRIC SERVICES INDUSTRY ASSETS $1,000,000 - $5,000,000 1995 (21 Establishments) $	%
Cash	1,004,621	2.9	11,881,272	3.0	2,174,092	3.1	337,900	8.8
Accounts Receivable	2,355,664	6.8	21,782,332	5.5	3,716,996	5.3	729,556	19.0
Notes Receivable	34,642	0.1	792,085	0.2	140,264	0.2	—	—
Inventory	415,705	1.2	7,524,806	1.9	1,262,376	1.8	241,906	6.3
Other Current	2,321,022	6.7	20,990,247	5.3	4,558,580	6.5	510,689	13.3
Total Current	**6,131,655**	**17.7**	**62,970,742**	**15.9**	**11,852,308**	**16.9**	**1,820,051**	**47.4**
Fixed Assets	20,092,430	58.0	247,130,458	62.4	42,920,784	61.2	1,785,493	46.5
Other Non-current	8,418,035	24.3	85,941,201	21.7	15,358,908	21.9	234,226	6.1
Total Assets	**34,642,120**	**100.0**	**396,042,400**	**100.0**	**70,132,000**	**100.0**	**3,839,770**	**100.0**
Accounts Payable	1,870,674	5.4	15,841,696	4.0	2,945,544	4.2	725,717	18.9
Bank Loans	103,926	0.3	396,042	0.1	—	—	—	—
Notes Payable	277,137	0.8	5,940,636	1.5	841,584	1.2	19,199	0.5
Other Current	2,043,885	5.9	28,911,095	7.3	3,716,996	5.3	218,867	5.7
Total Current	**4,295,623**	**12.4**	**51,089,470**	**12.9**	**7,504,124**	**10.7**	**963,782**	**25.1**
Other Long Term	13,995,416	40.4	161,189,257	40.7	31,489,268	44.9	952,263	24.8
Deferred Credits	554,274	1.6	26,534,841	6.7	2,665,016	3.8	88,315	2.3
Net Worth	15,796,807	45.6	157,228,833	39.7	28,473,592	40.6	1,835,410	47.8
Total Liab & Net Worth	**34,642,120**	**100.0**	**396,042,400**	**100.0**	**70,132,000**	**100.0**	**3,839,770**	**100.0**
Net Sales	15,307,938	100.0	98,982,050	100.0	28,172,354	100.0	1,581,575	100.0
Gross Profit	5,327,162	34.8	29,001,741	29.3	10,226,565	36.3	773,390	48.9
Net Profit After Tax	1,071,556	7.0	7,324,672	7.4	2,000,237	7.1	85,405	5.4
Working Capital	1,836,032	—	11,881,272	—	4,348,184	—	856,269	—

RATIOS	UQ	MED	LQ	UQ	MED	LQ	UQ	MED	LQ	UQ	MED	LQ
SOLVENCY												
Quick Ratio (times)	1.3	0.9	0.6	0.9	0.5	0.3	1.1	0.7	0.4	1.9	1.2	0.7
Current Ratio (times)	2.9	1.6	1.1	1.8	1.1	0.8	2.3	1.3	0.9	3.7	2.0	1.4
Curr Liab To Nw (%)	9.1	15.7	30.0	16.8	29.3	49.6	13.6	21.5	36.3	6.1	12.9	32.7
Curr Liab To Inv (%)	273.2	405.9	564.2	306.7	439.3	615.5	269.7	388.7	559.3	170.7	172.1	326.0
Total Liab To Nw (%)	76.6	120.5	186.4	124.6	177.7	230.5	107.1	163.7	215.3	44.9	92.9	175.0
Fixed Assets To Nw (%)	93.8	152.9	214.9	149.7	205.5	243.4	147.8	200.9	239.8	61.4	111.2	169.4
EFFICIENCY												
Coll Period (days)	26.3	34.3	47.3	25.6	34.7	46.7	24.5	32.1	41.3	20.3	33.2	50.9
Sales To Inv (times)	48.5	33.1	22.3	39.7	20.5	12.9	38.0	21.4	13.8	44.3	25.1	15.1
Assets To Sales (%)	158.4	226.9	305.4	179.5	250.8	358.6	194.4	242.9	300.0	20.0	172.3	262.2
Sales To Nwc (times)	14.0	6.9	3.1	19.9	7.8	3.0	18.3	8.5	4.0	19.6	12.4	4.2
Acct Pay To Sales (%)	4.6	6.3	8.8	5.1	6.9	9.5	5.2	6.6	8.5	3.8	6.6	9.5
PROFITABILITY												
Return On Sales (%)	10.8	6.9	3.8	11.9	7.9	4.2	11.0	7.9	4.4	8.2	4.4	2.1
Return On Assets (%)	4.8	3.0	1.6	4.4	3.2	1.8	4.6	3.3	1.9	3.8	2.5	1.2
Return On Nw (%)	11.4	7.0	3.5	12.2	9.5	4.9	11.9	8.7	5.2	11.2	7.5	4.3

	SIC 4911 ELECTRIC SERVICES INDUSTRY ASSETS $5,000,000-$25,000,000 1995 (225 Establishments)		SIC 4911 ELECTRIC SERVICES INDUSTRY ASSETS $25,000,000-$50,000,000 1995 (161 Establishments)		SIC 4911 ELECTRIC SERVICES INDUSTRY ASSETS OVER $50,000,000 1995 (614 Establishments)		SIC 4922 NAT GAS TRNSMSSN (NO BREAKDOWN) 1995 (105 Establishments)	
	$	%	$	%	$	%	$	%
Cash	536,703	3.4	619,161	1.8	22,681,350	3.0	14,150,396	5.2
Accounts Receivable	868,197	5.5	1,685,493	4.9	34,022,025	4.5	28,572,915	10.5
Notes Receivable	15,785	0.1	34,398	0.1	1,512,090	0.2	1,360,615	0.5
Inventory	268,352	1.7	447,172	1.3	14,364,855	1.9	4,081,845	1.5
Other Current	1,231,261	7.8	2,579,836	7.5	38,558,295	5.1	16,871,626	6.2
Total Current	**2,920,298**	**18.5**	**5,366,059**	**15.6**	**111,138,615**	**14.7**	**65,037,397**	**23.9**
Fixed Assets	9,818,514	62.2	20,363,504	59.2	474,796,260	62.8	159,191,955	58.5
Other Non-current	3,046,581	19.3	8,668,248	25.2	170,110,125	22.5	47,893,648	17.6
Total Assets	**15,785,393**	**100.0**	**34,397,811**	**100.0**	**756,045,000**	**100.0**	**272,123,000**	**100.0**
Accounts Payable	631,416	4.0	1,272,719	3.7	27,973,665	3.7	23,130,455	8.5
Bank Loans	—	—	—	—	—	—	272,123	0.1
Notes Payable	236,781	1.5	275,182	0.8	9,072,540	1.2	2,176,984	0.8
Other Current	631,416	4.0	1,616,697	4.7	46,118,745	6.1	29,389,284	10.8
Total Current	**1,499,612**	**9.5**	**3,164,599**	**9.2**	**83,164,950**	**11.0**	**54,968,846**	**20.2**
Other Long Term	6,598,294	41.8	15,994,982	46.5	362,901,600	48.0	67,486,504	24.8
Deferred Credits	126,283	0.8	412,774	1.2	51,411,060	6.8	18,232,241	6.7
Net Worth	7,561,203	47.9	14,825,457	43.1	258,567,390	34.2	131,435,409	48.3
Total Liab & Net Worth	**15,785,393**	**100.0**	**34,397,811**	**100.0**	**756,045,000**	**100.0**	**272,123,000**	**100.0**
Net Sales	7,393,449	100.0	16,063,280	100.0	115,905,078	100.0	73,195,999	100.0
Gross Profit	2,824,298	38.2	6,168,300	38.4	36,394,194	31.4	21,300,036	29.1
Net Profit After Tax	561,902	7.6	1,076,240	6.7	7,997,450	6.9	5,050,524	6.9
Working Capital	1,420,686	—	2,201,460	—	27,973,665	—	10,068,551	—

RATIOS	UQ	MED	LQ	UQ	MED	LQ	UQ	MED	LQ	UQ	MED	LQ
SOLVENCY												
Quick Ratio (times)	1.5	0.9	0.6	1.1	0.9	0.6	0.8	0.5	0.3	0.9	0.6	0.3
Current Ratio (times)	3.4	2.0	1.3	2.8	1.6	1.1	1.6	1.1	0.8	1.6	1.1	0.8
Curr Liab To Nw (%)	9.2	13.2	19.7	11.2	16.1	21.6	18.4	28.4	44.2	18.8	37.2	58.3
Curr Liab To Inv (%)	176.8	285.7	428.1	275.1	410.2	564.2	308.1	428.8	584.3	314.8	409.7	692.8
Total Liab To Nw (%)	67.8	119.5	170.4	94.8	134.5	183.6	145.8	188.6	234.7	67.1	145.6	246.3
Fixed Assets To Nw (%)	112.5	155.3	201.1	137.8	178.1	226.3	185.4	218.6	250.6	106.9	179.6	232.2
EFFICIENCY												
Coll Period (days)	25.9	33.1	41.3	23.8	31.4	38.4	24.3	32.1	41.6	29.3	44.9	57.3
Sales To Inv (times)	39.1	25.4	16.0	43.9	31.4	22.7	33.9	18.7	12.7	47.0	22.7	13.3
Assets To Sales (%)	181.6	230.7	273.3	185.2	222.4	264.9	204.6	254.5	331.1	110.0	219.1	380.3
Sales To Nwc (times)	14.0	6.9	3.2	13.7	7.9	3.9	24.6	9.8	4.7	17.6	6.9	3.1
Acct Pay To Sales (%)	5.1	6.3	7.9	5.6	6.5	8.0	5.2	6.8	8.7	4.7	7.4	11.8
PROFITABILITY												
Return On Sales (%)	10.3	6.9	4.2	10.4	6.9	4.2	11.4	8.5	4.6	17.0	6.0	2.1
Return On Assets (%)	4.8	3.3	2.0	5.0	3.3	2.1	4.5	3.3	1.9	5.7	3.5	1.5
Return On Nw (%)	9.8	6.7	4.1	10.6	7.6	4.9	12.5	10.1	5.8	13.6	9.2	3.3

	SIC 4923 GAS TRNSMSN DIST (NO BREAKDOWN) 1995 (83 Establishments) $	%	SIC 4923 GAS TRNSMSN DIST INDUSTRY ASSETS OVER $50,000,000 1995 (46 Establishments) $	%	SIC 4924 NTRL GAS DIST (NO BREAKDOWN) 1995 (237 Establishments) $	%	SIC 4924 NTRL GAS DIST INDUSTRY ASSETS $1,000,000 - $5,000,000 1995 (29 Establishments) $	%
Cash	4,574,752	5.2	9,452,544	2.4	4,361,949	5.8	300,750	10.8
Accounts Receivable	17,683,176	20.1	39,385,600	10.0	11,431,315	15.2	690,610	24.8
Notes Receivable	791,784	0.9	3,544,704	0.9	601,648	0.8	25,062	0.9
Inventory	2,199,400	2.5	12,209,536	3.1	2,707,417	3.6	108,604	3.9
Other Current	4,134,872	4.7	15,754,240	4.0	4,286,743	5.7	208,854	7.5
Total Current	**29,383,984**	**33.4**	**80,346,624**	**20.4**	**23,389,073**	**31.1**	**1,333,880**	**47.9**
Fixed Assets	40,556,936	46.1	222,528,640	56.5	40,009,603	53.2	1,083,255	38.9
Other Non-current	18,035,080	20.5	90,980,736	23.1	11,807,345	15.7	367,583	13.2
Total Assets	**87,976,000**	**100.0**	**393,856,000**	**100.0**	**75,206,021**	**100.0**	**2,784,718**	**100.0**
Accounts Payable	17,155,320	19.5	39,779,456	10.1	9,551,165	12.7	632,131	22.7
Bank Loans	—	—	—	—	300,824	0.4	11,139	0.4
Notes Payable	2,023,448	2.3	9,846,400	2.5	3,233,859	4.3	91,896	3.3
Other Current	9,413,432	10.7	36,234,752	9.2	7,971,838	10.6	203,284	7.3
Total Current	**28,592,200**	**32.5**	**85,860,608**	**21.8**	**21,057,686**	**28.0**	**938,450**	**33.7**
Other Long Term	18,826,864	21.4	126,821,632	32.2	17,673,415	23.5	392,645	14.1
Deferred Credits	4,574,752	5.2	30,326,912	7.7	4,963,597	6.6	47,340	1.7
Net Worth	35,982,184	40.9	150,846,848	38.3	31,511,323	41.9	1,406,283	50.5
Total Liab & Net Worth	**87,976,000**	**100.0**	**393,856,000**	**100.0**	**75,206,021**	**100.0**	**2,784,718**	**100.0**
Net Sales	120,308,944	100.0	295,353,000	100.0	66,959,271	100.0	4,118,700	100.0
Gross Profit	37,536,391	31.2	75,905,721	25.7	16,338,062	24.4	650,755	15.8
Net Profit After Tax	6,977,919	5.8	17,130,474	5.8	3,214,045	4.8	156,511	3.8
Working Capital	791,784	—	(5,513,984)	—	2,331,387	—	395,430	—

RATIOS	UQ	MED	LQ	UQ	MED	LQ	UQ	MED	LQ	UQ	MED	LQ
SOLVENCY												
Quick Ratio (times)	1.0	0.6	0.3	0.7	0.4	0.3	1.0	0.6	0.3	1.8	1.1	0.6
Current Ratio (times)	1.3	1.0	0.7	1.2	0.9	0.7	1.4	1.0	0.7	1.9	1.3	0.9
Curr Liab To Nw (%)	35.4	55.7	112.9	37.5	52.9	68.0	35.4	55.4	85.5	24.0	55.1	116.5
Curr Liab To Inv (%)	445.4	567.3	687.1	445.0	523.5	654.2	261.8	398.8	590.9	187.6	257.6	490.3
Total Liab To Nw (%)	90.7	172.6	231.1	136.1	172.2	208.0	104.6	178.6	219.0	40.1	93.1	183.0
Fixed Assets To Nw (%)	67.9	144.1	201.7	144.4	191.7	213.5	95.4	182.8	218.3	17.0	75.3	137.9
EFFICIENCY												
Coll Period (days)	28.1	38.0	49.3	26.3	38.0	46.6	25.2	35.8	50.0	27.9	39.6	48.7
Sales To Inv (times)	56.0	33.8	16.2	38.3	29.4	15.1	48.2	16.4	11.7	54.2	19.8	11.7
Assets To Sales (%)	51.0	117.4	177.3	111.5	153.2	206.7	89.5	126.7	152.9	58.0	89.0	118.8
Sales To Nwc (times)	36.2	22.2	10.6	28.8	19.8	8.0	47.1	12.3	6.8	37.1	14.7	4.4
Acct Pay To Sales (%)	7.2	10.1	13.7	7.0	10.5	13.7	5.7	7.9	11.8	7.6	8.5	10.3
PROFITABILITY												
Return On Sales (%)	8.0	4.2	0.8	8.4	5.5	2.4	6.8	4.7	2.8	4.6	2.9	1.5
Return On Assets (%)	5.7	4.0	2.2	4.7	3.6	2.2	5.6	3.9	2.7	6.5	5.0	2.5
Return On Nw (%)	14.9	11.0	6.3	11.8	10.4	7.3	13.9	11.0	7.2	18.7	9.1	2.9

SIC 4924 NTRL GAS DIST — INDUSTRY ASSETS $5,000,000-$25,000,000 — 1995 (35 Establishments)

	$	%
Cash	1,613,603	11.3
Accounts Receivable	2,998,731	21.0
Notes Receivable	14,280	0.1
Inventory	414,111	2.9
Other Current	699,704	4.9
Total Current	**5,740,429**	**40.2**
Fixed Assets	6,640,048	46.5
Other Non-current	1,899,197	13.3
Total Assets	**14,279,673**	**100.0**
Accounts Payable	2,627,460	18.4
Bank Loans	—	—
Notes Payable	1,013,857	7.1
Other Current	1,156,654	8.1
Total Current	**4,797,970**	**33.6**
Other Long Term	1,913,476	13.4
Deferred Credits	299,873	2.1
Net Worth	7,268,354	50.9
Total Liab & Net Worth	**14,279,673**	**100.0**
Net Sales	11,391,953	100.0
Gross Profit	1,936,632	17.0
Net Profit After Tax	854,396	7.5
Working Capital	942,459	—

RATIOS	UQ	MED	LQ
SOLVENCY			
Quick Ratio (times)	1.7	1.0	0.5
Current Ratio (times)	2.0	1.3	0.7
Curr Liab To Nw (%)	15.9	49.3	105.5
Curr Liab To Inv (%)	308.6	412.5	658.4
Total Liab To Nw (%)	27.8	104.8	171.1
Fixed Assets To Nw (%)	57.0	99.2	209.0
EFFICIENCY			
Coll Period (days)	28.1	48.9	58.6
Sales To Inv (times)	71.7	40.7	17.4
Assets To Sales (%)	29.4	92.5	135.5
Sales To Nwc (times)	20.5	5.8	2.9
Acct Pay To Sales (%)	6.3	9.4	12.8
PROFITABILITY			
Return On Sales (%)	10.2	4.2	1.7
Return On Assets (%)	8.2	6.0	2.8
Return On Nw (%)	16.7	11.9	7.5

SIC 4924 NTRL GAS DIST — INDUSTRY ASSETS $25,000,000-$50,000,000 — 1995 (20 Establishments)

	$	%
Cash	1,280,879	3.2
Accounts Receivable	7,004,806	17.5
Notes Receivable	40,027	0.1
Inventory	1,521,043	3.8
Other Current	4,122,828	10.3
Total Current	**13,969,584**	**34.9**
Fixed Assets	20,013,730	50.0
Other Non-current	6,044,146	15.1
Total Assets	**40,027,460**	**100.0**
Accounts Payable	6,444,421	16.1
Bank Loans	600,412	1.5
Notes Payable	720,494	1.8
Other Current	4,563,130	11.4
Total Current	**12,328,458**	**30.8**
Other Long Term	9,606,590	24.0
Deferred Credits	2,321,593	5.8
Net Worth	15,770,819	39.4
Total Liab & Net Worth	**40,027,460**	**100.0**
Net Sales	39,496,850	100.0
Gross Profit	8,807,798	22.3
Net Profit After Tax	1,342,893	3.4
Working Capital	1,641,126	—

RATIOS	UQ	MED	LQ
SOLVENCY			
Quick Ratio (times)	0.9	0.6	0.4
Current Ratio (times)	1.5	1.1	0.8
Curr Liab To Nw (%)	33.3	60.6	87.4
Curr Liab To Inv (%)	225.1	267.2	392.6
Total Liab To Nw (%)	106.7	181.5	216.9
Fixed Assets To Nw (%)	96.9	157.1	214.7
EFFICIENCY			
Coll Period (days)	21.4	34.1	45.6
Sales To Inv (times)	16.8	11.8	9.8
Assets To Sales (%)	72.4	107.1	134.2
Sales To Nwc (times)	50.1	12.1	8.5
Acct Pay To Sales (%)	6.8	7.9	11.5
PROFITABILITY			
Return On Sales (%)	6.0	3.3	0.5
Return On Assets (%)	5.1	3.4	1.3
Return On Nw (%)	14.8	10.2	3.3

SIC 4924 NTRL GAS DIST — INDUSTRY ASSETS OVER $50,000,000 — 1995 (128 Establishments)

	$	%
Cash	13,333,653	2.7
Accounts Receivable	41,976,315	8.5
Notes Receivable	987,678	0.2
Inventory	19,753,560	4.0
Other Current	25,185,789	5.1
Total Current	**101,236,995**	**20.5**
Fixed Assets	304,204,824	61.6
Other Non-current	88,397,181	17.9
Total Assets	**493,839,000**	**100.0**
Accounts Payable	29,630,340	6.0
Bank Loans	1,975,356	0.4
Notes Payable	16,296,687	3.3
Other Current	58,273,002	11.8
Total Current	**106,175,385**	**21.5**
Other Long Term	155,559,285	31.5
Deferred Credits	53,828,451	10.9
Net Worth	178,275,879	36.1
Total Liab & Net Worth	**493,839,000**	**100.0**
Net Sales	324,349,000	100.0
Gross Profit	106,062,123	32.7
Net Profit After Tax	15,568,752	4.8
Working Capital	(4,938,390)	—

RATIOS	UQ	MED	LQ
SOLVENCY			
Quick Ratio (times)	0.6	0.4	0.3
Current Ratio (times)	1.1	0.9	0.7
Curr Liab To Nw (%)	40.1	55.2	76.2
Curr Liab To Inv (%)	292.0	421.8	629.3
Total Liab To Nw (%)	159.1	191.7	228.0
Fixed Assets To Nw (%)	181.2	201.2	227.0
EFFICIENCY			
Coll Period (days)	24.8	34.7	46.0
Sales To Inv (times)	37.4	14.3	11.5
Assets To Sales (%)	119.9	139.0	157.9
Sales To Nwc (times)	53.2	15.4	8.0
Acct Pay To Sales (%)	5.4	7.5	10.3
PROFITABILITY			
Return On Sales (%)	6.8	5.5	3.9
Return On Assets (%)	4.3	3.8	3.0
Return On Nw (%)	12.8	11.2	9.0

SIC 4925 GAS PROD, DIST (NO BREAKDOWN) — 1995 (21 Establishments)

	$	%
Cash	2,424,912	9.8
Accounts Receivable	6,458,184	26.1
Notes Receivable	—	—
Inventory	1,039,248	4.2
Other Current	618,600	2.5
Total Current	**10,540,944**	**42.6**
Fixed Assets	10,392,480	42.0
Other Non-current	3,810,576	15.4
Total Assets	**24,744,000**	**100.0**
Accounts Payable	4,800,336	19.4
Bank Loans	—	—
Notes Payable	247,440	1.0
Other Current	3,761,088	15.2
Total Current	**8,808,864**	**35.6**
Other Long Term	2,919,792	11.8
Deferred Credits	618,600	2.5
Net Worth	12,396,744	50.1
Total Liab & Net Worth	**24,744,000**	**100.0**
Net Sales	50,587,165	100.0
Gross Profit	8,245,708	16.3
Net Profit After Tax	4,046,973	8.0
Working Capital	1,732,080	—

RATIOS	UQ	MED	LQ
SOLVENCY			
Quick Ratio (times)	1.1	1.0	0.4
Current Ratio (times)	2.0	1.2	0.8
Curr Liab To Nw (%)	15.7	40.7	83.6
Curr Liab To Inv (%)	143.5	215.5	570.2
Total Liab To Nw (%)	48.0	84.7	155.1
Fixed Assets To Nw (%)	23.6	98.3	164.5
EFFICIENCY			
Coll Period (days)	27.9	35.8	81.3
Sales To Inv (times)	58.9	27.1	12.0
Assets To Sales (%)	66.6	184.0	210.8
Sales To Nwc (times)	17.6	16.3	3.2
Acct Pay To Sales (%)	5.1	7.0	15.7
PROFITABILITY			
Return On Sales (%)	20.0	2.6	(0.5)
Return On Assets (%)	14.5	3.6	1.2
Return On Nw (%)	27.1	12.0	5.1

SIC 4931 ELEC,OTHR SVCS COMB (NO BREAKDOWN) — 1995 (63 Establishments)
SIC 4931 ELEC,OTHR SVCS COMB — INDUSTRY ASSETS OVER $50,000,000 — 1995 (37 Establishments)
SIC 4941 WATER SUPPLY (NO BREAKDOWN) — 1995 (664 Establishments)
SIC 4941 WATER SUPPLY — INDUSTRY ASSETS UNDER $100,000 — 1995 (34 Establishments)

	SIC 4931 No Breakdown $	%	SIC 4931 Over $50M $	%	SIC 4941 No Breakdown $	%	SIC 4941 Under $100,000 $	%
Cash	5,000,070	4.0	17,424,779	3.1	799,552	6.7	11,487	21.3
Accounts Receivable	7,625,107	6.1	20,235,228	3.6	465,411	3.9	6,094	11.3
Notes Receivable	250,004	0.2	1,686,269	0.3	23,867	0.2	701	1.3
Inventory	2,500,035	2.0	13,490,152	2.4	59,668	0.5	54	0.1
Other Current	5,500,077	4.4	23,045,676	4.1	632,482	5.3	4,314	8.0
Total Current	**20,875,293**	**16.7**	**75,882,104**	**13.5**	**1,980,980**	**16.6**	**22,650**	**42.0**
Fixed Assets	75,001,053	60.0	367,606,638	65.4	7,279,506	61.0	29,176	54.1
Other Non-current	29,125,409	23.3	118,600,918	21.1	2,673,130	22.4	2,103	3.9
Total Assets	**125,001,755**	**100.0**	**562,089,660**	**100.0**	**11,933,617**	**100.0**	**53,929**	**100.0**
Accounts Payable	4,000,056	3.2	16,300,600	2.9	238,672	2.0	4,422	8.2
Bank Loans	1,125,016	0.9	—	—	11,934	0.1	—	—
Notes Payable	1,500,021	1.2	8,431,345	1.5	202,871	1.7	4,692	8.7
Other Current	6,125,086	4.9	24,169,855	4.3	799,552	6.7	10,840	20.1
Total Current	**12,750,179**	**10.2**	**48,901,800**	**8.7**	**1,253,030**	**10.5**	**19,954**	**37.0**
Other Long Term	44,375,623	35.5	244,509,002	43.5	4,379,637	36.7	3,937	7.3
Deferred Credits	5,375,075	4.3	37,097,918	6.6	262,540	2.2		2.2
Net Worth	62,500,878	50.0	231,580,940	41.2	6,038,410	50.6	30,038	55.7
Total Liab & Net Worth	**125,001,755**	**100.0**	**562,089,660**	**100.0**	**11,933,617**	**100.0**	**53,929**	**100.0**
Net Sales	49,905,201	100.0	108,580,872	100.0	2,417,482	100.0	24,423	100.0
Gross Profit	15,720,138	31.5	34,745,879	32.0	763,924	31.6		—
Net Profit After Tax	3,393,554	6.8	7,166,338	6.6	215,156	8.9	488	2.0
Working Capital	8,125,114	—	26,980,304	—	727,950	—	2,696	—

RATIOS	UQ	MED	LQ	UQ	MED	LQ	UQ	MED	LQ	UQ	MED	LQ
SOLVENCY												
Quick Ratio (times)	1.5	0.8	0.4	1.0	0.6	0.4	2.9	1.2	0.5	3.1	1.0	0.4
Current Ratio (times)	2.7	1.2	0.9	2.6	1.2	0.9	5.6	2.5	1.0	3.1	1.5	0.7
Curr Liab To Nw (%)	8.1	17.1	35.1	8.8	24.1	36.9	3.8	9.2	25.1	5.4	46.7	94.9
Curr Liab To Inv (%)	230.5	365.9	543.6	216.5	365.9	532.5	232.8	412.5	671.9	—	—	—
Total Liab To Nw (%)	76.6	142.4	176.5	124.2	157.4	201.3	50.0	85.9	177.7	14.6	60.2	115.2
Fixed Assets To Nw (%)	101.8	167.2	213.6	142.3	179.5	213.8	84.1	103.5	217.5	60.6	88.9	103.2
EFFICIENCY												
Coll Period (days)	26.3	31.8	44.4	26.5	32.5	49.3	26.0	36.5	52.7	8.0	27.0	40.9
Sales To Inv (times)	30.3	18.7	12.8	20.7	17.0	11.0	68.4	39.4	24.1	50.7	50.7	50.7
Assets To Sales (%)	204.6	229.9	342.8	220.4	234.2	379.2	296.2	427.0	609.4	39.8	83.3	150.2
Sales To Nwc (times)	20.5	5.3	2.5	18.7	5.3	1.7	6.8	2.7	1.2	14.7	4.5	2.7
Acct Pay To Sales (%)	6.0	7.7	10.2	6.1	7.8	10.4	2.7	4.5	8.4	3.7	7.2	8.6
PROFITABILITY												
Return On Sales (%)	12.2	7.5	4.6	11.7	7.4	4.4	18.0	9.8	2.9	21.0	4.7	(6.9)
Return On Assets (%)	4.4	2.8	1.3	4.1	2.4	1.3	3.9	2.2	0.6	23.2	4.8	(2.8)
Return On Nw (%)	9.5	5.4	2.3	9.7	7.3	2.1	10.1	5.5	1.4	77.2	15.3	(1.5)

SIC 4941 WATER SUPPLY

INDUSTRY ASSETS $100,000 - $250,000 — 1995 (23 Establishments)

	$	%
Cash	43,531	30.4
Accounts Receivable	11,885	8.3
Notes Receivable	430	0.3
Inventory	—	—
Other Current	12,028	8.4
Total Current	**67,873**	**47.4**
Fixed Assets	60,284	42.1
Other Non-current	15,035	10.5
Total Assets	**143,193**	**100.0**
Accounts Payable	7,303	5.1
Bank Loans	—	—
Notes Payable	5,728	4.0
Other Current	16,324	11.4
Total Current	**29,355**	**20.5**
Other Long Term	18,186	12.7
Deferred Credits	—	—
Net Worth	95,653	66.8
Total Liab & Net Worth	**143,193**	**100.0**
Net Sales	45,172	100.0
Gross Profit	8,899	19.7
Net Profit After Tax	1,852	4.1
Working Capital	38,518	—

RATIOS	UQ	MED	LQ
SOLVENCY			
Quick Ratio (times)	9.5	2.7	1.3
Current Ratio (times)	12.7	3.0	1.3
Curr Liab To Nw (%)	6.6	12.6	63.8
Curr Liab To Inv (%)	—	—	—
Total Liab To Nw (%)	10.4	58.6	70.3
Fixed Assets To Nw (%)	51.7	71.9	100.6
EFFICIENCY			
Coll Period (days)	30.6	37.6	42.6
Sales To Inv (times)	751.5	751.5	751.5
Assets To Sales (%)	85.9	313.9	368.2
Sales To Nwc (times)	10.0	6.0	4.9
Acct Pay To Sales (%)	3.1	3.8	4.1
PROFITABILITY			
Return On Sales (%)	26.3	10.6	0.5
Return On Assets (%)	6.9	5.5	2.1
Return On Nw (%)	11.1	8.9	3.5

SIC 4941 WATER SUPPLY

INDUSTRY ASSETS $250,000 - $500,000 — 1995 (30 Establishments)

	$	%
Cash	35,221	9.4
Accounts Receivable	53,956	14.4
Notes Receivable	—	—
Inventory	1,873	0.5
Other Current	11,616	3.1
Total Current	**102,667**	**27.4**
Fixed Assets	242,428	64.7
Other Non-current	29,601	7.9
Total Assets	**374,696**	**100.0**
Accounts Payable	31,474	8.4
Bank Loans	—	—
Notes Payable	20,234	5.4
Other Current	57,328	15.3
Total Current	**109,037**	**29.1**
Other Long Term	80,560	21.5
Deferred Credits	375	0.1
Net Worth	184,725	49.3
Total Liab & Net Worth	**374,696**	**100.0**
Net Sales	131,729	100.0
Gross Profit	31,747	24.1
Net Profit After Tax	1,317	1.0
Working Capital	(6,370)	—

RATIOS	UQ	MED	LQ
SOLVENCY			
Quick Ratio (times)	3.2	0.7	0.2
Current Ratio (times)	3.7	0.8	0.3
Curr Liab To Nw (%)	8.1	37.0	84.3
Curr Liab To Inv (%)	427.8	641.3	694.9
Total Liab To Nw (%)	24.9	54.7	201.9
Fixed Assets To Nw (%)	53.2	117.6	252.3
EFFICIENCY			
Coll Period (days)	35.9	59.5	92.7
Sales To Inv (times)	260.1	50.2	35.0
Assets To Sales (%)	166.6	283.7	355.7
Sales To Nwc (times)	10.1	3.7	1.7
Acct Pay To Sales (%)	2.0	3.3	5.5
PROFITABILITY			
Return On Sales (%)	9.9	0.2	(4.4)
Return On Assets (%)	3.6	0.7	(1.3)
Return On Nw (%)	8.1	1.3	(2.9)

SIC 4941 WATER SUPPLY

INDUSTRY ASSETS $500,000 - $1,000,000 — 1995 (32 Establishments)

	$	%
Cash	118,197	15.3
Accounts Receivable	58,712	7.6
Notes Receivable	4,635	0.6
Inventory	773	0.1
Other Current	22,403	2.9
Total Current	**204,720**	**26.5**
Fixed Assets	524,547	67.9
Other Non-current	43,262	5.6
Total Assets	**772,529**	**100.0**
Accounts Payable	11,588	1.5
Bank Loans	—	—
Notes Payable	20,086	2.6
Other Current	66,437	8.6
Total Current	**98,111**	**12.7**
Other Long Term	265,750	34.4
Deferred Credits	6,953	0.9
Net Worth	401,715	52.0
Total Liab & Net Worth	**772,529**	**100.0**
Net Sales	208,822	100.0
Gross Profit	65,152	31.2
Net Profit After Tax	12,738	6.1
Working Capital	106,609	—

RATIOS	UQ	MED	LQ
SOLVENCY			
Quick Ratio (times)	8.5	1.9	1.0
Current Ratio (times)	11.1	2.7	1.2
Curr Liab To Nw (%)	2.6	8.9	41.3
Curr Liab To Inv (%)	211.1	222.6	517.5
Total Liab To Nw (%)	19.7	74.2	213.1
Fixed Assets To Nw (%)	64.3	104.3	188.5
EFFICIENCY			
Coll Period (days)	32.0	39.7	79.3
Sales To Inv (times)	210.9	147.4	83.8
Assets To Sales (%)	241.8	302.8	382.5
Sales To Nwc (times)	13.8	3.3	2.0
Acct Pay To Sales (%)	1.3	3.0	6.2
PROFITABILITY			
Return On Sales (%)	13.7	4.2	(4.8)
Return On Assets (%)	5.6	1.4	(1.0)
Return On Nw (%)	10.8	4.6	0.3

SIC 4941 WATER SUPPLY

INDUSTRY ASSETS $1,000,000 - $5,000,000 — 1995 (109 Establishments)

	$	%
Cash	223,479	8.3
Accounts Receivable	110,393	4.1
Notes Receivable	5,385	0.2
Inventory	13,463	0.5
Other Current	131,933	4.9
Total Current	**484,652**	**18.0**
Fixed Assets	1,777,059	66.0
Other Non-current	430,802	16.0
Total Assets	**2,692,513**	**100.0**
Accounts Payable	67,313	2.5
Bank Loans	2,693	0.1
Notes Payable	80,775	3.0
Other Current	201,938	7.5
Total Current	**352,719**	**13.1**
Other Long Term	977,382	36.3
Deferred Credits	48,465	1.8
Net Worth	1,313,946	48.8
Total Liab & Net Worth	**2,692,513**	**100.0**
Net Sales	703,271	100.0
Gross Profit	154,720	22.0
Net Profit After Tax	28,834	4.1
Working Capital	131,933	—

RATIOS	UQ	MED	LQ
SOLVENCY			
Quick Ratio (times)	3.1	1.3	0.6
Current Ratio (times)	5.0	2.5	1.0
Curr Liab To Nw (%)	5.2	9.0	28.1
Curr Liab To Inv (%)	160.7	274.7	488.5
Total Liab To Nw (%)	37.7	85.6	158.4
Fixed Assets To Nw (%)	83.0	121.8	215.9
EFFICIENCY			
Coll Period (days)	24.7	35.4	44.9
Sales To Inv (times)	48.0	28.8	19.2
Assets To Sales (%)	265.7	372.8	494.2
Sales To Nwc (times)	6.8	2.7	1.4
Acct Pay To Sales (%)	2.2	5.3	9.5
PROFITABILITY			
Return On Sales (%)	12.0	6.3	(1.4)
Return On Assets (%)	4.2	1.6	(0.6)
Return On Nw (%)	10.7	4.6	1.2

SIC 4941 WATER SUPPLY — INDUSTRY ASSETS $5,000,000-$25,000,000 — 1995 (232 Establishments)
SIC 4941 WATER SUPPLY — INDUSTRY ASSETS $25,000,000-$50,000,000 — 1995 (66 Establishments)
SIC 4941 WATER SUPPLY — INDUSTRY ASSETS OVER $50,000,000 — 1995 (138 Establishments)
SIC 4952 SEWERAGE SYSTEMS (NO BREAKDOWN) — 1995 (118 Establishments)

	$5M-$25M $	%	$25M-$50M $	%	Over $50M $	%	Sewerage $	%
Cash	555,693	4.5	1,058,999	3.1	3,737,855	2.6	1,510,807	7.3
Accounts Receivable	284,021	2.3	751,548	2.2	3,306,564	2.3	682,968	3.3
Notes Receivable	12,349	0.1	—	—	—	—	144,872	0.7
Inventory	74,092	0.6	102,484	0.3	718,818	0.5	41,392	0.2
Other Current	691,529	5.6	1,503,096	4.4	8,050,764	5.6	1,386,631	6.7
Total Current	**1,617,683**	**13.1**	**3,416,127**	**10.0**	**15,814,001**	**11.0**	**3,766,670**	**18.2**
Fixed Assets	7,199,306	58.3	19,779,373	57.9	93,158,841	64.8	13,348,912	64.5
Other Non-current	3,531,735	28.6	10,965,766	32.1	34,790,802	24.2	3,580,406	17.3
Total Assets	**12,348,724**	**100.0**	**34,161,266**	**100.0**	**143,763,644**	**100.0**	**20,695,987**	**100.0**
Accounts Payable	123,487	1.0	273,290	0.8	1,725,164	1.2	248,352	1.2
Bank Loans	—	—	68,323	0.2	143,764	0.1	20,696	0.1
Notes Payable	37,046	0.3	170,806	0.5	1,581,400	1.1	476,008	2.3
Other Current	555,693	4.5	2,049,676	6.0	7,188,182	5.0	1,759,159	8.5
Total Current	**716,226**	**5.8**	**2,562,095**	**7.5**	**10,638,510**	**7.4**	**2,504,214**	**12.1**
Other Long Term	5,100,023	41.3	14,860,151	43.5	54,055,130	37.6	6,912,460	33.4
Deferred Credits	209,928	1.7	546,580	1.6	7,763,237	5.4	62,088	0.3
Net Worth	6,322,547	51.2	16,192,440	47.4	71,306,767	49.6	11,217,225	54.2
Total Liab & Net Worth	**12,348,724**	**100.0**	**34,161,266**	**100.0**	**143,763,644**	**100.0**	**20,695,987**	**100.0**
Net Sales	2,199,802	100.0	5,584,452	100.0	26,355,141	100.0	3,784,921	100.0
Gross Profit	1,106,500	50.3	552,861	9.9	8,143,739	30.9	984,079	26.0
Net Profit After Tax	285,974	13.0	457,925	8.2	3,162,617	12.0	264,944	7.0
Working Capital	901,457	—	854,032	—	5,175,491	—	1,262,456	—

RATIOS	UQ	MED	LQ	UQ	MED	LQ	UQ	MED	LQ	UQ	MED	LQ
SOLVENCY												
Quick Ratio (times)	3.0	1.5	0.8	2.9	1.1	0.4	1.3	0.6	0.3	2.9	1.3	0.3
Current Ratio (times)	7.3	3.0	1.6	4.9	2.6	1.1	4.0	1.4	0.7	5.1	2.7	1.1
Curr Liab To Nw (%)	2.4	7.4	15.9	4.4	8.5	20.7	5.4	12.3	26.1	2.4	9.2	27.2
Curr Liab To Inv (%)	211.5	379.4	574.3	339.3	453.0	642.3	379.1	636.6	871.8	301.6	632.8	816.2
Total Liab To Nw (%)	61.2	83.4	133.8	71.9	91.2	179.6	49.0	113.1	229.6	29.0	62.3	107.9
Fixed Assets To Nw (%)	84.6	91.2	160.2	83.8	101.9	208.6	104.1	152.8	268.5	86.3	104.7	137.9
EFFICIENCY												
Coll Period (days)	24.8	36.5	57.7	31.1	39.1	49.3	25.7	36.2	51.4	34.1	47.8	80.9
Sales To Inv (times)	70.1	34.8	19.1	51.6	41.0	27.0	72.5	41.6	30.5	68.1	41.9	25.6
Assets To Sales (%)	368.2	455.2	651.6	465.2	511.8	726.4	376.9	502.0	742.9	322.2	620.3	733.6
Sales To Nwc (times)	7.5	3.1	1.1	4.4	2.7	1.9	4.4	1.6	0.8	3.3	1.4	0.8
Acct Pay To Sales (%)	2.2	3.9	8.7	3.0	4.5	5.5	3.2	5.0	8.0	1.8	4.5	8.0
PROFITABILITY												
Return On Sales (%)	20.6	12.0	3.6	16.5	9.8	4.1	18.8	10.7	6.5	19.4	9.6	(1.0)
Return On Assets (%)	3.8	2.4	0.8	3.3	1.9	0.5	3.3	2.5	1.3	2.6	0.8	(0.7)
Return On Nw (%)	9.1	6.2	1.5	7.3	5.5	1.5	9.9	5.2	2.5	5.9	2.0	(0.6)

SIC 4952 SEWERAGE SYSTEMS — INDUSTRY ASSETS $1,000,000 - $5,000,000 — 1995 (16 Establishments)

	$	%
Cash	304,376	7.6
Accounts Receivable	104,129	2.6
Notes Receivable	—	—
Inventory	—	—
Other Current	348,431	8.7
Total Current	**756,935**	**18.9**
Fixed Assets	2,687,321	67.1
Other Non-current	560,693	14.0
Total Assets	**4,004,949**	**100.0**
Accounts Payable	40,049	1.0
Bank Loans	20,025	0.5
Notes Payable	16,020	0.4
Other Current	312,386	7.8
Total Current	**388,480**	**9.7**
Other Long Term	1,886,331	47.1
Deferred Credits	64,079	1.6
Net Worth	1,666,059	41.6
Total Lib & Net Worth	**4,004,949**	**100.0**
Net Sales	627,690	100.0
Gross Profit	—	—
Net Profit After Tax	628	0.1
Working Capital	368,455	—

RATIOS	UQ	MED	LQ
SOLVENCY			
Quick Ratio (times)	1.7	1.0	0.4
Current Ratio (times)	3.1	1.8	1.5
Curr Liab To Nw (%)	7.5	23.9	61.9
Curr Liab To Inv (%)	819.4	819.4	819.4
Total Liab To Nw (%)	38.6	64.3	142.5
Fixed Assets To Nw (%)	84.1	92.4	143.2
EFFICIENCY			
Coll Period (days)	47.1	54.4	69.4
Sales To Inv (times)	—	—	—
Assets To Sales (%)	373.4	451.9	724.8
Sales To Nwc (times)	5.1	3.3	1.2
Acct Pay To Sales (%)	2.6	5.0	13.0
PROFITABILITY			
Return On Sales (%)	14.9	(2.3)	(11.9)
Return On Assets (%)	1.9	(0.4)	(1.6)
Return On Nw (%)	10.2	2.4	(5.4)

SIC 4952 SEWERAGE SYSTEMS — INDUSTRY ASSETS $5,000,000 - $25,000,000 — 1995 (36 Establishments)

	$	%
Cash	981,617	7.5
Accounts Receivable	222,500	1.7
Notes Receivable	130,882	1.0
Inventory	52,353	0.4
Other Current	994,705	7.6
Total Current	**2,382,057**	**18.2**
Fixed Assets	7,604,259	58.1
Other Non-current	3,101,909	23.7
Total Assets	**13,088,225**	**100.0**
Accounts Payable	78,529	0.6
Bank Loans	—	—
Notes Payable	431,911	3.3
Other Current	706,764	5.4
Total Current	**1,217,205**	**9.3**
Other Long Term	3,874,115	29.6
Deferred Credits	—	—
Net Worth	7,996,905	61.1
Total Lib & Net Worth	**13,088,225**	**100.0**
Net Sales	1,389,283	100.0
Gross Profit	—	—
Net Profit After Tax	104,196	7.5
Working Capital	1,164,852	—

RATIOS	UQ	MED	LQ
SOLVENCY			
Quick Ratio (times)	4.2	1.9	0.9
Current Ratio (times)	10.1	3.6	1.8
Curr Liab To Nw (%)	1.8	6.1	21.7
Curr Liab To Inv (%)	164.6	522.6	854.5
Total Liab To Nw (%)	27.7	62.8	85.1
Fixed Assets To Nw (%)	76.6	94.1	113.6
EFFICIENCY			
Coll Period (days)	19.4	40.7	80.0
Sales To Inv (times)	62.8	48.0	32.7
Assets To Sales (%)	462.4	611.2	745.6
Sales To Nwc (times)	2.1	1.5	0.7
Acct Pay To Sales (%)	0.7	1.9	2.4
PROFITABILITY			
Return On Sales (%)	11.9	2.8	(1.5)
Return On Assets (%)	1.1	0.3	(0.6)
Return On Nw (%)	2.9	0.4	(0.7)

SIC 4952 SEWERAGE SYSTEMS — INDUSTRY ASSETS $25,000,000 - $50,000,000 — 1995 (17 Establishments)

	$	%
Cash	1,955,732	5.9
Accounts Receivable	629,812	1.9
Notes Receivable	—	—
Inventory	—	—
Other Current	2,486,100	7.5
Total Current	**5,071,644**	**15.3**
Fixed Assets	23,601,374	71.2
Other Non-current	4,474,980	13.5
Total Assets	**33,147,997**	**100.0**
Accounts Payable	430,924	1.3
Bank Loans	—	—
Notes Payable	99,444	0.3
Other Current	1,624,252	4.9
Total Current	**2,154,620**	**6.5**
Other Long Term	10,839,395	32.7
Deferred Credits	132,592	0.4
Net Worth	20,021,390	60.4
Total Lib & Net Worth	**33,147,997**	**100.0**
Net Sales	4,775,528	100.0
Gross Profit	1,298,944	27.2
Net Profit After Tax	592,165	12.4
Working Capital	2,917,024	—

RATIOS	UQ	MED	LQ
SOLVENCY			
Quick Ratio (times)	2.6	1.4	0.6
Current Ratio (times)	3.7	3.0	1.7
Curr Liab To Nw (%)	6.2	9.2	14.5
Curr Liab To Inv (%)	—	—	—
Total Liab To Nw (%)	27.9	52.0	84.5
Fixed Assets To Nw (%)	83.3	106.1	128.0
EFFICIENCY			
Coll Period (days)	44.9	54.4	115.3
Sales To Inv (times)	376.1	145.1	43.0
Assets To Sales (%)	503.1	692.2	726.9
Sales To Nwc (times)	2.4	1.5	0.9
Acct Pay To Sales (%)	1.9	4.8	7.4
PROFITABILITY			
Return On Sales (%)	18.8	10.0	5.0
Return On Assets (%)	2.9	1.5	0.8
Return On Nw (%)	5.9	2.7	1.6

SIC 4952 SEWERAGE SYSTEMS — INDUSTRY ASSETS OVER $50,000,000 — 1995 (31 Establishments)

	$	%
Cash	5,895,723	5.6
Accounts Receivable	1,895,054	1.8
Notes Receivable	—	—
Inventory	210,562	0.2
Other Current	5,685,161	5.4
Total Current	**13,686,500**	**13.0**
Fixed Assets	71,801,484	68.2
Other Non-current	19,792,784	18.8
Total Assets	**105,280,768**	**100.0**
Accounts Payable	1,263,369	1.2
Bank Loans	—	—
Notes Payable	—	—
Other Current	8,948,865	8.5
Total Current	**10,212,234**	**9.7**
Other Long Term	35,163,777	33.4
Deferred Credits	105,281	0.1
Net Worth	59,799,476	56.8
Total Lib & Net Worth	**105,280,768**	**100.0**
Net Sales	13,216,776	100.0
Gross Profit	2,246,852	17.0
Net Profit After Tax	1,308,461	9.9
Working Capital	3,474,266	—

RATIOS	UQ	MED	LQ
SOLVENCY			
Quick Ratio (times)	2.8	0.6	0.3
Current Ratio (times)	4.8	3.2	1.2
Curr Liab To Nw (%)	2.6	5.7	12.8
Curr Liab To Inv (%)	448.5	630.7	649.1
Total Liab To Nw (%)	29.9	49.5	128.1
Fixed Assets To Nw (%)	100.5	126.1	163.5
EFFICIENCY			
Coll Period (days)	27.4	46.4	78.1
Sales To Inv (times)	46.4	30.2	22.4
Assets To Sales (%)	637.9	713.3	838.0
Sales To Nwc (times)	3.3	1.1	0.7
Acct Pay To Sales (%)	3.6	5.7	10.1
PROFITABILITY			
Return On Sales (%)	19.9	12.8	9.6
Return On Assets (%)	2.6	1.3	0.2
Return On Nw (%)	5.6	2.0	0.3

SIC 4953 REFUSE SYSTEMS

	(NO BREAKDOWN) 1995 (577 Establishments) $	%	UNDER $100,000 1995 (55 Establishments) $	%	$100,000 - $250,000 1995 (76 Establishments) $	%	$250,000 - $500,000 1995 (58 Establishments) $	%
Cash	101,648	9.4	11,898	25.4	16,947	10.0	38,251	11.8
Accounts Receivable	250,876	23.2	11,992	25.6	42,029	24.8	74,233	22.9
Notes Receivable	3,244	0.3	94	0.2	169	0.1	972	0.3
Inventory	33,522	3.1	2,202	4.7	9,829	5.8	9,401	2.9
Other Current	56,231	5.2	2,155	4.6	7,118	4.2	18,477	5.7
Total Current	**445,522**	**41.2**	**28,339**	**60.5**	**76,092**	**44.9**	**141,335**	**43.6**
Fixed Assets	495,264	45.8	15,505	33.1	72,703	42.9	157,219	48.5
Other Non-current	140,577	13.0	2,998	6.4	20,675	12.2	25,609	7.9
Total Assets	**1,081,363**	**100.0**	**46,842**	**100.0**	**169,471**	**100.0**	**324,163**	**100.0**
Accounts Payable	128,682	11.9	5,808	12.4	20,167	11.9	38,251	11.8
Bank Loans	2,163	0.2	—	—	678	0.4	—	—
Notes Payable	45,417	4.2	2,295	4.9	9,490	5.6	20,422	6.3
Other Current	154,635	14.3	7,307	15.6	22,540	13.3	36,630	11.3
Total Current	**330,897**	**30.6**	**15,411**	**32.9**	**52,875**	**31.2**	**95,304**	**29.4**
Other Long Term	275,748	25.5	10,352	22.1	40,673	24.0	87,200	26.9
Deferred Credits	4,325	0.4	—	—	—	—	648	0.2
Net Worth	470,393	43.5	21,079	45.0	75,923	44.8	141,011	43.5
Total Liab & Net Worth	**1,081,363**	**100.0**	**46,842**	**100.0**	**169,471**	**100.0**	**324,163**	**100.0**
Net Sales	2,278,202	100.0	317,268	100.0	498,413	100.0	946,161	100.0
Gross Profit	931,785	40.9	145,626	45.9	232,260	46.6	444,696	47.0
Net Profit After Tax	120,745	5.3	19,353	6.1	30,403	6.1	68,124	7.2
Working Capital	114,625	—	12,928	—	23,217	—	46,031	—

RATIOS	UQ	MED	LQ	UQ	MED	LQ	UQ	MED	LQ	UQ	MED	LQ
SOLVENCY												
Quick Ratio (times)	1.9	1.0	0.6	3.3	1.6	0.9	2.4	1.0	0.6	2.3	1.2	0.6
Current Ratio (times)	2.5	1.4	0.9	3.6	2.1	1.0	3.1	1.5	1.0	2.6	1.6	0.9
Curr Liab To Nw (%)	21.8	52.9	125.0	20.5	47.8	87.4	16.8	41.4	118.7	26.9	43.1	76.0
Curr Liab To Inv (%)	116.2	252.3	451.6	79.7	170.7	357.2	86.7	209.8	467.2	89.6	274.9	301.4
Total Liab To Nw (%)	45.6	118.0	219.0	18.0	49.1	190.1	38.2	105.9	199.1	50.9	80.1	152.8
Fixed Assets To Nw (%)	59.8	103.5	179.3	18.9	54.6	173.3	44.5	92.0	169.0	67.1	119.3	150.9
EFFICIENCY												
Coll Period (days)	29.7	46.6	66.4	23.4	26.3	59.9	16.4	31.4	60.7	21.8	34.0	48.4
Sales To Inv (times)	131.5	55.0	19.2	38.0	27.5	18.8	56.4	27.6	13.8	61.6	27.6	12.4
Assets To Sales (%)	32.0	51.8	86.7	7.8	16.2	30.4	20.8	32.3	46.7	26.9	36.5	52.4
Sales To Nwc (times)	27.6	12.9	6.6	49.6	15.8	7.7	44.4	16.9	8.4	18.1	9.3	5.5
Acct Pay To Sales (%)	2.8	5.7	9.3	2.0	3.2	6.6	0.7	3.6	7.1	1.4	3.3	6.9
PROFITABILITY												
Return On Sales (%)	10.6	4.8	0.9	11.6	2.8	(0.4)	13.6	3.7	1.4	15.0	9.3	1.9
Return On Assets (%)	16.6	6.8	1.2	38.0	7.4	(9.3)	28.5	12.5	5.6	27.4	12.2	1.3
Return On Nw (%)	50.4	18.0	4.8	77.3	44.4	12.6	59.8	27.6	8.8	74.8	25.1	7.8

SIC 4953 REFUSE SYSTEMS — INDUSTRY ASSETS (NO BREAKDOWN / UNDER $100,000 / $100,000 - $250,000 / $250,000 - $500,000)

SIC 4953 — REFUSE SYSTEMS — INDUSTRY ASSETS — 1995

Balance Sheet

	$500,000–$1,000,000 (103 Establishments) $	%	$1,000,000–$5,000,000 (148 Establishments) $	%	$5,000,000–$25,000,000 (86 Establishments) $	%	$25,000,000–$50,000,000 (11 Establishments) $	%
Cash	49,453	7.2	183,364	8.8	750,950	6.6	1,445,509	3.9
Accounts Receivable	187,509	27.3	520,922	25.0	2,207,338	19.4	5,707,905	15.4
Notes Receivable	2,061	0.3	8,335	0.4	22,756	0.2	185,322	0.5
Inventory	22,666	3.3	43,757	2.1	318,585	2.8	111,193	0.3
Other Current	36,403	5.3	122,937	5.9	546,146	4.8	1,334,316	3.6
Total Current	**298,092**	**43.4**	**879,315**	**42.2**	**3,845,775**	**33.8**	**8,784,244**	**23.7**
Fixed Assets	342,737	49.9	950,161	45.6	5,154,248	45.3	18,495,096	49.9
Other Non-current	46,019	6.7	254,210	12.2	2,378,009	20.9	9,784,981	26.4
Total Assets	**686,847**	**100.0**	**2,083,686**	**100.0**	**11,378,032**	**100.0**	**37,064,321**	**100.0**
Accounts Payable	91,351	13.3	266,712	12.8	1,365,364	12.0	2,446,245	6.6
Bank Loans	687	0.1	4,167	0.2	34,134	0.3	—	—
Notes Payable	32,969	4.8	79,180	3.8	329,963	2.9	222,386	0.6
Other Current	93,411	13.6	347,976	16.7	1,695,327	14.9	5,485,520	14.8
Total Current	**218,417**	**31.8**	**698,035**	**33.5**	**3,424,788**	**30.1**	**8,154,151**	**22.0**
Other Long Term	186,822	27.2	512,587	24.6	2,764,862	24.3	10,489,203	28.3
Deferred Credits	1,374	0.2	8,335	0.4	56,890	0.5	148,257	0.4
Net Worth	280,234	40.8	864,730	41.5	5,131,492	45.1	18,272,710	49.3
Total Liab & Net Worth	**686,847**	**100.0**	**2,083,686**	**100.0**	**11,378,032**	**100.0**	**37,064,321**	**100.0**
Net Sales	1,481,482	100.0	4,318,349	100.0	13,833,188	100.0	29,007,212	100.0
Gross Profit	680,000	45.9	1,917,347	44.4	3,485,963	25.2	11,573,878	39.9
Net Profit After Tax	74,074	5.0	168,416	3.9	926,824	6.7	1,450,361	5.0
Working Capital	79,675	—	181,280	—	420,987	—	630,093	—

RATIOS

	UQ	MED	LQ	UQ	MED	LQ	UQ	MED	LQ	UQ	MED	LQ
SOLVENCY												
Quick Ratio (times)	2.6	1.1	0.7	1.7	1.0	0.6	1.3	1.0	0.6	1.2	1.0	0.6
Current Ratio (times)	2.9	1.6	1.0	2.2	1.3	0.8	1.7	1.3	0.8	1.4	1.1	0.8
Curr Liab To Nw (%)	22.3	53.2	154.9	29.2	74.9	152.8	20.3	69.5	134.2	26.1	29.9	57.3
Curr Liab To Inv (%)	125.4	243.2	407.2	181.9	313.8	634.8	176.8	380.3	526.8	—	—	—
Total Liab To Nw (%)	55.8	119.7	278.1	62.4	132.9	254.6	57.2	140.0	241.8	33.4	86.1	118.0
Fixed Assets To Nw (%)	68.3	106.7	218.2	67.7	103.4	193.8	74.9	96.9	160.1	80.6	93.4	135.6
EFFICIENCY												
Coll Period (days)	32.1	43.3	58.6	28.8	44.5	62.8	40.0	54.2	71.2	49.8	57.5	67.5
Sales To Inv (times)	138.2	64.7	15.4	149.9	49.3	33.0	132.7	80.6	37.3	250.7	151.4	97.8
Assets To Sales (%)	31.8	43.3	57.3	36.0	53.7	74.8	61.1	79.6	118.8	75.0	153.6	240.1
Sales To Nwc (times)	27.1	12.6	7.1	27.4	14.5	6.5	20.2	11.5	4.6	38.4	11.2	10.0
Acct Pay To Sales (%)	1.9	4.4	7.2	3.0	5.8	8.5	4.4	7.7	12.1	4.1	5.6	10.1
PROFITABILITY												
Return On Sales (%)	9.2	5.4	0.8	9.2	3.7	1.0	9.8	4.5	1.6	8.5	7.7	4.7
Return On Assets (%)	14.8	7.9	1.8	19.2	6.3	0.6	8.1	5.7	2.5	6.0	3.4	2.5
Return On Nw (%)	47.9	24.2	6.9	58.3	21.2	1.9	34.8	12.9	5.4	12.9	5.9	4.6

SIC 4953 REFUSE SYSTEMS
INDUSTRY ASSETS OVER $50,000,000
1995 (40 Establishments)

	$	%
Cash	3,984,084	2.6
Accounts Receivable	18,541,314	12.1
Notes Receivable	153,234	0.1
Inventory	1,685,574	1.1
Other Current	9,347,274	6.1
Total Current	**33,711,480**	**22.0**
Fixed Assets	81,673,722	53.3
Other Non-current	37,848,798	24.7
Total Assets	**153,234,000**	**100.0**
Accounts Payable	7,968,168	5.2
Bank Loans	—	—
Notes Payable	2,758,212	1.8
Other Current	15,323,400	10.0
Total Current	**26,049,780**	**17.0**
Other Long Term	50,260,752	32.8
Deferred Credits	3,524,382	2.3
Net Worth	73,399,086	47.9
Total Liab & Net Worth	**153,234,000**	**100.0**
Net Sales	88,506,000	100.0
Gross Profit	22,480,524	25.4
Net Profit After Tax	3,540,240	4.0
Working Capital	7,661,700	—

RATIOS	UQ	MED	LQ
SOLVENCY			
Quick Ratio (times)	1.4	0.9	0.6
Current Ratio (times)	1.8	1.4	1.0
Curr Liab To Nw (%)	17.8	25.7	55.5
Curr Liab To Inv (%)	153.7	232.0	252.3
Total Liab To Nw (%)	47.0	131.8	175.5
Fixed Assets To Nw (%)	83.2	113.6	174.6
EFFICIENCY			
Coll Period (days)	58.1	69.4	90.2
Sales To Inv (times)	85.0	69.8	12.3
Assets To Sales (%)	136.8	210.7	306.0
Sales To Nwc (times)	29.4	8.6	4.2
Acct Pay To Sales (%)	5.9	8.5	10.1
PROFITABILITY			
Return On Sales (%)	10.1	5.9	0.2
Return On Assets (%)	5.3	3.2	0.5
Return On Nw (%)	12.8	6.3	0.2

SIC 4959 SANITARY SVCS,NEC (NO BREAKDOWN)
1995 (144 Establishments)

	$	%
Cash	72,329	12.3
Accounts Receivable	208,166	35.4
Notes Receivable	3,528	0.6
Inventory	14,113	2.4
Other Current	42,927	7.3
Total Current	**341,063**	**58.0**
Fixed Assets	203,461	34.6
Other Non-current	43,515	7.4
Total Assets	**588,039**	**100.0**
Accounts Payable	95,262	16.2
Bank Loans	—	—
Notes Payable	29,990	5.1
Other Current	109,375	18.6
Total Current	**234,628**	**39.9**
Other Long Term	117,608	20.0
Deferred Credits	588	0.1
Net Worth	235,216	40.0
Total Liab & Net Worth	**588,039**	**100.0**
Net Sales	1,353,624	100.0
Gross Profit	473,768	35.0
Net Profit After Tax	92,046	6.8
Working Capital	106,435	—

RATIOS	UQ	MED	LQ
SOLVENCY			
Quick Ratio (times)	2.7	1.2	0.7
Current Ratio (times)	3.5	1.4	0.9
Curr Liab To Nw (%)	28.3	78.5	204.7
Curr Liab To Inv (%)	145.3	353.4	508.4
Total Liab To Nw (%)	44.8	140.6	290.1
Fixed Assets To Nw (%)	30.6	70.8	166.7
EFFICIENCY			
Coll Period (days)	50.4	72.3	117.9
Sales To Inv (times)	135.7	50.9	25.0
Assets To Sales (%)	33.9	47.1	79.7
Sales To Nwc (times)	17.2	9.5	5.7
Acct Pay To Sales (%)	3.4	7.4	14.0
PROFITABILITY			
Return On Sales (%)	15.0	7.2	0.9
Return On Assets (%)	20.3	8.4	(1.5)
Return On Nw (%)	59.9	23.8	1.7

SIC 4959 SANITARY SVCS,NEC
INDUSTRY ASSETS UNDER $100,000
1995 (18 Establishments)

	$	%
Cash	11,556	24.9
Accounts Receivable	10,535	22.7
Notes Receivable	46	0.1
Inventory	1,439	3.1
Other Current	2,460	5.3
Total Current	**26,036**	**56.1**
Fixed Assets	15,455	33.3
Other Non-current	4,919	10.6
Total Assets	**46,410**	**100.0**
Accounts Payable	4,223	9.1
Bank Loans	—	—
Notes Payable	3,249	7.0
Other Current	15,222	32.8
Total Current	**22,694**	**48.9**
Other Long Term	7,333	15.8
Deferred Credits	—	—
Net Worth	16,383	35.3
Total Liab & Net Worth	**46,410**	**100.0**
Net Sales	262,677	100.0
Gross Profit	105,596	40.2
Net Profit After Tax	13,659	5.2
Working Capital	3,342	—

RATIOS	UQ	MED	LQ
SOLVENCY			
Quick Ratio (times)	2.9	0.8	0.2
Current Ratio (times)	2.9	0.8	0.5
Curr Liab To Nw (%)	28.9	64.0	332.3
Curr Liab To Inv (%)	356.7	501.3	603.5
Total Liab To Nw (%)	64.3	96.5	257.2
Fixed Assets To Nw (%)	50.2	93.9	199.7
EFFICIENCY			
Coll Period (days)	19.7	97.3	361.6
Sales To Inv (times)	59.6	48.1	36.5
Assets To Sales (%)	13.6	33.6	58.6
Sales To Nwc (times)	13.3	11.6	7.1
Acct Pay To Sales (%)	1.5	2.4	5.9
PROFITABILITY			
Return On Sales (%)	19.5	6.9	(3.2)
Return On Assets (%)	21.3	(4.6)	(7.7)
Return On Nw (%)	100.0	(8.5)	(8.7)

SIC 4959 SANITARY SVCS,NEC
INDUSTRY ASSETS $100,000 - $250,000
1995 (22 Establishments)

	$	%
Cash	27,120	14.7
Accounts Receivable	74,904	40.6
Notes Receivable	553	0.3
Inventory	2,398	1.3
Other Current	5,350	2.9
Total Current	**110,327**	**59.8**
Fixed Assets	69,185	37.5
Other Non-current	4,981	2.7
Total Assets	**184,493**	**100.0**
Accounts Payable	16,235	8.8
Bank Loans	—	—
Notes Payable	20,848	11.3
Other Current	35,238	19.1
Total Current	**72,321**	**39.2**
Other Long Term	30,995	16.8
Deferred Credits	—	—
Net Worth	81,177	44.0
Total Liab & Net Worth	**184,493**	**100.0**
Net Sales	483,013	100.0
Gross Profit	198,518	41.1
Net Profit After Tax	62,309	12.9
Working Capital	38,006	—

RATIOS	UQ	MED	LQ
SOLVENCY			
Quick Ratio (times)	3.3	1.5	0.8
Current Ratio (times)	3.7	1.6	1.1
Curr Liab To Nw (%)	32.6	63.4	192.4
Curr Liab To Inv (%)	160.9	182.5	204.0
Total Liab To Nw (%)	54.3	134.0	209.8
Fixed Assets To Nw (%)	26.4	55.5	147.7
EFFICIENCY			
Coll Period (days)	48.4	108.6	143.1
Sales To Inv (times)	178.7	165.3	100.8
Assets To Sales (%)	33.0	41.1	59.7
Sales To Nwc (times)	13.1	9.2	6.1
Acct Pay To Sales (%)	1.5	3.3	15.9
PROFITABILITY			
Return On Sales (%)	21.1	15.3	8.4
Return On Assets (%)	28.8	17.2	8.7
Return On Nw (%)	38.4	18.7	10.3

SIC 4959 SANITARY SVCS,NEC — INDUSTRY ASSETS $250,000 - $500,000 — 1995 (27 Establishments)

	$	%
Cash	38,072	11.3
Accounts Receivable	111,520	33.1
Notes Receivable	337	0.1
Inventory	5,391	1.6
Other Current	13,814	4.1
Total Current	**169,133**	**50.2**
Fixed Assets	156,667	46.5
Other Non-current	11,118	3.3
Total Assets	**336,918**	**100.0**
Accounts Payable	70,416	20.9
Bank Loans	—	—
Notes Payable	22,910	6.8
Other Current	32,007	9.5
Total Current	**125,333**	**37.2**
Other Long Term	69,742	20.7
Deferred Credits	337	0.1
Net Worth	141,506	42.0
Total Liab & Net Worth	**336,918**	**100.0**
Net Sales	807,218	100.0
Gross Profit	349,525	43.3
Net Profit After Tax	76,686	9.5
Working Capital	43,800	—

RATIOS	UQ	MED	LQ
SOLVENCY			
Quick Ratio (times)	3.6	1.5	0.6
Current Ratio (times)	3.6	1.6	1.0
Curr Liab To Nw (%)	20.4	109.9	181.7
Curr Liab To Inv (%)	291.6	299.5	307.5
Total Liab To Nw (%)	69.0	208.2	290.1
Fixed Assets To Nw (%)	67.5	85.7	210.3
EFFICIENCY			
Coll Period (days)	29.9	45.6	90.9
Sales To Inv (times)	125.8	97.6	52.8
Assets To Sales (%)	30.5	41.4	64.5
Sales To Nwc (times)	18.3	13.2	6.9
Acct Pay To Sales (%)	3.6	6.8	10.6
PROFITABILITY			
Return On Sales (%)	19.9	9.8	4.9
Return On Assets (%)	30.5	14.7	2.3
Return On Nw (%)	92.1	31.2	22.2

SIC 4959 SANITARY SVCS,NEC — INDUSTRY ASSETS $500,000 - $1,000,000 — 1995 (29 Establishments)

	$	%
Cash	65,564	10.0
Accounts Receivable	287,171	43.8
Notes Receivable	7,868	1.2
Inventory	11,802	1.8
Other Current	41,961	6.4
Total Current	**414,366**	**63.2**
Fixed Assets	213,084	32.5
Other Non-current	28,193	4.3
Total Assets	**655,642**	**100.0**
Accounts Payable	131,784	20.1
Bank Loans	—	—
Notes Payable	26,881	4.1
Other Current	96,379	14.7
Total Current	**255,045**	**38.9**
Other Long Term	159,321	24.3
Deferred Credits	656	0.1
Net Worth	240,621	36.7
Total Liab & Net Worth	**655,642**	**100.0**
Net Sales	1,473,689	100.0
Gross Profit	521,686	35.4
Net Profit After Tax	98,737	6.7
Working Capital	159,321	—

RATIOS	UQ	MED	LQ
SOLVENCY			
Quick Ratio (times)	2.1	1.4	1.0
Current Ratio (times)	2.5	1.4	1.2
Curr Liab To Nw (%)	36.5	87.4	250.2
Curr Liab To Inv (%)	310.5	475.6	492.0
Total Liab To Nw (%)	51.1	212.9	340.5
Fixed Assets To Nw (%)	33.1	100.5	165.3
EFFICIENCY			
Coll Period (days)	50.4	69.6	117.5
Sales To Inv (times)	87.7	53.0	23.2
Assets To Sales (%)	34.9	48.7	75.7
Sales To Nwc (times)	17.3	10.4	7.7
Acct Pay To Sales (%)	2.9	7.9	15.9
PROFITABILITY			
Return On Sales (%)	14.2	9.3	3.4
Return On Assets (%)	21.6	14.5	5.0
Return On Nw (%)	74.1	56.0	16.5

SIC 4959 SANITARY SVCS,NEC — INDUSTRY ASSETS $1,000,000 - $5,000,000 — 1995 (33 Establishments)

	$	%
Cash	167,946	10.0
Accounts Receivable	641,552	38.2
Notes Receivable	16,795	1.0
Inventory	28,551	1.7
Other Current	189,778	11.3
Total Current	**1,044,621**	**62.2**
Fixed Assets	419,864	25.0
Other Non-current	214,970	12.8
Total Assets	**1,679,455**	**100.0**
Accounts Payable	354,365	21.1
Bank Loans	1,679	0.1
Notes Payable	16,795	1.0
Other Current	334,212	19.9
Total Current	**707,051**	**42.1**
Other Long Term	411,466	24.5
Deferred Credits	1,679	0.1
Net Worth	559,259	33.3
Total Liab & Net Worth	**1,679,455**	**100.0**
Net Sales	3,195,308	100.0
Gross Profit	968,178	30.3
Net Profit After Tax	159,765	5.0
Working Capital	337,570	—

RATIOS	UQ	MED	LQ
SOLVENCY			
Quick Ratio (times)	2.0	1.1	0.7
Current Ratio (times)	3.0	1.4	1.0
Curr Liab To Nw (%)	50.8	98.5	219.7
Curr Liab To Inv (%)	286.2	385.1	540.4
Total Liab To Nw (%)	80.4	179.2	306.8
Fixed Assets To Nw (%)	33.8	58.9	138.8
EFFICIENCY			
Coll Period (days)	60.1	73.8	117.1
Sales To Inv (times)	111.4	39.6	22.2
Assets To Sales (%)	38.2	47.5	74.8
Sales To Nwc (times)	18.1	9.2	3.9
Acct Pay To Sales (%)	5.9	10.0	14.9
PROFITABILITY			
Return On Sales (%)	9.0	3.3	1.2
Return On Assets (%)	15.7	5.0	1.8
Return On Nw (%)	33.9	12.9	6.5

SIC 4961 STEAM AND AC SPPLY (NO BREAKDOWN) — 1995 (18 Establishments)

	$	%
Cash	1,153,687	4.5
Accounts Receivable	2,845,761	11.1
Notes Receivable	25,637	0.1
Inventory	307,650	1.2
Other Current	897,312	3.5
Total Current	**5,230,048**	**20.4**
Fixed Assets	16,305,443	63.6
Other Non-current	4,101,998	16.0
Total Assets	**25,637,489**	**100.0**
Accounts Payable	974,225	3.8
Bank Loans	—	—
Notes Payable	1,307,512	5.1
Other Current	3,102,136	12.1
Total Current	**5,383,873**	**21.0**
Other Long Term	8,896,209	34.7
Deferred Credits	487,112	1.9
Net Worth	10,870,295	42.4
Total Liab & Net Worth	**25,637,489**	**100.0**
Net Sales	13,554,865	100.0
Gross Profit	3,646,259	26.9
Net Profit After Tax	650,634	4.8
Working Capital	(153,825)	—

RATIOS	UQ	MED	LQ
SOLVENCY			
Quick Ratio (times)	1.1	0.6	0.5
Current Ratio (times)	2.1	1.1	0.5
Curr Liab To Nw (%)	22.3	35.7	87.3
Curr Liab To Inv (%)	204.1	446.4	653.3
Total Liab To Nw (%)	98.1	146.4	220.2
Fixed Assets To Nw (%)	130.0	197.5	236.2
EFFICIENCY			
Coll Period (days)	31.2	47.8	63.0
Sales To Inv (times)	140.5	36.0	24.2
Assets To Sales (%)	154.8	189.1	261.2
Sales To Nwc (times)	11.3	6.9	4.4
Acct Pay To Sales (%)	3.2	7.4	8.6
PROFITABILITY			
Return On Sales (%)	10.2	5.1	(0.5)
Return On Assets (%)	5.4	3.2	(1.6)
Return On Nw (%)	13.6	7.6	(4.8)

SIC 4971 IRRIGATION SYSTEMS

	NO BREAKDOWN 1995 (45 Establishments) $	%	$5,000,000-$25,000,000 1995 (15 Establishments) $	%	OVER $50,000,000 1995 (10 Establishments) $	%
Cash	1,735,271	16.0	1,876,261	17.3	8,179,531	9.3
Accounts Receivable	336,209	3.1	390,436	3.6	1,846,991	2.1
Notes Receivable	—	—	—	—	—	—
Inventory	292,827	2.7	75,918	0.7	351,808	0.4
Other Current	661,572	6.1	542,272	5.0	3,254,222	3.7
Total Current	**3,025,878**	**27.9**	**2,884,888**	**26.6**	**13,632,551**	**15.5**
Fixed Assets	5,444,412	50.2	5,053,976	46.6	57,520,569	65.4
Other Non-current	2,375,152	21.9	2,906,578	26.8	16,798,821	19.1
Total Assets	**10,845,442**	**100.0**	**10,845,442**	**100.0**	**87,951,941**	**100.0**
Accounts Payable	368,745	3.4	130,145	1.2	1,407,231	1.6
Bank Loans	—	—	—	—	—	—
Notes Payable	32,536	0.3	10,845	0.1	263,856	0.3
Other Current	650,727	6.0	466,354	4.3	3,078,318	3.5
Total Current	**1,052,008**	**9.7**	**607,345**	**5.6**	**4,749,405**	**5.4**
Other Long Term	3,069,260	28.3	2,559,524	23.6	38,171,142	43.4
Deferred Credits	86,764	0.8	140,991	1.3	527,712	0.6
Net Worth	6,637,411	61.2	7,537,582	69.5	44,503,682	50.6
Total Liab & Net Worth	**10,845,442**	**100.0**	**10,845,442**	**100.0**	**87,951,941**	**100.0**
Net Sales	4,853,980	100.0	1,923,769	100.0	8,386,348	100.0
Gross Profit	1,572,690	32.4	396,296	20.6	2,750,722	32.8
Net Profit After Tax	344,633	7.1	259,709	13.5	293,522	3.5
Working Capital	1,973,870	—	2,277,543	—	8,883,146	—

RATIOS	UQ	MED	LQ	UQ	MED	LQ	UQ	MED	LQ
SOLVENCY									
Quick Ratio (times)	6.4	2.4	0.7	7.9	4.2	1.4	4.4	1.8	0.8
Current Ratio (times)	9.2	3.8	1.6	9.0	4.4	3.0	5.0	2.1	1.5
Curr Liab To Nw (%)	3.9	8.1	13.7	3.6	6.1	11.4	3.5	6.6	10.2
Curr Liab To Inv (%)	223.8	453.0	747.7	215.9	292.2	396.4	719.8	856.4	909.3
Total Liab To Nw (%)	15.6	40.5	103.6	24.3	40.5	74.0	21.4	55.0	103.3
Fixed Assets To Nw (%)	58.3	76.6	126.5	60.3	78.8	109.0	76.5	111.4	177.1
EFFICIENCY									
Coll Period (days)	14.2	42.3	77.0	5.8	18.4	72.1	43.2	58.4	107.8
Sales To Inv (times)	63.4	31.9	12.8	67.0	48.8	19.4	59.8	29.3	15.7
Assets To Sales (%)	248.1	402.1	539.2	291.6	413.2	561.0	468.3	711.6	892.6
Sales To Nwc (times)	3.1	1.1	0.9	3.6	1.1	0.9	4.6	1.1	1.0
Acct Pay To Sales (%)	2.5	6.0	9.0	2.2	3.8	8.5	4.8	7.4	14.0
PROFITABILITY									
Return On Sales (%)	30.3	10.7	(2.2)	13.1	10.1	6.0	38.9	13.4	(11.6)
Return On Assets (%)	5.4	2.5	(0.4)	4.0	2.1	0.4	4.4	2.3	(0.8)
Return On Nw (%)	7.4	5.6	0.3	6.5	2.5	0.3	7.1	5.8	3.6